The Life and Times of Willie Velásquez
Su Voto es Su Voz

By

Juan A. Sepúlveda, Jr.

**With a Foreword by Henry G. Cisneros and an
Editor's Note by Henry A. J. Ramos**

Arte Público Press
Houston, Texas

This volume is made possible through grants from the Carnegie Corporation of New York, Charles Stewart Mott Foundation, the City of Houston through The Cultural Arts Council of Houston, Harris County, the Ewing Marion Kauffman Foundation, and the Rockefeller Foundation.

Recovering the past, creating the future

Arte Público Press
University of Houston
452 Cullen Performance Hall
Houston, Texas 77204-2004

Cover design by Phyllis Gillentine

Photos courtesy of the Henry Santiestevan Collection, the Labor Council for Latin American Advancement Collection, the Mary Louise Velásquez Collection, the Velásquez Family Collection, and the Southwest Voter Registration Education Project.

Sepúlveda, Juan.
     The Life and Times of Willie Velásquez: Su Voto es Su Voz / by Juan A. Sepúlveda, Jr.; with a Foreword by Henry G. Cisneros and an Editor's Note by Henry A. J. Ramos.
          p.   cm.
     ISBN 1-55885-419-3 (cloth : alk. paper)
     1. Velásquez, Willie. 2. Mexican Americans—Biography. 3. Civil rights workers—United States—Biography 4. Political activists—United States—Biography. 5. Mexican Americans—Civil rights—Southwest, New—History—20th century. 6. Mexican Americans—Suffrage—Southwest, New—History—20th century. 7. Southwest, New—Politics and government—20th century. 8. Southwest, New—Ethnic relations. 9. Hispanic Americans—Civil rights—History—20th century. 10. Hispanic Americans—Politics and government—20th century. I. Title.
E184.M5V4   2003
323'.092—dc21   2003050044
                                                                                                       CIP

3 4 5 6 7 8 9 0 1 2   10 9 8 7 6 5 4 3 2 1

Contents

Foreword

THE NIGHT THAT WILLIE VELÁSQUEZ was taken from us by cancer, his brother George stood by his bedside. George later told me that as Willie's last moments neared, he whispered, "Qué bonito mundo nuevo." His words translate roughly as, "What a beautiful new world it is!"

It is impossible to know precisely what Willie meant. Those of us who believe in the hereafter may surmise that Willie saw a glimpse of the spiritual world toward which he was moving that night. But he may also have been reflecting on the new world he had already helped create on earth and anticipating its beautiful progression. We now know that Willie's work—profoundly American, fair-minded, and full of love for the marginalized and striving—has created a better world of inclusion, of possibilities, and of dreams fulfilled.

Few Americans have had as much influence over American electoral participation and representation in the modern era as Willie Velásquez. Willie's efforts as a political organizer and builder of community-based institutions helped elevate American Latino voter participation to levels commensurate with our growing population numbers, following more than a century of institutionalized exclusion. Today, largely based on work Willie began, Latino voters and elected officials play an increasingly significant role in enhancing the nation's quality of life through the election of our public leaders and through interventions that shape policies.

Willie was raised in modest circumstances in San Antonio's historically Mexican American Westside. An active youngster and good son and brother, friends say that Willie was a late bloomer in traditional academic terms. But he was a product of the questioning sixties and a student of Catholic social values. These influences ultimately shaped him into one of the most effective social justice leaders and political organizers of our time. This volume, *The Life and Times of Willie Velásquez: Su Voto es Su Voz*, captures for the first time the impressive route that Willie followed to make a lasting mark on our nation's political system.

I grew up in those same times, in the same part of Westside San Antonio. I attended the same high school and also experienced the social and political transformations of the post-World War II era. As a result, I have a special appreciation for the forces that motivated Willie's progression from a son of a quiescent Latino neighborhood to one of the most visionary activists in contemporary U.S. history. As the first Mexican American politician elected as mayor of a major American city in 1981, I am also a direct beneficiary of Willie's work. So too are virtually all of today's many thousands of Latino elected officials who hold public office across the nation, representing districts that simply could not have been represented by Latinos in the era before Willie's work with the Southwest Voter Registration and Education Project (SVREP) took hold.

Willie Velásquez was a man of great purpose and passion for the public good. His achievements were the product of self-sacrificing commitment and prodigious hard work. His early years as a public leader—for example, as a founder of the progressive Mexican American Youth Organization, as well as of the nation's first Latino community development corporation, the Mexican American Unity Council—were influenced by the protest movements of the Civil Rights and anti-Vietnam War era. But the political underpinnings of his voter participation concepts were rooted in the traditions of the American immigrant experience. Willie believed deeply in American democracy and in the framework of self-governance that was cemented by America's founding fathers in the early American Republic. He believed in it so deeply that he committed his life to ensuring that Latinos and other traditionally excluded minority groups could be empowered to participate in the United States' modern democracy with full equality. His underlying strategy was to help make the political system and its leaders—non-Hispanic and Hispanic alike—accountable to grassroots constituencies in need.

His unrelenting commitment to a responsive political system required him at times to challenge those of us who were in elected and public leadership positions. We were officials with whom Willie shared clear cultural and ideological affinities, as well as a vision of Latino social and political progress. But in Willie's disciplined code of accountability, the worst public transgression for a Latino who was elected to help the disadvantaged was to instead strike a compromise for personal advantage at the expense of the people. This occasionally made for tense dealings between Willie and Latino officials he had helped elect. But he was right to push the envelope of political possibilities and he earned broad respect for his principles. Even conservative leaders, such as the staff of the Reagan White House, came to appreciate Willie's way of doing business. His integrity, his driving motivation to empower new Americans, and his commitment to the fundamental values of democracy were never questioned.

It has been fifteen years since Willie passed. He was still a young man just hitting his professional stride. There is no telling how much more of his magic he would have shared with us. Still, his legacy is large in the hearts and minds of those of us who knew him and who worked with him. It is important that Willie's valuable work and the enduring values which motivated it be explained to new generations of young leaders. Their lives have already been touched by Willie's, but they in turn can follow his example to touch the lives of others in profoundly positive ways.

This book is a valuable and timely contribution to the public record and one from which all Americans can learn. Arte Público Press and its Hispanic Civil Rights Series are owed gratitude for helping to bring forward—often for the first time to a significant national audience of contemporary readers— the stories of notable American Latino leaders such as Willie Velásquez. The series is a celebration of lives and beliefs that have helped make our country better and stronger. We do best as a nation when we translate our founding principles into tangible action in the present. That is the fundamental message of Willie Velásquez's life and of this important chronicle of tireless dedication and modern patriotism.

Henry G. Cisneros
Chairman and CEO
American City Vista, Inc.
San Antonio, TX

Editor's Note

DURING RECENT YEARS, WITH MAJOR support from the Charles Stewart Mott Foundation, the Ewing Marion Kauffman Foundation, and the Rockefeller Foundation, Arte Público Press has developed an important new book series highlighting Hispanic contributions to American civil rights. Through this series, Arte Público has published first time memoirs, biographies, and studies of the leading Hispanic figures and organizations that have defined the modern Latino social justice experience in America. As a result, Americans of all backgrounds—and especially younger Americans who did not experience the events recounted in series publications—are are being encouraged to better understand and appreciate the many contributions of Hispanic people to American democracy and quality of life.

As Latino Americans emerge to constitute our nation's largest minority population, it is more important than ever that their affirmative impact on American history and culture be captured in ways that inform more constructive intergroup relations and public policies. Many Americans, noting the significant proportion of the U.S. Latino community that is comprised today of newer immigrants, are surprisingly unaware of the long history of Spanish-speaking peoples in the United States. Many do not realize accordingly that Hispanic Americans have worked exceedingly long and hard to overcome institutionalized racism in many forms over the decades—and especially at the ballot box—precisely to mitigate and challenge the sort of hardships experienced now by too many present-day Latin American immigrants.

For many Americans, the long struggle of Latino people for political justice in America is simply not a part of the nation's collective consciousness. Unlike the experiences of other politically oppressed groups in U.S. history (Native Americans, African Americans, women, and various Asian American groups come to mind), Latino political history and exclusion are rarely subjects of civic discourse in American education or media reporting. Given the historical record, however, which remains still today largely devoid of Latino perspective on the issues, this is regrettably somewhat understandable. This, in turn, is precisely the situation that the Arte Público Press civil rights book series is intended to address.

In fact, the political situation of Latinos in the United States has only fairly recently allowed for widespread Hispanic participation and impact on significant national and regional governance. Prior to the late 1970s and early 1980s, Hispanic Americans were customarily inhibited from exercising their voting franchise as U.S. citizens owing to a variety of complex legal and informal barriers to participation, much the way African Americans were prevented from participating as a significant voting block under Jim Crow laws and customs throughout the American South. Only the aggressive organizing efforts of Latino leaders and groups formed in the aftermath of World War II created the space necessary to break down historical impediments to Hispanic voting.

Limited Hispanic voting in the United States prior to this period had contributed to decades of political neglect relative to U.S. Latino groups, especially in the Southwest, where Spanish-speaking people were most heavily concentrated. The manifestations of this sad reality included abhorrent indices of Latino disadvantage in education, housing, health, and employment. Throughout much of the American Southwest, Latinos were frequently banned from accessing public and private accommodations, such as movie theaters, public swimming pools, hotels, and eating establishments. Voting regimes that prevented Hispanics from being able to elect Latinos themselves or even to hold non-Hispanic officials more accountable to their interests were primarily responsible for enabling this inequality to continue.

The culminating effort to break through the most significant voting barriers and discriminatory practices facing Hispanics in the region was led by a young native of San Antonio, Texas, named Willie Velásquez. Velásquez, whose formidable leadership despite his relative youth included helping to establish some of the most important Latino rights groups of the modern era—such as the Mexican American Youth Organization (MAYO) and the Mexican American Unity Council (MAUC)—made his greatest mark as founder and executive director of the Southwest Voter Registration and Education Project (SVREP), during the mid 1970s until his untimely passing at age 44 in 1988. Through his life's work, and especially at SVREP, Velásquez helped to position Mexican American and other Hispanic groups as influential participants in American political life.

Now, fifteen years following his tragic early death, Velásquez holds a unique, although still insufficiently appreciated status in the pantheon of modern American civil rights figures. His work probably had more long-term impact on minority politics in the United States than any other person of his generation. Today, largely because of Velásquez's efforts, Hispanic Americans comprise one of the most important voting blocks in U.S. electoral politics, with growing and increasingly significant impact on elections in virtually every major U.S. city and state, and ever growing strategic influence on the nation's quadrennial presidential races. Yet, surprisingly, until now, Velásquez's formidable contributions to American civic culture have not been captured in a dedicated study of his life and work. This volume, in effect, constitutes the first major book ever produced on Velásquez as a man and as a public leader.

Former Rhodes Scholar and Velásquez protégé Juan A. Sepúlveda, Jr.'s biography of the man in the pages that follow here thus provides a long over-due, first substantial glimpse into the life and times of Willie Velásquez. Based on Sepúlveda's close personal relationship and exchanges with Velásquez during the SVREP founder's final years, and over a dozen years of subsequent research and writing, the book chronicles Velásquez's inform-ing influences, his landmark contributions to American public life, and his enduring legacy. It also examines the more complicated aspects of Willie Velásquez that even those who lived and worked most closely with him over the years rarely had occasion to encounter or discuss during his lifetime.

Sepúlveda's recounting reminds us that Willie Velásquez, like other epic figures of modern American history, was an individual of deep contradictions, personal challenges, and emotional limitations. These aspects of his persona and constitution dramatically affected his public successes and failures as much as his formidable skills and talents did. This is the story of both parts of his persona—the public and the private. To be sure, Sepúlveda's task in cap-turing Willie's many facets has not been an easy one. As a colleague of Velásquez during his brief lifetime, I remember him vividly as a man of epic presence. Whether at meetings we attended together with other Latino com-munity leaders, with President Ronald Reagan, or later at the Ford Foundation, Velásquez always made his presence felt. Sometimes he did so with highly developed humor, other times with wrathful commentary. In every case, though, Willie made his point in ways that were impossible to forget or to ignore. He was a man whose very demeanor suggested a profound sense of purpose to do the work of history.

Now, thanks to this volume, a record of his contributions to history exists in print. Numerous individuals helped to make this possible and warrant spe-cial attention here. First and foremost, Jane Velásquez, Willie's surviving widow, her children, and other members of the Velásquez family deserve spe-cial acknowledgement for their support of the project that culminated in this publication. Their patience throughout its completion, their respect for the author's independent reporting, and their assistance in corroborating facts and events all warrant the deepest appreciation.

Geraldine P. Mannion, chair of Carnegie Corporation of New York's Democracy and Special Projects Programs, also warrants special recognition and thanks. Through her efforts, Carnegie, which was a longtime supporter of SVREP during Willie Velásquez's leadership there, provided essential grant support to enable the publication of this work. We are most appreciative of this support, which reminds us of the significant role private foundations like Carnegie played in helping SVREP and other groups to gain initial impact in the struggle to gain Latino civic empowerment.

Finally, important Hispanic community leaders, including former San Antonio mayor Henry G. Cisneros, former SVREP director and Velásquez protégé Andy Hernández, National Council of La Raza president Raúl Yzaguirre, former MALDEF president and general counsel, Antonia Hernández, and former SVREP board member Henry "Hank" Lacayo, deserve special thanks for their support and encouragement throughout the long process leading up to this work's publication. We are exceedingly grateful to each of these individuals for their valued involvement and assistance.

There are few stories in the experience of the Mexican American people in the U.S. that match that of Willie Velásquez's in terms of their impact on our nation and its political culture. Arte Público Press is therefore especially proud to be able to feature this great leader's story as a central publication of our Hispanic Civil Rights Series.

Henry A. J. Ramos
Executive Editor
Hispanic Civil Rights Series
Arte Público Press

Author's Note and Acknowledgments

WILLIE VELÁSQUEZ WAS A GENUINE American hero. Through his tireless efforts over more than two and a half decades, he irrevocably changed the Latino political condition in the United States. Nearly one thousand voter registration and education drives and eighty-five successful voting rights lawsuits had put Willie and his organization, the Southwest Voter Registration and Education Project (SVREP), at the forefront of an almost unnoticed revolution taking place across the country by the mid 1980s. The body of work that Velásquez and SVREP accomplished resulted in a doubling of the number of U.S. Latino voters and elected officials during this period.

When I first met Willie, it was the fall of 1981. I was an 18-year-old idealistic freshman at Harvard College studying political science. Willie was a Fellow at the Institute of Politics, teaching a seminar on Hispanic political issues at the John F. Kennedy School of Government. He brought his firebrand style—passionate, charismatic, straightforward, and uplifting—to Cambridge and all of us, the Latino students, who interacted with him quickly fell under his spell. As many of us would later joke, "We had drunk the juice;" we became fervent believers and followers of Willie for life.

But it was not just the college students who Willie influenced and impressed. For more than twenty-five years, Willie had been converting, cajoling, and convincing hundreds of leaders from very different worlds—grassroots politics, the Catholic Church, foundations, minority activism, and others—to join his cause: the cause of working to improve the lot of Hispanic Americans and, in particular, Mexican Americans in the Southwest. Beginning in 1974, Willie took his fight to a new level, bullying SVREP into existence and imbuing it with a laser-like focus: to politically empower Mexican Americans through voter registration, education, litigation, and participation efforts.

When Velásquez died of cancer in 1988 at the youthful age of 44, his passing was highlighted nationally through scores of articles written by political insiders who were also believers in Willie's and SVREP's community-based approach to political power. His funeral was carried live on television in his hometown of San Antonio, Texas. And an unusually broad range of people—from seventy-year-old Mexican grandmothers who had volunteered

xiii

to go door-to-door registering Latino voters, to professional leaders in government, the media, and the nonprofit sector, to the president of the United States—paid their final respects to this American giant. In 1995, President Bill Clinton, recognizing the continuing legacy of the man's life's work, posthumously awarded Willie the Presidential Medal of Freedom—the highest honor given to civilians for exemplary service to the United States.

But, in the years following his death, most people across the country, including many residing in the Southwest, and even those who lived in his hometown of San Antonio, Texas, remained remarkably unclear about who this man was and why his work and his death had received so much attention. This book seeks to address the dearth of public knowledge about Willie's many contributions to American civic culture.

Willie's and SVREP's stories need to be told because their low-key, research-based, grassroots-led voter registration and education work helped dramatically to alter the political map of the Southwest. This work brought unprecedented numbers of Latino Americans to the ballot box and, more importantly, into American political life.

Willie used to say that SVREP did not do voter registration by press conference and, for that reason, its successful approach consistently took place under the radar screen. SVREP and Willie were not common household names. But, under Velásquez's leadership, the Project's tag line, "Su voto es su voz"—Your vote is your voice—became the rallying cry for large segments of the nation's emerging Hispanic community. And by the time Willie passed away in 1988, SVREP had risen to the top of the voter registration world nationally, serving as a model for political empowerment in disadvantaged communities that others sought to replicate within their own constituencies.

I was fortunate to have worked and lived with Willie and his family for two summers while I was in college. After meeting him in Cambridge, I was determined to come to San Antonio to see first-hand what Willie and SVREP were doing. When I contacted Velásquez and told him that I wanted to work with him for the summer, I received my first introduction to the nonprofit world. "We'd love to have you," Willie quipped, "but we just don't have the money." Stubbornly, I went home to Topeka, Kansas, and with the help of another San Antonio native, Father Ramón Gaitán, my former parish priest at Our Lady of Guadalupe Church, I was able to raise enough resources to join Willie in Texas for the summer. The only problem was I did not have a place to live. Father Gaitán assured me he could find a place for me with a group of nuns who lived on the outskirts of town. When Willie found out what I had arranged, he generously offered me a place to stay in his home.

Actually, it was in the backyard, in a garage apartment, where I joined an esteemed list of previous SVREP staffers who had also put in their time at the Velásquez residence because they had no other place to go. Because I was obsessed with politics and eager to take in as much as possible, I tagged along with Willie and followed him wherever he went. And because Willie loved politics as well and was willing to share his world with young people, he took me along for an eye-opening experience that changed my life. We had endless conversations that constantly crept into the wee hours of the morning, covering the widest range of topics imaginable—Latino politics, British history, the Aztecs, art, classical music, public policy, grassroots strategies, women, family, philosophy, and so on. And the real-life situations I witnessed—both the best and worst of politics—gave me a glimpse into what Willie and SVREP faced on a daily basis. As Willie would constantly tell me, "I betcha they didn't teach you that in your Harvard textbooks." And he was right. Little did I know that one day I would be writing a book about Willie's life and recalling those varied discussions and experiences for greater insight into who he really was and what truly mattered to him.

Like any individual, Velásquez was shaped by the informing influences of his youth. On the other hand, Willie showed little inclination for leadership during his formative years. In fact, his early life experiences combine to create a somewhat surprising picture of how he eventually came to be the quintessential Mexican American political activist of the 1960s, 1970s, and 1980s. It is this part of Willie's story—that is, the part that speaks to his grounding influences and motivations—that most heavily casts light upon the type of Chicano political activist Willie would eventually become and that most people, even those closest to him, knew very little about.

I know now that I also understood very little of this part of Willie's life before he passed. Even after the countless conversations we had during his lifetime, there was a vast set of stories that I had never heard until I reviewed every piece of paper that he kept in his office and personal files, and more importantly until I conducted extensive interviews with family members, friends, and foes who knew him through every stage of his life.

Before there was anything officially called "affirmative action," Willie was a working-class Mexican American college student who spent several summers working for the State Department. Prior to being inspired to choose a path of political activism because of the plight of *mexicano* farm workers, Willie was safely headed down the path of an international diplomatic career. At a time when there were few Latino elected officials, Willie, the college student, was developing close relationships with Latino congressmen, as well as state and local leaders. And while the Catholic Church suffocated the activist ambitions of many Mexican Americans, Willie found a willing partner in crime for his community organizing in the Catholic Church's Bishops' Committee for the Spanish-speaking. At bottom, Velásquez had decidedly moderate tendencies.

At the same time, Willie also had an uncanny knack of involving himself as a significant participant in many of the most progressive Chicano political developments of the 1960s and 1970s, such as the founding of the Mexican American Youth Organization (MAYO), the formation of the first Mexican American community development corporation (the Mexican American Unity Council), and the early organization of the Southwest Council of La Raza (now the National Council of La Raza).

All of these parts of Willie's life give us a better sense of what it meant to be a vital part of the Chicano political struggle and what it took for Willie to stick it out when so many others burnt out and gave up along the way.

Notwithstanding Willie's legend and unique skills (he was, at the end of the day, one of the most formidable and able political organizers of his generation), Willie and SVREP experienced more than their fair share of ups and downs throughout the years. This book seeks to capture the roller coaster story that was Willie's and SVREP's reality as they desperately fought, first to help the Latino community obtain political power, and then to exercise that power. In the end, it reveals the passionate journey of one of the twentieth century's most fascinating and influential agents of change at the grass roots: a Mexican American champion who dedicated his life to making our democracy true to its ideals. It is an extremely important story that, until now, has not been adequately told. I am thus extremely proud and humbled to be the first to publish Willie's story in book form.

I have many people to thank for their assistance and support in helping to bring this book to publication. Indeed, when I first sought advice from other biographers about what to expect in taking on the task of capturing the life story of someone who had not been written about in the past, one thing was clear: writing a biography is not something you do on your own. There is no way I could have completed Willie's story without the support of literally hundreds of people across the country.

I want to say a special thanks to Willie's family: Janie, his surviving wife; and his children, Carmen, Catarina, and Guillermo (Memo); as well as Janie's mother, Grandma Sarabia. Willie's story could not have been told without their backing and encouragement. Willie's mother, Mary Louise Velásquez, also deserves special recognition for sharing all she knew about her oldest son. Willie's siblings: his brothers, George, Ralph, and David, and his sister, Stella, added essential additional insight into the personal side of their brother, as did Willie's uncles, who introduced him to politics at an early age.

I know that the extended process of finally completing this long-anticipated volume has been a difficult one for Willie's family, both his immediate and extended relations, and I want sincerely to thank and acknowledge them for their patience.

This project was neither conceived nor completed the way most books are ordinarily written. When Willie learned that he had cancer, then San

Antonio mayor Henry G. Cisneros was helping Velásquez to develop his own book. In typical Willie fashion, he wanted to write about the *future* of Latino politics. The past was the past. Initiating a conversation about the ongoing potential of the Hispanic electorate and the role it should play in American political life was Willie's passion.

When I found out about Willie's writing plans and the challenges he would face with his cancer treatments, I knew he was going to need research assistance. I had just finished my first year of law school at Stanford University and was clerking at a Washington D.C. law firm, but I immediately knew that I wanted to join him, once again, to help him in any way I could. When I saw Willie, face-to-face, at the M.D. Anderson Cancer Center in Houston, Texas, I told him I wanted to take time off from law school to help him with his book. His instant reaction was to reject the idea. He said I was on the right track with my studies and the other opportunities I had been given and that I should not let anything get in the way. I thanked him for his selfless concern for my future and respectfully told him to reconsider the invitation. He said he would think about it.

A few days later, Willie called me and said that he had changed his mind. "Yes, you should come back home and help me out," Willie said, "plus, Memo (his youngest child and only son) would love to have you around again." I beamed with excitement. I could not wait to rejoin my mentor, the man who had done so much for me. Three days later, Willie was dead.

Shortly after Willie's funeral, I met with Mayor Cisneros and he talked about how important it was that we tell Willie's and SVREP's stories. He had heard that I was going to help Willie with his book and said he would be willing to help me work on Willie's biography. I said I would be honored and began the steps to prepare for the task.

I owe a great debt of gratitude to Henry G. Cisneros. This book could not have been done without his tremendous support. Henry believed in me and gave me a chance. He personally donated financial resources so that I could get started and he used his vast network of contacts and relationships to help me raise more funds to carry out my research and writing. He even lent me a place to write—a trailer home along the banks of the LBJ River outside of Marble Falls, Texas—that gave me the solitude I needed to begin my first draft of the book.

Another key figure who deserves recognition is Richard (Dick) Boone, formerly president of the Field Foundation and a long-time supporter of Willie and SVREP. While I was involved in developing this book, he became a treasured mentor to me. Boone helped me to gain a deeper understanding of the foundation world and opened doors to many individuals, organizations, and opportunities that facilitated both my completion of this book, as well as my own future professional path as an independent sector leader and consultant.

I am truly indebted to him for his treasured friendship and support.

While completing this work, I was also blessed to have a top notch crew of research assistants who helped me to strengthen and deepen our knowledge of Willie and the times in which he lived: Naomi López Bauman, Roshani Kathari, Manuel López, Candy Gregory, Kim Bielefeld, and Nancy Brune. I especially want to thank and single out Elaine Wolff, who became a partner and a friend in this and other major projects that I have taken on during recent years.

The staffs of the Southwest Voter Registration and Education Project and of the Southwest Voter Research Institute were remarkable supporters and gave me unparalleled access to all of their files, as well as to their many recollections of Willie. I want especially to thank Willie's successors, Andy Hernández and Antonio González, for their leadership and friendship.

I want to extend additional thanks to Stanford Law School, whose leadership understood the significance of this project and "bent" the rules a bit to allow me to take off fully three years to get started on it. I would also like to thank Professor Gerald López (now an instructor at New York University's Law School), who encouraged me, challenged me, and shaped my views relative to the book, while I was at Stanford.

After three years away from school, I returned to Stanford to complete my legal education and met Peter Goldmark, then president of the Rockefeller Foundation. In one of the toughest decisions I have ever had to make, I put Willie's book on hold when Goldmark and his associate Mark Gerzon offered me a unique job opportunity to help develop an exciting new national initiative for the foundation. I had completed extensive research, conducted more than two hundred interviews, and written three-fourths of the book's first draft. I convinced myself that I could accept the Rockefeller opportunity—a once in a lifetime job offer, while still working towards completing Willie's biography. I tried to work on the book in my free time, but law school classes, the Texas bar exam, and my work commitments to the Rockefeller Foundation left me very little concentrated time. In the end, for all practical purposes, I put the book on hold for nearly ten years. That is how long it took to develop, implement, change, and eventually create the type of national networks and professional work I lead today.

While I wish I could have completed this book earlier, in a positive way, the experiences and information I learned along the way make the final product a much better book than it likely would have been if published any sooner. During this time, I gained invaluable first-hand understanding and maturity that impacted the way I saw Willie and SVREP. I started and ran a nonprofit organization that was part of a national program. I saw the inside of the foundation world. I was given the task of learning the best practices and most innovative approaches being used in fields as varied as community organizing, leadership development, management, politics, the media, and the for-profit, nonprofit, and government sectors. These experiences had a major impact on how I now saw the challenges and obstacles Willie faced during his lifetime. I want, therefore, to thank Peter Goldmark and Mark Gerzon for offering me the opportunity to learn all of these things in such a direct, hands on way.

During 2001, I met Henry A. J. Ramos and Nicolás Kanellos of Arte Público Press (APP). They were the key to getting this book project completed. Ramos called me to ask about the status of my manuscript, which he expressed deep interest in publishing as part of a new Latino social justice history series he was editing for APP. He facilitated discussions between the Velásquez family and me, as well as Dr. Kanellos, his publisher, which enabled me to return to the project with the full support necessary to complete the job. I am extremely grateful to the leadership and staff of Arte Público Press for their professionalism and support in getting Willie's book published as part of the APP Hispanic Civil Rights Series.

In this connection, it is important to extend a special note of appreciation to my editor, Henry Ramos. Not only did he make this a stronger book with his keen eye and superb writing skills, but also he did it in a way that was challenging and fun. In doing so, he went well beyond the call of duty. I am truly grateful for his extraordinary efforts to ensure this book's publication.

As noted earlier, the book project was completed in a very different way than is standard for the industry. In essence, it often took on the properties of a SVREP organizing effort, with countless individuals and organizations donating time, resources, and leadership to make it possible. While I apologize in advance for not being able to list everyone who helped along the way, I would like to recognize many important contributors: Félix and Fifi Sánchez; Henry Muñoz; José Villarreal; Víctor Miramontes; Father Virgilio Elizondo; Josie Goytisolo; Oscar Sánchez and Al Montoya of the Labor Council for Latin American Advancement (LCLAA); Fred Meyer; Judge Nelson Díaz; Eliseo Solís; John Fisch; Tony Arnold; Governor Jerry Apodaca; former Congressman Esteban Torres; the late Lee Atwater; Frank Herrera, Jr.; Ronnie López; Dora Salinas; María Elena Torrralva-Alonso; Lionel Sosa; Jesse Treviño; Raúl Yzaguirre; Frank Gómez; Romeo Pérez; Jim Estrada; Lewis Tarver; Jorge Haynes; Emilio & Irma Nicolás; Manuel Rodríguez; Minnie García; David Garza; Larry Macon, Alice Guerra; and Juan Alvarez.

The following organizations awarded grants or made significant financial contributions to the book fund: the Tides Foundation; the Labor Council for Latin American Advancement; the National Association of Secondary School Principals; the Republican National Committee; Philip Morris U.S.A.; R.J. Reynolds Tobacco Company; the San Antonio Hispanic Chamber of Commerce; Anheuser-Busch; the Midwest Voter Registration Education Project; the Law Offices of Herrera & Vega; the William Penn Foundation; the Trull Foundation; Matthews & Branscomb; Edison Electric; Montemayor y Asociados; the International Bank of Commerce; LULAC No. 263 Scholarship Fund; Montoya & Sons Construction Company; A.J. Lowe & Sons; R & D Development, Inc.; and Rodríguez, Inc.

I would like to offer a special thanks to Charles Butt, Mike de la Garza, and the HEB grocery company for being the largest corporate contributors to the project. Their commitment to Willie's story and San Antonio, Texas, makes our community a much better place to live.

I am also especially indebted to Juan Andrade and the Midwest Voter Registration Education Project (now known as the U.S. Hispanic Leadership Institute) for all their help spreading the word throughout the heartland and for raising resources to help fund my research and writing through community fundraising events and individual donations.

Thanks also are due to Ramiro Cavazos for organizing a fundraising luncheon through the San Antonio Hispanic Chamber of Commerce.

Thanks are owed as well to former Massachusetts Governor and 1988 Democratic presidential nominee Michael Dukakis for headlining a book fundraiser in San Antonio, organized by attorney Frank Herrera, Jr.

I am particularly obliged to single out Chris Overbey, Robin and Carl Hardin, Allan Smith, and David Medina for their individual financial contributions. These are among my dearest personal friends. It means a lot when your friends support you, no matter what you are doing.

I also especially want to thank my family for being there for me at each and every step of the way—my mom, Aurora Jaramillo; my dad, Guadalupe Jaramillo; and my brother, Gary. Thanks for loving and supporting me.

And to my children, Michael and Victoria, I want to say thanks for keeping your dad laughing. I hope we leave you a better world than the one we inherited.

Finally, and most importantly, to my wife and best friend, Teresa, I give deepest thanks for standing by my side as my partner and equal throughout this journey. I can never repay her for all that she has done for me to support my efforts, in good times and challenging times alike. I look forward to having the rest of our lives together, however, to at least attempt to do so. More than any other factor or influence, her love has enabled me to see this longstanding project through to completion.

Introduction

WILLIE VELÁSQUEZ, THE FOUNDER of the Southwest Voter Registration and Education Project, lived a life that paralleled the experience of many young Chicano activists who tasted politics for the first time in the 1960s. But he was one of the few who had lasted beyond those times to make his mark on Latino politics. Now, in 1988, the end was drawing near, way too early for a man who had barely turned forty-four years old.

～ ～ ～

It was close to three in the morning, but the specific time didn't matter. The endless cycles of pain had started promptly after his operation and slowly, methodically, sucked life out of him. His wife, Janie, and his mother, Mary Lou, stood guard over him, sleeplessly, feeling him inching away from this world. Their empty, dazed stares and sagging eyes said it all—he wasn't getting any better.

For Janie, the picture was completely out of focus. Over nearly two decades of marriage, a marriage filled with extreme highs and lows, he had been the strong one. The one that made things happen. The one that made her laugh, that made her cry. The one who took care of her and the kids.

Now, overnight, she was thrust into the role of his caretaker, a responsibility she couldn't even manage for herself. "Most illnesses are in people's heads," he would tell her, "if they want to get better, they will." This was one time she desperately wished he'd be right.

Instead, he continued to writhe in pain. After nearly one thousand voter registration drives, eighty-five successful voting rights lawsuits, and a doubling of the number of Latino registered voters and elected officials over the past fourteen years, Willie Velásquez, the passionate, tireless, obsessive king of Latino voter registration efforts, was fighting to hang on.

Willie had just reached his forty-fourth birthday. Until now, he breathed, ate, and drank Chicano politics. For over twenty-five years he had been active in the Chicano political movement, having thrown himself naively into the thick of the battle at a tender, angry age. For Willie the movement sought one goal: self-determination, an idea whose roots were as deep as the birth

xxi

of the American nation. Yet it was an elusive aspiration that other groups labored and struggled decades to obtain. It was time, Willie believed, for Mexican Americans to take control of their own destiny as other immigrant groups had done in the past.

The first decade of Willie's involvement in Mexican-American politics coincided with the larger, turbulent movement of the 1960s. This time period was a whirlwind tour of duty for Willie, complete with lofty dreams, guttural realities, and a thirst for rapid change. The tension and excitement of the black civil rights movement triggered Willie and other young activists into examining the status of their own people, the Mexican Americans, in society, and fighting for their rights and needs. Watching the Texas Rangers brutally manhandle Mexican farm-workers fueled hatred for the way things were run and disgust with the people in charge. It called young activists into an immediate need for action. Allied with a group of older Chicano progressive politicos, this upstart band of irate youths was impatient with the political and economic realities of their times. They relentlessly attacked the institutions and politicians they held responsible for the unconscionable realities that continued to exist in the nation's barrios. They were seen as naive, disrespectful, misguided students by much of the Anglo population and by many traditional political actors in Mexican-American communities. They were branded as radicals, militants, communists, racists, and ultimately dangerous.

These were troubling times. They were fast paced, tiring, all-encompassing times that moved and functioned crisis by crisis. Endless heated political debates were matched by constant binges of beer drinking and chain-smoking. Yet, the Chicano radicalism of Texas was quite different from the militancy emerging on the streets of New York City, Washington, D.C., and Chicago. It was mild in juxtaposition to the riots and killings that increasingly accompanied social activism in other regions of the country. The verbal threats were as inflammatory as anywhere else, but the outright violence on the part of enraged Chicanos was, with few exceptions, nonexistent. The staid Texas landscape did not tolerate the excesses that were inflicting the large urban areas of the nation. Nonetheless, several Texas politicians and journalists gave emotional, patriotic speeches that exaggerated the threat and wrote apocalyptic columns warning their fellow Texans of the dreaded disease known as the Chicano political movement, consisting in their view of a group of infidels who were the devil's advocates seeking to destroy the good old lifestyle of the average Texan.

Willie, who shared the same ultimate goals as other young activists, emphatically differed on the strategies necessary to achieve a more just reality, urging pragmatic solutions to the problems of Mexican Americans. Strategic disagreements, along with clashing personalities, severely strained many of the early relationships Willie had developed in the Chicano political movement. With passions and emotions as raw as they could be, friendships forged during these times were constantly ruptured, leaving disturbing scars, scars that with time faded on the surface, but that persisted, deep down inside, forever more.

In early 1973, at the age of twenty-eight, Willie Velásquez concluded that hope for his people could be found in one simple but fundamental notion: constructing an institution that would politically empower Mexican Americans through voter registration, education, and participation. This wasn't an original idea. Political candidates, labor unions, and Latino organizations had attempted voter registration drives sporadically for decades in Mexican-American neighborhoods. Even the concept of creating an organization whose sole purpose was making Latinos politically active through the power of the ballot box was not an original idea of Willie's. Chicano leaders had been struggling since 1968 to create such an organization. Willie himself had been involved in ad hoc voter registration efforts while he was in college. The difference was that after hopping from job to job within the Chicano political movement—sometimes sidestepping land mines, other times being blown to bits—Willie finally had found the partner with whom he would spend the rest of his life: voter registration.

Choosing to work within the traditional two party system, Willie staked out a path distinct from many of his compatriots who were consumed with the creation of a third political party, La Raza Unida. With a clear directive in mind, Willie became the driving force behind the establishment of the Southwest Voter Registration and Education Project (SVREP). Having fathered this child in 1974, he spent the next decade and a half scolding, nurturing, guiding, and caring for this organization. Southwest Voter was Willie and Willie was Southwest Voter, pure and simple. Whether it was tackling the rural gerrymandering problem, pushing the notion that the quality of an elected official was more important than the color of his or her skin, or delving into international politics, SVREP's actions, directions, failures, and successes all bore the stamp of its founder.

Near the end of his life, many people declared Willie a visionary, a man ahead of his time, but many of SVREP's tried and tested political approaches didn't take shape without bitter opposition. Numerous leaders and individuals who were singing Willie's praise at the end of his life had, at one point or another in the past, tried to block his efforts. Now, in June of 1988, SVREP's founding father was dying at the M.D. Anderson Cancer Center in Houston, Texas. His sudden illness and impending passing created a rush of requests for public audience and visitation, by traditional allies and enemies alike, that crowded his hospital room, and later his home, in ways that ultimately could only drain his energies toward recovery.

As night crept on, the cycles of pain continued. Willie could neither rest nor eat. He managed only five to ten minutes of sleep at a time, faithfully jolted awake by the suffering; exhaustion was no match for the pain. He craved the "carne guisada" tacos he had eaten day after day, year after year, at Sulema's, a family-run Mexican restaurant near his office, but his body only sporadically allowed him to swallow a few pieces of ice. Late in the evening when the streams of well-wishers had finally gone home, his wife and mother took turns spoon-feeding him, harking back to childhood memories of "Billy," the mama's boy, in bed with the flu.

His movements were much slower now than the Willie of years past. The powerful "abrazos," hugs with which he used to greet women and children (men were given a half abrazo and a slap on the back), now sapped his energy. Out of habit he still ran a hand through his straight, raven-black hair, but not with the force or quickness of the past. Simultaneously, he babbled constantly about any topic, particularly politics, which had absolutely nothing to do with his physical condition. The external manner in which Willie invariably handled trying situations had not changed.

Internally, Willie wrestled with his mortality, as would anyone who had gone in for a simple physical only to learn he had cancer. On the outside, however, Willie acted as if he had a cold. It was the dispassionate controlled version of manhood that he had learned from his father, grandfather, and uncles, and that he wanted to pass on to his only son, Guillermo. When he asked his wife or mom to feed him some ice, it was not an outwardly terrified man seeking nourishment. It was a calm, steady voice that Willie typically used when asking for another tortilla to go with his rice, beans, and fajitas. The difference was that the voice was weaker, inwardly frightened, and struggling to come out.

Only rarely did Willie use the words cancer, illness, death, or any of their derivatives to describe his predicament. The closest and most seemingly comfortable phrase he used to relate his excruciating pain was, "You know, I really need to respect this thing," a statement more likely to come from a disinterested observer rather than the victim himself.

Numbed by the shocking news of his cancer, Willie's friends also were stunned by his casual, easygoing attitude toward his situation. Instead of repenting for all his earthly sins or contemplating the dark mysteries of the universe, Willie continued to talk politics. From his hospital bed he insisted on discussing the latest details of the 1988 presidential primaries or the status of ongoing voter registration campaigns as though nothing had changed.

Privately, Willie nonchalantly rattled off a list of things he still needed to do as though he was merely preparing a checklist of items to pick up at the grocery store: finish paying for the house, fix the house, take care of Janie, pay for the kids' education, write his book, and so on. Even the future took on a calm, dreamlike quality. "When Governor Dukakis wins the presidency, will he send me to D.C. or to another country such as Mexico? What kind of impact will the move have on the kids?" These were the types of questions

Willie was voicing publicly. After nearly four and a half decades one thing had not changed. Willie's deepest thoughts and emotions were still bottled up inside, only to surface occasionally when he let his guard down. Not even the prospect of death would change this.

Although there were signs of Willie physically changing and slowly deteriorating from 1986 through 1988, his hospital bed lacked the bodily image of the Willie who gazed hauntingly out from the cover of *Nuestro* magazine in March of 1979 under the title "Willie Velásquez—When this man comes to town, WATCH OUT!" The portrait painted in that picture is not the stereotypical vision Americans have when they think of political activists of the 1960s moving into the 1980s: ex-longhaired hippies protesting the Vietnam War, wearing psychedelic clothes, flashing the peace sign, and now making money in the mainstream. That wasn't Willie back in the 1960s nor was it he in the 1979 photo. If anything, the pose Velásquez strikes is more likely to be found on the cover of the National Rifle Association magazine: a stare daring you to take his political gun away from him.

Splashed across the front of *Nuestro* magazine was the rough, intimidating image of Mexican machismo. It was the standard Willie appearance, or at least the one he tried to cultivate. For a man who hated to take pictures, this was one of his favorites: penetrating pitch-dark eyes, one eyebrow slightly raised challenging you to confront his masculinity, a light slant in his eyes that led many of his friends to affectionately call him "Willie Fu," and his face full with a thick moustache riding across his upper lip, a moustache that he first donned in the 1960s, reminiscent, in his mind, of the commanding hairy faces of the Mexican revolutionaries Pancho Villa and Emiliano Zapata (a moustache that reminds his mother of the turmoil of the 1960s and for that reason, to this day, makes her despise moustaches).

His hands were clenched in a manner he typically used in speeches; his fingers entwined with knuckles jutting forward, his face resting upon his thumbs. Premature lines running across his forehead marked the stress of a man not yet thirty-five years old. His Indian-black hair was slicked back with the tonic of the barrio, Tres Flores, a potion that scared his son Guillermo whenever Willie threatened to splash it on him. There was absolutely no hint of a smile in his gaze; Willie was all business. The face that stared at the viewer was the look of a possessed man who had finally caught the person who had raped his mother years earlier. For Willie, it was the dignity of his people that had been raped over the years by various political tricks, deceptions, and devices, and for this he sought revenge.

Willie was no slave to fashion, yet the clothes he wore were important because they dictated the mannerisms he used. One journalist said he always knew when Willie was about to say something meaningful. If he were wearing a *guayabera* (a traditional shirt with short sleeves, four pockets, a full cut, and

xxvi   Juan A. Sepúlveda, Jr.

vents on the sides) he would put his hands in the front pockets of his shirt, and if he were wearing a jacket he would grab his lapels. In both cases, the journalist knew it was time to turn on his tape recorder.

Willie's style and dress combined with his oratorical skills produced a charisma that was appealing to both Latinos and non-Latinos. He had a transfixing cadence when he spoke. To some, it resembled a battle march, steady yet constantly building. For others, it was the deepness and strength that his voice projected that captured their imagination. With his left hand on his hip, Velásquez used his right hand to accentuate his themes by forcefully grabbing the air. He pointed at the audience, almost scolding them, when he spoke of the work still needing to be done.

The specific content of Willie's speeches changed over the years, but the central focus never varied. At SVREP's inception, the standard text centered on the notion that Willie and other Mexican-American leaders needed to listen more closely to their people. Once they did this, they would realize that it was the local issues—paving the streets, fixing the drainage system, and improving the schools—that were vital to the population, not larger national questions. In later years, the focus shifted to properly exercising the political power Mexican Americans were beginning to amass and reflecting upon the traditional immigrant experience they had lived.

These topics shared one crucial variable. The core of the message was aimed at validating and praising the experiences and opinions of the so-called uneducated, unsophisticated, lazy Mexican-American working-class population. It was this central idea, seasoned with Willie's mastery of Tex-Mex lingo, that instilled countless numbers of people with a sense of dignity and worth, inflaming them with a passion for political action. It was also a message that many white progressive leaders admired, particularly since, in their eyes, the word was coming from a street-smart barrio product who had taught at Harvard.

Willie carried his message to large numbers of "Mexicans" throughout the Southwest (Willie hated to use the terms Hispanic, Latino, Mexican American, or Chicano—to him everyone was Mexican). Still, the eloquent, charismatic voter registration king of 1988 was worlds apart from the reserved "Billy" of San Antonio's Central Catholic High School or the 1960s political organizer/fund-raiser whose words were few, bureaucratic, and stilted. His sedate insider style of the late 1960s and early 1970s is even more unconventional when contrasted with the fiery confrontational tactics used by the Black Panthers, the Brown Berets, the Student Nonviolent Coordinating Committee in its later years, and La Raza Unida.

Nevertheless, in 1988, after more than two decades plodding through the trenches, Willie was highly regarded by the Mexican-American communities he and his organization had politicized. He spoke their Spanish, drank their liquor, and articulated their potential. His leadership was easy for working-class Mexican Americans to accept because they saw Willie as one of them. Willie's lower-middle-class background made it natural for him to fit in and relate to the Mexican-American constituency he organized through SVREP, but this was only one facet of the man.

His experiences and opportunities created a person much more complicated, a Renaissance man whose duality mirrored life on both sides of the tracks. He loved Tejano *conjuntos* and Mozart, the Aztecs and the British, the Esquire Bar and "La Boheme," Pancho Villa and Disraeli, barrio women in tight clothing and public television.

His life straddled two worlds, poor and comfortable, realistic and idealistic, macho and intellectual, Mexican and American. His contradictory interests, beliefs, and actions seemed to parallel Octavio Paz's explanation of the origin of the differences between North America and Mexico, when he wrote: "It seems to me that North Americans consider the world to be something that can be perfected, and that we (Mexicans) consider it to be something that can be redeemed." For Willie, it was this struggle between his North American optimism and his Mexican realism that marked the life he lived and the work of his organization, Southwest Voter.

Now fifteen years following his passing, Willie Velásquez holds a unique, although still insufficiently appreciated status in the pantheon of modern American civil rights figures. His work has possibly had more impact on the long-term future of American politics than any other person of his generation. This work triggered an unprecedented mobilization of Mexican-American and other Latino voters in pivotal electoral states across the nation, including California, Texas, and Illinois, which play an increasingly critical role in electing our nation's presidents and setting our national agenda. As Latinos emerge to constitute America's new leading minority group with growing reach into other major states like New York, Florida, Georgia, Iowa, and North Carolina, Hispanic political influence in America can only become more significant in the years to come. In time, these states will produce important new political leaders of Hispanic heritage, who will become our future governors, members of the U.S. Congress and Senate, and, certainly one day, presidents of the United States.

Willie's work both envisioned these developments and facilitated their forward movement in time. This book chronicles Willie's life, his informing influences, his landmark contributions to American civic culture, and his enduring legacy. It also examines the more complicated aspects of Willie Velásquez that even those who lived and worked most closely with him over the years rarely had occasion to encounter or discuss during his lifetime.

Willie, like other epic figures of modern American history, was an individual of deep contradictions, personal challenges, and emotional limitations. He frequently tended to set goals that wildly exceeded reason and possibility, and then to focus on the disappointments of falling short rather than the advancements informed by his ambitious success benchmarks. These aspects of his persona and constitution dramatically informed his public achievements as much as his formidable skills and unique talents did. They are an essential part of the story that was his life.

This, then, is an important first effort to capture and assess the full measure of who Willie Velásquez was as an historically important public figure and as a man. The story of both Willies—the public and the private—offers critical insights and lessons related to effective grassroots community development, institution building, and minority empowerment in America. Willie's story sheds light on the nature and price of public leadership in American political life. It also informs an important new understanding of the quality and consistency of contemporary Latino community aspirations relative to established American traditions, dating back to the experiences of past significant immigrant groups of the late nineteenth and early twentieth centuries.

Willie's story, it turns out, is thus a quintessential American story. It is important reading, accordingly, for all who would aspire to better understand not only who Willie Velásquez was, but also who we are as Americans.

Chapter 1

IT WAS A LAZY SUNDAY AFTERNOON, 1949, in San Antonio, Texas, a city of over 250,000 inhabitants that postcards boasted was the second cleanest city in the country and the one with the lowest mortality rate. Nothing was special about this Sunday. Like countless other Sundays, Billy and the Velásquez family joined members of the Cárdenas family at Grandma Cárdenas's house for a Mexican barbecue.

Grandma Cárdenas lived on Lombrano Street in a tiny house that barely squeezed in all her children and their families when they visited her on these occasions. The smell and sound of the Mexican-American extended family lingered in the air as uncles opened beer bottles, meat sizzled, aunts chattered in a corner, and kids amused themselves with imaginative games.

One kids' game centered on brute strength. Billy, five years old, and his Sunday-at-grandma's playmates, challenged each other to the Herculean task of seeing who could pick up the largest rocks and throw them. After a few warm-up rounds, Billy decided to end the competition by attempting to move a huge stone. Billy budged the rock, lifted it a bit, and then it crashed, smashing his finger.

Billy's finger exploded with pain and he ran inside, crying, looking for comfort, as would any five-year-old. His mom wanted to pamper Billy, take care of him, and make him feel better. His father, however, intercepted his eldest child, spanked him, and told him to get back outside and stop his damn crying. To Willie's father, William "Willie" Velásquez, Sr., only helpless little girls cried, not Mexican boys, especially not Willie Velásquez's son.

At age five, Billy received his first lesson of many to come from his father (and others) that Mexican men should not reveal their pain, or deep feelings. To do so was a sign of weakness. Women were the ones who broke down, cried, and made fools of themselves. When that happened, it was the duty of a man to stand tall, both for his woman and his family.

Everyone could feel the throbbing of Billy's disfigured finger as he went back outside, held his hand, and whimpered quietly so that his father could not hear him. The men understood the need for a good spanking to keep a child in line, but this seemed a bit much. Billy's mom felt helpless because she

1

could not stand up to her husband, especially in front of the rest of the family. At times like this, she wondered how she and her husband had ever come together. They were two completely different people.

’ ’ ’

When Mary Louise Cárdenas met Willie Velásquez, Sr. again in 1941, he was a handsome, charming, and mesmerizing young man. The first time she met him in school, years earlier, she could not stand him. "I used to tell my mother there's this guy and I hate him. I had never heard the surname Velásquez so I thought he had added extra sounds to [the more common name] Vasquez to make himself unique."

At age sixteen, Willie, Sr., the fourth child of seven, left San Antonio for Winslow, Arizona. Stationed there with the Civilian Conservation Corps (CCC), he was one of 500,000 unemployed urban youths that the Roosevelt administration hired to work in semi-military environments planting trees, creating parks, and developing reservoirs. After two years with the Civilian Corps, Willie, Sr. returned home. His cousin, Beatrice, a friend of Mary Lou's, asked Mary Lou to walk into town with her. As they came to the Katy Depot, a train arrived carrying workers from the Tree Army camp. It was here that Mary Lou reencountered Willie, Sr. She was seventeen years old. He was eighteen.

After dating for a year, Mary Lou and Willie, Sr. decided to get married. Her father strenuously objected. How could she get married at such a young age? Didn't she realize what kind of family he came from? Why couldn't she marry a nice boy from the family's church? The more he pushed, the more she wanted to marry Willie, Sr. The situation also caused problems for Mary Lou's parents' relationship. Her parents fought because Mary Lou's father blamed his wife for not guiding their daughter more effectively in such an important decision.

Plans for the wedding went forward, but even up until the wedding ceremony Mary Lou was not certain whether her father would give her away. Her Uncle William had his only suit pressed and stood ready in case he had to step in. At the last minute, Mary Lou's father appeared at her wedding, tears streaming down his cheeks. Mary Lou also erupted into tears, and they strolled down the aisle together. On Valentine's Day, 1942, two months after the attack on Pearl Harbor, María Luisa Cárdenas and William Velásquez, Sr. were married at La Trinidad Methodist Church in San Antonio, Texas.

Almost immediately after getting married, Uncle Sam and World War II called and Willie, Sr. left his new bride for the army. Three months later, after he completed basic training, Mary Lou joined her husband at the headquarters of the Army-Air Force Tactical Center in Orlando, Florida, a major military installation. It was Mary Lou's first venture outside of Texas. There, she experienced the first of many jolts to come in her twenty-six years of marriage to Willie, Sr. Shortly after her arrival, a woman from the army came to their hotel room looking for Willie, Sr. The woman saw Mary Lou's wedding picture on the table and said she wanted only to confirm that Willie, Sr. was married. He had told her he was not and she did not believe him. Upon arrival in Orlando, Willie, Sr. had stopped wearing his wedding ring, claiming the gold had worn off in just three months; but it was his fidelity that was gone.

Mary Lou, dazed, repacked her bags. In the midst of her anger and hurt she could hear her father telling her not to get married. She was eighteen, almost broke, thousands of miles away from home, and lonelier than she had ever been. She braced herself for Willie's return and told him she was going back to Texas. Willie countered by calling the other woman a young foolish broad who was everybody's girl. She did not mean anything to him at all. She went around doing the same thing to other guys. He said it would never happen again. Mary Lou's defenses slowly withered away with each cliché of love, promise, and future that Willie, Sr. spit out. Her religion and upbringing reminded her that she was married for keeps, forever. Divorce or separation were not options. Still burned by his infidelity, Mary Lou tried to place it behind them and vowed to work harder on making the marriage last. He released a smile of relief and helped her unpack, again.

Things did get better for the young, inexperienced couple from the Southwest. Finding an apartment was extremely difficult, especially for enlisted men and their families. After living in a hotel room for a while, Mary Lou and Willie, Sr. stumbled onto a "Touch of Heaven", the Grove Hill Court Apartments run by the Eubanks, a former Port Orange, Florida judge and his wife who had recently moved to Orlando. With the price of a three-room dwelling averaging $15 or more a week, Judge and Ma Eubank had thirty rental units for enlisted men at $6 a week for three rooms and only $4 a week for two rooms. The Eubanks knew the problems enlisted men and their families faced with housing because two of their sons, a son-in-law, and their respective families constantly complained to the couple about the difficulty of finding affordable accommodations.

The Eubanks had five homes flanking a dead-end street named Grove Hill Court that they turned into apartments. During peacetime, resort tenants had occupied these houses. To Mary Lou, the buildings reminded her of Southern mansions she had seen at the movies. The endless number of rooms, the high ceilings with old-style fans, and the huge verandas made her feel as if she were living in the times of Scarlet O'Hara.

Mostly young couples occupied the apartments. They came from all parts of the country, many of them green from having left their homes for the first time. An air of informality and family existed, inspired by events like Ma Eubank's stork parties for expecting mothers and Judge Eubank's

Wednesday night hot dog roasts. As one sergeant from Pennsylvania said, "An evening in the Eubank living room is almost as good as a trip back home." The Eubank front porch served as an informal gathering point almost every night. After the men came home, the youthful couples would cling to each other, talking, joking, and singing. GI talk dominated the men's discussions: congratulations for promotions, complaints about service problems, the possibility of being sent overseas; the women talked about rationing, shopping, cooking, and jobs.

Mary Lou and Willie, Sr. lived in a one-bedroom kitchenette apartment. Often, Mary Lou's monthly allotment and Willie, Sr.'s meager wages did not make ends meet. Even with Mary Lou working at Woolworth's and later Yaldrew's Department Store, there were occasions when they ran out of groceries or quarters for the meter-run stove when the eggs or coffee were only half done. As fate would have it, other couples shared these experiences, so while the men ate at the base, the women shared what food they had with each other.

〜 〜 〜

On May 9, 1944, Mother's Day, William Cárdenas Velásquez, Jr., Mary Lou and Willie, Sr.'s first of five children, was born in a makeshift hospital established for the war in Orlando, Florida. Although married in Mary Lou's Methodist Church, Willie, Sr. wanted his children raised in the Catholic faith, so they baptized "Billy" at St. James Catholic Church in Orlando. To avoid confusion for her children, Mary Lou converted to Catholicism. To please her husband, they married again, this time "properly" in a Catholic Church. Living next door to the Eubanks made life easier as Ma Eubank loved to take care of Billy. Ma even woke up at night when she heard Billy crying, just to make sure everything was all right. Some women were jealous of the special treatment Billy received, including Mary Lou who wanted more time alone with her son.

Eight months after Billy's birth, the Velásquez's comfortable routine was jolted. Willie, Sr. was called to report to the European battlefield. Overnight they had to leave Florida. Mary Lou panicked, not knowing whether her husband would be granted an emergency leave to take her and Billy back home. Without a car, they could not take things to the post office to be mailed to San Antonio, so they gave many of their possessions to friends. Willie, Sr. was luckily granted a few days to escort his family to Texas before being shipped overseas. After saying a quick good-bye to her friends—the women who had coffee with her every day, the families that met on the veranda each night—Mary Lou, pregnant again, returned to San Antonio with her son and husband.

For half a year, Mary Lou waited for her husband to return. With Willie, Sr. in Europe, Mary Lou birthed her second child, Stella, on Father's Day, 1945. Willie, Sr. returned momentarily to Texas and then left for the Pacific Theater.

On Christmas Eve, 1945, Willie, Sr., finally released from the army, returned to San Antonio and joined his expanded family. He desperately desired a few weeks of rest and relaxation before seeking employment, but his older sister's boyfriend said he could help get him a job at the Swift Meat Packing Company if he could start immediately. Willie, Sr. wanted to be a tailor, but thinking of his family he could not pass up this waiting opportunity. He accepted the job and started working on January 11, 1945. Everything seemed normal again for the Velásquez family.

With the war over, Mary Lou and Willie, Sr. concentrated on finding a home for their growing family. Mary Lou's aunt owned a house and rented it to them, but this arrangement didn't last long. The city decided to build an expressway through their home and others in the area. As compensation, city officials moved the Velásquez's and other displaced families to different neighborhoods, stacking their relocated homes almost on top of each other, face to face, on dead-end streets. During the move, the Velásquez's lived with Grandma Cárdenas in tightly cramped quarters. After only a short stint in their re-situated house, Mary Lou and Willie, Sr. began to look for a new home just south of Culebra Avenue on West Laurel Street. This clean, untouched area would be Billy's new stomping ground and a place that would mark much of his life's journey. At age five, the house seemed like a castle to Billy, especially when he traveled around the nearby streets. It produced important memories and the sense of a center for him, even years after he had left home to pursue his college studies and career. As an adult, William C. ("Willie") Velásquez, Jr. paid homage to the house he grew up in when he returned to live there again with his own wife and children.

In the spring of 1950, the Velásquez's neighborhood felt like a brand-new car not yet driven. It was a modern subdivision located on the outskirts of town. It attracted Mexican-American working-class families that wanted to commence the upcoming decade with a slightly larger piece of the American pie.

It was not the suburbs, but it could be fairly described as a poor man's version of the Levittown planned community that captured and strangled American society in the 1950s. This scaled down rendition of the Levittown phenomenon was filled, street after street, with nearly identical single-family houses. Unlike the huge, sprawling houses of Levittown-type suburbs, however, the homes of Laurel Street and the surrounding area were built almost on top of each other. Unpaved streets and barren yards covered only with dirt filled the landscape. Yet, for kids like Billy, moving into your own home in previously unexplored territory was a mark of privilege.

Compared to the public housing project nearby, Billy's neighborhood was of higher-class status, but one most accurately described as lower middle class. The shiny modern houses contrasted intensely with the dim Menchaca Courts located only a few blocks away. Billy and his playmates envisioned the Courts as an area rampant with gangs, fights, knifings, drugs, evil, and mystery. They stayed away and automatically pointed in that direction when something was misplaced or stolen. The Menchaca Courts were the center of barrio life in the community. The pristine families of Laurel Street and its vicinity were outsiders at best and invaders at worst relative to the rooted culture of the projects.

Situated on an incline that led down to a creek, the Laurel Street community was a struggling family's dream. From the outside, the Velásquez house looked like it was on stilts and still under construction. There was no skirt around the house and passersby could see clearly and easily underneath the home. To enter the Velásquez residence, one crossed a dusty yard and a tiny porch, unless it was raining, in which case visitors walked across boards that spanned from the driveway to the entrance, hoping not to fall onto the mud-caked grounds. Entering visitors walked into a quaint living room where four-year-old Stella slept on a fold-out cot. To the right was Mary Lou and Willie, Sr.'s bedroom, and to the left was the kitchen. At the end of a narrow hallway was a second room where Billy and Grandpa Cárdenas shared quarters close to the only bathroom. Hot running water did not come with the house so family members relied on a stove kettle for such luxuries.

෴ ෴ ෴

Billy and the kids in the neighborhood lived wholesome lives filled with creative, imaginative entertainment and occasional bouts of mischief. The new subdivision in which they lived provided a large wooded area and creek that served as their surrogate playground. Culebra Avenue functioned as an informal borderline between the wealthier Anglos (and a handful of Mexican Americans) living to the north and the less affluent Mexican Americans located to the south. It was a border that Billy would not fully understand until he went to high school.

Toys were rare in the neighborhood so Billy and his pals turned to their active and slightly devious minds when they wanted to entertain themselves. They had kite wars where they sprinkled and glued crushed glass onto the tails of their kites, attempting to cut the lines of their opponents. They had spinning top battles where they replaced the original points of the top with a sharpened nail. The trick was to hit the opponent's top part of the spin and split it in half.

The outdoors also served as a natural outlet for their adventurous imaginations. With the creek dry, the kids tore up discarded cardboard boxes from new appliances and slid down the hill on them. Instant swimming pools appeared in the streets near their houses when rain, combined with a lack of drainage, sent cars helplessly floating by.

These are examples of harmless games devised by clean-cut all-American kids who lived day-by-day thinking of different ways to amuse themselves. Yet, while these childhood escapades nostalgically recapture the innocence of Billy's earlier days, they also reveal the continuing influences of what it meant to be a Mexican male. In traditional fashion, Billy and his gang of boys went hunting, fishing, and exploring while Stella and the other girls stayed at home with their mothers or played with dolls. With their bamboo poles and homemade slingshots, Billy and his buddies caught Rio Grande perch and knocked doves out of the sky for their mothers to cook for them. On those rare occasions that the girls and boys played together, the girls rendered a supportive role. Playing cowboys and indians, Billy and the boys battled each other in the thick of the weeds next to the creek. With the slaughter completed, the boys returned to civilization where the girls anxiously awaited them with their supper ready. Stella recalls the photographer who took pictures of the neighborhood boys dressed up in cowboy outfits sitting on a pony. When she asked Billy why he didn't smile, he told her that she was dumb for not knowing that cowboys don't smile.

Being stout, an older kid on the block, and not too bossy, Billy's respect level was high among his playmates. Donald Falcón, who later became a professional baseball player, remembers Billy as strong and quiet. Roger Segura, now an attorney, recalls him being aggressive and sort of the boss in the neighborhood. With more houses being built in the expanding neighborhood and new kids constantly moving in, Billy, Roger, and the older kids were increasingly looked up to because they knew the paths through the woods, where the drainage pipes were, and how to make bows and arrows.

〜 〜 〜

Billy started his education at H.K. Williams Elementary School, a predominantly working-class Mexican-American public school in the neighborhood. When the Velásquez family moved into their new neighborhood, Billy's mother hadn't realized she needed to register her son early so that he could attend Little Flower, the private Catholic school in the area. His mother regretted sending him to H.K. Williams, but having missed the application deadline for Little Flower, she had no other choice.

During this period, the Velásquez's added a third child to their growing family, another boy named George. Mary Lou began to think and concern herself more and more about her children's future, and especially their education. She became increasingly troubled by the sense that Billy's enrollment in public rather than private school could present safety and learning challenges for him that would unduly diminish his future prospects.

While Mary Lou worried about Billy attending the potentially dangerous and inferior public school, Willie, Sr. didn't see what the fuss was about. Why did his son need to go to a school where you had to pay? He recalled his father telling him that he was not going to be the president of the United States, so why should his son be any different? One of Willie Sr.'s brothers joined in on the chorus line of attack aimed at Mary Lou. He told Mary Lou and Willie, Sr. that as long as his kids were not as ignorant as he was, that would be enough schooling. Did Mary Lou think her family was better than everyone else?

For Mary Lou, the question was not whether her family was better than the others in the neighborhood. It was simply a question of ensuring for Billy and the rest of her children the best possible education. The poverty, poor school performance, and limited expectations of kids who attended H.K. Williams scared her. Many Williams' students seemed to her to come from homes where sons and daughters were pushed to get out of school quickly and where the minimal expectations of working at any job or getting married too easily equaled success. Frustrated by her own lack of education and life opportunities (she had only finished junior high), Mary Lou fought the men in her life for the direction of her little Billy. Her greatest fears never came to pass and Billy survived his initial school years at Williams unscathed. Mary Lou still did not want to take any chances. In third grade, at her behest, Billy transferred to the then newly established Holy Rosary Elementary School.

Housed temporarily in a three-room army barrack with primitive wood floors, Holy Rosary was a school not yet built. Barely a few years old when Billy and his sister Stella started there, Holy Rosary was a typical 1950s Catholic grade school. The faculty was predominantly Anglo and ruled by nuns in their imposing full-length habits. Based on its pre-Vatican Council II roots, Holy Rosary, a strict school, preached the fear of God and the damnation of nonbelievers. As an impressionable third grader, Billy intently listened as the nuns, at the height of McCarthyism, told horror stories of communists as the devil reincarnated. There was no doubt that the teachers and classes at Holy Rosary were a lot different from what Billy experienced in public school. Still, Billy, the deferential, diligent, quiet young boy would have no problem making the transition, and even if he did, no one would know because he was already mastering the art of keeping his feelings locked inside.

᪥ ᪥ ᪥

Holy Rosary was a good distance from the Velásquez house. Getting there required crossing two deadly, cluttered avenues and an assortment of winding streets. To Mary Lou, an inexperienced mother still adjusting to sending her first batch of kids to school, the thought of her precious little ones out there, alone, walking through a dangerous part of town sent nervous shivers down her back. When Billy and Stella first started classes at Holy Rosary, Mary Lou walked them to and picked them up from school, making sure nothing harmful would happen to them. This ritual lasted only for a short time, however.

One day, as Mary Lou prepared herself, again, to accompany her children to Holy Rosary, Billy, softly and assuredly told her, "Mom, you don't have to come with us; I'll take care of Stella. We'll be just fine. Don't worry." He didn't say it in a bratty, childish, "We can take care of ourselves now" voice. It was a serious, calmer sound that you'd expect from an older man, a tender father perhaps. It wasn't the first time Mary Lou had heard this tone. The first time she heard it she was having trouble with the vacuum cleaner. The stupid thing wouldn't start! No matter what she tried, it just wouldn't respond. Billy stood there watching his mother. When she walked away in disgust, Billy toddled over to the machine and carefully scanned it. After dropping it, beating it, twisting it, and kicking it, the vacuum suddenly eked out a breath of life. It was fixed! The noise startled Mary Lou and Billy nonchalantly handed her the nozzle and returned to being a helpless kid. "Here you go, Mom," he said.

Mary Lou's next recollections of Billy acting like a little man centered on him grocery shopping and beginning school. Unable to drive, Mary Lou needed to break her dependence on a man who was the most constantly absent person she had ever known, her husband. Many days passed when she couldn't go to the store because Willie, Sr. was nowhere to be found. Sick and tired of this nagging, growing nuisance, she carelessly turned toward her son and caught fragments of what he was saying. "What was that, Billy?" she asked. "I said that I'd go to the store for you," the little boy responded. Something told her not to let him go, but Billy's earnest gaze convinced her otherwise. At the store, Billy didn't blaze through the aisles like a reckless child. Instead, he took his time. He chatted with the workers as if he were a retired gentleman who had been coming to the store all his life, picked up the essentials, and went home. Inside the house, he placed the groceries on the table, handed Mary Lou the change, and returned to the habits and routines of any normal five-year-old.

These early signs of a level of maturity beyond his years would characterize Willie Velásquez's predisposition throughout his life.

〜 〜 〜

Billy especially loved his grandfather Fidel Cárdenas. When Grandpa moved into their house and shared a room with him, Billy saw him every day. Grandpa told him stories about his earlier life. How he studied art in Mexico and Denver. How he became a baker. How he co-owned the Firestone Tire Company out on Commerce Street. How his family was well known in the neighborhood because it owned the Cárdenas Brothers Garage on Pecos Street and was one of the few families to own a radio at that time.

Grandpa also advised Billy on topics that didn't matter much to a boy, such as how to treat girls. "When you accompany a woman down the street, you should always have her walk on the inside part of the sidewalk so that you can protect her from the passing traffic," he told Billy. "This is how a Mexican gentleman acts." Years later, when Billy and Stella walked down the busy street of Culebra on their way to Holy Rosary, Billy always insisted that Stella walk on the inside. "Why?" she asked as she tried to maneuver herself to the outside lane of the sidewalk. "Because if a car splashes us, I'll be the only one who gets wet, so get back over here!" he yelled at her.

Grandpa Cárdenas often took Billy fishing at Woodlawn Lake, a small pond a few miles away from the house. Along the way, Grandpa told Billy stories that only a grandfather could. Particularly frequent were magical stories about Mexico and its land and people. Later in life, Billy would reflect on these tales and understand why his grandfather never denounced his Mexican citizenship, although he volunteered to fight for America during World War I. At the end of the day, back in the house, Grandpa told Billy and Stella bedtime stories about sailors lost in colossal storms complete with sound effects.

The real life storm Grandpa Cárdenas did not tell Billy about was his rocky relationship with Grandma Cárdenas. Billy wondered why Grandpa was sharing a bed with him and not Grandma, but at that age the thought was merely fleeting. Billy only knew the happier moments of Grandpa's life. He did not know that Grandpa and Grandma had had an arranged wedding back in 1923. He did not know that Grandpa had flaunted his money and had lost it all during the Depression. He knew nothing about Grandpa's business partner at Firestone manipulating him to the point where Grandpa ended up working for him. And he did not know that in the midst of Grandpa's financial problems, Grandpa's younger brother was murdered. Set in his ways, Grandpa Cárdenas turned to other women and the bottle as a way to try to escape his pain.

Billy knew none of this, but his mother knew it all. She had grown up with it. Mary Lou knew that her mother's arranged marriage to a man fourteen years older had never worked. Perhaps the problems stemmed from what made her mother different from other young Mexican-American women who lived in Texas in the early 1900s. Although highly traditional, Mary Lou's mother was directed and highly educated. She had graduated from high school and attended a technical school, Durham Business School, while most of her companions stayed at home, married early, and raised children.

Matilde, Mary Lou's mother, put up with her husband's affairs, drinking, and financial problems for two decades. A divorce was out of the question because of the strength and fear instilled in her by her Catholic faith. After twenty years of hardships, though, Matilde had had enough. She separated from her husband and Billy gained a roommate.

Grandpa Cárdenas was a stubborn man. For a long time, he had an extremely hoarse voice and his wife and others tried to coax him into going to the hospital. Fidel refused. Finally, the day arrived when he could barely breathe and he asked to be taken to the local general hospital. He blamed his condition on the cold beers he had gulped while cutting the grass. The hospital staff did a tracheotomy, allowing him to breathe, but in the process they discovered that he had cancer. Shortly after his diagnosis, Fidel moved to a Veterans Administration Hospital in Houston, where he passed away in 1954. At age ten, Billy had lost his roommate, storyteller, and confidante. It was the first time anyone close to him had died. It affected him deeply and he wept openly, even though, being a Mexican man, he knew that he wasn't supposed to.

Chapter 2

AS BILLY NEARED THE END OF HIS years in grade school, he became more of a loner and a mystery to his classmates and friends. He didn't shut himself off completely from his old friends in the neighborhood or his new buddies in school. He did, however, spend less time with them and never had a true best friend, someone with whom he shared everything.

Things had changed when Billy transferred to Holy Rosary. Friendships had an unwritten limitation beyond Billy's control. The makeup of the student body and the strict discipline of Holy Rosary made it difficult to develop friendships there. At H.K. Williams, the student body was almost completely poor and Mexican American. Classmates lived all around you. Billy's class at Holy Rosary was mixed. In his class of fifty students, there were twenty-nine Anglos and twenty-one Mexican Americans. Coming principally from higher-middle-class backgrounds, most of the Anglos lived north of Culebra Avenue on streets with regal names such as Westminster or appetizing titles like Brandywine. The Mexican Americans, for the most part, resided on less grandly named streets south of the Culebra Avenue border and came from families whose working-class professions included meatpacking, mechanical maintenance, and janitorial services.

During the school day and in school-sponsored activities, the Anglo and Mexican-American students mixed freely. Yet, once the final school bell sounded, Anglo kids returned to their neighborhoods and friends, as did the Mexican Americans. Only rarely did the two groups interact socially.

The children did not hate each other. At that stage of their lives, most of Billy's classmates did not make distinctions between brown and white. They were too busy being kids. If there was any conscious separation, it stemmed from parents who wanted to keep their offspring close to home and away from trouble. In the same way that Billy and his neighborhood pals' parents kept them distant from the evil influences of the Menchaca Courts housing project, some Anglo parents did not want their children in "those neighborhoods" on "that side" of Culebra.

This subtle isolation affected Billy more than it did his Anglo classmates. While his Anglo schoolmates lived close to each other, Billy and his sister Stella and brother George were the only children in their neighborhood to attend Holy Rosary. In addition, Billy was older than most of his neighborhood buddies. As the years went by, he spent more time alone, building model airplanes, reading books, and outgrowing the neighborhood.

The only meaningful, interactive time Billy spent with his Holy Rosary classmates outside of school was in sports, especially baseball. When it came to playing—basketball, football, and baseball—Billy was either a captain choosing a team or one of the first chosen. On the baseball field, with thick glasses sliding down his nose, Billy was a third baseman with a golden arm who batted third in the lineup. He consistently stroked singles, not home runs, in a steady manner that matched his later political triumphs.

Billy's athletic prowess made him one of the "in" crowd, part of the jock group. Throwing, running, and jumping got him into the club, but it did not get him invited to many birthday parties or camping adventures in his teammates' backyards. Only rarely was Billy asked and given permission to spend the night with one of his Holy Rosary classmates. In return, few Holy Rosary students saw the inside of the Velásquez house or the stars from Billy's backyard. Mexicans hung out with Mexicans and whites socialized with whites— those were the unspoken rules of Holy Rosary School.

၆ၮ ၆ၮ ၆ၮ

At eight years old, Billy tasted politics for the first time, politics accented with a heavy dose of *machismo*. It started one innocuous Sunday afternoon at his grandmother's home and quickly grew into an addictive ritual for the wide-eyed kid. Just like countless other Sundays, Billy's parents and siblings joined the rest of the Cárdenas clan at Grandma's for a hearty meal and a chance to reunite as a family. After the traffic finally slowed at the entrance of the tiny house and everyone was present, the stale air occupying the house was gradually transformed into a feast for the senses as Grandma's cooking filled the atmosphere with pungent smells of Mexican herbs and spices. Polite, casual chattering entertained the family members until the serious business of eating commenced. Then, the men triumphantly marched to the table, respectfully following the lead of Grandpa Cárdenas. Once seated, the women served their men—hot tortillas, sizzling meat, ice-cold beer, more tortillas, and more beer—stopping only when the men's seemingly endless appetites were momentarily quenched. Seizing a break in the action, the women finally grabbed a few morsels for themselves.

With the sounds of dishes and silverware clanging, the family's women cleaned up after the men, who staggered into the front room for their traditional after-dinner talk. This signaled the kids to exit the house and begin their customary outdoor rampage. On this occasion, however, Billy snuck into the all-male assembly and planted himself in an inconspicuous corner, curious for the first time in his life to catch a few threads of the mysterious topics that his grandfather, father, and uncles would discuss for hours upon hours.

As the men's conversation grew more heated and passionate with the guzzling of each beer, Billy's presence went unnoticed—or so he thought. Actually, the older men were keenly aware of Billy's intrusion and silently welcomed his curiosity. The free-flowing discussion had remarkable range, moving from current issues to nostalgic wartime memories to bitter tastes of discrimination.

Billy listened intently as each participant in the conversation offered something unique to the exchange. Grandpa Cárdenas, the elder statesman of the group, painfully recalled the depths of the Depression, warning his sons and son-in-law that they would only mature in the emerging age of prosperity—characterized by shiny cars, glitzy radios, and spotless new homes—when they recognized the difference between inconveniences and true problems. Uncle George, a free-spirited military brat, who loved booze and arguments, was brutally frank and opinionated on every topic the group covered. Uncle Fred, a dreamer and optimist, saw something beautiful in everything and countered the largely cynical views advanced by the others. Uncle Frank, a poor man's Socrates whose comments were usually questions aimed at taking the exchange to another level, forced the others to reconsider their untested conclusions. Uncle Nero, a man's man with an inherently tough demeanor, remembered how hard things had been when he was growing up as a kid. Uncle Gene, a calm voice of reason, listened more than he spoke, offering only occasional comments aimed at healing and building the group's consensus. (Years later, he would run for political office, baptizing Billy in his first hands-on campaign experience as a high school student.) Finally, Billy's father, Willie, Sr., a meat cutter, brought a union bias to every issue and stance the group entertained.

Willie's first taste of the men's late-night musings was contagious. Being present for these sessions became important to him for the balance of his youth. Although each conversation of the family men covered different topics, they were marked by a certain ritualistic character with recurrent properties. The deliberations typically dragged on until two or three in the morning, by which time the men either had solved all the problems of the world or ran out of beer, sometimes both. If it grew excessively late and the arguments had not peaked, Billy would stay for the finale, sleep over at his grandmother's, and wearily drag himself to school the next morning.

As the months and years passed by, Billy gradually spent more time listening to his male elders' late-night conversations and less time growing up like other children. Something inexplicable, a force he could not control, compelled him to join the fierce debates. He felt blessed to be given permission to enter a world of adult wisdom, developed over time by the combined life experiences of his working-class family.

Billy's engagements with the adult world of politics and ideas, beginning in grade school and continuing until his college years, deeply affected him. As an adult reflecting back on those gatherings, Velásquez recalled, "Frankly, politics is something I've loved all my life. And I owe a lot of that to my grandfather, Fidel Cárdenas. He showed me that politics is all-pervasive in life and therefore must be dealt with passionately. . . . I remember clearly the intensity of [family] talks [during my childhood]. My grandfather, my father, and my uncles would talk passionately and forever about politics of all kinds. . . . It was a remarkable time. It wasn't until I got into college that I found people who expressed as strong an interest in politics."

ᥬ ᥬ ᥬ

Indoctrinated with a fear of God, religious tension also played a crucial role in Billy's intellectual and political formation. At Holy Rosary (and later in high school and college), Billy was bombarded with Catholic teachings and ritual. On the positive side, he was taught to have a Christian sense of mission and to serve the community. On the other hand, the regimentation and rigidity of the Church was alienating to Billy's natural boyhood instincts. The Catholicism Billy grew up with left little room for self-actualization. His time and focus were filled with required masses, prayers before classes, dietary restrictions on Fridays and before communion, and constant attention to a litany of sins that covered everyone's actions. Religion was being pounded into him. The sisters at Holy Rosary filled Billy and the student body with the fear of God and scared them into believing.

There is no doubt that guilt was an overriding factor in most Catholic students' lives during the 1950s and early 1960s. Billy was no exception. Spoonfed an extra dosage of old-time Catholicism because he attended grade school before the liberalizing impacts of Vatican Council II, Billy was not sure what things he was allowed to do. With the nuns constantly outlining all the possible sins (including a general disclaimer that covered anything not mentioned specifically), it became stifling to do anything. Ultimately, hiding was impossible because God knew everything. These dynamics created imposing pressures, anxieties, and fears for young Catholic school children.

For Billy, the same was true, but it was the ever-worsening relationship between his mother and father that caused Billy the greatest spiritual and practical challenges. Billy's mother did not drive, so the family depended on his father for transportation. But Willie, Sr. was sinking into an increasingly undependable mode, both as a husband and as a father. He often inexplicably disappeared for long periods of time for reasons having nothing to do with work or other legitimate responsibilities. With Willie, Sr. mysteriously absent on many Sundays ("I didn't know dad worked on Sundays," Billy's baby brother George would say), the Velásquez family did not attend mass regularly. The nuns constantly reminded Billy what happens to good boys and girls who stray from their obligation to worship the Almighty Father. The judgments of the Church were necessary and logical concerns to Billy. Beyond his concerns about the judgments of God and the nuns, Billy also had to manage his classmates' and neighborhood friends' growing questions and conclusions concerning why he did not show up for Sunday mass. In time, this became a source of consternation for him.

౿ ౿ ౿

Owing to these and other circumstances, Billy's relationship with his father worsened as he grew older. When Billy was younger, Willie, Sr. would occasionally round up Billy, George, and some of the neighborhood boys to take them fishing on the Gulf Coast. They piled into the Velásquez family car, talked about all the fish they were going to catch, and traded stories about the monster-size fish that barely eluded them last time they were there. They never caught much, but they had a great time casting their poles into a body of water that seemed endless (in stark contrast to Woodlawn Lake in inner-city San Antonio, where they could easily walk around the whole thing in an hour's time). As Billy prepared for high school, the fishing trips with his father became mere fragmented memories of days long gone.

Willie, Sr. did coach Billy's Holy Rosary baseball team for a few years and led them to the Catholic schools championship. (Holy Rosary's team was so good, in fact, that the rest of the area schools put together an all-star team to play them and still lost.) But while most of Holy Rosary's players looked up to Willie, Sr., a former all-around athlete, Billy suffered from coach's son syndrome: in order to please his father, his fielding, hitting, and running had to be twice as good as the other players on the team. As teammate Mike White recalls, "If we had to do it right, Billy had to do things extra right." While his teammates could see what was happening, Willie, Sr. was completely oblivious to the problem. Billy himself did not let his father know how he felt. It was not until he exploded into tears after a game, begging his father to forgive him for an error he had committed, that Willie, Sr. realized what he was doing to his son. Billy, rambling almost incoherently, said that he would not do it again, he promised, because he knew how much it meant to his dad that he play baseball. From that time on, Willie, Sr. would advise others never to coach their sons.

The diminishing fishing trips and disturbing baseball stories were only minor incidents in the troubled father-son relationship, compared to the shattering moment Billy experienced one day at the age of ten. The day had started like so many in the past. Billy and some of his buddies went exploring on their bikes. They went through the same motions they always did, played the same games, told the same jokes, and followed the same trails. It was nothing out of the ordinary, but for some reason they all seemed restless. They decided to go somewhere different, someplace new and exciting. They found new streets to terrorize, unchartered trails, and a previously unknown ballpark where men came together and played serious softball.

Tired of just riding all day, the boys decided to stop and watch the men playing ball. As they approached, one of Billy's friends yelled out to him, "Hey, isn't that your dad and mom?" Not paying much attention to the twosome, Billy glanced over to a loving couple in the distance, only to realize that it was his father with another woman. He slammed on his bicycle brakes and crashed to a halt. His blood quickly began to boil. What the hell was his dad doing out here with a strange woman? Shouldn't he be at work or taking his mom out somewhere?

The rest of the gang had kept on riding, moving closer to the field, when they stopped, turned around, and yelled at Billy. "Come on, let's go, what's your problem?" Billy didn't hear a word of it. In his mind, all he could think about were the countless number of times his mother and father stayed up late yelling at each other. During these altercations, Billy, being the oldest, had developed the habit of gathering up the younger kids in the most distant back room of their home. As he tried to comfort his sister and brother, he caught random phrases that came thundering from his parents' room. They never made much sense because he only heard bits and pieces. Now the pieces started to fit. All those times his dad said he was late because he was working were lies. He was out with other women, laughing and spending the family's money.

The more he dwelled on what was happening, the more he wanted to go over and beat his dad. Yet, at the same time, the jolt numbed him and he could not move. Gradually, he heard his friends' voices becoming louder as they began to shout in his face to gain his attention. "Hey, Billy, are you deaf or what? Are you coming along?" Billy snapped out of his daze and decided to keep his hurt and outrage hidden for another time. His dad had not seen him. Pulling seniority as an older kid, Billy nonchalantly responded, "Look, these softball games are boring. Let's just head home, okay?"

Forty-nine kids joined Billy on Sunday, May 23, 1958, for the graduation ceremony at Holy Rosary Elementary School. When Billy started Holy Rosary in the third grade the school was still under construction. Now, the campus housed two school buildings and twelve classrooms. Billy's class was the first to have its graduation in the modern Holy Rosary Church. Officially opened a month earlier, the octagon-shaped interior with its simple decorations and semicircular seating arrangement forced the students to focus on the plain altar of sacrifice. It was here that Billy received his diploma after six years spent collecting seventy-nine B's, thirty-three A's, eighteen C's, and claiming history as his favorite subject.

Mary Lou's belief that Holy Rosary would offer a more positive learning environment than public school for her children turned out to be correct. While the public schools were merely processing Mexican-American students through the system with an eye to helping them obtain limited job skills, Holy Rosary enveloped its students in an ambience of high expectations for their scholastic and professional pursuits.

Almost three-fourths of Billy's class professed college aspirations in his middle school yearbook. Whether Mexican American or Anglo, the adolescents who graduated with Billy had impressive goals extending beyond their years: Clifford Krisak already had his eyes set on attending college at Princeton; John Kleibrink envisioned becoming a mechanical engineer; and Robert Dashek planned to become a physicist. Albert Alcocer and Mariano Venzar wanted to study medicine. George Davila saw himself as a pharmacist and Robert Zepeda planned to study architecture. In this environment, it was virtually impossible for young Billy to lack initiative or important plans.

Only a handful of the Spanish-speaking public school kids would get through high school, while graduating from high school was a foregone conclusion for Billy and his private school classmates. At a time when only one in ten Mexican-American students finished high school, nearly 70 percent of the lower-middle- class Mexican-American pupils at Holy Rosary planned to go to college. Billy envisioned himself in college studying to be an engineer.

The likelihood of achieving this vision rested with his choice of high schools to attend. In 1958, San Antonio's Catholic boys' school network offered a handful of choices to Billy, but there were two that especially attracted Billy and his Holy Rosary classmates: Central Catholic and Holy Cross. In his eighth grade yearbook, Billy's plans included going to Central Catholic High School. More than half the boys in his grade school said they were going to either Central or Holy Cross. Of those, Central was mentioned twice as often as Holy Cross. Almost all the kids who said they were going to Holy Cross were Mexican American while Billy and one other boy were the only Mexican Americans talking about going to Central.

Central was the largest and oldest boys' private school in the state of Texas. Its roots trailed back to 1852 when a group of brothers and priests called The Society of Mary devoted their lives to spreading Christian education. Located downtown on St. Mary's Street across from its sister school Providence, Central attracted a predominantly Anglo student body running the gamut from lower- working-class Mexican Americans to young men from wealthy families who did not send their boys to the more exclusive

Texas Military Institute or east coast preparatories. Its faculty, curriculum, facilities, discipline, and long-standing tradition gave it the reputation of being the top Catholic high school in the city.

Holy Cross was a new, smaller, less expensive, somewhat unknown school close to Billy's house in the heart of the Westside where most of the city's Mexican Americans lived. Founded in 1957, Holy Cross found itself surrounded by vacant lots, an occasional grazing horse, and unpaved streets. Partly because of its location and its lower tuition costs, Holy Cross lured many Mexican-American students and had a student population for which the racial disparity in family financial standing was not as stark as at Central.

There were not any sophisticated calculations made by Billy or his mother weighing the advantages and disadvantages of a Central versus Holy Cross education. Billy's mother wanted only one thing for her oldest son, the best, nothing else. His father still wanted Billy in a free public school, but Willie, Sr. had long ago ceded to Mary Lou decision-making authority on such matters. In fact, Mary Lou knew almost nothing about either school. She had merely heard other mothers constantly referring to Central as the best and that was all she needed to hear. She enrolled Billy accordingly, vowing to get him through Central and to continue developing her family as the upper crust of their working-class neighborhood.

Unlike the nonjudgmental eight-year-olds he met upon transferring to Holy Rosary, Billy and his Central High classmates quickly became aware of the financial and ethnic differences present in their school. His uncles always talked about discrimination and racism, yet Billy escaped grade school without any major episodes slapping him in the face.

This changed at Central. During his sophomore year, while black college students staged sit-ins at a segregated Woolworth's lunch counter in Greensboro, North Carolina, Billy knocked heads with racism in the form of the class bully. Nearing the front of the cafeteria line after the customary protracted wait, Billy and some of his buddies stood patiently for their turn to be served. But the class tormentor, an Anglo, standing behind them in the line, decided he did not want to wait any longer. He cut to the front of the line in front of Billy and his friends. Billy, an average-sized kid, quietly and firmly asked the bully to go back to his space in line. The bully spit back some prejudiced slurs about 'goddamn greasy Mexicans' and unleashed within the reserved Billy a sense of anger and disgust that was new to him.

With his tough guy reputation on the line, the bully challenged Billy to a fight. Still fuming, Billy accepted. After school, the two brawlers made their way to an area near Woodlawn Lake, the lake where Billy and his grandfather used to fish. The Central boys started to line up behind the class bully, not because they hated Billy, but out of fear of the bully's retaliation if they didn't. No one backed Billy. The overgrown high school kid taunted

Billy one last time before the battle began. Sure enough, the mismatched fight between the football stud and the passive kid in thick glasses lasted only a few minutes. No one could believe it! Billy destroyed the guy. Observers were stunned. How did he do it? No one really knew (and they never would).

As fiercely as Billy exited his high school cocoon, he retreated just as quickly. As the days and months passed, his concerns necessarily took on a more serious and responsible tone that separated him from the juvenile preoccupations of his school classmates. Billy's priorities were focusing increasingly on family and related financial exigencies that pushed him to grow up faster than he should have had to. Hard work and considerable personal sacrifice became his constant companions.

↜ ↜ ↜

Billy's first job was at the De Hoyos gas station the summer after his freshman year in high school. One hot, dripping, San Antonio day, he cruised seven blocks over to 23rd and Culebra and asked for work. De Hoyos knew the boy was too young and inexperienced, but he needed bodies so he took a chance and hired Billy part-time. For almost forty hours a week, Billy washed cars, fixed flats, pumped gas, and turned his "part-time" position into full-time cash. From then on, whether by selling subscriptions to the *San Antonio Light* newspaper, hawking pots and pans door-to-door, manicuring lawns at Trinity University, or sweeping floors at the public library, Billy incessantly worked after school and during his summers. It was a collection of odd jobs that continued throughout his high school and college years.

Normally, work ended in time for him to get home around nine in the evening (at least during the school year). Totally exhausted, Billy hauled himself into the house, sat for a quick meal, and dreaded the thought of the homework he still had to finish (especially Latin).

How thrilling could it be to be fifteen years old and feel like you had the responsibilities of a man twice your age? In grade school, his mother's screaming and his father's increasing disappearances suffocated Billy, but he never fully realized the toll his parents' relationship was taking on the family. In high school, Billy slowly began to understand that not only was his father painstakingly breaking his mother's heart, but he was also playing Russian roulette with the family's financial situation. Between his drinking bouts and womanizing, it became increasingly uncertain each week whether his father would bring home a paycheck, and if so, how much of it would actually be left for the family's survival needs.

Escalating tension between his parents and his father's frequent absences drew Billy closer to his mother in a way that fulfilled both of their needs. She needed her oldest son to be a protective big brother and almost a surrogate father to her younger children. Billy knew that someone had to pay for his education and help with things at home. So at age fifteen, without complaining about not being able to live the life of a normal private high school kid and without being told he needed to grow up quickly, Billy prioritized work. His earnings went to pay for his schooling, and he even gave his mother a little extra to spend on herself. Willie, Sr. thought Mary Lou was spending this money on frivolous items while she was actually hiding it away to help support Billy through college. In this moment, Billy stepped into the patriarchal role he would play for his family the rest of his life.

∽ ∽ ∽

The problems at home, mixed with his new obligations, made Billy even more of a loner than he had been in grade school. He became the guy nobody would miss at class reunions; the picture in the yearbook nobody would remember. He did not completely shut himself off from high school life, but it came close to that. He played some B team baseball his sophomore year and dabbled with football his junior year until he broke his tailbone. In his senior year, Billy bowled, an activity not considered a true sport by the few boys who faintly recalled Billy as one of the first to be chosen for their athletic contests at Holy Rosary. He was singled out for good conduct his first two years (an award given to quiet, obedient students who needed something under their picture when they graduated). And he joined the Glee Club his last year, not from some burning desire to sing but because it was the only way his sister Stella could take part. If Billy had not been available to drive her back and forth from rehearsals, there would not have been any way for her to participate.

The frantic pace of Billy's life, with the emotional roller coaster his family was riding, affected his grades and attendance. Scoring consistently well on his annual standardized exams, Billy nevertheless finished only sixty-first out of a class of 187 with an 83 percent mark. Under Central's grading system, Billy was considered average. His top grades were in the social sciences—world and American history, geography, and sociology. He struggled through Latin, physics, chemistry, and college math. One can almost track the times family problems erupted beyond control by examining Billy's record. Religion, as he would later tell his daughter Catarina, was considered an easy class, a sure "A". When problems were not flaming at home, Billy averaged an eighty-nine in religion. During the rougher periods, his religion grades plummeted to the seventies; one semester he barely passed. In addition, the pressures of home and his work schedule led to thirty-one days of absence and eighteen times arriving tardy in his last two years.

When Billy graduated from Central on Sunday, May 20, 1962, at the

Municipal Auditorium, he seemed to be another obedient, quiet, untroubled Catholic school grad on his way to college. His grades were fair. His teachers gave him solid threes on those elusive qualities of leadership, honesty, initiative, dependability, and so on (which meant he was average). He was not a natural leader, but rather a loner. He did not date or socialize much, although he occasionally went to school dances. While he had been a part of the "in" crowd in grade school, he had now vanished into the "lost" crowd. Billy was a tired young man whose responsibilities and pressures were slowly eating away at him. In the same way that events during this period were heating up in the South with the freedom rides, Billy was boiling inside from the turmoil of his family's never-ending search for peace. Not completely aware of the force building inside him, Billy silently grabbed his diploma and anxiously waited for the fall to arrive.

Chapter 3

ST. MARY'S UNIVERSITY, THE quiet, traditional bastion of Catholic male education in San Antonio, set in the heart of the Mexican-American community, celebrated the opening of another school year with a solemn high mass. Beginning its 111th year of existence on this hot, muggy September 1962 day, Billy and hundreds of other new students made their way into Holy Rosary Church. Faculty members, dressed in their colorful academic robes, strolled down the aisle like a parade of peacocks. It was like stepping back in time. Four years earlier, Billy had graduated from grade school in this church. Now, at eighteen, he was here again, commemorating the opening of his college career.

Father Charles Neumann, president of St. Mary's, stressed the importance of unity in his address and downplayed the budding activism taking place across the country on college campuses. Neumann, a middle-aged, slightly balding priest who wore wire-rimmed glasses, looked as though he had spent his whole professional life at the same small-town parish. Foreshadowing the turmoil of the late 1960s, Neumann told the students that while each of them carried the responsibility of helping to shape society more in line with the teachings of Jesus, it was more important to concentrate on their studies. After college, there would be many opportunities to help bring about change in a sensible, civilized, and Christian fashion. The journey they were about to commence was not one of emotion but, rather, one of intellect. Invoking the proper role of Catholic education, while thinly veiling an attack on the activist approach of some faculty members, Friar Neumann implored his student body and teaching staff:

> We have come here to teach and to learn; we have not come to campaign, to whoop up partisan strife, to crusade for group interest, to band together in clannish separatism. . . . Few of these activities have their place even in the periphery of university distractions; most of them are unworthy of a university man. By them we should be losing not just our time but also that peace of heart that alone enables the mind to study.

For President Neumann and many older administrators and faculty members, St. Mary's was in the business of turning boys into men who carried with them the mark of a Catholic education. They were there to become Christian gentlemen.

No one, including President Neumann, knew exactly how to define a Christian gentleman. Like similar elusive terms, one knew it when one saw it, but to precisely describe its essence was nothing short of impossible. One thing was definite. In August 1962, the definition of a Christian gentleman was slowly being challenged. The customary notions of belief in and fear of God, not questioning elders of the church, and focusing on saving souls divorced from the earthly realities people faced, were increasingly being redefined by the spiraling violence of the civil rights movement and the liberalizing forces of the Second Vatican Council.

One tool St. Mary's used simultaneously to welcome and subdue its new students was a mandatory freshman orientation course. There, Billy—now increasingly known (like his father) as "Willie"—and his classmates learned effective principles of study and the function of student government. They also digested, again, the customs, rules, and regulations of the university, and, most importantly, the objectives of a college education at a Catholic institution. These required sessions set clear boundaries of expected campus behavior. Willie, like most of his freshmen classmates, received only a satisfactory mark for the orientation course, worth one-half hour of credit.

Under President Neumann, St. Mary's did not support the Kennedy-inspired notion sweeping the nation that action for its own sake was good. Unbridled progress had to be tempered with wise judgment and selective movement. While much of the country focused on meeting President Kennedy's challenge to serve the country, the administration at St. Mary's University praised former President Eisenhower's cautious, almost lethargic approach to governance when Eisenhower visited earlier in the year.

෴ ෴ ෴

In many ways, going to St. Mary's was like an extension of high school for Willie. He still lived at home, which meant he did not have to adjust to living on his own or surviving in a different city. The students seemed the same. Many kids who he knew from Central Catholic and Holy Cross had also decided to attend St. Mary's. Several Brothers now teaching at the university had instructed high school students at Central. St. Mary's was a Marianist-run institution, as was Central. All of this made St. Mary's very familiar.

This aura of familiarity certainly had its advantages. Yet for Willie and other working-class Mexican-American students on campus, the benefits and standing of being college students were significantly mitigated by the larger social inequalities and constraints of the day. Catholic institutions were not exempt from these biases. Ironically, the same Central Catholic High School that created high expectations for Mexican-American students to attend college also insidiously limited their options. Central counselors pushed many Mexican-American students to go to St. Mary's because it was a trusted institution where they would not have to make as many adjustments. Paternalistically, they knew these kids were not world travelers, had not lived away from home, and did not have the money to attend expensive schools. Therefore, Willie's high school counselors prodded him and many of his ethnic brothers to stay with the Marianists. Willie and his Central classmates accepted certain stereotypes that made St. Mary's their only viable option.

To its great credit, St. Mary's did offer a uniquely supportive environment for Mexican-American students. Unlike other schools in the region that either did not have any Mexican-American students or only a handful, St. Mary's had an established culture of ethnic diversity. President Neumann spoke proudly of this atmosphere, saying publicly on one occasion:

> [L]et it be recognized that St. Mary's is very conscious of the two main cultural strains—Anglo Saxon and Latin American—from which the fabric of history in this region has been woven. She looks upon it as part of her vocation to bring together these two cultures in the person of her students as well as of her faculty—persons who should best represent, she thinks, what is best in the cultures that are theirs.

This forward-looking perspective led to Mexican-American students taking leadership positions in many traditional college areas: student government, political clubs, fraternities, Reserve Officer Training Corps (ROTC), the college newspaper, and sports.

Despite these attributes, Mexican-American students at St. Mary's in the early 1960s were extremely deferential. Professor George Benz, one of Willie's economics teachers, recalls the typical Mexican-American pupil of the time as not excessively forceful or argumentative. The respectful "yes sir, no sir" attitude they developed at home, in school, and on the field in mandatory ROTC, continued in the classroom. This was not an exclusively Mexican-American attitude. Most of the students at St. Mary's received their education in a fairly passive manner, but many of the faculty felt the Mexican-American students were, generally speaking, more acquiescent in class.

∽ ∽ ∽

Studying at St. Mary's did not change much for Willie, initially. Still living at home, he started each day as he had in high school—exhausted from work, numbed from late-night studying, lacking sleep, skipping breakfast, and late for the bus to campus. Living at home during college, though, was slightly different than high school. Willie's hectic class, work, and extracurricular schedules were constantly at odds with those of his sister, his brothers (a new brother, Ralph, had been added to the family a few years following George's birth), and his father. Only his mother saw him somewhat regularly. In many ways Willie lived alone in a house full of people. For the Velásquez family, Willie became the most constantly absent person they knew, just like his dad had been for him. Everyone in the family knew that when not at home he was either studying, working, or at some meeting, but no one was ever completely sure what specifically he did at any of those places. Whenever things flared up with his father or when he just needed complete silence, Willie would spend the night with Grandma Cárdenas, who lived close to St. Mary's.

On campus, Willie found himself accompanied by over fifteen hundred students, an all-time high for St. Mary's. Predominantly filled with Anglo and Mexican-American Texans, the St. Mary's student body also included a large contingent of scholars from St. Louis and sixty-six foreign students representing seventeen different countries. There were even a handful of black students at St. Mary's. While this was not entirely unheard of at Catholic colleges of the early 1960s, because of the university's status as a Southern school it was seen to be well ahead of its time in the racial diversity arena.

Willie's tenure at St. Mary's also coincided with a major breakthrough in the school's gender diversity. After 110 years of admitting only young men, the Brothers and Fathers of the Society of Mary decided in that year to finally admit women to grace the halls of their beloved institution. Willie and most of his male classmates praised this radical departure, which had been opposed by some stodgier faculty members. The first class of St. Mary's women graduated seven individuals and produced a column in the college newspaper called "Miss Quote," which sought to provide a female perspective on campus life.

Suffering from typical freshman year uncertainty about what major or profession to pursue, Willie experimented with assorted introductory courses, ranging from English to physics to economics. He earned mostly B's and C's. Theology was obligatory for all Catholics at St. Mary's, as was two years of service in ROTC for all students. Four more years of religion made Willie and his Catholic classmates cringe, yet it was a requirement they were forced to accept. ROTC, on the other hand, intrigued him. The precision of the units, the clean-cut uniforms, the twirling bayonets, and the potential of receiving pay for duty in his last two years of school captured Willie's attention.

During his second year of studies, Willie's interests focused heavily on economics and politics, particularly international relations. Taking courses in international trade and economics, economic development, comparative economic systems, and American and Texas government, he immersed himself in subjects that his grandfather, father, and uncles had introduced him to through their many late talks during his youth.

In his undergraduate years, there were three professors who particularly aroused, prodded, and guided Willie's blossoming preoccupation with economics and politics. Ken Carey was a government professor specializing in international politics, who also served as a faculty advisor to the St. Mary's International Relations Club. Carey, a tall, slender, serious-looking man who always wore bow ties, was a strong Democrat in the Roosevelt New Deal tradition.

Bill Crane was an outspoken, liberal populist government professor. Born in Bethany, Louisiana, Crane was one of the most personable and well-liked professors at St. Mary's. He made it a policy to know the first names of his students, he would later reflect, "so that when I [met] them in the halls I [could] speak to them personally, not just as another face in the classroom." A highly motivational teacher, Crane made no effort to shield students from his political leanings and, like Carey, his love of the Democratic Party. Once, the crude Crane, in the middle of class, accidentally passed gas and without flinching blurted out in a heavy drawl, "Excuse me, I just voted Republican." Crane's philosophy thoroughly repudiated the established Catholic cultural view of conflict avoidance and favored a hands-on approach to learning. His applied theoretical bent found substance in one principal device: mandatory political involvement. Crane required his students to involve themselves in political campaigns of their choice. This was Crane's way of forcing his students to touch the abstract hands of democracy. It was also a way for Crane to funnel volunteers to his political friends.

Willie and countless others received their first true political baptisms because of Crane. To be sure, Velásquez had been involved in his Uncle Gene's school board race as a sophomore in high school, but that was the experience of a young, smart kid helping his family. Now, in college, he was becoming a political activist and observer. Whether it was Albert Peña's county commission battle or Henry B. González's congressional re-election, with Crane's encouragement, Willie was quickly becoming a bellwether of Mexican-American politics at St. Mary's.

A third professor who had significant impact on Velásquez's undergraduate education was Dr. Ludwig Mai, a professor of economics, faculty co-sponsor of the International Relations Club, and Dean of the Graduate School. Mai, a worldly, old-time German progressive with a modern penchant for global interconnectedness, brought a refreshing perspective to worldwide economic and political development that challenged the conventional views espoused by so many of America's universities in the post-World War II era. Mai's teachings encouraged Willie to look beyond American borders for a deeper understanding of the world order. Although the United States was a superpower, Mai taught his students, it did not have the answers to all global problems. Willie learned to examine other countries from their own historical and contemporary perspectives, not solely from an American view.

Mai, a hefty, jolly man who resembled Santa Claus with a cigar in his left hand, also ran a Friday night speakers' program, the International Relations (IR) Institute. Held in a cramped auditorium that seated only two hundred people, the IR Institute gave students two hours of credit and direct access to ambassadors, diplomats, and other government, business, and political leaders from a host of nations, including West Germany and South Texas's closest neighbor, Mexico. The IR Institute exposed Willie to influential people, ideas, and issues to which he would never otherwise have been introduced. This exposure was a source of profound interest and motivation to him, which in turn provided real direction in his ensuing pursuits. Under Mai's influence, Willie found a major: international relations; a calling: the diplomatic corps; and a perspective: global.

∽ ∽ ∽

After classes ended near lunchtime, students at St. Mary's University went in two distinct directions depending on whether one lived on-campus or commuted. Commuter students saw the on-campus folks as wealthy people who did not have to work. If they did it was to bolster their spending money and not to pay for their tuition. As one commuter student bitterly recalled, "We went to work and they went to play." What surprised Velásquez and the other Mexican-American commuter students was that there was a small group of rich Mexican-American pupils at the school. Willie had learned how money talked when he was in high school. There, many of his Anglo classmates paraded to school in their glistening new cars, wore the latest, flashiest clothes, and attracted the most beautiful young women. Now, in college, there were Mexican Americans from South Texas, from cities like Eagle Pass and Laredo, who cruised in shiny, spotless vehicles, wore nice clothes, and dated pretty girls. Sure, they did not have as much cash as their Anglo counterparts who could afford to live off-campus in apartments, but they had the same attitude. Although he was not too crazy about their sometimes pretentious attitudes, some strange curiosity about these well-to-do Mexican Americans perked Willie's interest: He liked the idea that some of "us" could be like "them."

For Velásquez and the other commuter students, the St. Mary's campus was the place one crossed on the way to or from work, stopping in between to take classes. Without any substantial loan or grant programs at St. Mary's, working after class was the only way commuter students could pay their college bills. With university costs spiraling upward each year, these part-time jobs became permanent fixtures.

Working crazy hours while going to school was nothing new for Willie. Ironically, with college classes ending near noon rather than three o'clock as class had in high school, he found himself with more free time. He did not completely shed his loner tendencies at St. Mary's. He still did not have a best friend or a serious girlfriend, but he crept out of his shell enough to become involved in various campus activities and leadership positions. These activities made him one of the more active commuter students at St. Mary's.

One such activity was the Marian Guard of St. Mary's, a troop of hardcore ROTC cadets who represented the university in parades and at competitions. Dressed in white gloves, a khaki military shirt that made him look like he was headed for a safari, and a helmet that featured the St. Mary's mascot (a rattlesnake), Willie showed off his gun twirling expertise as judges rated his group's style and precision. Led by cadets carrying sabers that harked back to the days of gentlemanly warfare, the Marian Guard captivated crowds and won respectful nods from former veterans. Kids stood especially mesmerized, daydreaming of one day wearing the spit-polished boots, immaculate uniforms, and military paraphernalia of the impressive cadets. With his adrenalin flying high and his heart pumping violently, Willie scanned the smiling faces and felt surprising pride in his affiliation with the ROTC.

It was Velásquez's fixation with politics, however, that increasingly took up most of his free time. Encouraged by Professors Crane and Carey, and struggling to find his political identity, Willie became active in the Young Democrats. By the end of his second year in college, he was a seasoned campaigner. For many Mexican-American activists, Willie was becoming a person to turn to for important information and guidance. He was also becoming increasingly involved with the International Relations (IR) Club, leading a St. Mary's delegation that represented Algeria in a Model United Nations conference. His work with the IR Club was more than a passing interest. At this stage in his life, Willie was more an internationalist than he was a Young Democrat. He was convinced that his future was in diplomacy, not the Democratic Party.

Velásquez's activism during his first two years of college was essentially conservative. He was not out on the street, beating down doors and organizing his neighborhood for reform candidates. His inclination was more likely to head a campus-wide effort to re-elect Democratic incumbent Congressman Henry B. González than it was to support a political outsider. He worked almost exclusively with college students, getting them involved in safe political campaigns and international activities that prepared them for careers in the foreign service. There can be no doubt that Willie's political beliefs were liberal, but his activities were squarely in tune with St. Mary's civilized, nonconfrontational, Christian gentleman approach. When Mexican Americans were staging a "first uprising" in the small Texas town of Crystal City in 1963, electing a full slate of Mexican Americans to the city council and taking over the political reins of the community, Willie's attention was focused more on how Algeria was voting in the General Assembly of the United Nations.

Willie was not rejecting his Mexicanness. Like most students of this era he was struggling with an identity crisis. The Mexican in him and the collegiate in him were still not at peace with each other. Trying to find his niche, Willie was in flux. He explored different possibilities and directions hoping to find the right fit. The Mexican Velásquez and the collegiate Velásquez ultimately came together in Willie's role as a charter member of Lambda Gamma, a Mexican-American fraternity.

Only a small fraction of the St. Mary's student body belonged to fraternities, but their presence dominated on-campus life. The Greek organizations were primarily social outlets for out-of-town students, but some commuters joined. To most commuters, frats either did not exist or were a nuisance.

Willie had not thought much about fraternities when he ran into Carmelo Lucio, a grade school friend who had gone to the rival Holy Cross High. "Hey, some frat guys asked us to play intramurals with them," Lucio reported to Velásquez. "Do you want to join us?" Willie thought about it, had some free time, and agreed to play. After the season was over, he and the other Mexican Americans who had played in the intramural league started to think about joining a frat.

When it came time to pledge, however, Velásquez, Lucio, and the rest of their sporting partners faced a dearth of membership invitations. Except for the Rattler Club, which invited a few of them to join, none of the other frats expressed interest. At the time, they felt as if they had been excluded solely because they were Mexican American. With hindsight, Lucio was able to acknowledge it was more likely because "we weren't the right kind of Mexican. We didn't have money or come from the right family. We weren't sophisticated like some of the others. Nobody wanted us."

The bitter taste of this experience led them to start their own fraternity: an all-Mexican-American fraternity. Willie had not felt so attacked for just being Mexican American since his sophomore year in high school when he fought the racist class bully. He was especially motivated, therefore, to start a new group that could embrace people like him and his friends; and he was convinced that such a group would be relatively easy to organize on campus.

It was tougher than he realized. First, the upstart group missed the school's incorporation deadline. The next time around they were rejected because their charter was completed incorrectly and they were instructed to redo it. They finally got it right on their third submission, which was accepted. After two years as an unofficial off-campus fraternity known as *Los Caballeros* (Spanish for "The Gentlemen"), Willie and his friends were now authorized to do business as a sanctioned campus frat. Their official name now became Lambda Gamma.

Lambda Gamma, which most people continued to call *Los Caballeros* anyway, was originally made up of twelve members, half from Laredo and half from San Antonio. It was exclusively Mexican American, although it later admitted Anglos and blacks. Lambda Gamma was considered a rogue fraternity. Its members were seen as outcasts, and the other, predominantly Anglo fraternities looked down upon them. Like so many ethnic organizations in American community life, the Mexican-American frat created a reinforcing space for its members that was simply not available in other venues. Lambda Gamma members learned and grew together in critically important ways, precisely by finding a healthy balance between their various cultural influences and realities. Lambda Gamma members from the border town of Laredo showed their San Antonio brothers what it meant to be Mexican while the San Antonio contingent introduced their Laredo allies to life as a Chicano.[1] Both groups helped each other to survive in the sometimes hostile, non-Hispanic world beyond the frat.

In the end, Willie enjoyed the idea of starting an alternative fraternity more than participating in and building one. As the years wound down on his undergraduate career, he spent increasingly little time with his Lambda Gamma brothers. His time was now spent instead almost entirely on classes, work, and politics.

෴ ෴ ෴

A Western Union telegram to Velásquez dated May 1, 1964, from Congressman Henry B. González read, "Happy to advise that you have [an] excellent chance for summer employment in [the United States] State Department. If interested, please advise at once." Willie responded immediately. Of course he would welcome the opportunity to work at the State Department. Dr. Mai and the Friday night international speakers' program at St. Mary's had already convinced him that he wanted to be a diplomat.

Three days later, another telegram arrived. He had been accepted! Willie felt like the luckiest person in the world. His feelings of fortune and accomplishment were grounded in the hard realities of the time. In 1964, Mexican Americans were almost completely ignored by the national government and affirmative action was an idea whose time had not yet arrived. In this context, Willie was truly exceptional. In one fell swoop, he was transformed,

---

[1]"Chicano" is the reference younger Mexican Americans used to describe themselves during the 1960s and 1970s. To be a Chicano meant to live both in the world of Mexican and American culture, without being fully accepted or embraced in either. The term typically carried political overtones and was a prideful statement that recaptured the Mexican past for a generation of people born in America.

moving from working the previous summer as a laborer at the Alamo Cement Company and as a janitor at a local library to working as an office professional at the U.S. State Department in the nation's capitol. Now he had the real prospect to start the career he had always dreamed of. Velásquez was enthusiastically on his way to Washington, D.C. for the summer.

For its part, the State Department was not so enthusiastic about having summer interns like Willie. In fact, its doors effectively had to be pried open just to let Velásquez and others like him in. During the early 1960s, there was only a small group of Chicanos working in Washington, D.C. Frequently, they met and brainstormed about how they could help with different Chicano issues and groups. One of their ideas was to bring young, promising Chicanos to Washington for the summer to work in a government agency. They wanted to give these young Chicano future leaders the same exposure and opportunities that Anglo students from Ivy League schools had received for decades. They knew how Washington worked. By getting these students into the system in ways that would enable them to start developing contacts at an early age, it would be easier for talented emerging Hispanics to succeed professionally in the future. Since several D.C. Chicanos worked in the vast State Department structure, they decided to target this agency. Initially, the Department did not even want to entertain the possibility of a program. But constant badgering by the small band of Chicano Department employees finally compelled agency officials to allocate to Mexican-American candidates nineteen spots out of a total summer program cohort of seventy-one interns.

Even with the positions guaranteed, the D.C. Chicanos ran into an unexpected problem. They could not find nineteen Chicanos willing or able to leave the Southwest for summer employment in Washington. Fearing the distance and the unknown, many Mexican-American parents did not want their young sons and daughters living so far away from home. Other families simply did not have the money to support their kids' travel to Washington. The D.C. group reintensified its efforts and made an even stronger pitch to secure talented Chicano students, using all the existing networks they had accumulated over their years in Washington. It was through this effort that Congressman González's office was contacted.

Velásquez was one of the first names González thought of when these jobs were brought to his attention. Willie was a good kid. He had chaired the St. Mary's Collegians for González effort without any major disasters, funneling numerous student volunteers into the campaign. He was a quiet, respectable young man trained in Catholic schools. He was deeply interested in international relations. He had even escorted the congressman's daughter Rosemary to her high school prom. And he was from the district. He was a perfect candidate for the congressman.

After Willie received word of his acceptance, González told him to find other interested students because spots were still available. Velásquez tapped into his St. Mary's connections and persuaded various people to apply. When all the decisions had been made, St. Mary's students had five of the nineteen positions. Velásquez had saved small amounts of money from his odd jobs and he used this to scrape his way to Washington. Both frightened and excited, he packed his car, which barely ran in town let alone on the highways, picked up his friend Luis Segura, and dashed off to Washington. Velásquez and Segura drove nonstop, hoping to save both time and money. A few days later, the St. Mary's duo arrived in the big city.

It was only the third time Willie had been out of the state of Texas. The first time he ventured out at age fourteen was to visit family in Iowa for two weeks. The second time, after his senior year in high school, he traveled to Mexico with his friend, Narciso Cano. Most of the Mexican-American students coming to intern in Washington that year also had limited travel exposure, and almost none had lived away from home. These Southwestern youths were hardly the worldliest group ever assembled, yet they faced an important task: they were Mexican-American pioneers in the nation's capitol and their success or failure would greatly impact the future of these special programs.

Upon arrival, the students were given placements for the summer. Ironically, the State Department, having been badgered into accepting the interns, did not want to stigmatize them by calling them minority or disadvantaged. Instead, they were hailed as "Spanish-speaking students . . . the first group chosen for bilingual abilities to be given a summer program of employment in the Federal Government." Most were given positions at Latin American desks. Velásquez, however, was assigned to British and North European Affairs and to the Canadian desk, a place where French, not Spanish, occasionally floated by. It was a far cry from the San Antonio public library, where he had swept floors the previous summer.

The political climate in Washington during the summer of 1964 was buzzing with the upcoming presidential election. It was a tense political time with the civil rights movement and the Vietnam War both beginning to boil. The Civil Rights Bill of 1964 had been signed into law at the beginning of July. Riots soon erupted in Harlem, however, and three of the first participants of Freedom Summer, who had pushed not only for the end of segregation but for the political enfranchisement of blacks, met a brutal end. In early August, President Johnson announced that American destroyers patrolling international waters in the Gulf of Tonkin had been attacked by North Vietnamese torpedo boats.

Velásquez and the other interns were not only around when all this was happening, but also had the chance to talk to government officials, ambassadors, college professors, and visiting dignitaries about these developments. As part of the summer internship program at the State Department, Willie and the other "Spanish-speaking" students were included in numerous official seminars, speeches, and receptions. Meeting the likes of Secretary of State Dean Rusk, Attorney General Nicholas Katzenberg, U.S. Ambassador to the U.N. Adlai Stevenson, and Presidential Press Secretary Bill Moyers was an electrifying experience for Velásquez and his colleagues. Most of the Chicano students were so overwhelmed by the heady atmosphere they rarely spoke at the briefings, choosing instead to listen intently and relying on their Ivy League-trained Anglo counterparts to ask all the questions.

One place Velásquez did not feel intimidated, however, was in Congressman González's office. Velásquez and the St. Mary's crew spent a great amount of time visiting with the congressman. Willie, who was closest to González among the interns, would stroll into the office with his sidekicks. The staff members knew them and made them feel right at home. After waiting for the congressman to have some free time, the young men would be escorted into his private office. There, they listened to González intently as he lectured them at length about the issues of the day. The all-American kids absorbed everything, now and then smiling to themselves. Barely twenty years old, they were sitting in the office of their hero, exchanging stories and laughs, and feeling for the first time in their lives like they were part of the "in" crowd.

Thousands of miles away from family, normal food, and a sense of security, the Mexican-American interns relied heavily on each other for support. They traveled to the official events as a pack and spent weekends touring, playing, and partying together. They even stumbled through some embarrassing moments collectively. At the first elegant dinner party the interns attended, Willie, sitting next to one of his St. Mary's friends, Frank Herrera, could not figure out why the table was set with so many knives, forks, and spoons. To complicate matters, there seemed to be some unspoken time limit on the dinner. Between a few bites of green vegetables and a smattering of words with one's neighbor, the waiters came and took away in waves each unfinished portion of the meal. At each turn, moreover, they would take away empty plates and replace them with new ones. It didn't make sense. "What's the story? Is there another dinner going on after ours? Or do the caterers have another gig somewhere?" Herrera wondered. The tension was too much. They decided to stop worrying about it, and to catch a burger later.

Then there was the group picture with Secretary of State Dean Rusk. As Willie and some of the other interns gathered to be photographed with the secretary, an unusually quiet Mexican-American student noticed that a woman was standing in the way about to ruin their picture. He hurriedly asked her to move, thinking to himself, who does she think she is? "Yeah, move it," the rest of them chorused en masse. The mysterious woman turned out to be Mrs. Rusk.

The summer in D.C. was an important time for Velásquez and his circle to be exposed to the finer things in life: ballet, classical music, museums, theater, and opera. There were moonlight cruises along the Potomac and special screenings of artistic films such as "Beckett." These events were part of the State Department's efforts to introduce the "culturally deprived" Mexican-American students to the sophistication of the East Coast. Most of these activities were not free, but were available at reduced rates. Even with the discounts they received it was difficult to afford all of the outings, especially with the modest amount of money they were paid as interns. Willie was accordingly selective in the cultural events he attended. "La Bohème," he wondered. "What's that all about? Well, I guess I should go to at least one of these opera things." And he did. For the rest of his life, Willie told his wife, kids, friends, and anybody who would listen that "La Bohème" was the best opera ever created. It was also one of the few he ever saw. Outside of its story, music, or performance, it was the fact that this was Willie's first exposure to opera, a dazzling introduction, which made "La Bohème" both magical and unforgettable to him.

The work at the State Department was not exactly challenging and in many ways the "disadvantaged" interns from Texas felt like glorified secretaries. They mainly took care of the many small tasks that required treatment by their offices. They answered questions from visitors and occasionally replied to correspondence from embassies and government agencies in other countries. Frank Herrera recalls a top assignment he was given where he had to put together a memo on the likes and dislikes of the Mexican president and his wife for a trip they were planning to the United States. Willie's most memorable assignment, the only one he ever mentioned in later years, was updating statistical information on Ireland.

While his work was less than demanding, it didn't really matter to Velásquez. He was engrossed in the State Department's culture and ambience. He learned about past great British statesmen and the courageous stands they took at crucial moments in history. He learned about the parliamentary system and how administrations were directly responsible for their actions and could not hide behind a House of Representatives or a Senate. He smiled broadly as he read the prim and proper correspondence that referred to the author's most bitter enemy as the "Most honorable respected gentleman from Lancashire". And he loved it all. At age twenty, the unpolished San Antonio Westsider was slowly becoming an Anglophile, a trait he would carry with him for the rest of his life.

After the summer, Willie was utterly convinced that government service was for him. While some interns quit early or reluctantly stayed for the duration of the program, Velásquez was disappointed to leave Washington. Willie reported, in his State Department profile, that after earning a Masters degree in economics from St. Mary's, he planned to enter the government either in the foreign service or another branch. His summer in D.C. had changed him. He was now a man of the world. While he packed, he thought about all the stories he would tell—the famous people, the fancy dinners, the funny accents. He stuffed his memories into his tiny car and headed back home.

Beaming from his successful tour of duty at the State Department, Willie filled his plate largely with international offerings in his final years of college. Convinced that he was bound for a diplomatic career, the barrio Westsider studied political geography, comparative government, diplomatic history of the U.S., international relations, and elementary French. Willie had made up his mind that he would someday return to Washington and diplomatic work. But events all around, even if not yet evident to him, were taking hold across the nation and the Southwest that would play a large and unanticipated role in Willie's trajectory. Brewing in the reaches just beyond Velásquez's daily pursuits was an incipient Mexican-American struggle for justice that would call him and others of his generation to action.

᭐   ᭐   ᭐

In the wee hours of the morning on May 3, 1965, in the desolate town of McFarland, California, home to the largest field of roses in the state, migrant workers began their day as they had for ages: on their knees, hands bleeding from the tiny cuts of the thorns, quickly trying to move from rosebush to rosebush (they were paid by the number of rosebushes they worked on). Today was different. With Zapata's revolutionary cry echoing in his head, "It is better to die on your feet than live on your knees," Epifiano Camacho slowly, defiantly, got up from his knees in the middle of the Mount Arbor Nurseries and screamed out the command. *"¡Huelga!* Strike!"* Eighty rose grafters, all with the same black scarred hands, joined Camacho and walked off the fields. Three people from nearby Delano had quietly organized the first strike known as the "War of the Flowers" and the "Strike of the Roses," César Chávez, Dolores Huerta, and Gilbert Padilla. It was small, but it prepared the farmworkers for the large battle to come.

At the end of 1964, Public Law 78, the Bracero Law, died. The act of Congress that had imported millions of Mexican farmworkers into the United States was no longer needed because mechanization of farms had decreased the amount of workers required. The Labor Department stipulated that any *braceros* hired would now have to be paid $1.40 an hour. In California, the domestic grape pickers received 20 to 30 cents less than this amount. Filipino grape pickers in the Coachella Valley went on strike in the early summer of 1965 and won increased wages from $1.10 to $1.40 an hour within ten days. Up north, in Delano, six to eight hundred Filipino grape pickers walked off the field on September 8, 1965, demanding $1.40 an hour or 25 cents a box. The growers started to bring in mostly Mexican strike-breakers, known as scabs, to pick the already rotting grapes. Larry Itliong, leader of the Filipino farmworkers, came to César Chávez for help. Without the Mexicans, the Filipinos were dead.

On September 16, 1965, Mexican Independence Day, more than a thousand farmworkers crammed into the Catholic church hall in Delano, California, to vote on whether to join the Filipino grape pickers in a strike against the growers. With the flag of the farmworkers flying, blood-red with a black Aztec eagle with squared wings, César Chávez, surrounded by a portrait of the Mexican revolutionary Zapata, demanded wages of $1.40 an hour for the workers. The crowd began to scream. *¡Huelga! ¡Huelga! ¡Huelga!* The vote to strike was unanimous. Eleven hundred Mexican grape pickers walked off the job on September 20.

Chávez and the farmworkers marched into battle with a few thousand poor Mexican and Filipino grape pickers, $85 in the union treasury, and an extremely formidable foe. Some tactics used by the growers and their supporters were harmless, like the city council condemning the *huelga,* Chávez, and the "outside agitators." But, as the strike dragged on, the intensity of the attacks grew and came from many different angles. Strikers renting homes from the growers were evicted. Scabs and undocumented workers continued to be brought into the fields. Picketers were harassed and some were physically abused. Workers sympathetic to the strikers lost their jobs. Growers started fabricated workers' groups that claimed they wanted to work without union representation. Chávez and the other strike leaders were arrested, not once but many times. By the end of the fall, with the sun setting earlier and earlier each day and the murkiness of winter creeping in, the strike fund and the strikers were nearly exhausted.

Steeped in the history of past failed labor movements, Chávez knew that his small union and scarce resources would not be enough to mount an enduring campaign against the growers. So Chávez appealed to the consciences and checkbooks of those religious and civil rights participants who were working to make other aspects of American life fair and equitable. Traveling to different colleges and cities, Chávez implored those with experience in confrontations to serve as picket captains until the grape pickers could be trained and pleaded with those who had money to contribute whatever they could to the cause of the farmworker. This urgent request struck the emotional chords of groups like the Congress of Racial Equality (CORE), the Student NonViolent Coordinating Committee (SNCC), Students for a Democratic Society (SDS), W.E.B. DuBois clubs, and hippies of all stripes. It touched clergymen of all faiths, especially Protestant ministers and a handful of Catholic priests. It also reached American labor when shortly before

Christmas, 1965, Walter Reuther of the United Auto Workers led a march down the streets of Delano, pledged the support of the AFL-CIO, handed the strikers a check for $5,000, and promised to give them this amount every month until the strike was finished.

The farmworkers' strategy of appealing to liberals, civil rights activists, clergy, and labor not only brought in volunteers and money, it also spread the news of the plight of the grape pickers nationwide. Willie Velásquez, like thousands of other Mexican-American (and other) students across the country, broke out of his cautious student mold and became intellectually and emotionally attached to the struggle of these workers, following them through articles, television reports, and stories blasted on Spanish radio stations. As a Mexican American and a Catholic, Velásquez knew deep inside the importance of having Our Lady of Guadalupe, patron saint of Mexico, as the lead symbol for the farmworkers as they marched three hundred miles from Delano to the steps of the capitol in Sacramento. He also silently understood the protesters' need to complete their march on Easter Sunday. While the urban Velásquez had never directly experienced the life of the Mexican farmworker, he vicariously transported himself to the fields through the media and steadily became more enraged with the mistreatment of his people.

As Willie became sensitized to the condition of farmworkers in California, his studies and activities in his senior year of college changed. They took on a more Mexican nationalistic tinge and community-based approach. He studied human rights, Mexican history, labor economics, and social philosophy. He became involved with San Antonio State Representative Johnny Alaniz's campaign for Bexar county commissioner against Ollie Wurzbach, a Southern redneck who politely and proudly used anti-Mexican rhetoric to attack Alaniz as "one of them bad meskins." The repeal of the Texas poll tax by a three-judge federal court in early 1966 changed voter registration laws and the way campaigns were run. This shift put Willie and hundreds of other campaign volunteers across Texas into the local neighborhoods, knocking on doors, trying to inform and convince people that they did not have to pay anymore to vote. This was the first campaign Velásquez spent large amounts of time working in the community, not isolated on campus. He was finally seeing politics the way Professor Crane wanted him to experience it—at the grass roots.

Velásquez's young, naive, idealistic political views received a jolt of cynicism in the late spring when Wurzbach squeaked by Alaniz with a victory margin of only five hundred votes and a liberal county judge, Charles Grace, was thrown out of office. Both campaigns used piercing anti-Mexican and anti-liberal messages to ruin Alaniz and Grace. After successful voter registration efforts in the minority communities, Velásquez, along with most progressive politicos, believed the Mexican-American community would turn out in numbers large enough to counter the ethnic scare launched by the conservative candidates. Many did, but not enough to stem the tide. These defeats left a bitter taste in Willie's mouth.

The farmworkers' strike in California and his first tastes of community politics struck a chord in Velásquez that momentarily seemed to knock him off course. Yet, these blossoming feelings were not strong enough—at least not initially—to lead him off the path he felt destined to follow: the career of a diplomat. On Sunday, May 29, 1966, at St. Mary's 114th annual commencement exercises, Willie received his bachelor's degree in international relations. Crossing the same Municipal Auditorium stage upon which he had received his high school diploma, Velásquez's life seemed to be in order. He made it through college with honors. His relationship with his father, while not great, was at least civil. He was headed back to Washington to work briefly at the Agency for International Development in its Food for Peace division. In the fall, he would return to start work on a Masters program in economics. The extended study course meant another two years of school, but he was convinced that once finished, he would all but be guaranteed a generous position somewhere in the U.S. diplomatic corps. "Who knows," he thought, "they might send me to England."

As people congratulated Velásquez and asked him about his plans, he repeated his well-conceived intentions again and again: Masters in economics, Washington, D.C., the diplomatic corps. He mentioned these plans so many times that he completely believed they could not be altered.

Little did he know that just hours away, in the boiling sun of the Rio Grande Valley, circumstances were unleashing a force that would forever change people's lives, including Willie's.

Chapter 4

CÉSAR CHÁVEZ SENT REPRESENTATIVES to the major cities of the United States to organize boycotts of Schenley Distilleries' products in early 1966 as part of a national strategy to garner needed support for California farmworkers. Eugene Nelson, one of Chávez's four strike captains in Delano, was sent to Houston in February to organize boycott efforts there. Cracking a large Southern city was no easy task, but Nelson's frustrations ended for a short time at least when Schenley abruptly came to terms with the California grape pickers. In Houston, local labor leaders prodded an enthusiastic Nelson to consider staying on to organize Texas farmworkers in the Rio Grande Valley. Against the advice of Chávez and the other California labor leaders, Nelson traveled to the Valley and formed the Independent Workers Association.

Nelson had written a book recounting the toils giving rise to the Delano strike, but conditions facing Texas farmworkers were the worst he had seen. Where California migrant workers were fighting to increase wages from $1 to $1.40 an hour, seasonal farmworkers in Texas received only 50 to 85 cents per hour. Almost half their "homes" did not have plumbing or hot water. In Starr County, according to the 1960 census, 75 percent of the inhabitants—many of them seasonal agricultural laborers—lived below the poverty line of $3,000 a year and one-third earned less than $1,000 annually. This made the area one of the poorest in the nation. According to Professor Claudio Arenas of the University of Texas Department of City and Regional Planning, Starr County was "for all practical purposes, an underdeveloped country . . . similar in economic problems to African and Asian countries." Nelson, who was not a seasoned organizer, had stepped into a nightmare.

In June 1966, the Texas farmworkers began a wildcat strike against eight major cantaloupe growers in Starr County demanding an hourly wage of $1.25. Within a few weeks even the *Texas Observer*, a liberal magazine, declared the strike a failure. Being near the border provided the growers with an almost inexhaustible scab force of undocumented workers. Recent heavy rains had damaged the melon crop, moreover, so the growers had less to lose each day of the strike. On the second day of the strike, District Judge Woodrow Laughlin imposed a temporary injunction against union picketing

40

of the targeted farms. Undaunted, Nelson and a small group of obsessed strike leaders vowed to go on organizing during the summer, with an eye to preparing a second attack against the growers in the fall.

From the outbreak of the strike, the farmworkers combined civil rights tactics with Catholicism, holding several short marches that ended with the celebration of mass or a prayer. On June 7, approximately 350 strikers and supporters marched eight miles from Rio Grande City to the Catholic mission church in Garciasville to draw attention to the strike and offer a mass on behalf of the farmworkers. Ten days later, around two hundred people marched in single file behind the American and farmworkers' union flags and a large portrait of Our Lady of Guadalupe, the patroness of Mexico and the farmworkers. They marched to the steps of the Starr County Courthouse singing "We Shall Overcome" in both Spanish and English and carrying signs that read simply "Justice." These marches and rallies were used to counter the injunction against picketing. As the strike began to crumble, union organizers turned to these events as a way to keep farmworker issues on the public agenda.

Mirroring Chávez's approach in California, the Texas farmworkers decided to march from the Valley to the steps of the capitol in Austin to promote their cause and ask the governor to call a special legislative session to mandate a $1.25-an-hour minimum field wage. On July 4th the farmworkers marched from Rio Grande City to the shrine at San Juan asking God to give them strength and courage in the difficult battle they faced. Members of the Texas AFL-CIO, local chapters of the League of United Latin American Citizens (LULAC), and the Hispanic veterans' organization, the American GI Forum, welcomed the marchers at the end of their journey. Engulfed in the strength of unity and camaraderie, with their adrenalin at a pitch, the marchers concluded that their effort should go forward beyond San Juan. After discussing various options, the group elected to continue the march, extending its trek almost five hundred miles to the governor's office in Austin. The Independence Day demonstration was thus turned into the official starting point for an epic march that would end on Labor Day on the steps of the state capitol.

The idea of a two-month-long march during the hottest time of the year when most farmworkers had already left Texas following the migrant trail now seems absurd. Nonetheless, on July 11, 1966, a small group of farmworkers and organizers, facing scorching temperatures, continued the journey.

Over a month and a half later, winding their way through New Braunfels, the pilgrimage met Texas Governor John Connally. Connally, steeped in consternation over the farmworkers' plans to demand a state minimum wage increase, sought a preemptive strike. There, on the highway, he informed the marchers that he would not meet them in Austin, stating: "I do not feel as governor of this state that I should lend the dignity, the prestige, of [my] office to dramatize [the] particular [cause for which you] march. . . . I want to make that clear." But Connally, the shrewd Texas politician, did not fully realize the thrust of the farmworkers' march. It was not limited to an hourly wage of $1.25. It went well beyond that. In essence, the march was about seeking and securing the human dignity and respect of Texas farmworkers. Connally's actions symbolized the Anglo power structure's disregard for the hopes and needs of many of his state's Mexican-American people. The marchers—tired, worn, hungry, and disheartened, to be sure—were never-theless injected with new blood by Connally's patronizing attitude. With a new burst of spirit, they rallied, picked up their pace, and anxiously pro-ceeded toward Austin.

As Eugene Nelson and the Valley farmworkers began a desperate, but futile attempt to strike against Texas melon growers, Willie Velásquez was thousands of miles away, locked in Washington bureaucracy, starting his sec-ond summer of work with an international agency. The Velásquez who returned to the nation's capitol was different from the wide-eyed kid who had made his first trip to the big city just two summers earlier. The exaggerated fear and excitement of being in a completely foreign environment was replaced by a cool, calm sense of belonging. He was confident, driven, and focused. He knew what he wanted. He was no longer a bumbling undergrad. He had graduated. He had been part of an experiment to bring Mexican-American students to D.C.; now he was part of the Washington scene. This was not just another summer job sandwiched between janitorial and meat-packing stints. It was a stepping-stone to his budding career in the Foreign Service. As farmworker supporters urgently collected food, clothing, and medical supplies for the strikers back home, Willie collected data for the Food for Peace program of the Agency for International Development (AID). Still, the import of the Texas farmworker struggle was not lost on him.

After finishing his second tour of duty with the federal government, Velásquez returned to Texas just in time for the conclusion of the Valley farmworkers' march to Austin. He had caught bits and pieces of reports con-cerning what was going on while in Washington, but he was not fully pre-pared for the tremendous fervor surrounding the marchers that met him when he arrived back home in San Antonio. Willie vividly recalled his introduction to the farmworkers' struggle at the end of his undergraduate studies when the Delano strike in California grabbed the national headlines, touched the con-science of many Americans, and converted countless students to the farm-workers' cause. Although he was surely moved by the California grape pick-ers' battle, which also included a dramatic march to the capitol of that state, the actions there had been far enough removed from his everyday existence to keep Willie's activism to a minimum. His position would begin to change with the conclusion of the Rio Grande Valley mobilization in Austin. Five days after confronting Governor Connally on the highway outside New Braunfels, sixty-five hundred marchers crossed the Colorado River bridge into downtown Austin and made their way to the steps of the Texas state capitol. Joined by thousands of supporters there and at another Labor Day rally, the marchers heard speeches from César Chávez, Senator Ralph Yarborough, Congressman Henry B. González, and State Senator Barbara Jordan. Fueled by an aura of near invincibility, the farmworkers and their backers then returned to the Valley resolved to carry on the battle.

Amidst the fiesta-like atmosphere, Velásquez's enthusiasm and sympathy were tinged by simultaneous feelings of disappointment. Unlike the earlier California march, which featured *campesinos*[1] telling their stories at the capitol steps, Willie quietly fixated on the sad irony that the Texas march offered not a single opportunity for farmworkers themselves to speak at their own rally.

This concern for inclusion of society's most disadvantaged voices in the emerging struggle for Hispanic rights would become a hallmark of Willie's work for the balance of his life. He would forevermore show skepticism and disdain for community initiatives that lacked grassroots ownership and authenticity. He would never forget the sense that movement leaders were at their strongest when they let the people speak for themselves.

⌁ ⌁ ⌁

The familiar feel of a new academic year called Willie back to St. Mary's in the fall of 1966. He joined almost sixty other students of the school's Masters program in economics. Then considered one of the top fifteen graduate economics programs in the country for international affairs, Velásquez was one of only a handful of Mexican-American students in St. Mary's predominantly white department. The course consisted of thirty hours of classes plus a thesis. While most of the program's students attended part-time, during the fall of 1966 Willie carried a full course load.

Still active in the Young Democrats, Velásquez attended many political gatherings. Increasingly, these engagements featured updates on the worsening situation of the Valley farmworkers and their strike. Bombarded with reminders of the poor living conditions facing migrant workers in Starr County, Willie, the city boy, could not escape the reality that the unfolding struggle between worker and grower was happening just a few hundred miles away. His moral instincts pulled on him to become involved. So did several

---

[1] *Campesinos* is Spanish for "farmers" or "farm laborers."

of his political colleagues. Catholic church leaders and labor activists who Velásquez met during his years at St. Mary's had already jumped into the struggle. They roused him to get involved as a volunteer. Willie signed on with the farmworkers, exhibiting the kind of innocence and blind devotion seen in many white liberals who volunteered to work in black civil rights organizations. In fact, he had no idea what he was getting himself into.

Willie's volunteer work on behalf of the farmworkers involved him in controversial activities for the first time in his college career. Many students laughed, jeered, and patriotically told Velásquez and his comrades to halt their communist-backed activities. Such resistance strengthened his resolve to support the farmworkers' campaign. Increasingly, Willie pursued field activities on behalf of the budding farm labor union, delivering food and supplies to Valley *campesinos* and their families. It was through these journeys that the sheltered city boy received a different political education than had been offered through the International Relations program he completed in college. Spending time with the strikers, Willie witnessed the stark realities of their condition and the tormenting treatment to which they were subjected by the Texas Rangers and local law enforcement officials. These experiences greatly influenced Velásquez. His formerly abstract concerns now had concrete expressions. It was akin to a religious experience for him. He could not believe the injustice he witnessed in the Valley and he vowed to do something about it.

৵ ৵ ৵

The Valley farmworkers' strike caused Willie to reevaluate the institutions, people, and ideas he had grown up with and forced him to take stands on issues that he had avoided in the past. His strong Catholicism, fostered by his Catholic school training, had generated an inconsistent dualism over the years. At one level, the teachings and culture of Catholicism told him to confront the injustices of society and smash them; at another level, they kept his people down, telling them, in effect, to accept their position in this world as they would be rewarded in the afterlife for their earthly troubles. Willie's progressive political views made him lean toward activism, but his mainstream activities never required him to grapple seriously with these opposing positions, until now. Consumed by the plight of the farmworkers, it was increasingly easy, under the circumstances, for Willie to reject the acquiescent traditions of Catholicism and to favor instead a more activist ideology of social change.

Velásquez was confident that the Church would ultimately follow suit, to support a society more in line with the teachings of Christ. After all, it was the Catholic Bishops' Committee's relief effort, "Operation Foodstuff," that had initially brought Velásquez and other starry-eyed college kids directly in contact with the farmworkers.

San Antonio Archbishop Robert Lucey had ardently championed the notion of Christian social responsibility in South Texas since his elevation to archbishop in March 1941. Lucey, a man ahead of his time, had recently been described by *Time* magazine as "the most socially conscious New Dealer in the Roman Catholic hierarchy." In the 1940s and 1950s, he championed the causes of Mexican Americans and migrant workers when most of America had ignored these groups. In 1944, Lucey pushed for the creation of a Catholic Church organization to tackle the growing problems of Spanish-speaking communities. The following year, he convinced the American Catholic Church hierarchy to approve his ideas and they named him executive director of the newly formed Bishops' Committee for the Spanish Speaking. The initial plan envisioned a roving headquarters that would spend two years in each of the seventeen dioceses of the Southwest. Instead, the Bishops' Committee never left the state of Texas and the scrutinizing eye of Archbishop Lucey.

The Bishops' Committee's original thrust was more religious and social, but it quickly became entangled with politics. The Valley farmworkers' strike brought the Catholic Church and Lucey immediately into the thick of the struggle. From the onset, Luccy's priests were participating in rallies, celebrating masses for the strikers, and leading marches to the Rio Grande City courthouse steps. The Bishops' Committee also organized "Operation Foodstuff" to transport thousands of pounds of groceries and other necessities to the strikers, thus providing critical backing for the workers' campaign.

Velásquez's direct engagement with the farmworkers' strike put him directly in contact with Lucey's priests and the Bishops' Committee. It was here that Willie saw Lucey and the Catholic Church taking a prominent role in the Valley effort. However, as time progressed and the intensity of the farmworkers' situation heightened, the aging archbishop exhibited a shifting set of priorities. No one who knew Lucey could reasonably question his solid, personal commitment to social justice, but at seventy-five years of age, his concerns for farmworker rights began to be outweighed by his belief that a handful of overzealous church representatives supporting the struggle were increasingly threatening Catholic institutional authority and hierarchy. On January 13, 1967, Lucey fired or, in the vernacular of the Church, "transferred" three persons whose pro-farmworker and pro-labor actions had become potentially destabilizing to his authority. Father Sherrill Smith was removed from the Social Action Department and was sent to a parish at the edge of town. Father Henry Casso was removed from his position as executive secretary of the Bishops' Committee and placed in a new position to fight urban problems—without an office or a budget. Erasmo Andrade, a Bishops' Committee field representative hired by Casso to help with the farmworkers' strike, was simply ousted.

Velásquez and other activists in San Antonio were stunned and disappointed by Lucey's actions. As Steve Privett writes in his work on Lucey: "It appeared that Lucey's proven courage to speak out against injustice was not matched by an equal tolerance for those who shared the courage of his convictions but opted for a more active modus operandi, with which the Archbishop was not in total agreement." In fairness, while arguably hasty and unnecessary, the Church leader's actions were not entirely irrational or unpredictable in their historical context.

When Lucey's activist priests had initially invaded the Valley in early June 1966, the diocese of Brownsville still had not replaced Bishop Adolph Marx, who had died the previous fall. By the end of June, however, Humberto Medeiros, previously assigned to Fall River, Massachusetts, had been installed in the position. Medeiros quickly opined that the confrontational approach used by Lucey's San Antonio priests was exacerbating the already tense situation in the Valley. He therefore politely asked Lucey to keep his priests at home. Respecting the bishop's wishes, Lucey promised to keep them out of the area. Bishop Medeiros's concerns were tied directly to Lucey's decision to reorganize the Bishops' Committee, which he thought would address the problem. On February 1, however, five San Antonio priests, including Smith and Father William Killian, reappeared in the Valley at a protest event and were promptly arrested along with five activists for disturbing the peace.

Lucey exploded. He decided to punish Smith and Killian by sending them to Via Coeli, New Mexico, a remote retreat facility for wayward priests who suffered from alcoholism, drug addiction, and sexual problems. On February 5, the Valley Farm Workers Assistance Committee, led by the jilted Erasmo Andrade, picketed the chancery and Lucey's home in protest of Smith's and Killian's banishment. Rejecting the advice of Casso and Smith to not picket, the angry group showed their disgust for Lucey by carrying protest signs and chanting antagonistic slogans such as "Lucey, How Many Pieces of Silver?" and "Lucey, Betrayer of Mexican Americans!"

With these controversies spiraling out of control, many members of the Catholic clergy felt that the Church in South Texas was self-destructing. Social activists, especially Mexican Americans, felt the archbishop had abandoned the farmworkers. Sensing things slipping out of control, Lucey turned to Father John McCarthy, a veteran of assorted War on Poverty programs, to get the Bishops' Committee effectively back on track working with the Spanish-speaking community nationwide, not just in Texas. McCarthy, who did not speak Spanish, saw the Bishops' Committee as a paternal organization of well-meaning Irish clerics. They were older priests who sometimes had problems dealing with others as intelligent equals. McCarthy recognized a changing attitude in the leadership roles of minority-focused organizations. Blacks were beginning to throw whites out of authoritative positions at their institutions and McCarthy sensed that the time of whites serving in those capacities had appropriately passed. Early in the new director's tenure, Father Bill Quinn, the Bishops' Committee field office representative in Chicago, asked McCarthy what program he planned to follow. Joking, yet essentially serious, McCarthy quipped, "I want to do three things. Fire you. Hire two Hispanics. And quit."

Velásquez's faith in the Catholic Church of South Texas was badly shaken during this period. Working closely with the Bishops' Committee under Casso and Andrade, he was bombarded with anti-Lucey sentiment. Andrade, whose perspective was clouded by his deep commitment to the farmworkers' movement, blasted Lucey's actions as nothing less than a betrayal of the Mexican-American people. Willie heard the criticisms of Lucey, to be sure, but his developing political pragmatism told him the Bishops' Committee still represented an important resource base that could effectively support Mexican-American community advancement. He continued to work closely with the Bishops' Committee even after Lucey had cleaned house. Andrade, unwittingly predicting the future, could only advise Velásquez to stay out of the archbishop's way.

The Valley farmworkers' strike took on a more professional look when César Chávez sent Reverend Jim Drake of Porterville, California and Gilbert Padilla, first vice president of the United Farm Workers Organizing Committee, to the Texas Valley in early 1967. Both men were veterans of the successful Delano strike and shared the belief that Eugene Nelson's failed attempt at a Valley strike in the summer of 1966 was the result of poor preparation. "To be honest," Drake reputed on arrival, "we at Delano have been somewhat lukewarm toward the movement [here], but [now] we're placing greater emphasis on Texas. In effect, we're starting the strike all over again."

The "new" strike promised to take the necessary steps to get the job done correctly. They worked on providing the striking workers and their families with services such as a credit union and insurance programs. They collected data on the history, operations, and income of one particularly egregious producer—La Casita Farms—to show Texas and the nation the insidious relationship between high profits and abused labor in the fields. In turn, they began a targeted boycott aimed only at La Casita and set up satellite boycott offices in Austin, Dallas, Houston, Corpus Christi, and San Antonio. Drake and Ernie Cortés, a graduate student from the University of Texas at Austin, organized these statewide offices and supporting leadership committees. Cortés, who had graduated from Central Catholic High two years before Willie, hired Velásquez to be the area boycott coordinator for San Antonio. Cortés wanted Willie because he was the most enthusiastic and supportive of the San Antonio college students volunteering with the farmworkers. Willie's job was to persuade community members to go to their local grocery stores and convince their produce managers to boycott La Casita Farms' products. He was thrilled to be working for the farmworkers in an official capacity and wore his five-dollars-a-week strike salary like a badge of honor.

∽ ∽ ∽

By the time Willie started his second semester of graduate studies, economics was already taking a back seat to his newfound activism. Against the backdrop of St. Mary's sleepy, civilized campus, Willie met four other Chicano activists whose heated talks of politics over cold beers would lead to the creation of the Mexican American Youth Organization (MAYO). MAYO would become one of the Chicano community's most important groups during this period, galvanizing young Mexican Americans in an explosion of activism and controversy that would rock conservative Texas and the staid Southwest.

The first of Velásquez's collaborators in MAYO's establishment was Ignacio "Nacho" Pérez. Pérez had recently come to be well known to Willie and others for spreading the gospel of the farmworkers to politically untainted St. Mary's students at Young Democrats' meetings. In 1965, Nacho's life changed when he heard Dolores Huerta, national vice president of the United Farm Workers (UFW), meticulously describe the desperate fight of the migrant worker. From that point forward, he fundamentally committed himself to the farmworkers movement and a life of social justice advocacy. On the second day of the Rio Grande strike, Pérez went down to see what was happening and did not come back, choosing instead to stay and help run the Bishops' Committee's warehouse for the strikers. Now he was back in San Antonio helping to raise funds for the farmworkers.

A second MAYO collaborator was José Angel Gutiérrez, a feisty, strident, self-assured first-semester graduate student in political science. Gutiérrez, a graduate of Texas A&I, had spent one semester at the University of Houston Law School before quitting and shifting his focus to his true love, politics. Raised in a small-town climate, he was the golden boy in high school—student body president, debate champion, and vice president of the Catholic Neumann Club. He broke out of his conventional shell, however, when he started college. There, under the tutelage of Charlie Cotrell, a young, dynamic, progressive A&I professor, Gutiérrez pursued a healthy menu of radical political activities to complement his studies.

Velásquez and Gutiérrez immediately sized each other up upon meeting. José Angel was by far the more aggressive and progressive of the two. He had participated in poll tax drives and drafted propaganda pieces for the mini-revolution that occurred in Crystal City when a slate of Mexican-American outsiders swept the city elections in 1963. Willie had dabbled in poll tax drives and after the repeal of the tax in 1966 had gone door to door registering voters in the barrios, but always in support of safe, moderate candidates. Gutiérrez had run for student body president at Southwest Texas Junior College and was tagged a racist for trying to cultivate the Mexican-American student vote. Velásquez, who had represented his fraternity on the St. Mary's student council, emphasized his involvement with the farmworkers. José Angel informed Willie that he was not at St. Mary's to be a part of a "rah rah" Catholic Joe College scene. He was there to get his degree and wake up a few folks. Willie, with flashes of his comparatively conservative past zapping through his mind—ROTC, Marian Guard, Model United Nations, the State Department—quietly nodded and then asked José Angel if he had told him about his work with the farmworkers.

A third cofounding member of MAYO with Velásquez was Mario Compeán, a product of one of the Westside barrio enclaves from which Willie's mother had tried to keep her son away during his youth. Compeán, small in stature and nonaggressive in style, was only beginning college in his late twenties when he got a call from Willie inviting him to attend a meeting. Compeán, who had the least amount of political experience of the five original MAYO members, had just recently met José Angel Gutiérrez. Gutiérrez had also asked Compeán if he wanted to attend a meeting. Gutiérrez's idea was to encourage Compeán to get involved in community organizing. Mario thought Willie's call was about the same meeting José Angel had mentioned. Compeán was thus caught off guard when the meeting he ended up attending turned out to be a farmworker assistance gathering led by Velásquez at the Bishops' Committee offices.

Compeán, who came from a migrant background and had been religiously following César Chávez and the farmworkers both in California and Texas, listened intently as Willie talked about assorted tactics to assist the strike—joining illegal picket lines, soliciting food and supplies, and stopping trucks and trains that carried produce from the Valley to the terminal market on South Zarzamora Street. Compeán, the novice activist, wholeheartedly jumped into the local efforts, but was unable to travel with supply-and-support caravans to the Valley because of work responsibilities and the inevitable challenges of his first year in college.

Juan Patlán was Willie's fourth co-founding member of MAYO. Patlán, considered to be the least ideological and most pragmatic of the organization's founders, had moved to San Antonio in January 1967 to work for the city. Upon arriving he ran into his old friend, José Angel Gutiérrez. Patlán and Gutiérrez had known each other since high school and together had attended Southwest Texas Junior College in Uvalde. Gutiérrez introduced Patlán to Velásquez, Compeán, and Pérez. Patlán, known as the technocrat of the group, was older, married, and out of school. This meant he could not easily spend time with the upstart group of activists. Nonetheless, in time, Patlán spent countless hours with them, plotting and strategizing MAYO's tactical development.

Inside the Roundtable bar, a college hangout just a few blocks away from St. Mary's University, Velásquez, Pérez, Gutiérrez, Compeán, and Patlán quenched their thirst and endlessly contemplated the burning political issues of the day. Except for Gutiérrez and Patlán, the five activists did not really consider each other "good friends." They did not get together just to have a beer, tell jokes, or catch up with one another. Rather, they came together to talk politics. They all suffered from activist's disease: incessant and tumultuous political activity. Their days became packed with meetings, discussions, picketing, demonstrations, drinking, dreaming, organizing, and more meetings. It was 100 percent politicking: Nothing else. Their exchanges took place everywhere. At the Fountain Room bar. At another bar. In the car. At somebody's house. In the car on the way to another bar.

These initial freewheeling sessions had natural distractions and limitations, however, which convinced the young activists to continue their discussions in more stable environments. The five highly motivated politicos decided to move their meetings away from bars and into more sober surroundings. Assembling at Woodlawn Lake, in the downtown park across from Santa Rosa Hospital, or in designated garages and backyards, they resumed their diatribes in a quasi-study group atmosphere.

Their discussion sessions were loosely structured get-togethers which especially featured exchanges about relevant books or articles they had recently read. In each case, they dissected, refined, and interpreted the presented ideas. Velásquez and Gutiérrez usually took the lead, suggesting what books to read and what topics to address. Gutiérrez tended to introduce more politically charged writings, such as those of black nationalists like Stokeley Carmichael, Eldridge Cleaver, and Malcolm X. Velásquez favored practical "how-to" organizing manuals, political classics such as Orwell's *Animal Farm*, and historical accounts of Mexico and the Aztecs. All of the group's members religiously followed the latest developments of the Valley farmworkers' strike and kept abreast of other Chicano actions taking place locally and across the Southwest. The quintet's discussions were not completely abstract; they often revolved around a standard set of questions that were intended to move the group toward greater concreteness and clarity: Who are we? Where have we been? Where are we going? Where can we go? How can we get there faster?

The MAYO five's discussions, debates, and often volatile relationships were largely informed by the diverse backgrounds that they represented. Willie, at one extreme, was mainly informed by the conventional touch points of his working-class, urban origins: a belief in liberal democracy, the core teachings of a socially activist Catholic Church, trade unionism, and a Democratic Party politics which made room for Mexican-American elected officials. José Angel, at the other extreme, was most heavily influenced by his early experiences in Texas's rural areas, which were characterized by exclusively Anglo-boss politics, the visceral suppression of Mexican people by the Texas Rangers, and a more dominating and oppressive rather than empowering Catholic Church. The other members of the quintet fell in between the poles represented by Velásquez and Gutiérrez, depending largely on their early life circumstances and experiences with institutional authority.

MAYO's founders shared common beliefs, thoughts, and experiences that cemented their determination to better things for Mexican Americans. They were furious with the debilitating conditions facing their people and restless with the inadequate pace of social change taking place in their communities. They were fiercely committed to speeding up the process of change and arrogant and idealistic enough to believe they could eliminate many, if not all, of the intractable problems that plagued the barrios and rural areas of South Texas. Their frustrations produced hard-core rhetoric, but little in terms of concrete solutions. The organization's five impatient founders were influenced and informed by the strides being made by the black civil rights movement, but their zealous identity as Chicanos directed their focus strictly to Chicano activities and not the black and antiwar campaigns sweeping across the nation's many college campuses. While they were more well-educated than the previous generation of Mexican-American leaders, they had all been slapped by discrimination in its various forms and they intuited that dramatic new efforts would be required in the years ahead to fully empower Americans like them. It was these commonalities that created an unwritten bond between the founders of MAYO that would carry them through the turbulent decades that were the 1960s and the 1970s.

At a time when strident calls for black power infiltrated the self-affirming yet separatist rhetoric of many civil rights crusaders, Velásquez steered a more liberal, mainstream course. Gutiérrez, Pérez, and especially Compeán, were enthralled by the bold, shocking statements of the Black Panthers and the Student Nonviolent Coordinating Committee. Patlán, ever the diplomat, tended quietly to side with Velásquez. A pattern quickly developed. As tensions mounted and discussions became lost in the undecipherable language of emotion, it was usually Velásquez and Gutiérrez who took to the center of the debate. As Gutiérrez recalls: "We went at each other like . . . roosters [in] flurries of skirmish and then we'd settle down."

After months of irregularly scheduled confrontational meetings, the group of five decided to come up with a name and a direction for their nascent organization. Gutiérrez suggested adopting a provocative and radical name because he wanted to acknowledge publicly the militancy boiling within the Mexican-American community. Other MAYO members rejected this reasoning and sought a less conspicuous identity. Pérez recommended that the group name itself the *Liga de Estudiantes y Obreros Nacionalistas* (LEON), Spanish for the National League of Students and Workers. LEON did not generate sufficient enthusiasm among the MAYO five, however, to secure its adoption. Velásquez suggested the name Mexican American Youth Organization (MAYO). Harking back to his Catholic school days, Velásquez felt that MAYO rolled off the tongue with the same innocence as the Catholic Youth Organization (CYO) with its images of polite little boys playing sports. The harmless MAYO label gave the organization's founders an innocuous identity from which to begin their work. They embraced this name, but realized that its anticipated cover might not last very long once they started promoting more militant agendas for social change.

In fact, conceiving the name MAYO was relatively easy. Deciding on a precise plan of organizational action was a more complicated matter that the charter members, in large part, accordingly chose to ignore. They did eventually incorporate, draft bylaws, establish membership requirements, and assemble a board of directors. They also effectively projected a certain division of labor and leadership roles. Newspaper accounts, for example, typically described Gutiérrez as the spokesperson, Velásquez as the fund-raiser, Patlán as the membership coordinator, and Pérez and Compeán as the grassroots organizers. These depictions of rigid organizational structure and responsibility exaggerated MAYO's formality. In fact, no one had official titles or clear job descriptions in the beginning. Such institutional conventions were downplayed in favor of raw motion. Scorched by a burning desire to correct all of the world's injustices, the impatient young MAYO founders boldly and naively craved to take on every problem that faced the Chicano community. They did not have the inclination or the discipline to set priorities. This created a hodgepodge approach for the MAYO five that often moved them from one issue to the next, without ever having completely addressed the last problem on which they had worked. In essence, then, MAYO began as a mercurial group of on-call Chicano activists prepared to do battle wherever their passions took them, and absent a great deal of attention to strategy or sustained investment.

During the spring semester, Velásquez and his MAYO associates were expelled from campus for leafleting on behalf of the farmworkers. Gutiérrez, Compeán, and Pérez had quickly developed a reputation on campus as diehard radicals because of the polemical stances which they aired frequently and without solicitation in the student cafeteria. Perceived by most St. Mary's students as zealots, they were usually ignored. Velásquez, interestingly, was not typically identified as an extremist. People who had spent their undergraduate years with Willie still pictured him as someone who marched with the ROTC Marian Guard, not the farmworkers.

Heightened tensions in the Valley farmworkers' strike marked the summer of 1967. Things worsened for the farmworkers as the Texas Rangers stepped up their indiscriminate arrests and "accidental" beatings of the strikers. Television crews documented the fear and rage that was present in the suffocating, sweltering Valley air. The strikers tried different tactics to hurt the growers. One especially bold tactic they considered was stopping the trains that took produce from the Valley to other locations for distribution.

At a huge mass meeting in Rio Grande City, with all the statewide support committees attending, the strikers discussed blocking the trains. The Rangers made it clear that anyone impeding the railroads would be dealt with in the strictest possible terms. Notwithstanding the imposing prospect of facing the full force of the Rangers' response, the strikers, feeling almost invincible in the righteousness of their cause, decided to proceed with a train stoppage strategy. At the point of decision, a call came for volunteers who would take the lead to see the new approach through. The proposed tactic would require a small handful of strike supporters positioning themselves in front of transport trains and establishing a human blockade that would hopefully prevent the trains from leaving their loading points. An eerie silence filled the room as a sudden hesitation overcame the action's planners. For a moment, it seemed as though the proposed train stoppage would not occur after all. Then, suddenly filled with a burst of immortality, three young men from San Antonio shot their arms into the sky, signaling their preparedness to face the trains and the Texas Rangers: Willie Velásquez, Ignacio Pérez, and José Angel Gutiérrez.

En route to the railroad tracks, the three MAYO members paused to think through what they were about to do. Would they be beaten? Would they die? Anything seemed possible. Thoughts of death flashed through their minds, some frightening, some heroic. Pérez promised his worldly possessions to Professor Charlie Cotrell and gave him his mother's phone number in case he did not return. Velásquez quickly put on his tough guy mask, refusing to reveal the real fear that was building within him.

As fortune would have it, Velásquez, Pérez, and Gutiérrez were greeted at the railroad tracks by television cameras and teams of journalists hungry to chronicle the idealistic young men's actions. With the cameras rolling and the prospect of public security looming large, the Rangers refrained from moving on the protesters. Still, their presence was formidable and the MAYO members were little match for the imposing, grower-sponsored train. The potential disaster ended in a draw with the train eventually departing and the Rangers quietly watching on the sidelines.

～ ～ ～

In June 1967, one month after MAYO selected its name and purpose, and as Mexican Americans continued to be largely ignored nationally, President Johnson reacted to the growing demands of the Mexican-American population. "The time has come to focus our efforts more intensely on the Mexican Americans of our nation," Johnson proclaimed at a public convening at the White House. With these words, the president created an Inter-Agency Committee on Mexican American Affairs and named Vicente Ximenes, a leading member of the American GI Forum Hispanic Veterans group, to head the effort. Johnson, boasting that the Inter-Agency Committee would be given the greatest priority, directed the Secretaries of Labor, Health, Education and Welfare, Agriculture, Housing and Urban Development, and the Director of the Office of Economic Opportunity to assist Ximenes in his work. Johnson informed the committee that its charge was twofold in nature: "To assure that Federal programs are reaching Mexican Americans and providing the assistance they need, and to seek out new programs that may be necessary to handle problems that are unique to the Mexican American community." The president specifically asked the committee to talk with Mexican Americans about their situation and then to report to him. "I will expect from you not just reports," he commented. "I want solutions. I may get too many of the former—but never too many of the latter."

The administration's action came after months of growing pressure from Mexican-American leaders who felt the White House was not following through on earlier promises. These leaders had been wary of the administration's grand talk dating back as far as December 12, 1965, when EEOC chairman Franklin Roosevelt, Jr. promised to investigate some eight hundred national companies that employed over 600,000 people in the Southwest but no Mexican Americans. No such investigation was ever pursued. Roosevelt's failure to fulfill his promise resulted in complaints. In March 1966, fifty Mexican-American leaders were invited to a regional EEOC conference in Albuquerque, New Mexico. Only one of five commissioners and a spattering of EEOC staff were present. Roosevelt did not attend. Infuriated, the fifty leaders, including Bexar County Commissioner Albert Peña, LULAC (League of United Latin American Citizens) President Alfred Hernández, American G.I. Forum President Agustín Flores, MAPA (Mexican American Political Association) representative Bert Corona, and Henry Muñoz of the Texas AFL-CIO, walked out on the bureaucrats. "Hell, we're the second largest minority group [in the country] and we don't have a Mexican American on the EEOC," declared Peña, the speaker chosen to announce the walkout. In fact, out of 150 employees at the EEOC only three were Mexican American and none of them held policy-making positions.

Soon after, Mexican-American leaders demanded that the president convene a White House conference on Mexican-American issues, to give them an opportunity to air their concerns and to propose specific federal interventions. Johnson agreed. The White House started planning a conference on Mexican-American concerns to soothe the aggravated leaders, only to have them bitterly complain that the administration was again dragging its feet. Indeed, nearly a year passed between the EEOC walkout and official White House confirmation that a national conference would finally be convened. Now with few resources and no enforcement power, the Inter-Agency Committee and Vicente Ximenes hastily prepared the groundwork for a White House convening.

❧ ❧ ❧

Summer employment lured Velásquez back to Washington, D.C. for a third time in 1967 but with a completely different attitude. Returning to the Agency for International Development (AID), Velásquez's dreams of a diplomatic career seemed less urgent than when he first caught Potomac fever in the summer of 1964. Since then, the plight of the farmworkers and his increasing political involvement with Bexar County Commissioner Albert Peña and Texas State Senator Joe Bernal, redirected Velásquez's focus from the East Coast of America to the Westside of San Antonio. He returned to D.C. almost out of habit, barely hanging onto the idea of being a career diplomat. He felt guilty leaving Texas and all the work that needed to be done in the Valley and in the barrios, even if only for three months. His departure from Texas was low key. He did not spend any time explaining the specifics of his absence to his MAYO associates. He just told them he was leaving for a summer job, nothing else. They would not understand.

He did not completely understand either. The novelty and the quirkiness of the Washington scene had worn off. Fancy meals, famous people, and flashy lifestyles did not mesmerize Velásquez as they had when he was twenty years old and fresh to D.C. Now, a more seasoned young man of twenty-three, Velásquez was more interested in changing the world than simply his address.

❧ ❧ ❧

After what turned out to be the least electrifying internship of his three summers spent in D.C., Willie visited with Congressman Henry B. González, the man who had been his political inspiration and benefactor. The courtesy call began with the typical formalities but then quickly developed into an uncomfortable and relationship-altering exchange. Velásquez, the UFW convert, politely suggested that González back César Chávez and the migrant workers struggle. "No, I can't do that, it's out of my district," González responded without missing a beat. Willie was shattered. He did not understand how a prominent national Mexican-American elected official could ignore the desperate calls of his people. Was it that difficult for González to take a moral stand for what was right? The intensity of Velásquez's beliefs blocked his comprehension of González's precarious political position. Willie at twenty-three still saw issues in the absolute and did not grasp the subtleties and constraints facing early Mexican-American elected officials like González. For him, the world was black and white. Either you supported the farmworkers or you did not. There were no other possibilities.

The dialogue, slightly strained, continued. Velásquez, ever the well-mannered young man, thanked González for helping him along his career path. The congressman asked him about his plans for the future. Willie calmly mentioned that he was going back to Texas to help the Mexican-American people. His response was at once steeped in admirable conviction and the hint of naiveté that often accompanies the passions of young people. González urged Velásquez to stay away from the congressman's enemies, specifically mentioning Peña, Bernal, and City Councilman Pete Torres. Velásquez respectfully opined that these were "good people, doing something." González warned the unsuspecting idealist that he could no longer support Willie if he associated with these individuals. Velásquez did not fully understand the ramifications of González's statement. He left the congressman's office, for the last time, puzzled and with a sense of moral indignation. At age twenty-three, Willie's relationship with his first political mentor was crumbling. From this point on, Velásquez and Congressman González would become bitter ideological and political opponents. Their break would haunt Willie for the rest of his life.

〜 〜 〜

Just as the dreams of becoming a career diplomat no longer captured his fancy, Velásquez's interest in graduate economics waned as his need to promote progressive reform on behalf of the Mexican-American people grew. The fall of 1967 marked his second year of graduate studies. He survived the first year carrying an almost full load of classes, earning slightly above a B average. Combined with his ever-soaring host of political activities, Velásquez felt numbed, almost burned out, from the furious pace he had kept up in his first year of graduate school. There was no way he could keep up this tempo and retain his sanity. Something would have to give and it could not be his activism. He decided to put economics on hold to pursue his activist interests with the full weight of his faculties and undivided attention.

His drift from the Masters program in economics did not mean that Willie gave up intellectual pursuits altogether. In fact, he simply replaced his economics textbooks with writings of Spanish historian Bernal Díaz de

Castillo, Mexican novelist and philosopher Octavio Paz, radical labor leader Ricardo Flores Magón, and a mix of comparable thinkers dealing with the history and people of Mexico.

At a time when many black and Chicano activists ousted liberal whites from leadership positions in their organizations, exposing them to accusations of racial separatism, Willie became obsessed with the writer José Vasconcelos's notion of *la raza cósmica*, the cosmic race. Vasconcelos argued that racially mixed peoples were superior to racially pure groups, in direct contrast to emerging neo-Nazi and biological determinist concepts. Velásquez developed his own version of the cosmic race theory. His view was grounded in a belief that racial mixing made it more possible for society to build on the best qualities each group had to offer. For Velásquez, this meant that Mexican Americans could help to create an American Southwest where culture fusion produced a higher order of people. It was an optimistic idea that he pondered and promoted for the rest of his life.

No one in the movement really shared Willie's attraction to Vasconcelos and the idea of a united higher race. "What the hell does that have to do with helping folks in the barrio?" his Chicano activist friends would ask. More and more, the movement's adherents sought to call attention to the particular needs and interests of Chicanos through increasingly ethnocentric and strident efforts. Out of loyalty more than conviction, Velásquez reluctantly supported these efforts even though he essentially believed that outlandish confrontations were not always the best way to promote change. Yes, it caught people's attention, but did it guarantee improvements? Willie's MAYO co-principals Gutiérrez, Compeán, and Pérez did not embrace his more accommodating approach to politics. Piecemeal reform, working within the system, using the Democratic Party, and relying on established labor leaders were ideas that became more and more repulsive to these and other radical Chicano leaders. Willie's heart was in the right place, his MAYO colleagues believed, but more drastic action was needed.

᳓ᜥ   ᳓ᜥ   ᳓ᜥ

As the MAYO organizers continued forward in their passionate advocacy, the Ford Foundation cautiously pursued efforts to promote expanded public and institutional attention to the nation's largely ignored Mexican-American people. Back in 1965, as the problems of Mexican Americans were still boiling under the national radar, the foundation, led by its public affairs director Paul Ylvisaker, had commissioned a series of community surveys and needs assessments led by three proven Mexican-American leaders: Dr. Ernesto Galarza, a writer and longtime labor activist from San José, California; Dr. Julián Samora, head of the sociology department at Notre Dame University;

and Herman Gallegos, a community activist from San Francisco. The trio was asked to examine the problems of Mexican Americans in the Southwest and to help the Ford Foundation and other private funders determine what might be done to bring Mexican Americans together to solve these issues.

Two years prior to this arrangement, the foundation had approved a groundbreaking grant totaling nearly $600,000 to support an academic study of Mexican Americans by the University of California at Los Angeles scholars Leo Grebler, an economist; Joan Moore, a sociologist; and Ralph Guzmán, a political scientist. The goal of the Grebler study was to educate elected officials, policy planners, and institutional and civic leaders about the nation's second largest minority group and its dramatic need for social, political, and economic investment support. While information concerning Mexican Americans was desperately lacking, many Mexican-American leaders were wary of Ford's motivation. The foundation's Mexican-American advisors were also somewhat skeptical.

Sitting in Ylvisaker's New York office, Gallegos cynically asked whether the consultant team was supposed to go out, conduct a study, come back, and tell him that Mexican Americans needed an NAACP.[2] After a pause, Gallegos was stunned at the answer. Ylvisaker, responding not like a stodgy, cautious Foundation administrator but more like a high school football coach, told him that he and his colleagues should go wherever—and do whatever—was responsibly necessary to learn about Mexican-American community needs in order to advise the foundation intelligently about what it could do to be responsive. With this blessing, the three designated experts divided the territory and plunged deeply into the field, only rarely meeting to compare their findings.

Gallegos met Bexar County Commissioner Albert Peña through his work on the Ford Foundation project. Peña told him that if he really wanted to know what was going on in San Antonio he needed to meet with young people. Taking Peña's advice, Gallegos set up a session with MAYO's Velásquez and Patlán in the fall of 1967. Meeting at Karam's, a Mexican restaurant on the Westside of San Antonio, Gallegos, Velásquez, and Patlán filled themselves with Jax beer and nickel tamales. They discussed the stark realities facing Mexican Americans in South Texas. Gallegos listened intently as the two MAYO leaders described the particular problems of Mexican Americans in the barrios of San Antonio: lack of social and political empowerment; physical deterioration of the area; inadequate schools; and no meaningful possibility for upward mobility. Gallegos knew that Velásquez and

---

[2]The National Association for the Advancement of Colored People (NAACP) is the nation's leading African-American civil rights organization.

Patlán were undoubtedly enraged by these hard realities of Mexican-American community life in San Antonio, but he was impressed by the young men's enthusiasm, intelligence, and composure. They did not seem crazed like one bitter young Chicano Gallegos encountered in Fresno, California, who shook his fist at him and said, "If you bastards don't move any faster, you'll find footprints on your back."

Gallegos sensed Velásquez and Patlán were responsible, dedicated activists. Wanting to advance their prospects to gain the Ford Foundation's interest, he asked whether their organization had a 501(c)3 status. They had no idea what he was talking about. It was as if he were speaking a different language. And he was. It was the vocabulary of nonprofit organizations, foundations, and War on Poverty programs that provided influence and money to those with little of either. Without promising any money from the Ford Foundation, Gallegos went on to explain the intricacies of setting up a 501(c)3, a tax-exempt nonprofit organization, and the financial role foundations play in supporting such groups. The inexperienced young interviewees soaked up Gallegos's knowledge. For some time now, MAYO's charter members had dreamed of creating an organization that would tackle directly the problems of the barrio. They were tired of more established Mexican-American leaders and groups who they felt did not focus enough energy on the root causes of the Mexican-American predicament. Bursting with hope, the two activists could not wait to report their findings to their colleagues and begin working on obtaining their own 501(c)3 designation. After discussing Gallegos's visit and his suggestions, MAYO's group of five agreed that Willie would lead the project. Velásquez had just recently turned his volunteer work with the Bishops' Committee into a part-time paid position, although, in reality, he was working full-time hours. He had ingeniously tapped committee resources to help the farmworker cause as a volunteer and then picked up the pace even more as a staff assistant. Now he could turn his zeal and the Bishops' Committee's assets into a tax-exempt group that would empower Mexican Americans themselves to tackle the problems of the barrios.

Father John McCarthy, acting director of the Bishops' Committee, trusted Willie to use the organization's resources wisely for actions on behalf of the Mexican-American community. McCarthy liked Velásquez. He picked Willie up every morning and they drove to work together. Instinctively, they were good friends. In addition, though both were intensely serious and dedicated, they could easily share laughs about their movement-inspired predicaments and dilemmas. Now, as McCarthy prepared to hit the road again looking for an appropriate Mexican American to run the Bishops' Committee, he felt confident that Willie would wisely keep himself busy with his latest scheme to help the cause.

In October 1967, a month after Velásquez officially began working for the

Bishops' Committee, McCarthy finally found a Mexican-American priest to run the organization. Father Miguel Barragán, although a youthful priest, was nevertheless a seasoned veteran of Mexican-American affairs in Northern California. Barragán promptly joined forces with Velásquez, his part-time employee who knew the ropes of the office and the politics of the territory. Barragán quickly supported Willie's efforts to incorporate a tax-exempt organization and to secure foundation funding. They put together a steering committee and a proposal-drafting group for the new, more ambitious organization they hoped to create from MAYO. Choosing the name the Mexican American Unity Council (MAUC), the original MAYO leadership group was impanelled as a board of directors, along with a few sympathetic Anglo college professors and well-respected citizens, in order to demonstrate broad community representation and legitimacy. On November 16, 1967, MAUC was incorporated. Less than a month later, the group received notification of its federal tax-exempt status. The concept that Velásquez and Patlán had been encouraged to develop by Ford Foundation consultant Herman Gallegos was now a reality.

Things at Ford had changed, however, since Galarza, Samora, and Gallegos began their commissioned studies there in 1965. Paul Ylvisaker left the foundation in 1966. McGeorge Bundy, an insider in the Kennedy and Johnson administrations had become president of the foundation. Mike Sviridoff, a UAW (United Auto Workers) man who had just helped start New York City's colossal social services agency, the Human Resources Administration, had been appointed vice president. Both Bundy and Sviridoff knew little about Mexican Americans and were hesitant to jump recklessly into unchartered areas. The Mexican-American consulting trio recommended that Ford provide money directly to established local groups scattered across the Southwest, as the best way to improve conditions in the nation's needy Mexican-American communities. In this way, Ford could work directly with diverse grassroots community organizations and leaders in the most responsive possible fashion. Ford officials rejected this approach feeling that it was too risky. The foundation had not worked extensively in the Mexican-American community and it wanted to move slowly, strategically, and with a degree of distance from the field that would minimize its exposure if things did not go well. Some Southwestern towns had experienced groups already working extensively in the barrios or in the fields, but most did not: Even the most experienced of the established groups, moreover, tended to be relatively young and untested. Ford decided that to be serious about solving the problems of the Mexican-American people and to exercise due diligence in its efforts to do so, it needed to develop a regional intermediary organization that could take the lead to coherently organize and fund Mexican-American community-building efforts across the Southwest. The effort would be structured to help participating organizations feel like they were part of a larger

Mexican-American game plan and not just isolated entities working in Los Angeles, Phoenix, the Rio Grande Valley, or San Antonio. With this concept in mind, foundation officials charged Galarza, Samora, and Gallegos to assemble a group of nearly twenty-five Mexican-American leaders of the Southwest to discuss the possibility of creating a new institution dedicated to advancing Spanish-speaking community interests across the region. With planning support provided by the Industrial Union Department of the AFL-CIO, the National Council of Churches, and the Ford Foundation, the organizing group of union men, local politicians, and community activists met several times, frantically trying to figure out how they could form a group Ford would fund significantly over the long term. Someone suggested the new organization should be called a council. Henry Santiestevan of the UAW took out a legal pad, scribbled "Southwest Council," and showed it to the others. Dr. Galarza took the pad and added the final touch: "of La Raza." The Southwest Council of La Raza was thus born. Now, like MAYO and MAUC, all it needed was money and a plan of action.

ᗌ ᗌ ᗌ

Planning for a White House conference on Mexican-American affairs was becoming mired in political and logistical complications. Mexican-American leaders had requested and been promised a White House event to underscore the importance of the proceedings. Now, suddenly, the event was being planned as a series of Cabinet hearings to be convened in El Paso, Texas. Given the already significant delay in gaining presidential follow-through on the idea of a national event to address Mexican-American concerns, many community leaders felt additionally let down by Johnson's handling of the matter. They saw the proposed El Paso hearings as nothing more than a political device to generate support for Johnson's assumed re-election bid in 1968. More progressive and militant leaders questioned Johnson's commitment to begin with and doubted anything would be implemented from the hearings. These leaders were especially angered that more progressive community advocates, such as Reies López Tijerina, a land-grant activist from New Mexico, were not invited. Some leaders, moreover, including César Chávez, although invited, refused to attend owing to concerns about the proposed gathering's integrity. Instead of merely demonstrating outside the Cabinet hearings to protest the inadequacies of the presidential convening, concerned activists decided to hold their own grassroots conference in El Paso at a nearby location. Barragán, Velásquez, and another San Antonio activist drove to El Paso, squeezed into a single motel room there, and joined almost six hundred others for the alternative La Raza Unida (United Race) Conference at the Southside Sacred Heart Parish Hall.

The Cabinet Committee Hearings and the La Raza Unida Conference contrasted the old with the new, the mainstream with the progressive, and the patient with the restless. Approximately one thousand delegates gathered at finer area hotels and the University of Texas at El Paso during October 26–28, 1967, to participate in the administration's hearings. On Friday evening, the group heard Vice President Hubert Humphrey proclaim, "Our purpose is grander than simply guaranteeing every Mexican American the opportunity to achieve a decent American standard of living. . . . We are talking about providing a material basis on which a cultural tradition that is precious to America can grow and flourish." The somber delegates responded with kind yet guarded applause. Fifty-two Mexican-American leaders presented their plans for tackling a host of problems in reserved, monotonous, ten-minute bites as they testified before four Cabinet officers and the Director of the Office of Economic Opportunity. Highlighting the symbolic hearings was a surprise appearance by President Johnson, who had been busy meeting with Mexican president Díaz Ordaz to resolve a long-standing land controversy over the Chamizal area, a disputed territory between the United States and Mexico located not far from the conference site. After reminiscing about his teaching days in Cotulla, Texas, Johnson told the crowd: "We are moving forward. Nobody knows better than you know how far we have to go. . . . A lesser people might have despaired. A lesser people might have given up a long time ago. But your people didn't give up. They believed. They believed that they were full-fledged citizens of the greatest nation on the earth, even if others didn't always treat them as such." As with Humphrey, the audience respectfully applauded the president's words.

No one doubted that the El Paso Cabinet Committee Hearings were a major historical event in the largely ignored history of the Mexican-American people. No such event had ever occurred in the history of the nation. The group heard major addresses from the president and vice president of the United States, and many seasoned community leaders from across the Southwest testified before top administration officials. Major problems affecting Mexican Americans across the land were made starkly clear to these leading national policy makers, in some cases for the first time. Novel policy interventions were seriously pondered to address the issues. Yet none of this was sufficient to placate the pulsating anger emanating from the impatient conference huddled on the other side of town. The tediousness, formality, and even-temperedness of the Cabinet Hearings paled in comparison to the roaring, raucous alternative conference being held by scorned activists and irate youth at the Southside Sacred Heart Parish Hall. The Laredo, Texas delegation defiantly marched into El Paso carrying a sign that read: "TODAY WE PROTEST, TOMORROW REVOLUTION." Speakers like United Steelworkers' leader Maclovio Barraza taunted President Johnson's claim that

Mexican Americans were moving forward. "It is not enough!" Barraza roared in a speech before the alternative gathering. "It barely touches the many problems that beg attention. Our people are saying that before we shout 'Viva Johnson', there better be a 'Viva la Gente Mexicana' (Long Live the Mexican People). Mañana is too late." Following Barraza's remarks, some young Chicanos participating at the protest gathering produced placards that warned "MAÑANA IS HERE!"

Taking his turn at the podium, Willie informed conference participants about the evolving work of MAYO with a stilted academic speaking style that seemed more appropriate for the Cabinet Hearings. Parts of his presentation contained abstract thoughts and theoretical strains that many participants did not understand. Reading from his notes and rarely looking up, Willie peppered his remarks with the pompous terms and phrases an insecure individual uses to try to impress his listeners. Still, the boisterous audience applauded courteously. "I could tell he was a college graduate," quipped one commentator attending the conference, "because he didn't make complete sense."

The La Raza Unida Conference was both crucial and successful because it brought together Mexican-American activists who, until then, had been largely isolated from each other. Fledgling organizers and groups were infused with a burning sense of hope having learned that they were not alone in their efforts. Participants from the White House Hearings left El Paso with promises of a report of the proceedings, whereas Velásquez and other participants attending the alternative gathering of activists left with promises of cooperation and a cry of unity. They now shared a common identity as a movement that was gradually sweeping through the barrios and fields of the Southwest.

As the White House Hearings drew to a lifeless close, the boisterous and boiling outsiders of the alternative conference staged a march and rally in the St. Mary's Church gymnasium in the barrios of El Paso. With a strange and overflowing mix of characters—old-time hardened, cynical organizers; progressive politicians who loved to prick the conservative establishment; audacious men of the cloth who preached the gospel of God's work on earth through community action; and frenetic, naive young dreamers—the participants committed their aims and claims to writing in the following terms:

On this historic day, October 27, 1967, La Raza Unida, organized in El Paso, Texas, proclaims the time of subjugation, exploitation and abuse of human rights of La Raza in the United States is hereby ended forever.

La Raza Unida affirms the magnificence of La Raza, the greatness of our heritage, our history, our language, our traditions, our contributions to humanity and our culture. We have demonstrated, proved and again affirm our loyalty to the Constitutional Democra-

cy of the United States of America and to the religious and cultural traditions we share . . .
We reaffirm a dedication to our heritage, a bilingual culture, and assert our right to be members of La Raza Unida, anywhere, anytime, and in any job.

With swelling enthusiasm, Velásquez and Barragán promised to keep the momentum flowing by agreeing to organize a follow-up meeting in San Antonio.

〰 〰 〰

Working from his stronghold at the Bishops' Committee's office, Velásquez immersed himself in planning a follow-up to the conference held in El Paso. That gathering, which countered the White House Hearings, generated tremendous enthusiasm that Willie wanted to build on and harness for coordinated attacks against the problems facing Mexican Americans across the Southwestern region. The El Paso assembly of La Raza Unida brought some six hundred people together and Willie hoped he could at least match that figure. Using the Bishops' Committee's mailing list and contacting organizations he had worked with in the past—the Texas Council of Churches, the Texas AFL-CIO, LULAC councils, G.I. Forum chapters, the Valley Farm Workers Assistance Committee, and other Catholic groups—Willie hustled to get the word out about the upcoming conference in San Antonio. With other MAYO members largely committed to activist projects on other fronts, Velásquez had to assume most of the logistical organizing of the event himself. He mailed huge numbers of letters, spent endless hours on the phone, mimeographed propaganda for the delegates, and did everything else necessary to bring the conference together. His efforts paid dividends.

On Saturday, January 6, 1968, some twelve hundred delegates, twice the number who attended the El Paso conference, converged on John F. Kennedy High School in San Antonio for the second La Raza Unida Conference. They came to hear speeches by Dr. Ernesto Galarza and Texas State Senator Joe Bernal, to discuss the problems facing the Mexican-American community, and to reach consensus on how they should tackle these issues. Galarza opened the conference proclaiming that henceforth, Mexican Americans would no longer tolerate second-class status and unacceptable circumstances in their communities. Now, Galarza asserted, "Mexican Americans are . . . uniting to improve their living standards through education and voting." Senator Bernal closed out the proceedings with a call for good old-fashioned American political involvement as the key to improving things for the Chicano. "When every Mexican American of voting age has properly registered," said Bernal, "then he can elect Spanish-speaking citizens in his community to vital offices." Imploring the audience to vote accordingly, Bernal concluded with the imperative: "Elect your friends and defeat your enemies." Posters of Mexican revolutionary Emiliano Zapata joined cries for unity and a triumphant revolutionary fervor at the conference. The promise of the new year brought forth bold and sometimes doctrinaire ideas to transform the Mexican-American population's situation soon, before things got out of hand and neighborhoods exploded. At the end of the day, the delegates called for Mexican-American political empowerment through massive voter registration efforts, teaching Mexican Americans how to use voting machines, and investigating areas where Mexican Americans were being barred from voting by manipulation or intimidation. In education, they called for abolishing the Texas state rule forbidding any language but English in classrooms, requiring Texas teachers to learn Spanish, and expanding college financial aid programs for Mexican-American students. All told, the delegates considered over two hundred resolutions covering issues related to civil rights, the war on poverty, community organizing, and the image and identity of Mexican Americans in Anglo-American society.

Most participants at the second La Raza Unida Conference, as in El Paso, left the gathering feeling that it was a staggering success. Velásquez, the coordinator, had a different sense of the event. Willie acknowledged that the convening helped to keep the drive alive in many who had attended the El Paso gathering and that it had brought important new people to the table. At the same time, though, the San Antonio conference produced disturbing notions and remarks, from his perspective. Some delegates brought such hostile feelings toward Anglos, they were unable to distinguish that some white Americans were in fact sympathetic to their cause. Other activists suggested protest tactics including sabotaging leading public utilities and facilities (such as the wires of the San Antonio Public Service Board or the computer system at Kelly Air Force Base).

Velásquez was also disappointed that few if any grassroots Mexican Americans from the poor and working classes were encouraged to inform discussions at the conference. Remembering the absence of farmworker participation in past rallies on their behalf in the state of Texas, he worried middle-class and college-educated leaders were unduly defining the agenda. Willie had another vision for the movement. Yet, with the crowd wildly screaming ¡Viva la huelga! ¡Viva la causa! ¡Viva la Raza Unida! and demanding that other events be planned, Velásquez focused on the lingering problems of the Mexican-American people and prepared to organize the next La Raza Unida Conference.

Laredo, Texas was the site of the third La Raza Unida Conference. Held on March 24, 1968, nearly one thousand people attended, including nearly fifty MAYO members. Velásquez, hoping to avoid another event that talked for the poor and the working class but did not include many of them in the actual proceedings, announced, "All moderators and coordinators for the Laredo conference will be people from the disadvantaged barrios, who for the first time in their lives will have the opportunity to voice their problems and anger for not having been able to be assimilated in the mainstream of American society." Velásquez hated the elitist attitude some Mexican-American leaders shared, thinking they had to do things for the poor, uneducated people in their barrios. In many ways this was the same complaint the Mexican-American leaders had against Anglo politicians and other institutions that did things for them, rather than with them. These Mexican-American workers knew what they wanted. They just needed a chance to air their sentiments. Willie, now going by the title of statewide coordinator for La Raza Unida, sent five thousand invitations to the poorest areas in Laredo, hoping to convince residents and leaders from these areas to attend. A highlight of the Laredo gathering for Velásquez was the participation of residents from sixteen of the town's most needy barrios and their prominent role in shaping the conference.

෴ ෴ ෴

The La Raza Unida Conferences of 1967 and 1968 successfully brought more isolated Chicano political activists together and infused them with the settings and resources necessary to create lasting working relationships. Unfortunately, the rhetoric of the activists was beginning to give their movement a separatist tinge. Calling for loyalty to La Raza before anything else, the participants were increasingly seen by some (and Anglos especially) as reverse racists—segregationists who were against white people in general. In fact, some La Raza members were so angry that they wanted absolutely nothing to do with Anglo Americans. Such individuals expressed rage against whites and virtually all of the institutions they led, from government agencies and private foundations to business institutions and even the Catholic Church. Still others, including Willie, had a different view. They saw the La Raza Unida call as a way to make things better for Mexican Americans without categorically being against all things Anglo.

This nuance was largely lost on Velásquez's employer at the Bishops' Committee, Archbishop Robert Lucey. Lucey despised the anti-Anglo and anti-Catholic Church rhetoric that was emerging from some quarters of the La Raza Unida membership. He knew, moreover, that the Bishops' Committee was closely associated with the La Raza Unida effort because of Velásquez's involvement as state coordinator. Extremely displeased, Lucey consulted with Father Barragán, director of the Bishops' Committee, and instructed him to fire Willie. Barragán was stunned, but it was clear the archbishop had made up his mind. Barragán told Willie he had to let him go.

Velásquez laughed, thinking about what Erasmo Andrade told him a year earlier when he started the job. Velásquez told Barragán to watch out, warning him that he would be next.

Losing his job was surely a financial crisis, but more importantly for Velásquez, it created a practical political problem. Without the job, he had no more ready access to what seemed like endless resources at the Bishops' Committee. Barragán would still let him occasionally use the phones, mimeograph machine, and mailing privileges, but he would not have the free rein that helped him organize the Raza Unida conferences or important MAYO and MAUC activities. With things going the way they were, moreover, it was very likely only a matter of months before Lucey would fire Barragán for doing the same things Willie had been doing. This would mean a complete drain of resources for the impatient activists. What would they do to survive?

Willie's mother hoped that he would get back to school to complete his Masters degree. Velásquez had become so lost in his community activism that his economics studies took a permanent backseat to it. In his second year of graduate studies, Willie took three incompletes out of the four courses for which he registered. The only class he completed was one outside of his degree program, a government course with the activist professor Charlie Cotrell covering political thought from Marx to the present. For all practical purposes, Velásquez's graduate student career had ended.

In the spring of 1968, Willie registered for two courses from which he hoped to secure decent grades. Professor George Benz, a political animal who came from a German immigrant family background, taught one of the courses. Benz, academically known as an economic institutionalist, was in fact a debunker who sought to expose the misuse of ideas by people seeking expedient results. A gruff teacher who had roughly a dozen commandments for his students to follow, Benz scared his students and they rarely challenged him.

One day Benz nonchalantly called Willie over to his desk. He told Velásquez that he had read his paper and could not believe how smooth it was. It was so smooth that he wanted Willie to know that he would be watching him carefully on his next paper. Willie's response to the veiled plagiarism charge was respectful. He did not cause a big scene; he merely denied that he had done anything wrong. The work was completely his.

Benz did not have to worry about a next paper. There never was one. After the peaceful confrontation with the professor, Velásquez dropped out of school. Part of it was hurt pride and part of it was the realization that the Chicano political movement had ended his graduate studies a long time ago. There were still massive amounts of work to be done in the barrios and that was more important than any pointless degree, Willie rationalized. But all he could hear in his head was his mother repeating again and again, "Once you drop out, it is like you never started."

Velásquez never went back to school. Years later, ironically, Benz tried to persuade him to write a thesis on the economics of voter registration, promising it would be enough to secure his Masters degree. Velásquez refused the suggestion, saying he no longer had time. For the rest of his life, Velásquez boasted publicly that he left graduate school to work for César Chávez, the farmworkers, and a strike salary of five dollars a week (all things he actually did while still in school). He repeated the story so many times that he started to believe it himself. Over the years, though, he could never get Professor Benz and his casual accusation of cheating out of his head.

Chapter 5

SIDNEY LANIER HIGH SCHOOL HAD THE reputation of being a solid inner-city school that had avoided the excessive problems of disorder, vandalism, and truancy that dominated many other barrio schools in San Antonio. More students graduated from Lanier than from the city's other predominantly Mexican-American high schools. Situated in a stable Mexican-American working-class community, Lanier seemed the last place a student uprising would occur.

During 1968, however, student council elections, the harmless annual popularity ritual that most high school students ignore, triggered a narrow, youthful rage in a handful of Lanier students. Teachers involved with the elections did not approve of some of the students nominated. A battle ensued between these teachers and student leaders at a meeting designed to resolve the resulting elections impasse. When the meeting reached a boiling point, the teachers abruptly ended it. A confrontation ensued and the rebellious student representatives were swiftly expelled. In response, another group of Lanier students belonging to a neighborhood club initiated a series of after-school meetings to deal specifically with the conflict. The administration reacted by threatening to expel any and all students who attended these gatherings. Confused, the Lanier students turned to the people running their neighborhood center for advice: the Mexican American Youth Organization (MAYO).

Willie Velásquez met with the outraged kids and calmly listened to their grievances. When the students finally exhausted their litany of concerns, Velásquez inquired about the larger conditions facing students at the school, beyond the student council problem. The students recounted the hard realities of their dismal educational experience: the lack of positive books and teaching content about Chicano history, the enforcement of English-only school language policies, the absence of basic college prep courses, and the disrepair of many school facilities.

Velásquez persuaded the students to create a coordinating committee that would formally address the problems they had enumerated. The students, accordingly, decided to focus on four major objectives: adding courses that presented the positive civic contributions of Mexican Americans, terminating the rule forbidding Spanish on the school grounds, creating advanced placement and college preparatory courses, and modernizing the school's equipment used to teach vocational skills. Student council elections quickly took a backseat to the larger educational concerns facing Mexican-American students at Lanier. Having articulated their concerns, the Lanier students now focused their sights on the school's administration, to demand change. Edgar Lozano, an articulate, bright, football player, who belonged to the local neighborhood club, was chosen to chair the reform campaign. Knowing that school finance was based on daily student attendance rates, Velásquez and MAYO recommended that the students use the threat of a walkout as a bargaining tool vis-à-vis the Lanier school administrators. If the call for greater educational opportunity and relevance did not awaken administration officials on the merits, the students would hit them where it hurt most: their school revenue base. The battle was joined.

After tense weeks of back and forth grappling, division appeared everywhere. Chicano students became increasingly estranged from their Mexican-American school officials and teachers. Parents divided into those who blasted the student organizers as "extremists" and those who staunchly supported their childrens' valiant undertaking. As the conflict unfolded and community leaders weighed in on both sides, the Lanier student committee gained the blessing of several local Catholic priests and Mexican-American politicians, such as County Commissioner Albert Peña, who commented to the student leaders when he met them: "Our generation didn't have the courage to speak out. You are brave." Such support bolstered the Lanier students' credibility and filled them with confidence.

The pivotal moment in the campaign took place at a local Catholic Church hall located near Lanier in a hastily called meeting of students, parents, and school officials. More than five hundred people attended the meeting. Students expressed their grievances in highly emotional, yet sophisticated terms. Each testimony had a clear message. The students wanted respect for their culture and stronger educational opportunities for themselves and their younger brothers and sisters who would someday also attend Lanier. The students made a compelling case for important reforms in school policy and pedagogy. Attending parents and community leaders roundly supported the students' cause. Administration officials had little choice. Out-maneuvered and themselves impressed by the students' preparation and persuasiveness, the administration gave in to their core demands.

The success of the Lanier High School confrontation created a momentum and expertise that MAYO could export to other venues. Velásquez and the MAYO activists, accordingly, continued to make themselves available to assist aggrieved students and families seeking educational and political reforms across South Texas. In each case, MAYO stayed in the background. It was the students who led the charge. It was their school issues and their passions that would publicly fuel the battle.

At Edgewood High School, another predominantly Mexican-American inner-city school in San Antonio, approximately six hundred students walked out complaining that many of their teachers were not certified and that deteriorating facilities at the school were not only potential firetraps, but also symbols of the school district's basic lack of respect for Mexican-American students.

Later in the year, the MAYO-supported school protest movement penetrated the Rio Grande Valley, where some 150 students, provoked by two of their classmates' expulsion for refusing to cut their hair, walked out of Edcouch-Elsa High School. They presented a list of grievances to local school officials dealing with issues ranging from students' rights and curriculum concerns to school language policies and migrant worker educational opportunities.

School walkouts detonated throughout the Southwest in 1968. By leading and engaging in these protests, Mexican-American youths joined a nationwide search for expanded equality and justice. For MAYO, the walkouts were a critical platform for elevating public and institutional attention to the long-standing inequalities facing Mexican-American youth. They were also important educational and organizing tools for Mexican-American students and their families, many of which were politicized for the first time in the walkouts.

～ ～ ～

The frantic, nonstop lifestyle of the Chicano political activist, and in particular the original MAYO group, was driven by more than an altruistic zeal to organize the Mexican-American community and solve its problems. It also stemmed from a self-centered need for purpose and position among passionate and talented individuals who had been arbitrarily excluded from conventional power centers. One way to compensate for the tension this dynamic inflicted was to give in to the frequent craving for pleasurable excess. Hard work was not offset by light play. Hard work was reinforced by hard living. This did not mean that political work was curtailed to drink heavily or dance the night away. It meant that sixteen-hour organizing days were often topped off with a heavy dose of alcohol. Tired of pumping all their beer-drinking money into the coffers of assorted bar owners, the leading members of MAYO and other local Chicano political activists decided one day to invest some money to establish their own club.

It was decided that Willie would run the establishment, located on Highway 90, which they called the DMZ (Demilitarized Zone) bar. The DMZ was, in essence, a hard-core after-hours dive. Music, drinking, and dancing were constants there. The festive club had one problem: it did not bring in money. Too often the co-owners brought in their friends, treated them, or gave them credit that never was paid. As a result, the DMZ bar lasted less than six months. Velásquez and his political colleagues learned the hard way that they were not savvy businessmen. The failed venture forced Willie especially to refocus on his passion for politics.

Ever since Velásquez and fellow MAYO member Juan Patlán had met with Herman Gallegos, the Ford Foundation consultant, to discuss the creation of the Mexican American Unity Council, Willie had pushed fervently to get this new entity going with the help of Father Miguel Barragán. As early as January 1968, one week after he coordinated the La Raza Unida Conference at Kennedy High School, Velásquez and Barragán had submitted a formal proposal to Ford. They asked for money to cover a mishmash of activities that lacked a core of programming and that sought to piecemeal each barrio problem to death. It was painfully obvious that Velásquez and Barragán were entirely new to the world of philanthropic funding.

Based on Herman Gallegos's recommendations, Ford Foundation staff was predisposed to fund the Unity Council concept, but only as part of its larger national strategy to develop a regional intermediary organization that in turn would help to develop more locally based groups through pass-through grants and technical assistance. This meant that the Unity Council now had to wait until the nascent Southwest Council of La Raza was funded before it could receive Ford Foundation support. Fortunately, Father Barragán was heavily involved in the proposal-writing for the Southwest Council and he kept Willie informed of developments along the way. Following months of back and forth negotiation and proposal review, the Ford Foundation finally awarded the Southwest Council a start-up grant of $630,000 in early June 1968. Ford staff, honoring earlier promises, enumerated one of the Southwest Council's core objectives as "providing grants for community cooperative activities related to central problems in the region's Mexican American barrios and neighborhoods." That same day, at a special board meeting of the Southwest Council held in El Paso, the Unity Council received a sub-grant of $110,000 to commence work in the barrios of San Antonio. The Unity Council was the first local council to be funded by the Southwest Council of La Raza, but the early support came with important strings attached. The Unity Council had to expand its board to include a broader representation of the San Antonio community. At the time, the Unity Council's board was nothing more than MAYO's founding leaders and their closest academic and political friends. In addition, the Unity Council was again requested to clarify the specific program priorities it planned to support with its new funding resources. Its latest proposal was still too vague to inspire Ford's and the Council's confidence that MAUC would be a strategic program administrator. Shortly after these requests, Bexar County Commissioner Albert Peña and MAYO member Ignacio Pérez both withdrew from the MAUC board to make way for more diverse representatives of local barrio groups, but the Unity Council's program objectives remained as elusive as ever.

≈ ≈ ≈

By the time the Unity Council grant was approved, Willie no longer spent much time with the original members of MAYO. The days of their endless political discussions were long gone. Their growing differences on ideology and strategy pushed them onto separate paths. Gutiérrez, Compeán, and Pérez still felt strongly that confrontation, shock, and hard-core militancy was the only way America was going to be awakened. Velásquez—and to a lesser extent Patlán—continued to believe in a more mainstream course, clinging to the belief that Mexican Americans could most improve their lives not by screaming and threatening, but rather by diligently organizing for economic and political empowerment in ways that drew on basic American values and did not alienate the larger Anglo community. In many ways, the differences in approach between Velásquez and the other MAYO founders mirrored the distinctions that existed in the black civil rights movement between the more moderate approach encouraged by Dr. Martin Luther King, Jr. versus the more radical direction espoused by the Black Panthers and the Student Nonviolent Coordinating Committee.

The growing schism between MAYO's founding members was amplified by the Southwest Council's sub-grant of $110,000 to MAUC. The grant was met by jubilation on the part of MAYO's more radical founding members. They saw it as an opportunity to channel money to MAYO's core organizing agenda. They counted on controlling the board and staff in ways that would ensure MAYO's will. But this was not meant to be. In fact, out of necessity to meet the Ford Foundation's requirements, Velásquez had structured MAUC to be far more independent of the MAYO organization than his cofounders would have liked. Ford and its advisors were committed to a more moderate and inclusive organization that would be able to seek methodical changes, slowly and over time. They insisted on organizational integrity, diversity, and measure. Velásquez was accordingly accommodating to ensure MAUC's continuing consideration, but along the way he failed in important respects to apprise his MAYO colleagues of resulting concessions to Ford and the Southwest Council, which ultimately diminished MAYO's ability to control MAUC and its newfound major resources. Indeed, Willie's concessions ensured that MAYO would not have a voting majority on MAUC's board nor significantly influence the Unity Council's community grant-making.

Gutiérrez, Compeán, and Pérez were infuriated to learn only after the fact that their plans to control MAUC would not be realized. They felt betrayed by Velásquez. How could this happen? At one point, Gutiérrez, unable to hold back his anger, lashed out at Velásquez, "You know, I don't trust you from now on, man, because you're out there," he chided. "I already know that you're going to go and take this thing off on its own instead of supporting us."

Given their frustration and sense of betrayal, Gutiérrez, Compeán, and Pérez were determined not to let Velásquez slide in unchecked when it came time to select an executive director for the Unity Council. For a time, a stand-off ensued as the disgruntled MAYO founders attempted to block Willie's appointment. Eventually, a compromise was reached. Willie Velásquez would be MAUC's first executive director; but, at the insistence of the rebuffed MAYO leaders, Juan Patlán, the most diplomatic and steady of MAYO's founding leadership, was also appointed as deputy director. Gutiérrez, Compeán, and Pérez were confident that Patlán would counter Willie's more independent attitude and keep them informed of the Unity Council's activities. Gutiérrez, who from the beginning days of MAYO was constantly competing with Willie, left the fateful meeting with a challenging promise to Velásquez: "First chance I get, I'm going to try to move you out!"

෴ ෴ ෴

In August, the Mexican American Unity Council received an advance of just over $18,000 from the Southwest Council of La Raza to begin operations. Soon, MAUC opened an office on the Westside of San Antonio. The Unity Council quickly became the center of incessant community activity. Located on the second floor above the Progreso drugstore on Guadalupe Street, MAUC's headquarters facility cried out for cleaning, repairs, and attention. Eventually, the office was repainted and modestly decorated with progressive posters and paraphernalia.

The Unity Council's first barrio grant was directed to the Edgewood Concerned Parents Association on September 10. The money, totaling just under $5,000, was earmarked for office rental and partial salary payment for a coordinator. The Edgewood Concerned Parents presented a proposal seeking to address roughly the same objectives that Edgewood students had demanded four months earlier when they walked out of their classrooms in protest: the right to speak Spanish on school grounds, improvements in the quality of education at Edgewood, including the addition of courses portraying the positive contributions of Mexican Americans to society, and programs aimed at lowering the dropout rate.

Other community groups were funded before the end of the year. These were not traditional Mexican-American organizations. They were raw, fresh groups rising directly out of the barrio experience. They included Barrios Unidos (an organization composed of seven barrio councils, funded primarily to bring about educational reforms in the San Antonio Independent School District similar to those sought by groups like the Edgewood Concerned Parents Association); La Universidad de los Barrios (a highly controversial school-without-walls program that attempted to help reform barrio gang members); and the Committee on Voter Education and Registration (COVER) (an effort to encourage barrio citizens to become more active in voting and political participation through voter registration block walks and rallies).

Despite continuing admonishments from both the Ford Foundation and the Southwest Council of La Raza to establish a coherent program agenda, MAUC was slow to institutionalize a clear-cut strategy. Many goals and objectives existed solely in Willie's head and could not be found written anywhere. Juan Patlán quickly realized that MAUC's program was being defined by "pretty much whatever kind of vision Willie woke up with that day. One day it would be education, the next day it would be housing, and the next day it would be community organizing." Willie was the thinker, conceptualizer, and cheerleader. Patlán did the paperwork.

The Unity Council's entire oversight and control structure under Velásquez was certainly loose. MAUC typically offered advice and technical assistance but essentially encouraged its community grantees and partners to tackle problems as they saw most fit. This did not mean the Unity Council would fund and hide. Velásquez and Patlán showed up to confront officials, the media, and other powers that be whenever MAUC grantees requested them to do so. Yet, they tried to let the neighborhood groups lead whenever possible, knowing this was the only way barrio organizations and leaders would learn to do things for themselves in the future.

On important nuts-and-bolts fiscal and institutional management issues, Velásquez was especially tuned out. His philosophy was that responding to human need and emotion was paramount to all else: "minor" things like bookkeeping and finances were secondary considerations. Willie's approach to management scared Patlán, but when confronted with these concerns Velásquez replied sharply in what would become a denial-based, imperative for the balance of his organizational life: "Details, details; don't bother me with details, just get it done!"

Willie's expediency relative to organizational administration did not prevent MAUC from gaining quick traction in its substantive work. During its first six months of operation, Unity Council-sponsored groups successfully pushed for the abolishment of the "no Spanish on campus" rule for all seventeen of San Antonio's public school districts. Teacher sensitivity and training sessions were started at Our Lady of the Lake University for barrio teachers. New bilingual materials for curriculum changes were introduced into classrooms. Groups like the Cassiano Park Neighborhood Council developed adult basic education programs. Taking a cue from the War on Poverty term "Maximum Feasible Participation," which spoke to the goal of optimal community engagement in public projects, Barrios Unidos pressed for grassroots representation on the committees and executive board of the local Model Cities program. And the barrio voter registration project, COVER, helped to increase the city's Mexican-American voter base from 198,000 to 246,000. In short, barrio residents were becoming markedly more active in many political, economic, and educational decision-making processes that, prior to MAUC's intervention, had locked them out for decades.

〜〜〜

While MAUC's early victories and ongoing projects kept Velásquez going, growing problems with grantees made life increasingly difficult for Willie. These groups and their leaders had never had access to power and resources. With the Unity Council grants they abruptly gained some of both and in many cases abuses resulted. The newly created "barriocrats," as some came to call them, often simply replicated old power dynamics and repressive practices inherited from the Anglo hierarchy of the past. Instead of alleviating problems in their neighborhoods, some emerging Chicano community leaders exacerbated the oppressiveness of the barrios. In the past, barrio residents had to cast their anger at abstract notions of affluent Anglos living across town in huge mansions; now, in some areas, they were forced to refocus their consternation on inflated Mexican-American egos residing only a few houses away. Deep-seated splits among various community groups and between certain organizations and the Unity Council eventually began to stifle progress. Board meetings became shouting matches where neighborhood groups fought over money and prioritization. Funds were not used improperly, but money was wasted and sometimes spent in ways that were questionable relative to the Unity Council's purposes. With time, the Unity Council was becoming discernibly less unified.

〜〜〜

Five silent months had passed since Willie and three of his MAYO comrades had broken trust over the funding of the Unity Council. Each day brought a deepening division between the former allies. While they all continued the struggle for barrio justice, they no longer fought together. The personal scars opened by their confrontation had not healed and their shared stubbornness to seek their own resolution left each of them on edge. As the divide solidified, Juan Patlán decided to try to help smooth out the differences between Velásquez and Gutiérrez, Compeán, and Pérez. Patlán had always been the mediator of the five original MAYO members, especially playing the buffer role between Velásquez and Gutiérrez. He felt it was time to try something to break the growing pressure that kept these two key movement leaders from actively working together.

Patlán thought that a small peace offering in the form of a Unity Council mini-grant to MAYO would begin to mend the shattered bonds between the Chicano activists. At first, Willie rejected the idea, but Patlán persisted. He pushed Velásquez to work past his pent-up anger and growing personal conflicts with the MAYO leaders to see the merit and the practicality of supporting their work. He knew that, at the end of the day, Willie would be rational and fair. Accordingly, Patlán pressed Velásquez hard on the matter, invoking MAYO's undeniably essential work in the movement as his justification.

"Look, Willie, I know you aren't too crazy about those guys," Patlán told Velásquez, "but you've got to admit, what MAYO is doing out there needs to be done and they're the only ones doing it." In the end, Willie agreed with Patlán; MAYO had a vision that was a necessary part of the movement plan and, even if he did not agree completely with MAYO's leadership, it needed to be carried out.

In early December 1968, the Unity Council granted MAYO just over $8,500 for a six-month period to work on improving education for Mexican Americans in San Antonio and the Rio Grande Valley. The grant, which was to be used to organize more school walkouts and reforms, was a relatively important one in MAUC's and MAYO's experience to that point in time. Of the slightly more than $36,000 in community grants that MAUC allocated in its first six months of operation, the MAYO allocation was its largest single mini-grant.

While the grant only mildly thawed out the strained personal situation between MAYO's founding members, it did make it easier for them to respect each other's work going forward; even if only at a distance. But, as subsequent events would soon reveal, the growing distance between Willie and his increasingly contradictory MAYO co-founders remained vexingly small in the perception of San Antonio's political elite.

In January 1969, under the banner of the Committee for Barrio Betterment, Compeán of MAYO, Dario Chapa of LULAC del Barrio, and C. H. Alejos, vice president of the Laredo Street Council, all Unity Council grantees, announced their intentions to run for city council. Compeán proclaimed the slate's strategy in predictably controversial terms: "Together with my fellow candidates, I shall pursue a course plotted to overthrow the gringos and their vicious and oppressive political machine, which is the Good Government League."

Willie's conscientious abstinence from the city elections to avoid conflict of interest allegations was not enough to protect him or the Unity Council from responsive assaults. Less than two weeks into the protest campaign, Mayor Walter McAllister, himself a product of San Antonio's Good Government League and a notably crusty, vigorous, and opinionated old man, commenced harsh attacks on the challengers and the Unity Council. Invoking a strategy of guilt by association that would later be joined by Congressman Henry B. González, McAllister accused the Unity Council and the Ford Foundation of undue political meddling and alleged misuse of tax-exempt monies for partisan political gains. The attack-driven effort to tie the Unity Council to subversive political activity was relentless and effective. No matter how rationally or diplomatically Velásquez argued that the Unity Council was not involved with the protest campaigns, they were inextricably linked in the minds of many San Antonians.

In fact, Unity Council mini-grants did indirectly facilitate these campaigns. COVER had supporters going door to door with Unity Council funding to register barrio residents to vote, and also used Unity Council support to start service programs for the candidates' neighborhoods. More generally, the Unity Council helped Compeán, Chapa, and Alejos (and, for that matter, dozens of other activists) to develop a relationship with the barrio community that they could now strategically tap for partisan political campaigns. To suggest that the Unity Council intended all of this, however, would be to give too much credit to Velásquez, whose vision for the organization was still very elusive and unsettled in his head. Nevertheless, the city elections of 1969 revealed that MAUC was having a serious (even if not fully calculated) impact on established power relationships in and around San Antonio. This growing impact, in turn, would inspire further resistance down the line from increasingly more formidable adversaries.

༄ ༄ ༄

Del Rio, Texas, a town of 25,000, where slightly more than half the population was Mexican American, was slowly changing its character in the late 1960s. The city's first Mexican-American mayor was elected, as was the county's first Mexican-American commissioner. Five of the seven city councilors were now Mexican American. Mexican-American businessmen were beginning to thrive and were taking a more active role in the community. Although it had taken decades to come, social progress was finally creeping into this sleepy South Texas border town.

In 1968, the Del Rio War on Poverty agency took on several members of the federally supported VISTA (Volunteers in Service to America) Program. Later Del Rio was selected as one of only five locations in the country where a trial Minority Mobilization program would be tested. The purpose of the Minority Mobilization program was to train local people to help VISTA create barrio self-help projects that would inform community residents of available government and private services, and how to access them. The experiment in Del Rio was small, involving at its height only eight VISTA volunteers and ten Minority Mobilization trainees.

The tiny group of community activists quickly began to rile more conservative residents of Del Rio. Community activists became heavily involved with militant youth, and especially the local chapter of MAYO. Unlike San Antonio, where most of the bad-mouthing of MAYO came exclusively from the Anglo side of town, in Del Rio, the attacks came from both Anglos and Mexican Americans, who were led by Arthur González, a local attorney. Many Mexican Americans felt that they had waited too long for improvements to take place and, now, being on the verge of finally seeing needed reforms, they did not want young radicals destroying their momentum. Their concerns stemmed mainly from the VISTA trainees' involvement with MAYO. The VISTA and Minority Mobilization participants, the complainants held, were violating federal rules precluding them from being politically active in the communities they were serving.

In February 1969, following months of constant bickering, the Val Verde county commissioners asked the Del Rio community action agency to discontinue its local VISTA and Minority Mobilization activities. A bitter four-and-a-half-hour town meeting was held with approximately seven hundred people in attendance to resolve the matter. The agency elected to continue the program, but did fire one VISTA worker and two Minority Mobilization trainees for inappropriate involvement in MAYO activities. The meeting's outcomes satisfied neither the advocates nor the opponents of the federal community action programs. The matter could not be left to stand as a tie, however, and subsequent events would see the controversy elevated to state and national proportions.

Contending that the poor were being politically exploited, Del Rio's county commissioners voted unanimously in March to ask Governor Preston Smith to discontinue the programs. Smith, in private gatherings with Del Rio citizens, had earlier indicated a need for local officials to request state intervention before he could do anything. MAYO publicly protested the move and threatened to demonstrate. Four days later, the Mexican-American-dominated city council of Del Rio passed an ordinance similar to one in Birmingham, Alabama that the U.S. Supreme Court had struck down during the height of the black civil rights movement. It prohibited parades and demonstrations without city permits. Defiantly, MAYO organized a march in clear violation of the ordinance. The demonstration ended quickly when over sixty law enforcement officers from Del Rio, Eagle Pass, Ozuna, Rocksprings, Sonora, and Bracketville were brought in. Thirty-one people, mostly kids in their mid-to-late teens, were arrested.

On March 18, State Senator Joe Bernal, State Representatives Carlos Truan, Merle Smith, and José Uriegas, AFL-CIO representative Henry Muñoz, and leaders of VISTA and MAYO (including José Angel Gutiérrez), met with Governor Smith to resolve the expanding conflict. The encounter ended with nothing but more bitterness between all of the combatants.

For Velásquez, much was at stake in the Del Rio situation. The fundamental need to prevent actions such as those taken against MAYO and its community-action agenda there presented more than a question of protecting MAYO; it went deeper. Much of the work the VISTA and Minority Mobilization people were trying to do was the same as the Unity Council was promoting in the barrios of San Antonio. Velásquez believed that if the VISTA and Minority Mobilization programs teaching the needy how to help themselves could be dismantled in Del Rio, MAUC could easily be next on the list. Mexican Americans everywhere could then be blocked from efforts to improve their lot through community organization and self-help. With these thoughts in mind, Velásquez brought State Senator Bernal, Father Henry Casso, Commissioner Albert Peña, and others together to brainstorm a plan of attack. True to the times, it was agreed that a huge march would provide the right response.

Willie's and the Unity Council's deep involvement in the planning of the Del Rio march further strengthened the perception that the Council and MAYO were inseparable units. Velásquez, using the masterful, behind-the-scenes organizing techniques he had learned during the La Raza Unida conferences and the early school walkouts, was one of the march leaders. Held Palm Sunday, March 30, 1969, the mobilization included well over two thousand marchers protesting Governor Preston Smith's and the Val Verde county commissioner's attempts to discontinue Del Rio's VISTA and Minority Mobilization programs. Marching to the county courthouse, the protesters taped a manifesto to the door that read in part: "We feel compelled to warn the U.S. Congress that unless legislation is enacted to protect the VISTA principle of self-determination from arbitrary interference by state and local officials, the entire concept of volunteer service, whether at home or abroad, will be prostituted in the eyes of those idealistic fellow Americans who participate in it."

Senator Edward Kennedy wired his support, telling the protesters, "My strong conviction is that the nation should listen to what is being said in Del Rio." The march was not just a convention of radicals. Liberal Catholic priests, members of the Texas state legislature, respected union officials, and principals of moderate Mexican-American organizations, including Dr. Hector P. García, the founder of the veterans-based American G.I. Forum, lent their support to keeping the VISTA and Minority Mobilization workers in the county.

Unfortunately, much of the rhetoric at the march was excessive. Various speakers made comments that offended more moderate supporters. Instead of focusing solely on VISTA and Minority Mobilization programs, some of the presenters angrily threatened the larger community with militant statements and threats. Gutiérrez, representing MAYO, shocked the crowd assembled at the Del Rio Civic Center when he harshly delivered his point: "We have been oppressed for too long and we will tangle with the *gringo* anywhere he wants to go."

Henry B. González was the target of many protest organizers. They seethingly denounced the congressman's recent charges made at a speech in McAllen that their organizations were infiltrated by "flaming radicals of Mexican descent who had just returned from Cuba and were heavily indoctrinated with racial hatred of the *gringo* imperialist."

The outraged demonstrators publicly demanded that the congressman offer proof of his charges. González later responded by saying his remarks were distorted by the demonstrators. He had not accused the march leaders of being communists; rather, what he had said was that "MAYO for a year or so was infiltrated by students and others from California and these students [had] been subsidized for trips to Cuba by Castro." He had not said that any Texas MAYO members had gone to Cuba. González then went on record to blast MAYO for distributing racially divisive pamphlets, both in Del Rio and in San Antonio.

Willie could sense that something dangerous was brewing in the zealous rhetoric of the marchers and the conspiratorial language of the congressman. Years down the road, he would look back on the Del Rio march and call it "the most significant march and demonstration by Chicanos in Texas history," but that day, Velásquez was most impressed and concerned by the growing civic discord that was increasingly characterizing Mexican-American community political life. The moment was marked by angry, ugly, impatient inclinations ready to explode in a million different directions. Congressman González felt the same way and quietly waited for the young leaders of MAYO and the Unity Council to stumble, hoping to be there to make sure they would not get up again.

Chapter 6

ON THE VERGE OF TURNING A QUARTER of a century old, Willie nostalgically reminisced about his relationship with Congressman Henry B. González, his first political mentor. From the time Willie was growing up in the shadow of the barrios, González was his role model, hero, and inspiration, as he was to many children and adults in the Mexican-American neighborhoods of the Alamo City. When Willie was Billy, nine years old, curiously listening and tasting politics for the first time with the men in his family, González was one of the few Mexican-American politicians' names he heard. Having been elected to the San Antonio city council in 1953, González quickly became a household name—either revered or despised because of his bold, iconoclastic, liberal style. The Mexican-American community loved and respected González because many times he was their lone voice for justice. Those who detested him—mainly those outside of the community—had different names for him. "Nigger lover," was applied when González pushed to end public segregation in San Antonio in 1956 and spent twenty-two hours and two minutes on the floor of the Texas Senate filibustering against a package of segregation bills in 1957. "Dirty, radical, Meskin'," was invoked when he introduced a minimum wage bill in 1956 for thirty cents an hour. "Damn Commie," was attributed to the congressman for most things he did or said that aimed to help his people. González's passion was helping the downtrodden, the voiceless, and the neglected. It was this vision of González that attracted Willie to the congressman.

There was no getting around it; Willie was one of González's boys. Velásquez was a bright, energetic, compassionate, Catholic-trained kid from the Mexican side of town when González first met him. Willie even had taken González's daughter Rosemary to her high school prom. At St. Mary's, Willie headed Collegians for González in the congressman's successful 1964 re-election bid. The following summer, González brought Willie to the big city for a stint at the State Department. Thanks to González, this once-in-a-lifetime opportunity grew into three summers in the nation's capitol and a possible career for Willie in the American diplomatic corps.

A misunderstanding between the naive, idealistic kid and the seasoned politician marked the end of Willie's last summer in Washington, but it was nothing that should have necessarily resulted in a fundamental split. González did not explode when Velásquez told him he was going back to San Antonio to help his people (and some of the congressman's political adversaries) instead of pursuing a permanent career with one of the international agencies. Rather, González, although clearly disapproving, behaved like a father reprimanding a slightly rebellious son—lecturing him and hoping that eventually he would see the light. Willie was caught up with the fervor of the times. It was just a phase, González thought, sooner or later he would have to grow up.

But since the fateful encounter in Washington the gap between the community activist and the veteran politico had steadily continued to grow. Now, at the close of the decade that had brought them together (the 1960s), it was becoming increasingly clear that Willie and the congressman were playing on different teams.

᭞   ᭞   ᭞

In 1969, in the well of the U.S. House of Representatives, Congressman González began a crusade that would make the next few months the longest ones Willie had lived in his short, hectic twenty-five years. Two days after his MAYO co-founder Mario Compeán shockingly woke up the San Antonio establishment in the April city elections by falling just a few hundred votes short of forcing longtime Mayor McAllister into a runoff, González made his first attack against what he perceived to be the growing threat of unchecked Chicano militancy. Under the title "Race Hate" González began his speech saying, "There is no greater poison of mind and spirit than race hate." He then described the grassroots activists as poor, misguided, militant Mexican Americans "becoming the purveyors of the hate they denounce; they are themselves the personification of the unspeakable evils they declaim against; and they are themselves the ultimate tragedy of racism."

González's attacks preyed on the expanding fears of many Americans who felt the country was collapsing and under siege by uncontrollable fringe elements, including minorities who seemingly wanted blood revenge for every act of discrimination bottled up in America's past. The congressman used the national mood, filled with visions of violence, anarchy, and revolution to link his newest political enemies, MAYO, and his older adversaries to these exaggerated images.

González wanted to warn his fellow congressmen and the rest of the nation about the true nature of MAYO's potentially destabilizing impact. Challenging the notion that MAYO's benefactors and supporters were good guys fighting for the poor Mexican American against the wretched Anglo who diabolically plotted to keep the Mexican oppressed, the congressman publicly characterized MAYO's leaders as individuals who were "drawing fire from the deepest wellsprings of hate." As proof, González offered for the congressional record a quotation from *El Deguello*, the San Antonio MAYO newspaper, which underscored the harsh rhetoric and excesses the activists were using to energize their followers: "The gringo took your grandfather's land, he took your father's job, and now he's sucking out your soul. There is no such thing as *mala suerte* (bad luck); there is (sic) only *malos gringos* (bad gringos)."

González realized that some of his political enemies in San Antonio supported MAYO and its activities and he wasted no time in making these individuals accessories to his allegations of that organization's racial misconduct. Trading jabs daily with Bexar County Commissioner Peña and State Senator Bernal, González publicly charged that both were basically motivated to attack him in order to gain his congressional seat.

Peña and Bernal saw González's racial diatribes aimed at MAYO and themselves as nothing more than a smoke screen to discredit the Chicano movement, as well as dilute any small influence they might have. Although they had no real power, especially compared to González, they felt the congressman was threatened by their growing stature and relevance in the barrios. Peña charged: "It is becoming more and more obvious that anyone or any group organizing on behalf of the civil rights of Mexican Americans, if not cleared with [Congressman González], are suspect." Bernal added, "It all seems to be a case of paranoia. He does not seem to feel he has job security and anyone disagreeing with him . . . he sees with distrust and suspicion." Both Peña and Bernal were appalled that González was using McCarthyite guilt-by-association strategies against them. Bernal remembered having earlier defended González against the smear campaigns that labeled him a "pinko" and a "Commie" for his liberal stands. Now Bernal was on the uncomfortable receiving end, his patriotism challenged by the die hard liberal congressman from San Antonio for whom he had once stood up.

Velásquez closely followed the escalating barbs being thrown back and forth between González, Peña, and Bernal as an interested observer, but with no desire to engage as a participant. Irrevocably, this changed on April 8, when González, at a legislative seminar in New Braunfels, Texas, attached Willie, the Unity Council, and the Ford Foundation to his list of targets associated with spreading racial hatred and radicalism. Grouping Willie with Peña, Bernal, and other activists he characterized as "self-imposed leaders," González criticized the Ford Foundation for giving such large amounts of money to their cause, and for unwittingly enriching and promoting them rather than more legitimate grassroots leaders. None of the Chicano activists, the congressman charged, "had ever interested themselves in what they condescendingly [called] *el barrio* until Ford Foundation money became available." González predicted that when the Ford money ran out, these leaders would go back to their comfortable homes and not the barrio. Although personally scarred by these statements, Willie was not overly concerned with González's comments about him or the Unity Council. In his mind, the positive impact of the Unity Council's efforts in the barrios completely overshadowed the occasional use of angry rhetoric by activists; surely, reasonable observers would see it similarly, he felt. If things cooled down for a while, Willie thought, the Unity Council's continuing successes would douse González's attacks and everything would be normal again.

∽ ∽ ∽

Velásquez's hopeful and idealistic beliefs were smashed two days later when MAYO held a press conference to respond to González's accusations and to set forth MAYO's purposes and direction. On April 10, Gutiérrez, in a cold, calm, professorial tone, opened up the MAYO press conference demanding that the journalists report the entire text of his opening statement and the question-and-answer period. Surrounded by Compeán, Guerrero of *La Universidad de los Barrios*, and Juan Rocha of the then recently formed Mexican American Legal Defense and Educational Fund, José Angel Gutiérrez unemotionally read MAYO's prepared statement. It began by blasting federal government and church-related programs as insufficient to bring about rapid social change for Mexican Americans. It went on to assail the cultural genocide of La Raza brought on by gringos and their institutions. The statement marched on with forceful language screaming for Mexican Americans to take control of their destiny, totally separate from the Anglo world. "We will not try to assimilate into this gringo society in Texas," Gutiérrez asserted, "nor will we encourage anybody else to." In answer to Congressman González's attacks, Gutiérrez proclaimed MAYO's resistance to fight against other Mexican Americans. "MAYO will not engage in controversy with fellow Mexican Americans regardless of how unfounded and vindictive their accusations may be." Ending in the same, even, calculated voice, Gutiérrez predicted that some Mexican Americans, the true believers interested in ending the oppression of their people "will come together, resist, and eliminate the gringo."

The dozen or so local journalists who came to hear MAYO's response to Congressman González's accusations immediately pushed Gutiérrez to clarify MAYO's broad generalizations.

"What is your definition of a gringo?" one of the attending journalists inquired.

"A person or an institution that has a certain policy or program or attitudes that reflect bigotry, racism, discord, and prejudice and violence,"

Gutiérrez responded.

"Is Congressman González a gringo?" another reporter asked.

"He has demonstrated some tendencies that fit into that category," replied Gutiérrez, unwittingly rescinding the policy made public just minutes before about not attacking fellow Mexican Americans.

"Are a majority of Anglo-Americans gringos?" the journalists pressed further.

Without pausing, Gutiérrez fired back, "According to the Kerner Report (the Johnson administration's commissioned study of U.S. race relations that followed the worst episodes of racial unrest in the 60s) we could say yes to that question."

"What exactly do you mean by the phrase 'eliminate the gringo'?" the journalists wanted to know.

"You can eliminate an individual in various ways," Gutiérrez quickly explained. "You can certainly kill him, but that is not our intention at this moment," José Angel asserted. "You can remove the base of support that he operates from, be it economic, political, or social. That is what we intend to do."

The reporters were not satisfied: "If nothing else works, you're going to kill all the gringos?" they asked.

Gutiérrez sought to sidestep the question, stating: "We'll have to find out if nothing else will work."

The journalists insisted further, "And then you'll kill us all?"

Gutiérrez started to answer, then went after the newsman in a subtle way. "If it doesn't work . . . I'd like to add . . . that if you label yourself a gringo then you're one of the enemy."

The exchange continued and it seemed for a moment as though Gutiérrez had successfully deflected the reporters' jabs. Yet, minutes later, Gutiérrez was pushed again on the question of killing gringos. Flustered by the continuing onslaught, Gutiérrez defiantly stared down the reporters and replied, "If worse comes to worst and we have to resort to that means, it would be self-defense."

The next editions of the local papers ran predictably unsympathetic and sensationalist recounts of the press conference: "MAYO Head Warns of Rioting, Violence"; "Elimination of Gringos May Become Necessary, Gutiérrez tells S.A. Press Conference"; "We'll Crush Any Gringo Who Gets in Our Way."

When Willie saw the headlines he was furious. How could Gutiérrez have been so naïve and stupid? he thought. Eliminate the gringo? Kill the gringo? What was he thinking?

Velásquez knew Gutiérrez's remarks would deeply intensify the attacks being directed to the Unity Council, as well as other Chicano organizations and activists in the city. Still, Willie thought he could help to moderate the resulting damage. He started by taking a positive public posture. When reporters asked how *he* felt about Anglos, Willie replied: "San Antonio and the nation are full of good Anglos who pay taxes, vote, and treat all persons equally." Unfortunately, this is not what the press was looking for. Lacking bite, Velásquez's soft, healing statement was buried deep in an article that otherwise accented the more colorful, threatening remarks of the militant MAYO representatives.

The day after the newspapers trumpeted Gutiérrez's alleged calls to kill the gringo, Congressman González quickly condemned the remarks as "false, noxious, and poisonous drivel" and publicly challenged Peña and Bernal to disavow their support for MAYO, Gutiérrez, and his statements. Then González told the press about three threats that had been made on his life in the last week. While he received threats regularly, González said he was singling out these recent ones because they had "the same threatening tenor as statements made by José Angel Gutiérrez." These comments strengthened the public's image of MAYO as an extremist organization constantly planning subversive activities (and now possibly plotting political assassination).

೭ ೭ ೭

On Saturday, April 12, two hundred neighborhood residents crammed into Cooper Junior High School to hear Willie talk about the ongoing work of the Unity Council and to voice their opinions on the recent charges made by González. In glaring contrast to MAYO's press conference, Velásquez answered the congressman's attacks by appealing to deeply held, fundamental American values.

He spoke of the Unity Council's mission "to work with . . . Mexican American barrio inhabitants to initiate a social and economic self-help program to lift themselves up by their bootstraps with private sources of funding so as not to be a tax burden." Willie felt these ideas appealed to the American spirit that was borne of the nation's immigrant traditions and Protestant work ethic. He also wanted to touch people's indignant self-interest, letting them know that their precious tax dollars were not being wasted on any of the Unity Council's programs.

Wrapping himself in the flag, Willie respectfully asked González to name the alleged extremists and criminals who had infiltrated the MAYO organization and the movement more generally. Velásquez then harkened back to the McCarthy anti-communist excesses of the 1950s, recalling that many innocent lives were destroyed by expedient and baseless charges. Now, he argued, Congressman González was using these same tactics. Velásquez's presentation intensified as he angrily stated, "In all our collected efforts, in working for César Chávez's union in Rio Grande City, in working with the Bishops' Committee for the Spanish Speaking, in working in Crystal City, in working with the students at Lanier and Edgewood and barrio gangs, NEVER were we called traitors to our country!" The audience exploded with approval. This was definitely not the language of separatism or racism.

In closing, Velásquez listed the inhumane conditions existing on the Westside of San Antonio and declared, "The Mexican American Unity Council strives to let the people determine for themselves what their problems are and determine for themselves what to do about them, in the great American democratic tradition." The attending community members roundly applauded Willie's public-spirited, positive, and uplifting words.

Willie felt that the Unity Council's response to González had been successful that evening because it answered his charges without lowering itself into a González-bashing statement. Velásquez never lost control of his cool, collected demeanor as he read his prepared remarks. He avoided the temptation to call González a gringo or a tool of the Good Government League, advising instead, "We respectfully warn the public to beware of public officials who misrepresent the anguish and frustrations of the barrio people." Willie's remarks were followed by supporting comments by various community members. Guadalupe Ibarra, youth chairman of the Cassiano Park Neighborhood Council, softly stated, "It is a shame that our Congressman is fighting Mexican Americans who come to help us help each other." Other speakers invited the congressman to come observe the many good works Chicano activists were doing in the neighborhoods. At the meeting's conclusion, Velásquez and other Chicano organizers breathed a deep sigh of relief, hoping the community's support would help to get González off their backs and allow them to concentrate on their programs again.

⌇ ⌇ ⌇

Killing gringos was the last thing the Ford Foundation wanted to see in the media coverage of their funded programs in Mexican-American communities. Ford was tightly locked in a battle with Congress when the MAYO episode exploded. The recent infusion of large amounts of private foundation money into controversial public arenas like educational desegregation and reform, and voter registration had led Congresswoman Edith Green of Oregon to introduce strict legislation in Congress that would significantly bar Ford and other funders from supporting political activities or campaigns amounting to "lobbying" or "influencing" with an eye to informing public policy. By some estimates, these changes in the federal tax laws governing the work of foundations and other tax-exempt organizations would outlaw nearly 70 percent of Ford's current programming in their National Affairs and Social Development sections, leaving the foundation, some experts believed, with "little to do with its wealth but hand it out to symphony orchestras, Community Chests, and Ivy League schools."

The dual tension of the Vietnam conflict and the rapidly deteriorating racial situation across the country created an environment in which conservatives sought to control what they saw as radical threats to the nation. For Congressman Wright Patman, foundations were a large part of the problem. Patman, one of the leading congressional forces behind the attempt to curtail foundation activity, was a feisty, seventy-six-year-old down-home Texas congressman who had been crusading for several years against what he perceived to be irresponsible liberal groups. Patman's distrust of the liberal foundation world was evident in his statements on the floor of Congress: "What are the Ford and Rockefeller Foundations . . . really up to? . . . Are they on the road to becoming political machines? . . . Does the Ford Foundation have a grandiose design to bring vast political, economic, and social changes to the nation in the 1970s?" Patman intended to force the foundations' hands through federal action that would either significantly regulate their activities in certain areas or compel them to pay taxes.

Four major events helped Patman in his latest bid to strangle Ford, the largest of his targets. First, there was Ford's involvement in a New York City school decentralization experiment that tried to increase the participation levels of African-American and Puerto Rican parents in the policy-making decisions of their schools. The program led to raw conflict between middle-class Jewish administrative and teaching professionals and poverty-stricken black and Puerto Rican parents whose children filled the schools in the Ocean Hill-Brownsville area of Brooklyn. A hostile, citywide school strike resulted and John Lindsay's run at a second term as mayor was threatened by a significant drop in support from Jewish voters who had backed him in his first election. Ford was singled out for creating this chaos.

Second, Ford Foundation-supported voter registration work in Cleveland with the local chapter of the Congress of Racial Equality (CORE), came to be interpreted by many observers as a blatantly partisan effort to elect Carl Stokes the first black mayor of the city. Ford gave CORE $175,000 to do community work including voter registration. An estimated $30,000 was used for voter registration efforts targeted almost exclusively to the African-American community of Cleveland, resulting in approximately twenty thousand new registered minority voters. Stokes defeated incumbent Mayor Ralph Locher by eighteen thousand votes in the Democratic primary and then squeezed by the Republican nominee Seth Taft by a scant sixteen hundred votes. Though there were three major voter registration efforts going on simultaneously in the local black community, the white establishment in Cleveland blamed Ford and its grant to CORE for unfairly tilting the political balance in their city.

The third major event inspiring Congressional objection was Ford president McGeorge Bundy's performance before the House Ways and Means Committee in February of 1969. The week before his testimony, Bundy and the Ford Foundation had been embarrassed by a *New York Times* article which reported that eight grants had been given to prominent staff members of the recently assassinated liberal U.S. Senator Robert F. Kennedy "to ease the transition from public to private life." Personally approved by Bundy, the awards gave "up to a year of leisure and freedom from immediate financial concerns." This put the essentially conservative committee in a highly discriminating mood. Instead of being deferential, Bundy brought a somewhat arrogant and condescending attitude to the congressional hearing. The former Kennedy and Johnson administration official talked down to many of the committee members and flippantly answered several of their questions. Congressional members from both sides of the aisle denounced Bundy's testimony and responded by inserting even stricter conditions, known as the "Bundy provisions," into proposed anti-foundation legislation before them. Foundation leaders and observers saw Bundy's encounter with the Ways and Means Committee as a major setback to the philanthropic field. One commentator characterized Bundy's testimony as "a personal Bay of Pigs and . . . a political disaster for the entire foundation industry." Another top foundation executive commented publicly: "I admire greatly what Mac has achieved at Ford but in my opinion most of the punitive aspects of the (anti-foundation) bill can be directly related to his behavior at the hearings."

The fourth and most recent episode undermining Ford's standing among moderate and conservative congressmen was the growing crisis surrounding the foundation's involvement in Mexican-American communities. Traditionally, Ford's philosophy and approach had built on three proven precepts: fund the moderate middle, replicate successful model programs, and put money in the hands of proven people. None of these practices governed the funding of projects in the untested Mexican-American community. By funding the moderate middle, Ford meant established groups such as the NAACP, the National Urban League, and the Southern Christian Leadership Conference in the black community—groups that walked and talked the language of accommodation and working within the system. As Mike Sviridoff, Ford's watchful Director of National Affairs said, "We're not interested at Ford in raising hell and we're certainly not interested in revolution."

Ford made a bold decision when it decided to enter the unknown realm of the Mexican-American world at a precarious time in its own existence. When news hit of the raging battle going on between foundation subgrantees like MAYO and the Unity Council, on one hand, and the influential Congressman González, on the other, top Ford officials became uneasy and alarmed. Hoping to diffuse the escalating confrontation, Sviridoff called Siobahn Oppenheimer, the Ford program officer in charge of the Southwest

Council grant and its sub-grantees, to the foundation's "Tenth Floor," the court of power where Bundy and his top officials were housed. Sviridoff told Oppenheimer to meet with Chicano leaders and find out what really was happening in San Antonio. To avoid adding East Coast fuel to the Texas fire, Ford decided the first investigation would take place in secret, away from the battlefront, in the deceptively sleepy city of Phoenix, Arizona, headquarters of the Southwest Council.

Oppenheimer, affectionately known as "Oppy" by her foundation colleagues, was highly familiar with local organizing and community action programs in and around New York, but the world of Chicano activism was relatively new to her. As her plane landed in Phoenix, Oppenheimer collected her materials, mostly raging newspaper articles about alleged Mexican-American revolutionaries, and told herself to "Think brave and look cool." Not knowing exactly what to expect, Oppenheimer was startled when the two Texas radicals she was scheduled to interview, Velásquez and Gutiérrez, showed up with neatly cropped hair, all-American outfits, and thick glasses. Dipping into their Catholic training, they respectfully called her "Ma'am," politely took her bag, and prepared to leave the airport. "My God, [these] are the sort of young men you hope your daughter will bring home," Oppenheimer thought to herself.

Oppy's initial meeting with the Chicano leaders to ascertain their side of the story dragged on for eight hours. Velásquez, Gutiérrez, Herman Gallegos (now director of the Southwest Council), Miguel Barragán (now a Southwest Council field representative), and Alex Mercure, director of an agricultural project known as HELP, rehashed in great detail all of the contested events and developments that had recently taken place. Oppenheimer tediously explained what could and could not be done with Ford funds, explaining to her hosts: "(Ford) cannot be associated with any group that professes or practices violence, racism or any illegal or subversive activities. We can only support nonpartisan small "p" political activities—and maybe not for long on that one—and we do not favor community organization without goals and issues that lead to hard programming."

Velásquez and Gutiérrez frankly defended their actions and presented Oppenheimer with examples and evidence of the many positive contributions the Unity Council and MAYO had made to San Antonio's barrios. Oppenheimer found herself developing a quick understanding that the alleged San Antonio radicals were in fact passionately committed young Americans who simply wanted to improve the dire circumstances of their people. She saw them as relative innocents by New York standards. They had not started any riots, burned any flags, or taken over any buildings. They looked more like college nerds than revolutionaries. In her post-review report to Sviridoff, Oppenheimer called Velásquez and Gutiérrez "young, clean cut, articulate, bright gentlemen. They really fit no stereotype of the raging dangerous militant. If we walked (San Antonio Mayor) McAllister around [Brooklyn's] Bed-Stuy [neighborhood] for a couple of days, he'd go home [and] clasp his militants to his bosom." In the end, Oppenheimer strongly recommended that Ford continue to support Chicano community advocacy efforts. "In my mind, the decision we must make is whether we can afford *not* to support justifiable programs that are consistent with our priorities. . . . If the critical issue is whether [controversial] incidents may occur [as a result of us funding this work], we could end up funding nothing."

∽ ∽ ∽

The very same day Oppenheimer met secretly with Velásquez, Gutiérrez, and representatives of the Southwest Council, Congressman González had dramatically stepped up his assault on MAYO and the Unity Council by unleashing what would become a relentless avalanche of attacks on the floor of the House of Representatives. Over a two-week period, González would speak on six separate occasions on the wicked ways of militant Chicano racists. On April 15, González reiterated the dangers of reverse racism that in his estimation permeated the Chicano movement. He also underscored allegations of a growing potential for violence in more radical movement quarters, citing Gutiérrez's 'kill the gringo' remarks before the House as evidence for his concerns.

The next day González engaged the Ford Foundation in the thick of the battle. Chastising Ford staff for being irresponsible, González, in a patronizing tone, stated, "I do not believe that it is wise to hand a child gasoline and matches but this is what has been done." González did not accuse foundation principals of deliberately funding racists; he conceded in fact that they probably had the greatest of intentions when they funded the Southwest Council and its sub-grantees. But he assailed, "rather than fostering brotherhood, the foundation has supported the spewing of hate, and rather than creating a new political unity, it has destroyed what little there was, and rather than creating new leadership, it is simply financing the ambitions of some men who are greedy and some who are ruthless and a few who are plainly irresponsible." González then resurrected the notion of *La Universidad de los Barrios* as a place where Mexican-American gang members carried out drinking bouts, wild activity, and terror. Finally, without mentioning Willie by name, González went after the Unity Council director saying, "The Council is headed by a very young and peculiar man whose attitudes appear to be more or less racist." It was the most negative accusation González could plausibly share about Velásquez because he was one of the few original MAYO members who had not turned to harsh, intimidating, separatist language in the growing confrontation with the congressman.

On April 22, González continued his public campaign to discredit Chicano activists and their supporters as instigators of interracial hatred and demagoguery, commenting on the congressional floor: "I cannot accept the belief that playing at revolution produces anything beyond an excited imagination; and I cannot accept the belief that imitation leadership is a substitute for the real thing."

The congressman continued his personal attack against Willie by adding three new dimensions to his prior repertoire of charges: Willie was handing out Unity Council money only to friends; he was too young to know what was best for the people in the barrios; and the barrio residents were not even a part of deciding what the Unity Council did. "It is questionable to my mind that a very young and inexperienced man can prescribe the social and political organizations of a complex and troubled community; (The Unity Council's money) is actually being spent . . . to employ friends of the director and his preconceived notions. The people who are to be united apparently don't get much say in what the 'Unity Council' is up to." Calling the militants "architects of discord" and "prophets of doom," González predicted that, in the end, only those who spoke with conviction and integrity would still be around while the others who merely rambled with passion would be long gone.

In addition to his speeches on the House floor, González wrote to Wilbur Mills, the powerful chairman of the House Ways and Means Committee, asking him to investigate the growing problem of Chicano militancy. Mills responded by writing his friend "Mac" Bundy at Ford, asking him, in effect, what the hell was going on in the foundation's thinking and actions relative to Mexican-American community activism. González also passed on as much unfavorable information about movement leaders as he could to fellow committee member Wright Patman. He hoped his fellow Texan Patman, the avowed opponent of the liberal foundation world, would attack Ford for promoting reverse racism. The congressman also requested that the comptroller general comprehensively review War on Poverty programs in San Antonio and asked the IRS to examine Ford Foundation-supported projects in his district, with the idea of exposing any excesses relative to political activities.

In a press conference held April 28, González further attacked Willie, personally attributing to him the birth of Chicano reverse racism on account of his role fifteen months prior in organizing the January 1968 Raza Unida Conference at Kennedy High School, where twelve hundred people assembled to discuss community concerns. The idea of gathering to discuss ways to help the poor did not bother González. What upset him was that the conference had opened the door, in his view, for outside agitators to infiltrate San Antonio: Communist-trained individuals who "came for the purpose of inciting disturbances and riots." González challenged Velásquez "to tell us who these people were who for the first time came to our area."

Later that day in the chamber of the House, the bleeding-heart liberal

González was joined by several conservative congressional colleagues as he stepped up his campaign to warn America of the emerging Chicano radicalism. Resurrecting proven anticommunist attacks of the early cold war era, González tried to link the militants with Cuba's Fidel Castro, arguing that many MAYO members copied Castro's manners by wearing berets, beards, and fatigues. González wanted these radicals stamped out, now, not later when they had a chance to recruit more racists to the fold. "I believe the best time to kill a snake is before it begins to rattle," he stated. Congressman O. C. Fisher of San Angelo, a conservative who rarely agreed with González on anything, joined in and praised the San Antonio congressman for "having performed a very timely service to our country." Congressman Abraham Kazen of Laredo warned the public of the hate mongers "advocating violence and the overthrow of the rule of law." Congressman Kika de la Garza of Mission chimed in, saying these angry young men did not want justice; they wanted to get even. Finally, Congressman J. J. Pickle of Brownsville voiced the need for some sort of congressional control of the irresponsible foundation world. González then took another stab at Willie, asking aloud how the Ford Foundation could give such large amounts of money to someone who had never had a regular job.

On April 29, González returned to his pulpit with fresh information and alleged direct proof that several of MAYO's founders were on Ford payrolls and that many MAYO members either directly or indirectly received assistance from Ford-funded sub-grantees. Under the heading "Foundation Responsibility II" González cautiously covered his bases and claimed that of the seven grants MAUC had made to date, three supported groups headed by MAYO members and a fourth grant assisted a voter registration effort run by "an old ally of a local politico who often addresses MAYO meetings," and who was a board member of the Southwest Council—Bexar County Commissioner Albert Peña. With this recount, González sought to inspire a public outcry against MAYO, its leaders, and their various benefactors and supporters.

On May 1, González took to the congressional floor one last time and reiterated his disgust for *La Universidad de los Barrios* and its so-called gang program in a speech entitled "Ford Foundation Plus San Antonio Equals Murder." González indirectly held Ford executives responsible for recent incidents of mismanagement, crime, and violence that allegedly took place at the MAYO—and Unity Council—supported youth center. González closed by stating it was a shame that Ford money had been wasted on such a frivolous program when it could have gone toward helping to solve the real problems that existed in his district.

᪐ ᪐ ᪐

The spring of 1969 seemed a painful eternity for Velásquez. He felt violated by González's relentless assaults. His entire life had been upended, thrown into a chaotic state of uncertainty. The congressman's attacks paralyzed the Unity Council's activities. From the first allegations charging misuse of foundation funds, Velásquez had been put on the defensive. Even the supportive Southwest Council of La Raza was now demanding detailed reports on everything the Unity Council had done, was doing, and would do, going forward. Ford requested still additional documentation. Every day slowly blended into the next as Willie spent most of his time reacting, responding, filling out forms, checking figures and expenditures, copying, reporting, verifying, and then filling out still more forms.

On one level, Willie could understand González's concerns. He was worried about political power and control in his district. Many politicians around the country were feeling the same pinch from community action programs established by the War on Poverty. These innovative projects created new power centers in neighborhoods that lacked direct links to any politician or loyalty to established individuals and institutions in the larger community. Groups like the Unity Council were tinkering with the existing balance of power in the barrios. These unknown quantities made González and other politicians across the nation nervous. They just did not know how much the balance possibly could be changed by these groups and did not really want to find out.

Congressman González knew that none of this could have happened without the resources of the Ford Foundation. Without this money, the barriocrats were nothing more than unarmed agitators. The Ford money generated fresh, small pockets of influence in the barrios. Even though the amount given to the Unity Council and its neighborhood groups was never enough to truly impact the complex interconnected problems that plagued the Mexican-American neighborhoods, it was enough to stir things up.

What Willie could not understand, however, was the knee-jerk hostility built into González's reaction, which seemed grossly exaggerated and out of proportion relative to what was actually occurring. Willie was also disappointed and confused by the congressman's unwillingness to consider the beneficial impact and potential of the work being done by Chicano activists in the barrios. Why wouldn't he give them the chance to prove themselves? Did he see them as that big of a threat? Militants from other communities around the country had in fact caused murders, riots, and extreme violence, but none of that had happened in Texas with the Unity Council and MAYO. They were not burning down buildings or instigating riots like the ones that had taken place in Detroit and Watts in the past few years. Given these realities, Willie simply could not understand the congressman's motives.

Hoping to dispel continuing misapprehension and misinformation stemming from González's aggressive campaign to discredit the San Antonio movement, Willie decided to hold a press conference on the last day of April 1969, to set the record straight. Looking battered, worn out, and feeling mentally taxed, Willie took a deep breath, and began the press conference by stating: "[Congressman] González has made many charges over the last few weeks, and now we think it's time to produce the facts." Velásquez presented a list of thirty-two organizations that attended the Raza Unida Conference he had organized fifteen months prior, which González was now touting as the beginning of reverse racism in the Mexican-American community of Texas. Listing groups such as the Texas Council of Churches, Texas AFL-CIO, LULAC councils, G.I. Forum chapters, and the Valley Farm Workers Assistance Committee, Velásquez pointed out that the organizations invited were compiled from lists of Catholic groups he had worked with while he was at the Bishops' Committee for the Spanish Speaking. Frustrated by what he felt were trumped-up charges brought up over a year after the event took place, Velásquez rhetorically asked González, "There were some twelve hundred people at the meeting. Is González suggesting we should [have checked] everyone on their patriotism before [permitting them] to attend the meeting?" In a burst of virulent Mexican machismo, Willie closed the press conference by defiantly challenging the congressman to stop using his congressional immunity on the floor of the House of Representatives where he was making false, wild charges. "We have sent him a letter asking that if he has a problem we will be glad to discuss it with him anytime, anywhere," Willie concluded. Velásquez left the press conference wondering how soon it would be before González began his next round of fire.

৵ ৵ ৵

Conservatives blasting the Ford Foundation was a normal and relatively manageable occurrence, but when Congressman González, a die-hard liberal, came after the foundation, Ford executives knew they had a problem. Near the end of May, Sviridoff phoned González seeking a meeting with the congressman to discuss his concerns about the Unity Council, MAYO, the Mexican American Legal Defense and Educational Fund (MALDEF), and the other San Antonio groups receiving money from Ford's coffers. Outside Washington at the time, González responded to the Ford message by sending a six-page letter saying they should not meet until Ford fully understood his position. Restating the arguments he had been making on the floor of Congress and in the media, González presented his case. He added an important new contention as well, alleging that the multiple layers of people and groups involved with Ford-funded projects made it possible for local activities and their sponsors to "use tax free money for [political] purposes that are not legitimate under the terms of the grants." None of this was simply abstraction for González. He accused Willie and his colleagues of campaigning against him. Yet González the congressman had no way of proving whether this was done on their free time or on the expense of the Ford Foundation. "Further," González went on to observe, "since Velásquez has many outlets, it is impossible to trace which of his activities are legal and which are not."

A few weeks later at the Occidental Restaurant, González discussed the issues over dinner with Ford representatives Sviridoff and Oppenheimer, community labor leaders Paul Montemayor and Henry Santiestevan, and Herman Gallegos of the Southwest Council of La Raza. Sviridoff flatly told González that Ford already had the reactionaries after them and now with a liberal on their back, the anti-foundation legislation was strengthened. González did not cave in to the pressure. He was not as harsh with them as he was in his speeches, interviews, and letters, but he still firmly held his ground. Santiestevan and Montemayor reminded González of the tremendous support labor had given him and tried to convince González of what they were trying to do with the Southwest Council and its affiliates. González did not budge. He wanted to see some changes. That was the only way he was going to be satisfied.

◡ ◡ ◡

In the midst of the MAYO controversy, the Southwest Council of La Raza asked Ford's approval to make an additional sub-grant to MAYO out of its remaining funds. Ford delayed making a decision and finally requested the Council's Gallegos to have Peña, Velásquez, and Compeán fly to New York so they could discuss the latest developments in the dispute with Henry B. González and his congressional allies. In New York, the contingent made its way up to Sviridoff's office on the famed "Tenth Floor." Once inside they exchanged the usual pleasantries and moved straight to the business at hand. Peña, who did most of the talking, did not mince words and quickly tried to put Sviridoff on the defensive. "Is it true that you all are going to cut off these young men for the work they are doing? If it's true, all I can tell you is that you are the most chicken-shit outfit I've ever heard of in my life!" Sviridoff did not hesitate. Yes, it was true; no more Ford money would go to MAYO. Ford, reacting the way it usually did with controversial programs, decided it was in the foundation's best interest to cut all ties to MAYO and its inflammatory talk. The San Antonio community leaders all tried to convince Sviridoff and Ford to change their mind, to help them continue their work, but it was too late. The decision stood. The Ford Foundation, after having been a pioneer in funding Mexican-American community organizing activities, had finally caved in to the false and exaggerated accusations of powerful political forces.

Compeán, speaking for MAYO, strongly condemned Ford's action back in San Antonio, unwittingly underscoring the foundation's rationale for discontinuing MAYO's support by stating: "Political involvement is necessary in order to continue our programs." The MAYO leader topped off his comments by calling Ford a "gringo" institution, cementing in the minds of many San Antonians the perception that MAYO was a purely separatist and extremist organization.

Willie was himself outraged and felt bitterly disappointed by Ford's refusal to stick it out with MAYO. In his eyes, it was his ex-political mentor González who made this all possible. Willie naively felt that MAYO's actions as a group should be separated from what individual MAYO members did on their own. MAYO did not run for office, Compeán did. But Velásquez was only fooling himself. At a time when any suspect group was closely scrutinized, it was impossible for activists to take off one hat and put on the next without someone accusing them of being the same organization hidden behind a new name.

Cutting itself off from MAYO was the easier half of the battle for Ford in its attempt to get its Mexican-American grantees under control. The tough part was making sure stricter rules for the Southwest Council and its affiliates were implemented. Ford executives had been pushed to the brink by the MAYO situation, and they were going to do everything they could to make sure a repeat performance did not occur in the broader Mexican-American portfolio of the foundation. Before Ford staff would even consider refunding the Southwest Council, it had to make corrective changes in internal structure and local program strategy. Following these adjustments, Ford demanded that the Southwest Council strengthen its monitoring of local programs and increase its ability to provide technical assistance to more inexperienced groups. It also requested the Council to cut back on its expanding program activities and to focus on only three or four key areas. Ideally the areas would be "hard" programming such as housing and job training rather than controversial "soft" activities like community organizing and voter registration. Once these priorities were established, the local affiliates needed to restructure themselves to run projects in line with the new objectives.

Ford also had special requests and conditions for the Unity Council relative to continued funding, including another round of board diversification (to ensure as broad and representative a group of community leadership and views as possible) and a discontinuation of its work in the Rio Grande Valley.

The Southwest Council and the Unity Council suddenly felt the winds of change steadily closing in on them. Their earlier dreams of doing whatever was needed to solve neighborhood problems were fading rapidly, yet there was still so much to do. With everything in flux, Velásquez and his Chicano movement allies braced themselves for an uncertain future.

Chapter 7

WILLIE FELT LIKE HE HAD BEEN BEATEN raw. The relentless attacks had numbed him. The spiraling stacks of bureaucratic foundation forms and reports had drained him. The Ford Foundation's response to the crisis had deeply disheartened him: MAYO would not be funded again. The San Antonio movement had hit a formidable wall, inspired by the controversy involving Congressman González and other adversaries. It was an extremely discouraging time for Velásquez and his fellow movement leaders. In the midst of this turmoil, however, an unexpected ray of hope came to Willie. Her name was Janie Sarabia.

Willie remembered interviewing Janie in the fall of 1968 on a community television program he had co-hosted. Then a young VISTA volunteer, she talked about the VISTA minority mobilization effort and how people could get involved. Half a year later, the attractive community organizer surprisingly popped back into Willie's life when he visited longtime labor activist Franklin Garcia's home to watch televised election returns with other Chicano politicos. Afterwards, the activists went to the Alaskan Palace, a Mexican club packed with the sounds of clashing billiard balls and blaring *conjunto* music. It was there that Willie had his first intimate conversation and dance with his future wife. A few weeks later, Willie called Janie for a date. Their first formal night out together would greatly define the couple's future terms of endearment.

Willie and Janie's first date was not the passionate, romantic, starry-eyed tale of two destined lovers finally finding one another and losing themselves in each other's arms. This was May 1969, the heyday of the Chicano political movement. Instead of a candlelight dinner for two, Willie took Janie to a Methodist convention meeting where he was trying to get funding for the Unity Council.

The entire evening was a nerve-wracking, horrible experience for Janie, a shy, Kansas-reared Latina who had grown up in a poor migrant farmworker family. She hated public receptions and small talk. She did not know a soul in the crowd. She could not think of anything to say to Willie. All of this made her nervous. As the evening drifted on, Janie's nervousness was replaced by a sense of failure. When she said good night to Willie later that night, she was certain that he would never call her again.

Janie was completely wrong. Willie was quickly falling in love with her. He liked her light-brown hair and funny midwestern accent. He liked her commitment to the Mexican-American people. But, most of all, he loved the way she made him smile and laugh. Her natural sense of humor and upbeat personality made everyone feel relaxed and at home. Willie, ever the serious one, needed someone exactly like Janie to force him to enjoy life and to laugh out loud. He had not been looking for a serious girlfriend when he asked Janie out. His community work was his true love, but her presence tugged at his dormant heart in profound and unexpected ways.

Willie and Janie were still not dating exclusively when he decided to have a surprise birthday party for her in June. It was her twenty-second birthday and no one seemed to remember; none of her close friends or colleagues were anywhere to be found. In coordination with Willie, Gilbert Rico, a VISTA friend, asked Janie to the movies to quietly celebrate the occasion. After the show, they decided to go by Janie's apartment to see if her roommates were back and to get something to eat. As she strolled in, all of her VISTA friends startled her with loud choruses of "Surprise!"

It was the first surprise birthday party anyone had ever thrown for Janie in her entire life. As she thanked her roommates, they told her that she really needed to thank Willie Velásquez, who was not even there. Willie, always the organizer, had planned the whole thing and had given them money to put everything together. "Willie?" Janie asked, "Well, then why isn't he here?" At that precise moment, Willie burst through the door followed by an eight-piece mariachi band that serenaded the birthday girl with beautiful love songs for the balance of the evening. This was definitely more romantic than going to a meeting with a bunch of Methodists, Janie thought to herself.

Janie's relationship with Willie up to this point was relatively casual. There were no commitments. They enjoyed each other's company, but they could see other people if they wished. Now things began to become more serious; in time, too serious for Janie. Willie wanted something more than an occasional date, but Janie was not sure what she wanted. After going through the dizzying possibilities in her head, she decided the best thing she could do was to back off from the relationship. She needed some distance. She needed to think. Willie accepted Janie's call for space and agreed dejectedly not to bother her anymore.

During the weeks that followed, however, Janie could not fill the void Willie's absence created. It was as if someone had reached into the deepest recesses of her soul and taken away what brought her joy. She had made a huge mistake. Now, unable to suppress her longing for Willie, she wanted him back. She sent him a card saying she was sorry about the way she had acted. She wanted to be friends again; maybe they could start seeing each other once more. Willie received the card and responded by tracking Janie down at a local community meeting. He marched up to her during the meeting and told her that if they were going to see each other again, he wanted it to be exclusive, just them and no one else. Janie hesitated and then answered yes with her heart instead of no with her head. In time, the two would marry and start a family. Willie had now seemingly managed to get his personal life on track. But the challenges of his public commitments and responsibilities would only continue to grow as the 1960s came to a close.

꒜   ꒜   ꒜

In the midst of Congressman Henry B. González's charges that *La Universidad de los Barrios* was nothing more than a center for gang members to continue their wild ways, Velásquez envisioned a plan that would turn the alleged ruffians into entrepreneurs and ease concerns about MAUC's involvement with the gangs. Formally known as *Las Industrias de La Universidad*, Velásquez's program consisted of gang members and school dropouts developing and running small for-profit businesses. These businesses would give the youth managerial and business skills they could transfer to other jobs and leadership venues.

MAUC's first entrepreneurial foray involved the development of a fast-food Mexican restaurant called *El Chaleco* (after the multicolored Mexican folkloric vest of the same name). *El Chaleco* was to be run by twenty former gang members with the help of several college students. The proceeds from the venture would support efforts to encourage school completion by area Hispanic youth. Community businessmen would serve as advisors to the project, which received start-up loans and gifts from local churches totaling $28,000.

The restaurant's successful commencement portended good things to come. City Councilman Pete Torres and County Commissioner Albert Peña were guest waiters for the opening, which saw over one hundred people pack into the tiny establishment in the brief two hours it was open for business on its first day of operation. A deep sense of fulfillment and relief took hold in Velásquez, but it would be sadly short-lived.

Ironically, fresh on the heels of the Unity Council's battle with Congressman González, MAYO co-founders José Angel Gutiérrez and Mario Compeán resurfaced to further complicate things for Willie. From their platform as founding Unity Council board members, they became bent on firing Velásquez for attempting to take the Unity Council down a new path, away from the thick of the political battle. The flimsy, unspoken truce that forced the original MAYO associates back together to fight Congressman González's attacks had snapped easily. The anger and leeriness the dissatisfied MAYO co-founders had expediently shelved was now back in the fore-front of their minds. Gutiérrez and Compeán now wanted Willie out. They saw him turning the Unity Council into nothing more than another conventional social service agency that offered Mexican Americans false hopes and dependency. The Unity Council board erupted in contention with members divided over the organization's appropriate direction going forward. Constructive talk was lost, drenched in a pool of pettiness.

Velásquez, the man who could handle anything, could no longer handle the Unity Council. González's relentless attacks on Willie and the Unity Council's alleged misdeeds, Gutiérrez and Compeán's blistering assaults on Willie's leadership and the organization's direction, and the MAUC Board's constant bickering, all had finally whittled Velásquez down. He was burnt out, broken, and irrevocably taxed. The organization he had fathered was on the brink of being destroyed. Days crept by and blurred together, with Willie paralyzed, unable to force himself out of bed and into work. He had had enough. It was time for him to move on.

Willie's formal departure from MAUC was bittersweet and graceful. While acknowledging the imminence of changes he clearly must have regretted, he vowed his continuing support for MAUC's future work and leadership. "It is with deep regret that I submit this letter of resignation to the Board of Directors of the Mexican American Unity Council," Willie penned on November 11, 1969. "The Unity Council is entering into its third year of operation and will be moving in a new direction. In all fairness [it is best that I] resign now and allow [others to determine and manage] the structure that will have to be set up to deal with the new conditions. . . . Whatever job I take you can be assured that I will do what I can to assist the Unity Council to accomplish its goals." With these words, Velásquez's days running MAUC were over.

ᔐ ᔐ ᔐ

In 1970, the promise of a new year and a new decade seemed far away from Willie's new reality. He was without a job, without direction, still living at home, and numbed by everything that had happened at the Unity Council. He floated around in a daze like a champion prizefighter who had been beaten for the first time and did not know what to do with himself. The one constant source of comfort and hope for Willie during this otherwise confused and unhappy time was Janie. Willie was madly in love. Not long into the new year, with his life still in relative disarray, he asked Janie to marry him.

Janie could not understand why Willie loved and wanted to marry her. Although they had been seeing each other exclusively for almost five months, they still only knew each other on a surface level. They came from different backgrounds and had little in common. Willie was the serious, Catholic-trained, college-educated, well-read intellectual who grew up in a modest, but new home on San Antonio's Westside. Janie was a gregarious, insecure, twenty-two-year-old whose childhood memories were molded by picking cotton, sugar beets, cherries, and whatever else needed to be picked on the migrant worker trail. Moving from state to state, Janie's "homes" ranged from a cleared out animal barn sectioned off from other families' "homes" by cardboard to an abandoned ice skating rink. Janie thought the differences were too great. Sooner or later, Willie would want someone smarter, more secure, more grown up, and more sophisticated.

"I know enough," was Willie's only response to Janie's concerns. He had found the right person and nothing else mattered, he told her. "Don't sweat the details," Willie nonchalantly commented when Janie pointed out that he had no job, no money, and no definite plans. Willie, ever confident, even in moments when the evidence suggested cause for caution and concern, proposed forging ahead. Challenging conventional wisdom and Janie's underlying apprehensions, Willie and Janie married on June 12, 1970.

 босу   босу   босу

Early in 1970, several San Antonio student activists formed the Chicano Coalition of College Students (CCCS) hoping to support and unite Mexican-American students on the campuses of San Antonio College, St. Mary's University, and Our Lady of the Lake University. Willie's brother George and Janie played large roles in forming the coalition. They dreamed of assisting more Chicanos to go to college, helping them to pay for their education, and sensitizing them to the plight of Mexican Americans in the barrios and in the fields.

The coalition dabbled in political action, but rarely with real focus or consistency. It was not a highly centralized organization that met frequently or efficiently saw through programs and change strategies. In fact, on those infrequent occasions when coalition members tried to do something as a group, it was usually hastily put together, not well thought out, and unsuccessful.

Most of the students involved in CCCS were avid supporters of MAYO and the Unity Council and deeply resented Congressman González's attacks on these groups. One month after their organization was formed, González was invited to speak at St. Mary's University. The CCCS members saw the upcoming event as a chance to embarrass the congressman. They decided the most effective way to get their message across would be to walk out on González's speech as a form of protest.

True to form, their grand plans to humiliate González were matched by feeble organizing efforts. In the end, planning for the proposed action consisted of each student informally, almost nonchalantly, passing the word to his or her friends that a walkout was going to take place. No clear scheme was devised to orchestrate and manage the protest effort. CCCS members and their campus and community supporters would just show up, sit together, and walk out once the congressman started to speak. It was that simple.

Willie heard about the planned action from George and Janie but did not think much about it. He would attend to support the efforts of his brother and soon-to-be wife, and to passively witness the hoped-for public humiliation of his former mentor turned nemesis; but otherwise Willie had no real role in shaping or organizing the walkout.

Shortly after seven in the evening on February 27, 1970, more than a hundred students, faculty, and interested community members assembled in the Scholasticate Auditorium at St. Mary's University to hear Congressman González speak. Many in the front rows sat poised to walk out on the man they considered a traitor to his people. Willie sat in the second row directly behind his brother George. A few journalists who received anonymous tips about the walkout watched the clock and the crowd hoping to capture the protest as it unfolded.

After a short wait, the congressman arrived. He made his way to the stage coming down the auditorium's left-hand aisle. Passing the first rows of seats, González instantly recognized the hate-filled faces of his young enemies. At once, he sensed he was walking into a trap. In essence, he was right. Roberto Garza, a St. Mary's student who was part of the walkout plan, began the program by telling the audience about the role of the University Speakers' Committee. He then haltingly introduced the congressman. "Ladies and gentlemen, we're going to start this meeting. Here is Henry B. González." As González took the podium amidst a combination of applause and grumbling, his aide, Albert Bustamante, hurriedly passed out literature from the Congressional Record documenting the congressman's positions and his efforts to help the Mexican-American community.

González began his speech by admitting that prior to his arrival he had not been aware that St. Mary's had advertised his discussion topic as "The Condition of the Chicano in South Texas." Had he known, he reported, he would have strongly objected. He was not a Chicano or a hyphenated American, the congressman asserted; he was an American, period.

González, feeling entrapped, then initiated a full-fledged attack on the naivete and futility of Chicano activism. Relentless and condescending in his remarks, like a father lecturing his wayward children, the congressman launched into a litany of one-line critiques of the movement. "Politics doesn't exist in a vacuum"; "Petty politics is irrational"; "A minority is not a majority", "Some so-called Mexican American leaders don't know what they're doing"; "Pride in race is a slender hope, indeed, for political achievement." González then steadfastly criticized the Raza Unida third-party concept (a then popular notion among many Chicano political activists), saying its limited and racist appeal would not develop into an effective change strategy for Mexican Americans.

Ten minutes of the congressman's rambling commentary was enough for the activists. Following the lead of those in the front rows, they began to walk out as González feverishly continued. Abruptly, registering what was happening, the congressman paused and taunted the protestors, asking them where they were going. "*¡Cabrón vendido!* (You son-of-a-bitch sellout!)" replied several of the departing audience members. The congressman could no longer contain his anger. He unleashed a barrage of guttural expressions more suited to the reaction of a hostile sports fan to a rival team's actions than an elected official addressing his local constituents: "*¡Pendejos!* (idiots!)," "*¡Babosos!* (dummies!)," "*¡Bola de animales!* (bunch of animals!)." Willie's brother George, one of the last to walk out, responded thunderously, screaming back at González: "We don't want to hear you anymore!"

The now livid congressman fired back in Spanish, "*¿Por qué te vas pendejo? ¡Si eres hombre ven para acá; si eres gallina vete con los otros!* (Why are you leaving, fool? If you're a man, come over here; if you're a chicken, go with the others!)" George, a hotheaded, six-foot tall, two-hundred pound, twenty-year-old, could not take González's baiting. He broke off from the group walking out, and quickly made his way back towards the stage, hollering incoherencies and curses at the congressman. As George made his way onto the stage, González's aide, Bustamante, intercepted him, forcefully planting both of his hands onto George's chest and challenging him to retreat. "What the hell are you doing on the stage?" Bustamante roared. "Get off!" "Henry B. told me to come up here, so I did!" George responded angrily. "So, what kind of speech should I give?" González asked George, taunting his would-be challenger. George turned slightly to respond, but before he could, Bustamante cracked him against the jaw on the left side of his face, snapping his head back like a toy doll.[1] González then jumped into the physical fracas using his aide as a shield, trying to hit George, cursing him, and demanding that he get off the stage.

Protest supporter Albert Gámez and Willie promptly rushed for the stage to get George off as quickly as they could. Gámez threw himself between Bustamante and George hoping to break up the scuffle. Willie moved to help Gámez and his brother when González immediately recognized him and threateningly blurted out: "There's that loudmouth! Take off your glasses!

---

[1]Bustamante's sucker punch anointed him forever afterwards with the nickname "Pistolero" (gunslinger), a name he would proudly carry with him into his own political career as a county commissioner in 1972 and then as a congressman in 1985.

Willie, if you take one step further I'll knock the shit out of you!" Velásquez froze and in a split second all the assaults, depression, frustration, anger, exaggeration, sickness, and pain that he had gone through because of the congressman reverberated through his body. Willie intensely peeled off his glasses, handed them to Gámez, and prepared to end the conflict once and for all. While those close to him knew that Willie had a stubborn, feisty streak, this street-level posturing with González was out of character for him. Given the congressman's standing as an elected federal official, moreover, it was quickly obvious to Willie's more levelheaded allies that there was no way a physical confrontation with González could possibly end well for Velásquez.

Janie and some other women shrieked, "This is exactly what he wants you to do; don't do it, Willie!" Willie, too enraged to hear their warnings, focused his energies on accommodating the feisty congressman's invitation to scuffle; just as Willie moved in, however, his fellow protestors restrained him and whisked him out of the auditorium, defiantly shouting "¡Viva La Raza!" as they left the scene.

The entire episode had lasted no longer than a few minutes, but its implications and significance were profound and lasting for all concerned. A St. Mary's student stood up and apologized to the congressman for the actions of the departed Chicano radicals. González regained his composure and went on with his presentation telling the remaining audience members: "These thugs are not nearly as tough as some I've faced in the past. . . . [They will never succeed] by inducing fear or advocating violence in our democratic structure. Fear breeds distrust, which undermines the democratic process. Violence by the few against the many is foolhardy and can result only in tragedy for the innocent."

The convening participants who stayed on to hear these remarks remained stunned. They still could not believe what had just taken place. Many were shocked and appalled that a U.S. congressman would taunt his detractors and use the vilest language heard on the streets of the barrio in a public forum. Others applauded the congressman's ability and willingness to stand up to the protestors and give them a dose of their own confrontational medicine. Commenting later on the evening's events, González announced in his most manly of voices: "I have never tolerated an insult from anyone and if someone calls me a *vendido* (sellout) and I'm not, he's going to get a fight. . . . If I had wanted to hit him (Velásquez), I could have and he would have known he had been hit. He would have ended in one of those seats in the front row. . . . I never turn the other cheek."

As the next morning's newspaper headlines predictably sensationalized the St. Mary's incident, Willie dejectedly prepared himself for the worst. The few months of relief from the relentless personal attacks by González had turned out to be only a temporary lull in his devolving relationship with the congressman who had once been his hero and mentor. Fulfilling Velásquez's fears and expectations, González wasted no time singling out Willie as the instigator of what he characterized as an orchestrated attempt by the "hippie-types" to bully and humiliate him, and by extension the majority of San Antonio voters who had elected him to Congress. He knew that he could use Willie's momentary lapse of self-control to further discredit his political ene-mies at MAYO, the Unity Council, and *La Universidad de los Barrios*, as well as their benefactors. "Paid organizers for Albert Peña . . . racial fanatics . . . a known felon . . . MAYO hotheads. They were all sitting there like a row of coiled rattlesnakes poised to strike," González reported to the press, describing the faces of rebellion and contempt for public order he saw star-ing at him from the front rows of the Scholasticate Auditorium.

After formally apologizing to González for the unfortunate uproar, the St. Mary's University's Speakers Committee voted nearly unanimously to invite MAYO's Compeán and Gutiérrez to appear the following week at a public forum to offer their perspective on the condition of the Chicano in South Texas. The university laid down strict guidelines to prevent further mayhem, requiring Compeán and Gutiérrez to respond to questions from a four-person panel that included two professors and two students, and tightly controlling the number of people admitted to the assembly.

On the evening of March 6, 1970, a standing-room-only crowd packed into the student center to hear the MAYO leaders. After most of the auditori-um had filled and the speeches had begun, campus security guards refused to allow anyone else into the event. A struggle ensued, however, when Nacho Pérez, another of the MAYO co-founders who had arrived late, tried to force himself and other locked-out MAYO members into the proceedings. A secu-rity guard wrestled him out. In response, many in the audience clamored for the doors to be reopened and for the excluded MAYO members to be per-mitted to enter. Both Compeán and Gutiérrez left the stage to go to a door where they recognized MAYO members trying to enter. Compeán screamed at the campus guards securing the door: "Let them in!" After a few crazed minutes, Brother Victor Naegele, the program's moderator, reluctantly requested the guards to let them all come in. Gutiérrez, now back on stage at the podium, quickly played up the point that people were trying to walk into instead of out of the session—inferring a higher relevance and moral ground for the progressive youth perspective than that offered by establishment lead-ers like Congressman González.

The MAYO response to González was otherwise a non-event. Compeán and Gutiérrez forcefully detailed MAYO's goals and predictably attacked their enemies. Both especially blasted González and older Mexican-American organizations such as LULAC and the American G.I. Forum for not doing enough to confront institutionalized racism and for not incorporating the young in their work. "All they want us to do is lick stamps and move chairs," Gutiérrez charged. "If the people that can change things don't, we will..." he asserted.

The MAYO-focused follow-up session to Henry B. González's remarks during the prior week failed, ironically, to provide any meaningful opportunity for Willie to publicly discuss his near fistfight with the congressman, nor to challenge his many accusations that Willie and his movement allies were fanatics and felons. Willie had no choice now but to forcefully react to the congressman on the public record through press interviews and published statements. Attempting to challenge González's exaggerated claims, Velásquez asserted: "Those in the walkout weren't thugs. They weren't riffraff. They were clean kids or they wouldn't have been there. The riffraff don't go to speeches. These are the kinds of kids who are presidents of their classes and officers of the Young Democrats." Several weeks later Willie sent a formal rejoinder to González that was printed in the local paper on April 16. In this letter, Velásquez called on the congressman to retract his statements at the first St. Mary's forum that had forced "innocent persons to suffer . . . public abuse." Velásquez went on to clarify that of the thirty-three individuals who had walked out on González's speaking engagement at St. Mary's—all of whom the congressman had characterized as idiots, dummies, and animals—"five were seminarians studying for the priesthood, seven were teachers, three were social workers, four were law students, two were professors, eight were students, one girl was formerly studying to be a nun, and three were workers." Willie closed by saying, "It was indeed a sorry sight to see the congressman from San Antonio calling the people vile names, accusing people . . . and worst of all remaining silent about his errors."

At a press conference closely following these comments, Willie stated in the most serious terms: "A personal attack on me has been made by the congressman and I am going to respond. [From this point forward . . .] every time Henry B. González does something wrong, I'm going to be right there and I'm going to correct it." With that declaration, Willie launched a lifetime effort to discredit González.

Although the political quarrels that erupted in the late 1960s and early 1970s between González and his many activist detractors were more or less resolved in later, calmer times, the same cannot be said of the relationship between González and Velásquez. Their memories were too long, and the wounds they inflicted upon one another were too deep. Willie had been a part of the González political family early on but had poisoned the relationship from the congressman's standpoint in ways he could never forget or understand. While they never again confronted each other publicly as they had in the late 1960s and early 1970s, their animosity toward one another grew, year after year, for the rest of Willie's life.

∽ ∽ ∽

Shortly after marrying in June, Willie and Janie found an unexpected but welcome opportunity to gain needed relief from the heated political environment of San Antonio and Willie's recent unemployment. Following a short job training stint in California that took longer than expected to complete because Willie had to have an emergency appendectomy along the way, the newlyweds prepared to move to Phoenix, Arizona where, somewhat ironically, Velásquez would soon start a new job as community services officer for the Southwest Council of La Raza. Notwithstanding the tensions that had sometimes emerged between Willie and the Southwest Council during the battles involving the Ford Foundation and Congress over MAUC's and MAYO's work, the Council's executive staff, now led by former Ford consultant Herman Gallegos, understood well Velásquez's organizing and political skills. It did not take long for the Council to see a unique hiring opportunity when Willie left MAUC and began to flounder in the wake of still another contentious episode with Congressman González. The move to Arizona would help to substantially strengthen the Southwest Council's leadership and technical assistance capacities while at the same time giving Willie a more national stage to apply his energy and vision. The move to Phoenix would also offer Willie and Janie a healthier and more independent setting in which to consolidate their new marriage, enabling them, or so they planned at least, to distance themselves from many of the stresses that had characterized their situation in San Antonio.

Sadly, owing to new unexpected challenges, Willie's and Janie's first year of marriage in Arizona turned out to be an excruciatingly taxing period for the young couple, notwithstanding their high hopes and expectations for the move. Willie's new job kept him on the road over 80 percent of the time. In his all-too-frequent absence, Janie felt trapped in the couple's apartment, a depressing unit with an invariably dark living room. She was spending most of her time crying. With no job of her own, no close family members or friends to call on, and only scattered time with her new husband, Phoenix left Janie with little joy or comfort. In time, she became despondent and chronically insecure. Her worst doubts and fears about being married to Willie, articulated at the outset of their relationship, were beginning to materialize.

Indeed, it was becoming apparent that Willie and Janie had come into their marriage with quite different expectations. Willie was looking for the perfect housewife—a traditional mate who would stay at home and raise children, nurture and support him, and remain happy and uncomplicated in the process. He thought that Janie's insecurities would somehow magically disappear once they landed in Phoenix. A good dose of marriage would make her grow up quickly, he thought.

Janie was not sure what she expected, but it was not this. She wished Willie would give her some sort of signal, good or bad, anything at all, to let her know how she was doing in her new role as his wife. She felt like she was auditioning for a part in a play. Was she acting right? Doing the right things? Saying the right words? She desperately needed and wanted Willie to reassure her. But the demands and strains of his heavy workload and travel made him anything but accessible to her. He had little time or patience to focus in any meaningful way on Janie's problems or needs. Increasingly, as she would reach out for help and support, he would become impatient with and even angered by her appeals.

As the relationship became more strained, Willie introduced a tactic that he would perfect over time both to punish Janie for her growing neediness and to avoid contending with her specific challenges—the silent treatment. During moments of contention, Willie would simply ignore Janie, making her feel as if she did not exist. He would go on with his daily rituals as if he lived alone. The stoic quality of his demeanor, possibly intended to bolster her strength by making her more independent, in fact forced Janie deeper into bouts of depression and insecurity. While the couple would learn to manage and even accept these behaviors (however painful and dysfunctional), the essential disparity between their emotional needs and coping skills would never be resolved. At the end of the day, Willie's ways and ideas would dictate the terms of the marriage. Janie would have to follow with no real standing to challenge or renegotiate this unstated but clear contract.

At the end of 1971, the Southwest Council made a critical strategic decision to relocate its headquarters office to Washington, D.C. The move would enhance the organization's prospects to influence national policy, to generate funding, and to grow. While Willie's substantive work would change very little as a result of the move, the abrupt and unanticipated decision called upon Janie once more to make supportive adjustments to accompany Willie with no questions asked. As in so many similar situations throughout their relationship, she would do so notwithstanding large questions, uncertainties, and associated inconvenience.

Willie, although committed to make the move in order to continue his important work at the Council, was himself not convinced that it made good sense. While he understood that Washington, D.C. was the national center of important government policy making and government contracts in the Council's core programming areas (housing, economic development, and civic participation), he felt that the organization was risking dislocation from needed action—and, by extension, legitimacy—in Mexican-American neighborhoods across the Southwestern United States He simply did not see, therefore, how the move to D.C. would enhance the Southwest Council's role and standing in the Chicano movement.

Although he was not thrilled about the move to Washington, on a personal level Willie and Janie's relationship greatly improved on the East Coast. Unlike Phoenix where the couple knew almost no one, they quickly established friendships (often with fellow Texans) and spent more time going out together socially. This helped to make Janie more relaxed and happy. In addition, the move enabled Janie to re-engage constructively in political activities. She became an active volunteer at the Democratic National Committee and then later with the George McGovern presidential campaign. She was no longer sitting alone in a dark, dreary apartment waiting desperately for Willie to come home.

With 1972 in full gear, Willie began to feel the weight of two years of tireless work and travel throughout the Southwest. Although he loved his work, he was no longer learning and growing sufficiently for it to keep him as enthusiastic and engaged as he wanted to be. In addition, he realized there was not much room for professional growth at the Southwest Council that would finally be appealing to him. In the near term, Willie saw his chances to move into the executive director's position as slim to none. And even if that were not the case, he was not sure that he wanted to spend his time leading an organization which, in his eyes, was moving closer to Washington, D.C. power elites and further away from Chicano communities across the Southwest. It was time for him to consider seriously some fresh alternatives.

Willie was torn between two options: trying to gain admission to Harvard Business School or heading back to the Southwest to do community work. Narciso Cano, a close friend from high school, was attending Harvard Business School and did everything he could to persuade Willie to join him. Cano knew of Willie's background in economics and his desire to help the Mexican-American people; he thought these interests would merge perfectly in a setting like Harvard. Willie was tempted by the idea. He sent his St. Mary's transcript to Harvard and took the graduate business school qualifying exam. In the end, however, he could not bring himself to apply. He understood the significance of having Harvard on his resume (especially since so few Mexican Americans did in those days), but his interest in an Ivy League pedigree paled compared to his desire to serve the community now, not a couple of years down the road. His obsessive need to be a community activist made Willie feel guilty about even thinking of going to business school. He would be placing himself even further out of touch with people in the Southwest if he spent an additional two years studying in Cambridge. Long gone were his aspirations of foreign service and diplomatic adventure. Willie's now deep-seated political and organizing passions told him that he needed to go home and re-engage in the Chicano struggle at the grassroots community level, but he was not exactly sure how and where to land, in order to follow through successfully on his instincts.

Still unsure, Willie and Janie returned home to San Antonio to visit family and friends during Easter 1972. Janie was now four months pregnant. She was glowing with expectation. An earlier pregnancy in Phoenix had resulted in a miscarriage. Family and community celebration thus accompanied this child's anticipated arrival.

Even though she had quickly adjusted to Washington, D.C. (unlike Phoenix), Janie wanted to raise her children in Texas. This additionally motivated Willie to break away from the Southwest Council and get them back home so that their children could be raised on tortillas and Mexican pride.

Owing to her earlier unsuccessful pregnancy, Janie's doctor in Washington told her to stay off her feet while visiting San Antonio, but she felt awkward spending her brief time in San Antonio being bedridden at her mother-in-law's. She did not want to worry or inconvenience family and friends back home, so she tried to move around during the visit and to rest only when she felt the need.

One day, however, as Willie was preparing to play golf with his father, Janie told him that she was not feeling well. She begged him to stay with her. Willie, not grasping the gravity of the situation, told her not to worry. He would be back before she knew it. She knew what that really meant, though, from experience: Willie's response was a cover for a few holes of golf followed inevitably by large quantities of beer out on the town. She asked him again to stay with her, but Willie was clearly on his way out the door in all but physical form. Janie, though increasingly weak and frightened by her failing condition, did not want to embarrass Willie by having a temper tantrum in his parent's home. She sadly and begrudgingly braced herself to go it alone in his absence. Willie once again assured Janie that he would return soon and then headed off with his father, leaving her by herself for the day.

As the day passed Janie's condition worsened. She became weaker and queasier. Suddenly, severe cramping attacked her body and she began to fade into and out of consciousness. Nobody was there to help her. Janie managed to get her friend Esther Anguiano on the phone, but there was little Esther could do at a distance except try to calm her down. Janie got off the line and her agony continued. By the end of the day, she had miscarried for the second time.

Janie's second miscarriage was an especially traumatic experience. It ravaged her body and left an enormous void in her spirit. She wondered if she would ever be able to have a family. She hated losing another child; but even more so, in that moment, she hated Willie. At a time when she truly needed him, he was nowhere to be found. From her perspective, the experience provided a harsh reminder of what was fundamentally missing in her marriage.

～ ～ ～

Back in Washington, D.C., in October of 1972, Willie wrapped up his tenure at the Southwest Council of La Raza and prepared to return to San Antonio. Herman Gallegos, the Council's executive director, sought to facilitate Willie's return home by offering him the opportunity to run a social services agency aimed at assisting elderly Mexican Americans. The project could be based in San Antonio and developed by Willie from there. Willie was ecstatic. Not only would this get him closer to the action in South Texas, but it would also give him the chance to mold his own organization, something he had craved since his days running MAUC. Willie had admired and respected the Southwest Council's CEO from the first time he met him during Gallegos' stint as a senior consultant to the Ford Foundation. Willie was then an inexperienced political activist with MAYO. In a sense, Velásquez idolized Gallegos. He was the only Mexican American Willie knew who wore classic suits, ate exotic foods, and could select the right wine for any culinary occasion. After weeks of preliminary discussion, Gallegos gave Willie the go-ahead signal on the seniors' project. Everything was set. Willie and Janie could finally leave the East Coast and reclaim their roots back home.

The couple hastily returned to San Antonio. They did not have a place to live so they stayed temporarily with Velásquez's parents. Reinvigorated by the idea of being home, Willie, without delay, feverishly began to set things in motion for his new job. He called the woman who he had employed as his assistant in Phoenix, and asked her to move to San Antonio to work for him again. She gladly accepted, packed her belongings, and made her way to Texas. He rented space in Arnold Flores's cramped union offices. Flores, a streetwise labor organizer, had known Velásquez since the mid-1960s. In Flores's office space, Velásquez began to map out logistics and a preliminary plan to support the new advocacy project for Mexican-American seniors.

A few weeks later, however, Willie's new project slowly began to unravel. The done deal was becoming undone. Gallegos abruptly stopped returning Velásquez's phone calls and referred him instead to a staff underling who proved unable to do anything to support Willie's plans. After stringing Willie along for weeks, Gallegos and his Southwest Council staff abruptly delivered crushing news: Authorization to proceed with Willie's new organization was being revoked.

The project's cancellation was dropped on Velásquez like an unexpected air strike; it seemingly came out of nowhere. Gallegos explained the messy situation as a product of the harsh vagaries of the business world. The planned organization was intended to be a for-profit venture. At the eleventh hour, it ran into difficulties securing the necessary financial backing to ensure its start-up. Gallegos was sorry it ended this way, but that was the cruel reality of the commercial capital market. Willie was furious. Gallegos had assured him just weeks earlier that everything was good to go. Now Velásquez stood alone, without a job, without money, and without any security.

The job loss could not have come at a worse time. Willie's employment woes, combined with growing personal problems, left him teetering on the edge. His parents had recently separated and divorced after many years of marriage, and his own marriage remained fragile.

Flores offered Willie part-time work writing union proposals, developing new projects, and offering advice. This kept Willie floating, but with the likelihood of long-term employment looking dismal, Velásquez was sinking faster and faster each day. He started spending most of his time with hardcore union men. This made him an even more macho character than he had been in the past. He often stayed out drinking until all hours of the night.

Nineteen seventy-three loomed on the horizon like a plague waiting to strike. Willie was once again without a real job. He did not have the means to support his wife or their continuing hopes to start a family. His parents were no longer together. His relationship with Janie was waning again. He was depressed and scared. Willie's triumphant return to San Antonio had vanished before it could even start. In effect, his situation in recent years had gone from bad to worse. Velásquez had hit rock bottom, the lowest point of his young life, and he was nowhere close to being clear about how to pick himself up again.

Chapter 8

EARLY VOTER REGISTRATION EFFORTS IN the Mexican-American community resembled manipulative fiestas. In effect, they were just that. Anglo machine politicians were adept at drawing out Mexican-American voters just in time to gain needed support, but with little reciprocity. As the elections drew closer, word quickly spread throughout the barrio that an enormous party was going to be held in the plaza that evening. After toiling another seemingly endless day, many workers in the community put on fresh shirts, caressed their hair with hints of tonic, and dragged themselves (and their families) to the gathering. People closed in on the fiesta from all directions. Feelings of celebration and happiness, steadily growing, saturated the air. Feverish dancing, slightly off-tune renditions of classic Mexican songs, and the alluring scent of free tamales and beer complemented the festivities. This intoxicating liveliness was inevitably interrupted by a hired hand with a rickety old blow horn, who would yell out in a Spanish that lacked conviction: "Welcome, friends, I hope y'all are enjoying yourselves. Remember, this fiesta is being brought to you courtesy of Harold Smith, Democratic candidate for sheriff. On Tuesday, vote Smith for Sheriff!" (or whatever the candidate's name and desired office).

Soon thereafter, the candidate, hating every minute of the necessary charade, would take the stage branding a huge Texas-size grin. Addressing the crowd in barely comprehensible Spanish, the candidate would then implore his guests to support his candidacy: "Thank you very much. Tomorrow you vote. I need votes. Please give me votes. Enjoy the party. Thank you very much."

After Smith's brief plea for support and some polite but guarded applause, the political boss's team would announce a raffle prize. All the new voters would frantically search for their stubs and assigned numbers as the barker, retaking the microphone on stage, blurted out the winning ticket number for a giant bottle of tequila. The night would stagger on with the faceless prospective voters finally giving in to exhaustion and returning to their modest homes and apartments. On election day, like cattle being led to the slaughter, many of these purchased supporters would cast their votes for candidate Smith, giving him the needed boost to put him in office. Smith, now sheriff, would return to ignoring Mexican Americans until his reelection

115

bid rolled around. Everything was normal again.

This all too familiar scene was taking place throughout the Southwest with each state and region adding its own appropriate local touches. In the 1950s and 1960s, various Mexican-American rights and justice organizations sought to change this crass use of their people for political gain. Groups in California, like the Community Services Organization (CSO) and the Mexican American Political Association (MAPA), and, in Texas, like the League of United Latin American Citizens (LULAC), the American G.I. Forum, and the Political Association of Spanish-Speaking Organizations (PASO), held significant voter registration and education drives hoping to make the Mexican-American vote a strong, respected, independent voice. They had several prominent successes. In Texas, there was the Viva Kennedy campaign that helped push John F. Kennedy to victory in 1960 and the election in 1963 of an all-Mexican-American slate to the city council of Crystal City (a sleepy town that Anglos had always dominated). In California, there was the election of Edward Roybal of the Los Angeles City Council to Congress in 1962. Unfortunately, many of these early efforts at political reform suffered from a scattered, hit-or-miss approach that centered on particular candidates and highly localized races. These efforts, however, did not translate into statewide or regional gains for the Mexican-American community. The reform campaigns also lacked the legal firepower to tackle structural barriers and impediments faced by Mexican Americans in exercising their right to vote.

The obstacles Mexican Americans faced relative to unfettered political participation covered an impressive array of exclusionary approaches. In certain Southwestern towns, Mexican Americans were herded to the polls by their political bosses under the threat of losing their jobs if they did not vote the right way. In other cases, literacy tests were introduced to discourage Spanish speakers from voting at all. Texas, until 1966, required its citizens to pay a poll tax of $1.75 per person, making voting disproportionately costly and impractical for many in large, poor Mexican-American families. When the poll tax was outlawed, Texas lawmakers responded swiftly by imposing a mandatory scheme that required Texans to register to vote every year, well in advance of each election cycle, in order to discourage Mexican-American participation. Some towns incorporated the use of separate voting boxes for Mexican Americans to facilitate tampering in the event of undesired electoral outcomes. And, across the Southwestern United States, creative boundary drawing, or gerrymandering, divided Mexican-American neighborhoods into districts that more closely resembled abstract modern art paintings than political jurisdictions, divorcing the ethnic community from any potential political power.

As the 1960s drew to a close, these were the harsh circumstances and political realities that Mexican-American community advocates faced in their quest

to secure fairness and equal opportunity in local, state, and national elections.
In the summer of 1968, when the Ford Foundation awarded $630,000 to the newly created Southwest Council of La Raza, it planted the seeds of coordinated activism within the Mexican-American community that for the first time would alter the political balance of the region. The Southwest Council's founders were brash, ambitious, energetic activists who had swallowed a heavy dose of the frenetic idealism of the 1960s. Inspired by the flourishing work of the Voter Education Project (VEP) in the African-American community, leaders of the Southwest Council dreamed of incubating a Mexican-American version of VEP that would create a feared and respected, autonomous Mexican-American vote. Local affiliates of the Southwest Council had earmarked money for voter registration and education campaigns, but these were largely isolated and limited efforts. A broad-based regional strategy and capacity to educate, register, and mobilize Mexican-American voters in the Southwest was simply lacking. The anti-foundation climate created by congressional leaders like Henry B. González and the Tax Reform Act of 1969 (which severely restricted nonprofit "political activities") significantly discouraged the Ford Foundation and other private funders from directing seed capital to overtly political work like voter registration, so Mexican-American leaders had to look elsewhere for support to develop the capacity to mobilize and leverage Mexican-American participation in regional electoral processes.

One of the very few alternatives to private foundation support for progressive community initiatives then, like now, was financing by organized labor. Ironically, many of the Southwest Council's founders and allies came from union backgrounds and retained strong ties to the labor movement. These leaders pushed hard to seek support from their friends in labor across the Southwest and the Midwest, where Mexican-American and other Hispanic workers were increasingly organizing. The quest for expanded Mexican-American political mobilization turned out to complement the labor movement's need to expand its own political base. It was the United Auto Workers (UAW), therefore, with an unrestricted $10,000 grant, that breathed life into the idea of a political arm of the Southwest Council. Henry Santiestevan, a journalist for the UAW and a founder of the Southwest Council, was given the money by Bill Dodds, a feisty, shrewd labor man and devoted fan of Pancho Villa, who believed in the Mexican-American struggle for justice. To demonstrate his commitment to Mexican-American community empowerment, Dodds gave the donation to Santiestevan without conditions and told him to do what he felt was best for his people.

Santiestevan and the other Southwest Council founders were relieved. The support from Dodds dramatically augmented their capacity to pursue community-focused political aims with a degree of independence that would not otherwise have been possible. Already, other would-be financial backers, including foundation officials, had talked to them about starting a registration and education effort to help Senator Robert F. Kennedy's presidential bid and, after Kennedy's assassination, Hubert Humphrey's campaign. While most of those involved with the creation of the Southwest Council personally supported these Democratic candidates, none of those interested in creating a Mexican-American voter registration and education project wanted to start a group that compromised itself from the beginning by focusing on purely partisan short-term goals. They wanted instead to focus on unencumbered community empowerment and political engagement activities that would have lasting, positive impacts on Mexican-American electoral representation.

Santiestevan presented the UAW check to the Southwest Council's executive committee in Los Angeles on September 9, 1968 and was promptly named chairman of the newly formed standing committee, PREP, the Political Research and Education Project. PREP quickly became a high priority for the Council and its leaders. With a small amount of money, a chairman, an advisory group, and a simple, ill-defined notion of increasing Chicano political clout, PREP boldly dove into unexplored waters.

᠅ ᠅ ᠅

Timing, as always, plays a crucial role in political ventures, and the Southwest Council picked an especially difficult moment to move more prominently into the voter registration and education field. In late 1968 and early 1969, nonpartisan voter registration groups were hanging on by the thinnest of threads in a reactionary climate that sought to severely curb their activities and influence. Ford's funding of the Cleveland chapter of CORE, where an estimated $25,000 went to support voter registration efforts almost exclusively on the African-American eastside of the city, had only recently helped to unseat Mayor Ralph Locher. The resulting shift in Cleveland's political balance inspired an uproar and mainstream accusation of unfair dealing. Locher, a white incumbent who lost to Carl Stokes, a black candidate in the Democratic primary, lamented the outcome in the press, stating: "When [foundation] grants of new money are made for registration drives in limited areas, this is not in the fair play tradition of this country or the Democratic or Republican parties." Locher's sentiments were echoed by white establishment political insiders across the country who were suddenly concerned about losing their clout. Such leaders in turn made their views widely known to Congress that private foundation engagement in the field was in need of severe curtailment.

In response, Texas Congressman Wright Patman, the self-appointed crusader trying to crush the powerful uncontrolled universe of foundations, pushed hard to force private grant-making institutions completely out of the political arena. Along with Henry B. González and other concerned congressional representatives, Patman sought powerful new legislation to proscribe foundation support for lobbying and other "political activities."

The Ford Foundation, with the rest of the foundation world, was put on the defensive by Patman and his congressional allies. Ford warned its grantees that it was now even more imperative than ever that they be on their best behavior and avoid any activity that could be labeled too "political." For the Southwest Council, this meant that PREP would have to be pursued with utmost caution and responsibility. While this dampened the spirits of those involved with PREP, it did not douse them. Still, for the time being, PREP was shelved as a priority and subjected to heightened Foundation scrutiny.

ᔕ ᔕ ᔕ

Siobahn Oppenheimer, Ford's program officer in charge of the Southwest Council, sternly warned Council leaders to change their relaxed attitudes toward sub-grantee voter registration and education activities. In addition, Oppenheimer and Ford required each grantee (and sub-grantee) to follow strict voter registration guidelines developed for the Southern Regional Council (SRC) and VEP. Ford hoped these new rules would keep Southwest Council affiliates in line and serve as an example to Congress that foundations could regulate their voter registration programs without legislative interference.

After a few bitter months of relative inactivity, the Southwest Council cautiously began to resurrect PREP. PREP's advocates understood Ford's fears and decided to tread slowly and methodically in their quest for a political division of the Council. With the future of foundation-funded voter registration groups still being debated in House and Senate committees in Washington, VEP, the leading black voter registration organization in the South, was emerging as a model of how registration groups should be run. Highly effective, but appropriately low-key and nonpartisan in approach, VEP found a way to advance minority voter gains without inspiring the wrath of mainstream political powers, as both CORE and MAYO had. PREP leaders understood the practical and symbolic significance of VEP, and turned to VEP experts for strategic advice and direction.

Armando de León, a clean-cut, efficient, military-brat-turned-activist who served as the Council's staff attorney, was dispatched by the PREP leadership to meet with VEP officials. He was instructed to acquire any and all information that might help to speed up Council efforts to get an effective voter mobilization unit off the ground and running across the Southwest. De León arrived in Atlanta on June 30, 1969 and combed through the VEP offices, grabbing copies of every form, report, booklet, and instruction sheet he could get his hands on. For five-and-a-half hours, de León politely interrogated his VEP hosts, asking them every question possible about registration and education work, soaking up each reply, and recording copious notes. De León was intrigued by the way VEP distributed project funds. Instead of providing sub-grants in lump sums like the Southwest Council did (which thereafter severely diminished grantee accountability to Council concerns), VEP allocated funds on a phased basis, awarding sub-grantees only upon achievement of certain concrete goals and objectives, including avoiding public controversy. This meant more bureaucracy for VEP partner groups, but also much more control for the sponsoring VEP organization and, by extension, its benefactors. VEP's staged payout strategy kept everyone out of trouble and could do the same for PREP.

As de León's visit drew to a close, Vernon Jordan, the dynamic director of VEP, offered additional helpful suggestions for PREP. First, grabbing a stray piece of paper, Jordan carefully drew for de León a copy of the VEP structure and its relationship to the SRC, advising PREP to reformulate its governing committee into an advisory body; according to Jordan, this would give it more flexibility. Second, Jordan advised de León that PREP should not spin off from the Southwest Council. Instead, it should remain affiliated with the Council in order to benefit from its leadership and infrastructure, unless and until subsequent congressional action required separation of the two organizations. Finally, Jordan offered two suggestions that would help to make the IRS happy and protect the Southwest Council's tax-exempt status. To begin, he encouraged de León to implore his Council colleagues to drop the word "Political" in PREP and change it to something like "Civic" or "Citizens." The name change would minimize undue scrutiny of the Council's voter engagement work by stripping the patently political aims of its work from its name and public representations. Next, Jordan recommended that PREP develop educational, citizenship, and leadership programs. This would help to make the organization's work seem less threatening and objectionable to leaders and institutions. It would also help to broaden the benefits and long-term impacts of PREP's work, Jordan argued. Instead of being seen as merely an organizing tool to take over the Southwest, with Jordan's modifications PREP would look more like the League of Women Voters. Its work would be much more geared toward democratic enhancement rather than radical rabble-rousing.

De León furiously noted Jordan's suggestions, profusely thanked him and the VEP staff for putting up with his relentless queries, and promptly returned to headquarters to brief Southwest Council of La Raza board chairman, Maclovio Barraza, on his findings. De León's visit to VEP's offices in Atlanta would have a significant impact on Mexican-American voter mobilization in subsequent years. In effect, it would establish the essential framework upon which the Southwest Voter Registration and Education Project would later be built.

〜 〜 〜

President Nixon signed the Tax Reform Act of 1969 into law in December. With that stroke, Ford instructed the Southwest Council to concentrate on safer, "hard" investment programs in areas like housing, economic development, and education in order to continue receiving foundation funds. In addition, according to Ford program officer Oppenheimer, the Southwest Council would have to discontinue its voter registration activities, or spin them off to be continued by a separate and independent nonprofit organization. PREP's organizers were not completely surprised; they had seen signs of Ford's reluctance to get involved with a political arm for some time.

At a suspenseful Southwest Council board meeting in late 1969, the Council's trustees, many of them also PREP directors and/or champions, reluctantly voted to accept Ford's recommendations to emphasize "hard" programs and to spin off PREP as a separate, unaffiliated nonprofit organization. PREP's principal advocates had mixed feelings about having to spin off from the Council. Many felt certain this was the end of the line, believing that recent changes in federal law made it virtually impossible to commence effective voter mobilization activities. The new guidelines, targeted especially to unions and other progressive groups were, in fact, formidable, requiring registration organizations to be completely nonpartisan and to be active in at least five states. In addition, such groups were highly prohibited in their use of and access to funds. They could not work during just one election cycle, and they could not receive more than 25 percent of their funding from any single source. By congressional design, the barriers to entry prohibiting organized labor, and by extension new groups, from engaging in minority voter empowerment were erected to be highly controlling and, indeed, discouraging.

Nevertheless, those still most heavily committed to creating a Mexican-American voter registration and education outfit, including Board Chairman Barraza, attorney de León, and Executive Director Gallegos, remained stubbornly optimistic. Despite the many growing federal disincentives to voting rights advocates, they vowed to fight on, believing it would not take much effort to resuscitate PREP as a strong, freestanding organization. Seeing more obstacles than opportunities going forward, Santiestevan respectfully resigned as chairman of PREP.

〜 〜 〜

For the next one-and-a-half years, PREP laid dormant as an unincorporated association. Southwest Council Board Chairman Maclovio Barraza remained determined to bully the concept into existence, but with no one formally charged or funded to shepherd PREP's application for independent tax-exempt status, progress was slow to take hold. Time slipped by as assorted consultants and committed individuals worked only irregularly on PREP's development, stumbling often in the absence of a clear and continuous path to pursue. Barraza in Tucson, de León in Phoenix, and Gallegos in San Francisco dutifully moved the sporadic work forward with three broad goals in mind: First, they sought to secure for PREP exempt status so that it could qualify for private financial support without having to be liable to pay taxes; second, they sought to generate operating funds to initiate voter registration work; third, they sought to engage PREP in existing ad hoc registration efforts so that it could be seen as a player, rather than a mere observer. Barraza kept the work moving forward through monthly discretionary contributions of $1,000 from his United Steelworkers union.

De León agreed to head up filing PREP's application for tax-exempt status. Gallegos, now recently resigned as executive director of the Southwest Council, was brought on as a consultant to raise funds for PREP. Barraza pursued opportunities to engage PREP in real-life voter registration and education campaigns, to build its credibility and track record on the ground.

Utilizing an array of part-time field consultants and other sporadic contractors, the group's leaders forged ahead with all deliberate speed. PREP's first engagement involved a modest, but in retrospect risky contribution to the Raul Castro for Governor Campaign in Arizona, a highly emotional but ultimately futile attempt to elect a Mexican American as chief executive of a key southwestern state that PREP organizers felt they simply had to support. Though PREP only contributed $1,000 to Castro's election effort, the donation could have ruined PREP's IRS exemption application for being tied directly to a political candidate. Fortunately, the small donation never came to public light nor otherwise impeded PREP's continuing forward movement. Subsequent PREP awards, more in keeping with the spirit of evolving federal law, went to nonpartisan campaigns and broad-based educational materials, in both Spanish and English, urging Mexican Americans to make their voices heard through the ballot box.

On June 8, 1971, PREP was officially incorporated in Arizona as the Citizen Voter Research Education Project (CVREP). Two days later, a board of directors was selected with Barraza listed as president, Gallegos as vice president, and de León as secretary-treasurer. Representatives from the southwestern states of Arizona, California, Colorado, New Mexico, Texas, and nearby Utah filled out the new board as members at large. The machinery to formally enable Mexican-American leaders to legally undertake voter registration and education activities with tax-exempt status appeared to be moving forward without undue external encumbrance. CVREP officials gained confidence that IRS exemption would be a mere technicality, following the group's successful incorporation in Arizona. De León, writing to a potential funding source said, "There is no reason to suspect the IRS [will] do anything

[but] grant us our tax exempt status . . . we have very carefully tailored this program so as to assure a tax exempt status." Gallegos added, "VEP in Atlanta establishes a good precedent and our [careful approach] gives us every reason to believe that our application will be granted." With this mind-set, the CVREP leaders focused their attention on fund-raising and program development. Unfortunately, IRS approval of CVREP's tax-exemption request would prove far more complicated than anticipated.

Exactly three months after CVREP was formally recognized, de León sent its application for tax-exempt status to the Los Angeles regional office of the IRS, where he had successfully processed other exemption requests in the past. A month later, however, IRS agent John Bloxham telephoned de León to inform him that CVREP needed to send additional information by November 11, 1971, before any final decision could be made. De León responded immediately with ample time before the IRS-imposed delivery deadline. But de León's submission did not secure the hoped-for approval. On November 9, the IRS notified CVREP officials that their bid for a 501(c)3 tax-exempt status was denied. The denial shocked and disappointed the CVREP leadership team, but it did not dampen their spirits. Undaunted, CVREP's leaders prepared themselves to make adjustments needed in their application for a quick resubmission. But behind-the-scenes considerations at the IRS would slow and confuse the process considerably during early 1972. Out of nowhere, the Los Angeles office informed de León that it was no longer handling the CVREP case; rather, CVREP's application had been sent to the national IRS office in Washington, D.C.

No one ever could give de León and CVREP a clear and satisfactory explanation for the transfer. All de León knew was that the CVREP file was in D.C., and IRS officials wanted still more information on the organization's plans. As the new year plodded along, CVREP officials were beginning to sense that something was very wrong at the IRS. In public, they continued to act like the exemption was just around the corner. But, by May, they finally began to grapple with the notion that their plans for a Mexican-American voter registration project might never happen. After a half year of denial, those closest to the daily developments (or lack thereof)—Barraza, de León, and Gallegos—all sensed their hard work and dreams slipping away. They could not hold off potential benefactors or partners much longer with talk of the exemption being just around the bend when all they were getting from the IRS personnel was further stalling and delay.

Instead of giving up entirely, the CVREP organizers desperately sought a plan, any kind of plan, which would somehow get them into the 1972 presidential election cycle. They pursued a temporary merger with VEP, asking the leading African-American group to serve as its fiscal agent until CVREP received its own tax-exempt status. CVREP leaders thought that VEP's executive committee could make a decision quickly; but over one month passed before VEP was able to take official action. By the time VEP eventually agreed to serve as CVREP's fiscal agent, only six weeks remained before the November 1972 presidential elections. Even for the highly committed CVREP leaders, it was too late in the campaign cycle to play any meaningful role by this point.

By the fall, the chilled atmosphere surrounding CVREP's efforts to get into gear moved closer to a deep freeze. Forced to watch another election cycle from the sidelines, the heavily liberal, Democratic, pro-union CVREP leadership group stood meekly silent as Richard Nixon smashed George McGovern in his re-election bid, capturing the electoral vote by a margin of 520 to 17 and garnering over 60 percent of the popular vote. With time and hope both running out for CVREP, its leaders anxiously awaited a reply from the IRS on their latest and final application revision. Gallegos's letter to Carnegie Corporation of New York—one of CVREP's most coveted prospective benefactors—captured the ominous moment with all that was on the line, stating: "I believe that three years of hard work are now at stake. The IRS has promised to make its ruling within 24 hours of receiving a summary work plan from CVREP along with letters of commitment from 5 or more tax exempt organizations. . . . Since 1969, CVREP has worked to meet an urgent need among Spanish speaking citizens of the Southwest. All that work and $61,000 of committed funds will hang in the balance when (the) IRS makes its ruling."

Despite the considerable efforts of its backers, CVREP was denied IRS tax-exempt status for a second time on November 22, 1972. The IRS decision was based on the fact that CVREP had been receiving more than 25 percent of its support from one source: the United Auto Workers. CVREP's leaders were paralyzed. Shattered by the IRS's decision, they struggled to maintain the tiniest of hopes in the morass of technical language that accompanied the agency ruling. What they did not have for the moment, however, was the money, stamina, or drive to continue the battle without pause. They were exhausted. As the end of the year approached, therefore, they begrudgingly decided to cleanse their systems of the bitter taste of a second IRS rejection and to clear their minds for yet another attempt during the coming new year.

In order to achieve success moving forward, Barraza and the others felt CVREP needed a change of some sort to break the scent of resistance hovering over its problematic efforts to date. They decided to hire an additional consultant, not another floater who saw CVREP as a secondary or tertiary priority, but rather someone who would make the project the most important priority in his work. They wanted new blood; someone who was young, energetic, unselfish, committed, and brash enough to throw himself completely into reversing the chaos and disillusionment in which CVREP found itself mired. In short, they wanted someone like Willie Velásquez.

~~ ~~ ~~

Velásquez was at the bottom of the barrel, desperately searching for the right group to get him back onto the frontlines of the Chicano movement, when Barraza asked him to come on board and unleash his talents at CVREP. Willie's life was in shambles. He was barely surviving on part-time work with his friend Arnold Flores. His wife Janie was expecting and he did not have the financial resources to take care of her and a child. His parents' recent divorce still haunted him and left him filled with deep-seated anger toward his father. Barraza's offer seemed like a gift from God, coming when Velásquez's scattered activist interests and growing personal challenges demanded some type of focused response.

Barraza had a deep confidence in Velásquez based on firsthand observation. He recalled Willie from his early days heading the Unity Council, from his feisty battles with Congressman González, and from his brief but impressive staff work at the Southwest Council. He saw Willie as a prototype of the new Chicano leader: well-educated, committed to the cause, and able to speak the language of the people. He was especially attracted to Willie's reputation as a survivor and an organizer who could live on lean budgets and yet still make things happen. For his part, Willie admired Barraza's brash leadership style and saw him as a pioneer in the Chicano struggle. He relished the Southwest Council chairman's real commitment to developing young leadership at a time when many older leaders were trying to shut out new voices and perspectives. Willie also liked Barraza's Mexicanness. He remembered going to cantinas to drink with Barraza and, after a few rounds, watching him bellow *corridos* that brought to life the trials and tribulations of assorted Mexican folk heroes. Willie looked forward to working with Barraza. He knew that he would learn a great deal from the longtime labor activist and also that he would be given considerable space to do what was necessary to get the job done. Velásquez, accordingly, signed on with Barraza and CVREP for an initial period of one-half year at $600 a month in salary.

Velásquez's position made him CVREP's principal consultant. His most important assignment was to secure sufficient financial commitments for CVREP to qualify for tax-exempt status under the IRS's cumbersome rules governing nonprofit voter engagement activities. Fund-raising and proposal writing thus became Willie's primary responsibilities. But, as fate would have it, ever larger procedural and political considerations eventually came into the picture that severely stymied the project's forward movement. On the procedural side of the equation, CVREP's presumed standing to qualify for IRS tax-exempt status as a voter registration and education project was seriously questioned by logical allies in the field. During early 1973, for example, Adrian DeWind, an attorney recommended by Ron Brown of the National Urban

League, surprisingly informed CVREP's de León: "[Based on the facts presented, rather than merely denying the application,] the IRS could have ruled that [CVREP] is a section 501(c)3 which has made taxable expenditures subjecting the organization to a tax and the managers to possible penalties." DeWind then concluded: "If my fears that the CVREP is itself a private foundation and that more than 25% of its support came from another private foundation, you may be in a position where the [best] thing you can do is to start all over again with a new organization which will not get itself into this kind of problem." Instead of rationally considering this recommendation made by someone sensitive to minority concerns, de León and the CVREP leadership criticized and rejected DeWind's suggestion. Velásquez, still fresh to the whole operation, filed DeWind's advice away in the back of his mind.

Sadly, for CVREP, DeWind's advice would turn out to have been well founded. On the political side of the equation, CVREP's development became increasingly mired in the pettiness and paranoia of the Nixon White House. In time, the project's fate would be shown to have been manipulated for political reasons by the administration, but not before irreparable harm had been inflicted upon it.

ᔕ ᔕ ᔕ

The rest of 1973 flashed by like a blur for Velásquez. He worked at a sizzling pace that reminded him of his earliest days in the Chicano movement. At one moment he would be locked away in the back room of a borrowed office, feverishly scratching away at a revised CVREP proposal. Later on, he would be on the road trying to organize local CVREP chapters. In between, Willie would meet with anyone—representatives of VEP, foundations, liberal groups—who could help to make CVREP a reality. With CVREP's union-based funding dwindling rapidly, Velásquez was paid only when extra money was available.

With his wife Janie at home again and pregnant, this posed severe challenges for Willie. In light of the couple's premature losses with two prior unsuccessful pregnancies and their recent financial and marital hardships, Willie wanted desperately to provide a more comfortable and nurturing life for his budding family. At the same time, he savored the thrill of sacrificing for the cause, of living on the edge, and of never knowing when he would get his next check. To him, living paycheck to paycheck was a psychological rite of passage that tied activists even closer to the movement. It armed them with a sense of moral superiority in a world where rampant self-interest was increasingly taking center stage.

Ironically, Velásquez's return to the hectic, workaholic world of Chicano politics initially turned out to be just what he needed to diminish the growing gap between his public and private commitments. It fundamentally resuscitated him. It gave him newfound energy and purpose. It lifted him up and excited him. Willie's renewed spirit in turn spilled over into his relationship with Janie as the time drew nearer to the birth of their first child. Willie was starting to let Janie know where he was and when he would be getting home. He cooked for the two of them when Janie was afflicted by a serious kidney infection and high fever only five months into her pregnancy. He even took Lamaze classes with Janie and prepared himself to be an active partner in the birth and rearing of their expected child.

Janie went into labor on May 25, 1973. Willie was her coach at the hospital where she endured seven agonizing hours of contractions, one minute apart. When everything ended, Willie and Janie were blessed with a daughter, Carmen Maria, named after Janie's mother Carmen and Willie's mother Maria, both strong women. Carmen's birth was the happiest moment in their almost three years of marriage, coming just months after their bleakest hours. Sadly, the couple's bliss would turn out to be relatively brief.

Janie was hoping that Willie would settle down for good once Carmen was born. Instead, he quickly reverted to his fully absorbed, activist lifestyle. He pounded out long hours of work while increasingly ignoring Janie and their little girl. Janie, the young, inexperienced mother, felt Willie's absence to the core of her soul as she tried to raise their daughter alone. He casually blew off planned family gatherings and dinner parties, blocking out their existence, leaving Janie to feebly explain his truancy while he kept working through the night.

From Willie's point of view, he had to keep pushing. He was so close to securing the financial commitments the IRS required to grant CVREP's exempt status that he could allow nothing to stop him until he succeeded. By mid-October, Velásquez was convinced that he had secured five guaranteed support pledges that would allow CVREP to successfully resubmit its exempt status request.

CVREP formally submitted its application to the IRS for the third time on December 20, 1973, at a specially arranged meeting in Washington, D.C. with responsible IRS staff. A frank exchange between the parties resulted in CVREP's representatives introducing a sensitive question: Had any political motives of the Nixon administration played a role in CVREP's arduous journey through the IRS's qualification process? CVREP's concern was fueled by earlier congressional testimony of John Dean, Nixon's legal adviser, before the Senate Watergate Special Committee. On June 29, 1973, Dean presented the committee with White House memos written in 1970 and 1971 indicating that attempts were being made to force the IRS to take administrative actions against "left wing" and "activist" organizations whose views the White House found offensive. CVREP leaders linked this broader revelation with statements made before the Senate committee by William Marumoto, a White

House assistant, confirming the Nixon administration's use of punitive tactics against Mexican-American and other Spanish-speaking groups. Marumoto admitted that, as part of Nixon's 1972 re-election bid, the Spanish-speaking division of the Committee to Re-elect the President had engaged in a policy of neutralizing groups that did not support the administration.

The CVREP leaders intuited that they were among these targeted entities, owing to their ties to progressive labor and community groups, as well as Republican fears that they would register too many Democrats if successfully operated. Herman Gallegos reported having met with Latino Republicans over a year earlier and being advised that CVREP was too Democratic and needed quickly to add Chicano Republicans to its board in order to gain the administration's backing. In exchange for CVREP's cooperation and partnership, the Latino Republicans pledged to do all they could to help the budding voting project secure its exempt status. Now it appeared clear to Gallegos and his CVREP colleagues that their would-be Republican friends had duped, misled, and otherwise successfully kept them out of the 1972 presidential elections.

The attending IRS representatives sought to reassure the CVREP officers. While they acknowledged that there had been some White House interest in CVREP's case, they rejected the notion that political motivations had been responsible for the organization's failure to secure IRS exempt status. At the meeting's close, the IRS representatives assured the assembled Mexican-American leaders that CVREP would be treated fairly and equitably, especially considering recent public disclosures concerning administration attempts to coerce the IRS to play politics.

The CVREP leaders left the meeting dazed, but hopeful that they would finally receive a positive response from the IRS within the next few weeks. But on February 8, 1974, their hopes were dashed. The IRS had denied CVREP's application for the third time. The CVREP team was absolutely shocked. The IRS ruled against CVREP again, ostensibly because the labor-oriented Greatness Fund, one of the sponsoring groups that had made a commitment to support CVREP, was not itself an exempt organization. This meant that CVREP was one funder short in meeting the federally required number of pledges necessary to receive tax-exempt status. In effect, CVREP's legal standing to undertake federally approved voter registration and education projects was barred on the basis of a technicality.

While a fatal application flaw technically ruined CVREP's chances to obtain exempt status, CVREP's leaders felt certain that political antagonists—the Nixon White House, Latino Republicans, and the IRS—were more likely at work to deny their various submissions and appeals. They also knew that it was virtually impossible to produce concrete evidence proving their suspicions.

After five-and-a-half years of unrewarded effort and sacrifice, CVREP was inching closer to a premature demise and its backers and advocates were not sure there was anything else they could do. After a brief period of reflection and scenario analysis, Chairman Barraza reluctantly announced that CVREP was dead.

Velásquez was extremely upset. He deeply respected Barraza, but he could not accept his conclusion. Willie was not ready to let the idea of a Mexican-American voter rights organization die. Over the past year, Velásquez had blindly put stock in his belief that a group like CVREP had to be established. Failure was not an option, from his perspective. He informed CVREP's leadership group that he would not stop, that he was going to make this thing happen. They did not even have to pay him, he reported; all he wanted was their support. Barraza did not believe Velásquez would succeed, but there was something in Willie's voice and look that resembled a man possessed, so the Southwest Council board chairman reluctantly gave Velásquez his blessings to continue the struggle. Gallegos and de León also saw the fire in Velásquez's belly and offered their support. They knew this was absolutely the last chance they had to create a community organizational capacity to expand Mexican-American political participation for some time to come. If it did not happen now, it probably would never happen during their lifetimes. History would hastily write them off as obscure failures, and Mexican Americans would continue to be abused and manipulated by both major political parties.

After two crazed months of scrambling to decide what CVREP's next move should be, Velásquez returned to a plan the organization's leaders had prematurely spurned over a year earlier. With encouragement from Mario Obledo, a former general counsel of the Mexican American Legal Defense and Educational Fund, who Willie brought on board to help with legal advising, Velásquez decided that it was time to start over with a fresh organization. Velásquez and Obledo agreed to shut CVREP down, therefore, and to set up a brand-new organization based out of Texas. The new group, christened the Southwest Voter Registration and Education Project (SVREP), was incorporated one week after Willie's thirtieth birthday. It boasted a headquarters address that also doubled as the Velásquez residence.

In order to gain IRS exempt status, SVREP, like its precedents, faced stiff review hurdles. Its initial request was denied and forwarded to the IRS national headquarters for additional review. Willie and his colleagues knew this path well. But, this time, Velásquez truly would not be denied. He feverishly added detail to what was basically the same application CVREP had submitted. He dropped the Greatness Fund as a financial supporter and added three new sponsors he had galvanized in case any remaining funders turned out to pose a problem for the IRS reviewers.

Eight weeks later, on July 24, 1974, the nearly six-year ordeal was over.

SVREP was granted its 501(c)3 tax-exempt status. Velásquez and the others wildly celebrated the long-fought victory. Their anguish and frustration had been transformed into newfound energy that eagerly awaited work still to come. Velásquez, in a letter to Chairman Barraza, turned the near nightmarish experience into a positive lesson for the movement: "The son-of-a-bitches at the IRS gave us an unnecessarily hard time; however, I think it only served to strengthen our resolve to found the organization and get on with the job before us. In this sense, it has served to make us a tougher organization with a clear sense of how far our enemies will go to destroy us and an equally clear understanding of our own tenacity."

The establishment of SVREP as a going concern under the federal tax laws was a monumental accomplishment, to be sure. It required a level of commitment and staying power that was effectively superhuman. But Willie knew, more than most, that the battle to empower Mexican-American voters had not concluded with SVREP's victory in obtaining IRS tax-exempt status; rather, it had only really just begun. Indeed, time would prove that even tougher hurdles and challenges lay ahead for Willie and his allies in the months and years still to come.

Chapter 9

SVREP'S SUCCESS IN OBTAINING TAX-EXEMPT status in early 1974 transformed Velásquez instantly. His doubting and stifling worries were replaced by a newfound strength. Overnight, he went from being an underpaid, overworked consultant seeking to sell a floundering concept to an executive director of an exciting new organization with great promise. But the intoxication of SVREP's administrative and procedural victory gaining official legitimacy to commence operations paled in relation to the sober, tedious, day-to-day actions necessary to achieve its mission.

For the rest of 1974 and the entirety of 1975, Willie committed himself to building an enduring and effective organization. His concerns ranged from the mundane to the sublime, covering everything from determining how best to organize SVREP's office and staff to identifying which approaches would most successfully turn organizational theory into action relative to Mexican-American political empowerment. The small amount of remaining funds available to SVREP through its labor-based grant support meant the staff would be necessarily lean and low-paid. At a minimum, Velásquez felt SVREP required, in addition to himself, an analyst, a field organizer, and an administrative assistant. The harder part of the equation was determining how most strategically to structure the substantive work these staff members would focus their energies on.

After meeting in Atlanta with VEP officials and analyzing his past, ad hoc voter registration efforts, Willie was convinced that research was the most crucial element in laying the groundwork for SVREP's success. VEP leaders told him that if they could start over with the knowledge they had acquired over the years, research is where they would begin before jumping into direct organizing. Velásquez also recalled author Penn Kimball's assessment of the Mexican American Unity Council's registration efforts in the late 1960s in his book *The Disconnected*. Kimball's thorough examination of the Unity Council's support of COVER (the Committee on Voter Education and Registration) concluded: "Regardless of the expenditure of substantial amounts of money, energy, and emotional appeal, an untargeted registration effort was simply not effective in doing the job in San Antonio in 1969." Kimball then revealed what Willie now in retrospect understood to be the better approach: "It is always more rewarding to go hunting where the most ducks are likely to be. . . . Registration continues to be a retail type of business even when conducted on a wholesale scale. The [imperative] is to identify, sort, and organize the names and addresses of unregistered voters in a form that lends itself to systematic contact by workers in the vineyard." Such attention to data and detail had never defined Mexican-American voter registration efforts. For all the sweat and passion Mexican-American activists had expended in earlier drives, their lack of research killed them. Their inability to target more precisely led to a hodgepodge registration approach where time, money, and effort were wasted. SVREP now had to find a better way to carry forward its work, in Willie's carefully studied judgment. To do that, he felt, research would have to serve as the essential prerequisite to action.

In August of 1974, just weeks after receiving SVREP's exempt status, Velásquez pushed to find a researcher who could help the organization immediately develop an informed field strategy. He talked to his progressive academic allies, asking for hungry, intelligent students who might be capable and interested. Charlie Cotrell, the St. Mary's University professor who had helped to inspire Willie's grassroots activism recommended Andy Hernández, a Trinity University student who had worked in Joe Bernal's unsuccessful bid for re-election to the Texas state senate. Velásquez had also worked on the Bernal campaign and vaguely recalled Hernández. Cotrell told Hernández that Willie was looking for research help and that he had given the SVREP director his name.

Hernández, a relative anomaly among Mexican Americans for being raised as a Methodist and for being politically active since his teens, was then a twenty-one-year-old political science enthusiast entering his senior year at Trinity. Following Cotrell's lead, he quickly called Velásquez and said he was interested in SVREP and the research position. Willie told Andy to come by his office to talk. The impressionable student was immediately awed to learn that Velásquez even had an office; hardly anybody in the grassroots Mexican-American political sphere had such luxuries. But Hernández's awe was short-lived. In fact, SVREP's headquarters was a small borrowed space at the Mexican American Unity Council, buried deep in a back corner. When Willie greeted Andy and welcomed him to SVREP, the physical reality of the organization was anything but impressive. A folding table, two chairs, and a phone comprised the entirety of Velásquez's "office." This was Hernández's introduction to SVREP.

Hernández was quickly moved, however, by Velásquez's excitement. A certain glow radiated from Willie's face; his bubbling attitude filled the otherwise vacant room. Andy could sense Willie's passion and purpose, his commitment and his impatience. He knew somehow from the start that the conversation with Velásquez would not assume the properties of a conventional job interview. In fact, it was not much of an interview at all. Willie was not interested in wasting time interviewing and reinterviewing prospective candidates. Cotrell and significant people in the Bernal campaign had given Hernández exceedingly high praise. That was enough for Willie, who wanted to get SVREP's work off the ground as soon as possible.

After some small talk, Velásquez launched into politics, asking Hernández to explain why Bernal had lost his re-election bid by a mere ninety-nine votes. The Trinity University senior was relieved. He had been studying that question extensively and felt he could answer it without any problems. He quickly cited various statistics, political variables, and theories that could be offered as possible explanations. Willie occasionally shook his head and mumbled "Mmm, uh huh."

Suddenly, Willie politely interrupted Andy's dissertation and advanced his own interpretation of Bernal's defeat, based on raw power, "Andy, the reason we lost was we ran out of Mexicans [at the polls] and we're going to keep on losing until we register them [and bring them out to vote]." He then boldly predicted that SVREP was "going to build the biggest voter registration organization the Mexican community had ever seen." SVREP, Willie asserted, would exist for ten years, electing more "Mexicans" than ever to office, and transforming a meek, almost nonexistent political voice into a powerful, respected, and feared vote. As Willie spoke, he became more and more animated about SVREP's prospects. His voice became louder and stronger. He spoke about voter registration with the passion and conviction of a religious convert.

Even Hernández, a staunch believer in Mexican-American political potential, found it hard to share Velásquez's optimism and certainty concerning SVREP's possibilities. Willie's dreams and hopes for SVREP were evolving precisely as the progressive wing of Mexican-American politics in San Antonio was on the decline. In recent years, three leading local flag bearers of the liberal cause had been defeated—former City Councilman Pete Torres, former County Commissioner Albert Peña, and former State Senator Joe Bernal. The historical moment, therefore, seemed not at all to support Willie's plans. SVREP's little, borrowed office and paltry resources, moreover, made it clear that the organization was highly unlikely any time soon to emerge as a significant change agent in the regional political equation. Hernández was, accordingly, dubious.

When Willie walked Andy out at the conclusion of their meeting, he offered Hernández the job as SVREP's researcher. The position would begin on a part-time basis, but would surely present rewarding, indeed historical opportunities for the young student, Willie asserted. Andy, thinking over the situation, was initially coy with Willie, telling him that he was considering other outstanding offers. Willie, demonstrating his integrity, begrudgingly advised the young Hernández to accept one of the other jobs, assuming it would give the Trinity senior full-time work, because SVREP simply lacked the resources to offer him anything but part-time employment; the full-time job opportunities,

Willie advised, would surely give Andy the better start out of college. In reality, Hernández had no other offers to consider. He also surmised that Velásquez, however far-fetched in his thinking, was one of the most compelling and forward-thinking political activists that he had ever met. He intuited that Velásquez might actually be capable of making meaningful headway on the issues. Before even realizing it, Hernández was informing Willie that while his "other offers" were good enough, the SVREP position felt more stimulating and challenging to him. He would accept Willie's offer, therefore, and could start immediately. Velásquez, always a step ahead of the pack, wasted no time. He immediately assigned Hernández to investigate and document the living conditions of the Mexican-American working-class population in San Antonio. Hernández began his work with SVREP shortly thereafter, sharing Velásquez's dingy loaned office, slaving away at a tiny table facing a wall, and listening to Willie's frequent complaints about the Unity Council administrative staff's reluctance to type up his many long funding proposals, memos, and reports. In this way, the Catholic-trained Velásquez and the middle-class Methodist Hernández began a relationship that would produce unprecedented political gains for Mexican-American and other Latino voters across the United States.

After successfully recruiting Hernández to guide SVREP's research activities, Velásquez hired Aurora Sánchez to be his administrative assistant in October 1974 and Robert Cabrera to be his field assistant in January 1975. Sánchez, also a product of the Bernal campaign, had been working for the recently defeated state senator at the Commission for Mexican American Affairs. Velásquez and Cabrera knew each other from their high school days when Willie attended Central Catholic and Robert attended Holy Cross in the barrios of the Westside. The two had both gone on to St. Mary's University where they were involved in the same activist circles. Cabrera was working temporarily at his father's boisterous meat market on Guadalupe and Navarro Streets in the heart of the barrio when Willie recruited him to join SVREP.

Velásquez and Cabrera met at the Esquire Bar, a cantina that brought the flavor of the Westside to downtown San Antonio, to talk about SVREP and their organizing dreams for the Southwest. Willie talked about Cabrera traveling around Texas and other Southwestern states to organize targeted registration efforts, and the tremendous impact they could have on the face of politics in the region. Willie knew of Robert's deep commitment to the community and he played to that sensibility. After a few rounds of beer, Cabrera was raring to go into the field on SVREP's behalf.

Shortly after hiring his foundational team, Velásquez and SVREP board member Arnold Flores inspected a half-dozen potential permanent headquarters' sites before settling on a space located above the Majestic Theater on East Houston Street in downtown San Antonio. There were other buildings Velásquez and Flores wanted to rent, but it quickly became apparent that

Willie's former links to the strident Mexican American Youth Organization, his battles with Congressman González while heading the Unity Council, and his early ties to the radical Raza Unida party made him an unwelcome guest to many of the city's more conservative building owners. This troubled Velásquez, both because he felt he had moved away from those groups long ago and because an unduly militant image attributable to Willie could substantially impair SVREP's progress throughout the region on various fronts.

Like its Unity Council's predecessor, the new SVREP headquarters office was small and extremely austere. Its furnishings were quite old and limited. Boxes rather than file cabinets housed the organization's paperwork. The lone typewriter in the office was rented. Willie's office contained only the barest of essentials: a table, a couple of chairs, and a phone. Hernández sat at a modest desk situated in an open space area of the main office entrance, and Sánchez occupied a spot cramped up against Velásquez's door. Eventually, the arrangement proved too limiting in terms of productivity and morale, and SVREP moved to another floor in the Majestic Building with additional space and more generous furnishings inherited from Velásquez's ally and role model, Albert Peña.

Having Peña's furniture in the SVREP office was bittersweet. On the one hand, Velásquez bragged about sitting in the former county commissioner's chair and using his desk. He was proud indeed to be a benefactor of someone he believed was an authentic exemplar of the kind of progressive elected leadership SVREP was trying to advance through its work. Yet, having Peña's things in the SVREP office also symbolized the impending downfall of the aging politician. SVREP was able to acquire Peña's items only because after being ousted from office the ex-elected official was having serious financial problems and recently was forced to close his law practice. SVREP's office furniture, inherited from the venerable Peña, was thus a cold physical reminder of the human cost of Mexican-American political activism in Texas and other Southwestern states, where progressive community leaders were often ultimately consumed by mainstream retaliation and/or the effects of unrelenting personal sacrifice. Peña's demise embodied the unsavory reality that the politics of change were immensely brutal and demanding. In the mid-1970s, Willie could not fully comprehend that these same dynamics would one day factor in his own personal journey. Ironically, he was too busy focusing on SVREP's development to even imagine that possibility.

៦ ៦ ៦

As 1975 began, Velásquez moved aggressively to consolidate a strong governance and programmatic base for SVREP and to expand the organization's funding support. Since securing SVREP's exempt status, Willie had spent just under $17,000 to get an organizational structure in place. All things considered, this was a remarkably modest sum for an ambitious new organization with significant regional and national plans. Still, SVREP's bank account was dangerously thin and extreme economy was an essential and necessary imperative, from Willie's standpoint, for the project to have a fighting chance to achieve its potential. Cost saving efforts thus complemented every element of SVREP's early work and governance.

Planning for the first SVREP board meeting exemplified Willie's commitment to keep costs to a bare minimum. Los Angeles was chosen as the meeting site because three of SVREP's four board members also served on the board of the National Council of La Raza (formerly, the Southwest Council of La Raza), which was slated to hold its own board convening in Los Angeles at the same time. By scheduling SVREP's meeting to coincide with the National Council's gathering, Willie knew he could avoid having to pay for most of his board members' travel, as their expenses were largely being covered by the Council. Through his stringent use of resources along these lines in 1975, Willie was able to achieve nearly $28,000 in savings, enough to support nearly six months of now full-time work for his staff and to launch SVREP's first voter registration efforts.

SVREP's first board meeting as a legitimate national nonprofit organization was held on January 17, 1975, at the Los Angeles International Hotel. The founding board members assembled on this historic occasion included: Maclovio Barraza, the board chairman, whose unflappable commitment and labor connections had kept PREP, CVREP, and SVREP alive during some of the worst of times; Arnold Flores, Velásquez's inseparable partner and local San Antonio labor leader, who served as SVREP's vice chair; and Armando de León, the legal counsel and faithful follower of Barraza, who had also been instrumental from the beginning in assisting SVREP's formation and now served as board secretary and treasurer. Willie held the final remaining seat on the SVREP board, which was reserved for the organization's executive director.

Velásquez proposed adoption of a straightforward core organizational goal for SVREP: "to assure the development of a comprehensive six-state nonpartisan voter registration, voter research and educational program that [would] substantially increase . . . voter registration levels . . . in the Southwest, particularly [among] Mexican American[s], Indian[s] and other minorities." Unlike the far-reaching and ultimately unwieldy goals of organizations like MAUC or the Southwest Council, which from their incipiency had targeted virtually all the ills of the Mexican-American community, Velásquez wanted SVREP to be driven by a laser-sharp focus: expanding minority political participation in the Southwest. By centering energy and resources on this single aim rather than dabbling in a multiplicity of realms, Willie felt that SVREP could alter the course of history for Mexican Americans by substantially increasing their representation as voters and public officials. A highly targeted and coherent focus would force SVREP to produce, in Willie's estimation. It would heighten its public accountability and provide a tangible set of benchmarks against which to assess progress and impacts. SVREP would either increase the number of Mexican-American registered voters and elected officials or it would not. In either case, it would be judged accordingly. It was that simple.

Velásquez additionally proposed that SVREP's initial program activities should concentrate on research and efforts to test different voter registration strategies in a small number of locations across the Southwest. To advance this work, he suggested establishing an advisory committee of Chicano scholars who would critique SVREP's research and registration methods. The SVREP board embraced Willie's recommendations, but Barraza warned him about the need to build a legitimate base of program operations, not merely a presence, in the field. This would require sustained and meaningful work in each target community that SVREP engaged, and campaign activities of consequence in at least five states in order to meet the IRS guidelines for exempt status as a voter registration organization. Barraza did not want SVREP to become merely a research entity nor a predominantly Texas-focused operation. Willie nodded in agreement, commenting that SVREP's approach would have to be highly pragmatic and adaptable to varying local conditions across the Southwest in order to address Barraza's legitimate concerns.

In fact, SVREP really had no choice but to proceed experimentally. Having never actually implemented a voter registration campaign, it had no proven approach to draw on; and, therefore, no unifying organizing model to offer to local partner communities relative to how best to conduct a winning voter mobilization campaign. Under these circumstances, Velásquez's emphasis on pragmatism and adaptability, an approach that essentially envisioned partner localities employing the methods best suited to their respective environments, and an "anything goes if it works" attitude, would have to do until SVREP gained enough registration know-how to determine the most cost-effective and impactful ways to promote Latino voter empowerment. Until then, the local partner groups would have to stumble through the learning process hand in hand with Velásquez and SVREP. Wishing the approach could be more sure and scientific, but recognizing that this was the best they could do, the board concurred with Willie's assessment and vested its confidence in his ability to learn quickly on the job.

∽ ∽ ∽

With board approval of his major plans, Velásquez and the SVREP staff returned to San Antonio with a full plate. As time passed, Willie settled into a strenuous work routine. On most days, he rushed into the SVREP office around half-past eight in the morning, his adrenalin already at a pitch. Almost immediately after arriving, Willie was on his way out, driven as a creature of habit by uncontrollable forces, to a nearby family-run Mexican restaurant for daily morning tacos. Affectionately known as "taco time" by the SVREP staff, Willie spent thirty to forty minutes consuming *carne guisada* tacos and the latest financial news from the *Wall Street Journal* or *Business Week*, thinking, brainstorming, and bracing himself for the long and challenging hours to come before quitting time. Here, isolated from the constantly ringing phones and the confines of the office, he dreamed up new directions and a larger focus for SVREP as beef stew dripped unnoticeably from his tacos onto the table below. With his food and thought cravings satisfied, Velásquez returned to the SVREP office with his bearings straight.

Back in his office, the pace and tenor of Willie's days promptly shifted to nerve-wracking, nonstop marathons. Most of his time was spent conducting high-stakes, fast-paced business on the phone. Willie would telephone his board vice chair and confidant, Arnold Flores, daily—sometimes up to three or four times. They planned meetings with potential SVREP supporters and made arrangements to get together for additional strategy sessions in person over cocktails after hours.

Velásquez also typically called his board chairman, Maclovio Barraza, daily, to inform him of SVREP's evolving activities and to ask for his guidance concerning new plans and ideas. Often Barraza challenged Willie's inclinations, sometimes with abrasiveness. As the elder Barraza talked, Willie listened intently to the union man. Somewhat ironically, the normally independent and strong-willed Velásquez rarely retaliated or contested, even when Barraza dressed him down. He had too much respect and admiration for Barraza, and too much confidence in his wisdom to question the steadfast board chairman's judgment.

Beyond his intensive interactions with Flores and Barraza, Willie engaged heavily in external lobbying efforts. He unleashed a barrage of ideas and appeals on foundation executives, labor officials, and Mexican-American community activists. Hour after hour, Willie used his telephone as a primary weapon to advance the Hispanic voter registration movement, pleading in conversation after conversation to gain more funding and support for SVREP projects.

When not politicking or otherwise cajoling on the phone, Willie would often lock himself away for long periods of time writing and rewriting proposals or reports for foundations. An important aspect of this work was educating and informing private benefactors about the harsh realities and disadvantages facing Mexican Americans in the Southwest. Most of the major funding institutions that had any potential interest in SVREP's work were based in and around New York City or selected midwestern cities. Accordingly, foundation staff professionals tended to have some awareness of African-American community needs, and in some cases Puerto Rican claims, but few intimately understood Mexican-American community history or circumstances.

Andy Hernández's research quickly emerged as a critical ingredient in Velásquez's campaign to gain funder appreciation of the project's important and timely work. It also helped to bolster SVREP's strategic program planning by enabling Velásquez to make more informed judgments about where most productively to target the organization's precious resources.

Like many political leaders and practitioners, Willie was convinced that information was power. He felt that SVREP could never know too much about its target population. He wanted SVREP's work to be driven by rigorous analysis of facts and data, not merely gut feelings and assumptions. Hernández pulled information from wherever he could: the census bureau, journals, magazines, newspapers, published and unpublished reports—anything that would give SVREP more facts and data. In due course, he found himself working on an exhaustive list of research projects concerning the Mexican- American electorate. His studies were not complicated regression-laden reports, but rather somewhat crude, rudimentary stabs at creating a case, and a base of strategic information, for SVREP voter registration efforts. What this work lacked in sophistication it more than made up for in utility. As one early voter registration coordinator related, "SVREP's research work was great. It was the first time we had anything like it. And with the little money we had it helped us get the most bang out of our bucks." This was exactly what SVREP wanted from its one-man research team, useful information that would help SVREP spend its money wisely.

Getting this data was a tedious task slowed down many times by uncooperative county officials. Hernández was literally counting by hand the number of Mexican-American registered voters and elected officials in different areas of the Southwest. He would overlay census data on precinct maps, find the predominately Chicano precincts, and then go to the courthouse and count the raw numbers of Mexican-American registered voters, one by one, for hours at a time—every single voter in every single Chicano precinct. There were no computers or lists of Spanish surnames to draw on at the time. If a name sounded Mexican to Hernández, he tallied it. These numbers were then compared with the voting age population to give SVREP an estimate of the unregistered Mexican Americans in each jurisdiction. This information, in turn, gave SVREP's field staff and local partners an idea of where potential new Mexican-American voters could be found.

Although SVREP's data consisted of nothing more than informed guesswork and estimates, Velásquez felt obliged to report them as precisely as possible. If Hernández estimated that there were 131,249 potential Mexican-American voters in Bexar County, Texas, SVREP would report the figure exactly that way. There was no rounding off. Willie was convinced that the more precise SVREP's figures, the more likely they were to be accepted by external audiences. Velásquez was not only concerned about increasing SVREP's soundness and rigor as an applied research outfit in order to maximize the value of its data for field activists but he also knew that SVREP's work would inspire resistance and detractors, and he wanted as much as possible for the organization's research activities to favor precision over generality. He felt this would minimize attacks on SVREP's claims and position the organization as an honest broker in the field.

Notwithstanding these inclinations, there were times when Willie's own integrity waned relative to reporting the facts based on honest analysis. On one occasion, Velásquez told Hernández to include noncitizens in an analysis of potential Mexican-American voters to bolster the case for SVREP's work. When asked why he wanted to inflate the numbers with ineligible entries, Velásquez told Hernández: "Anglos aren't smarter than you are, Andy. If they challenge it, then they are going to have to go through all this work. They won't do it. We've been denied all these years; it's okay if we fudge a little." At bottom, from a tactical standpoint, Velásquez hoped that by presenting a potentially larger Mexican-American electorate he could convince private grant-makers, and especially more liberal funders interested in expanding the power of the Democratic party and minority communities, that SVREP's work was urgently needed.

In addition to occasional fudging of this sort, Hernández was often concerned about the methodological limitations of his work. His methods were highly unscientific and based on relatively dated (1970) census figures. All of this significantly exposed SVREP to potentially devastating challenges from those who, for a variety of reasons, might take issue with its evolving work and agenda. Fortunately, SVREP's initial low profile meant that few people were even positioned to be aware of its research activities, let alone to critique them.

SVREP's desperate need for grant support to help fuel its start-up activities in the field presented nagging problems that haunted Velásquez and SVREP every step of the way. His development strategy was simple and relatively clumsy: He applied for funding from any foundation, labor council, or progressive group he knew of, utilizing a single, standard proposal text that he updated every now and then with new statistics and ideas. The disadvantage of this approach was its failure to address the varying program interests and specializations of targeted grant-making institutions. In addition, Willie's early proposal submissions were simply not well presented; wordy, long, and typically neither clear nor compelling, these appeals were antithetical to the needs and customs of program staff at the more established national grant-making institutions.

Richard Lawrence, of the Cummins Engine Foundation, critiqued one of Willie's early SVREP proposals and helped Velásquez see these problems: "Your introductory statement is the first thing someone sees when reading the proposal and [yours] has absolutely no value. . . . Your description of the elements of the problem are very detailed and very long and in most cases not really very engrossing. . . . My impression is that the proposal is too full of what appears to be a kind of term paper collection of quotes, data, and graphs." These harsh comments were exactly what Willie needed in order to make adjustments that could enhance SVREP's competitiveness. Unfortunately, in response, Velásquez, partly because of time restraints but largely out of pride and stubbornness, chose to make only minimal revisions to improve SVREP's proposal.

SVREP's fund-raising efforts during its first year of operation were, not surprisingly under the circumstances, highly ineffective. Willie's undisciplined approach resulted in many rejections and a paltry $68,700 in support from eleven funding sources during the first half of 1975. Grants ranged from $1,000 to $15,000 and included gifts from funders such as the Field Foundation, the AKBAR Fund Foundation, the United Methodist Church, the San Antonio Catholic Archdiocese, and various labor groups. SVREP expended just under $60,000 getting started that first year, but directed only $4,900, or approximately 8 percent of its budget to fieldwork. The lack of more substantial field activity posed special problems relative to SVREP's efforts to attract the support of the nation's most significant and influential grant-makers. These funders, including the Ford and Rockefeller Foundations, wanted to support more proven organizations with strong programs and infrastructure. They were especially reluctant to fund unknown quantities, a cautionary position that had been strengthened during the turmoil of the late 1960s when many leading foundations faced unsettling congressional scrutiny and interference for funding militant groups. SVREP, being an unknown quantity, was denied funding from these sources time and time again initially, largely on account of the perception that with no available track record to draw on, supporting the upstart voter group would be too risky.

Velásquez resented the unwillingness of established foundation leaders to help SVREP get started and he grew more and more bitter with each rejection. "It seems that we are fated to suffer more than just the birth pangs of this project," Velásquez wrote in October 1975 referring to the struggle to raise funds. The curse of being resource poor was something that would torment SVREP for years to come. By June of 1975, Willie was already negotiating loans with George Casseb and the Westside Bank to pay for things like the production of public service announcements. His experiences to date had made him highly skeptical of the largely East Coast foundation establishment. He imputed a sense of hostility to SVREP from many in the funding world, writing at one point: "It seems [the larger funders] believe that [a Chicano group] can organize nothing significant unless the idea originates with [them]. We want to show them that in fact Chicanos [themselves] can form significant organizations." Building on this line of logic, Willie desperately tried to devise strategies that would enable SVREP to raise its own sources of funding, independent of the "Eastern givers," but this proved futile for the most part. Whether he liked it or not, SVREP was ultimately dependent on the support of large Eastern grant-making institutions, both for its immediate existence as well as its future development.

〜 〜 〜

The pressures of Willie's responsibility as the founding executive of SVREP were beginning to manifest themselves in ways extending beyond occasional slips on research methodology and laments about organized philanthropy. In important ways, his entire persona was transforming. He was becoming more compulsive, more aggressive, and more moody. Velásquez's exceedingly high expectations of staff created a tense and pressure-filled work environment at SVREP. Willie, a workaholic and perfectionist, set an impossibly high performance benchmark. He generated a smothering amount of work for SVREP staff members, and showed little sensitivity when they could not measure up.

Velásquez hoped his own limitless energy and drive would serve as a model for his employees, and at times it did. Aurora Sánchez later recalled the strength of Willie's contagious attitude. His passion and belief in SVREP's potential was so deep that his team felt moved to help him in every way humanly possible. He would often race out of his office, waving his latest draft funding proposal, and scream that SVREP was going to be the greatest thing in the world for the Mexican-American community. Sánchez and the others believed him. Willie made them feel like history was being made and they were playing a key role in the process. The most mundane task was elevated to crucial importance; each project took on special urgency.

Such exaggerated excitement, though, was simply impossible to maintain. Willie felt he had to try, however, to do just that if SVREP was going to succeed. To ensure that outcome, he ruled SVREP as a benevolent dictator, controlling every detail and decision in the organization and demanding the utmost of his tiny staff.

Velásquez's controlling nature, however, caused great anxiety for SVREP staff members. Staff meetings lacked give and take. They were primarily sessions for Willie to dole out additional assignments and unrealistic delivery deadlines. In between meetings, Willie would often change staff responsibilities midstream, taking an established line of work in an entirely new direction. There were also occasions when an irritated Velásquez would come storming up to staff members, throw a stack of work papers back at them, and sternly comment as he walked back toward his office: "This is not done right, fix it," or "That's not how I told you to do it, do it right this time." He rarely took time to point out specifically what was wrong with a staff product he did not like or to suggest constructively what changes could be made to satisfy him.

Velásquez's gruff early management style at SVREP focused narrowly on getting things done, producing substantial results, and making SVREP an effective organizing tool. In the beginning this approach resulted in SVREP's small staff of four generating tremendous amounts of work. But slowly, almost unknowingly, their passion and enthusiasm was drained. Willie's attempts to maximize impact and to accelerate results, for the least amount of money possible and in the shortest amount of time imaginable, finally had its limits on a human level.

The immense strain and tension of getting SVREP going created a Willie who subjected his staff to dramatic mood shifts. On occasion, he used the silent treatment on staffers in the same way he treated his wife Janie. There were even episodes when Velásquez would go days without speaking to anyone in the office, with the staff having no clue why he was acting that way. Then, suddenly and unexpectedly, from one day to the next without explanation, he would appear at the office, loud and cheerful. At first, the SVREP staff did not know how to handle Willie's often dark mood swings. In time, however, they learned to cope by simply not taking them personally and hoping that they would be short-lived.

Periodically Willie's staff would put in long overtime hours and work weekends. In general, though, they worked weekdays until half-past five or six in the evening. Velásquez, on the other hand, typically kept going into the night virtually every day of the week. When quitting time finally arrived, he often rendezvoused with Arnold Flores, his closest of friends, for evenings packed with smoking, drinking, laughter, and politics. This was Willie's way of handling his growing strains and pressures. Instead of relaxing in a low-key fashion, he often pushed his body and mind to the limit.

Willie's after-hours gatherings with Flores were neither mere drinking binges nor vacuous bull sessions. Typically, their conversations advanced SVREP's strategic work. On occasion, the pair entertained foundation representatives or union officials. During festive meals and evenings out on the town past midnight, Willie and Arnold would try to sell SVREP to both current and prospective benefactors, who invariably knew little about Mexican Americans or their political alienation. In these instances, many new friendships of value to SVREP were cemented.

Velásquez and Flores had two favorite hang-outs: the Gunther Hotel bar, for no other reason than it was across the street from the SVREP office, and the Esquire bar, a toned-down version of a barrio cantina located in the heart of the city. Of the two, the Esquire was the preferred watering hole. It was customarily packed with people of all stripes. During lunchtime and in the early afternoon, the Esquire attracted respectable downtown businessmen in pinstripe suits. As night fell, however, the Esquire inevitably became more and more Mexican. Laborers stopped by after work to drown their memories of another harsh and thankless workday. Washed-up musicians straggled in, plopped themselves in lounge booths, and plucked meaningless notes from rickety guitars. Middle-aged, single Mexican women, caked in makeup, reeking of cheap perfume, and dressed in sleazy clothes found their way to bar stools in hopes of meeting someone special. This was the Esquire after dark.

Foundation representatives and other SVREP visitors loved the Esquire because it made them feel like they were somehow closer to the grassroots and in touch with a slice of barrio life. In fact, the colorful drinking hole did have a certain quality of local authenticity, rawness, and even danger. On one occasion, Velásquez, Flores, and Barraza experienced this firsthand during an informal executive committee meeting at the Esquire. As the three leaders discussed recent developments of their nascent voter registration group, an inebriated patron worked hard to gain Willie's attention. Velásquez and the other two men ignored the drunk and continued their discussion. But the mumbling souse would not be denied, and he persisted to seek Velásquez out. Willie, annoyed by the man's perseverance, sharply told the interloper that he was trying to conduct a meeting and asked him to get lost. Shortly after the executive committee recommenced, Willie's newfound antagonist returned. Sneaking up from behind, the man smashed a beer bottle over Velásquez's head, inflicting a deep gash. Instead of rendering Willie to the floor unconscious, the impact seemed to inject him with a surge of power. Willie attacked the man like a possessed spirit. He unleashed a barrage of anger and punches that made him look like a madman. He had not felt this much rage since his parents were divorced. Velásquez could not stop pounding the man. It was as if a deep dark force had taken control of his actions. Barraza and Flores ultimately managed to drag Velásquez away from the drunken provocateur, but not before Willie had inflicted a serious physical price in retribution for the assailant's unannounced attack.

Such was the passion and the precariousness of Velásquez's early days as SVREP's founding executive. Everything was for keeps. Willie, driven by a restless resolve that was now beginning to incur higher and higher costs, would be stopped by nothing and no one. Neither the accepted standards of survey research, the whims of national foundations, the growing concerns of his staff, nor the vagaries of his colorful after-hours stints would prevent him from seeing through SVREP's potential to transform Mexican-American political history. Willie's commitment to his cause was remarkable and highly impressive. On the other hand, his inclinations were putting him increasingly at risk of spiritual, personal, and physical harm. Like a high-stakes gambler, Velásquez was aiming for a record roll of the dice. Unfortunately, as only time would tell, he was unwittingly betting with his ethics, his family, and, ultimately, with his health as collateral.

Chapter 10

AFTER SVREP'S TREACHEROUS BATTLE to obtain IRS tax-exempt status, Velásquez took an extremely diligent and proactive posture in his dealings with federal tax officials. Technically, SVREP had until the end of 1976 to establish a working presence in at least five states, in order to meet IRS requirements to operate as a legitimate nonprofit voter registration group. But Willie did not want to take any chances. Prior experience with the agency had thoroughly convinced him that its staff would do anything necessary to prevent SVREP from becoming an effective catalyst for change in the region. Anticipating the worst, Velásquez was determined not to give federal authorities any potential ammunition to hinder the project's work going forward. If the IRS wanted SVREP to be working in at least five states by December 1976, Willie would develop organizing campaigns to meet that threshold by June 1975, fully a year-and-a-half in advance of the agency deadline. This in turn would absolutely underscore that SVREP was a genuine regional outfit.

The goal of initiating five geographically distinct pilot voter registration projects by the summer of 1975, however, was brutally ambitious, especially considering SVREP's thinly staffed and poorly resourced operation. Willie unleashed Robert Cabrera, his lone field assistant, to lead the aggressive Southwest organizing effort barely one month after he started working at SVREP. Not having any readily available "how-to" manuals on organizing local Mexican-American voter promotion groups, Cabrera was able to tackle each state with only his past experiences, common sense, and a deference to local leadership as his artillery. Every obstacle and triumph along the way became part of the accumulated history and learning that SVREP would carry into each new organizing venue.

Using SVREP Board Chairman Barraza's immense contacts from his lengthy labor and political career, and Velásquez's still strong network from his days organizing on behalf of the Southwest Council, the project was able to gain a quick foothold in the required five jurisdictions. The organization thus commenced local registration drives in Texas, Colorado, California, Arizona, and Utah during early 1975. The project's efforts in Texas, California, and Arizona especially reflect the range of insights and results that SVREP achieved through these formative campaigns.

Not surprisingly, SVREP's initial registration efforts targeted Velásquez's hometown of San Antonio. Willie's record of community engagement and his strong network of key local contacts gave SVREP unusual advantages in its Texas organizing efforts.

In order to initiate its Texas campaign, SVREP organized an introductory community meeting in late January 1975. Slightly over sixty San Antonians representing approximately forty different groups and the public at large attended the gathering and signed on to help with the local drive. After speeches by various leaders and an explanation of the campaign's major aims and objectives, the participants formed three subcommittees—one for strategy, one for operations, and one for voter education.

In early February, the group elected a reluctant Olga Peña as chairperson of the San Antonio drive. Peña, the ex-wife of former Bexar County Commissioner Albert Peña, had a long history of walking the streets of the barrios stirring up support for an assortment of progressive political candidates. In exchange for commitments by other Mexican-American community leaders to play a large role in the campaign, Peña signed a contract with SVREP to chair a four-week registration drive with a modest $1,000 start-up grant.

SVREP staff was assigned to support the San Antonio group's three subcommittees. Andy Hernández and Cabrera were detailed to the strategy subcommittee, which decided to target registration efforts on the heavily Mexican west- and southsides of San Antonio, as well as on the city's predominantly African-American eastside. Cabrera and Aurora Sánchez helped the operations group to set up outreach offices in each area, to hire three coordinators familiar with the target neighborhoods, and to assemble a working budget. Hernández and Cabrera also worked with the campaign's voter education subcommittee, which galvanized the region's Spanish-speaking media, particularly local radio stations, to sponsor public affairs messages highlighting the importance of Mexican Americans registering and voting.

Reliance on the Spanish-speaking media would become a centerpiece of SVREP's tactics in the years to come. Andy Hernández's early research showed that Mexican Americans received most of their political information and news through the Spanish media. These data encouraged Willie, not only for their advantageous applications to his grassroots strategy and the need for economical organizing investments (the Mexican-American media were a far cheaper distribution vehicle than the mainstream media in virtually every major market of concern to SVREP's strategy), but also because, in effect, Hernández's early research on the efficacy of the Spanish media for Mexican-American community engagement relieved pressure on Velásquez and SVREP alike to rely on mainstream media to mobilize the minority vote.

Willie simply did not trust the region's Anglo-run newspapers, radio, and television stations to provide evenhanded treatment of SVREP's work and aims in their reporting. He feared instead that the English media would construe SVREP's pro-American, pro-democratic registration efforts as subversive activities aimed at taking over the Southwest—a position that could only prod the Anglo community to resist and discourage the project's success. In a letter to a funder in 1975, Willie spelled out SVREP's concern this way: "The issue of registering Mexican Americans, Native Americans, and other minorities in the Southwest is a hot one for politics in the [region] and as a result we are maintaining a low profile in the first year of our operations."

Velásquez's strategy was informed by author Penn Kimball's analysis of failed registration drives in and around San Antonio during the late 1960s and early 1970s. These campaigns, ironically, had typically resulted in higher registration rates in unorganized Anglo communities than in targeted Mexican-American neighborhoods. A large part of the problem was the highly discernible and viscerally challenging nature of past minority voter initiatives. Kimball's analysis alerted Willie to the proven downside of highly visible mobilizations targeted to minority voters. According to Kimball: "[E]xperience in the [field] has shown that a publicized effort to register minority-group voters often triggers a countervailing reaction within the majority." Willie etched Kimball's analysis in his mind and cemented it with his own growing political suspicions of Anglo community motivations to create a signature strategy for SVREP's early national work: Spanish media only and an overall low profile in the general community.

SVREP's resulting dependence on the Spanish media complemented Velásquez's personal worldview of Mexican Americans operating in a relatively isolated, separate barrio reality that connected only rarely and superficially to the ways of the larger society. The community's overwhelming reliance on Spanish media for news and information reflected this reality. Recognizing this alerted Willie and SVREP to the strategic advantages of being able to educate and mobilize prospective new Mexican-American voters largely out of range of the Anglo community's control or direction. One of Willie's favorite sayings was "If we [Mexican Americans] started a revolution tomorrow and announced it on Spanish radio, we'd be the only ones to know it was happening."

SVREP's first registration attempts in San Antonio ultimately relied on two intensive weekend mobilizations involving volunteer workers from leading national organizations like LULAC and the American G.I. Forum, various neighborhood nonprofits, local student clubs, and regional labor associations. The campaign resulted in the registration of nearly three thousand newly eligible Mexican-American and African-American voters in Bexar County. These new voters included, at one extreme, seventeen-year-old Rodolfo Ortiz, who would be eighteen before the next election cycle, and eighty-eight-year-old Leonato Reyna, at the other.

Two methodologies dominated the San Antonio group's campaign: roving door-to-door registrations at people's homes in the targeted neighborhoods and site-based registrations at central locations like shopping malls and public events. Both approaches produced positive results, but the campaign's successes were mitigated by certain obvious shortcomings. These included the unanticipated reluctance of many more middle-class volunteers to engage people in the city's neediest minority neighborhoods, the lack of support training to prepare volunteers to be more effective registrars, and the absence of more generous funding and institutional wherewithal to do the job at maximum capacity.

Owing to these variables, SVREP's first voter registration drive, though on balance successful, produced mixed results. On one hand, the campaign-inspired increase in the number of registered minority voters was not much more than recent drives had produced in San Antonio's barrios. On the other hand, the San Antonio mobilization generated important insights, lessons, and organizing protocols that would help to guide and inspire future gains in Texas and elsewhere. Perhaps the most interesting aspect of SVREP's inaugural effort, though, was its relatively stealth nature. In fact, surprisingly few people involved with the coalition—either as volunteers or observers—saw it as a SVREP initiative. By design, the campaign produced no SVREP signs, bumper stickers, or posters to indicate that it was a project-sponsored phenomenon. Defying history and conventional political practices emphasizing mainstream media and brand-oriented public engagement techniques, SVREP and Velásquez thus effectively made their Southwestern debut almost without anyone noticing. This essential strategy and style of operation would significantly shape SVREP's work to transform Mexican-American politics throughout the Southwest in ensuing campaigns.

SVREP ventured into the huge, sprawling, and daunting Los Angeles basin to commence its next significant voter registration drive. California, the country's largest state, representing almost 10 percent of the national population and housing more Hispanics than any other jurisdiction in the United States, was an essential battleground in SVREP's quest to alter the balance of political power in the Southwest. Latinos, who made up 16 percent of the state's population and were the largest California minority group nevertheless suffered from abysmal political participation rates. Hispanic rights and justice leaders nationwide understood that Latino California had to be targeted and given tremendous resources in order more proportionately to exercise its political voice. Los Angeles County alone, according to SVREP estimates, was home to some 1.3 million Chicanos, or 19 percent of the total Southwestern Hispanic population. Gaining a stronger visibility and role in shaping the politics of the region could only substantially advance the national Hispanic community's and SVREP's fundamental objective during these years: to establish Latino voters as a key factor in American politics.

Historically, California had implemented a series of flexible voter registration laws that gave SVREP much greater room to maneuver than it had ever had during the campaign in Texas. California encouraged registration year round, rather than only during certain designated periods. Almost any citizen residing and eligible to vote in the state could become a deputy registrar with legal power to register voters door-to-door or at convenient sites such as local grocery stores or shopping malls.

In this relatively favorable legal environment, voter registration drives were nothing new to Latino neighborhoods of California, especially in East Los Angeles where a long line of primarily candidate-driven efforts had taken place for years. Dating back to 1947, when members of the initially unsuccessful campaign to elect Edward Roybal to the Los Angeles City Council founded the Community Services Organization (CSO), East Los Angeles had been a constant target of political organizing. CSO, for example, launched a massive voter registration effort in 1948–49 under the direction of Henry Nava that resulted in thousands of newly registered voters in the city's ninth council district. Riding the crest of enthusiasm generated by these drives (as well as the changed electorate), Roybal, in 1949, defeated the incumbent city council member from the ninth district by a two-thirds margin—making him the first Mexican-American city councilman in Los Angeles since 1881. CSO registration efforts, aided by Fred Ross and the Industrial Areas Foundation, continued in the greater Los Angeles area until the 1960s, when the CSO then switched its focus from political action to service-oriented programs in areas like health care, leadership development, and citizenship promotion.

Other grassroots voter mobilization organizations and individual political campaigns emerged sporadically during this period to register and organize Mexican-American voters in southern California. These efforts, mostly based on the city's heavily Mexican-American eastside, were largely sporadic and volunteer-driven. Nevertheless, they had produced knowledge, networks, and strategies that Willie realized early on would be vital to SVREP's success in the region. Velásquez, wanting to draw upon this expertise to advance SVREP's aims in East Los Angeles, sought the assistance of the Reverend Antonio Hernández of Clelland House. Hernández, a Presbyterian minister, had been running social justice programs and community centers in the East Los Angeles area for almost three decades. During recent years, under Hernández's leadership, Clelland House had become synonymous with eastside community action because it housed and otherwise supported so many neighborhood activist groups. Willie had known Hernández since the late 1960s when they both directed community organizations funded predominately by the Ford Foundation through the Southwest Council of La

Raza. Hernández's group at the time, the Mexican American Community Programs Foundation had organized one of the largest registration drives ever undertaken in East Los Angeles, adding an estimated thirty thousand new voters to the rolls during the 1968–1969 campaign cycle.

Willie understood that a strategic alliance with Hernández would dramatically enhance SVREP's prospects for a successful southern California campaign. With Hernández's support, SVREP would have the benefit of a proven infrastructure and local knowledge base to draw from. It would also have much enhanced local credibility and access, as well as a trusted partner on the ground in the region. All of this compelled Willie to push hard for Hernández's collaboration. Fortunately for Velásquez, Hernández agreed to work with SVREP to help it build a presence across Los Angeles County, notwithstanding the project's embarrassingly scant resources. SVREP could muster only $1,200 for an initial three-month countywide organizing effort. By comparison, the six-month drive Hernández directed in 1968–1969 had spent roughly $12,000 working almost exclusively in East Los Angeles. Under these circumstances, every effort would have to be made to mobilize southern California Hispanic voters through highly disciplined and economical community organizing efforts. In short, movement activism more than money would have to be generated in Los Angeles' barrios in order for SVREP to make a meaningful difference in the region. Velásquez and Hernández surely had the commitment and the community-based organizing experience to inform meaningful gains in the field. But, in the end, their lack of financial wherewithal and institutional capacity would make their burden an especially heavy one.

Willie envisioned each local community operating its own registration drive with a central coordinating office established in East Los Angeles directing the overall county effort. John Barba, a Hernández protégée, was hired as SVREP's lone paid staff person to undertake the daunting task of coordinating the Los Angeles area drive. Barba had met Reverend Hernández during the Los Angeles school blowouts in 1968 and was still only a college student when he accepted the Los Angeles position with SVREP. For approximately one year, Hernández and other leaders of the Los Angeles project struggled to keep Barba going by raising tiny amounts locally to add to SVREP's initial, meager support, but they were not very successful. Barba's hardship was exacerbated by SVREP's still evolving and often cumbersome fiscal and programmatic reporting requirements. Notwithstanding his exceedingly low-paid salary, the upstart Los Angeles County SVREP staffer was constantly under pressure to document his activities and his project-related expenses. Typically, these obligations impeded Barba's capacity to attend to pressing local circumstances and to receive timely reimbursements for his out-of-pocket coverage of project campaign costs. These bureaucratic encumbrances had discouraging effects on Barba's morale and campaign leadership during important moments in the California campaign, but Velásquez and other SVREP principals, still trying to develop the project's work in other venues with limited staffing and funding, were less than sufficiently attentive to the young organizer's plight.

Despite SVREP's back office dilemmas and constraints, the Los Angeles County Voter Registration and Education Project was officially launched on June 7, 1975, almost four months after initial organizing meetings were convened in southern California. Fiscal problems and organizational difficulties, already evident in the campaign, did not constrain SVREP from establishing a wildly unrealistic goal of registering 500,000 new California Hispanic voters by Cinco de Mayo of 1976. Local steering committee members, consisting essentially of holdovers from Reverend Hernández's well-funded registration drive of 1968–1969, saw the 1975–1976 mobilization as an extension of their earlier work. They falsely believed that they would have even more resources than in the past to register eligible voters in communities surrounding the heavily Hispanic East Los Angeles area. When it became apparent that this would not be the case, the Los Angeles leadership drastically decreased its campaign registration target to 150,000 new Chicano voters by July of 1976. Even still, this adjusted target remained vastly out of reach given the campaign's severe limitations of available funding and manpower.

Sponsors for the Los Angeles County drive included many of the state's top Mexican-American officials, such as State Assemblymen Richard Alatorre and Art Torres, California Health and Welfare Secretary Mario Obledo, and Los Angeles School Board member Julian Nava. Except for Obledo, however, these well-connected politicos offered relatively little tangible campaign support. Instead, they wholeheartedly endorsed the drive, giving it added public legitimacy, but they essentially looked to SVREP, along with community activists and volunteers (most of them affiliated with Hernández's community center), to fuel the campaign's success. The resulting lack of campaign access to the organizations and funds amassed by these community political leaders proved to be another major impediment to the drive's traction in southern California. It pressed SVREP and Barba to rely very heavily on a rapidly decreasing grassroots base, owing to the incipiency of a less progressive public spirit following more than a decade of citizen activism.

Growing public and volunteer apathy, combined with the financial woes of the Los Angeles venture, forced the SVREP-sponsored drive to severely cut back its organizing scope. Instead of its originally envisioned countywide scheme coordinated by a central office in East Los Angeles, SVREP had to settle for a hit-or-miss approach in a handful of targeted areas. Barba concentrated almost exclusively on his territory, East Los Angeles, while token efforts were feebly attempted in selected neighborhoods of El Monte, San Pedro, the San Fernando Valley, and West Los Angeles. The rest of the county was left virtually untouched. Not surprisingly, the drive fell far short of even its organizers' drastically adjusted goal of 150,000 newly registered Mexican-American voters in Los Angeles County. In the end, the campaign produced only about the same level of increase as Reverend Hernández's earlier solo efforts had produced, raising serious questions about SVREP's value-added.

Reverend Hernández knew Velásquez and deeply valued his and SVREP's partnership in the 1975 drive. Secretary Obledo was also a strong friend to Willie and SVREP's efforts in California. These endorsements helped the Texas-based voter registration advocates with many important southern California Latino leaders, but many others saw Willie and SVREP as mere outsiders with little to bring to the table.

In the end, Velásquez was baffled and frustrated by SVREP's first move into California. He had hoped to achieve far more there. While the drive was successful in the limited area of East Los Angeles, the campaign showed virtually no traction to significantly crack any of the outlying Chicano areas in Los Angeles County. Willie's growing inclination was to focus future efforts around election cycle drives outside of East Los Angeles as a logical response. Reverend Hernández advocated supporting a nonpartisan, year-round voter registration office located in the heart of East Los Angeles. Reaching no conclusive agreement concerning which strategy to support going forward, Velásquez left California, giving Hernández another $3,000 to support continuing registration work in the southern California region. The two men agreed to continue to talk about deepening SVREP's involvement there, including, perhaps, the development of a Los Angeles branch office of SVREP, staffed by a full-time, year-round organizer.

SVREP's early work in Arizona focused on Pima County, which included the state's second largest city, Tucson. Targeting Tucson and its surrounding areas was significantly facilitated by the fact that SVREP's chairman, Maclovio Barraza, was a local native with a long history of partnering effectively with area labor and community activists. Barraza's strong local base and credibility generated an immediate cadre of willing partners for SVREP's Arizona effort, which was solidified in early March 1975.

The organizers of the Pima County drive brought considerable mainstream political experience to SVREP's aid. Hector Morales, who served on the Tucson city council from 1965–1968, was chairman of the registration effort. Richard Martínez of the Barrio Education Center acted as field coordinator. Other active leaders in the campaign had political baptisms dating back to 1957 when John F. Kennedy visited Tucson in anticipation of his 1960 presidential campaign. These individuals were active in registration and get-out-the-vote work for Kennedy and found the work easy to do because of Kennedy's ability to inspire people of widely diverse backgrounds. Kennedy's Catholicism, charisma, and compassion had powerful appeal for

Mexican Americans in particular. Many were drawn to the Democratic Party by the young senator's quest to become president, and this bolstering of the state's progressive base was applauded by Anglo party leaders. Being associated with Kennedy thus made it easier for leading Tucson Mexican Americans to start supporting Chicano candidates (such as Arnold Elias) for state legislative positions in the early 1960s without the threat of being labeled radicals, militants, or communists.

These Tucson politicos continued their mainstream work in 1964 with Lyndon Johnson's presidential campaign and in 1968 with Robert Kennedy's bid for the presidency. Through these efforts, they sought to establish in Arizona an expanded space for Mexican-American political representation and participation that would help to make state policies more responsive to the plight of grassroots community needs. But, at bottom, Arizona was an intensely conservative state, and by the mid-1970s the glow of John Kennedy's new frontier had long ago subsided, even among working-class Mexican Americans in Tucson, a traditional Democratic Party stronghold in the state.

When Morales made an unsuccessful bid for a seat on the Arizona Corporation Commission in 1974, his advisors and supporters immediately interpreted the cause for his campaign's failure as a lack of political sophistication. Their consensus analysis was that they had overdepended on grassroots mobilization efforts and had not been sufficiently attentive to emerging, more modern campaign techniques. The times had changed, they surmised. Community organizing no longer created the benefits it had in the past. If they wanted to move the Mexican-American community ahead politically, they inferred, it would be necessary to master more media—and opinion poll—driven strategies. This was the approach that many of the Tucson politicos hoped SVREP could help them to develop in 1975.

Velásquez, who was seen by the Arizonans as a down-to-earth, deep-thinking technocrat, quickly challenged their inclination to resort to fancy media and survey polling tactics as the way to further the cause of Mexican Americans in Pima County. Instead, he argued that more informed door-to-door registration canvassing at the grassroots level would produce the most significant increases in future Mexican-American voter participation. This, he argued, would require targeted demographic research and efforts focused on precincts that would most likely produce the greatest receptivity to Chicano political mobilization. After much debate and additional discussion, Morales and other Tucson leaders deferred to Willie's conviction and organizing expertise, and agreed to tackle the barrios one more time. They signed a $1,000 contract with SVREP for a nine-week registration and education drive beginning March 10, 1975, and established a baseline goal to register fifteen hundred new Mexican-American voters. Building on SVREP research and their own political knowledge, the experienced Tucson activists targeted city precincts 18, 19, 48, and 49, as well as the outlying areas of Marana to the north and Sahuarita to the south, with the highest priority directed to the barrio areas of Tucson.

Getting started was not as easy as the campaign organizers anticipated. With all their combined political experiences, many of them still held romantic notions of going into the barrios, registering their people, and getting them out to vote without much effort. They badly underestimated the hard work necessary to do effective door-to-door registration work, and they were especially slow to identify and train required field personnel. As a result, the campaign quickly fell behind schedule in obtaining needed volunteer deputy registrars. The drive's launch was thus delayed by one month. Eventually, when things were set in motion, the Pima County group attracted housewives, copper miners, student activists, schoolteachers, and a handful of small businessmen to augment the legion of community and political organizers already committed to the cause.

In addition to the drive's late start and truncated timeline, other problems mired the Arizona group down. The state's established Democratic Party elites, including some Mexican Americans, for example, resented the Pima County effort because it was not cleared through or controlled by them. While the party leaders did not actively sabotage the drive, their lack of support cost the Pima County group needed backing and legitimacy in certain community leadership circles.

Another obstacle was convincing many grassroots Mexican Americans that their vote actually would have an impact. SVREP had encountered this problem in all its opening drives, but it took on a different meaning in Pima County. In many areas of the Southwest, Mexican Americans had no faith in their electoral power because they had never been able to elect one of their own to any position. This was not the case in Tucson. Tucson voters had elected Mexican Americans to various offices, but had seen little positive change as a result. Campaign leaders tried to explain that change of the type they needed and sought required continuous, long-term community mobilization and engagement. But community members asserted the need for better jobs and schools now, not twenty years down the road.

A smaller, more affluent segment of the Mexican-American community was opposed to the work of the Pima County registration drive for still other reasons. This group, made up of leading community businessmen and professionals, many if not most of them Republicans, saw the boisterous organizing effort as a radical intervention that was disrupting the subtler, quieter movement of middle-class Mexican Americans, such as themselves, into the mainstream of Tucson society. Their belief was that the SVREP-supported campaign risked backlash by forcing unduly aggressive changes down the dominant society's throat. They also suspected that SVREP's claims of nonpartisanship were in fact a cover to support what was a decidedly Democratic Party agenda.

Resistance to the Pima County effort from both establishment and grass-roots quarters, coupled with the campaign's troubled start, produced a less than successful outcome. A few days before the official close of the effort, campaign principals reported to Willie and his SVREP team that they were slightly over budget and still three to four weeks away from reaching their goal of fifteen hundred new voters. The sheer enthusiasm of campaign volunteers carried the drive forward for a month beyond its expected closing, but even with this additional surge the Pima County group never quite reached its registration goal.

෴ ෴ ෴

Virtually against all odds, as the summer of 1975 commenced, Velásquez and SVREP had achieved the unthinkable: establishing a presence in five states, fully a year-and-a-half before the IRS eligibility deadline to establish the project's protected status as a tax-exempt voter organization. SVREP's first drives were by no means stellar examples of how to conduct effective voter registration campaigns in Latino communities. Nevertheless, Velásquez felt momentarily relieved. SVREP's experimental period had ended without any major catastrophes. Its search for the best techniques and approaches to support Hispanic voter registration was far from over, but even with highly mixed results, at least the project had successfully launched activities outside of Texas in other states that were also critically important to its core mission. These first drives in turn, for all their successes and failures, laid the essential groundwork for an ongoing learning process that would constantly push SVREP to re-evaluate its starting assumptions and techniques.

These initial ventures also produced grassroots political organizing standards that would become synonymous with SVREP's longer-term work and legacy. For example, SVREP's introduction of research data, crude though it was, offered a more efficient way of doing voter registration canvassing. Prior to SVREP, many Mexican-American communities held registration drives that targeted areas based on an impressionistic sense of where unregistered Hispanics lived. SVREP changed this approach by producing research reports based on recent census and voting information that reliably estimated the number of unregistered Hispanics in a particular vicinity and showed more precisely where these new voters could be found. This manipulation of census data and voting statistics, though sometimes imperfect, especially early on, greatly added value to the organizing effectiveness of grassroots voter registration and education efforts in Latino (and other minority) neighborhoods throughout the region, and eventually the nation. Errors in the analysis and application of data became less frequent over time and were greatly outweighed, even in earlier stages, by the net benefits to local groups to more accurately determine where to place sparse resources for the most cost-effective impact possible.

Another distinctive practice informed by SVREP's early work was the nonpartisan use of coalitions of community and civic organizations to lead local drives, rather than establishment leaders or political candidates. Through this approach, SVREP sought to avoid turf battles by including any individual or group that wanted to encourage increased Hispanic voting. It also took a coalition-building approach to create a feeling of assurance in partner states and localities that its sponsored registration drives finally belonged to the community, not the same old group of politicians and organizational power-brokers who usually dominated the scene. SVREP's first registration drives instantly revealed that in practice the ideal of mitigating past rivalries by including all groups into a unified front worked only occasionally. But its coalition-based process did stimulate new groups and people to challenge more traditional political actors in their communities and this helped to encourage new ideas, new leadership, and new participants in the local political process.

In a sense, early skeptics of SVREP's ostensibly unbiased, inclusive approach were correct to suspect that its agenda was not limited solely to increasing the Hispanic electorate. Willie also wanted to develop a more progressive Chicano politics, one that unequivocally advanced the interests of working-class Mexican Americans. Andy Hernández, SVREP's first research director explained Velásquez's intentions along these lines as follows: "We were training [disadvantaged grassroots] people to think about voter registration, politics, and campaigning in different ways. It wasn't civic duty stuff for Willie. It was all about creating the conditions out of which we could win." In reality, Velásquez's aims were overwhelmingly favorable to the Democratic Party. According to Robert Cabrera, SVREP's first field director, "[SVREP's] blanket invitation to any Chicano group in [a given target] area meant [that] 99 percent of the [participants] who showed up [represented] some type of Democratic Party-aligned group." This meant that from the beginning Willie and SVREP used the tricky mask of nonpartisan coalition-building to cultivate a Hispanic electorate with a definite pro-Democratic Party leaning.

The most important objective for Willie, however, was expanding the political clout of the Mexican-American population, not the Democratic Party. For Velásquez, the Party was merely a means to an end, a vehicle that would carry the Mexican-American population to a higher level of political participation and clout. Eventually, it would be necessary to have Hispanics represented in highly visible positions in both parties, Willie thought, but for the time being SVREP had to harness the Democratic Party as the vehicle that could most rapidly attract large numbers of Mexican-American voters. The Mexican-American people already had a strong, established base of affection for the Democrats, and with La Raza Unida Party on the decline and still relatively few Hispanics involved with the Republicans, SVREP set its early sights on pursuing the path of least resistance. SVREP's highly decentralized and limited financial resources made it utterly dependent on volunteers for the success or failure of its early voter registration campaigns. The project's initial drives accented this reliance because the tight timetables under which they were implemented did not allow SVREP to properly train its unpaid workers. SVREP had not yet produced a how-to handbook for its volunteers or developed a training protocol that taught the necessary skills workers required to be effective in the field. In its initial drives, SVREP was merely a conduit, passing extremely small sums of money to Chicano network allies, assisting as possible in campaign strategy, and hoping something fruitful would result. In some cases the drives worked, but in the main, campaign target goals were not met.

Some community observers thought the answer to SVREP's reliance on untrained volunteer workers was more money and staffing. With more money, SVREP could hire more people, making each project less dependent on volunteers and more reliant on paid staff. Willie adamantly disagreed with this assessment, arguing that "[w]hat registers people is not large sums of money, but rather a large number of volunteers. For this reason we [will continue] our policy of organizing coalitions composed of all the key elements in the community and funding them for [essential] expenses." Willie knew that if SVREP wanted to be a productive regional registration outfit, and not just another paper entity, it had to generate worthwhile materials and training sessions that could guide SVREP's volunteers and also make SVREP more accountable for what transpired in the barrios. Willie and the SVREP staff experienced frustrating problems with the organizing efforts in Los Angeles, Tucson and, to some extent, in their own backyard of San Antonio. Until they took more control of the instructional process, the number of voters registered in their drives was destined to rise and fall without them having much to say about it. Willie wanted to address this challenge with SVREP's second cycle of drives scheduled to begin in July of 1975. But much remained largely beyond his control. His largest problem was convincing local groups that SVREP was an ally and an asset that was going to be with them for the long haul. Sadly, many of these groups had been burned by others in the past who had demonstrated little or no follow-through. These experiences left many community activists bitter and cynical about the likes of SVREP, which after all had no history, no track record, and ultimately no legitimacy in the barrios of the Southwest. Each drive going forward would slowly build SVREP's image and credibility in the field, but only time, a lot more hard work, and a great deal of patience would convince the people of its ultimate value. Willie, begrudgingly realizing these hard realities, braced himself for the lengthy journey and the beginning of SVREP's second year in existence.

Chapter 11

SVREP MOVED INTO ITS SECOND YEAR of existence in July of 1975 having established a token presence in five states, but much work remained to be done to maximize the organization's reach and efficiency, as well as its impact on the forthcoming 1976 national elections cycle. Initial efforts in the field obviously had left much to be desired. Willie had scraped together slightly less than $70,000 for SVREP in its opening season from an assortment of smaller, liberal foundations, church funds, and labor sources. In the organization's initial five state drives, however, after salaries and administrative costs were accounted for, only about $5,000 was actually directed to registration work in the field. This represented less than 8 percent of SVREP's total expenditures for the entire fiscal year, a percentage that would have to increase dramatically if SVREP wanted to become a credible player in the voter registration arena. SVREP carried just over $9,000 into its second year of operations and had ambitious plans to expand its registration activities in the barrios of the Southwest.

SVREP launched six more voter registration drives during the second half of 1975, bringing its grand total for the calendar year to eleven. With the exception of Fort Bend County, Texas, a slumbering community located thirty miles outside of Houston, SVREP concentrated all of its efforts in urban areas, mainly in Texas. Targeted sites included Austin, Houston, and El Paso, as well as San Jose, California, and Phoenix, Arizona. No new registration work was commenced in New Mexico, where Hispanics made up 40 percent of the population—the highest percentage of any state in the nation.

Various problems plagued these second-stage drives. SVREP had to battle strict purging laws in Texas that had decimated the number of Mexican Americans registered to vote. Under these laws, legally registered but recently inactive voters were periodically and systematically removed from eligible voter rolls, typically without notification. Houston had lost 28 percent of its Hispanic electorate to purges and Austin had Chicano precincts in which more than two thousand voters out of a total of thirty-one hundred were taken off the rolls. As a result, SVREP volunteers had to spend an inordinate amount of time re-registering Mexican-American voters who had not voted in recent elections.

The net effect was no significant increase in the relative share of Hispanic voters in Texas. In California, SVREP's San Jose organizing committee relied too heavily on site registration and special events such as community picnics, rather than more difficult, tedious, and effective door-to-door registration efforts. The strategy there produced considerable activity, but it had little reach into local communities and ultimately led to very few new registered voters.

The Arizona campaign was effectively derailed when it suffered the early tragic death of Bob Pastor, a popular Justice of the Peace who had played a significant role in establishing the drive. The issue of bilingual voting also ironically distracted the Arizona coalition. Conservative forces in the state challenged the use of Spanish in local and state elections to discourage expanded Hispanic civic participation, particularly among primarily Spanish-speaking citizens. The challenge should have been a plus for SVREP's Arizona coalition to galvanize Hispanic registration. Instead, the issue pushed SVREP's effort there to become embroiled in highly technical activities and philosophical debates that distracted attention from actual community registration and voter mobilization activities. Unwittingly, the Arizona campaign became mired in efforts by its leadership—at great cost in time and resources—to defend the right to bilingual English/Spanish ballots in the courts and the media. The ultimate result was a less than satisfactory impact on Hispanic voter registration and electoral participation in Arizona.

Happily, not all of SVREP's early campaign efforts were doomed to failure or lack of any meaningful forward movement during the second half of 1975. El Paso, for example, achieved significant gains as a result of SVREP's efforts there. Building on a strong union of Chicano labor leaders, educators, students, housewives, and the League of Women Voters, SVREP's El Paso coalition was able to add nearly seventeen thousand Mexican Americans to the city's registration rolls. This impressive result, clearly a product of growing leadership and learning in the organization, gave Willie, his colleagues, and their supporters a critical sign that effective voter registration mobilizations were possible to employ in larger, more complex metropolitan cities.

SVREP's first registration drive held outside an urban setting was also its last effort of 1975. Fort Bend County, Texas, a sleepy hideaway nestled just south of the sprawling metropolis of Houston, turned out to be Velásquez's favorite campaign of the eleven originated during that year.

Fort Bend County, whose two major towns were Rosenberg and Richmond, had been a strong center for Ku Klux Klan activity in the 1920s and 1930s. It had also remained fiercely segregated until the late 1960s when the federal government interceded. With African Americans making up nearly 17 percent of the county and Mexican Americans almost 27 percent, the minority community of Fort Bend County comprised nearly half of the total population. Long-standing racial hatred aimed at blacks also spilled over to hatred aimed at the county's poor and working-class Mexican Americans. Only one Mexican American had ever been elected to office in the county's history. A large part of the problem was the dearth of eligible Hispanic voters. In 1975, more than half of the county's nine thousand Mexican Americans were not registered to vote. Earlier that year, a young Mexican-American attorney had lost a close race for the Fort Bend School Board. His nearly successful and highly dynamic candidacy, however, sparked a revival of Mexican American community political interest that led local leaders to seek SVREP's partnership in order to gain much needed and long overdue political representation.

Fort Bend County project director, Dora Olivo, who Willie would later nominate to serve on the SVREP board of directors, recalled, "When we started the project in December 1975, even though we had given out advance publicity to the community at large and personal contact was made with city and county officials, there was still a lack of cooperation from the elected [leaders], some being very negative." Such lack of support was not limited to the Anglo officials. According to Olivo, "Some members of our community were [also] skeptical and some churches gave us a cold response." Nevertheless, by the time the Fort Bend County campaign was winding down in April of 1976, most local churches, the media, and the community as a whole had come to embrace it as a positive endeavor.

The Fort Bend County coalition was able to mitigate public and institutional skepticism through the depth of its sincerity, its contagious enthusiasm, and its creative incorporation of important aspects of Mexican culture. The local group, which effectively supported both door-to-door and site registration strategies, supplemented its work with clever usage of time-tested slogans, songs, folk dances, and plays drawn from important community experiences, ranging from the Mexican revolution to the farmworker organizing campaigns of the 1960s. In the spirit of these traditions, the campaign also used Spanish as a galvanizing element, at once motivating and educating community residents.

The campaign slogan, plastered over all its materials, was *"¡Despierte! ¡Regístrese! ¡Y Vote!"* (Wake up! Register! And Vote!). A traditional Mexican *corrido* (a song that captures a special moment or event and preserves it for later generations) was composed to advance the effort. Entitled *El Despierto de Fort Bend* (The Awakening of Fort Bend), the *corrido* chronicled the entire registration drive, beginning with the people in the barrios deciding they were fed up with not having a voice, continuing through the hard work of registering the community, and finally realizing its fullest strength. Velásquez enthusiastically wrote the Cummins Engine Foundation about the *corrido*. "You will share with us, I am sure, the satisfaction of knowing that the Foundation's contribution has been immortalized in the folk music of the Mexican people," he boastfully reported.

Solidarity meetings were periodically organized to bolster the campaign's reach and community relevance. Such meetings typically included barrio high school students, dressed in colorful, native costumes, performing ancestral dances from Mexico such as "El Jarabe Tapatío" and "Pavido Navido". Local youth also presented social message plays at these gatherings, with titles like "Las Dos Caras del Patroncito" (The Two Faces of the Boss) and "Los Vendidos" (The Sell-outs) to inspire community awareness and interest in empowerment efforts such as the campaign. Volunteers interviewed leading political candidates for the local bilingual newspaper *Las Noticias de Fort Bend* and asked them about issues Chicanos wanted addressed.

When the drive ended, over twenty-three hundred Mexican Americans were registered to vote, a countywide increase of nearly 60 percent, with some towns tripling their number of eligible Chicano voters. For the first time ever in Rosenberg's history, a Chicano judge was elected. By every important measure, the Fort Bend campaign was an overwhelming success.

Willie was captivated by the blatantly prideful expression of working-class "Mexicanness" that radiated from the small towns that made up Fort Bend County. He compared their leaders to "[brash] young *gallos* (fighting roosters) flexing their muscles." For the first time since SVREP began its work, Willie actually saw his vision taking shape in Fort Bend. The campaign's principals there were not polished political operatives, like those who had headed most of SVREP's campaigns in the large cities. Rather, they were ordinary people who had grown tired of their second-class status and diligently rallied to do something meaningful about it. Through their creative energy and dedication, Velásquez experienced a renewed sense of assurance and confidence that SVREP's work was indeed poised to reshape the political balance of the Southwest in historically significant ways. In a letter to Olivo, Willie observed, "The success that you are having in Fort Bend is being duplicated in many places throughout the Southwest. There is no question that we are participating in an historical awakening of Chicanos throughout the [region and the nation]. Everywhere our people are beginning to question old injustices and working to improve ourselves through the ballot box." While somewhat overstated on its face, Willie's message to the Fort Bend County project director spoke to the undeniable fact that SVREP's work was beginning to put in motion changes in Hispanic community political engagement that would alter the face of American electoral politics.

෫ ෫ ෫

An especially important task facing Velásquez and the newly constituted

SVREP as this work evolved was the need to augment its board of directors. When SVREP held its first board meeting in Los Angeles in January 1975, the board consisted of only four individuals: Chairman Maclovio Barraza, Vice Chairman Arnold Flores, Secretary-Treasurer Armando de León, and Willie. Barraza, the formidable United Steelworkers leader, and de León, the hard-working, faithful attorney from Phoenix, had been working on the creation of a Mexican-American voter registration organization since 1968. Flores and Velásquez were best friends, a tandem that seemed to do everything together, whether it was politics or partying. They were a tight-knit group that had few problems collaborating, but they understood that the board would have to expand if SVREP was to gain respectability, as well as succeed.

SVREP's key foundation sources, both current and prospective, including especially Field, Carnegie, and Ford (which had at the time still not yet supported SVREP's program), were the most persistent advocates of organizational efforts to establish a diverse and prominent board of directors. Key staff of these institutions advised Willie that a board composed of leading Mexican Americans, Native Americans, blacks, and Anglos, both men and women, from every American political bent would best enable the organization to be taken seriously. It would also help SVREP to raise money and secure the best available thinking about how to move the field and the larger society on its issues. The SVREP officers were also committed to the notion of assembling a "star" board consisting of at least a few famous individuals, particularly entertainers, who would give the organization instant credibility and recognition. But when Willie finally recommended new candidates to join the organization's founding board, his suggestions strayed widely from the lofty criteria SVREP's founders had earlier considered. Vikki Carr, the well-known Mexican-American singer, and Vernon Jordan, then president of the National Urban League, were the only two legitimate "stars" Velásquez included on his initial list of proposed nominations. Carr was only half-heartedly pursued. Jordan, however, was someone Velásquez desperately wanted on the SVREP board. The influential African-American leader had given Willie and the other SVREP founders invaluable early support and advice when they were trying to establish the project and Willie never forgot that. In addition, it was not lost on Velásquez that Jordan was immensely connected to important U.S. labor, business, foundation, and political leaders who could be huge assets to the fledging SVREP. After Jordan declined because he was already overextended, Willie did not give up and tried, to no avail, to get Jordan to reconsider his decision.

When it became clear, to Willie's great dismay, that Jordan would not be available to serve, Velásquez developed a second target list of prospective big-name nominees. Father Theodore Hesburgh, president of Notre Dame University, former U.S. Senator Ralph Yarborough, and United Auto Workers leader Leonard Woodcock were among the individuals considered. However, when all was said and done, surprisingly little effort was made to court and secure commitments from any of these leaders.

In the end, Willie created an expanded board consisting primarily of "friends" or people from the larger civil rights/activist community that he could trust and who he knew believed in the same dreams he did. This new cohort of SVREP board leaders included: Rubén Valdez, Speaker of the Colorado House of Representatives and a distinguished labor leader; Leonel Castillo, city comptroller of Houston; Lucy Valerio, head of SVREP's registration efforts in Utah; the Reverend Monsignor George Higgins of the U.S. Catholic Conference of Bishops; Vilma Martínez, president and general counsel of the Mexican American Legal Defense and Educational Fund; and Wilbur Atcitty, an elder of the Navajo Nation. (Wiley Branton, a controversial civil rights attorney, was asked to serve just months after this expansion group was selected, to round out SVREP's board augmentation campaign.) These people were not nationally known stars or household names, but they brought much to the fore that would serve SVREP well. They were individuals deeply respected in their fields and by political activists in their respective communities. They were people who wanted the same things for Mexican Americans and other disadvantaged American minority groups: equal opportunities, expanded national recognition, and the real-life prospect of these groups achieving their fullest human potential. All felt good about the work they were doing to make these ideas concrete realities throughout American society. With this group of new SVREP directors, then, Willie could feel the basis of an enduring organizational consensus, a pulling in the same positive direction, a focus on the larger picture and not egos; this was exactly the type of board dynamic and composition he thought SVREP needed.

Willie's newly expanded board of directors would substantially increase SVREP's credibility and impact over time, but, in the short term, the battles on the ground facing Velásquez and his fledgling organization would increase. More often than not, ironically, the battles in question would involve logical allies rather than conventional antagonists; that is, for example, Latino labor and community leaders, rather than reactionary Anglo leaders and institutions, as might be expected.

෴ ෴ ෴

SVREP became embroiled in a bitter fight with national Latino union executives in late 1975 over Latino labor's lack of financial support for SVREP, a battle that would haunt Velásquez for years to come. The tragic irony of this development was that, for all practical purposes, the house of labor had built SVREP. PREP, the embryonic predecessor to SVREP, had originated with a $10,000 grant from the United Auto Workers in 1968. After PREP was forced to spin off from the Southwest Council of La Raza in the aftermath of the Tax Reform Act of 1969, the United Steelworkers' (USW) had kept its successor organization, CVREP, alive, almost single-handedly. Through the persistent prodding of SVREP's founding board chairman, Maclovio Barraza, himself a seasoned steelworkers' executive, the union provided nearly $60,000 over a four-year period in small monthly contributions, enabling SVREP's founders to establish the project as a viable Mexican-American voter registration group. Without this regular injection of resources, there would not have been enough money for the organizational, fund-raising, and legal work necessary to sustain SVREP in its formative stages.

Willie's own strong labor background made the impasse with Latino labor leaders especially difficult to swallow. In college, his involvement with the United Farm Workers (UFW) and the farm labor strike in the Rio Grande Valley had transformed the impressionable student from a campus-based participant into a lifelong community activist. Willie's fellow MAYO colleagues used to complain that Velásquez was more of a trade unionist than he was a Chicano militant. His later work in the early 1970s with Arnold Flores brought him directly in contact with various San Antonio unions—representing workers, negotiating on their behalf, drafting propaganda for them, and getting drunk with them—and this made Willie crave even more for a lifetime advocating on behalf of the Mexican-American working class. These experiences, especially after the heady times of the farm labor movement, greatly affected Velásquez. Flores, and others who knew Willie closely, consistently remarked that, deep down, Velásquez harbored a not-so-secret desire to become a labor organizer.

Willie truly admired the strides the labor movement was making to incorporate Mexican and other Spanish-speaking Americans, but he was disappointed that Latino workers had never joined together to promote their own agenda within organized labor circles. Velásquez's pragmatism warned him that Hispanic workers could not indefinitely rely on the gracious hearts of top non-Latino labor leaders for progress. Rather, to make progress on their own terms, Willie believed Latino labor leaders would have to become more strategically connected, purposeful, and aggressive. They would have to learn to organize and advocate as a single unified entity, rather than as merely a loosely joined hodgepodge of union representatives.

This was not an original idea, but it was one that had not been actively pursued in San Antonio. As a result, and because Flores fundamentally shared Velásquez's views, he and Willie had joined briefly to create the San Antonio Chicano Organizers (SACO) in the early 1970s. Through training and organizing, they wanted to replicate César Chávez's success uniting Mexican rural workers in an urban setting, hoping to speed up the process of change for Chicano workers in the city. Similar Latino-based labor organizations were appearing throughout the Southwest and as far away as New York. Unfortunately, Willie's increasing involvement with the formation of SVREP took him away from SACO and no one joined Flores to fill the void left by the dynamic Velásquez's departure. As a result, SACO slowly disappeared from the scene and Willie transferred his passions for working-class training and empowerment to the voter registration arena.

Just a few months following SACO's demise, the Labor Council for Latin American Advancement (LCLAA) was founded in Washington, D.C. in November of 1973. Spurred by aims such as those espoused in the work of regional groups like SACO, LCLAA committed itself to advocating on behalf of Latino laborers nationwide, through more integrated organizing efforts that transcended distinct union claims and sectors. LCLAA's formation thus created unprecedented opportunities for crosscutting union campaigns and voter registration work that could radically help to increase Latino vesting and clout in American society. On the other hand, LCLAA's leadership was fundamentally loyal to liberal Democratic Party and generalized trade union interests. Accordingly, their agenda was neither neutral nor necessarily fully consistent with the emerging SVREP's larger, and at least ostensibly, nonpartisan mission.

Still, LCLAA's arrival on the scene made it an important and potentially formidable SVREP partner and benefactor. The early composition of the new labor association suggested, moreover, that its relationship to the upstart SVREP would be an especially close one. Sadly, in the end, this early promise was left unfulfilled in ways that would ultimately prolong the U.S. Mexican-American/Latino community's political disenfranchisement and underscore disturbing splits within progressive Latino leadership circles.

LCLAA's first slate of officers and board members included founding SVREP Board Chairman Maclovio Barraza, who was elected to serve as the organization's secretary-treasurer. Barraza, the longtime steelworkers union official with a deep commitment to the Chicano movement, had been heavily involved in LCLAA's conception. It had been his lifelong aspiration to devise such an association, and indeed to lead it as chief executive. Unfortunately, for Barraza, his candidacy to serve as LCLAA's first executive director fell short. He was bitterly disappointed when he lost out to fellow steelworker Paul Montemayor, whose health was already beginning to deteriorate by the time he arrived in Washington to lead LCLAA. Barraza's consolation prize, namely, the appointment to LCLAA's executive board committee, was hollow and brought him few prospects for meaningful clout in shaping Latino labor's first national venture. Having lost this bid to lead LCLAA and being disenchanted with the Southwest Council (now the National Council of La Raza), which he had chaired since its infancy, Barraza turned his focus to SVREP. But the erstwhile labor leader's unsuccessful quest for LCLAA's executive director job would portend encroaching divisions between SVREP and the Labor Council.

Velásquez wholeheartedly endorsed the LCLAA concept of a unified Latino labor front. Since SVREP's inception, he had envisioned making organized labor and Chicano worker groups central partners in the project's registration campaigns. Robert Cabrera, SVREP's field organizer, had no problem with this directive because he too had a strong labor background, having been active in a San Antonio teachers' union prior to joining the project's staff. Now, SVREP could collaborate with local LCLAA chapters to tap their leadership, organizing, and volunteer resources in ways that would fundamentally complement Willie's desire to infuse SVREP's field approach with a more far-reaching, no-nonsense, nuts-and-bolts quality.

In most cases, in fact, LCLAA's local chapters became essential fixtures of SVREP's grassroots campaign work during both groups' formative years. While SVREP was building lasting relationships with local LCLAA chapters and their members, however, the project ran into unanticipated early problems with national LCLAA leaders. Barraza had been taking Velásquez to LCLAA meetings to present SVREP field reports and to seek financial help, but after months of trying they had nothing to show for their effort and investment. In time, Barraza, seizing on his credibility and deep network of contacts in the field, was finally able to squeeze modest labor support for SVREP's work indirectly through LCLAA; however, receipt of these dollars involved some minor shortcuts in LCLAA's funding application and processing phases, and the SVREP chairman was ultimately slapped on the wrist for circumventing proper channels by Montemayor who wrote his steelworker brother, "In the [future], we [look] forward to a better understanding of procedures amongst ourselves for any future requests." Such experiences created deep and growing concerns for Velásquez and Barraza alike.

Velásquez's uneasiness sprang from SVREP's ongoing struggle to gain some semblance of financial stability. He had always envisioned labor unions providing a major and relatively unrestricted source of funding for SVREP. SVREP's deep labor roots coupled with the African-American voter registration group VEP's history of strong union backing convinced Willie that Latino labor would endorse and support his organization as a matter of course. LCLAA's formation bolstered Willie's confidence that this would be the case, by creating a more consolidated network of Latino leaders from across the nation for SVREP to tap. He did not assume that money for SVREP would necessarily come directly from LCLAA, even though he hoped some of it would. His expectations were rather that mainstream labor leaders would be interested in (or at least amenable to) backing SVREP in a major way, and that LCLAA leaders would help the project to secure their support.

LCLAA national leaders, however, had an entirely different sense of SVREP's grant-worthiness. Purely from a self-interested point of view, LCLAA's leaders questioned why they would want to fund an untested organization that did not exclusively target union workers and Democrats, or even help it to gain access to the larger community of labor funders. Given LCLAA's decidedly partisan Democratic and union organizing interests, SVREP's blanket approach to registering Hispanics was simply too risky for its tastes. Hank Lacayo of the United Auto Workers, one of the top Latino labor leaders in the country, would later explain, "LCLAA . . . leaders saw Willie and Southwest Voter as unguided missiles. They feared losing control of him (and) weren't sure what direction he'd take next. The result was they couldn't trust or fund him."

Over time, LCLAA's resistance to support SVREP exasperated Willie, particularly as the project's forward movement became complicated by lack of funding. Velásquez had been devoting sizable portions of his time to fundraising, with little success, and the resulting financial pressures and programmatic limitations were beginning to wear him down. Utterly frustrated by SVREP's unhealthy condition and LCLAA's unwillingness to assist, Velásquez vented his rage by lashing out at the Labor Council's leaders, blaming them for SVREP's fiscal woes and publicly chastising them for failing to open doors for SVREP in the larger labor community or to provide even modest support resources from its own substantial coffers.

Willie's perception that LCLAA's support resources were enormous was a gross exaggeration. In fact, LCLAA barely had enough money to keep itself running. The union collaborative had only been operating for less than a year before SVREP received its tax-exempt status and was still trying to consolidate its operation as a viable entity when Velásquez commenced his public challenge concerning LCLAA's failure to support SVREP. Labor Council officials sought to communicate these points to Willie, but the now-hardened community organizer was not satisfied with LCLAA's explanation. Rather than stepping back and toning down his rhetoric, Willie escalated the assault on LCLAA, relying increasingly on personal attacks against its chief executive, Montemayor, who Velásquez had decided was the main impediment separating SVREP from LCLAA's needed financial support. Willie's concerns about Montemayor were not entirely unfounded as it turned out, but his aggressive public protest against LCLAA—and Montemayor in particular—deepened the growing wedge between SVREP and the Labor Council.

Velásquez's substantive charges against LCLAA were twofold in nature. First, in extensive letters to the SVREP executive committee and close political allies, Willie accused Montemayor of spreading lies concerning labor policy in funding independent voter registration groups. According to Velásquez, Mario Obledo, a staunch SVREP supporter and California's Secretary of Health and Welfare, had approached his friend Montemayor about union resources for SVREP. Montemayor flatly told Obledo in response that labor groups affiliated with LCLAA did not give money to autonomous voter registration outfits. Willie noted in his letters, however, that the African-American-focused VEP had long received huge amounts of funding from labor, with many of the sources being unions represented on the Labor Council. Montemayor discounted the assertion that his stated position on labor funding policy was factually inaccurate until Willie showed him an official list of VEP's financial backers, which indeed included numerous LCLAA-affiliated union groups.

Second, Velásquez accused Montemayor of calculated efforts to block and discredit SVREP in the organized labor universe. The allegation was based largely on information Willie had received from representatives of various international unions to which SVREP had applied for funding. According to those sources, Montemayor had counseled strongly against them supporting SVREP. Velásquez concluded from this that Montemayor and other LCLAA leaders were proactively casting doubts about SVREP in the minds of allied union officials who decided where charitable labor support would be directed. Willie considered this a fundamental violation that warranted even more aggressive public campaigning against Montemayor and LCLAA.

SVREP Chair Barraza and Secretary Obledo both tried to ease the growing polarity between SVREP and LCLAA that was now increasingly embodied in the personal contest between Velásquez and Montemayor. Barraza had had sharp disagreements in the past with his steelworker brother Montemayor over what labor or political candidates to support, what tactics to employ in labor disputes, and what grander vision Chicanos should pursue into the future, but none of these disputes had ever been blown out of proportion or taken place outside of labor leadership exchanges. He did not appreciate Montemayor and LCLAA refusing to promote SVREP, but the last thing he wanted was Willie declaring war on LCLAA. Seeking to mitigate the potential for an irreparable split, Barraza directed Willie to cease his attacks on LCLAA and Montemayor because, as Arnold Flores recalled, "Mac understood that you only use [fighting] words when you're about to get a divorce, and the last thing Mac wanted was a divorce from Latino labor." Mario Obledo also sought to intervene as a moderating force on SVREP's behalf, sending handwritten notes to Montemayor pleading with him to help SVREP secure funding, and to Hank Lacayo of the UAW, calling SVREP probably the most important organization ever founded by Mexican Americans. "If SVREP succeeds, as it must surely do," Obledo wrote to Lacayo, "then we can all be proud of at least one great accomplishment in our lives."

These reasoned appeals for calm and recognition of SVREP's potential in the big picture of Mexican-American struggles for justice in society, unfortunately, were not enough to bridge the now-gaping divide between SVREP and LCLAA. At a Texas AFL-CIO meeting in Dallas, the budding conflict between Velásquez and Montemayor came to a head. They confronted each other in the lobby of the hotel where the conference was being held. Each man violently told the other what he thought about the entire situation, with Montemayor ending the fracas on brutally definitive terms: "As long as I'm director (of LCLAA), you're not going to get *any* money from labor!" With that, the two men parted.

Eventually, Montemayor and LCLAA did give SVREP a small project grant in 1976 to partially defray SVREP's cost to produce a report on Latino voting in that year's presidential election. But the deep divisions between SVREP and LCLAA would never fully be resolved in Willie's lifetime, and the logical alliance that should have characterized both groups' work in the field was accordingly never fully realized.

෴ ෴ ෴

Willie's impatience and fierce determination to develop SVREP into a major national political force led him to push the organization faster than it was equipped to go throughout most of his tenure as executive director. This was especially the case in the start-up phase of SVREP's work and during the early years of its evolution. Velásquez was simply unbending in his will to propel the organization to greatness and unwilling to be slowed in this quest by conventional constraints or notions of cautious incrementalism. He believed that people who wanted to make something happen badly enough, could and did—including and up to changing the course of history. For Willie, it was not a question of timing, but rather one of conviction and persistence. In his mental construct, man was not a prisoner of time or outside forces, but rather a molder of fate given the proper level of determination and commitment. With this attitude, Willie forged through life, relentless in his pursuit to tackle problems that could not wait for time to resolve in its own due course.

Actualizing SVREP's historic potential in southern California was one of the major problems that Willie wanted to tackle during 1976. SVREP's initial voter registration campaign in Los Angeles County had been overly ambitious and poorly funded, resulting in a huge disappointment. This time around, Willie vowed to tackle the region's immense concentration of Mexican Americans, the largest of any in the nation, using a drastically different approach than had been employed in 1975. At the same time, he had no clear and specific alternative strategy in mind, and knew that he would ultimately have to rely on southern California Latino leaders to help guide him. Velásquez accordingly re-established his prior alliance with the evangelical Reverend Hernández and the other SVREP supporters in Los Angeles to devise a new way to unleash tremendous untapped Latino voter potential there. Reverend Hernández immediately resurrected his recommendation that SVREP open a permanent, year-round voter registration office in East Los Angeles that could also expand SVREP's readiness and capacity to assist drives throughout the Southwest. Velásquez's gut reaction was to reject Hernández's suggestion. SVREP barely had enough money to operate its small shop in San Antonio, and Los Angeles was a far more complicated terrain whose scale and political nuances were formidable and intimidating, even to Willie.

On the other hand, Willie knew that if SVREP was ever to attain the status of a truly effective national player, it would have to make a sizeable dent in California. He also understood that gaining needed support for SVREP's work and aims among California Chicanos would ultimately require a meaningful presence there, particularly in Los Angeles. By establishing a southern California field office, Velásquez ultimately realized, SVREP would signal its intention to make a long-term commitment to the area and significantly increase the organization's prospects to achieve its larger goals. In the end, despite lingering worries about the possible administrative and financial headaches SVREP would face, Velásquez embraced Hernández's recommendation and agreed to establish a SVREP branch office in East Los Angeles.

From the onset, SVREP's Los Angeles field office was only sparingly funded and fraught with challenges that left Willie second-guessing his decision to move into California. Problems began with the selection of a staff person to manage the office. The Los Angeles contingent of SVREP volunteers who had coordinated the organization's prior drive was under the impression that its leadership would form the basis of SVREP's Los Angeles office and that someone among its ranks would be hired as SVREP's regional director. Velásquez saw things differently. He wanted to hire a native Californian with movement credentials, to be sure, but he wanted it to be someone he could be assured would be loyal to him and who would be able to bring a more global than parochial view of SVREP's work to the region. Through an old United Farm Workers connection, Willie was introduced to Jackie Arispe, a young student activist who had earned her political stripes working with the farmworkers. Velásquez, who was quickly impressed by Arispe, asked her to direct SVREP's California office and she accepted without hesitation. Unfortunately, the young director would come under immediate fire once employed, due to a combination of factors ranging from her inexperience in the field to unrealistic expectations about what could be reasonably expected from a fledging field office operating on a shoestring budget.

To begin, Arispe encountered legitimacy problems because, though a Californian, she was neither from nor known in the East Los Angeles area. Not surprisingly, therefore, many of her early moves were clumsy by the standards of Eastside community leaders and volunteers. She puzzled many in the community when she opened the SVREP office in nearby Monterrey Park, for example, rather than deep in the heart of East Los Angeles. Her lack of managerial experience, moreover, considerably slowed SVREP's ability to craft and implement a grand design for Los Angeles County that could meaningfully impact Latino voting. Arispe's limitations immediately inspired ire both at SVREP's national headquarters office, as well as in the surrounding Los Angeles community.

SVREP national staff was upset with Arispe because it had not been receiving periodic reports she had been requested to provide on the progress of the Los Angeles project. Arispe was supposed to be sending monthly summaries of her work but rarely did. Willie reacted by demanding that Arispe submit biweekly accounts of her activities or face dismissal. Arispe responded with more frequent reports, but these mostly highlighted the Los Angeles group's lack of traction and strategic impact. This increased Willie's consternation with the newly hired Los Angeles director, as well as his anger with himself for ever having agreed to open a southern California office. Instead of sympathizing with Arispe's untenable position—not having enough money or manpower to have much success—SVREP responded by tightening its grip on her actions: increasing her reporting and justification burdens relative to project activities and every manner of office expenses.

By August 1976, SVREP's Los Angeles office problems had become a primary topic of concern at the organization's annual board meeting in Las Vegas. Magdalena Lona, Norma Alvarado, and Nellie Armenta, all board members of the Los Angeles project, attended the meeting and bitterly complained about their working relationship with Arispe, saying that was the brunt of the problem and demanding that SVREP fire her immediately. The demand that SVREP introduce a staffing change underscored the hard reality that local Los Angeles leaders wanted greater control over the project's leadership, finances, and strategy in southern California. Even though SVREP attempted wherever possible to adhere to local guidance and advice, the California project leaders wanted still more decision-making authority and leverage relative to SVREP's resources. These demands and expectations, coupled with the lightening rod posed by Arispe's credibility and capacity issues, as well as continuing fund-raising challenges concerning the Los Angeles office, made the relationship between SVREP and the Los Angeles project an increasingly thorny one.

SVREP board members deliberated to consider an appropriate way to address the Los Angeles leaders' concerns. Vice Chair Flores suggested that the Los Angeles office be treated more like a franchise than an affiliate, with local leaders and staff (rather than SVREP headquarters personnel) assuming primary responsibility for fund-raising, staffing, and program strategy.

SVREP, in turn, would supplement local efforts by providing direct funding to needy, selected neighborhoods demonstrating the greatest likelihood to register and mobilize Latino voters. While most members agreed with Flores' proposal, some felt that discontinuing the Los Angeles partnership might be the better response. In the end, the board decided to work toward an immediate short-term remedy for the Los Angeles operation in its existing form, realizing that an office closure or a major change in strategy would either prematurely prevent SVREP from achieving desired advances in California or give the appearance that it had caved-in to pressure from Los Angeles board members. In order to gain a quick handle in the Los Angeles situation, it was agreed that Barraza and Velásquez would conduct an emergency meeting with Arispe and, based on the results, recommend specific corrective steps that ideally would enable SVREP to maintain its Los Angeles presence with greater local support and impact.

Two weeks following the SVREP board meeting in Nevada, and after visiting with Arispe, Velásquez informed the Los Angeles project's leadership that the SVREP southern California office would be closed as of December 31, 1976. SVREP board member Arnold Flores's recommendation would be put into effect; from now on, only a selection of the most promising and effective Los Angeles neighborhood registration efforts would receive SVREP financial support in southern California.

The difficulties SVREP encountered in Los Angeles during the 1976 election season mitigated its impact on Latino voter mobilization in November, but even despite this, outcomes in the field were relatively favorable to progressive community groups and interests. Latino-friendly candidates, including newly elected President Jimmy Carter, were successful throughout California and Latino voters did in fact play a strategically important role. This was especially the case in Los Angeles County.

Over 16,500 new voters were registered by the SVREP-supported Los Angeles project during 1976, an increment that proved to be meaningful in important local, state, and national races. Willie, however, who had expected SVREP to have a far greater impact, was underwhelmed by the outcome. In a report to board members and financial supporters in March of 1977, a disappointed Velásquez assessed the Los Angeles campaign experience in stark terms: "We have had uniformly bad results. . . . The steering committee was mostly concerned with delivering people rather than registering voters. . . .The idea of housing a full-time person there did not produce the voters registered per dollar expenditure that we are looking for. . . .On the whole, Los Angeles was our biggest disappointment (of the year) and was keenly felt by staff." For the second time in its short history, SVREP had struck out in Los Angeles.

Despite major disappointments in the labor funding arena and in southern California and other early field campaigns, SVREP dramatically increased its fieldwork during 1976, expanding its portfolio from eleven reg-istration drives to forty-two throughout the Southwest. This jump in field activity was accompanied by significant fund development gains totaling over $160,000 in contributions in fiscal year 1975–1976 (compared to just under $69,000 for 1974–1975), and by substantial boosts in direct funding to grassroots campaign efforts, totaling over $46,000, or slightly more than 29 percent of total expenditures in 1975–1976 (compared to only about $4,900 or approximately 8 percent of 1974–1975 outlays). SVREP's greatly expand-ed coverage in 1976 was heavily Texas-based with more than half of its efforts—twenty-three in total—launched in the Lone Star state. But the proj-ect also organized important campaigns in other key Southwestern states, including eight registration drives in California, four in Utah, three each in Arizona and New Mexico, and one in Colorado. By the end of 1976, SVREP had registered over 150,000 Mexican Americans to vote since it started its first drive in 1975.

The furious work pace that SVREP pursued at Willie's behest during its first two years of existence claimed an important casualty in late 1976: Robert Cabrera, SVREP's field director. Velásquez fired Cabrera near the end of the year because he no longer did much work. In fact, Cabrera was com-pletely burned out. Since early 1975, Willie had deployed SVREP's lone field operative at a blistering, nonstop tempo to organize voter drives throughout the barrios and farmlands of the Southwest. The heavy demands of this work did not significantly trouble Cabrera initially, but following his marriage in December of 1975, he wanted, not surprisingly, to spend more time at home in San Antonio with his new wife. Owing to the demands of his work at SVREP, however, and the heavy stakes associated with the Novem-ber national election cycle, Cabrera spent most of 1976 on the road. Trying to find a healthy balance between the relentless organizing demands of his job at SVREP and his newfound domestic impulses and needs finally proved impossible for Cabrera. By mid-1976, he was physically and emotionally exhausted. He started to avoid important work responsibilities. He came to dread the thought of going back on the road. He desperately needed a break.

True to character, Willie was less than sympathetic to Cabrera's waning commitment to SVREP's work. For Willie, his longtime friend's personal needs, though not unimportant, could only be secondary to SVREP's organi-zational needs. For Willie, it had become clear that Cabrera would have to be relieved of his duties. But implementing his decision would be difficult for Velásquez. He had never been one for dealing with sensitive personal con-troversies or emotions and Cabrera was much more than just an employee to Willie because of their formative history together—riding the bus to St. Mary's University, drinking together, arguing about politics. Now things were different, though. They were no longer friendly peers. They were boss

174 Juan A. Sepúlveda, Jr.

and employee.

Willie dreaded telling his friend that the end was at hand in relation to their partnership at SVREP, and he tried to push off the inevitable conversation that would make this clear to Cabrera for as long as possible. But the burden of withholding from his friend grew heavier and heavier. Finally, Willie had to tell his colleague, buddy, and field director that it was time for him to leave. Cabrera agreed, confessing what Velásquez had long known: He was tired. Willie announced Cabrera's departure to the SVREP board, not as a firing, but as a resignation in October of 1976.

Cabrera's departure, coupled with the unforeseen problems of SVREP's impasse with leading Latino union representatives and the Los Angeles office closure, would usher in an important new chapter in the project's evolution. SVREP would enter 1977 having lost a great deal of its original innocence and starry-eyed optimism. It would confront inevitable new responsibilities with its growth and increasing demand for its leadership in the national field.

In the years to come, SVREP would have to become much more institutionalized to meet its expanding responsibilities and to accommodate growing grassroots need for its expertise. It would also have to demonstrate continuing improvements in the ratio of dollars spent for administration versus registration campaigns and in the return on investments in the field. These imperatives, ironically, would push SVREP in its next generation of activity to rethink its early focus on places like San Antonio, Denver, Los Angeles, Tucson, and Salt Lake City, which were assumed to promise great rewards based on the presumed logic that focusing on big states and cities would necessarily maximize the project's propensity to produce big numbers and big successes. In fact, SVREP's early experiences in these places produced some important gains, but more often than not, the results were big headaches and disappointments.

The mixed outcomes in these venues would compel SVREP to question its early tactics and to focus much more of its second generation activities on smaller towns and more remote areas. These theaters of engagement called out to SVREP for three concrete reasons. First, demand for the project's partnership from such places was growing exponentially by the end of 1976; this alerted Willie and his team that the need for SVREP's work was actually much greater than anticipated outside of the large population centers that had been the focal points of early project investments. Economy was a second, practical reason for SVREP's next generation focus on more remote communities of the Southwest. By working in an assortment of smaller communities, the project could funnel its limited resources into more places with a greater chance of having direct impact, rather than concentrating dollars in massive jurisdictions like Los Angeles where SVREP's scarce funds were instantly swallowed up and the effect of its registration efforts were ambiguous at best. A third calculated reason for shifting resources and attention toward smaller venues was Willie's evolving belief that it would simply be less complicated to score victories in those places compared to the larger urban centers that SVREP had begun targeting. Following the lead of Chicano activist organizations, such as the La Raza Unida Party in the Texas Rio Grande Valley, SVREP would seek in its next iteration of work to focus on smaller towns where Mexican Americans made up a majority of the population. By arousing untapped voter strength in these places, SVREP could literally encourage overnight political takeovers by Latinos, based solely on sheer numbers. Once this process was duplicated in sufficient order, SVREP could rapidly increase Mexican American political participation and representation in ways that would transform American regional and national policy, from the ground up.

The road going down this path would not be easy, but SVREP's turn to the grassroots and small-town America would in fact increase its value added and impact in the unfolding scheme of national Latino community political empowerment. As SVREP pursued this work, it became more and more evident to Willie and his project colleagues that change and forward progress were indeed attainable. Increased organization, use of research, data, and analysis, and the development of energetic new leadership were the essential ingredients of the change SVREP sought to encourage. On the other hand, it would also become increasingly clear to Willie and his followers that community mobilization by itself could not alone reshape the region's political landscape. Instead, a minefield of institutionalized barriers targeted to Latino voters, including gerrymandered districts, uneven voter eligibility requirements, and outright ballot tampering would first have to be challenged successfully for SVREP's impact in the field to be fully maximized.

Chapter 12

THERE WAS A TIME EARLY IN SVREP's history when Willie himself wondered if there was something wrong with Mexican Americans, especially those isolated in the rural trenches of the Southwest, who simply showed no inclination to vote. He realized that there was always going to be a portion of the Latino population (just as in the general body politic) that did not want anything to do with politics, but he was left confused and frustrated by how widespread voter apathy appeared to be among Latinos all across the Southwest. Velásquez was not alone in his critical view of Hispanic political engagement. Many of SVREP's early local partners in Mexican-American communities across the Southwest also tended to blame their own people for their lackluster voter participation. In time, however, experience in the field revealed to Velásquez and his local leaders on the ground that there was actually something remarkably rational about Hispanic voter abstinence in many parts of the region.

For generations, Latinos across the Southwest had been effectively discouraged from voting by a combination of *de facto* and *de jure* impediments to the unfettered exercise of their franchise. In addition to outright intimidation (ranging from the threat of lost employment to serious physical injury or lynching), Latino citizens were excluded from electoral participation by a range of insidious institutional constraints that effectively prevented them from gaining their full political voice. Gerrymandered districts, uneven voter eligibility requirements, and outright vote tampering were among the methods used to marginalize Latino voters and diminish their electoral clout.

By witnessing these strategies at play through his early work at SVREP, Willie came to comprehend that many Latino voters were simply disinclined to vote out of a conscious recognition that they often had more to lose than to gain by doing so. Even in the best cases, moreover, where Latino voting was relatively unencumbered on the surface, hidden systematic impediments—often supported, or at least tolerated, by Anglo-controlled public authorities—simply reduced going to the polls to an exercise in futility. By encountering these realities firsthand in SVREP's work, Willie began to realize that Mexican Americans were not a bunch of political losers, but rather unfortunate victims of sophisticated and intentional measures designed to discourage their democratic engagement.

Having developed this understanding, Velásquez was able to help important grassroots Latino political and community activists across the Southwest to see that true voter empowerment in their neighborhoods and communities required more than mere voter registration. What was needed in addition was a complementary series of interventions to educate and activate Latinos around the need for comprehensive electoral reform, as well as reinforcing legal and policy challenges to the established exclusionary order.

Grabbing a napkin at a restaurant table or bar, Willie would underscore these imperatives to unwitting SVREP clients and collaborators by writing down the number of registered voters in their particular districts of interest. He would then show them, in effect mathematically, that no matter what they did, even if they registered all the Hispanic voters in their county and every one of them voted, they could not win any seats. It just was not possible. The district lines had been drawn in a way that weakened the Mexican-American vote with the endorsement and application of laws that typically had been on the books for generations. (Medina County, Texas was one of Willie's favorite examples because it had not redistricted since 1896, even though it was required to do so by law every ten years.) In some cases, rigged election outcomes were supported by the Latino community being dispersed across multiple districts so that it would not be a majority in any county jurisdiction. In other instances, the Mexican-American electorate would be crammed unnaturally into a huge, sprawling district with many thousands of voters, enabling the occasional election of a Latino official, while the overwhelming balance of other districts would be assured very small numbers of Hispanic voters, making these latter jurisdictions virtually guaranteed seats for Anglo politicos.

When measures of this sort were not used, a range of other exclusionary tactics was employed. These included selected purges of county voter rolls to diminish Hispanic voting eligibility, literacy requirements that disadvantaged Latino voters, and until only recently poll taxes that required poorer Hispanic citizens to pay qualifying fees for the right to vote. If none of these regimes proved sufficiently effective, Anglo vote counters would simply undercount Latino votes cast (or over count Anglo votes cast) in order to ensure continued mainstream electoral dominance—even when Hispanics constituted an overwhelming local population majority.

By revealing these normally undetected realities to SVREP's core constituents, Willie changed their fundamental understanding of the problems facing Latino voters and of the work that needed to be done to address those problems. In doing so, he triggered a newfound resolve in the Latino political community of the Southwest to once and for all surface and eliminate the many systemic impediments to Hispanic civic engagement in America.

෨ ෨ ෨

How to practically secure Latino electoral justice became clear to Willie only through a cumulative series of discussions he had with various activist lawyers, especially voting rights attorney Joaquín Ávila of the Mexican American Legal Defense and Educational Fund (MALDEF). Willie had met Ávila shortly after the Harvard-educated attorney started working for MALDEF in San Antonio. The two men instantly became good friends, spending countless hours laughing, drinking, and talking politics at the Esquire bar and other local cantinas. Velásquez had a deep fondness and respect for Ávila because the MALDEF attorney symbolized to him the best and brightest of the Mexican-American people. Willie especially appreciated the fact that, upon completing his law degree, Ávila had returned to help his people, rather than proceed to a lucrative career in a corporate law firm, which would have been an easy and logical pursuit given his impressive Ivy League credentials.

Ávila's first impressions of Velásquez were of someone deeply committed to his work, someone who had clear and straightforward objectives. Years later, the respected civil rights lawyer would reflect, "Everything was simple for Willie: There were good guys and bad guys. He knew that some elected officials would never change, so the only way [he felt] you could change things was through the electorate."

A natural bond was formed between Velásquez and Ávila, and by extension SVREP and MALDEF. During one of their many after-hours bar discussions, the activist and the lawyer pooled their experiences and knowledge and posited theories about why SVREP was having problems in rural counties across the Southwest. After reviewing the circumstances, they concluded that while many factors were likely involved to explain the relative lack of Latino political participation and success throughout the region, some type of legally actionable obstacle was most likely at play. They were just not sure which constitutional or voting rights violations might establish the strongest case for the purpose of crafting winning legal challenges to the multiplicity of barriers in effect that played a role in discouraging Hispanic voter participation and political empowerment.

The history of voting rights cases since the passage of the Voting Rights Act of 1965 and the various amendments to that legislation ratified by Congress in 1975 offered SVREP and MALDEF an array of overlapping legal options in their quest to challenge the barriers facing Mexican-American voters. Each alternative possessed its own advantages and disadvantages. By pursuing an extension of special provisions of the Voting Rights Act to Southwestern states like Texas, SVREP and MALDEF had three major legal precedents upon which they could rely. First, there were strong informing cases under which at-large election schemes—wherein all voters in a given city, county, or school system voted for and elected en masse all of the officials in their jurisdiction—could be challenged in favor of a voting scheme in which local officials would respectively represent voters of various diverse and demographically representative districts. For minority groups, the move from at-large elections to single-member districts typically enhanced opportunities for fairer representation by formalizing clusters of ethnic voters with shared interests to elect persons of the same racial or cultural origin. Such an approach, endorsed by prevailing federal law, would afford inherent gains to underrepresented Hispanic voters, if applied across most or all of the Southwestern United States.[1]

---

[1]In the 1973 Texas case of *White v. Regester* the U.S. Supreme Court held that multimember districts in Dallas and Bexar Counties (which included San Antonio) violated the Fourteenth Amendment guarantee of equal protection and mandated single-member legislative districts for these counties. *White v. Regester,* argued successfully by Dave Richards and George Korbel, was brought forth by African-American and Mexican-American plaintiffs contesting portions of the 1970 Texas House of Representatives reapportionment plan. The Court found certain shared problems of both minority groups. They suffered from historical discrimination, political underrepresentation, and bad treatment "in the fields of education, employment, economics, health, politics and others." Each group also had its own distinct obstacles. African Americans in Dallas County had to face a white-dominated slating group that controlled Democratic Party nominations, while Mexican Americans in Bexar County suffered "from a cultural and language barrier that (made) participation in the community processes extremely difficult." The Court went so far to say that this "cultural incompatibility" of the Mexican American, combined with an historical poll tax and "the most restrictive voter registration procedures in this nation," had denied Mexican Americans political access "even longer than [African Americans had been] formally denied access by the white primary."

The number of black and Mexican American state legislators in Texas increased significantly after *White v. Regester* as did the number of at-large voting cases attacking local election methods used by many city councils and school boards. The problem with the White decision however was its lack of precision in outlining principles the plaintiffs had to produce. Outside of past historical discrimination and socioeconomic indicators, the *White v. Regester* opinion relied upon "factual findings" that one voting rights scholar said, "in reality, were unexplained assertions of indeterminate weight." Civil rights attorneys James Blacksher and Larry Menefee called the *White* principles "difficult to catalogue" while voting rights scholar Abigail Thernstrom went further and said, "they lacked coherence."

The Fifth Circuit in another at-large case, *Zimmer v. McKeithen,* just three months after *White v. Regester,* tried to remedy this problem by holding that "the Fourteenth Amendment's guarantee of equal protection was violated whenever minority plaintiffs could show some combination of primary and 'enhancing' factors." The court considered primary factors to be "lack of minority access to the slating of candidates; a "tenuous" state policy (backed by neither tradition nor persuasive reason) underlying the preference for at-large voting; and a history of past discrimination that limited political participation." These elements were considered "enhanced" when they were united with any mix of ingredients that included "large districts, a majority vote requirement, a prohibition against voting for less than a 'full slate,' and an absence of sub-districts, such that all candidates running at large could reside in one neighborhood—affluent and white, for instance."

The *Zimmer* decision gave potential minority plaintiffs a more clear-cut sense of what they needed to prove in order to overturn at-large election schemes.

The problem from Velásquez's and Ávila's perspective was that ensuring widespread application of relevant special provisions in even a few needy jurisdictions would require inordinate amounts of time and resources to prepare. In 1976, given the still significantly limited assets available to SVREP and MALDEF, it could easily take several (or even many) years before the full benefits of any at-large litigation challenge along these lines would be realized. Willie and Joaquín were unenthusiastic to pursue unduly prolonged and piecemeal litigation of this sort. They wanted instead to identify an intervention strategy that would create a more global impact in a shorter period of time.

A second option available to SVREP and MALDEF was to pursue a series of Section 5 preclearance cases. Section 5 was a provision of the Voting Rights Act that required covered jurisdictions to acquire federal approval of any changes in "voting standards, practices, or procedures." Because various key jurisdictions in Texas and other Southwestern states were covered by the act, important suspect counties across the region contemplating proposed annexations, redistricting plan amendments, or voting rules changes could be compelled to obtain Justice Department or U.S. District Court approval. This was an appealing alternative for SVREP and MALDEF for its promise of relative ease and quickness. All the two organizations had to do was show that any or all suspect jurisdictions had made electoral system changes since 1975 without obtaining preclearance. This would force the covered governing body (or bodies) to submit plans to the Justice Department, where SVREP and MALDEF leaders could press to secure at least some "safe" Hispanic seats. Velásquez and Ávila would eventually discover, however, that a major problem with Section 5 was that it only affected a tiny fraction of the rural counties in Texas and nearby states. This fundamental diminution of the law's reach effectively took it off the strategy board that Velásquez and Ávila were developing.

The third major legal possibility—and ultimately the preferred strategy for SVREP and MALDEF to consider—was to activate a "one person, one vote" line of cases that would, in effect, promote activation of a principle of representation for comparable numbers of people. This principle was formulated in a series of reapportionment cases involving districts that were unequal in population, but similar in the numbers of government officials they elected. The cornerstone of this case law was *Reynolds v. Sims*, a 1964 U.S. Supreme Court decision that held: "legislators represent people, not trees or acres." Consequently, the court found, it was the number of people an elected official represented that mattered, not the actual physical size of the represented jurisdiction. The net impact of these rulings for Latino voters was to give them an anchor upon which to successfully challenge all manner of voting impediments that resulted from laws or practices whose ultimate effect was to disproportionately diminish Latino voting clout relative to other groups in the same jurisdiction.

These lawsuits, while not as quick and easy probabilities for success as Section 5 cases, were typically much less difficult to win than at-large election challenges. According to José Garza, another MALDEF attorney at the time, "The difference between one person, one vote cases and at-large cases was like night and day." In fact, the relative advantages of pursuing these cases were numerous from SVREP's and MALDEF's perspective. Instead of years, it was possible to complete one person, one vote preliminary research in several weeks, evidentiary preparation in a month or so, and a successful trial in a few days or weeks. After a victorious verdict, moreover, plaintiffs would typically be asked either to participate in the redistricting process or, at worst, at least to help ensure via review and comment the creation of equitable district lines. Given these many considerations, Velásquez and Ávila decided to emphasize efforts to test the one person, one vote method. County commissioner districts in their home state of Texas offered the most logical place to begin, since those counties uniformly housed four seats allegedly comprising one-quarter of each county's total population.

While the courts did not issue any magical, ironclad, numerical signposts for triggering successful one person, one vote challenges, Velásquez and Ávila felt that a Latino population disparity of 10 percent or more between similarly situated demographic districts was a reliable indicator that the relevant district lines should be redrawn to ensure more consistent and equitable representation.

Neither SVREP nor MALDEF had sufficient manpower to undertake wholly new investigations designed to identify suspect jurisdictions for possible one person, one vote challenges. But, fortuitously, Andy Hernández, SVREP's one-man research department, was already collecting data on counties for voter registration targeting plans that Velásquez and Ávila agreed would advance their tactical assessment of suspect county commission districts. While they knew the courts would not recognize these data as indicators of a valid one person, one vote challenge (only population figures would suffice), registration statistics were easier for SVREP to gather in the field, and they would at least give preliminary guidance as to which counties were most likely to be worth attacking. Hernández, the young, hardworking research associate, quickly went to work assembling the relevant information, physically counting, jurisdiction by jurisdiction, all the registered voters by hand and analyzing the overall findings with an eye to uncovering especially egregious practices.

SVREP's sketchy preparatory analysis revealed outrageous differences in the number of registered voters in the county commissioner districts they examined; so outrageous, they believed, that the lines had to have been drawn with conscious intent to dilute the voting strength of Mexican Americans. By this they meant that the district lines were manifestly designed in such a way that it was virtually impossible for a Mexican-American candidate to win. Perhaps the most informative jurisdiction they investigated was Sutton County, a rural Texas hideaway that SVREP field reports called, "one of the most racist and segregated counties in . . . Texas." Eligible voter data assembled by Hernández, primarily from the city of Sonora, showed that the county's two largely Anglo precincts had 1,200 voters and 650 voters, respectively, while its two heavily Hispanic precincts *combined* had a grand total of only 55 registered voters. Velásquez and Ávila expected racial variations to exist, but neither one of them thought that what they would uncover would reflect inequalities of such great magnitude. Findings along these lines from Sutton County and the other Texas counties SVREP studied provided strong evidence of probable civil rights violations, powerful enough at least to convince Velásquez and Ávila that they had potentially struck gold.

〜 〜 〜

Velásquez and Ávila used 1976 and early 1977 to prepare SVREP and MALDEF for a successful entry into the one person, one vote anti-gerry-mandering arena. Much to their surprise and satisfaction, the relative timing of the proposed campaign seemed suddenly to be perfect when Dr. Charlie Cotrell and others of the Mexican American Equal Rights project were able to score a historic local election victory in San Antonio, successfully getting voters there to approve a wholesale change in the city council elections from an at-large system to a purely single-member district scheme. The San Antonio victory made Willie even more emphatic to pursue similar victories in the rural regions of the state. He redoubled SVREP's efforts to complete Andy Hernández's preliminary case-by-case jurisdictional analyses by hand counts, pushing his staff to its absolute limits. He prodded Ávila and other MALDEF principals to ready themselves for the ensuing battle as well. Finally, Willie waged an aggressive fund-raising campaign designed to generate needed project support to finance the work SVREP and MALDEF proposed. At the close of 1976, following near misses at the Norman and Cummins Engine Foundations, he was finally able to secure a $20,000 grant from the Field Foundation to support SVREP's and MALDEF's rural voting rights partnership in Texas. By March 1977, Willie was informing his board members and funders that SVREP and MALDEF were investigating twenty-four Texas counties and—in an important departure for the normally stealth-minded Velásquez—that an early June press conference was being planned to announce their findings concerning possible Latino civil rights violations.

On Saturday, June 4, 1977, SVREP and MALDEF co-convened a press conference that identified Comal, Edwards, Guadalupe, and Sutton Counties as possible violators of the one person, one vote principle. The two leading Latino rights groups also signaled their intention to target these jurisdictions for remedial actions in the courts. Medina County was also mentioned as a probable one person, one vote transgressor, but it was not included as one of the targeted counties.

Velásquez and Ávila presented their concerns to attending press professionals in compelling terms. "They say Mexican Americans don't register and don't turn out to vote, but there are extenuating circumstances," Velásquez told the journalists. "SVREP studies indicate that because of malapportionment and gerrymandering Mexican-American voters in these counties are not allowed to exercise their full potential." Ávila added that minority voters in these counties, primarily Mexican Americans, had been packed into one district or were spread into two or more districts, thus diluting the Mexican-American vote. "This process has had the effect of preventing Mexican Americans from electing members of their own communities," Ávila remarked. "In some counties," he continued, "you can register every single Mexican American, but because of institutional lines—gerrymandered commissioner's precincts—you will never have a minority elected." The media event generated considerable press coverage of the issues and raised the ire and defensiveness of Anglo political leaders across South Texas.

County officials from Guadalupe, Comal, and Medina Counties reacted to the charges brought against them by SVREP and MALDEF, alleging in varying degrees of civility—and culpability—that the two Latino rights groups had unfairly singled them out. In a press interview, Guadalupe County Judge Pat Baker, seeking to take the high road, acknowledged Latino voting issues in his county but appealed to SVREP and MALDEF to work with, rather than demonize, local leaders to find a constructive solution. "We've got almost all the Mexican Americans in one precinct now," Baker reported. "We've talked about redistricting several times, but we just don't know how to do it. If they (SVREP and MALDEF) can tell us how we can do it, we'd be glad to. We're open to negotiations on this thing." Comal County Judge Max Wommack was not as accommodating, claiming Comal had redistricted eight years earlier to bring it in compliance with the one person, one vote standard. "I don't believe in gerrymandering and we don't have it here," Wommack said to reporters. Then, jabbing back at SVREP and MALDEF, Wommack accused the two groups of hypocrisy for wanting to draw their own racially driven district lines, stating for the record that, "What *they* want to do is gerrymander!"

Medina County Judge Jerome Decker was the most adamant of the county officials replying to SVREP's and MALDEF's charges, commenting to the press: "I'm not about to negotiate with them. I'm not going to give them the time of day!" Unknowingly playing right into SVREP's and

MALDEF's hands, Decker proudly boasted that Medina County's precinct lines had not been changed since the county was formed in the 1800s. By his logic, this fact should exonerate local officials allegedly supporting unfair electoral practices, since gerrymandering, according to Decker, did not exist in the nineteenth century. Decker concluded that he would make adjustments after the 1980 census if necessary, but in no way would he be bullied to do so under pressure from SVREP and MALDEF.

SVREP and MALDEF spent the summer of 1977 initiating legal challenges and negotiations to inspire electoral reforms across South Texas. A combination of some early successes and raw determination (informed by the righteousness of Latino civil rights claims in the offending jurisdictions) heartened Willie. In a letter to David Ramage of the New World Foundation in late August, Velásquez reported that two counties had lost to SVREP and MALDEF in court, three were currently negotiating with them, and another three were being evaluated for possible later action. Velásquez confidently predicted that of those last three counties, two would definitely "cave in to negotiations." While they were still unsure how much process, time, and money would be required, Velásquez vowed to Ramage that SVREP and MALDEF would "take on three [jurisdictions] at a time until they are all fixed."

Notwithstanding these initial positive factors, in reality, forward progress on SVREP's and MALDEF's campaign was severely slowed by multiple impediments. Reviewing public records by hand to establish presumed violations in the field and dealing with uncooperative county officials drastically bogged down the foundational research required to carry cases forward with some confidence of their ultimate success. With hopes of expediting this work, the technology-poor SVREP appealed to Hank Lacayo of the United Auto Workers, asking him for permission to use the union's computers to conduct data analysis in support of potential lawsuits. The union leader's inability to assist presented a major setback and another wedge between SVREP and its logical allies in organized labor.

Recalcitrant county officials and records keepers presented especially thorny barriers to SVREP's research in the field. Either directly or indirectly, these individuals let SVREP know that it would have to uncover the requested field data without much assistance from them. According to Arnold Flores, SVREP's Vice Chairman, "Some counties refused to give [information] to us, some refused to let us in the courthouse, and some just said they didn't have the information."

Beyond these essentially external challenges, internal developments at SVREP also impeded progress on the campaign. Shortly after SVREP and MALDEF announced their program, Andy Hernández, Velásquez's first— and now his most trusted—employee, resigned his research position to attend the Perkins Theological Seminary in Dallas where he would train to become a Methodist minister. Velásquez entrusted the task of finding a new researcher to Hernández, and Andy hired Choco Meza, a former Raza Unida activist who had just graduated from Willie's alma mater, St. Mary's University. Meza was a quick study and ultimately an effective replacement for Hernández, but Andy's unique knowledge of the field and Willie's intuitive confidence in his work would be sorely missed at a crucial time in the SVREP/MALDEF voting rights campaign.

Shortly after Hernández's departure, Velásquez also lost the daily companionship and trusted advice of his board vice chair and dearest friend, Arnold Flores, when Flores was tapped for a special position at the Immigration and Naturalization Service (INS) headquarters office in Washington, D.C. Flores had been unexpectedly called to serve there by fellow SVREP board member Leonel Castillo, the former Houston city comptroller, who President Jimmy Carter had just appointed to head the INS. Castillo, who was SVREP's treasurer, resigned his position from the SVREP board along with his other affiliations, while Flores surrendered all of his board posts except his SVREP seat. Willie and Arnold would continue to talk occasionally on the phone and exchange new bits of information through the mail, but with Flores consumed in the nation's capitol, it would simply not be possible for the two men to eat lunch together several times a week or frequently to talk politics and drown their frustrations at the Esquire bar. Flores's and Castillo's move to Washington would effectively diminish Willie's access to key Texas-based leaders who he could otherwise rely on for counsel and advice concerning the evolving partnership with MALDEF to forge voting rights gains in the Lone Star state. For Willie, pursuing the campaign without Flores's direct involvement, in particular, would be like fighting with one arm tied behind his back.

In order to achieve success in its voter rights collaboration with MALDEF, SVREP ultimately needed to produce reliable population data to show the disparities facing Hispanic citizens across Texas relative to the Anglo population, in terms of political participation and representation. But securing this information, even from the U.S. Census Bureau, proved remarkably elusive. The primary problem for SVREP and MALDEF was that the Census Bureau used units of measure called enumeration districts to record and track rural populations because the limited density of these areas did not warrant using more compact census tract data. As a result, Bureau enumeration districts were so vast that they universally transcended county voting district lines. This made it virtually impossible for SVREP and MALDEF to rely on the Bureau's statistics for legal purposes absent requesting census officials to tabulate population figures for each county district of interest through the production of what was called split enumeration district data. Fortunately for SVREP and MALDEF, the Bureau reported that it could produce the required data, but this good news was followed by disappointing revelations for the two groups. SVREP and MALDEF would have to pay for the data they required. In addition, the Bureau's fees would be considerable. In November of 1977, Willie estimated the cost of obtaining this information for all the counties they were targeting at over $75,000.

In due course, Velásquez learned of an even greater obstacle to the campaign: the scope of the problem. The number of probable one person, one vote and gerrymandering violations being uncovered was growing at such an alarming rate that SVREP and MALDEF alone would likely not be able to attack them all completely for years. Both organizations knew the problem was serious, but no one had expected it to be nearly so far-reaching. The total number of suspect counties examined on a preliminary basis had jumped from four in June to twenty-four in August; then from forty-six in September to sixty-six in October. Choco Meza, her predecessor Andy Hernández, and various MALDEF paralegals had now scrutinized nearly seventy rural counties in Texas and every last one of them showed signs of systematic weakening of the Mexican-American vote because of how the jurisdictional lines were drawn.

The unexpected vast sum of likely lawsuits resulting from this work forced Velásquez and Ávila substantially to rethink their strategy of challenging offending jurisdictions through lawsuits. They knew that, logistically, it would be nearly impossible for SVREP and MALDEF to take every one of these counties to court, so they leaned increasingly toward pushing for out-of-court settlements. To help responsible county officials see the advantages of settling out of court, Willie proposed a united front organizing approach that would scare them into negotiating. Velásquez's idea was to encourage as many Mexican-American lawyers and rights organizations as possible to support SVREP's and MALDEF's voting rights litigation work.

In order to advance this agenda, Velásquez and Ávila enlarged the pool of attorneys working with them and formed an ad hoc Lawyer's Committee on Reapportionment. In addition to SVREP's and MALDEF's staffs, the committee included former MALDEF attorneys, Texas Rural Legal Aid (TRLA) personnel, private practitioners, and others with an extensive background in voting rights litigation. The mainstays of the group were Velásquez, Ávila, Luis Segura, who had accompanied Willie on a trek across America back in 1964 when they worked for the State Department, Jesse Botello, a former MALDEF lawyer, and George Korbel, a feisty, independent attorney with deep experience in the field.

The Lawyer's Committee greatly expanded SVREP's and MALDEF's capacities to selectively threaten and, when necessary, bring legal action against the most suspect counties in South Texas. By widening the network of support for this work, moreover, the committee attracted a growing number of leading Hispanic organizations and associations to join the fray.

The committee's work during 1978 produced seven lawsuits against Texas rural counties and a major show of solidarity at a Mexican Independence Day press conference. Representatives from LULAC, the American G.I. Forum, the Texas AFL-CIO, IMAGE, and the Mexican American Women's Caucus joined SVREP and MALDEF at the press conference, which produced precisely the sort of Latino community unity and resolve that Willie hoped would frighten county officials into settling out of court. Speaking before the assembled gathering, Velásquez reported that since June of 1977, SVREP- and MALDEF-supported litigation efforts had resulted in favorable court orders or negotiated settlements involving fifteen counties. "The significance of reapportionment, we believe, is that for the first time we can have the impact we ought to have," Velásquez said, pointing to Crockett County as a prime example. In Crockett, pressure from SVREP and MALDEF had led to a court-ordered reapportionment which was immediately followed by a massive voter registration campaign in the county's Mexican-American neighborhoods. At the next election, owing to new county commissioner lines and a reinvigorated Chicano electorate, 95 percent of the Mexican-American community was registered to vote; nearly 90 percent of those Mexican Americans actually voted in turn, resulting for the first time ever in the election of two Mexican-American county commissioners in a jurisdiction where the Latino community comprised a clear minority (only 37 percent of the county population).

The SVREP-MALDEF voter rights campaign produced important and impressive gains, to be sure, and it galvanized Latino and progressive groups to come together in extraordinary fashion. But these significant accomplishments were mitigated by various difficulties and challenges (many of these unanticipated by the campaign's supporters) that became increasingly evident in the course of SVREP's and MALDEF's collaboration.

Two especially critical problems that emerged during this period were: first, the unexpected wide-ranging and often remarkably creative resistance of many of the jurisdictions that SVREP and MALDEF targeted; and, second, both MALDEF's and the Lawyer's Committee's ultimate inability to provide SVREP with the dedicated, in-depth legal support that it required to advance the campaign, owing to resource limitations and commitments on other fronts.

Many of the offending counties that SVREP and MALDEF challenged responded by suggesting or imposing costs for local Mexican Americans who supported the upstart rights groups. Many grassroots Chicano families in these counties relied on local governmental largesse for jobs and opportunities that they desperately needed. Supporting civil rights advocacy aimed at the Anglo powers-that-be in control of these resources and benefits thus left an important segment of the region's Hispanic people vulnerable to threats of direct or indirect retaliation. SVREP's and MALDEF's personnel and allies could aggressively advocate for change in the most remote and exclusionary areas of the contested counties with the luxury of leaving them at the end of the day absent fear of possible direct consequences for their livelihoods or safety. Back home in San Antonio, these activists were relatively secure and out of reach. But rural Mexican Americans inclined to demand change faced a different set of circumstances. The relatively limited economic and other opportunities available to them were largely contingent upon their continued good relations and indeed their continued relative subservience vis-à-vis the dominant Anglo community. The resolve of many mainstream county leaders and officials to counter SVREP's and MALDEF's challenges through subtle and not-so-subtle local intimidation of Mexican Americans, therefore, was a frequent strategy to neutralize grassroots support for progressive reforms.

In some cases, local Anglo obstinacy was cloaked in seemingly benign terms. In Edwards County, for example, leading Anglo officials encouraged Mexican-American residents to withdraw a lawsuit developed with the support of SVREP and MALDEF by offering to support the development of a new community park, expanded city employment opportunities, and other public benefits. Other challenged counties, however, were simply defiant in the face of the coalition-based voter project. Among these jurisdictions, some simply refused to negotiate with SVREP and MALDEF concerning the sharing of any political power whatsoever. In at least one case of this sort, Anglo community reaction to the prospect of Hispanic political empowerment was so strong that it defied common logic and decency. In Aransas County, located on the Gulf of Mexico, the supporters of an Anglo candidate for Justice of the Peace, who had recently died, urged voters in newspaper ads to elect him over his SVREP- and MALDEF-supported Mexican-American opponent anyway. They did, "maintaining," Velásquez remarked, "the highest standards of the Texas political tradition by electing a dead man [so that] a live Mexican wouldn't serve."

Despite the engagement of MALDEF's Ávila and other leading legal experts in the campaign, SVREP found itself frequently lacking needed support on matters that ultimately only civil rights attorneys could help it to resolve. Ávila and other MALDEF attorneys were deeply committed to the Texas voting rights work, but they were also stretched on many other fronts. MALDEF's litigation portfolio spanned a broad range of other critical issue areas affecting the national Mexican-American community's rights and opportunities in America. These included education, employment, and criminal justice matters for which the organization was considerably more well-funded at the time. It was finally a matter of practicality that MALDEF could simply not justify committing the resources Velásquez and SVREP felt it should to advance the Texas voting rights campaign. Over time, MALDEF's limited capacity to intervene at the required level of depth was amplified by the similar constraints of other legal experts on the Lawyer's Committee team. Lacking funding to support their time on the campaign and being pulled like MALDEF to address burning community needs in other fields, these attorney-experts left Willie and his SVREP colleagues feeling overlooked and abandoned more than just occasionally. These circumstances frustrated and deeply concerned Velásquez. They left SVREP with a formidable and complex litany of field responsibilities absent sufficiently reliable technical expertise to do the job.

As the year came to a close, Willie could no longer condone continuing the campaign as things were. He was sensitive to MALDEF's and the Lawyer's Committee's constraints, and he knew they were doing the best that they could given the considerable limitations and obstacles they faced. But Velásquez knew the campaign could not optimize its successes without SVREP securing more accessible and responsive legal support on the ground; he felt that he could no longer rely on MALDEF and the Lawyer's Committee alone, going forward.

Willie's solution was to push for SVREP support and hire its own attorney to oversee the voting rights project—and related SVREP litigation—on a full-time basis. Velásquez recommended this strategy to his board members and funders in late 1978 and early 1979. "We are putting such a priority on redistricting that we must absolutely deliver," Velásquez noted in his fall 1978 board report. "Already with the modest amount of cases that have gone to court, we have overloaded MALDEF's ability to handle the load," he continued, raising the rhetorically framed concern: "What will happen when we begin suing all over the Southwest?" Willie additionally implored his board and benefactors to seriously consider the litigation backlash that was starting to develop in the field as another justification for SVREP to support in-house legal capacity. "We also have to protect our people from lawsuits such as are now beginning to occur when Mexican Americans win," he argued. "Our credibility will suffer if we can't defend those people who stick their necks out (to advance our campaign and organizational aims)." Velásquez was not exaggerating the problem. One irate rancher, in fact, had sued the chair of one of SVREP's local registration drives for $1,000,000—a frivolous and extreme, although real example of the frustration the campaign was creating for some Anglos in the countryside—because Mexican-American elected officials had taken over the school board.

Initial reaction to Willie's proposal for a SVREP legal arm was fraught with uncertainty, hesitancy, and skepticism. MALDEF General Counsel Vilma Martínez, a native Texan who also served on SVREP's board, told Velásquez and the other SVREP board members that she did not feel Southwest Voter should be expanding into new arenas, such as litigation, when it still had not yet even established itself doing basic door-to-door registration work in California and other states outside of Texas. Some SVREP board representatives accepted Martínez's comments at face value while others felt her remarks stemmed from an ulterior motive to keep SVREP out of the litigation business. MALDEF, since the late 1960s, had played a leading role in the major legal casework for Latinos nationwide. Other legal aid societies, local Latino groups, and private practitioners had done, and continued to do, legal work on behalf of Latinos, but none of them had developed the resources, credibility, or accumulated experience that MALDEF possessed. The last thing Martínez wanted, in the estimation of observers, was another competitor that could possibly diminish funding that MALDEF needed to support its essential work.

In fact, Martínez's concerns were much less parochial and much less based on a personal clash of visions relative to SVREP's and Velásquez's proposed new approach. Rather, the MALDEF chief executive was simply convinced that SVREP's best and highest use of its limited resources was to focus on its core competencies—namely, voter registration and education. In her judgment it would be better for SVREP to leave the legal work to more established litigation nonprofits, like MALDEF, that had built their capacities over the years precisely to support effective community-based legal challenges to Mexican-American voting rights infringements.

Although various SVREP board members (and funders) interpreted Martínez's position as a veiled way to neutralize SVREP's legal ambitions, no one questioned that the tension created by Willie's proposal would be quickly and amicably resolved. Notwithstanding the fact that Martínez and Velásquez were both strong-willed individuals, they deeply respected each other and shared an irrepressible commitment to the cause of Mexican-American community justice. For these reasons, they were bound to find a way to meet minds on the matter of supporting voter rights campaign needs in South Texas. Under the circumstances, however, MALDEF attorney Ávila played a key role in expediting a resolution that addressed both his boss's and Willie's concerns. Ávila fundamentally trusted Willie's judgment and felt confident that SVREP's entry into the legal world would be an asset, not a threat, to MALDEF and the voting rights project going forward. Ávila, who would ultimately replace Martínez as MALDEF's general counsel largely as a result of her great confidence in his skills and judgment, conveyed these sentiments to Martínez, and MALDEF wholeheartedly embraced SVREP's attempt to join the legal universe of minority rights organizations.

ᔕ ᔕ ᔕ

Shortly before the end of SVREP's fiscal year in 1979, Willie received word from the North Shore Unitarian Society that it had approved a $20,000 grant to help SVREP support its own litigation work. Velásquez was ecstatic. He immediately began to search for someone to fill SVREP's newly devised attorney position. Based on reconnaissance and feedback of SVREP staffers, San Antonio native Rolando Ríos emerged as the lead candidate for the job. Ríos had worked as a paralegal at MALDEF before entering law school and now, having recently graduated, he was currently looking for a legal position in San Antonio. Ríos, fresh out of Georgetown Law School, had recently passed the Texas bar exam and had been working temporarily for the Austin Legal Aid Society for several months. A decorated Vietnam War veteran and former Holy Cross High School basketball star, Ríos was ironically in the process of applying for a voting rights job with MALDEF when he was contacted by Velásquez. Willie invited Rolando to his house for a leisurely Sunday brunch where the two could get to know each other and talk about SVREP's legal plans. Velásquez also asked Andy Hernández to join them. Hernández, who had left SVREP in 1977 to study Christian ministry, had been returning to do special projects for Willie during his summer breaks ever since, and was now slowly becoming an important confidant to Velásquez. Willie no longer saw him as a naive, starry-eyed recent college grad, but rather as a seasoned politico who could be trusted to provide strategic counsel and advice.

In typical Velásquez fashion, well in advance of the Sunday brunch gathering, Willie had already made up his mind that he wanted to hire Ríos. The meeting merely offered an opportunity for Velásquez to sell SVREP's ambitious and still undefined litigation goals to Ríos in a way that would excite and convince him to accept the challenge. Within the first hour of their conversation, it became crystal clear that Ríos would enthusiastically accept the job. Willie made it virtually impossible for the young new law school graduate to consider any other option. In effect, he offered Ríos an already funded position, a substantive legal agenda that promised to make historic contributions to the Mexican-American people, and a weighty position title—legal director, which even though clearly overblown (Ríos would have no department or staff to support him) could only appeal to a young attorney looking for his first permanent job.

While his working relationship with Ávila, MALDEF, and the rest of the Lawyer's Committee was excellent, Willie now felt released from his prior need to depend on them primarily for legal counsel. SVREP would still have to rely heavily on Joaquín Ávila's expertise, especially during Ríos's initial introduction to the field, but because SVREP now had its own lawyer it could act with much greater flexibility and speed to advance the campaign through bold, aggressive, and unbridled attacks on Texas rural counties that were violating Mexican-American voting rights.

192 Juan A. Sepúlveda, Jr.

Willie wasted no time with Ríos. Within four months, the young attorney was trying his first federal case in Corpus Christi, Texas. SVREP's legal agenda was simple, direct, and yet markedly different from that of MALDEF, TRLA, and the private practitioners. SVREP was concerned with only one item, voting rights cases, and nothing else. While the other groups and individuals had diverse practices and priorities that changed over time, SVREP was wedded to those cases alone that would increase the chances for Mexican Americans to gain political influence. This meant Ríos and SVREP, while continuing to coordinate their activities with the Lawyer's Committee, had the freedom to pursue their own plan at their own pace.

Shortly after Ríos was brought aboard as SVREP counsel, the Lawyer's Committee was expanded and still more new blood was drafted into the ongoing struggle against suspect voting practices and election schemes in Texas. José Garza, fresh out of law school, Raul Noriega of TRLA, Rolando Romero, and two women, Lucilla Sánchez and Erlinda Walden, joined the group of researchers, attorneys, and organizers who made up the ad hoc litigation team. Much of the continuing success of this group stemmed from a combination of Ávila's able leadership and knowledge, and the youthful spirit of the new committee members. Ávila's voting rights track record clearly positioned him as the elder statesman of the committee, the point person who effectively directed the junior members of the team. He even guided and directed much of Ríos's earlier work with the absolute approval of Velásquez. Things ran fairly smoothly with the seasoned Ávila informing the committee's work and cohesiveness along these lines.

By mid-1979, with a collection of experiences between them, good and bad, memorable and laughable, the Lawyer's Committee on Reapportionment had figured out a set of options that gave Mexican Americans a winning game plan for challenging one person, one vote and gerrymandering violations of controlling federal law. Their first step involved preliminary research, conducted mainly by SVREP, to assess the jurisdictional composition and geographical scale of rural county districts based on voter registration data. If in particular cases the results demonstrated potential violations, Lawyer's Committee representatives would arrange meetings with local Mexican-American community leaders to present the information, instruct them on their legal options, and help them devise appropriate response strategies based on local priorities. More often than not, the rural Mexican-American leaders would opt to challenge local authorities, usually by authorizing the committee to assist them in initiating a lawsuit.

The findings of SVREP's preliminary analyses were then presented to county officials along with a polite encouragement to consider the many benefits of an out-of-court settlement, including economies of time and money, minimization of local rancor and bad publicity, and increased likelihood of

more mutually agreeable outcomes for all concerned. Most counties confronted with these considerations, and knowing already for the most part that they
were in violation of the law, opted to settle. When the Lawyer's Committee
filed suit against the most stubborn and egregious violating counties, it won
nearly every single case, resulting in brand-new county district lines, many
designed by SVREP and MALDEF, that fundamentally advanced prospects for
increased Hispanic voter participation and representation. The litigation victories were followed immediately by voter registration drives aimed at tapping
the swelling momentum of change. Massive get-out-the-vote campaigns then
completed the process with the outcome typically being the election of Mexican-American officials, often for the first time in county or local history.

By the time the SVREP/MALDEF-led voting rights strategy had fully
played itself out in the mid-1980s, visible and striking changes had occurred
across rural Texas. According to MALDEF attorney José Garza, "Mexican
Americans during the late 1970s were about 19 or 20 percent of the population in Texas but were less than 6 percent of the elected officials on the county commissioner courts. . . . By 1982 and 1983, when we saw the effect of
(our) lawsuits, with new plans being drawn and new people getting elected,
we were 10 to 12 percent—almost a 100 percent increase in a matter of five
years. . . . It was just incredible!"

The changes inspired by the Lawyer's Committee for Reapportionment in
the Texas rural county political structure were impressive, and Velásquez made
sure that his board members and funders were acutely aware of SVREP's role
in this mini-revolution, but he was far from satisfied. There was still plenty of
unchartered territory to explore. Texas county commissioner lines were only
the tip of the iceberg. There were other, arguably even more important jurisdictions to attack—including city councils and school boards—and other key
Southwestern states that suffered from many of the same problems that existed in Texas. And now that Mexican Americans were winning for the first time,
important new questions entered Willie's mind that he knew would require
careful consideration and thoughtful response in the future SVREP's work was
helping to create. What were all these Mexican Americans going to do in
office? How would they avoid becoming mere token voices or worse yet conventional protectors of the status quo in county politics?

Velásquez realized that the overnight litigation and electoral achievements
inspired by the Lawyer's Committee's work in rural Texas would not translate
into overnight substantive changes for the small-town Chicanos who lived
there. That would take time (as this was a long-term empowerment movement,
after all, not a quick fix) without a deeper, more meaningful set of substantive
aims beyond electing individuals with Spanish surnames. Willie's logical side
knew this, but still he somehow had to reconcile it all with his characteristic
impatience and his deep desire to see everything move forward much faster.

Chapter 13

SVREP MANAGED TO SURVIVE THROUGH its early years without a comprehensive communications strategy and with surprisingly sparse attention paid to the English-speaking media across the Southwest. Willie's skepticism of the mainstream media's balance and objectivity, dating back to his formative years as an activist, informed this arm's-length approach to Anglo journalists. By comparison, the project selectively pursued publicity through the Spanish media, which Willie saw as an effective and safe means of spreading the news on its latest efforts. In most instances, however, SVREP maintained a low profile in the public media to avoid the potential of conservative backlash, as well as the danger of creating false expectations of the organization's capacities in the Mexican-American community.

In December of 1976, SVREP's executive committee, pushed by Velásquez, implemented an important change in course, deciding that it was time to promote fully the project's activities through conventional media strategies. SVREP already had completed nearly fifty registration drives since its founding, helping an estimated 160,000 Mexican Americans to register and vote across the Southwest. In the process, the organization and its leaders had learned a great deal about how to implement effective registration campaigns, including how to educate and motivate Latino communities throughout the region to engage in political processes that had long been set up to diminish their participation. But the lessons and implications of SVREP's work were still not widely recognized, either in Mexican-American communities that had not yet benefited from the project's growing expertise or in mainstream quarters, where Mexican Americans continued to be viewed as politically disinterested or inconsequential. In a letter to Rick Casey, a progressive freelance journalist who, like Willie, was a St. Mary's University graduate, Velásquez wrote: "The [negative] image of the Chicanos nationally, particularly in politics, is a great burden that has impeded our progress. Perhaps we can do some work that will begin educating the country about Mexicans and begin remedying this problem."

In an attempt to forge an effective media strategy, Velásquez asked Casey to help SVREP develop its communications capabilities, focusing

194

especially on its capacity to serve as a national clearinghouse on Mexican-American politics for journalists and policy researchers. Casey assisted Willie to lay the groundwork for SVREP's communications department, helping him to craft a strategic outline for the organization's public education work and to identify a communications assistant who could implement it. A key element of Casey's proposed strategy was the development of a regular publication series that would enable SVREP to brand its work in the public media arena, while at the same time consolidating its base network of political and community activists. Lydia Espinosa of Austin's Chicana Research & Learning Center was hired in early 1977 to staff SVREP's communications work accordingly.

Espinosa, a sociologist trained at Notre Dame University, looked forward to shaping SVREP's communications program. Her first major assignment was to help Willie create the *Southwest Journal*, a bimonthly publication that would highlight impending issues affecting SVREP's work and also serve to inform local leaders and organizations involved with SVREP of project-related plans and activities across the Southwest. In introducing the journal to SVREP's funders and board members, Velásquez announced that it was time for the organization to break out of its media shell. "Latinos are being ignored because we are too quiet and are not assigning skilled people to the job of bringing Latino issues to the national forum," he asserted in a Spring 1977 report.

Willie's analysis of the need for SVREP to aggressively augment its communications work was undeniably grounded in the realities of American political and public life. Without a strong communications presence in the mainstream culture, Hispanics would never be able to realize fully a level of public comprehension and sensitivity that would facilitate their political integration in American civic life. Velásquez fundamentally understood this and saw SVREP communication efforts as a necessary intervention to address the problem. Unfortunately, Willie's strong desire to help put Mexican Americans on the political map through more assertive public media engagement was not matched by his availability or clarity of approach, nor by the necessary resources to make SVREP's evolving communications strategy all that he wanted it to be. He provided little guidance to Espinosa and became increasingly disengaged from her work as demands on other fronts consumed him.

A contributing factor in this dynamic was Espinosa's lack of journalistic and press experience. More a scholar and a writer than a media professional, the young researcher was poorly prepared for the large and arguably unrealistic communications agenda that Willie wanted SVREP to develop. In time, the combination of Velásquez's competing commitments on other fronts and Espinosa's journalistic inexperience resulted in a media campaign that never fully developed. Willie, increasingly pressed for time, was finally unable to articulate a clear core message around which to anchor project communications and related fund development activities. Nor was he able to avail himself of staff-driven ideas or initiatives intended to move SVREP's media work forward. Finally dejected, Espinosa lasted only until the end of 1977. Having served just under a year, she left SVREP feeling that she never really had the opportunity to fulfill Velásquez's grand designs because the new communications department's needs and ideas were constantly being tabled in lieu of more pressing projects, usually field-related. SVREP's media work was substantially abbreviated after Espinosa resigned. Willie let the position remain open for half a year before hiring a replacement. The second time around, Velásquez opted for a trained communications expert.

Pam Eoff, a Masters degree graduate in communications from the University of Texas at Austin, was hired as SVREP's communications staffer in June of 1978. Eoff was employed largely because Willie was impressed with her media credentials, which included a Master's thesis on Mexican television programming and experience teaching college courses in television production and scriptwriting in Spanish. During her three-year tenure, Eoff took SVREP into areas it had not ventured before, including the production of Spanish radio programs called "Avances" and "Pláticas del Barrio," which featured community activists and political leaders representing the Mexican-American population. Under her watch, the *Southwest Journal* was expanded and new public service announcements were produced for television and radio broadcast. Eoff also helped the project to document its media impact by collecting stories and reports that mentioned SVREP and recording the number of times SVREP personnel appeared on radio or television. These were substantial contributions to SVREP's media savvy and visibility, to be sure.

With Pam Eoff's able efforts to establish a public communications presence for SVREP in mainstream as well as Hispanic community media, Willie was able to direct SVREP's attention in late 1978 to the implementation of a major shift in its field strategy. Now, in addition to focusing on organizing efforts intended to register and educate voters, SVREP would also set its sights on helping Latino and other minority and progressive political candidates to win elections. After nearly 180 registration drives throughout the Southwest, some bringing historic gains to previously untouched rural areas, Velásquez was convinced that SVREP's door-to-door registration approach and its expanding litigation experience provided the accumulated standing and capacity to inform lasting—rather than merely incidental—political victories and policy reforms.

Willie wanted logically to focus on winning elections because he felt that, in general, Mexican-American elected officials were more likely to be responsive to the needs of the Chicano community. He knew this would not be the case across the board, but the scattered political successes of SVREP's registration drives to date already presented models of the class of Mexican-American elected official Velásquez hoped to cultivate—the type that rejected business as usual and raised the level of political dialogue in their communities. Raul Flores, sheriff of Reeves County, Texas, was a prototype of what Willie had in mind when he talked about winning elections. Flores replaced A. B. Nail, who Willie often reminded people "had the reputation of being the most redneck anti-Mexican sheriff in West Texas." Flores, a former professor of law enforcement at Sul Ross College in Alpine, Texas, who held a Master's degree in criminal justice and insisted that his deputies have a Bachelor's degree and at least five years of experience, brought the right set of credentials and values to his position, according to Velásquez. Flores's academic training, his professionalism, and his commitment to the community made him the type of candidate that would be elected in a pure meritocracy. In Willie's worldview, Flores was precisely the sort of individual that the Mexican-American community needed to elect.

A pioneering strategy for SVREP to encourage expanded electoral opportunities for candidates like Flores to seek and successfully gain office was educating Mexican Americans on how to participate in party caucuses and delegate selection. Although primary and general elections involving citizen voting were the most visible and fundamental components of U.S. democratic life, Velásquez and his team at SVREP had quickly learned that the behind-the-scenes workings of the major party hierarchies had much to do with who ultimately was advanced to run successfully for public offices throughout the region and the nation. Without the support and financial backing of the major parties, electoral victory was a rare outcome indeed. Expanding Mexican-American/Latino influence in the party selection processes was, therefore, increasingly seen by SVREP as a critical necessity in the quest for Spanish-speaking political empowerment. SVREP first acted on this realization in Colorado in 1978, at the Democratic state party caucuses and achieved tremendous results. During this period, SVREP financially supported thirteen sites for voter education drives that included training sessions on the secrets of the Colorado delegate selection process. As a result of this work, almost 12 percent of the delegates ultimately selected that year were Chicanos. This was more than double the previous record for Chicano delegate selection in Colorado and came extremely close to mirroring the 13 percent Hispanic share of the total state population at the time.

The successful effort in the Colorado delegate selection process encouraged Willie to build SVREP's fieldwork increasingly around more sophisticated strategies designed to elect and empower Mexican Americans with progressive inclinations. In order to advance these strategies, Willie recruited and hired Bill Calderón, a twenty-five-year-old political advisor and professional musician, who had been working with the political consulting group of Reimer, Kaplan, Duncan & Young for over a year. Calderón's shrewd political sense and experience with more modern techniques of campaigning and organizing convinced Velásquez that he could help SVREP's various ad hoc coalitions to be much more effective in local elections. Shortly after securing Calderón to staff SVREP's next generation field operations, Willie formalized SVREP's new approach, informing his board and benefactors in writing of his rationale and planned foci going forward: "As we go back to the coalitions for our second and third campaigns, the people require more in-depth training in the skills necessary to do a [better] job registering voters and getting the vote out. [Accordingly, we will be adding new sections to our] organizing manual dealing with targeting, voter identification techniques (phone and mail) and get-out-the-vote [strategies]." Velásquez, in his usual manner, unleashed his new field director on the Southwest with precious little guidance, except the clear mandate to develop a field program that Calderón felt would be most appropriate for positioning Mexican Americans to have a stronger bearing on the winning of elections.

In addition to making important departmental and directional changes, Velásquez also moved at this time to expand the groups SVREP worked with in the Southwest. Even though SVREP had not done as much organizing as it would have liked in Mexican-American communities of the Southwest, Willie believed that it was important, both symbolically and strategically, to reach out to both Native Americans and African Americans in the region. Velásquez proudly characterized Native Americans as "Indians" in the same way that he referred to his own people as "Mexicans." He hated to use the term Native American because, for him, it carried the same connotation as Hispanic. To Willie, these were referents that sounded like Anglicized, governmental creations, void of any feeling. (In some respects, he was correct, as the terms Native American and Hispanic were the official U.S. government usages to describe indigenous tribal and Spanish-speaking people in America on census and other public reporting forms.)

Velásquez's decision to work in Indian communities was especially heartfelt. Since SVREP's inception Willie had envisioned working with the various Indian nations because he felt a kindred spirit with them, a shared history and experience in important respects. Like many old-time Chicano activists, Velásquez felt more Indian than Spanish in his mestizo makeup and this bonded him spiritually and emotionally with the pre-European peoples of North America. In Willie's eyes, Mexican Americans and Indians were two of the most oppressed and forgotten groups in the country. As he saw it, however, most Americans—including influential policy makers and foundation executives—understood minority problems and civil rights claims almost exclusively in terms of African-American community needs. While

Velásquez did not deny significant, continuing black inequality in America, he knew that being thousands of miles away from the power centers of the Eastern seaboard meant Mexicans and Indians were just as far away when it came to securing needed recognition and support in their own right. It was therefore imperative in Willie's view for SVREP and the different Indian groups to make themselves better known to the Eastern establishment.

For Willie, SVREP's mission was not limited to politically empowering Mexicans and Indians; he hoped its impact would be larger and more far-reaching. Velásquez envisioned a future in which, by amassing political influence and power, Native and Latino groups would help to moderate U.S. policy making in ways that would both heal old historical wounds and encourage improvements in public problem solving. Velásquez explained these ideas to several East Coast funders, calling political participation "a natural step in the progress of Mexican Americans and Indians toward regaining the positions of honor and respect we used to enjoy in the region." According to Velásquez, the restoration of honor and respect were vital to rebuild the self-image and political vitality of both Mexicans and Indians in the Southwest. By working together, they would accelerate the attainment of these goals and simultaneously offer American society needed new ideas and talent in the public decision-making arena.

Research was the fundamental starting point of SVREP's work in Native-American areas, just as it had been in Latino neighborhoods of the Southwest. SVREP had a great deal to learn about Indian communities before being positioned to commence drives in them that could produce meaningful outcomes. Velásquez and other project leaders needed to deepen their staple of relationships and trust in the Native communities of the region. SVREP board member Walter Atcitty, himself an Indian and an essential advisor to SVREP on Native issues, had been a major asset to the organization since its early days. His counsel and encouragement helped Willie to work toward developing the project's targeting of and engagement with tribal groups. As fate would have it, however, Atcitty was killed in a car accident early in 1976. His death was a substantial loss to Velásquez and to SVREP in general terms, but especially with respect to the project's continuing forward movement in Indian country, Atcitty's sudden, unexpected absence was a substantial setback.

Another factor bearing on SVREP's relatively long lead time in generating work in Native-American communities was the absence of express tribal interest to seek the project's partnership and technical assistance. Atcitty had certainly helped to open important doors for SVREP in Indian leadership circles, but it was not until after his passing, somewhat ironically, that the inquiry for support of a Native-American registration drive came to Willie and his project colleagues during the late summer months of 1976. The Arizona Inter-Tribal Council, based in Phoenix, saw the success of SVREP's

Maricopa County drive earlier that year and approached SVREP about commencing a drive targeted to its members. With eighteen different tribes present in the greater Phoenix area, the Council felt that it could add two thousand new Indian voters to area rolls, and possibly even many more.

Regrettably, SVREP was not sufficiently prepared to maximize the impact of its intervention on behalf of the Inter-Tribal Council, given the extremely tight time frame that it had to work with prior to the November elections. Its community research had not been completed, moreover, and SVREP personnel had not yet developed a sense of what registration devices would work best in Native communities. Finally, rather than tailoring its intervention to unique Indian needs in and around Phoenix, SVREP unthinkingly offered Council elders its usual mix of supports, including a small cash grant of $1,525 and eight weeks of standard training, technical assistance, and campaign advising. In the end, not surprisingly, the fate of the campaign was basically left in the electorally inexperienced hands of local ad hoc coalition leaders, including especially the drive's chairperson, Floyd Bringing Good. Bringing Good and the Council's SVREP-supported local coalition labored strenuously, but encountered predictable obstacles that exceeded their capacities (and SVREP's) to overcome. After two months of genuine effort and hard work, the drive fell far short of its goals, resulting in the registration of only about 250 new Native voters. Velásquez was deeply disappointed by SVREP's initial drive in the Native-American community and pledged to develop a more responsive and informed Indian strategy for the future. Bringing Good, who had been working on Indian causes since the late 1960s, was recruited to join the SVREP board of directors and immediately began working with Willie to draft plans for more successful SVREP forays into the Indian world.

SVREP organized a second Indian registration drive in 1977 in Bernalillo County, New Mexico, which encompasses the city of Albuquerque and its surrounding areas. While the results were not spectacular, nearly five hundred new Native voters were registered, twice the number of SVREP's first Indian venture. As importantly, however, the Bernalillo County drive connected Velásquez and SVREP for the first time to Gerald Wilkinson, the person who would become SVREP's most influential and valuable ally in the Indian political world during the project's organizational apex in the 1980s. Wilkinson, a Duke University-trained Cherokee, had been executive director of the National Indian Youth Council (NIYC) since 1969, an organization that had developed effective programs and activities touching virtually all aspects of Indian community life. NIYC sponsored programs for ex-offenders, young people, and emerging legal and social justice advocates. It supported litigation work, an environmental education program, a film and documentary series, and off-reservation Comprehensive Employment and Training Act (CETA) programs targeted to Indian groups. Now, with

SVREP's support, Wilkinson proposed to start a voter registration entity to mobilize and empower Native-American groups across the United States. Relying heavily on Wilkinson in New Mexico and Bringing Good in Arizona, SVREP made a huge push in 1978 to help initiate this effort by organizing eleven Native-American drives in their respective states. Ex-Texas State Senator Joe Bernal, now a regional action director for the VISTA program in the Southwest, was able to commit federally sponsored volunteers to some of the New Mexico sites.

The larger number of campaigns produced critical challenges for SVREP and its Indian community partners, mostly related to circumstances particular to the Native-American communities targeted. There was the historical problem of many tribes in the target communities discouraging their members from voting in non-tribal elections because of past (and in some cases continuing) unhappy experiences with the U.S. government. For many of the older Navajo Indians who were predominant in the region, moreover, the inability to read or speak English substantially discouraged participation in the SVREP-supported effort. Another major challenge in gaining Native participation in the campaign was the terrain. In certain cases, reservation-based Indians would have to travel nearly one hundred miles on decrepit roads in order to vote, a significant practical disincentive to registering and participating. These multiple deterrents, along with the severe conditions facing many Indian groups in the area, including poverty, few job opportunities, high rates of alcoholism, and poor education considerably reduced Native interest in political participation. Nonetheless, SVREP's involvement and perseverance brought an unprecedented sense of hope and potential to Indian leaders and communities involved in the Arizona and New Mexico campaigns. Wilkinson captured this sentiment in a letter to Velásquez in the summer of 1978, thanking SVREP for its hard work and partnership: "Your interest in Indian people has given us a whole range of possibilities we never thought possible for us." Highly moved by Wilkinson's gratitude and partnership, Willie redoubled SVREP's commitment to help expand Native-American voting potential.

After Bill Calderón began work as SVREP's field director, the project's activities and achievements in Indian country evolved considerably, extending to new reservations, different tribes, and more effective outreach strategies (including the development of compelling public service announcements in an assortment of Native tongues). Calderón also took a more hands-on approach to SVREP's engagement in Native-American communities than the project had taken to date in Mexican-American communities. In some cases, the new field director spent considerable time in the field working side by side with SVREP's Indian partners, both to teach and to learn about how best to expand Native-American political participation and representation. This more engaged approach helped to enhance SVREP's impact and value added in Native communities.

When Bringing Good's term on the SVREP board of directors expired in 1978, it was unnecessary for Willie to undertake an extensive search for a leading Native American to replace him. Velásquez looked immediately to Gerald Wilkinson. He deeply admired Wilkinson's quiet yet firm presence, his dedication to his people, and his vision of Indian empowerment through comprehensive organizing and leadership development work. He also knew that Wilkinson would keep SVREP focused on promoting an Indian game plan as a part of its core organizational strategy. Wilkinson accepted Velásquez's invitation to join the project's board and his involvement with SVREP immediately gave the organization precisely the boost in its approach to Indian community organizing that he had hoped for. SVREP's Indian work was now well on its way.

SVREP's relationship with the African-American community, and in particular the Voter Education Project (VEP) based in Atlanta, Georgia, was deeply rooted and dated back to its founders' earliest attempts at organizing a voter registration outfit. Beginning in 1968, when the idea for a SVREP-type group was first proposed by board members of the Southwest Council of La Raza, through the summer of 1974, when SVREP finally received its tax-exempt status, VEP had served as the singular model that the organization's leading protagonists wanted to emulate. Since its beginnings in the early 1960s, VEP had established itself as the nation's leading minority voter registration group. It had amassed a tremendous track record of political success built on immense struggles and against unbelievable odds. VEP's effectiveness made it a favored cause of much of the progressive foundation world because its efforts were bringing meaningful change to black neighborhoods of the nation's most racist and conservative Southern states.

The Mexican-American leaders of the Southwest, who during the late 1960s wanted to establish a community-based Hispanic voter engagement entity, were clearly inspired by VEP's successes, and they relied almost exclusively on VEP's structure and approach in formalizing the organization that eventually became SVREP. In the process, Maclovio Barraza, Armando de León, Arnold Flores, and Velásquez spent hours upon hours probing VEP director Vernon Jordan and members of his staff for mundane details, practical information, guidance, and support. They made it clear to potential funders and the IRS that they were seeking to clone the VEP prototype in ways that would address Mexican-American community needs for expanded democratic participation. After Jordan left VEP to head the National Urban League, the Mexican-American leaders who founded SVREP continued the association with him and his replacement, John Lewis, soaking up as much of their accumulated knowledge and experience as possible.

When SVREP ultimately gained IRS approval to begin operations,

Velásquez was quick to heap praise upon Jordan, Lewis, VEP, and the Urban League for sticking by the project and giving it the strong early foundation for success. Velásquez's gratitude to these African-American community leaders and institutions was real and profound. Throughout his final years, Willie consistently pointed to César Chávez's work with the farmworkers and effective black civil rights leaders and organizations as two of the main reasons why the political consciousness of Chicanos had been raised during the 1960s and 1970s. In Willie's estimation, the strategic lessons and priorities of African-American advocacy efforts had been extremely instructive to Chicano leaders of the time, including especially himself. He focused in particular on VEP's many impressive successes as a source of guidance and inspiration because they offered tangible expressions of change and opportunity for the black community that he believed SVREP's work could make equally real and powerful for Mexican Americans and other emerging minority groups.

Willie's sense of appreciation and solidarity relative to black social justice and minority rights leaders compelled him early on in SVREP's development to seek formal alliances with VEP and African-American community leadership representation on the project board. He tried desperately, but ultimately in vain, to gain Vernon Jordan's agreement to serve as a SVREP director, begging him repeatedly, to no avail, to reconsider, even after Jordan had graciously declined.

After failing to persuade Jordan to join SVREP's board, a year passed before Willie pursued another major progressive black political actor to serve on the project board. In April, and again in August of 1976, Velásquez asked Wiley Branton, a leading African-American civil rights attorney, to consider being nominated. But Branton, who had financially supported SVREP during its formative campaigns by drawing on multiple sources from his extensive national network of social justice donors, was initially hesitant to accept. Like Jordan, and many other top-notch activists, Branton was overbooked and did not know if he would be able to make SVREP board meetings. He offered Velásquez a compromise, telling him he could assist SVREP informally from his base in Washington, D.C. but would not join the board because of his many other commitments. Willie rejected this idea, saying that SVREP wanted him on its board even if he could not attend every directors meeting. In pressing his cause forward, Velásquez vigorously urged Branton to consider the strategic import of Hispanic and African-American leaders like themselves coming together as partners in ways that would ensure greater cooperation rather than competition into the future. Writing to Branton in the summer of 1976, Willie appealed to the erstwhile black civil rights activist in the following terms: "We must realize the need to work hard at developing and maintaining a harmonious working relationship between our people. . . . To not work at it is to invite trouble in the future." Branton was taken aback and compelled by Velásquez's keen strategic insight, as well as his clear commitment to ensure meaningful African-American leadership involvement in SVREP's work. Following much reflection and further conversation, Branton agreed to accept SVREP's board invitation in the spring of 1977.

Shortly after Branton's appointment, SVREP and VEP discussed the possibility of working together on a multisite campaign. The notion of a significant black-brown coalition in the field was fueled by Branton's input and SVREP's latest foray into Eastside San Antonio politics. While since its formation most of SVREP's organizing work had been conducted in Mexican-American neighborhoods, there had been occasions when it ventured into the black community. In fact, SVREP's first registration drive ever in San Antonio had included an organizing component staffed by a longtime African-American activist and targeted to black citizens on the east side of town. Now, in late 1977, SVREP was targeting additional black districts of San Antonio, using the talents of Abram Emerson, a young, well-connected grassroots leader in the local African-American community. Emerson's hard work and energy accelerated Willie's thinking about pursuing an alliance with VEP to promote African-American registration and voting in San Antonio and other cities.

Willie's proposed approach was simple. SVREP and VEP would choose places they both wanted to organize in any case and they would coordinate efforts in those areas, sharing costs and mobilizing their respective leadership resources in ways that would optimally benefit both groups' core constituencies. VEP officials liked the concept, but stressed the need for clear and formal divisions of labor and cost sharing. After going back and forth on the notion for over three months, they sent Velásquez a draft partnership agreement that mapped out responsibilities for both organizations. Willie signed the papers in July of 1978 without even reading them and mailed a copy back to VEP, including a brief cover note that contained the following telling observation (which clearly delineated the extent of his commitment to work with VEP): "you could have put anything into that agreement or nothing, and I would have signed it anyway."

The joint agreement called for SVREP and VEP to split the costs of Emerson's salary. Emerson was to recommend ten to twelve cities in Texas where black-brown coalitions were most likely to succeed, and VEP would primarily fund the drives. Texas was chosen as the sole target state because it turned out surprisingly to be the only one in which both groups operated meaningful campaigns. SVREP would support fees and administrative costs for Emerson and would also cover his travel expenses. Collectively, SVREP and VEP would promote local fund-raising strategies for their united campaigns and sponsor gatherings and seminars involving African-American and Mexican-American leaders to improve the two groups' relations and develop longer range joint campaign plans in other venues. Velásquez considered this pioneering endeavor critical to both organizations and their main constituencies as they looked to the next decade. In one joint convening of each group's lead representatives, Willie underscored the import of making the partnership a priority by echoing the sentiments he had shared with Wiley Branton to secure his agreement to join the SVREP board of directors, stating, "I don't want to sound ominous, however, it seems to me that if we don't do something, Mexicans and blacks are going to find themselves in opposite camps, working against each other. . . . We cannot afford to let this happen. An historic opportunity is before us, we must do everything in our power [working together] to do what is right."

VEP officials responded enthusiastically to Willie's sense of passion and urgency, which to their ears harkened back to the heady days of their earlier movement years. Unfortunately, within only a few months of formalizing their proposed joint venture, serious problems emerged in the SVREP-VEP partnership. VEP's financial situation took a sudden severe downturn that prevented it from meeting its partnership commitments. VEP informed Velásquez that its money problems would not likely improve before April or May of 1979, after the Texas election cycle had ended. Willie worried deeply about the potential negative fallout that might follow from VEP's unanticipated financial problems. Highly public kickoff events recently convened in Atlanta and San Antonio had helped to create significant regional and national interest in the unprecedented intergroup partnership. Pulling back from the effort before it effectively got off the ground would expose both SVREP and VEP to potentially devastating questions of credibility among important funders, journalists, and political activists. In addition, VEP's pullback put additional financial pressure on SVREP to carry a larger cost burden to see the campaign through at a time when the project was for the first time gaining a semblance of fiscal security. Even the risk-taking Velásquez knew that it would not be possible for the project to fill the void left without unreasonably risking SVREP's own solvency. At the same time, he wanted desperately to have something positive to show the world; SVREP and VEP had committed themselves to taking on the joint campaign on behalf of improved black-brown relations and political influence in America. His answer was to cut the number of drives to six, to lower the amounts of grants provided to participating local coalitions, and to reduce the total number of site-based technical assistance trainings offered. SVREP agreed in turn to pick up all costs associated with this slimmed down version of the partnership.

Velásquez was extremely disappointed by these developments and confided in his staff and closest Mexican-American community allies that he felt VEP had let him down. But he maintained unusual resolve in his commitment to advance to the fullest possible extent what could be spared of the partnership with VEP. "We will do everything we can to turn this situation around and make our first coalition attempt successful," Velásquez told Patricia Hewitt of Joint Foundation Support, one of the main financial backers of the SVREP-VEP joint venture. In order to make good on his promises, Willie heavily involved himself in the campaign, personally committing time to it that involved even more substantial sacrifices than were customary for the highly driven activist.

In the end, Velásquez kept his word and SVREP completed six Texas registration campaigns targeted to prospective African-American voters in Dallas, San Antonio, Edna, Bryan, Austin, and Houston. As part of the campaign, SVREP and MALDEF also supported several litigation efforts that favorably impacted black neighborhoods in some of the communities targeted by VEP under the partnership. Most of the drives produced marginal results in relation to SVREP's and VEP's heavy preliminary goals, but the partnership did substantially introduce SVREP to the politics of important African-American communities and leaders of the Southwest. In addition, the SVREP-VEP collaboration, in spite of its failure to fulfill its ambitious informing aims, established an important and forward-looking precedent in the formation of stronger black-brown political coalitions. By daring to cross racial lines to promote needed civic engagement in needy African-American *and* Mexican-American communities, Velásquez and SVREP demonstrated their progressive and humanistic inclinations, their deep appreciation of early African-American leadership support for their efforts, and a principled, practical commitment to intergroup coalition-building. Under Willie's leadership, values and tendencies of this sort had come to establish themselves as hallmarks of SVREP's approach to the world. Not long from now, they would help to distinguish the project in national political discourse and elevate Hispanic-American civic participation in unprecedented ways. Still, the bridge to that awaiting future would be neither quick nor easy to cross. In fact, much to Velásquez's growing dismay, the price of admission to achieve the greatness he sought for SVREP would continually increase at every step of the way.

The first five years of SVREP's life were electric. In that short period of time, Willie's unbending energy and nonstop barrage of new ideas, new programs, and new directions caused great havoc at SVREP's headquarters, but it also put SVREP on the map. By the close of the 1970s, the project had organized over two hundred registration drives in dozens of Chicano and other disadvantaged communities across the Southwest. Its work with MALDEF, TRLA, and other progressive attorneys to develop a rural litigation strategy was quickly transforming the Texas countryside. *Nuestro* magazine presented SVREP with its 1977 award for most impressive political achievement of the year for its efforts to organize voters in Mexican-American neighborhoods. SVREP was on the move. Despite having suffered its share of early losses, frustrations, and setbacks, SVREP's dedication and relentless forward movement had earned it growing respect within as well as outside of the Mexican-American community. Increasingly, SVREP's influence extended beyond the neighborhoods and communities in which it primarily worked to leading foundation executives, grassroots activists, and progressive politicians.

SVREP's rapidly growing stature during these early years, however, did nothing to erase insecurities growing inside of Willie about the organization's still low profile and stature among the nation's major political actors. In public and in private, Willie presented an image of strength and self-confidence so powerful that few people could have believed he was not entirely satisfied with SVREP's growing public profile and reputation. Yet behind the macho, rough-riding exterior was a hidden, frustrated side of Velásquez that dreaded SVREP's continuing status as nothing more than a nameless, faceless non-entity among important mainstream political players. Willie had worked too long and too hard on SVREP to not have it respected and acknowledged for what it had accomplished in its still short life span. Velásquez kept his concerns concealed deep within himself, only rarely revealing them, but when he did it quickly became obvious that Willie was not the utterly secure individual his public image projected.

In the fall of 1978, Willie's insecure and paranoid side burst into the public domain in a less than becoming way following a harmless oversight by Hamilton Jordan, President Jimmy Carter's chief of staff, and other presidential aides. The Carter administration, in an effort to regain its waning popularity, decided to convene a series of town hall meetings to tap public sentiment and local leadership for guidance. San Antonio was one of the sites chosen as a barometer of the American pulse.

In the haste of planning the San Antonio convening, Jordan and his staff inadvertently overlooked Velásquez and SVREP on the White House invitation list. At the last minute, the Carter staffers were advised by numerous San Antonio leaders that Willie should be included in the proceedings. The overwhelmingly southern White House event organizers knew very little about Velásquez or his group, but he sounded like exactly the type of grassroots leader they wanted at the gathering. They quickly tried to contact Willie to request his participation. But Velásquez, his ego severely bruised, never responded. Instead, he fumed and sulked about the White House oversight to the point of losing some of his renowned self-control. Willie decided that he simply could not let his anger go unaddressed. As the Carter staff wrapped up the San Antonio assembly and began planning arrangements for their next stop, Willie locked himself away in his office and hurriedly scribbled a rambling letter to Jordan about the entire mess. The tone and content of the letter was comparable to other angry, emotionally charged messages he had dictated or handwritten before and then decided not to send after coolly reflecting on the potential consequences. Often, Velásquez vented his frustrations on paper as a form of therapy, but this time he actually sent his emotion-laden thoughts to the president's chief of staff, as well as forty-five Mexican-American leaders across the nation. The disjointed tirade blasted Jordan and the Carter administration for intentionally barring SVREP from the event. Willie, reminiscent of the Nixon days, then went on to accuse the Carter staff of having developed a blacklist of organizations, including SVREP, that had been deemed enemies of the president.

Chairman Barraza and other SVREP board members and supporters were appalled and concerned that Willie would send such a letter to Jordan. Most wished in secret that Velásquez had consulted them before rashly mailing his letter to Jordan. Some of Willie's allies were even directly critical of his actions. Chuy Ramírez, a political pal from the Rio Grande Valley wrote Velásquez, stating in the plainest of terms, "I was not impressed with your letter to Hamilton Jordan . . . the letter should never have been sent!" Only a handful of SVREP friends wrote letters of support to Jordan backing Velásquez's sentiments and, even among those who did, no one advocated or attached any credibility to Willie's claim that Carter had a blacklist that included SVREP.

Barraza knew he had to do something to remedy Velásquez's uncontrolled outburst so he summoned Willie, Houston political leader Ben Reyes, and Rick Hernández, one of the few Mexican Americans in the Carter administration, to his home in Tucson to determine how the entire episode had occurred and might best be resolved. They discussed the specifics of the San Antonio mishap but mostly ended up focusing on larger concerns about the Carter administration. Velásquez, now substantially less animated than when he addressed Jordan in his letter, still nevertheless expressed a strong view that the Carter folks had a blatant disregard for the Mexican-American people and their organizational efforts. From the outset of the Carter presidency, Willie had been an ardent critic of the administration's Latino policy. He constantly attacked Carter's record of Hispanic appointments and his Justice Department's lack of swiftness to help SVREP and MALDEF advance their voting rights work in rural Texas counties. It was these complaints coming from the nonpartisan SVREP that made Velásquez suspect he was not favored at the White House.

In terms of appointments, Carter had actually done more for Latinos than most presidents before him, but Willie expected far more from the Democratic administration. While not as adamant as Velásquez, the other participants at Barraza's summit (including Hernández, the presidential appointee) also expressed concern about the Carter White House. In large measure, the Tucson summit of Chicano leaders convened by Barraza surfaced issues that would soon reveal themselves to have reach beyond the

Mexican-American community relative to the Carter presidency. In fact, Carter was increasingly facing doubts about his viability to seek and gain a second term in office by this time. Not only were more conservative Americans gaining irreparable discomfort with the former Georgia governor, but also progressive Democrats like Willie and his fellow grassroots activists were becoming substantially disillusioned with Carter. With more than a year to go before the traditional commencement of the presidential re-election campaign, many Americans were beginning to see him as a one-term officeholder. During this period, many on the political left began to contemplate the real possibility of a successful bid to challenge Carter's re-election within the Democratic Party. The most commonly mentioned challenger to Carter was Massachusetts Senator Edward M. (Ted) Kennedy. Kennedy's popularity and standing in Mexican-American communities well surpassed that of any major national political figure of the day, owing largely to the legacies of his tragically assassinated older brothers, John and Robert Kennedy.

Many Mexican-American families, regardless of their political bent, loved the Kennedys. Like so many other working-class ethnic groups, Mexican Americans had been captivated by the charm, presence, Catholicism, youth, vigor, energy, and hope that John F. Kennedy projected in his bid for the presidency. The depth of affection for Kennedy among Mexican Americans was especially profound. The mythical Irish-American poll reached such immense status during and after his presidency that his portrait was often hung side-by-side in barrio homes with pictures or statuettes of Our Lady of Guadalupe, a sign of ultimate penetration into the hearts of Mexican-origin families.

Mexican Americans became especially endeared to the man and his family when Kennedy favorably mentioned Mexican Americans during his heavily contested presidential debates with Richard Nixon. This marked the first time that any significant national candidate had ever mentioned, let alone noticed, this long-forgotten minority group. Hundreds of Mexican-American political novices received their campaign baptisms through so-called Viva Kennedy clubs that were organized across the Southwest to advance JFK's presidential prospects. These clubs not only introduced national politics to many Mexican Americans, but, in the end, they also played an important role in the tight Texas race where Kennedy sneaked by Nixon to secure the presidency. These clubs showed the Kennedys and other leading white political insiders (both Democrat and Republican) that Mexican Americans could be a crucial swing vote.

The Kennedy mystique was accordingly etched in the memories of multitudes of Mexican Americans. They recalled JFK stumping on the campaign trail and smiling easily during the presidential debates. San Antonians remembered the president's visit there the day before he was assassinated. The dapper president joked, laughed, and connected effortlessly with the people he encountered that day, both Anglo and Mexican American. The elegant First Lady spoke briefly in Spanish to demonstrate respect for the language and traditions of the city's heavily Mexican Westside. The president's assassination in Dallas left a deep hole in the souls of Mexican Americans across the nation, an emptiness they shared with the rest of the country and the world.

After JFK's tragic death, the Kennedy aura continued with his younger brother, Bobby. He also had the distinctive Kennedy style: the handsome boyish looks, the charisma, the drive, and the compassion. RFK brought additional (and especially younger) Mexican Americans into the Kennedy fan club. He supported César Chávez and the migrant farmworkers, breaking bread with the union leader to end a highly publicized fast intended to underscore the plight of farmworkers seeking collective bargaining rights. He also sent uplifting messages of support to Chicano marchers in the tiny Texas town of Del Rio when they were fighting to keep VISTA workers in the town's Mexican-American neighborhoods against the wishes of reactionary local Anglo officials. But, like his older brother, Robert Kennedy was gunned down in his prime by an assassin during a presidential campaign swing in the West. Mexican Americans again mourned along with the nation and the world at the senseless killing of yet another leading member of the Kennedy family.

Now, more than ten years later, still another Kennedy, Ted, was preparing to run for president. Ted Kennedy did not command the same spellbinding adoration and awe that his felled older brothers had possessed, but he was still a Kennedy. The prospect of the Massachusetts senator effectively challenging the increasingly unpopular President Carter produced a groundswell of dormant Kennedy enthusiasts on the political left—true believers who felt that Carter's relative conservatism and failing policy initiatives were dooming the Democratic Party to national rejection and a shameful retreat from its established traditions.

Velásquez was one of those believers. "Can you imagine what Chicanos could do under Kennedy?" Willie would ask his friends, beaming with thoughts of all that might be possible with another Kennedy in the Oval Office. He had fallen under the spell of the Kennedys back when he was a teenager and President Kennedy had challenged Americans to serve the nation. He became a full-blown devotee after Bobby Kennedy joined the farmworkers movement just as Willie himself was coming into his own as a community activist. And now, with another Kennedy making a bid for the presidency, Velásquez prepared himself to become an active backer.

But the idea of actually leaving SVREP and taking an official campaign position was something Willie had never considered until UAW official Henry Santiestevan privately suggested the possibility. Caught off guard by the proposition, yet intrigued by the potential, Velásquez agreed to quietly pursue the options. Throughout the process, however, Willie remained ambivalent.

Part of him flew to Washington, D.C. to begin negotiations with the Kennedy camp, but a big part of him never left San Antonio and SVREP. In private, Santiestevan and Velásquez met with a couple of Kennedy aides to offer Willie's services in return for a prominent role in the senator's presidential campaign. The Kennedy staffers were pleasantly surprised and intrigued by the offer. They liked Willie's style and expertise and could certainly use his talents and contacts in crucial states such as Texas and California. They agreed to meet again and discuss more fully the range of possibilities. Willie was cautiously optimistic.

Back in Texas, Willie continued to have major doubts about signing up with the Kennedy campaign, but he calmly persisted in taking the steps necessary to prepare SVREP for his potential departure. His most important task was finding someone to lead SVREP in his absence. Willie reached out to two fellow Chicano activists who had gone through the politically charged times of the 1960s and 1970s with him, although not always on the best of terms—community organizer Ernesto "Ernie" Cortés and La Raza Unida Party founder José Angel Gutiérrez.[1] By offering SVREP's top spot to each of them, Willie surprised both men and showed them that the political differences they had with Velásquez were greatly outweighed by the high esteem and respect he had for them.

SVREP's fragile and tax-exempt status, however, quickly stifled Willie's brief flirtation with the Kennedy campaign. After five years of struggle and sacrifice building the organization's base throughout the Southwest, the last thing Velásquez wanted, upon reflection, was to jeopardize SVREP's progress by leaving it prematurely, and possibly to someone unable to ensure its forward movement. At the same time, Willie could not simply remain at SVREP and become engaged as an active Kennedy campaign official. Under federal tax law, neither SVREP as an organization nor Willie as its chief executive could legally be involved in partisan political activity without jeopardizing the project's tax-exempt status, upon which the organization's entire private fund-raising eligibility rested. Given all these considerations, in the end Willie did not have a choice: A public role supporting the Kennedy camp was completely out of the picture. Velásquez would have to settle for supporting Senator Kennedy's presidential bid indirectly and quietly on the sidelines as an informal advisor and resource. In the main, his attention and focus would have to remain with SVREP's continuing developmental needs.

ஸ்ஸ்ஸ்

---

[1]As fate would have it, neither Cortés nor Gutiérrez agreed to replace Velásquez at SVREP when Willie approached them in separate conversations on the possibility, though they were both flattered and intrigued by the offer.

Willie's decision to remain at SVREP was a necessary relief for the organization. With the project's rapid expansion in recent years, and funding always elusive, SVREP was suddenly facing its most challenging period to date. Its evolving work and effectiveness had generated enormous demands across the Southwest by this time, in literally hundreds of communities. Yet, owing to the vagaries and uneven schedules upon which the project's core foundation funding sources made their grants to SVREP, there was simply not enough funding in hand to meet all the organization's commitments. The project desperately required Willie's leadership and his established credibility to weather the storm.

Velásquez responded with a solution that had the short-term benefit of keeping SVREP's work alive, but the longer-term impact of compromising the project's fiscal integrity: borrowing. Willie was so adamant about supporting the growing demands and needs of local coalitions that he began to take out small loans to cover their drives rather than make them wait until SVREP's next round of funding was secured, which was often after the current election cycle. Velásquez saw each of these local registration campaigns as historical opportunities existing only for a particular moment in time. If SVREP did not fund them straightaway and engage them precisely when local leaders said their communities were primed for action, SVREP—and Hispanic and other minority Americans everywhere—would lose that precious instant forever. From Willie's perspective, accordingly, SVREP's impending fieldwork was infinitely more important than any temporary lull in its financial wherewithal. Not surprisingly, SVREP's creditors and funders would come to see it differently in time.

In addition to Willie's community-driven passions and his associated fiscal rationalizations, there can be no doubt that SVREP's growing financial burden was fundamentally linked to the cumbersome requirements and scattered cycles of foundation grant-makers. Like all nonprofit voter registration groups, SVREP was almost exclusively dependent on private foundations for financial support and was thus at their mercy when it came to grant approvals and payments. At one extreme, there was a certain predictability to the madness. Velásquez knew that, in general, foundations interested in political participation were most likely to make their largest grants in years leading up to presidential elections. Midterm elections generally received the next highest allocations and off-year races usually garnered the smallest awards. While each foundation had its own agenda, this essential arrangement reflected a consensus belief—based on common logic—that it made sense to concentrate money in voter registration and education campaigns associated with national elections, especially presidential contests, because heightened media exposure and overall interest levels would combine to touch a larger segment of the population.

The unpredictability of this pattern was the constantly changing levels of resources the foundations made available to the field for each election cycle. Here there appeared to be little rhyme or reason. Foundation giving might change from one campaign to the next based not only on the type of elections SVREP was targeting, but also on highly variable factors, such as the status of recent foundation market investments or the political persuasion of foundation trustees and senior staff. The net effect of having to organize around so many unpredictable factors was that SVREP could never definitively plan for the future. In some ways, this suited Velásquez's freewheeling management style, but it also led to persistent uncertainty. The problem was amplified by the often shifting interests of foundation program officers.

Velásquez's experiences with the foundation world had taught him that program staff were inordinately faddish and dominated by an East Coast mentality. The foundations had short-term attention spans, Willie believed. They seemed always to be in search of popular new issues and causes, rather than consolidated investment approaches designed to inform lasting changes over a longer period of time. It reminded Velásquez of many of the politicians he had come to know over the years, whose philosophies ebbed and flowed according to the latest public opinion polls. One never knew how long an issue would remain fresh and interesting to the foundations. One day voter registration might be the "in" thing, the next moment it could be considered passé. What bothered Willie most was that there was not much he could do to counter this reality. In his mind, it was *The New York Times*, *Time* magazine, the television networks, think tanks, federal government agencies, Ivy League schools, and other centers of influence, all based solidly in the East, that fed the foundations fresh topics and anointed the issues and groups that should be considered most relevant. The worldview of these institutions inherently focused the funders on problems and groups along the nation's East Coast. Being locked away in San Antonio, Texas, was, for Velásquez, similar to being banished from the kingdom of gold.

Some nonprofit social justice organizations learned quickly to adapt their objectives to those being pursued by the various foundations at any given time. Their resulting chameleon like behavior positioned them strategically to seek support to address the latest foundation craze, whatever it might be. Willie despised this approach and had long vowed that he would never allow Anglo easterners, no matter how well intentioned, to dictate SVREP's agenda. But the project's growing financial pressures and the sheer reality of its reliance on foundation funding would now challenge his ability to take a hard line in this connection.

In late 1979, Velásquez warned SVREP board members and their supporting institutions that the project was in serious financial trouble. "This fiscal year has been the most difficult we have had since the project began," he reported, adding, "A great number of requests (for drives) have come in . . . and people confidently expect us to be able to help. . . . Had it not been for our reserve of $30,000 carried over from last year, we would not [presently be] able to operate." With just half a year left in its fiscal cycle, SVREP was projecting a budget shortfall of nearly $120,000 and was considering cutting its fieldwork roughly in half, from 125 campaigns to only 69.

Many SVREP contributors did not think the project's situation was as desperate as portrayed by Velásquez. The colossal deficits Willie was reporting were still merely hypothetical shortages. SVREP had not accumulated any actual debt from previous years and timely budgetary adjustments were a logical response to the problem. In fact, much of the shortfall stemmed from the fact that Willie had dramatically increased SVREP's operating budget from around $250,000 in 1978–1979 to over $430,000 for 1979–1980 in anticipation of foundation funders pouring massive amounts of new resources into the 1980 presidential election. Hoping for the best, Velásquez had designed a plan that greatly expanded SVREP's registration and education projects, accordingly. Unfortunately, Willie substantially miscalculated foundation enthusiasm to support voter promotion activities in conjunction with the 1980 elections. Rather than deepened concern and interest in supporting a massive voter registration and education blitz across the Southwest, philanthropic leaders demonstrated a fairly lackadaisical approach to support organizing related to the upcoming national elections. The net effect was substantially less funding availability than Willie had banked on.

Velásquez understood that SVREP's proposed budget for 1979–1980 was ambitious, but he also knew the project could handle its proposed expansion and that Mexican-American communities throughout the Southwest would expect it to. In its first years, SVREP's low profile meant that very few communities asked for its help and SVREP was accordingly able to meet virtually all of the requests that it received. Now, at the beginning of 1980, even with its continuing limited media exposure, SVREP had to turn down many prospective campaigns because it simply lacked the resources to accommodate the demand for its work. With new resources and new staff, however, Willie was confident that SVREP could effectively take its work to a needed next level of scale. What upset him most was the timing of the foundations' inclination to step back from the 1980 campaign. SVREP had received only slightly more funding by the midpoint of its 1980 fiscal year than it had at the same time the prior year, an election off-year and historically a low point in foundation funding cycles for voter registration work. The swelling sentiment for activism and change in barrios across the Southwest was being lost, Velásquez lamented. Instead, he and SVREP were becoming increasingly mired in fiscal deliberations and woes related to a now growing deficit. Reporting to his board and benefactors in January 1980, Willie wrote: "Our anticipated deficit has increased by $56,000 in the last month. The total [annu-al] shortfall now projected will be $179,669.08. As a result . . . all SVREP field operations may have to end soon. No registration drives will be organized after March 15th if we cannot resolve our funding shortfall." Velásquez and SVREP were now at the end of the line, as they saw it. Absent several significant interventions by funders, they would have to prepare for the worst.

One month later, at the end of February, SVREP had miraculously scraped by again, avoiding disaster by receiving $41,000 from the North Shore Unitarian Society and $5,000 from the United Steelworkers. These grants allowed SVREP to support all twenty-nine of its ongoing projects at full funding levels, as well as several additional sites that had received organizing and training assistance but were still awaiting mini-grants. Willie was ecstatic that SVREP had been lifted out of the financial graveyard by these awards. Though the project still faced a projected deficit of $145,000, even after receiving the Unitarians' and the Steelworkers' support, he realized that, if needed, he could easily dispose of the remaining shortfall with modest cutbacks and some innovative accounting techniques. The important thing for the moment was that the project could now forge ahead assured that it could honor in full its current, outstanding community commitments. Responding to the need for additional budget adjustments to make up the remaining shortfall, Willie slashed SVREP's budget by almost $85,000 at the end of March, transforming the deficit from a six-digit figure to a mere $18,500. In the next few months, he cut additional projected expenses and SVREP drew closer to eliminating its projected over-expenditure. By the end of the 1980 fiscal year, SVREP had managed to raise over $310,000, which was over $120,000 less than it had originally projected and only $56,000 more than it raised the previous year. The conventional notion of there generally being more money available in presidential election years proved to be true, but nowhere near Velásquez's hopes and expectations. At the end of the day, SVREP reported its first ever deficit—$8,500; but to Willie's great satisfaction, the organization managed to avoid financial ruin, while it expanded its work and investments in the field. All told, SVREP allocated more than $90,000 in community grants and technical assistance during 1980 and organized 121 campaigns—only four short of what the project had planned under its original, much larger budget. While many of the additional campaigns the project supported did not receive the funding they had hoped for from SVREP, and while resources were inadequate to run drives in all of the areas project staff had originally targeted, 1980 marked the first time that SVREP had completed more than one hundred drives in a twelve-month period. Velásquez was particularly proud of this achievement.

Regrettably, SVREP's favorable change in fortune during the final stretch of the 1980 campaign helped Willie further to rationalize his dangerous practice of "funding" registration drives when there was absolutely no money in the bank. The last minute bailout and accounting maneuvers that enabled SVREP to avoid disaster in 1980 fueled a false sense of confidence in Willie that he could continue to play with fire. Velásquez now began to commit funding to local campaigns even when SVREP's bank accounts were bone dry. He did this because he fiercely believed that somehow, somewhere, someway, he would eventually secure funding sufficient to cover these commitments. The mission of SVREP and the needs of local communities requiring the project's guidance and support meant much more to Willie than any textbook lesson in fiscal responsibility. These were SVREP's entire reasons for existing, as Velásquez saw it. Little did he realize at the time, though, that the project's growing practice of smoke-and-mirrors financing would ultimately have grave consequences for the organization's and his own personal health and well-being.

∽ ∽ ∽

In the midst of SVREP's 1980 financial crisis, Willie turned to another questionable coping mechanism to manage the stress of the situation. He created another external enemy to build his days around—just as he had positioned Congressman González, the IRS, and the Carter administration as enemies in the past, in order to explain away difficulties that he confronted in his work. This time, he sought out a second round of challenges targeted to another past enemy: organized labor. Following up on his earlier critiques initiated during the project's formative years, Velásquez now attacked a large portion of the labor movement, accusing the unions again of irresponsibility for not helping to advance SVREP's mission with more generous contributions. By revisiting his anger toward the trade unionist movement, Willie created a tangible nemesis that he could publicly blame for SVREP's financial predicament. His monthly financial reports to board members and supporting institutions now featured "The American Labor Movement" as a highlighted potential funding source with the biting figure of zero dollars sarcastically placed next to its name.

Willie's renewed attack on organized labor pitted SVREP against prominent national Latino union officials, including especially Hank Lacayo, the Community Action Program (CAP) director of the United Auto Workers union and a strong supporter of the Labor Council for Latin American Advancement (LCLAA)—the labor organization that Willie most ardently contested in prior years for not supporting SVREP's work. The earlier problems Velásquez faced with Paul Montemayor, LCLAA's first executive director, did not vanish when the aging Montemayor retired from the LCLAA in the spring of 1977 because of illness. LCLAA was now a more established association and was receiving larger amounts of funding from mainstream labor sources to support Latino community organizing and empowerment efforts. SVREP, however, was still not seeing a drop of LCLAA money and this continued to infuriate Velásquez.

For someone who had grown up in a working-class neighborhood, buoyed by early exposure to trade unionists and later direct labor organizing experience, Willie, as SVREP boss, showed remarkably little sympathy to labor when it came to his problems raising money from the unions and working with the LCLAA. Instead of dealing with things the way they were, Velásquez's passion and idealism pushed him to operate from the reference point of how he felt things ought to be. SVREP's work was so important for Latinos, Willie believed, that labor, especially Latino workers, should wholeheartedly support it. Willie felt he could successfully preach this message to labor leaders because his constituency was grassroots Latino voters and their families, and most of them were working class.

Latino labor leaders were unsympathetic to Willie's position because they felt he was masking SVREP's self-interest behind the facade of a mythical pro-labor constituency. In their view, when SVREP sought labor funding, it was asking for SVREP, not for the Latino population. Bill Dodds, a political operative with the United Auto Workers (UAW), saw Willie's problem in obtaining labor support as a result of the different attitudes and objectives the two groups pursued. "Some of these guys (labor leaders) are very hard nose counters," Dodds would later explain. "They felt that while you could get a fair degree of votes from the Hispanics, [in fact] the black minority [probably] gave a far [higher] percentage [to the] Democratic [candidates labor leaders wanted to win] than did the Hispanics." According to Dodds, therefore, "it was just a [straightforward] mathematical calculation. Willie was trying to build a movement. Labor was trying to win elections."

During 1980, Willie channeled his significant consternation with Latino labor leaders into a highly personalized contest against Hank Lacayo, one of the most powerful Hispanic labor executives in the country. Lacayo was a traditionalist who had worked his way up the ladder to head the UAW's political division, CAP. Soon he would assume the presidency of the LCLAA, Willie's longtime labor community nemesis. Lacayo was a realist, a bottom-line politico who understood and thrived in the behind-the-scenes horse-trading that informed decision making in Democratic Party politics. By his own admission, he was flamboyant and suffered from a sensitive ego. In his earlier years as a steward, Lacayo developed a reputation for being a maverick. Many over the subsequent years came to characterize him as arrogant and impatient. His impatience sometimes got him into trouble, but it never killed him because his strong street sense always pulled him through. Ultimately, Lacayo came to be known as someone who simply had to be reckoned with.

Many people resented Lacayo and some hated him with a passion, but most believed that in a crunch he would produce, he would deliver for you. The union leader had produced important though relatively modest grants for SVREP in the $10,000 range during 1977 and 1978, but Velásquez nevertheless felt slighted. He was convinced that Lacayo could and should do more to assist the project. He was also embittered by the fact that Lacayo was visibly unimpressed by SVREP's work and disinclined to make its business a priority. In recent years, numerous calls placed by Willie and his staff to Lacayo's office—for consideration to gain in-kind access to union computer programs, expanded organizational support, or introductions to other important labor contacts—had fallen on deaf ears. Lacayo often simply did not respond or was considerably delayed in his reply. This outraged Velásquez, who interpreted Lacayo's approach as a personal affront.

By the beginning of 1979, Velásquez was at the end of his rope with Lacayo. At a meeting in San Antonio, Willie told SVREP's executive committee about his inability to reach the UAW leader, saying that he no longer wanted to spend valuable time trying to get him on the phone. Maclovio Barraza reassured his protégé that Lacayo would help SVREP, encouraging and advising him to reach out to the labor official one more time.

Velásquez waited another nine months before reinitiating contact with Lacayo. But his communiqué was anything but friendly. In a short, curt letter Willie informed Lacayo that he regretted the UAW was not able to help SVREP with computer time nor its needed additional support for efforts such as the project's Texas redistricting work. Velásquez then lamented the UAW official's failure to respond to SVREP communications, reporting pointedly, "My notes from June 30, 1978 show that in the previous year we had called seventeen straight times without a return call from you. This not only attests to your busy schedule, but also gives you the distinction of being the only person in the country who does not return my calls."

Lacayo did not take kindly to Willie's words because he felt he had helped SVREP as much as he could. He responded in writing a few days later, reminding Velásquez: "It is a matter of record that the UAW is among the very few labor unions that have chosen to work with your organization, and I would like to take full credit for making that possible." Lacayo went on to accuse Willie of never sending him enough information to process SVREP's earlier requests for access to union computers. He then challenged Willie's accusations about the number of calls placed to him recently, asserting that, according to his own very accurate records, Velásquez had only called him six times during 1977 and 1978. Lacayo closed by saying, "I do not mean to engage in a letter writing contest with you, but I do think the record should be set straight; because, as you know, I do not deal in personalities. . . . I trust the foregoing will lay to rest personal vituperations."

Lacayo's response to Willie did anything but end the unfriendly and increasingly petty exchange between the two men. Velásquez, now fuming over Lacayo's letter, sat down and immediately ripped off a reply, telling Lacayo among other things that he was amazed at the labor leader's characterization of SVREP's 1975–1976 computer request as inadequate. Willie went on to challenge Lacayo in the most direct terms possible, taking their contest to an undeniably personal level, writing, "It would be a miscalculation on your part to interpret our courtesy and deference to you in the past as a sign of weakness or obeisance. We extend that courtesy to everyone, regardless of station. Nonetheless, no one has permission to take liberties with our sensibilities, the quality of our work or the veracity of our statements, including yourself. I am not in the habit of receiving letters like the one you [just sent me], so I am sending it back to you. I do not expect any similar correspondence in the future."

Willie decided to approach Bill Dodds, another UAW executive, and as it turned out, ironically, not a fan of Hank Lacayo's, to see if he could possibly help SVREP to maneuver around Lacayo for union financial support. At their initial meeting, Willie hit Dodds with his standard East Coast pitch, telling him about the necessity and historical importance of SVREP's work, rattling off numbers and statistics about the Latino electorate, and emphasizing the deep grassroots nature of SVREP's campaigns. Dodds was impressed with Velásquez's presentation, but his past experiences with other promising groups that turned out to disappoint in the end put a check on his enthusiasm. Several times in the past, Dodds had fallen prey to the skillful, articulate, mesmerizing tactics of organizers without organizations. Since then, he had learned to be skeptical of every new group's claims until he actually saw its work in action. SVREP was no exception. Before he committed himself to do anything for Velásquez, Dodds wanted to see SVREP's work for himself.

Dodds had spent a year in the Air Force some years back stationed in Wichita Falls and San Antonio and was therefore curious to see how SVREP was dealing with the Texas he had known. He came to SVREP's headquarters and was relieved to see Willie in his natural setting rather than on automatic pilot, reciting his polished presentation for potential funders. Dodds visited with Velásquez and the SVREP staff and watched Willie operate in his daily element. After the workday closed, Velásquez, Dodds, and several SVREP staffers retired to SVREP's second office, The Esquire bar, for beers, business, and bonding. Dodds loved it. It gave him the perfect chance to catch a glimpse of the unofficial Velásquez, the relaxed Willie who talked about ideas, books, movies, history, women, and of course, politics. By the end of the evening Velásquez and Dodds were acting like long time friends, drinking, laughing, and plotting strategies through which SVREP could crack labor's reluctance to fund it.

Dodds returned to Washington committed to helping Willie and SVREP to gain more generous and less onerous UAW support. In a confidential memo to his boss, UAW President Douglas Fraser, Dodds wrote: "I don't think I've been so excited and impressed by anyone or anything since the early civil rights days as I was by Brother Velásquez and his absolutely first rate staff. While I know he and Hank Lacayo have had sort of an up-and-down relationship, the fact that they've received thousands of dollars from various groups but not one damned penny from the labor movement concerns me deeply." Dodds later met with Fraser privately to discuss helping SVREP and Fraser agreed to meet with Velásquez. Dodds quickly told Willie and the SVREP crew about this breakthrough but warned them to not let anyone know about it because if Lacayo found out, SVREP would have a much more difficult time securing additional UAW support. A month later, ironically, SVREP received a $5,000 general support contribution from Lacayo's CAP fund.

Dodds had warned Velásquez all along the way to pretend they had not become friends if Willie wanted to make any headway with Lacayo; but word soon spread of their alliance. Once Lacayo found out that Velásquez was trying to circumvent him by going through Dodds, he became outraged and vowed to shut out SVREP even more in the future than he had in the past. There was no love lost between Lacayo and Dodds. In fact, the two men disliked one another considerably. Lacayo believed that Dodds had both tried to stop him from gaining his post as National CAP Director, as well as bad-mouthed him in conversation with Lacayo's prior boss, Leonard Woodcock, during the Carter campaign. He saw Dodds as nothing more than a limousine liberal who gave lip service to progressive groups and leaders, but did not really have the juice or the intention to deliver anything to them. In an interview during the early 1990s, Lacayo described his assessment of Dodds in the following pejorative terms: "Dodds made mile wide statements with half-inch commitments." Even prior to the brewing contest involving SVREP, Lacayo, who was especially dangerous when he combined his anger with righteousness, had alerted Dodds that he was "going to get him" because there was not room enough at the UAW for the both of them. Dodds, for his part, saw Lacayo as nothing more than a flashy boss man who liked to throw money and his clout around. Dodds also disliked Lacayo's more conservative bent politically and his consequent tendency to distance himself from more grassroots groups and causes, like SVREP.

With Willie and SVREP now even more neutralized with Dodds' intervention than they had been prior, and no end in sight to the stalemate between Lacayo and Velásquez, Arnold Flores decided to act as peacemaker in the growing dispute. Flores was the perfect person for this role. He was Velásquez's dearest friend and he had become close to Lacayo through his work in the Carter administration as an assistant to former SVREP board-

member-turned-INS-commissioner, Leonel Castillo. Knowing both characters well, Flores surmised that the only way to work out their differences
would be to compel the two gladiators put down their weapons and talk. Flores negotiated diligently to arrange a meeting for that purpose, and Velásquez
and Lacayo begrudgingly agreed to work toward a truce.

In the process, Flores pushed to create a tangible manifestation of the
two adversaries' newfound understanding. Behind the scenes, in conversations with SVREP Board Chairman Maclovio Barraza, Flores suggested that
SVREP offer Lacayo a peace offering in the form of a seat on the project's
board. Barraza approved of the idea, agreeing with Flores's estimation that,
properly mined, Lacayo's impressive contacts could be turned into large
favors and funding for SVREP. Notwithstanding progress toward healing the
old wounds with Lacayo, Velásquez's response to Flores's proposal was predictably negative; he blew up. "Bullshit! I don't want that son of a bitch on
my board!" Willie replied.

Eventually, Flores, Barraza, and even Bill Dodds were able to persuade
Velásquez to temper and rethink his objections. With time, Willie gained
greater comfort with the idea of organized labor having a stronger institutional stake in SVREP's work by virtue of having someone like Lacayo on
the project board. Lacayo showed his commitment to advocate more strongly for SVREP by contributing still another $5,000 from the UAW shortly
after he was elected president of LCLAA. Velásquez and SVREP reciprocat-
ed this gesture by honoring Lacayo and all the LCLAA national officers at a
public reception in San Antonio. A few weeks after the event, Willie formally nominated Hank Lacayo to serve on SVREP's board of directors and
Lacayo accepted.

As time passed, Velásquez and Lacayo realized they were more alike than
they were different. Although their Mexican-American *machismo* prevented
them at all costs from apologizing for their past sins against one another, they
found ways through indirect dialogue and humor to gain mutual respect and
understanding. Willie drew heavily on his well-developed sense of irony to
tease Lacayo while acknowledging the union leader's formidable character.
"Hank, I've been throwing everything at you and you're still standing," Willie
would lament in jest. "Goddamn man, don't you have any sense? Don't you
know you were supposed to fall down?" Lacayo would respond in kind:
"Willie, I've done the same thing to you. I've slammed a lot of doors in your
face." Years later, Lacayo would aptly characterize the two men's delicate relationship, commenting with a mile-wide grin: "Willie and I treated each other
like two porcupines making love; we were very careful with one another!"

Velásquez's second major battle with Latino labor and one of its top
leaders had come to an end. Advisors close to Velásquez, especially Flores,
had convinced him to place practicality on an even level with his well-formed

but often stubborn principles. The result was greater support from the UAW and organized labor at a critical juncture in SVREP's evolution. This was a welcome development that positioned the project to enter the 1980s from a position of relative strength—or at least one much more likely to prove sustainable than the track Willie and the organization had been on earlier.

〜〜〜〜〜〜

The past year and a half had been the most stressful Velásquez had experienced at SVREP. The burgeoning problem of bringing racial gerrymandering suits with MALDEF in the rural counties of Texas and SVREP's lack of resources to balance them all was weighing heavily on Willie's mind. The failed coalition effort with the African American Voter Education Project had left a strong taste of disappointment in Willie's mouth. The outburst directed at Hamilton Jordan and the Carter administration's town hall meetings debacle still riled Velásquez to the core. Finally, barely surviving SVREP's most severe financial crisis to date and another round of battle with organized labor left Willie praying for some sort of fundamental reprieve. Through all of this, Willie had been pushed closer to the edge than ever before at any time in his professional life. By any system of accounting, the final years of the 1970s had been extremely taxing for Velásquez and his organization.

But all of that was quickly fading from memory now. By the close of 1980, SVREP was back on top. Financial ruin had been avoided. The Lacayo and labor difficulties were being worked out. The litigation victories in Texas, though hard-fought and consuming, continued to roll on without major setbacks. SVREP completed its largest number of campaigns ever in one fiscal year, organizing 121 successful registration drives across the Southwest. Suddenly, miraculously, everything Willie had been working and sacrificing and hoping for was beginning to take shape. SVREP was now evolving into a highly effective and respected organization whose work was poised to change the face of American politics and history.

Early picture of Willie ("Billy") with his mother, Mary Louise Velásquez. (Photo courtesy of the Mary Louise Velásquez Collection)

Willie with wife, Jane, his brothers George, Ralph, and David, and his sister Stella. (Photo courtesy of the Velásquez Family Collection)

Willie with wife, Jane, and their children, Carmen, Catarina, and Guillermo. (Photo courtesy of the Velásquez Family Collection)

Willie with SVREP staffer Hilbert Ocañas before a Southwest Voter poster. (Photo courtesy of the Southwest Voter Registration Education Project)

Willie (second from left) with Southwest Voter Research Institute Central American delegation. (Photo courtesy of the Southwest Voter Registration Education Project)

Willie (third from left) participating in a Southwest Voter litigation press conference in Texas. (Photo courtesy of the Southwest Voter Registration Education Project)

Willie at SVREP press conference with then San Antonio mayor, Henry G. Cisneros, seated to his left. (Photo courtesy of the Southwest Voter Registration Education Project)

Willie speaking at SVREP press conference in Los Angeles. (Photo courtesy of the Southwest Voter Registration Education Project)

Willie in SVREP staff portrait shortly after discovering he had cancer. (Photo courtesy of the Southwest Voter Registration Education Project)

Willie (second from left) with United Farmworkers' leader César Chávez and other Latino labor leaders. (Courtesy Labor Council for Latin American Advancement Collection)

Willie applauding Vice President George Bush at kick-off of National Hispanic Voter Registration Campaign. (Photo courtesy of the Southwest Voter Registration Education Project)

Willie (standing, second from left) with African-American and Latino labor leaders. (Photo courtesy of Henry Santiestevan Collection)

Chapter 14

JUST AS SVREP WAS OVERCOMING its most serious organizational challenges to date, Maclovio "Mac" Barraza, Willie's anchor and the project's founding chairman, died of a heart attack during labor negotiations with the Magma Copper Company in Phoenix, Arizona. He was only fifty-three years old. He began working in a copper smelter at the age of fourteen, became an underground copper miner at sixteen, left for a short stint with the army at age eighteen during World War II, and then returned to the copper pits and started a stellar labor career that would last for three decades. Mac had recently decided to slow down and had purchased a home in Magdalena, Sonora, in the north of Mexico where he and his family could rest. For the past thirty years, Chicano and labor causes came first, his family second. But he would never get the chance to make it up to his family for neglecting them. Barraza's passing cast a net of despondency over the Chicano and labor communities of the Southwest. With his passing, one of the nation's most unsung but important Hispanic community leaders was gone.

For Willie, the Arizona union leader's death was devastating. Barraza was Velásquez's hero. He was the father figure Willie never had growing up. Willie revered the elder Barraza for his great common sense and wonderful negotiating skills. He always saw the felled labor negotiator as being bold and courageous enough to take risks when they were necessary to achieve a larger goal. He learned how to navigate the political party world from Mac, a staunch Democrat who hated Republicans, had problems with La Raza Unida Party members who sought a separatist path, and deeply believed in working within the two-party system. Willie respected Barraza's willingness and desire to mentor young activists, like himself. These were the things that Velásquez especially appreciated about the man and tried to emulate in his own life.

In memorial services and private gatherings across the Southwest, Barraza's passing was noted by those he left behind and especially those leaders with whom he worked most closely to advance social change. The leading Hispanic foundation advisor and founder of the National Council of La Raza, Herman Gallegos remembered Barraza mixing hard work and play seamlessly, belting out Mexican *corridos* in different cantinas in the region following long hours of intense community politicking, his energy contagious, his presence inspiring. Armando de León, a fellow Arizonan and Barraza protégé, recalled Mac as a man of great principle and integrity, who preferred to work one-on-one or in small group settings on behalf of the poor and needy. All who remembered Barraza acknowledged plainly that his passing left a huge void in the Chicano political landscape that could never be filled.

Willie and his wife Janie attended Mac's funeral in Tucson, Arizona, the longtime home of the Chicano labor activist. The packed church more closely resembled a Chicano activist reunion or a labor conference than it did a burial. Everyone from Willie's and Janie's political pasts had been drawn together again, if only for a short time, to say their final good-byes to Barraza, rekindle old ties, and recommit themselves to continuing the struggle ahead.

Velásquez exchanged solemn greetings with the various Mexican-American politicos and trade unionists who crammed into the pews of the church. The Catholic funeral mass filled him with recollections of his childhood religious training and the incipiency of his career as a social advocate. He remembered his early meetings and work with the deceased Barraza, and how the union leader had helped Willie to build his character and his professional capacities. He recollected Mac's dependability and his commitment to the cause. He recalled talking to Mac daily and never making a major decision for SVREP without Barraza's input guiding him; he suddenly felt very alone.

At the gravesite, the ferocious Arizona sun beat down upon the attending mourners. A band of mariachis played sad songs of life and death. A soft-spoken priest recited the final rites as dirt was sprinkled over Barraza's casket. Tears streaked down Willie's reddened face. His beloved mentor and friend was no more. Willie had no idea how he would go forward without Mac by his side. It was a future he had never pondered.

SVREP listlessly dragged itself through the balance of the 1980 presidential campaign. There were scattered local elections throughout the Southwest that inspired SVREP, but, unfortunately, an unexpected number of these races did not produce victories, leaving many Latino communities searching for answers. Part of the problem, to be sure, was Willie's and SVREP's low spirits in the aftermath of Mac Barraza's passing. But something even darker and more sinister seemed to be at work, too. In fact, during the 1980 national elections, Americans took a hard conscious turn to the political right. Much of the past decade's apparent concern about righting social wrongs, encouraging minority opportunities, and promoting an activist government was thrown overboard by voters. Now, the American electorate seemed to be moving in precisely the opposite direction. By electing the conservative former California governor, Ronald Reagan, to the presidency and sweeping Democrats out of control of the U.S. Senate for the first time in a generation, American voters rejected much of what SVREP stood for. Going forward, for the foreseeable future, American governance would be defined by substantial retrench-ments in civil rights, equal opportunity, and government social spending. These changes, in turn, would radically alter the landscape of public debate in America, turning policy discourse decidedly to the right after nearly twenty years of largely Democratic Party rule in the nation's capitol.

In this shifting political environment, SVREP suddenly became the tar-get of an increasingly reactionary Anglo press corps throughout the South-west. Especially among newspapers and radio stations located in small, rural areas where SVREP was running registration drives and initiating gerryman-dering lawsuits that were anathema to the ruling white elite of the region, Velásquez and SVREP were subjected to a barrage of attacks that character-ized them as anti-democratic, anti-freedom, anti-fair play, and most of all, anti-American. Having been on the political defensive for nearly a generation, the newly revived upholders of American conservatism were particularly zeal-ous in their efforts to attack their enemies, both real and perceived. In rural Texas, SVREP and its allies were high on these individuals' enemies lists.

In Mathis, Texas, SVREP's San Patricio County registration project was accused of "buying" an election because it directed $135 of SVREP funding to support its local, nonpartisan campaign work there. After winning anoth-er racial gerrymandering suit in the West Texas county of Crosby, moreover, local journalists responded to SVREP's triumph by dredging up as many negative associations as they possibly could muster. Crosbyton's newspaper editor, Jim Reynolds, reflected the conspiratorial, populist chord of the terri-tory, lamenting and belittling SVREP's efforts there on the grounds that "the federal judge who issued the order is paid by the federal government and the organizations which instigated the suit [including their attorneys], operated with a federal grant." Another West Texas paper, *The Ralls Banner*, invoked "big government" fears to malign SVREP and Federal District Judge Halbert Woodward, who presided over SVREP's successful voting rights challenge in that jurisdiction. In a comment to its readers, the paper alleged that the judge should be more accountable to local majority will, rather than outside agitators. The commentary closed by listing Woodward's address, his work and home phone numbers, and a series of statements and questions intended to suggest that SVREP and federal law enforcement officials were commu-nists or otherwise un-American.

Willie was enraged by the media negativity that the 1980 elections pro-duced concerning much of SVREP's work across the Southwest. Rather than ignore the press, as he had mostly tried to do in the past, Velásquez decided to address the project's critics head on in a series of selected responses. One person who Willie particularly targeted for response was Afton Richards, publisher of *The Ralls Banner*. Richards had recently written various articles and a letter to Velásquez denouncing SVREP's actions and calling its leaders and followers traitors to their country and their Catholic faith. In pointed correspondence, Willie went after Richards for implying that SVREP's work was communist-inspired. He told Richards about the outrage of Mexican-American veterans when the article was read to them because they were active participants in SVREP's so-called communist plot. Velásquez, personally insulted by Richard's veiled attacks on Mexican-American patriotism, then pointed out that Chicanos in the military had earned more Medals of Honor per capita than any other American ethnic group. "We've never had a turncoat," Willie reported to *The Ralls Banner* newspaperman, "yet your paper associates us with being part of a communist plot because we want to eliminate through the use of the courts the outrageous gerrymandering found in West Texas." Turning Richard's claims of Chicano un-Americanism on its head, Willie then observed, "How odd that we have not found one county [in the region where you reside] with lines drawn to the advantage of Mexican Americans." Velásquez went on to close by explaining to Richards the inevitability of SVREP's work, letting the anti-SVREP journalist know that there was nothing he could do to stop the historical sea change that was redefining political reality in the Southwest:

> As a newspaper owner you can print untruths about us, which you have; you can arouse one side of the community against the other and you can even make the faithful application of the Constitution of the United States of America appear to be a communist plot. You can do all that, but it will be to no avail because the basic decency of Americans will eventually win out. You will find that Christian leadership will sooner or later assert itself and say, "Yes, the Mexican American community has a point, maybe we ought to listen to them." This is inevitable and it is also inevitable that civic and some political leadership will also rise and ask questions about the equitable drawing of county commissioner lines. And the result of all this will be the application of true democratic principles and a democracy that is truly representative of its citizens.

What troubled Velásquez most about the rash of negative post-1980-election media coverage targeted to SVREP was its breadth. Willie had not seen as much anti-Hispanic sentiment and news coverage since the Raza Unida days of the late 1960s and early 1970s. Anglo leaders and institutions across the Southwest suddenly now appeared to be moving backwards in their acceptance of increased Mexican-American political participation and power sharing. Velásquez, like so many other progressive community leaders, was taken aback and caught off-guard by this unexpected shift in direction.

Intellectually, Willie understood that the situation called for a strong response from the left and grassroots minority anchor organizations like

SVREP, in particular. His proposed remedy was to work aggressively toward expanding Mexican-American community political skill and sophistication. Relying on the sheer force of Latino numbers in any given area would not suffice; there also had to be a more concerted attempt at creating a potent, progressive political leadership and following in Latino communities. This is where SVREP's focus and investment would rest increasingly in the aftermath of the 1980 presidential campaign. But, emotionally, Willie was reeling and poorly positioned to forge ahead. Now that Barraza could no longer be called upon to keep him focused, Velásquez felt lost. Confused, tired, striking out at his enemies at times, but not having enough energy to plough ahead, Willie became deeply discouraged. Movement toward a second-phase SVREP agenda to create a progressive political force in Latino communities of the region was consequently slow to take shape.

Willie's problems were amplified, ironically, by the ascendance of his best friend, Arnold Flores, to replace Barraza as SVREP board chairman. Almost instantly, Velásquez and Flores clashed in their new roles. Since Flores had returned to San Antonio after serving in the Carter administration, the two longtime buddies had sought to revive their close connection. But things had changed. Willie and Arnold were no longer free-spirited, heavy drinking, political enthusiasts who enjoyed spending more time together than they did with their wives and children. Time and distance had created a new and much less equal and carefree reality around them. Now, they were thrust into a completely new relationship, one in which years of teamwork, equality, and friendship were suddenly replaced by serious public responsibilities and an awkward hierarchy in which Flores was effectively overseeing Velásquez and SVREP. It was particularly hard for Willie to make the adjustments necessary to accommodate Flores's evolving role. He felt increasingly violated by Flores's inclination to review or second-guess SVREP's day-to-day management decisions, something his predecessor Barraza had never done. In retaliation, Willie began to withhold information from Flores that would ultimately appear on board dockets, much to the new chairman's surprise and chagrin. Within months, things reached the point where Velásquez and Flores rarely spent any time together that was not absolutely required. Their entire relationship became stilted and SVREP began to suffer from the fallout.

Velásquez's problems soon spread to his staff. The informing characteristics of SVREP's initial office culture—the feelings of SVREP being a small tight-knit family, the sense of unity and common purpose among staff and board members alike—were now slipping away. In their place, sadly, a factionalized, self-protective, and distrustful organizational reality was emerging. Part of the problem stemmed from staff uncertainty about how to manage the crumbling relationship between the former close friends, Velásquez and Flores. Aurora Sánchez, one of SVREP's original staff members, recalls particular problems emerging after Flores's elevation to the SVREP chairmanship when he began calling SVREP staff members to give them his own directives absent prior consultation with Velásquez. Staff, of course, accommodated his requests, also without consulting Willie, partly because Flores was now chairman, but more importantly because he was their friend. To SVREP workers, who had known the new board chair for many years, Flores was less a board official and more like an old buddy with whom they felt comfortable drinking beers and trading gossip after hours.

Because of their historically casual relationship with Flores, SVREP staff members were often likely to tell him when asked what had happened that day at the office and what Velásquez had done or said about different subjects. Typically, their reports were unthinking and somewhat naïve relative to Flores's shifting allegiance and proximity to Willie. When Velásquez refused at times to take Flores's calls, for example, staff would sometimes tell the new chairman that Willie was in the office but chose not to talk to him. Flores quickly perceived the benefits of his long-standing affiliation with the SVREP workers and tried as much as possible to use them to his advantage. He would convince SVREP staff members to tell him where Velásquez was at a given time or what he was doing. In the process, he began shrewdly to fill their heads with thoughts that chipped away at Willie's reputation and authority.

Velásquez hated this arrangement for obvious reasons. As former SVREP Executive Assistant Sánchez remembers it, "Willie wanted us to treat [Flores] as [a nosey] board member [saying,] 'you're not going to tell him anything unless I know about it.'" Willie began to reprimand staff members for blindly carrying out the new chairman's requests. He would frequently remind them that he was the executive director and that merely because Flores called and asked for something did not mean they were supposed to drop everything for him. Soon, they would first have to clear the chairman's requests with Velásquez before any follow-up action could be taken in response to Flores's directives.

Willie's problems at the staff management level deepened when he was forced to discipline Sánchez for her public endorsement of candidates in the San Antonio city elections during early 1981. In an unintended but clear violation of SVREP policy, Sánchez had allowed her name to be included as an official supporter of Henry G. Cisneros's historic mayoral bid and Alfonso Peeler's district one council race. When Velásquez learned of her endorsements, which were now part of the public record, he exploded. Trapping Sánchez behind closed doors in his office, Willie bombarded her with admonitions. His screaming and yelling reverberated through the entire office, "Goddamn it, Aurora, you should know better than this! . . . You have to straighten up! You never talked to me about this or ever gave me the courtesy of hinting you were going to do this. In fact this is a serious breach of the protocol we have developed in this office regarding activities of this sort by the staff." When the dressing down finally ended, Sánchez exited Velásquez's office in tears.

What disturbed Velásquez even more than Sánchez's endorsements—which gave SVREP's worst critics fodder to prove their claims that the project was merely a political machine, rather than a nonpartisan pro-democracy outfit—was the fact that, consciously or not, the SVREP staffer chose to go behind Willie's back in her political maneuvering. In Velásquez's paternalistic mind-set, this was another example of SVREP's endangered family culture. Instead of discussing her options in advance with the entire SVREP family—and seeking Willie's advice in particular—the wayward Sánchez had struck out on her own. From Velásquez's standpoint, she had become caught up in the rush of the moment without thinking through the full impact of her decision on the whole organization. For Velásquez, this revealed that SVREP was no longer an upstart organization whose progress was first and foremost tied to hard work and close ties. It had grown, matured, and was now beginning to lose important pieces of its innocence. Now, individual staff members were getting ahead of Willie, acting like free agents, and unwittingly putting SVREP at risk with the IRS and in the court of public opinion. To Willie, SVREP was still and always a family, but internal relationships were becoming painfully strained, distant, and problematic.

Barely a week and a half following the Sánchez reprimand, Willie had another antagonistic encounter with a staffer that further underscored the incipiency of an internal breakdown at SVREP. SVREP Research Director Choco Meza faced off with Velásquez in a showdown that resulted in her unexpected resignation. Meza had developed a close relationship with Velásquez over the almost three-and-a-half years she had been working with the project. During that time she had become more than an analytic investigator; in fact, she was now an obsessed advocate of SVREP's cause and a warm friend of Velásquez. Meza loved her job and devoted her complete energy to it, sometimes bordering on the extreme. On occasion, she would spend the entire evening at the SVREP office, working feverishly into the night, crashing for a few hours, and waking up frazzled, her clothes wrinkled, her eyes bloodshot red. Her deep commitment to SVREP's work was undeniable.

Over the years, Meza had demonstrated her loyalty to Willie and SVREP, in part, by mastering the art of covering up for her boss. Normally, she was guilty only of telling harmless half-truths on Velásquez's behalf, such as informing his wife, Janie, over the telephone that he was tied up in an office "meeting" when he was actually relishing a cold, late afternoon beer across the street at the Esquire bar with some political buddies. When this happened, Meza would rush over to the famed watering hole and remind Willie of some overlooked but important personal commitment—a baptismal practice, a school function, or perhaps an early dinner engagement.

During the early weeks of 1981, Willie and Meza hit a large wall in their otherwise friendly and mutually supportive relationship. The problem developed when Velásquez asked Pam Eoff, the soft-spoken SVREP communications director, to help him edit Meza's report on Latino voting in the 1980 presidential elections. Both Eoff and Velásquez took a red pen to Meza's writing without including her in the original editing process, a fairly standard procedure in developing publications for broad external distribution. When they finished making changes in the report, they presented them to Meza for review and correction. Meza vehemently disagreed with some of the proposed alterations and saw others as unnecessary. She incorporated several of the changes suggested by Velásquez and Eoff but omitted those that she felt were unwarranted. As far as Meza was concerned, her revised text constituted SVREP's final product.

Velásquez saw things in a different light. To him, the report was not finished. He ordered another session of editing by both Eoff and himself. Meza was outraged. Not only did she consider the additional edits unnecessary, but also she saw Willie's continuing lack of confidence in her product and judgment as professionally degrading. Much of the conflict resulted from a clash of personalities between Meza and Eoff. The strong-willed Meza had long harbored a dislike of Eoff, who she saw as nothing more than a stereotypically subordinate and passive female. Worst of all, from Meza's standpoint, Eoff was an Anglo. It seemed finally wrong to Meza that a white woman should be charged to chronicle the official record of Latino voting, which she herself, a Chicana, had tracked and analyzed. Thus, even with all of the non-Latina Eoff's well-established liberal values and credentials, it was hard for her counterpart Meza to swallow the fact that Willie had charged a *gringa* to polish her work.

Meza stormed into Willie's office and angrily confronted him about the situation. Velásquez's impatience and disinterest, however, were immediately obvious. The research director instantly caught herself and realized that she was wasting her time. Willie's lack of availability to listen to, let alone meaningfully address, Meza's concerns unleashed a deep well of latent resentment in the SVREP research director, which she could no longer contain. Now, enraged by Willie's lack of receptivity to her concerns, Meza unwittingly opened a door she had not intended to by half seriously suggesting that maybe it would be best for her to leave SVREP. Not in the mood to be bothered by Meza's flippant remark, Velásquez, without blinking an eye, responded, "Okay, then leave." The whole exchange took no more than a minute, but it was a minute that changed the entire course of things for Meza and SVREP.

Meza left Willie's office distraught. Tears flowed from her uncontrollably as she slowly came to grips with her unrehearsed, unplanned resignation. Her work at SVREP, the Chicano cause, these things were much more than just a means to a paycheck for Meza. They embodied her entire persona and purpose in life. They gave her reason, direction, and a sense of pride that were suddenly all subject to being undone. Meza was beside herself with hurt and confusion following the exchange with Willie.

SVREP lawyer Rolando Ríos and Field Director Bill Calderón tried to mediate the conflict by encouraging Velásquez to rethink Meza's departure, but Willie, ever stubborn, would not have it. Instead, with only the briefest of warnings, he rounded up the entire SVREP staff with the exception of Meza for a crucial, one-item staff meeting. When everyone settled into the SVREP conference room, Velásquez tersely announced that Meza had quit and that he had accepted her resignation. That was it, nothing else. No other topics. No question-and-answer period. No miscellaneous business. Just Choco's departure. Velásquez then abruptly dismissed the staff to continue with their preparations for an upcoming board meeting, which was convening in just two days.

After the initial shock of her fateful exchange with Willie subsided, Meza crafted an official letter of resignation for Velásquez. By the time she finally put down her pen, her letter had blossomed into a three-page critical review of the nearly four years she had worked at SVREP. "My resignation does not come forth because of this single incident," she wrote. "It is yet another one added to [many] that have occurred during my employment." She went on to accuse Velásquez of treating her in a disrespectful and condescending manner that he had never employed with male staffers, including ruthlessly yelling at her when he wanted to make a point. "You have done this in the presence of other staff members, friends, and even my own family," she asserted. Meza finally faulted Velásquez for being dictatorial with staff generally and for not appreciating the long hours she and other SVREP staffers had put in over the years in demonstration of their loyalty to Willie's and the project's goals. Once she felt comfortable with the wording, having read each sentence again and again, Meza handed the draft to her secretary to be typed and formally submitted to Velásquez.

But even prior to receiving Meza's letter, Willie had already decided to ask her to remain at SVREP. Prodded by some of his board members, including Chairman Arnold Flores, to reconsider the decision to part with Meza, and realizing that he had acted hastily, Velásquez strolled into his departing research director's office to seek her agreement to stay onboard. Meza was stunned by the gesture and moved to reconsider her departure on condition that Willie reinsert all the numbers and original analysis she had wanted included in the contested report Velásquez and Eoff had edited. Velásquez quickly agreed, if Meza in turn would immediately commit to stay with SVREP. Meza stalled, but quickly relented when Willie broke into a silly, childish series of pleas intended to convince her to stay: "Tell me to stop breathing. Tell me, count to fifty and I won't breathe. Just tell me you won't leave, Señora!" Velásquez had always affectionately called Meza "Señora" and now with Willie laughing, grinning, and acting like a kid, she could not resist the temptation to return to the job she had never really wanted to leave in the first place. Velásquez thanked her and suggested that she take a short two-week vacation.

Minutes after Willie left her office, Arnold Flores called Meza. The new SVREP chairman wanted to know if she had accepted Willie's offer to return to her job as the project's research director. She said yes, she had. Flores paused and then told her that she had made a mistake. He had been in the union business a long time and had seen this scenario play out a number of times. In four months, Flores solemnly predicted, Meza would be out of a job. Meza did not appreciate the eerie warning nor the chairman's involvement in the matter.

Flores's prediction proved to be remarkably accurate. Velásquez's and Meza's relationship never fully regained its previous closeness. Instead, Willie increasingly distanced himself from his old friend and worried in private about how she might be able to hurt him with all the information she had accumulated on him over the years. Indeed, Meza had learned a lot about Willie's personal side, much more than most people, and this vulnerability scared Velásquez. It was not that he had deep, dark, horrible secrets to hide. He just did not like the idea of anyone having easily misrepresentable knowledge about him that they might indeed try to inflate, alter, or otherwise manipulate to his or SVREP's disadvantage. Velásquez's somewhat paranoid concerns about Meza's potential to slander him were reinforced when, one night, at a post-work SVREP drinking session, Willie asked Aurora Sánchez to tell him what Meza had been saying about him lately. Sánchez reluctantly told the inebriated SVREP leader that Meza had in fact called her one evening, obviously upset with Velásquez, and without solicitation had told her about "the real Willie Velásquez," flaws and all. Sánchez did not understand Meza's motives in telling her about many of Willie's personal shortcomings, but she knew from her own experiences with Velásquez that he did not cherish the idea of anyone knowing of or reporting his private affairs. After his concerns about Meza were verified, he stopped socializing with her altogether.

Within months, as Flores had predicted, Velásquez called Meza into his office and told her that upon reflection he had decided after all to accept her letter of resignation. This time, it was obvious that Willie's decision to part ways with Meza was real and irreversible. The two did not really even waste time discussing what had changed Velásquez's mind. It was simply clear that Meza's days on the project staff were over.

Willie's reliance on Meza's earlier letter of resignation to release her the second time around was almost surely legally suspect. But Meza knew that even if she successfully challenged Velásquez's decision, it would only further strain their now near fully broken friendship. She knew, moreover, that she had lost the essential will and trust to remain at SVREP in any case. All

Meza could do now was cry. She was three months pregnant. She no longer had a job. What would she do? Meza and others close to SVREP's work and history wondered how Willie could so coldly handle someone who had been such a close ally and friend.

Velásquez did not see the matter as a question of friendship. To him, it was all strictly about business. Meza could no longer inspire Willie's confidence nor fulfill his sense of obligation to the SVREP family. For these reasons, she had to go. Ironically, Velásquez wrote a glowing letter of recommendation for Meza to use in pursuing new employment when she left SVREP. The letter emphasized her integrity, loyalty, and conscientiousness. Its fundamentally affirmative tenor was largely at odds with Willie's decision effectively to fire Meza. Concerned about the possibility of responsive legal action and also out of concern for the longtime female SVREP employee, Vilma Martínez, one of Velásquez's toughest board members and a labor attorney, called Meza to ascertain her inclination to respond via legal or other action. The now former SVREP research director assured Martínez that she had no intention to go that way. To her way of thinking, it was time to move on. Willie had dodged a bullet of sorts but lost another once dear colleague and friend in the exchange with Meza. On every front now, it seemed, the walls of the world he had built at SVREP were closing in all around him.

⌐ ⌐ ⌐

Against the backdrop of SVREP's growing internal struggles, the mayoral race in San Antonio was shaping up as a key bellwether in the quest for Chicano political opportunity. Henry Cisneros, a thirty-three-year-old, Harvard-trained, three-term city councilor was hoping to make history by becoming the youngest and first Mexican-American mayor ever elected in San Antonio. His opponent, John Steen, a millionaire businessman who had made his money in the insurance industry, had also been a city councilor for six years. Steen had flirted with running for mayor in 1977 and again in 1979, but chose not to when his own polls showed that he did not stand a chance against the incumbent, Lila Cockrell. With Cockrell deciding for personal reasons not to seek a fourth term in 1981, both Cisneros and Steen quickly offered their candidacies to replace her. Cisneros's charisma, flair, and intelligence garnered immediate national media attention. The articulate and personable Mexican-American politician—who spent more time talking about economic development than civil rights—was already being crowned a likely future national candidate, even before the successful conclusion of his quest to become mayor.

Cisneros benefited from a large outpouring in support of his candidacy from Chicano activists in the city, though many of them harbored questions about the young city councilman's commitment to Mexican-American neighborhoods in light of his strong association with Anglo political and business leaders. Robert Cabrera, SVREP's first field director, recalls Cisneros, Velásquez, and himself discussing Cisneros's initial bid for a city council seat back in 1975. According to Cabrera, Cisneros told Velásquez at that time that he was considering running on the ticket of the Good Government League (GGL), San Antonio's elite political machine, which had been quietly helping to elect carefully selected, moderate reform candidates to office since 1955. Chicano community activists hated the GGL. They perceived it as an exclusive, Anglo-dominated clique that presumptuously spoke for rather than through needy Mexican-American and African-American grassroots constituent groups. It was the GGL that Velásquez and so many of the angry, young Chicano politicos of San Antonio had attacked in the late 1960s and early 1970s for holding back the city's move to a more progressive politics. Willie tried to convince Cisneros that he should circumvent the GGL and instead rely on SVREP to advance his council race through aggressive city-wide registration and education drives. Cisneros appreciated the advice and Willie's offer, but said he *wanted* to run with the GGL because he knew he could win with them, while relying on SVREP would be more uncertain.

Velásquez begrudgingly understood and accepted Cisneros's concerns in 1975. At the time, SVREP was a fledgling outfit that had not yet attempted a single registration drive. To bank on an untested group would have been not only risky, but also plainly unwise. Willie respected Cisneros's political astuteness, which over the years since had proven remarkably solid. Now, Cisneros, still closely allied with the GGL, was poised to become the next mayor of San Antonio, the nation's tenth largest city.

But, while clearly proud of the young politician's prospects, Willie and other community activists in San Antonio felt uncomfortable in the fact that the promising city council member often appeared to be split between his loyalties to his people and the city's predominantly Anglo business interests. Willie knew that the burden of keeping Cisneros honest would fall upon the entire Chicano activist community. As Velásquez saw it, the activist community would have to press Cisneros to leverage compromises for the city's Mexican-American community, both as a viable candidate and as mayor, if elected. But even the most progressive skeptics of Cisneros's candidacy, including Willie, knew that the young councilman's quest to be elected mayor was vital to the national Latino community's evolution, and therefore an essential cause for all to support.

In order to help Cisneros's cause, while honoring IRS constraints on 501(c)3 nonprofit political activities, SVREP quietly decided to stage an intensive four-week registration drive followed by a voter education effort that would play an indirect, but decidedly sympathetic role in promoting the young councilman's mayoral bid. SVREP was now well prepared to see this balancing act through with success. For some time, it had been strategically sponsoring nonpartisan voter registration campaigns that coincided with local elections in which SVREP's major stakeholders and partners shared an interest to elect Mexican-American or progressive candidates. Velásquez painstakingly mapped out the limitations of SVREP's activists to avoid being accused of partisan activity, while at the same time doing everything humanly possible to mobilize community voters in support of candidates with a grassroots focus and sense of accountability. The ultrafine line between nonpartisan and partisan action had long been effectively straddled by American labor groups and business, Democrats and Republicans. Velásquez did not create this method of political organizing. He merely made it available to the Chicano community, in hopes of better positioning it to play a meaningful, participatory role in the American electoral system.

The 1981 San Antonio voter registration drive was one of SVREP's largest and most fervent efforts of the year. Led by Rita Elizondo, the campaign lasted four weeks and included two weekends of heavy door-to-door registering. The first weekend was plagued by rain and drizzle, but sixty-five volunteers were still able to register nearly seven hundred people. The second wave of canvassing was even more successful, owing to better weather, more volunteers, and even larger numbers of newly registered voters. Many of the drive's organizers joined the Cisneros campaign as volunteers after the registration deadline had closed in early March and helped with get-out-the-vote efforts in the very neighborhoods they had canvassed for SVREP.

In the citywide mayoral election, Cisneros destroyed Steen and a third minor candidate, Dr. José San Martín (who garnered little support), by capturing more than 60 percent of the vote on April 4, 1981. Velásquez immediately wrote to SVREP financial backers and board members, telling them about the significance of Cisneros's election and the impact it could have on other races in the Southwest. Willie gleefully shared SVREP's preliminary analysis of the San Antonio mayoral race. SVREP's statistics underscored a record turnout of voters with Mexican Americans showing a much higher turnout rate than either Anglos or African Americans. Forty-four percent of the Mexican Americans registered to vote actually voted compared to only 38 percent of eligible Anglo voters and 30 percent of registered blacks. SVREP estimated that Cisneros received nearly 95 percent of the Mexican-American vote, which accounted for about two-thirds of his final vote total. Cisneros also picked up 75 percent of the black vote, but even more significantly, he collected nearly 40 percent of the white vote with some predominantly Anglo areas giving him nearly half of their votes cast. Cisneros's broad appeal and commanding victory was indeed an amazing feat, given the torrid history of racial and ethnic relations in and around San Antonio.

SVREP received its share of congratulations for the important supportive role it played in facilitating the Cisneros victory. Letters poured into its headquarters from many parts of the city and the region, thanking SVREP's leaders and staff for increasing the San Antonio Mexican-American electorate and for playing a role in assuring Cisneros's historic triumph. Velásquez appreciated the kudos, but was careful not to claim credit, large or small, for the outcome of the Cisneros race. It cannot be denied, however, that SVREP's contributions to the Cisneros victory were significant and a long time in coming, to be sure.

SVREP's style had always been low-key and this was especially true in its hometown of San Antonio. There is no doubt that the Cisneros campaign inspired SVREP to organize a particularly aggressive voter registration drive that was designed to help the promising city councilor win. But first and foremost on Willie's and SVREP's radars, always, was the critical importance of slowly and methodically building a stronger Mexican-American electorate in San Antonio, as well as throughout the Southwest. This was a long-term proposition that was larger than any single candidate or race. SVREP, in effect, was quietly laying the groundwork for a grassroots revolution in the politics of the largely Hispanic Southwest. Few even really noticed what SVREP was up to. Only a handful of people knew, consequently, that SVREP's work netted a gain of several thousand more Mexican-American voters for the 1981 city elections over the prior election cycle; even fewer realized that SVREP had been consistently increasing Hispanic voter participation since its creation in 1975. The few thousand voters registered over the project's four-week campaign in San Antonio paled in comparison to the overall work SVREP had done in the city during the prior six years. The 1981 mayoral elections gave rise to the project's eighth registration campaign in San Antonio and these efforts played a crucial part in enlarging the registered Latino voting population of the city by over forty thousand to some 153,000 voters that year. It was SVREP's long-term organizing work, therefore, that mainly contributed to the successful Cisneros campaign of 1981 that, in years hence, would create similar possibilities for other Hispanic politicians who truly wanted to do substantive things for the Mexican-American people.

ᑲ ᑲ ᑲ

The Cisneros triumph was a watershed moment in Latino politics and Willie was certainly moved by the national excitement that it generated; but personal circumstances prevented Velásquez from fully availing himself of the festive post-election celebrations that were taking hold across the Southwest. At home, Willie and his wife Janie were experiencing problems that stemmed from now a decade of increasingly irreconcilable differences in their personalities, priorities, and professional commitments. Willie, consumed by his work at SVREP, was rarely able to make quality time for his family. Often, he was closed off from Janie and their three small children, Carmen, Catarina, and Guillermo. It appeared increasingly as if Janie and the kids had been somehow abandoned or forgotten by Willie for large chunks of time. Janie, open, emotional, and gregarious by nature, was beginning to experience feelings of growing insecurity and low self-esteem for never seemingly being able to gain Willie's care or attention anymore. Willie, strong, self-confident, logical, and tightly controlled—at least on the outside—dominated the relationship. Over time, he lost patience with Janie for not being more content and self-sufficient in their marriage, and for not being able to better manage the multiple responsibilities time had imposed on her as a wife, mother, and daughter. All of this made for a considerable amount of volatility in the Velásquez marriage. As Janie later recalled, "The good times were really good times, and the bad times were really bad." High and low, hot and cold, black and white, the Velásquez union increasingly gave little middle ground.

With Willie's encouragement and her mother Carmen's enthusiastic agreement to offer daycare for the Velásquez kids, Janie decided to accept a seasonal job as a census tracker. The temporary position would help Janie to regain her sense of self, while enabling her indirectly to help advance the Mexican-American cause by quantifying the community's recent growth in ways that would ultimately inform needed changes in federal districting schemes, funding allocations, and appointments to important offices and commissions.

Janie's work with the Census Bureau from March through October of 1980, however, turned out to be extremely demanding. Long hours (often extending into late evenings away from home) and growing responsibilities on the job stretched her bone thin. She wanted desperately to be the perfect parent, wife, and daughter. But time and circumstance increasingly prevented her from feeling successful on any level. She was simply increasingly being pulled away from meaningful contact with her family, precisely when she wanted and needed family connections the most. At the time, in addition to her newfound job responsibilities, Janie continued to assume the major family responsibilities, often to compensate for her growing inaccessibility to her loved ones. Because she felt guilty about leaving Carmen, Catarina, and Guillermo with her mother while she slaved away with census business, she would frequently drive across town to have dinner at home and then struggle back to the census office near Kelly Air Force Base to complete unfinished work, sometimes until midnight. At the close of each day, she would drag herself home, sleep for a few hours, wake up early to get the Velásquez children ready for school, push Willie out of bed and into the shower, and then head off to work again. This nonstop schedule was quickly draining Janie. She was exhausted and deeply unhappy.

During the summer, Janie's crazed working hours at the Census Bureau began to match Willie's at SVREP. The couple drifted even further apart. Their unrelenting schedules meant they were spending almost no time together. They communicated less and less with one another, and their brief, fleeting exchanges became more mechanical and transactional than loving and intimate. In effect, Willie and Janie were becoming strangers to one another.

Willie began to stay away from home even more than usual, normally choosing instead to frequent the Esquire bar after hours with his friend, MALDEF attorney Joaquín Ávila, and anyone else who wanted to join them. "It's hard to go home when there is nothing to go home to," a disheartened Velásquez told a SVREP staffer in a rare flash of personal transparency during this period. Ironically, the problems evolving in the Velásquez household would intensify rather than subside when Janie finally concluded her work at the Census Bureau.

Rather than regaining a sense of common ground and family unity following Janie's stint at the Census Bureau, the Velásquez's found themselves unexpectedly divided even further by the onset of a deep depression in Janie that provoked a skeptical and mean-spirited response from Willie. The problem manifested itself on a seemingly harmless shopping outing. Janie had taken the Velásquez's oldest daughter, Carmen, to K-Mart to pick up some odds and ends. At the end of the otherwise routine and uneventful visit to the store, the mother and daughter made their way to the checkout counter to purchase their items. Suddenly, without explanation or warning, Janie was shaking violently. The clerk, immediately sensing some sort of danger, asked if she was alright. Janie, unable to answer, was quickly rushed to a seat. Uncertain what to do, the store staff called for an ambulance. With each passing minute as the ambulance made its way to the shopping center, Janie felt worse and worse, her heart now racing as if she were having a heart attack. A powerful surge of fear rocketed through her body like a blast of radiation.

The ambulance finally arrived and took Janie away. After examining her and finding nothing physically wrong, however, the hospital medical staff contacted Willie, told him what had transpired, briefed him on his wife's condition, and asked him to pick her up. Willie arrived at the hospital in an angry and impatient mood to escort Janie home. During the entire ride home, he did not say a word to her. He was upset that she had let something like this happen. Willie had long considered Janie to be suffering from nothing more than human weakness, something for which he had absolutely no sympathy. He was convinced that Janie's condition was purely imagined and not in any way serious. Pampering her would only encourage her to fall back on this type of behavior in the future, Willie believed.

But Willie was wrong. As the next several months progressed, Janie's mysterious condition worsened. A new round of attacks caused disturbing side effects—she lost large amounts of weight and experienced excruciating headaches, stomach cramps, and diarrhea. Janie became paralyzed by her predicament, afraid to leave the house because she never knew when another attack might take place. She finally felt that she had no choice but to undertake another round of medical tests to determine what might be causing her physical and emotional difficulties. She rarely laughed or smiled anymore, as was her lifelong custom, and she found herself strangely on the outside looking in at family parties and public events that she attended. She was no longer Janie, but rather just a shadow of the happy-go-lucky person she used to be.

Janie's decision to return to the hospital for additional medical assessment in the spring of 1981 caused Willie to become even more displeased with her. Convinced that her condition involved exaggerated hypochondria and still wedded to treating her through his own version of tough love, Willie refused to visit Janie during her entire hospital stay. Occasionally, when the two spoke over the phone, Janie spent most of the time crying and apologizing to Willie for not being a good wife, a strong parent, and a normal person. Throughout the entire ordeal, Willie reacted coldly to Janie's cries for understanding and forgiveness.

Janie anxiously awaited the results of her supplemental medical tests while Willie became more and more convinced that they would reveal nothing serious. During the last days and hours leading up to the medical staff's conclusive diagnosis, the stress and anticipation became so great for Janie that she desperately began to pray that something tragic would in fact be discovered within her—an unknown disorder, an unpronounceable infirmity, an incurable disease—anything that would confirm the validity and severity of her suffering over the last endless months. But it was not to be. When the attending physician finally arrived to share the outcome of Janie's tests, he could only report that there was absolutely nothing physically wrong with her. He suggested that she seek psychological counseling, in hopes of making things more bearable again in her life going forward.

Janie reacted to the doctor's clear bill of health like someone who had just been told she only had a year to live. She was mortified, especially by the idea of having to face Willie. Her sense of humiliation and defeat now began to surpass her feelings of anger and disappointment toward Velásquez. Janie's hopes for a kinder response from Willie were abruptly shattered upon their return from the hospital. Willie's impatience with Janie's unsubstantiated ailments had now reached a boiling point. "If you want to get better you will. It's all in your head!" he yelled in a disapproving and condescending voice.

Janie's response was both apologetic and resentful. She tried to make Willie understand that she did not want to be in this condition. Whatever it was that was inside was dictating to her; she had no control over its power. Did he really think she wanted to go through this type of distress? As Willie continued to ignore her pleadings, however, Janie became increasingly unsettled by his insensitivity and inflexibility. She wondered how the man who professed to love her and with whom she had been through so much could abandon her at such a time of need. The more she thought about how Willie had treated her, in fact—not visiting her in the hospital, harassing her on the phone, ignoring her calls for sympathy and a bit of understanding—the more she resented him. She tried to keep these ugly thoughts out of her mind, but she could never fully let them go. Something had fundamentally changed in the Velásquez's personal equation. For the next years, Willie and Janie would circle around the meaning of this change, but mostly they would revert to old roles and patterns to avoid painful confrontation, unless and until roused from their growing distance and denial by raw necessity.

᭝   ᭝   ᭝

By early 1981, Velásquez was weary and fatigued. Years and years of highly pressure-packed public engagement, stressful institution-building, and growing personal and marital challenges had finally caught up with him. Willie *needed*, and now even wanted, a break. Maclovio Barraza's death, his disintegrating friendship with Arnold Flores, continuing fund-raising and staff dilemmas at SVREP, and most of all his problems with Janie at home— all conspired to alert Willie that he desperately needed a change.

Velásquez was not tired of SVREP or its mission. He was just burned out—mentally and physically taxed in a way that he could no longer sustain the current course of things. In order to continue to serve SVREP well in the long run, he needed to take space from it in the short run by pursuing a discernible change in scenery and daily routine. He did not know where he would go—Spain, Mexico, perhaps New Mexico—or what he would do, though he talked more about writing books and exploring ideas than searching for inner peace or resuscitating his marriage. In any case, Velásquez was clear that he had to do something different for a while, and soon. If he didn't, he knew that he could lose more than mere interest in his work; he could lose his mind.

During the spring, therefore, unbeknownst to all but his family and his closest public allies, Willie concluded an agreement with Harvard University's Institute of Politics (IOP) to spend the fall in Cambridge, Massachusetts, teaching, studying, and writing as an IOP Fellow. The stint at Harvard would give Willie the break he so desperately needed, as well as help to heal the wounds of more than fifteen years of "unfinished academic business" dating back to his never-completed Masters studies at St. Mary's University. All in all, it would prove to be a timely and necessary respite from the increasingly stressful life he had created for himself in San Antonio at SVREP.

Chapter 15

VELÁSQUEZ WAS ECSTATIC ABOUT GOING to Harvard. His sense of the possibilities for both personal renewal and intellectual growth was extreme. The grassroots political organizer envisioned himself researching and writing a book on Hispanic politics that would be a primer for organizing in the Southwestern states and inform readers generally about Latino political issues and opinions. In the process of developing this work, he would teach a related course and expand his network to include important new individuals who knew little or nothing about SVREP or Chicano politics, but who could become key supporters of his work and vision. The Harvard community attracted many of the nation's best and brightest policy practitioners and analysts, opinion leaders, and progressive donors, after all. Willie wanted to penetrate this crowd in ways that would serve his own and SVREP's longer range interests. He saw his sabbatical semester at Harvard, then, as a way not only to gain a needed, temporary release from his current burdens, but also as a means to position himself, going forward, as a more respected and legitimate political actor in the Southwest. On every level, the opportunity to spend the final months of 1981 on the Harvard campus fundamentally appealed to Willie. By late summer, he simply could not wait to get to Cambridge.

Janie was not as optimistic as Velásquez about uprooting the entire family from its familiar surroundings in San Antonio. In fact, she was scared to death at the prospect of moving to New England. Her continuing physical and emotional challenges had actually worsened since her battery of hospital tests had given her a clean bill of health. Much to Willie's dismay, she was now seeing a psychiatrist at the Brady-Green Clinic, who diagnosed her as severely depressed. Janie's psychiatrist informed her that the inexplicable nervous episodes she had been suffering were known as panic attacks. The seemingly uncontrollable outbursts of fear and paralysis were brought on by the accumulated stresses of her recent past. As Janie delved into her memories and feelings, she uncovered an intense sadness. She still harbored a deep resentment toward Willie for neglecting her needs. She lamented his constantly being away from home, his tendency to place business over family priorities, and his refusal or inability to provide greater financial security for

241

her and their children. Janie's psychiatrist believed that all of these issues were combining to immobilize her both physically and emotionally. To address the problem, Janie began taking prescription anti-depressants and seeing her therapist extensively. Knowing of Willie's sensibilities, however, she minimized his knowledge of her therapy sessions and withheld from him altogether her use of anti-depressants to cope with her increasing emotional difficulties. In time, Janie's condition stabilized around this routine and she regained a brief moment of comfort; but it was sadly short-lived.

When Willie announced his fantastic news that the family was going to Harvard, all Janie could think about was her growing dependency on psychiatric care in San Antonio and the renewed pain and uncertainty the proposed move to the East Coast might reintroduce in her life. The last thing she needed or wanted now was to be thrust into a thoroughly unknown environment where she would have to grapple with her unresolved issues and continue her secretive medication regimen alone. Not being able to reveal anything about these fears to Willie, since he was the cause of so many of them, she tried instead to find other excuses to keep her and the children in San Antonio, but Willie would not listen to any of it. The Velásquez family was headed for the Ivy League, whether Janie liked it or not.

〜 〜 〜

At the end of August, the entire Velásquez clan, including Willie, Janie, their three children, and Janie's mother, Carmen, packed up their belongings, threw a small trailer on the back of the family's 1974 Delta 88, and headed east. The early portion of the trip was nothing spectacular as they flew through the Deep South trying to make it to Washington, D.C. as soon as possible, so that Willie could conduct a few meetings with selected foundation officials, liberal supporters, and politicos. Janie and her mother prepared a Mexican feast at the home of Peggy Simpson, a Texan journalist based in D.C., and they celebrated in typical Southwestern style. The next stop for the Harvard-bound Texans was New York City, where Willie met with Leslie Dunbar, an old friend of SVREP's and the former chief executive of the Field Foundation.

The family's stays in both D.C. and New York City were largely devoid of family sightseeing and tourism. The two stops were all about business from Willie's standpoint. For the other family members, Washington and New York City were foreign and intimidating places that they were merely pleased to survive along the way to New England.

In early September, with Labor Day approaching, the family finally arrived in Boston, tired and worn from the hectic trip. They made their way to the home of family friends who had agreed to house and orient them during their first several days in the area. Staying with friends appeared to Janie to be a welcome reprieve from the inherent discomforts of traveling on the road. For days she had been fighting off a nasty flu, taking aspirin at every opportunity to tone down the effects. Unfortunately, the added stability provided by friendly surroundings could not mitigate Janie's growing illness and discomfort. Only a few short evenings into the family's initial visit, her condition worsened considerably. With her physical well-being declining rapidly and her fever rising to dangerous levels, Janie could not sleep. Her head and body were pounding with pain. Desperate for relief, she quietly made her way to the bathroom, being careful not to wake anyone up, and began searching for another aspirin to soothe her bursting head. In her groggy state, she fumbled around the bathroom sink and medicine cabinet. Suddenly, she felt dizzy and paralyzed. She was quickly fading out of consciousness. Terrified, but rapidly losing strength, she eked out a faint cry for help: "Mom, I'm not feeling well." In the next instant, she was free-falling to the ground, crashing her head on the toilet on the way down.

Janie's crushing fall awakened the entire household. Her mother, Carmen, was instinctively the first to arrive on the scene to provide care and comfort to her fallen daughter. Janie was as pale as a ghost and her motionless, twisted torso spoke to the severity of her fall. Upon finding their mother unconscious on the bathroom floor, the Velásquez children began to cry and scream uncontrollably. Willie dashed in, flustered and scared, yet determined to keep his head so as not to make a bad situation worse. He called for an ambulance and helplessly waited with the rest of the household for what seemed like an eternity for the medics to arrive.

Emergency medical professionals finally arrived and promptly administered aid, snapping Janie out of her unconscious state with smelling salts. Realizing that her situation was serious, they dashed her off to the hospital with Willie by her side, sirens blaring. The rest of the entourage of family members and friends followed closely behind in the Velásquez's car, worried and praying for Janie's well-being. Inside the ambulance Janie slowly started to regain her senses. She strained to focus on what was happening as the ambulance staff asked her various questions. "Are you on any medication?" they probed. Janie paused, still extremely weak and increasingly aware that her cover was about to be blown. Defenseless and broken, she reluctantly revealed that she had been taking prescription anti-depressants. Willie, taken aback by Janie's response, was left stunned and angry. He had virtually no idea that Janie had been withholding this information from him. He suddenly felt like he was married to a complete stranger. How long had she been hiding this from him? How could he not have suspected? What else did he not know? His dueling emotions, worrying about Janie's condition and at the same time feeling betrayed by her, engulfed Velásquez for the balance of the trip to the hospital. He did not say a word the rest of the way. For Janie, however, he did not have to. She could read the anguish and frustration on his face. Willie was never good at hiding his emotions, even if he thought he was controlling them all the time.

Janie was hospitalized for four days. Her malady actually turned out to be a serious case of strep throat. Massive doses of aspirin, which she had taken to attack her high fever, had combined with her anti-depressant medication to make her situation even worse. Janie's mother, Carmen, and the kids did all they could to lift Janie's spirits, but Willie presented a formidable, stoic obstacle to her healing and emotional well-being. He strolled into Janie's hospital room silently and authoritatively during visitation hours. Long vacant pauses marked their time together. Janie could sense Willie's disapproval and consternation, even absent conversation. Just as he had shut down emotionally in the ambulance on the way to the hospital, he became closed off to her during her convalescence.

The more Willie rehashed the series of events leading to Janie's illness and fall, the angrier he became. As a result, Willie showed almost no love or caring for Janie as she struggled to regain her health and her dignity. Instead, he unleashed a barrage of obnoxious attacks on her that opened still more wounds in the couple's unraveling marriage. He berated her for being weak and unable to manage problems that, as he saw it, millions of other people faced daily and dealt with without the help of drugs or psychiatrists. Janie sat in her bed, trying her best to deflect or ignore Willie's assault, but ultimately he made it impossible for her not to feel his wrath, his utter disapproval, and his almost complete lack of sympathy.

Janie left the hospital in Boston with renewed apprehensions about the decision to temporarily leave San Antonio. The dramatic revelations about her regimen of prescription anti-depressants that resulted from her seizure and hospitalization had resurfaced fundamental problems in the Velásquez marriage. Willie had proven even less supportive of Janie now than when her problem first surfaced in San Antonio. The situation appeared to be going from bad to worse. In every aspect, it seemed, Willie's and Janie's relationship had reached a crisis point.

Nevertheless, some profound, unexplained impulse told Janie to stay with Willie. This was fortuitous for Velásquez, who, despite his consternation and disapproval concerning Janie's condition, emphatically rejected the notion of a separation. In fact, Willie fundamentally wanted Janie to be well and able again to radiate the lightness and laughter that had made him fall in love with her years before. He wanted his family to be happy and whole. Finally, Willie wanted Janie to experience and share with him the rich journey that his path was beginning to offer them, a journey that her current circumstances could only threaten.

Although awkward in his emotions and harsh in his words, Janie knew

that Willie was afraid to lose her. She knew that his emotional and psychological challenges were at least as great as her own and that much of what
motivated his defensiveness in life was fear. Indeed, Willie was so adamant
about Janie not being weak precisely because his own deepest fear in life was
finally being weak himself. A mutually held but unstated understanding
between the two helped them to forge ahead together, establishing a delicate
truce that would be tested but never fully broken during the balance of their
stay in Cambridge and in the years that followed.

᭡   ᭡   ᭡

The first few days of the fall semester at Harvard were memorable ones
for the Velásquezes. They spent their initial nights on campus in the John F.
Kennedy suite at Winthrop House, a temporary stopover before Willie found
a more permanent dwelling for the family. Living in the Kennedy quarters
was an unexpected gift for the Chicano activist who playfully referred to JFK
as "El Santo" (The Saint). The Kennedy suite filled Velásquez with a sense
of treasured history and a link to the felled president who continued to inspire
countless Mexican Americans.

With assistance from the IOP staff, the Velásquez family finally secured
an apartment across the Charles River near the Harvard Business School in
Soldier's Field Park. Janie and her mother forced smiles on their faces as they
walked into the tiny apartment for the first time, nostalgically recalling what
they had left behind in Texas. The entire place consisted of only four small
rooms and a modest bathroom. Two bedrooms were assigned to the kids and
Grandma Carmen. A third tiny room adjacent to the kitchen (a room that
more appropriately should have been a study) uncomfortably accommodated
Willie and Janie. The fourth room, an open, all-in-one dining and living room
space, rounded out the family's new quarters.

Within days, it became clear that the apartment was simply too small to
comfortably house them. Janie pressed Willie to seek alternative living space
more appropriate for the children and her mother. There were larger, empty
apartments in the complex below the one they were occupying, but Willie
refused to discuss with IOP officials what Janie considered to be a reasonable
request for additional space. Willie had been ingrained with the ethic of sacrificing on behalf of the cause for so long, bordering on the absurd in Janie's
opinion, that his conscience would not allow him to feel entitled to pay raises, fringe benefits, or other accoutrements of professional life, let alone larger living quarters for his fellowship. In an almost twisted way that increasingly jeopardized the welfare of his family, Willie came to associate sacrifice as
a badge of honor in relation to his purity and standing as a social justice
leader. In ways both large and mundane, Velásquez would deny himself and

his family essential comforts that few others would even consider doing without, in the name of advancing the movement. He came to consider even the pursuit of his own and his family's most natural and harmless dreams as somehow selfish, egotistical, and inconsistent with his social responsibilities. On the other hand, Velásquez was typically prepared to advocate and fight for Mexican-American community access to the good life with everything he had. For Willie, the cause came before himself, before Janie, even before the Velásquez children. As Janie would later recall, "He could do it all for the masses, but not for Willie Velásquez or his family." Willie's refusal to seek larger living space for his loved ones in Cambridge unleashed renewed strains in his relationship with Janie. It also portended challenges on other fronts that would further complicate the family's Ivy League experience.

Almost immediately, there was a stark contrast in the lives Willie and Janie led at Harvard. Janie's days quickly became little more than a seemingly endless parade of taking and picking up the kids from schools and day-care centers, worrying about her mother, trying to improve her own condition, and wondering about her crumbling marriage. She took Carmen to Catholic school in the morning, then returned to pick up Catarina and drop her off at her half-day kindergarten class. Guillermo stayed at home with Grandma or was dragged along by Janie during her daily routine. In between, Janie would coax her mother out of the apartment and they would spend their time shopping at the grocery store or doing laundry. A few hours later, she would reverse her parental ritual, picking up Carmen and Catarina before preparing supper for the family with her mother. The perpetual demands of Janie's family responsibilities left little time for her to attend to her own individual interests and needs.

The day-to-day reality of Janie's life in Cambridge thus ended up being nothing like what she thought her Harvard experience would entail. Her early images of life in the Ivy League setting across the river from Boston included her having occasional opportunities to dabble in Harvard's vast bastion of knowledge. She wanted to sit in on courses and lectures, to meet interesting people and leading thinkers, and to learn about East Coast life. Her demanding domestic schedule, however, largely precluded these possibilities.

Now and then, the Velásquez family did get out for some local sightseeing—visiting old revolutionary towns, stomping through the Boston Commons, eating at Fanueil Hall, and visiting the aquarium. Janie, her mother, and the kids universally enjoyed all of these experiences and felt enriched by them. But, on balance, joyful adventures were rare for the family and easily muffled by a daily reality that lacked most of what they knew and treasured most. They missed Texas. They missed the warm weather, the feel of their old neighborhood, the smell of Mexican food in the air, the sounds of everyday Spanish surrounding them as they walked down the street. They missed home.

Willie, on the other hand, was happily integrating himself into the stimulating IOP and Harvard environment. Every activity and event, it seemed—including everything from lunches and breaks to chance meetings and study groups—was consumed by discussions of politics and he loved it. Willie was like a child set free in a candy store at the Kennedy School. Any new political idea or contact he wanted he could have, it seemed. Any resource or reference he needed was there. It was all for the picking, just as he had hoped and envisioned it would be.

Janie, increasingly weighed down by family responsibilities, participated in few of the orientation activities the IOP organized for its Fellows and their spouses. She did, however, attend the IOP Fellow's welcome dinner, an important, semi-formal event involving many of the Kennedy School's most prestigious and important faculty and patrons. Though intimidated by the idea of sitting around chatting with seasoned politicos, academics, intellectuals, and donors—especially when she saw herself as nothing more than a housewife (and a poor one at that)—Janie was nevertheless determined to participate. She wanted to show her support for Willie, gain insights into the institutional culture of Harvard, and add a layer of Hispanic diversity to the prestigious gathering (which, but for her and Willie, would otherwise have been entirely absent). She also looked forward merely to having a rare and much needed evening out with her husband, away from her mother and the kids.

Janie's plans for an enjoyable evening with her husband at the IOP welcoming dinner were quickly complicated when, upon arrival, the Velásquezes learned that they had been assigned seats at different tables. She found it difficult to understand why they were not seated together. Perhaps the predominantly East Coast couples and Ivy League veterans were tired of talking to each other and wanted to spend the evening meeting new people and discussing unusual topics, she speculated. Whatever the reason, Janie was suddenly terrified to be off by herself, left to her own inadequate devices to charm and otherwise contend with a crowd of strangers. She felt the sensation of every passing minute, as if a large clock were ticking loudly inside of her. She truly wanted to be herself, relish the company, and actively absorb the amazing conversation that surrounded the evening, but she finally did not know how to get started. She did not want to act the wrong way, say inappropriate things, or otherwise transgress any of the mysterious protocols that governed these types of events. Wanting at all costs not to do anything that might embarrass Willie, Janie quietly disappeared into the woodwork, choosing to watch the party as if she were on the outside looking in, rather than actually participating. In contrast, Willie thoroughly savored every sip, morsel, and exchange of ideas that complemented the dinner. Straightaway, Janie could not miss Willie's happiness and content from across the room—

his bellowing laugh, the intensity of his stare, his gestures sweeping and confident. Though far from home and new to the ivory tower world of Harvard, Velásquez was remarkably in his element here.

When dinner ended, the feast continued with potent but pleasant after-dinner drinks and the pungent aroma of imported cigars. This was civilized behavior, the proper way to introduce another bumper crop of political practitioners to the esteemed halls of Harvard. Janie loosened up somewhat as the evening progressed and ended up having a delightful visit with the people who kept her husband company during the day. This Harvard stuff wasn't all that bad, she thought to herself; if only she could steal some of the magic of the evening and bring it back to their dingy apartment, the Velásquez's fragmented relationship and Cambridge might be made tolerable.

∽ ∽ ∽

Unfortunately, Janie's hopes for an improvement in circumstances did not materialize. Sadly, in fact, things progressively got worse as the weeks passed. Barely a month and a half after moving to Cambridge, Janie was at a critical breaking point. Tensions between her and Willie had reached an all-time high and were showing no signs of easing anytime soon. From the onset of Janie's panic attacks, almost a year earlier, Willie and Janie had done little to deal with the impact of her condition on their marriage, and they had done even less since arriving at Harvard.

Janie had long ago given up trying to engage her husband in any serious discussion concerning her deepening depression and their slowly deteriorating marriage. It had grown impossible for her even to bring up these topics due to the predictability of Willie's inevitable rejection. She knew that he hated people who were not strong enough to confront and solve their own difficulties, and that was how she saw herself. Without Willie even saying a word, Janie felt the immense pressure of his disapproval and rejection. There was no more tenderness in him for her, no room for sympathy, no inclination on his part to offer comfort to ease her turmoil.

Now, Janie could no longer ignore Willie's lack of compassion. She gradually stopped pretending to herself and others that everything was normal and well in her marriage. She was tired of hiding her pain and acting as though everything was fine. The time had come, she decided, to make a major change in her life.

No longer able to sustain the pretense of the contented Mexican-American wife away with her family on sabbatical in Cambridge, Janie concluded that it would be best for her, her mother, and the kids to leave the intellectual environs of Harvard. She phoned her sister, Carmen, in her home state of Kansas and made arrangements to relocate to the Midwest, along with

Grandma, her two daughters, and her son. She organized a U-Haul trailer and set a date for her brother-in-law Bill to fly into Boston from Wichita, Kansas, in order to escort the departing family members back to the rural communities of her youth. There, she hoped to concentrate on taking care of herself. After all the details of the move were nailed down—costs budgeted, tickets purchased, and logistics coordinated—Janie prepared herself for the difficult task of telling Willie what he did not yet know: she had decided to go home. It would be one of the most difficult things she would ever have to do in the entire course of their relationship.

As expected, Willie did not think it was a good idea for Janie and the other members of the family to abandon him in Cambridge. He was angry and upset with Janie for even contemplating such a move, let alone arranging everything without meaningfully consulting or even warning him. He was livid. Hoping that his heavy mood and obvious anger would be enough to change her mind, Willie made his disapproval brutally clear. This time, though, for the first time, his pressure tactics did not work. Janie was resolved to go in a way that even Willie could not deny.

After it became apparent to Willie that Janie was actually leaving, the soon-to-be-estranged couple distanced themselves even more by not talking to each other at all. Janie worried whether her decision to go home to Kansas to save herself and her children would work, but quickly regained her conviction that she had no other choice than to flee. She knew that this was not the last time she would see Willie or deal with him, and she fundamentally harbored fantasies of a joyous reconciliation, in time; yet in her most honest moments she sensed this was the end. Divorce had to be the next step in this tragic affair. She felt shut out by Willie because she did not think or do things the way he wanted her to, but in seeking to accommodate him over the years she had ceased being her own person. Divorce or no divorce, Janie was now convinced that her only hope for the foreseeable future would be to keep Willie locked out of her mind and to focus instead on her own needs.

Bill, Janie's brother-in-law, ultimately arrived in Boston and helped Willie stuff the family car with all of Janie's, her mother's, and the kids' belongings. Owing to the situation, Bill did not say much to anyone in hopes that his relative silence would help to mitigate the intensity of everyone's underlying anxiety. Everyone tried to remain strong. In the end, though, Janie's departure with her mother and the kids was sad and stressful. As they finally prepared to leave, Carmen, Catarina, and Guillermo began to cry. None of them wanted to leave their father behind. Willie gave his kids huge, powerful hugs, hoping they would last through the completion of his fellowship at Harvard. His eyes watered and emotions welled up inside him, but he caught himself when it came time to bid Janie farewell. At that point, cool as ice, indifferent and detached, he whispered a good-bye to her and stepped back away from the packed car to watch his family drive away. As soon as they were gone, a profound sadness overtook Willie. It finally hit him. He was alone now, all by himself in a foreign environment where he would find ample feeding for his intellectual passions, but little medicine for his troubled soul.

〜 〜 〜

A definite uneasiness and uncertainty plagued Velásquez now. He was torn. On the one hand, he was free to do whatever he pleased because there were no longer three children, a wife, and a mother-in-law locked away in a puny apartment, depending on his every move to organize their own activities and emotions. For all practical purposes, Willie could pursue all of the Harvard experiences his heart and mind desired unencumbered by immediate worries about his family's many issues and needs. At the same time, though, Velásquez was haunted by the sheer severity of what was happening to his family. Janie had left him in a state of devastation and confusion, and he still was not certain what had taken place or precisely how it had come to this. He tried hard to hide the anguish he was feeling from the rest of the IOP Fellows and staff, but it was obvious to many of them that something was wrong in the life of the usually jovial Texan.

As was typical of IOP Fellows' classes, Willie's group was a sophisticated and urbane cast. It was, however, a relatively eclectic lot by IOP standards in its composition. According to Terry Donovan, the IOP Fellows program director at the time, "It was not the typical northeast political mainstream-dominated group that usually filed in and out of the IOP." Instead, the cohort consisted primarily of minorities, women, and internationalists whose interests spanned an unusual array of topics and a wide range of fields in often nontraditional ways. Cleta Deatherage, an Oklahoma state representative and feminist political powerhouse, conducted research and a course on the new federalism of the 1980s and its potential impact on states. Ellen Hume, an accomplished journalist formerly employed by *The Wall Street Journal*, probed the relationship between the media and government in a study group called "Media Politics: How Newsmakers Manage the News." Eddie Mahe, a conservative Texan, used his expertise as a Republican political consultant and former executive director of the Republican National Committee to examine the status and direction of American political parties in the 1980s. Percy Wilson, who had recently served as Peace Corps director in Sierra Leone, conducted a study group entitled "The Impact of U.S. Foreign Aid on Africa's Development." Finally, Yao Wei, a former executive in the Ministry of Foreign Affairs of the People's Republic of China, conducted research and lectures on the recent evolution of U.S.-China relations from a Chinese perspective.

Busy schedules and disparate interests kept the IOP Fellows from engaging in deep relationship-building and interaction during Velásquez's semester at Harvard. Most of their exchanges were informal—a quick conversation in the halls, a short hello and good-bye entering and exiting the Kennedy School building, an occasional cup of morning coffee—but there were some more formal gatherings, such as weekly luncheons with Harvard professors and other notable guests, that consolidated the Fellows in lively discussion and recurring occasions to catch up with one another. While it was difficult for Willie to attend all of these gatherings, owing to his heavy heart as well as his busy research and lecture schedule, sheer curiosity for knowledge and learning brought him to most of them. With Janie and her mother gone, moreover, the IOP Fellows' lunches offered Willie the opportunity to fill his often empty stomach with a decent meal from time to time. In between bites of ham and cheese sandwiches and potato salad, Willie often attended and participated in discussions led by leading intellectuals and world political figures, such as Ellen Goodman, a columnist with *The Boston Globe*; Laurence Fouraker, president of the Boston Museum of Fine Arts; William Shannon, a former U.S. ambassador to Ireland; and Benigno Aquino, a political exile from the Philippines (who would soon sadly lose his life trying to save his country from the evils of the Marcos regime).

Even though Willie never became extremely close to any of the other fellowship participants or the IOP staff, most of them genuinely liked Velásquez because he exuded a refreshing quality of authenticity and grounding that was rare at Harvard, and especially at the Institute of Politics. Ellen Hume later recalled Willie being refreshingly informal and unpretentious. Whether he was coolly puffing away on a cigarette or downing a few beers in a seedy bar near Harvard Square, Velásquez was easily the least "Harvard" of his entire Fellows' class. He never tried to change or adapt to gain acceptance while in Cambridge. He merely stayed true to himself.

Fellows Director Terry Donovan remembers Willie's Southwestern style of dress and his biting humor. Velásquez would stroll into the Institute wearing jeans, boots, and a white guayabera (a traditional Mexican shirt), an outfit that would go entirely unnoticed almost anywhere in San Antonio, but which could not be missed at pristine Harvard where bland business wear dominated the fashion tastes of the ruling East Coast elites. Upon arrival, he would sarcastically poke fun at Harvard traditions and Northeastern snobbery, two of his favorite targets of ridicule during the sabbatical semester at the Kennedy School. Over morning refreshments he would proceed to announce flippantly to anyone listening nearby that he was pouring himself a cup of coffee and eating a croissant. The word "croissant" was always grossly exaggerated and severely bludgeoned by the time it finally left his mouth. The IOP staff and Fellows loved Willie's irreverent outbursts because

they allowed everyone to laugh at themselves and the otherwise sanctimo-
nious surroundings of Harvard.

Hume has called Velásquez "the least polished of all [the IOP Fellows in
their cohort], but also the closest to the earth" because of his grassroots ties.
His unpolished edges meant that many of the more sophisticated IOP Fellows, who felt they knew so much more than the brash Mexican American,
did not hang on every word Velásquez uttered. This was in stark contrast to
the usual reverence Willie received in Latino neighborhoods across the
Southwest. On the other hand, Velásquez clearly posed a welcome "reality
check" on his more urbane fellowship classmates, because, unlike any of
them, he came from the "real world" of community politics, the most basic
level of political influence that exists in any governance or electoral context.
While the other Fellows had more experience in the larger arenas of American and world politics, no one among them could doubt they lacked the
hands-on wisdom that Willie had accumulated on the ground over the years.
For many, in fact, Velásquez's vision and commitment to his work and people served as an inspiration that there were still a handful of activists battling
community problems in their most raw form, up front and on the streets.
Most agreed that the Institute did not have enough individuals like Willie
passing through the classrooms and corridors of the Kennedy School.

Willie's IOP study group, entitled "The Chicano Movement in American
Politics," was largely based on content and ideas flowing from prepared
remarks and media sound bites that he had been delivering for years across the
Southwest. The bulk of his course centered around talks by several of his political buddies from back home. He cleverly relied on them, not only because of
their substantive expertise on Chicano political (and related) issues, but also
because with his family now in Kansas he wanted to share his time at Harvard
with old friends and pals who were familiar and comforting to him.

Velásquez brought Texas State Representative Paul Moreno of El Paso,
an old-time liberal Democrat who chaired the Chicano Legislative Caucus,
to Harvard to talk about how he won elections, what he stood for politically,
and how the caucus was doing in Texas. Other leading figures in the Mexican-American political movement of the Southwest followed, including José
Angel Gutiérrez, one of the original members of MAYO and founder of the
La Raza Unida Party. But, always one to think about the big picture,
Velásquez did not limit his course content or speakers solely to Chicano perspectives or voices. Willie also invited Gerald Wilkinson, now a SVREP
board member and head of the National Indian Youth Council, and Gene
Locke of the Human Organizational Development Corporation of Houston to
speak, respectively, about issues in Chicano/Indian politics and Latino/black
coalition-building possibilities.

Twenty-six students preregistered for Velásquez's noncredit study group and almost all of them were Latino students, predominantly Mexican Americans. Many were members of a student association known as the Harvard-Radcliffe Raza group. Most knew little or absolutely nothing about Velásquez or SVREP, and simply were thrilled that one of their own was now teaching at Harvard, even if only for one semester. Coming mainly from the Southwest, these budding activists were frustrated by the physical and mental distance between Harvard and their Mexican-American communities of origin in California, Texas, New Mexico, and the other states from which they emanated. Velásquez symbolized a direct link to the homes they had left behind on their voyage to the East Coast. His work and ideas also fed the deep longing many of these students had for one day returning to their neighborhoods in order to help their people.

The first real occasion for the Raza group to meet Velásquez in a private, intimate setting was at a reception the students sponsored on September 24, 1981, in his honor. The event was organized at the Phillips Brooks House, a facility nestled in Harvard Yard that was known for accommodating many of the university's community action organizations. Willie gave a rousing rendition of his standard SVREP stump speech, complete with references to local concerns, notions of self-determination, and an historical opportunity in political participation that Chicanos were on the brink of seizing. Once he had the students utterly mesmerized, Willie told them that they all had an even greater responsibility to the Chicano cause than members of his generation, precisely because of the amazing opportunities Harvard would open up for them. If SVREP and the Chicano political movement were to succeed, he concluded, it would be on account of the commitment of young Mexican-American students, like those in the Raza group, to be strong enough to stand up for what Velásquez felt was the most crucial part of the Chicano struggle for justice—political empowerment.

Many of Harvard's Chicano students were forever converted by Velásquez's remarks. Willie was used to preaching to the choir. He had done it endlessly in his career, but these Ivy League students were uniquely ripe for the picking. By being active members in the Harvard/Radcliffe Mexican-American student association, these young adults were already openly professing their desire to promote their culture, their beliefs, and the hopes of their people in mainstream institutions. Velásquez now became a powerful outlet to deepen their commitments to become change agents in the national Mexican-American community's efforts to crack the rigid political status quo that blanketed the Southwest.

For the balance of his stay at Harvard, Velásquez thus served as an important role model for the Mexican-American students and spent a great amount of time with them. In addition to teaching them in his study group, he spent quality time, one-on-one, with various students, helping them with research projects, reports, theses, and career-planning issues. He also frequently took groups of them out for beers at Charlie's Kitchen, a greasy, traditional dive located just around the corner from the Kennedy School. There, Willie and the students discussed any and all things, laughing the chilly nights away in the company of frosty beers, smoky rooms, and nostalgic thoughts of home and family.

In addition to these informal exchanges with students, Willie augmented his teaching and IOP engagements with efforts to fill his intellectual appetite still further with new knowledge and ideas. His large demand for intellectual development and learning led him to spend a great deal of time by himself exploring the classrooms, libraries, and bookstores of Harvard and Cambridge. He audited courses on Meso-American anthropology, Spanish literature, Cuban and Latin American history, and a law school offering on Central American investment. He lost himself for hours upon hours in the massive stacks of Harvard's libraries, reading about the history of immigration to the United States and how immigrants integrated themselves into American political processes. At many of the surrounding area bookstores he bought large bags of books on subjects he loved, subjects as diverse as British political history, Aztec civilization, and Irish and Italian immigration. Unlike most of the Institute Fellows, Willie would spend countless hours locked away in his office on the second floor of the Kennedy School, just reading.

For the other Institute Fellows, the time at Harvard was a chance to take distance from work back home or to network for new employment possibilities. Velásquez's situation was different. His powerful ties to home, however—SVREP, Texas, and the entire Southwest—made it impossible for him to completely shelve the work he left behind there. As much as he could, he continued to be engaged on SVREP issues. He faithfully worked the phone, checking in with colleagues and friends in San Antonio to find out what was happening. He also occasionally flew to Washington and New York City to meet with SVREP funders and supporters. In addition to trying to stay even with current issues at SVREP, Velásquez spent time at Harvard thinking about the months and years to come. His fellowship gave him the luxury to daydream about SVREP's future and to develop many ideas for the organization's growth. These ongoing preoccupations with SVREP's work during his time at Harvard meant that Willie's fellowship never became a true sabbatical; he never finally allowed it to provide a thorough break from the grind that had been suffocating him. Rather, the IOP Fellows program merely offered Willie a relative pause, a temporary lessening of his tremendous workload back home. This was Willie's version of getting away from it all. It was the most his obsessive spirit would allow himself.

After Janie, her mother, and the kids left for Kansas, Willie and Janie quickly settled into a pattern of biweekly telephone conversations that enabled Velásquez to catch up with what his family was doing out on the plains. When the kids would talk to Willie, he would tell them stories about the freezing weather in Cambridge and they would tell him how they all missed him immensely and wanted their whole family to be together again back home in Texas. In times of minor crises, the kids would often scream out for their father. When Guillermo, the youngest and only son, was bitten by a relative's German shepherd, he simply refused to stop crying until he spoke with his father; no one else could replace Willie in calming the boy.

Janie sensed things slowly working out on these calls. She knew that Willie truly missed her and the kids. He would often mention to her how he hated the idea of them being apart from him, and he would gently count down the number of days left to fulfill his commitment at Harvard, after which he could be reunited with his family. Janie was genuinely encouraged by these developments, but overall Willie remained resistant to dealing with the core issues that had led her to leave him. When push came to shove, Janie simply could not convince Willie to dig below the surface when it came to his issues about her and her illness. The several long, drawn-out talks they had on these topics seemed to replay themselves like an irritating, broken old record. Janie would do most of the talking and Willie would half listen. As best she could, Janie would explain why she suffered the way she did, why she needed to take anti-depressant medication, why he had to accept this, and most importantly, why she felt that he had abandoned her when she most desperately craved his love and understanding. Willie would skillfully dodge all the issues, using seemingly logical arguments to lay responsibility for the problem squarely on Janie. Willie's predictable retreat from the heart of the matter and his cold efforts at logic made Janie cry, but not as often nor as despondently as she had in the not-too-distant past. Janie was saddened, disappointed, and depressed by Willie's continuing lack of openness and affection, but she did not fall apart like she used to under these circumstances. From the minute she left Willie standing outside on the street in Cambridge, Janie had pledged to take care of herself, no matter what that meant. Willie's latest withdrawal only hardened Janie in her quest to get well and fend for her children, without Willie if necessary.

Janie and the kids adjusted as well as they could to their temporary home in the Midwest. For Janie, however, the toughness of being in Kansas was easily outweighed by the tremendous advantages she had acquired. Most importantly, she was with her family, a place where she could be pampered and cared for while she worked on her recovery. She did not have to worry about taking care of Willie or hiding her pain. At her sister's house, she could just be herself, complete with all her ailments, imagined or real. With her mother and her sister Carmen doing most of the washing, cooking, cleaning, and other mundane chores, Janie could once and for all concentrate on herself. In this supportive atmosphere Janie was slowly but surely becoming stronger—strong enough, in fact, to finally accept that Willie would never change. But just as she concluded that her husband simply could not be persuaded to have a change of heart, something unanticipated happened during the final weeks of Willie's fellowship at Harvard.

In fact, it happened in such an unplanned manner—thoroughly independent of all the yelling, screaming, explaining, and crying she had gone through with Willie—that Janie could only believe some higher power had intervened on her behalf to quell Willie's unyielding doubts about her medical condition. One innocuous day in Cambridge, in a moment of temporary boredom, Velásquez, the voracious reader and constant seeker of knowledge, casually picked up a copy of *Time* magazine. He nonchalantly shuffled through its pages when he unexpectedly came across an important medical article on panic attacks. The report attempted to separate the myths from the truths behind this disorder and it authoritatively dispelled the idea that such episodes were purely fictitious creations of the mind. It mentioned recent advances made in understanding the illness and noted that there was evidence certain chemical imbalances in the brain could trigger attacks. Finally, the *Time* article reported that some of the world's most intelligent, famous, and successful individuals had suffered from this ailment.

The scientific data presented in the article backed the claims Janie had been futilely trying to explain to Willie for months and, now that he had read corroborating claims in a leading national publication, he realized that he had reacted improperly by denying the validity of her illness. Janie, of course, was overjoyed by Willie's change in perspective. It signaled new ground and fresh possibilities for their listless relationship. Of course, the couple still had much work to do to have any hope of repairing their marriage, but the *Time* magazine article helped to create needed, positive energy upon which they could build.

৶ ৶ ৶

With Christmas and the close of his sabbatical semester rapidly approaching and his family so far away, Willie desperately wanted to go home. As the month of December marched on, he told Janie that he really wanted to be back in San Antonio with the family for all the festivities of the holiday season. She agreed, believing that it would be great for the entire Velásquez gang to be reunited at Christmas. Willie immediately flew to Kansas, picked up his wife and kids, and rushed them back toward their old house and, hopefully, as Willie envisioned it, their old comfortable way of life. Janie was ecstatic about her family being together again, though she fully understood that she and Willie still had considerable unfinished business to work through before they were all out of the woods.

As soon as the car door opened in their Texas driveway, the joy of the holiday season overtook the Velásquezes and it did not let up until after the New Year. Everyone was so delighted to be home that all the unhappiness and problems of the past few months got compartmentalized in their distant memories. The Velásquez family swiftly focused on last-minute shopping for presents, searching for the perfect tree, and hosting the annual SVREP office party (complete with festive tamales, frosty beer, and strange mixtures of classical and *conjunto* music). It was, remarkably, like any other Christmas at the Velásquezes: nonstop, tiring, and fun.

Willie and Janie cheered in the new year in 1982 with joy, hope, and largely incompatible views of where they stood in their rocky relationship. With the holidays behind them, Janie was hoping to pick up where they had left off, working diligently on resolving their problems and differing expectations. In her mind, the cheer of Christmastime and the beginning of another year had not erased the still thorny issues they faced nor the looming potential of a divorce. Willie, on the other hand, truly believing that everything was getting back to normal between them, did not feel the same urgency to rehash the past or delve still deeper into their issues. In fact, Velásquez was still handling the couple's difficulties in the same way he always had: by simply not dealing with them.

Chapter 16

Back at the SVREP office, a fresh, reinvigorated Velásquez returned to work at the beginning of 1982, feverishly prepared to attack the next set of challenges facing the organization. He officially announced his re-engagement in correspondence to his board members and financial supporters, stating enthusiastically, "I am happy to say that I am back in San Antonio and hard at work [after] a four month leave at Harvard. What I learned at Harvard is . . . how much I really like this job!" His buoyant return to the helm, however, masked the personal and organizational turmoil that had pushed him into taking distance from SVREP and Texas in the first place: a conundrum that was suspended during the sabbatical semester at Harvard, but which now still hovered over him, unresolved. The coming year would test his mettle no less than others before it.

The most pressing professional challenge Willie faced upon his return was his increasingly troubled relationship with his former best friend and current board chair, Arnold Flores. Ever since the tragic, startling death of Velásquez's mentor, Maclovio Barraza, SVREP's founding chairman, Willie's and Arnold's tight-knit, brotherly relationship had rapidly deteriorated. Flores's elevation to Barraza's former position as SVREP board chair marked the beginning of the end for Willie and Arnold. While, theoretically, Willie's time at Harvard provided a cooling-off period for the two men and an opportunity to work toward a reconciliation to serve the project's best interests, in fact, the brief interlude had only distanced them further from one another. Now, with Velásquez back in San Antonio, it quickly became clear that the two proud Chicano leaders would not be able to address their issues without a confrontation. They would have to fight it out. Anything else would have violated their sense of themselves as Texans, as Mexicans, and as men.

SVREP's vice chair, Rubén Valdez, was one of the few board members who knew in depth the serious problems existing between the formerly inseparable *compadres*, Velásquez and Flores. Ever since Barraza's death, Valdez had been irregularly meeting with the battling activists to mediate their growing conflict with only enough success to keep the two feisty combatants from declaring an all-out war on one another. Within the first months of Willie's return to SVREP from Harvard, it became apparent to Valdez that SVREP's best interests required a closed-door summit that would bring Velásquez and Flores together to once and for all resolve their issues.

In order to encourage reconciliation, Valdez arranged for the estranged SVREP leaders to meet on neutral ground. Willie and Arnold begrudgingly agreed and they rendezvoused with Valdez in the border town of El Paso, gathering behind the closed doors of a downtown hotel room to work out their differences. Valdez encouraged the two antagonists to bring forward their most candid and serious concerns in a spirit of responsibility and mutual respect. But as soon as he laid down the conversation ground rules, the pent-up poison that had been accumulating between Willie and Arnold flowed freely from both of them. There were no introductory niceties. Rather, it was all-out warfare from the opening bell.

In the end, Valdez's envisioned peace summit never had a chance to succeed. Neither Willie nor Arnold was there to bargain, compromise, or make up. They were there to fight. For nearly half an hour, the two went at each other, exchanging accusations and unpleasantries. As the encounter unfolded, they became more and more petty with one another, more and more hurtful.

Flores expressed deepest frustrations over Willie's lack of deference to him—a deference he believed was owed to him by virtue of his position as SVREP chair. Willie was most angered by Flores not giving him room to run SVREP as he saw fit (the way Maclovio Barraza had before Arnold). More than anything, the meeting underscored that the two men's positions were finally irreconcilable. Reduced to the lowest common denominator, Flores threatened to go to the full SVREP board to have Willie fired unless he would bend. Velásquez wanted no part of Flores anymore. He had had enough. "I'm going to leave. I can't live with this anymore," he said, getting up to end the meeting and, by implication, his tenure at SVREP.

Valdez quickly stepped in before the situation spiraled totally out of control. With all of his conviction and paying due respect to his fellow board leader Flores, Valdez boldly stated the obvious. Willie simply could not be allowed to resign, to leave the project. The fate of Mexican-American political standing across the Southwest hung in the balance, Valdez reminded them. After nearly eight years of building the organization that was now SVREP and securing unprecedented gains in Latino civic participation in the process, Velásquez had simply become invaluable. Without him, there could be no SVREP as people had come to know it. Willie *was* the project. Flores, listening intently to Valdez's impassioned assessment, reluctantly agreed and slowly left the room stating his intention to step down as SVREP chair.

The bitter hotel room showdown in El Paso ended with a forced resolution that terminated Velásquez's and Flores's professional relationship, and more significantly, squashed what little was left of their friendship. To most of the remaining members of the SVREP board, Flores's decision to resign came as a large and unexpected surprise. None of them were aware of the depth of the substantial divide that had come to separate Arnold and Willie; none were made aware of the El Paso confrontation until well after the fact— well after its decisive outcome had been cemented, that is. Flores followed his decision to leave the SVREP chairmanship by resigning from other important boards on which he sat, the very same day. Turning increasingly inward, he faded from the national Hispanic leadership scene to focus on family and private pursuits, but no doubt mortally wounded at the level of his heart by the course of events that had unfolded between him and Willie. In early February 1982, Flores's resignation as SVREP's second board chairman was officially announced. No fanfare, no explanations, no regrets: just a simple announcement marking the beginning of a new stage in SVREP's organizational governance.

〰 〰 〰

With the Flores situation finally resolved, Velásquez tried to refocus his energy on SVREP's day-to-day operations. Much to his dismay, he returned to the helm only to confront renewed financial challenges that threatened SVREP's effectiveness and viability. Within only weeks of reassuming control of the project following his sabbatical at Harvard, Velásquez was warning SVREP's benefactors and friends that the project was once again in deep financial trouble. In a letter to Eddie Ball of the United Steelworkers dated February 19, 1982, Willie reported SVREP's shortfall and resulting cutbacks in fieldwork in Texas. Dejected by the absence of local funding prospects to fill the shortfall, Willie expressed his frustration to Ball, lamenting: "We have never been able to raise any money in Texas to finance our efforts here."

Velásquez attributed SVREP's persistent financial problems mainly to a dramatic increase in requests for voter registration drives in Indian communities of the Southwest, particularly across the state of New Mexico. SVREP's recent legal activism in New Mexico had spurred many local Indian groups to seek funding and training for grassroots voter mobilization efforts and Willie felt compelled to convert these campaigns into discernible gains in Indian political clout. Interest in the Indian areas to undertake voter registration work had never been so pronounced and he wanted to build on the region's nascent Native-American activism. Ironically, as fate would have it, Native demand for SVREP's intervention and assistance rapidly began to outstrip the project's capacity to respond. The unexpected uprising in Indian community solicitations caught SVREP off guard and ill prepared financially. "I am at my wits end trying to fund the Indian campaigns," Velásquez declared in a letter to Karen Padget of the Youth Project, a staunch financial supporter of SVREP's work during this period. Willie's deep sense of responsibility to fulfill grassroots hopes and expectations in Indian country meant he was prepared to do whatever he could to beg, borrow, and otherwise release money for SVREP.

Willie's pleas were always based on SVREP's desire (which he saw as an obligation) to strike when things were hot, before they cooled down and historic opportunities were lost forever. Increasingly, he resorted to imploring friends and allies in the national funding community to accelerate payments due on approved grants, to make up the difference relative to SVREP's own budget shortfalls or those of its partner communities in the field. This "you've gotta' help us now" approach was nothing new to foundation officers and private donors. They had encountered it many times in recent months as a plethora of progressive nonprofit groups struggled to contend with the harsh new funding and political realities created by Ronald Reagan's New Federalism. With Reagan's election to the presidency, many of these groups, formerly beneficiaries of federal contracts and grants, were defunded or severely cut back. In addition, many of their substantive agendas were seriously challenged by Reagan's proposed policies, a threat that in its own right required expanded resources to combat. The net effect was an increasingly challenging and aggressive fund development environment.

Velásquez, like other desperate and possessed nonprofit directors of the era, used a language of urgency and necessity, filled with fiery rhetoric and powerful symbols, to advance his case, believing in his heart as he did so that every funding request was a do-or-die proposition for SVREP and its grassroots allies in the field. His growing demand to current benefactors to release approved grant funds to SVREP on an accelerated payout schedule in order to address increasing activity in the field became an issue during early 1982—one that even Willie himself acknowledged (though not without rationalization and friendly justification).

In the spring, for example, Velásquez wrote the Veatch Fund to request an advance payment on a pre-approved grant, saying, "I hope our sometimes urgent requests for funding do not become a burden for you. It is just that our successes in the courts open up opportunities that must be seized. And, as you can tell, we have been doing a lot of seizing lately." The timeliness and impact of SVREP's work made these otherwise awkward donor appeals entirely acceptable to Willie. His self-effacing, down-home humor and his clear dedication to the cause, moreover, made most benefactors amenable to assist. But even Willie's effectiveness in cajoling donors to release funds as early as possible during this period was not enough.

As SVREP entered into its 1982–1983 fiscal year, Velásquez knew full well that its carryover reserves would be exhausted long before the project could possibly cover all of the season's planned registration campaigns. For

one of the first times in its brief existence, SVREP had run a real deficit during the previous fiscal year, not just a paper one based on expected revenues.
This reduced the project's fund balance for the start of the 1982–1983 fiscal
year to slightly more than $10,000. Notwithstanding growing uncertainties in
the national funding environment and SVREP's own dangerously thin collateral, Willie was so consumed by the prospects of SVREP's Indian organizing efforts that he ill-advisedly took out loans to make sure the voter registration and education drives occurred. The Center for Community Change, a
progressive outfit whose leaders had known Velásquez since his MAYO days,
loaned SVREP $10,000, as did Project VOTE!, a new voter registration
group that Willie had been helping in its infant stages. Velásquez tried to
rationalize this borrowing to other SVREP contributors, claiming this was
the first time SVREP had ever taken out loans, when in fact it was not. Begging for understanding, Velásquez assured concerned donors that this would
be the last time the project would ask for special treatment. "I do not antici-
pate that SVREP will ever again find itself in this situation (taking out loans).
We run a tight organization that is cost effective and prudent about its financial practices," Willie wrote to one of SVREP's largest individual contributors, Ann Roberts of the New York-based Rockefeller family. In reality,
Velásquez was making borrowing to cover SVREP's costs a standard operating procedure that leading foundations and donors would eventually challenge, both for their own sanity and to preserve Willie's and SVREP's fundamental integrity.

The blind passion to make SVREP's field projects a top priority even at
the price of taking out loans when funds were not sufficient to cover costs
had repercussions extending beyond putting the organization on an unsound
financial management footing; it also caused significant personnel difficulties and morale problems for SVREP, particularly as the scale of Willie's fiscal gambling grew. In the past, he had made pledges to community leaders
when he clearly did not have the money on hand or even the prospect of new
resources, but the amounts were typically small—usually in the $500-$5,000
range—and Willie was confident that he could cover those promises down
the road. Velásquez's impatient spirit led him to believe that somehow, someway, the funding would take care of itself. Buoyed by this certainty, Willie
had no problem writing hot checks, putting off paying SVREP's bills, and
cutting back on his own fringe benefits so that SVREP's fieldwork could
continue to move with as few postponements as possible. Several SVREP
staffers had questioned this practice privately, but few confronted Velásquez
with their concerns. Now, however, Willie's financial shortcuts were beginning to reach a level and regularity that some SVREP staffers, for their own
integrity and conscience, could no longer simply allow to go unchallenged.

Aurora Sánchez, Willie's administrative assistant and early hire at the project, took an especially principled stand against his questionable fiscal practices when, one day, Velásquez casually asked her to co-sign various checks for him, totaling some $25,000. It was standard procedure to have two people sign off on SVREP's checks and Willie needed Sánchez's signature so that he could honor certain field support commitments he had recently made. Sánchez knew SVREP's financial numbers better than anyone else and was, therefore, well aware that the organization could not cover the amounts Velásquez wanted her to approve for allocation to the field. In the past, she had given in to him in these situations, afraid to challenge his strength and authority as SVREP's CEO; while she hated the custom, the fudging had never been too extreme. This time, though, she could not merely go along with Willie. Sánchez politely expressed her misgivings to Velásquez and returned to her work without signing the proposed payment checks.

Willie pushed her again, this time more forcefully, reminding her who was boss, but Sánchez would not budge. Willie exploded and demanded that she sign the checks. Once again, Sánchez refused, telling her irate chief that she did not want to be part of any fraud that might endanger herself or SVREP. The exchange deteriorated into a shouting match with Sánchez holding steadfast and Velásquez finally walking away, unsatisfied and unsure of what to do next.

The next day, Willie marched silently into his office, carrying obvious unresolved anger in his expression. He ordered Sánchez to join him and to take a memo. Sánchez entered the office and prepared to record Willie's memorandum. But, within seconds, Velásquez jettisoned her recording assignment and lost all control. He began berating and yelling at Sánchez, calling her stupid and ignorant and accusing her of never having done anything right at the office. He continued on his rampage, listing out loud her faults and forcing her to write them down like a child under the heading "8 out of 10 things I do not do right." Sánchez was frightened by Willie's onslaught, yet could tell from his conduct that he was not completely in control of what he was doing or saying. She wanted to run away and cry, but she drew on every amount of strength she had stored inside of her to maintain her composure and avoid making things even worse. When Willie abruptly ended his tirade, he curtly instructed Sánchez to leave his office and resume her duties.

Sánchez did not know what to do. Willie's utter hostility had caught her totally off guard. There was only one thing she definitely knew; she could never work for Willie again. That evening, she drove to Austin, interviewed for a job with Ann Richards' campaign for state treasurer, and accepted the position on the spot. She resigned from SVREP the next day. When she told Velásquez she was leaving, he acted as if nothing unusual or unpleasant had taken place between them the day before. He said he was thrilled for her and even offered to help her write a plan to address what the Richards' campaign needed to do in the Hispanic community. Sánchez, not fully comprehending Willie's clear denial in the situation, just sat and watched as Willie haphazardly threw some ideas together on paper. He then handed his notations to Sánchez and wished her good luck. She left the SVREP office, still not quite sure what had happened between them.

Velásquez's tantrum with Sánchez offered another sad manifestation of his waning sense of judgment when it came to managing both his organization and his emotions. While it was easy to admire his dogged determination to advance SVREP's work and leadership in the field as much as possible, his growing flirtation with organizational mismanagement and personal hostility directed to those who had once been his closest allies was slowly taking both him and the project closer and closer to the edge. Harry Wexler, a senior financial consultant for the Ford Foundation, grasped Velásquez's restless pattern. He tried to warn Willie to catch himself when Velásquez asked him for advice on pushing the foundation to give SVREP an approved grant payment earlier than scheduled. Wexler urged Velásquez not to press Lynn Walker, his program officer at the foundation, for the money, because she was currently reviewing the entire nonprofit voter registration field for Ford, and Wexler wanted Walker to see SVREP as one of "the most stable and best managed [groups of its kind in the nation]." To request the advance payment, Wexler warned Willie, would unnecessarily raise concerns at Ford by underscoring "the fact that you have a temporary funding problem that may limit your capacity to make early commitments to local voting coalitions."

Willie backed off this time, but there would not always be a Wexler around to temper his hunger. For Velásquez, the work still to be done in the field was all that mattered; everything else was secondary. If he had to lose staff, cut his insurance payments, or take a risk that not enough money would actually be raised, that was fine. He could live with those chances, since up to this point, his gambles had basically paid off, at least as Willie saw things.

৶ ৶ ৶

Observers on the outside could only be impressed by the project's exceptional output and results, to be sure. After having paid heavy dues over eight years of sweaty, low-key, backbreaking voter registration work, SVREP had clawed its way to the top by the fall of 1982, capturing one of the best reputations in the nation for its work. The project's leadership and staff became known across the country as experts and authorities on the issues, the ones people turned to for advice when they wanted to start their own voter registration organization. Velásquez had gained a reputation for being one of the few established voter registration leaders who was willing to help build new registration outfits. Many registration directors were not inclined to encourage new groups to form because they were worried about their own survival in a political and funding context that was not producing bountiful support resources. Even though the national nonprofit voter registration universe was made up of a relatively small number of organizations, the limited amount of available funding in the field meant that any newcomer was a likely competitor.

Willie saw things differently. To him, the growing numbers of activists seeking to replicate SVREP's work were potential collaborators. He saw their aspirations and dreams as natural complements to the work SVREP had begun in the progressive world of grassroots politics. Nostalgically, he also saw his own past in their unbridled passion. He recalled the battles SVREP had been required to wage to gain its own existence. He also remembered with appreciation the vital role the African-American-focused Voter Education Project (VEP) had played in supporting the project's early development. Without VEP's care and guidance, SVREP could easily have been lost in the dust-bin of failed historical opportunities. But VEP's leadership had a certain vision that enabled it to offer help where others would have closed the door; Willie, having been the direct beneficiary of VEP's benevolence, never forgot that. It was this recognition of VEP's kindness and charitable impulse that made Velásquez feel he had a responsibility to support new and emerging groups whose goals and objectives involved giving political voice and representation to those who had little of either commodity.

In 1982 and 1983 three groups approached Velásquez for help in starting citizen participation outfits. One was a Latino organization based in the Midwest hoping to emulate SVREP; another was a project headquartered on the East Coast that planned to register people through government agencies; the third was an Hispanic outfit based in California that wanted to emphasize media use. Of these, Velásquez was most heavily involved with the creation of the Midwest Voter Registration and Education Project (MVREP). It also was the one that caused him the most unwanted headaches and unanticipated tensions.

Willie had always dreamed of expanding SVREP's work into the rich, untapped areas of the Midwest. He recognized that Mexican Americans were becoming a significant population cluster in the region owing to a combination of historical and continuing migration patterns. They followed the migrant trails, the railroad construction and meatpacking jobs, and the auto industry to cities and towns that otherwise had little experience with Latino Americans, from Kansas to Iowa and from Illinois to Minnesota. The size of Willie's challenge to organize across the Southwest and the even greater difficulty of raising funds to develop a Midwest strategy for SVREP did not allow Velásquez to venture in this direction. But with MVREP's introduction onto the scene, Willie saw a unique opportunity to help mold, direct, and shape successful Hispanic voter empowerment efforts in the region, based on the lessons SVREP had learned in its work over the years. As it turned out,

Velásquez was hardly alone in his desire to play a role in advancing Latino voter engagement in the Midwest.

Another individual keenly interested in brokering support to develop Hispanic voting capacity in the region was Raúl Yzaguirre of the National Council of La Raza (NCLR), formerly the Southwest Council. Yzaguirre, a product of the Texas Rio Grande Valley, was firmly implanted in the Washington, D.C. scene, having worked there since the mid-1960s on numerous Latino causes. Since the late 1970s, he had been discussing ways to organize effective voter registration efforts in the Midwest, primarily through the National Council's affiliates in the region. Yzaguirre felt a close kinship to SVREP because of the Southwest Council's role in planting the seed for the project's initial development in 1968. At the same time, he felt strongly that his organization, rather than SVREP, was in the best position to incubate a Midwest voter promotion strategy. SVREP, he felt, was developing a bad reputation for the research it was producing because it did not meet the standard levels of polling and analytical quality generally required by key groups, including policy practitioners, applied scholars, and leading journalists. Yzaguirre also saw SVREP as too closely aligned with the Democratic Party, even though it was ostensibly a nonpartisan group. Finally, he did not feel that SVREP's board of directors was as connected to the Midwest as was his own board, which included several executives of NCLR affiliates based in the region.

Still another person preoccupied with the notion of developing a Latino-focused, Midwest voter project was Juan Andrade, a native of West Texas. Somewhat ironically, Andrade had worked for three-and-a-half-years as the Texas state director for the VEP in the early 1970s before relocating to Columbus, Ohio, in 1974. After a short stint as director of Ohio's Spanish-speaking Committee, Andrade struck out on his own as a freelance consultant. Then, in September of 1979, he visited Velásquez at the SVREP headquarters to inform him that he wanted to set up a Midwest voter education and registration organization. It was one of a number of ideas Andrade was chasing at the time, but it was the closest to his heart. He wanted SVREP's help and support to make it happen.

Willie, inherently warm to Andrade's concept, but mindful that given its growing financial and organizational concerns SVREP was in no position to offer him material sponsorship, diplomatically informed the Ohio transplant that the National Council was also interested in establishing a Midwest voter registration project. He suggested that Andrade and NCLR join forces and promised to assist them in any way he could. Andrade thanked Velásquez for his time and immediately contacted the National Council to follow up.

Elisa Sánchez was the National Council staffer who had been assigned to explore organizational options for NCLR to support voter education work in the Midwest. When Andrade contacted her to discuss his interest in organizing the region, the two quickly hit it off and came to the conclusion that a collaboration building on NCLR's credibility and back-office support capacity, on one hand, and Andrade's knowledge of the region and the issues, on the other, offered a more likely formula for success than either of them trying to go it alone. In early 1980, therefore, Sánchez asked Andrade to write a prospectus for NCLR to support a research study on the potential of the Hispanic vote in and around Chicago. Andrade agreed and was hired as a consultant. His work was then used to generate a grant-supported project of the National Council to establish the case for Latino-focused voter organizing in the region.

It took over a year, but NCLR was finally able to obtain funding for the Midwestern Hispanic voter participation study from the Chicago-based Joyce Foundation. A longstanding trust relationship between NCLR President Raúl Yzaguirre and Joyce Foundation Director Chuck Daly helped to leverage the foundation's support of this work, which would help to direct regional private funding attention to Latino political participation in the Midwest for years to come. By this time, Sánchez had left the National Council to take the helm of the Mexican American Women's National Association (MANA). Lupe Saavedra, a vice president for the council, inherited Sánchez's responsibilities for the Midwest voter project. With the Joyce grant secured, NCLR's Yzaguirre called Velásquez to seek reassurance about Andrade's capacity to see the Midwest project through. With so much at stake and no real personal experience to draw on relative to Andrade's work, Yzaguirre felt himself having eleventh-hour reservations about collaborating with him. Willie reiterated his strong support for Andrade and told Yzaguirre that SVREP would give him its full support in hiring him and pursuing a Midwest organizing strategy. Relieved, Yzaguirre contracted Andrade and sent him to San Antonio to consult and train with Willie and his staff before commencing work in Chicago.

Andrade left his family in Columbus, Ohio, following the brief training stint at SVREP and moved to Chicago to carry out the study. He worked out of the National Council's regional office which was on the brink of being closed, owing to Reagan administration budget cuts of key labor and education programs that supported the office's work in recent years. The only person left on staff was Rey González, a Chicago native, who served as NCLR's regional director. Working long hours and relying heavily on the assistance of local Latino community leaders in and around Chicago (including especially NCLR's González), Andrade accumulated strong and compelling evidence of the need for expanded regional investment in Hispanic voter participation. By the end of 1981, Andrade had finished his study and a published report including his findings was released with great fanfare at a National

Council press conference. Yzaguirre flew to Chicago for the report's public release and highlighted its contents. The report showed both disturbing levels of Latino electoral nonparticipation, as well as vast potential for improved engagement through community education and organizing.

The Midwest study sponsored by NCLR and completed by Andrade significantly elevated public and institutional attention to the issues all across the region. It established a solid foundation for Andrade and NCLR to build on going forward and for a time it seemed as though the marriage that had unwittingly brought these parties together was made in heaven. All of this changed rapidly in 1982, however, when Andrade and the National Council started clashing at almost every turn over questions of agenda control and strategy. Velásquez became a crucial sounding board for Andrade as the latter's relations with NCLR and its president, Raúl Yzaguirre, soured.

Willie was not interested in massaging egos or choosing sides as the divide between Andrade and Yzaguirre grew. What mattered most to him was finding a quick resolution in the best interests of Latino communities and voters across the Midwest. In addition, notwithstanding Velásquez's own strong views and opinions, he was committed to avoid telling Andrade what to do. Instead, he listened intently to the former Texan's concerns and carefully walked him through the pros and cons of alternative scenarios, based on his own experiences; but Velásquez never advocated for Andrade to follow any particular path. As Willie saw it, only Andrade himself and his closest allies were finally positioned to make those choices.

One of the most significant divides emerging between Andrade and Yzaguirre concerned board composition for the new Midwest project they proposed to create together in order to address Andrade's Joyce-supported study findings. Yzaguirre envisioned the nascent Midwest Voter Registration and Education Project (MVREP) being closely tied to NCLR leaders, both at the national and regional levels. He wanted MVREP's board to be filled with people from all walks of life and every political persuasion. He envisioned the board containing as many as fifteen members, including representatives from both political parties and various corporations. Andrade had altogether different board criteria in mind. To begin, he wanted MVREP to operate with significant autonomy from NCLR. Andrade, moreover, wanted more grassroots people on his board, as opposed to political party professionals and corporate operatives. Finally, as a progressive Democrat, the new MVREP executive was loathe to include conservatives in the mix.

Stark differences in perspective over direction and leadership composition especially came to light when Andrade proposed to include Hank Lacayo on his board, with Velásquez's strong encouragement. Lacayo, one of the top Latino labor leaders in the country, had earlier clashed with Willie, but the two had reconciled. Now, Lacayo, a powerful player in the Midwest for his executive work over the years with the United Auto Workers, was an increasingly helpful member of SVREP's board of directors. Lacayo and Yzaguirre, however, were not on the best of terms. Their relationship had soured considerably over time as their respective paths to power took them to very different places. Lacayo, a staunch trade unionist and Democrat, felt that Yzaguirre had rejected the National Council's labor roots in recent years and was now sleeping with the left's natural enemy, the Republicans, by appeasing Reagan administration officials and appealing to corporate leaders (most of them conservatives) to mitigate the devastating effects of Republican budget cutting on NCLR programs and Latino community life. Yzaguirre, for his part, felt that Lacayo's partisan views and aggressive approach would undercut the kind of measured, bipartisan and technocratic approach that he firmly believed MVREP needed to institutionalize in order to be successful in the prevailing political and funding environment.

In the end, the differences separating Andrade and Yzaguirre became so great that even Willie, the one individual with strong relations all the way around, could not bring them together. By the spring, Andrade had lost patience with Yzaguirre and the National Council altogether. He began to plan for a clean break with NCLR and the development of MVREP as a fully independent entity, unbeholden to Yzaguirre.

Andrade's plans to strike out on his own, however, came as a great surprise to NCLR principals. At Yzaguirre's instigation, Armando de León, the National Council's legal adviser and a co-founder of SVREP, called Andrade at the height of the growing conflict to talk about and work through the ongoing obstacles preventing the two sides from getting together around MVREP. To his shock, Andrade informed de León that he had already filed an application to incorporate MVREP as an independent entity that was wholly unattached to the National Council. The NCLR attorney was stunned because Yzaguirre had him working contemporaneously on incorporation papers for the Midwest project. "Andrade didn't [consult or inform us]," de León would later remember. "Instead he just did an end around and formed his own [organization] and set up Lacayo as chair. Raúl (Yzaguirre) was stunned when it happened so fast."

In fact, Andrade had commenced the process to incorporate MVREP in April of 1982. He was disappointed that NCLR principals had to discover his plans in a manner that caught them off guard, but he did not finally regret what he had done. Years later, Andrade would explain his rationale in the following terms: "Hispanics in the Midwest did not need someone in Washington pulling their strings. We [did not want to be] an arm of a Washington-based organization. We [wanted to be] independent. . . . How [could] we implement a community-based agenda when the agenda was going to be set at the national level?" What Andrade had wanted, in short, was supportive technical assistance from NCLR to establish MVREP as a freestanding regional entity, not a subsidiary relationship that would tie the organization to the Council's larger national agenda and bureaucratic requirements. Yzaguirre felt bitterly betrayed. "Out of nowhere, Juan calls and resigns, says he's already incorporated Midwest Voter, that Hank (Lacayo) was going to be chair, and good-bye," Yzaguirre remembers. "I was extremely pissed off. My initial reaction was to go after this guy and tear him [apart]." Willie phoned Yzaguirre immediately after he learned what had happened and said he understood Yzaguirre's anger and was sorry that things had turned out as they had. At the same time, he asked Yzaguirre to let go of his resentment in the best interest of all concerned and to find ways to support MVREP's important efforts to increase Hispanic voting clout in the Midwest. Begrudgingly following Velásquez's advice, Yzaguirre eventually wrote a diplomatic letter of support for MVREP, listing some of the Council's reservations but wishing the new organization well in its important work. Years later, Yzaguirre would blame himself for what happened, saying that he did not keep close enough tabs on Andrade's moves. Times had been busy for the National Council, especially owing to its efforts to contest the Reagan budget cuts and the eventual closing of its Chicago office. Even in the context of these many challenges, however, NCLR had not given Andrade the attention he deserved, Yzaguirre would ultimately acknowledge.

The sudden and tumultuous break with Yzaguirre and NCLR did not stop Andrade; if anything, it fueled him even more to turn MVREP into a working outfit. "We didn't have time to sit around and sulk. We had to get moving once the decision was made to break from the Council," Andrade later reflected. In order to help the group move forward, Willie put Andrade in contact with Silverstein and Mullins, a Washington, D.C.-based law firm that did excellent pro bono work for progressive groups. Lawyers from the firm ultimately helped MVREP to secure formal tax-exempt status and to establish an organizational infrastructure. The founding board consisted of three individuals who Andrade felt he could trust completely: Lacayo, the powerful trade unionist; Rey González, the former Chicago field director for NCLR, who ironically had supported Andrade through the entire ordeal with the Council; and SVREP's Velásquez. In May 1982, less than a month after filing for incorporation, MVREP's founding board members gathered at Chicago's O'Hare airport for a whirlwind meeting. The gathering resulted in decisions to officially charter the organization, to name Andrade as executive director, and to place Andrade on the MVREP board. The new board members also discussed the group's tax-exempt status, as well as the likely backlash MVREP would face for its break from the National Council.

Everyone agreed that money and effective fund-raising would be the essential ingredients of MVREP success going forward. They all also concurred that establishing a friendly temporary home for MVREP was essential to help stabilize the fledging organization while it awaited its legal incorporation. Velásquez stepped in to help the group on both fronts, agreeing to serve as MVREP's treasurer and chief fund-raiser and also to house the Midwest project temporarily as a sponsored entity of SVREP. Shortly after MVREP's founding meeting at O'Hare, Velásquez thus formally designated SVREP as fiscal agent for the Midwest project, pending final resolution of its tax-exempt status. He also cajoled the up-and-coming mayor of San Antonio, Henry Cisneros, to write a fund-raising letter of support for MVREP, which—along with Willie's own substantial fund development efforts—helped the new organization to generate more than $150,000 in support revenues in its first fiscal year.

MVREP's eventual success, notwithstanding early obstacles and impediments, was hard-fought and bittersweet. Sadly, the whole episode left scars that would be impossible to heal in the short term. Yzaguirre and Andrade would never fully reconcile. As far as Yzaguirre was concerned, the National Council, not Andrade, had created MVREP. Andrade, on the other hand, felt that MVREP was ultimately able to succeed not because of, but rather in spite of, NCLR. For Velásquez, it was all just another example of Latinos fighting each other rather than working together. With the final resolution of the matter put behind everyone as 1982 came to a close, he could only hope that the bickering was over and that the important work of Latino community building could begin anew.

Chapter 17

Willie's return to the organizational and political fray following his fellowship semester at Harvard proved rocky throughout 1982. Personal and professional conflicts on every level seemed to surround him, often pulling the voting rights leader in directions that ultimately terminated longstanding friendships and alliances. These developments underscored the increasingly high stress, high stakes realities of working on the front lines of social change. They reflected the substantial costs involved in advancing the struggle for justice on behalf of systematically marginalized Latinos and other minority populations across the Southwest. The respite Willie had hoped for in going to Harvard never fully materialized. The rough-and-tumble, pull-and-haul of the world he was now a leading player in would give no pause. Nor would Velásquez's response to the expanding pressures and power dynamics that marked his reality help him to mitigate the conflicts all about him.

In some measure, Willie's own unbending and relentless approach in all aspects of his life substantially exacerbated his woes. His restless, dogged, and uncompromising need to forge constant change on behalf of disenfranchised minority communities in the region had now become so central a part of his constitution that family, old friends, traditional allies, and even his own happiness and well-being were diminished to secondary importance in his personal construct of priorities and values. All of these factors combined to make Velásquez a sometimes difficult and unpredictable character, even to those who knew him best and cared for him the most.

On the other hand, Velásquez's raw determination and singularity of focus were the fuel that pushed SVREP into the vanguard of progressive political change by 1982. Despite huge impediments created by limited financial wherewithal and significant mainstream and institutional resistance, Willie's leadership and vision were quietly changing the political equation of the Southwest and the nation. Educating, registering, and mobilizing Hispanic and other poor minority groups on an unprecedented scale, SVREP was increasingly transforming the face of American civic culture. County after county, district by district, SVREP and its legal partners—including groups like the Mexican American Legal Defense and Educational Fund

(MALDEF) and Texas Rural Legal Aid (TRLA)—were now sweeping over the stubborn past of Texas's predominantly rural areas, toppling the strongholds of power that had systematically excluded Mexican Americans and others. From these efforts, a generation of "firsts" was born—the first Mexican Americans, Indians, and blacks elected to key public positions in decades and in many instances for the first time ever in the region. While the work of SVREP and its various organizational allies was far from done, it had by now directly impacted a huge portion of the Southwest political scene. José Garza, one of the maverick MALDEF attorneys, later recalled the unbelievable success they were having at this juncture: "We were so successful during that time that after the 1980 census was released, all we had to do basically was monitor. Everyone was redistricting on their own. Of the 254 counties in Texas, 249 counties voluntarily redistricted knowing someone would come after them if they didn't."

SVREP and its allies in the field quickly followed these victories at the county level by breaking down additional barriers in subsequent years, securing Latino and other minority gains by combating exclusionary at-large election schemes affecting local school boards and city councils. The project complemented these gains by bolstering its regional community organizing capacities through the development of so-called Regional Planning Committees (RPCs) that worked to hold elected and appointed officials of the region—both Hispanic and non-Hispanic—accountable to the needs and interests of poor minority communities.

෴ ෴ ෴

Challenging at-large election schemes that effectively excluded non-whites from key local offices by diluting the influence of minority voters was a substantial proposition under the evolving standards of review imposed by courts hearing alleged violations of the federal Voting Rights Act. In 1980, the U.S. Supreme Court's ruling in *City of Mobile v. Bolder* radically reduced the chances of winning at-large challenges from slim to none. The court's decision substantially augmented the costs and complexities involved for community advocates seeking justice via the legal system by increasing the burden of proof required to prevail to a near unattainable level. *Mobile* held that any challenge to an at-large system or any other election procedure would have to prove that the intent of creating or maintaining it was to place minorities on an unequal footing with the majority community. Under the new standard, it was no longer enough that an electoral system had the visible impact of being unfair to minorities; rather it had to be the active aim of its drafters to exclude minority groups, in order for it to be struck down. A "smoking gun" standard was established where minority plaintiffs effectively had to catch discriminatory city officials or school board members with a pistol in their hands, smoke slowly rising from the barrel, and bullets clearly designated for the minority community permeating the organized system.

Most black and Latino legal proponents knew that racism had become more subtle in recent years and that it was nearly inconceivable that they would ever apprehend public officials in the act of overt racial exclusion. It just did not happen that way anymore. SVREP's legal staffer, Rolando Ríos, understood well the obstacles involved in proving intent on such a high threshold level as now required by the courts and advised Velásquez to stay away from at-large challenges altogether. Willie heeded his lawyer's advice in the short term, but, never one to stand still, he actively prepared SVREP for potential future at-large challenges, starting with efforts to research and document the extent of the problem on local school boards. SVREP's Ríos, aided by paralegal Gladys Alonzo, thus investigated the impact of at-large systems by measuring the number of Chicano elected officials charged to oversee Texas school governance. Testifying before the House of Representatives' Subcommittee on Civil and Constitutional Rights, Velásquez revealed SVREP's findings, reporting the following to members of Congress: "there are forty-two school boards in Texas with 50 percent or more Chicano students and no Chicano elected official. Another thirty school boards with 50 percent to 91.5 percent Chicano students have only one Chicano school board member. The number of Chicano students must rise to an average of 89.1 percent before Chicanos begin having appreciable representation at the school board level. The reason for this is the at-large election scheme." The Supreme Court and Congress had both maintained that minority groups were not guaranteed proportional representation by the Voting Rights Act, but Velásquez and SVREP knew that the exceedingly limited incidence of representation of Chicano elected officials at the school board level was a strong indicator of a systematic problem and not merely a matter of accident or chance.

During the first half of 1982, SVREP, MALDEF, TRLA, and a host of other voting rights supporters joined efforts to extend and amend the Voting Rights Act of 1965, with an eye to addressing continuing electoral imbalances across Texas and the Southwest. Much to their surprise, they were able to secure most of the changes in law they were seeking by the summer. In what was to become a linchpin for SVREP and other organizations fighting at-large election systems, Congress amended Section 2 of the Voting Rights Act in ways that, for all intents and purposes, balanced the legal intent requirement established by the Supreme Court's *Mobile* ruling with opportunities for plaintiffs to prevail merely by demonstrating that a method of voting had an invidious result sufficient to invalidate it. In effect, the congressional action did not eliminate the *Mobile* intent standard for constitutional cases, but it did give SVREP and other minority advocates the option to rest their suits on the amended Voting Rights Act, thus enabling their cases to be judged by the "results" yardstick developed in pre-*Mobile* decisions. The amendments to Section 2 of the Voting Rights Act, and subsequent favorable court rulings, such as *Rogers v. Lodge* (which overturned a Georgia election scheme without even requiring proof of discriminatory intent), created the conditions for SVREP and other groups now to aggressively challenge at-large election systems. SVREP's prior research showing strong evidence of electoral injustice affecting Latino school board representation in Texas convinced Willie to bolster the organization's research capacities in ways that would substantially support its evolving legal strategy. To that end, Velásquez recruited Dr. Robert Brischetto, a non-Latino scholar with strong applied research and policy experience, to head SVREP's research department. With the addition of Brischetto, SVREP emerged by the fall of 1982 as the leading Latino rights organization in the country with real capacity to combine legal work with community organizing and sound supporting research.

Building on this potent combination of factors, Velásquez and SVREP's lawyer, Rolando Ríos, began to size up opportunities to pursue an at-large challenge that would gauge SVREP's future ability to win such suits on a broader, strategic level. TRLA had already taken the lead by initiating a suit challenging the at-large school board election scheme in Beeville, Texas on the same day the *Rogers* Supreme Court decision was announced. The impatient Velásquez did not want to wait idly for the results of the TRLA action; he wanted action now and felt that by applying still more legal pressure through SVREP's own independent litigation, he could accelerate the rate of change needed in the region.

In September of 1982, therefore, SVREP decided to make the city of Lubbock the first target of its unfolding legal strategy, building on a well-developed case that had been working its way through the judicial review system for several years with the support of a surprisingly able and committed cadre of community activists. *Jones v. City of Lubbock* was an at-large challenge that had been filed in 1976. Following nearly three years of waiting and original trial proceedings, the plaintiffs were defeated in 1979. Refusing to go away, however, the plaintiffs chose to challenge the trial court ruling and had been seeking an appeal hearing before the Fifth Circuit for almost three years when they joined up with SVREP.

Velásquez was immediately enthused about the prospects of forging a legal victory in Lubbock and became quickly enamored of the people there who SVREP would be representing in its first at-large challenge. Willie had a deep admiration for the Chicano activists of the High Plains of Texas. He loved the energy, enthusiasm, and drive of the Lubbock folks. He cherished their earthiness and their willingness to take on the establishment. He respected and related to their deep commitment to the cause. They were a hungry, restless, irritated group of citizens who wanted progressive change now.

A key leader and motivator of the Lubbock contingency was Eliseo Solís, a community activist who had experienced firsthand the injustice of electoral vote-rigging in recent years as a county political candidate. Solís's campaign following was largely comprised of grassroots community members who were beholden to neither of the major political parties nor any of Lubbock's political elite. They were true political outsiders who wanted to forge a different path in local and regional governance. Most had their roots in the controversial La Raza Unida Party and carried about them symbols of the radical past that scared so many Texans, especially in the Panhandle area—wild clothing, long hair, unkempt beards, pro-farmworker bumper stickers, and an outward attitude of skepticism toward the status quo. They were, accordingly, hated by the local white establishment and mistrusted at best by traditional Mexican-American community leaders.

In 1980, Solís chose to seek an open county commissioner seat when two other potential progressive Chicano candidates decided at the last minute not to run. Solís, knowing his chances of winning were slim, wanted nevertheless to make a statement with his campaign. He ran on principle, mounting a campaign that was decidedly staffed and fueled by Chicano radicals. The upstart Solís and his backers wanted to fundamentally challenge many of the county's sacred-cow policies and knew that in doing so they could not rely on traditional Mexican-American political leaders for support. In response, they pounded the dusty streets of Lubbock County, going door to door in SVREP-like fashion to build a base of appeal. The grassroots campaign found surprising traction and received an unexpected jolt when Solís took the lead over his leading Anglo contenders in the first round of balloting: Solís-1,052; Dunn-846; Lancaster-760. The surprise primary outcome elevated Solís to an entirely new level, thrusting him into the role of a serious contender rather than a mere bystander. During the final round flurry of runoff campaigning, Solís came up short, losing to Dunn by 107 votes, with the victor capturing 1,309 ballots compared to Solís's 1,202.

Solís and the band of Chicano outcasts who supported him were sorely disappointed by the close loss and skeptical that it could have been achieved without some form of ballot tampering or other illegalities. Solís had seen the Mexican-American community's voting power used, abused, strangled, and stifled too many times in the past and he wanted to make sure that his close campaign defeat was not a repeat performance of good ole' boy Texas politics. At lunchtime one day shortly following the election, Solís and a dedicated backer visited the county courthouse and found evidence of suspicious voting irregularities. They found Republican voters participating in the Democratic primary, unregistered voters casting ballots, and residents from outside of Lubbock County adding their votes to the contest. In total, they counted 134 illegal votes cast against Solís. Since he had lost by only 107 votes, Solís's supporters now felt robbed of a triumph they never thought they had a chance of winning. Solís and his backers later approached one of the county election officers, showed him a copy of the election laws, and said the jurisdiction was in violation of the law. In a scene reminiscent of a bad Western movie, the bureaucrat gazed into Solís's raging eyes, paused for dramatic effect, and cynically told him that the book of election laws did not apply to "Mexicans."

Solís immediately contacted SVREP's Ríos, described the situation, and asked for help. The Lubbock leaders did not have significant resources to contest Solís's election results, but they were confident they could prove their allegations of impropriety. Ríos agreed and SVREP took on the case, aided by Tomás Garza, a Lubbock attorney. To save money, Solís and his support base of Chicano radicals personally subpoenaed 128 people instead of paying the local sheriff $7 per person to serve papers on each recipient. Walking through neighborhoods they had never before visited, serving subpoenas to shocked Anglos, Solís and his crew were universally greeted by disapproving and disbelieving stares that made them feel as if they were a gang of criminals, rather than a group of law-abiding citizens trying to reclaim a tainted election. Unfortunately, for Solís, his preliminary legal challenge failed when the trial court found that only eighty-one votes of those contested by his campaign were illegal, narrowing the loss to twenty-six votes, but still keeping Solís out of office.

Though the county election results were not overturned, Solís and his backers had made a strident and powerful statement that they were not going to stand by and watch business as usual cheat them of their rights. They were determined to serve as a watchdog especially and increasingly in the city of Lubbock, where minority exclusion was particularly pronounced. Keeping the Lubbock officials honest and making sure the Chicano community's ever-increasing voice was not lost in the halls of power became a rallying point for Solís and his budding political organization. Willie loved this sense of popular activism bordering on hostility, and it was precisely these inclinations that he wanted to tap in SVREP's first at-large case. By joining Solís's forces with the protagonists of the long-contested *Jones* case, Velásquez sensed that he had found the winning combination that would be required to establish a beachhead for attacking at-large election schemes all across the Southwest.

The trial began on January 10, 1983, with SVREP and Ríos taking the lead for the plaintiffs, representing both the African-American and Mexican-American communities of Lubbock, which lacked meaningful political representation despite comprising fully one-quarter of the city's nearly 175,000-person population. From the outset, SVREP and its allies faced stiff opposition. Travis Shelton, the past president of the Texas State Bar Association, was retained by the city, as was James Brewster, another top-notch lawyer in the region, in order to bolster the defense's prospects for victory. Local newspapers, radio stations, and other media largely backed the city's position that the at-large system in place did not dilute black or Hispanic ability to participate fully in the local political process. Many traditional Mexican-American leaders also opposed the *Jones* litigation, in most instances because they did not want to be associated with the "radical" forces—including SVREP—that were spearheading the case.

During the trial, SVREP offered updated information on the extreme, racially polarized voting (a strong indicator of intergroup electoral disparity) that existed in Lubbock. Its evidence showed irrefutably that, with painfully few exceptions, Anglos simply did not vote for Mexican Americans or blacks, and vice versa. SVREP's research director, Bob Brischetto, served as the plaintiff's expert witness. His supporting data were so powerful that the defendant's expert, Dr. Delbert Taebel, was himself compelled to admit that with such high correlations in racial voting patterns, polarized voting did in fact exist in Lubbock. The best Taebel could manage in his testimony on behalf of Lubbock was the dubious qualification that, even with such convincing evidence, he did not feel ethnicity was an overriding factor in explaining the city's pattern of political representation. While explanations having to do with factors other than racial exclusion and inequality were certainly plausible, even the judge in the case was left unmoved by Lubbock's defense, which simply defied common sense.

On January 20, 1983, Chief Judge Halbert O. Woodward of the Northern District of Texas thus ruled in favor of the plaintiffs, concluding that "the at-large election system in Lubbock results in an abridgement or denial of the right of minorities to vote." Woodward went on to observe that according to the evidence provided, the answer to the question "Do the members of the two classes of minorities . . . blacks and Mexican Americans, have less opportunity than the other members of the electorate to participate in the election process and to elect members of their choice?" was clearly yes, given the court's review of relevant factors and circumstances required by Supreme Court case law and the newly amended Section 2 of the federal Voting Rights Act. While Woodward concluded that Lubbock did not have anything equivalent to a candidate slating process that patently denied access to racial minorities, he did find overwhelming proof that the elected officials of Lubbock were administering an electoral system that was finally unfair to its minority citizens. This reality, coupled with important historical and contemporary facts brought out at trial, ultimately killed the city's defense. In fact, Lubbock's history of official discrimination; the effects of discrimination in areas such as education, employment, and health; its high levels of racially polarized voting; the fact that no African American or Mexican American had ever been elected to the city council or mayor's position; and the controversial finding that a discriminatory intent existed when the at-large system was established, all made the plaintiff's case easily the stronger one.

The *Jones* victory was a dramatic breakthrough for SVREP, MALDEF, TRLA, and other minority voting rights advocates because it was the first successful at-large case tried under the newly amended Voting Rights Act. In Velásquez's eyes, the *Jones* case was a watershed for the Mexican-American community because it sent out a distinct message warning other local political bodies of what awaited them if they chose unreasonably to uphold and defend their entrenched at-large systems. The impact of the *Jones* decision, Velásquez hoped, would be to scare cities and school boards into settling at-large disputes out of court, rather than having to finance and sustain lengthy discovery procedures and trials they were now far less likely to win. Velásquez wrote to SVREP financial supporters to advance this theory, reporting, "The effects of the case (*Jones*) are already being felt. Only two weeks after our decision in Lubbock, Federal District Judge George Kazen ruled for MALDEF forcing the Corpus Christi Independent School District to also go to single-member districts. Within another few weeks we expect a similar ruling in Beeville, Texas, regarding the Beeville Independent School District. The latter case was handled by . . . Texas Rural Legal Aid."

Velásquez's bold predictions eventually proved true, but in the beginning progress was mitigated by the unknown quantity of what remedies SVREP and the other voting rights advocates could negotiate. The establishment of pure single-member district plans was their ultimate goal, but political realities and the inevitability of necessary compromise usually resulted in mixed plans—election systems that incorporated both single-member district seats and at-large positions. Velásquez and Ríos understood well the inherent conservative nature of the Texas political environment and stretched the system as far as it would go. "We weren't compromising our values by accepting mixed plans. It was the best thing we could get at the time," Ríos later recalled. "It was incremental progress, not as much as we would've liked, but it was better than the old at-large system." As SVREP's principals knew only too well, winning a case completely on the merits did not in any way guarantee a satisfactory remedy. For Ríos, SVREP's point person making the judgment calls on the plans offered, the guiding principle was to salvage the best plans possible in the immediate context and then slowly to push harder and further in the long-term for better arrangements as the number of favorable suits being won by the entire voting rights community increased.

The *Jones* decision buoyed Velásquez and inclined him to redouble SVREP's efforts rather than rest on the laurels of its victory. His immediate reaction was to steamroll ahead full blast and to tackle other localities. Reflecting on SVREP's successful record of negotiating settlements with county officials concerning racial gerrymandering, Willie saw absolutely no reason why SVREP and its allies could not replicate this approach with cities and school boards regarding their exclusionary at-large systems. In true Velásquez style, therefore, the SVREP chief, just weeks after the Lubbock victory, declared open warfare on Texas's cities and schools, boasting that the voting rights community had plans to attack as many as one hundred jurisdictions believed to be in violation of federal Voting Rights Act provisions.

Velásquez spoke with such forcefulness and commitment when he visualized the potential impact of at-large challenges that, at times, he seemed to forget that SVREP, for all of its growing importance and impact, still only had a one-person litigation department backed by one paralegal or that MALDEF and TRLA had their own limitations. Willie's dreams were exactly that—hopes, ideals, possibilities—and while he knew it would be extremely difficult, if not impossible, to take on the number of cases that needed to be tackled, he could not help but bask in the optimistic glow of what lay ahead. After the tough times he had faced since returning from Harvard, Velásquez was now bursting with faith. He knew that SVREP's forward movement from here would offer new hope and possibilities to communities where Mexican Americans and other minorities made up 30 to 40 percent of the population and did not have any elected representation. With a true chance of winning elections, Willie knew that Chicanos and other historically marginalized groups would rally, register to vote, and turn out like never before. He had seen it before and could already imagine even greater successes going forward.

In April of 1983 a Mexican American and African American were elected to the Lubbock City Council for the first time in the city's history, thanks to the newly created single-member districts that SVREP's court victory in *Jones* made possible. Willie knew this was only the beginning. Electing these new minority political representatives made him smile and worry simultaneously. Getting them elected, though surely an accomplishment, was suddenly now less important to Velásquez than ensuring their responsiveness and accountability to their grassroots constituents. The challenge of holding these new minority elected leaders to the highest standards of constituent responsiveness thus became a significant focus for SVREP following *Jones*.

෨ ෨ ෨

Developing active Regional Planning Committees (RPCs) was Velásquez's response to the problem of holding Latino and other minority elected officials accountable to their constituencies. The RPCs were meant to be groups of key Mexican-American political actors, all living in different areas of a particular region, who would bring their expertise and passion to

the fore in discerning and advocating constituent needs and targeting responsive organizing and voter registration drives. In grand style, Willie
announced in mid-1983 that SVREP eventually planned to form fifteen
RPCs throughout the Southwest made up of some one thousand influential
Mexican-American leaders.

For Velásquez, the RPCs were the next logical step in developing
SVREP's field capacities. At the beginning of its history, SVREP relied almost
exclusively on Willie's personal network and on ancillary contacts he and
other staffers made in the course of their work. While this worked fairly well
before SVREP became more established in the grassroots world, it became
increasingly more difficult to respond effectively and optimally to the large
number of localities requesting aid from the organization as its visibility and
standing increased over the years. This created an ongoing dilemma for
Velásquez. He had always prided himself for working toward social change
from the bottom up, but now he found himself occasionally having to make
decisions about where SVREP should work based on nothing more than sec-
ondhand information gathered by his field director and others who were not on
the ground, as such. There is no doubt that Willie trusted his knack for sizing
up such situations, but he felt immeasurably more comfortable in situations
where local folks could tell him directly whether or not SVREP needed to run
a drive in a particular census tract of the Southwest that they knew intimately.
For awhile SVREP toyed with the idea of posting regional coordinators, individuals trained by SVREP and placed in charge of their home turf, but the idea
proved unworkable for its prospective overreliance on single individuals and
the inevitable unevenness of those individuals' commitment, availability, and
skills. Willie knew that SVREP needed a more potent approach, one that built
on more collective grassroots leadership development.

Shortly after commencing the RPC strategy, Willie devoted one of his
monthly progress reports to board members and benefactors to the RPCs,
outlining several rationales for the new entities. First, the RPCs would set
priorities for where SVREP should hold registration drives. "Instead of staff
making determinations about where we should work," Willie reported, "the
committees [will] counsel SVREP on where we should work, when, and who
it is locally that really gets the job done. In this way, important campaigns
[will not] fall between the cracks because we don't know about them or they
don't know about us." Second, the RPCs would allow local leaders to network and develop closer ties. "It is curious that even in politically sophisticated areas like South Texas the people don't know each other completely,"
Willie observed, adding, "There are great benefits in all [of us] getting to
meet and understand ourselves."

The third and fourth reasons for SVREP to support the nascent RPC
structure, according to Velásquez, was to create necessary platforms for

building a strong regional political agenda and keeping elected officials honest relative to addressing the needs and interests of their grassroots constituencies. These were the core reasons why the RPCs were important to Willie. By bringing grassroots leaders together in the RPC structure, SVREP provided a framework for them to go beyond organizing isolated voter registration drives to discussing issues and planning other political efforts on a far more coordinated and strategic level.

In order to advance this work, the SVREP research department began providing RPCs with polling results of the Chicano electorates in their respective areas to enable RPC leaders to see how closely in tune they and SVREP were with the evolving views of their constituents. The first time SVREP did this, it found that the RPC leaders in South Texas, South-Central Texas, and the Texas Coastal Bend, while slightly more progressive than the average Mexican-American voter in their region, closely mirrored the views of the general Latino electorates in their respective areas. Willie hoped that this type of information and reconnaissance capacity would keep the RPC leaders grounded and closely connected relative to the issues their communities considered most important to them.

As the RPC leaders became more comfortable with each other and their community-driven political advocacy imperatives, they began to ask SVREP for research on the voting records of politicians who represented them. Many were shocked at how miserably the Mexican-American community had been served by these legislators and vowed to address the issue. Velásquez placed the blame squarely on the shoulders of his people, arguing, "This has come about mostly as a result of neglect on the part of us Chicanos. Quite simply, it is our own fault that the political system has produced legislators with such abominable records." Willie knew full well that community disengagement was only part of the story, but it was one explanation that he hoped would enrage and motivate the RPCs into action, and it did. The Texas RPCs, the first organized, quickly branched out and started to forcefully question elected officials and potential candidates on why they had taken certain stances and what they promised they would do for the Hispanic community in the future. Many of the target officials and candidates subjected to these tough, questioning community advocates had never been pressed in this way.

Willie relished the exchanges. Watching different politicians, both friends and foes, squirming from the point-blank questions of the SVREP field leaders, made him feel good about democracy. To be sure, these dialogues were hardly the most sophisticated interchanges Willie had ever seen. Many of the community leaders' comments, in fact, were no more than crude statements of frustration, but they symbolized American politics at its best for Velásquez, filled with ups and downs, heated debate, hard-fought compromises, and a sense of real public participation in local problem solving.

∽ ∽ ∽

It had been slightly less than a year and a half since Willie had returned from his emotionally mixed fellowship experience at Harvard to the harsh realities of his personal life. One of the overriding reasons that he had sought to leave Texas in the first place was to cleanse his soul, refresh his vitality, and come to grips with where he and SVREP needed to go in the future. Instead, the roller-coaster ride in Cambridge only deepened his frustration and his reappearance in San Antonio only heightened the levels of stress he had hoped to conquer, or at least minimize.

It was in the midst of this silent crisis that Velásquez reached deep down inside and doggedly charted an expanded course for SVREP, one centered on the development of an effective at-large litigation strategy and the other on a new democracy-building tool called the Regional Planning Committee. These were not logically instituted changes. They were not propositions offered by SVREP's board, which Willie tended to use only as a supportive body, not a creative one. They were not responses to newly found financial resources; SVREP would be lucky to break even at the pace it was moving, and the RPCs generated little new revenue for SVREP initially.

These developments were triggered by nothing less than Willie Velásquez's deep inner need and thirst for movement. Action was the only answer for Willie's seemingly incurable rut. Even after some of his major problems dissipated and SVREP plodded forward, returning to its character-istic frantic pace, Velásquez still was not satisfied. Being stuck in the same routine was tantamount to inaction for Willie, no matter how much good it produced. At the end of the day, he was simply not capable of just going through the motions. His essence craved change, new ideas, new challenges, and a chance to will forward another level of SVREP growth. These were the qualities that made Willie who he was and that pushed SVREP to greatness, even in times and places where it was unlikely to be obvious to anyone, including Velásquez, that success was in fact a possibility.

Chapter 18

BY THE BEGINNING OF 1983, WILLIE HAD developed a strong, favorable reputation among progressive foundation officials for his gritty and passionate presentations on the urgent need for voter registration and education activities in Latino and other minority communities. The liberal foundation leaders loved his unflinching convictions and authentic, down-home Tex-Mex flavor. They appreciated his common sense, his cogent and compelling political analysis, and his keen vision about how to expand American democracy through minority voter mobilization. His positive standing among benefactors was now making Willie a regular fixture on the foundation speaking circuit.

In April, Velásquez was invited to speak at the Council on Foundation's annual meeting in San Francisco at a session called "Empowerment: Personal Stories of Strength." Speaking on the panel with fellow activists Harry Bowie, head of the Mississippi Institute for Technical and Economic Resources in McComb, Mississippi, and Lois Marie Gibbs, president of the Citizen's Clearinghouse for Hazardous Wastes in Arlington, Virginia, Willie lived up to his reputation. He touched the audience of grant-makers with his customary humor and his fire-and-brimstone political analysis. But it was another, later, and less formally programmed conference gathering, organized by the Ad Hoc Funders Committee for Voter Registration and Education, that made Willie's participation at the San Francisco meeting most memorable and significant.

The Funders Committee consisted largely of a relatively small band of progressive grant-makers who were SVREP's core supporters: Dick Boone of the Field Foundation; Karen Paget of the Youth Project; David Ramage of the New World Foundation; and Margery Tabankin of the Arca Foundation, among others. These proactive foundation executives brought a decidedly left-leaning perspective to their work and wanted more of the organized philanthropic field to bring its vast resources to the aid of groups like SVREP that were seeking to make democracy a more tangible reality for historically marginalized populations across the United States. Frustrated by the larger field's relative disengagement from this work, the committee's leadership decided to host an eleventh hour, unofficial meeting of funders at the San Francisco conference to discuss opportunities to expand the base of private support available to groups like SVREP. They especially wanted Willie to participate as a leading spokesperson for the cause. They knew that the Chicano leader from Texas would be able to lift the sights of benefactors standing on the sidelines, while reinforcing the commitment and rationale of already engaged foundations to deepen and redouble their pro-voting rights investments.

Willie enthusiastically agreed to participate at the Ad Hoc Committee's meeting, expecting a modest group of his most ardent supporters and perhaps a small handful of prospective converts to make up the audience. Much to his surprise, the gathering turned out to be something altogether different than Velásquez had planned for. Willie found a jam-packed room at the belatedly scheduled meeting that was buzzing with excitement. There were more than seventy interested funders represented at the gathering. Velásquez stood at the meeting hall's entrance in disbelief: half shocked, half puzzled, and crammed in with a throng of mostly unfamiliar faces. For a moment, he wondered if he was in the right place. He had never known there were so many foundations interested in voter registration. On the contrary, he was used to counting the number of foundations who would even consider supporting registration work on just his two hands with fingers to spare.

In fact, most grant-makers *were* disinclined to support voter promotion activities on account of fear that doing so would invite undesired federal oversight of their work. These fears, arguably exaggerated, did, however, have a basis in recent national and field history. As Tom Wahman, formerly of the Rockefeller Brothers Fund, would later explain, "There had been less than a dozen foundations who had put money into voter registration and education work after the Tax Reform Act of 1969. Congress slapped foundations on the wrist [at that time for engaging in so-called 'partisan political activities'], not much more than that; but it [certainly] intimidated [many private grant-makers]."

The overwhelming turnout of benefactors at the Ad Hoc Committee's San Francisco gathering appeared to signal that an important sea change was in the works relative to donor interest in voter empowerment activities. What caused this shift to occur, however, was not at all clear to Velásquez or anyone else in attendance. The Field Foundation's Dick Boone, one of the central players in the attempt to expand resources for voter registration work at the time, believed there were multiple, converging agendas at play that finally defied any simple explanation. "To the surprise of us all, people came and filled the room" he would later observe. "It was beyond our wildest expectations and to this day I'm not sure why it happened. . . . People can say they [came] for this reason or that, but [I don't think anyone really knows why we all] came together."

Indeed, the funders in attendance at the Ad Hoc Committee gathering seem to have been motivated to participate for a range of reasons. Notions of social justice, political reform, and concern about expanding conservatism in U.S. policy making appear in retrospect to be the unifying factors that galvanized them into action. Boone and most of the funders representing the smaller, more progressive foundations in attendance were especially concerned about political empowerment for minorities and low-income people. Others wanted to use voter registration and education efforts to rally expanded public involvement on specific liberal issues, such as nuclear disarmament, reproductive rights, economic justice, and Central American policy. Tangled with all of these considerations, for many of the donors, was the expectation that increased registration and education support would have a dramatic impact on liberal voter turnout, hopefully leading to a dramatic change in who was getting elected on all levels, from the local school board to the White House.

Concerns about regaining the White House were especially strong among the progressive members of the Ad Hoc Funders Committee in the wake of Ronald Reagan's commanding presidential victory in 1980. Many of the ideas and agendas that the committee's members and their grantees had pursued since the reform-oriented 1960s were now being threatened by the decidedly conservative policies of the Reagan administration. By mid-1983, when the Ad Hoc Committee convened, Reagan's policies were beginning to have tremendous impact on national governance and the economy. Radical cuts in federal spending and oversight led to a major recession and regulatory rollbacks that especially hit hard at traditional liberal constituencies. The Reagan budget cuts, in the words of historian James MacGregor Burns, "slashed toward the heart of the New Deal, Fair Deal, and Great Society domestic programs—education, health, housing, urban aid, food stamp programs, the National Endowments for the Arts and for the Humanities, the Corporation for Public Broadcasting, and even federal subsidies for school meals." All of these developments were anathema to members of the American political left, including most of the grant-making executives who made up the Ad Hoc Funders Committee on Voter Registration and Education. Reagan was seen as an enemy of minorities, women, the peace movement, farmers, students, and the poor.

With the Reagan administration aggressively seeking to press public policy to meet its stated conservative goals, voter registration and education activities emerged in the minds of progressive and liberal benefactors as one of several potential strategies to mitigate the Republican Party's growing strength by increasing the political leverage of poor and minority communities. In addition to expanding progressive voter registration and education grant-making, other left-oriented funding agendas began to develop at this time around an array of grant-maker coalitions concerned with issues of environmental protection, pro-choice, legal services for the poor, nuclear disarmament, and federal budgeting, among others. The Ad Hoc Funders Committee gathering enabled the nation's small handful of leading voter mobilization grant-makers to expand their reach to more significant philanthropic leadership institutions, such as the Ford and Rockefeller Foundations, as well as other funders who were not yet engaged in the field. Practitioner testimonials from field leaders like SVREP's Velásquez helped to strengthen the case for a more concerted philanthropic effort to promote minority voter empowerment.

Discussion at the special conference session was rich and wide-ranging. Clearly, the size and nature of the gathering spoke to a growing conversation among foundation funders concerning their strategic options in the political advocacy arena. Gratefully, from Willie's standpoint, the funders were not only speaking among themselves. Most of them had also been speaking in recent months with executives of the leading national and regional minority voter registration groups, including SVREP in the Latino community and VEP and Operation Big Vote in the African-American community.

The funders came away especially impressed by the strategies and impacts that Willie and SVREP had been effectively pulling forward. By the time they assembled in San Francisco, many had come to see SVREP as an essential leader and asset in the national voter mobilization equation. They wanted to help SVREP and other organizations like it to expand their capacity on a much broader level. By all accounts, SVREP was establishing the template that leading funders wanted to become the standard for the field.

Velásquez was encouraged by these discussions, though he was never fully convinced that private funding levels for these groups would actually rise dramatically as a result. The last thing Willie wanted to do, however, was to give the foundations an excuse to sit on the sidelines, rather than push to make big things happen. For Willie, it was a critical moment in American political history. The success or failure of groups like SVREP would have much to do not only with the nature of minority participation in U.S. governance, as he saw it, but also with the quality of American life through the final decades of the twentieth century. The moment was huge in his assessment. It represented an historical opportunity for private grant-makers to think on a larger and more coordinated scale about their pro-democracy work and to launch what time would reveal to be one of the greatest democratic experiments the country had ever seen.

◠ ◠ ◠

Willie returned from the Council on Foundations meeting inspired, but not exactly sure where he wanted to take SVREP. From the beginning of the year he had been pushing hard to increase the project's funding base, challenging both current and potential supporters to help him address growing difficulties that lay ahead as a result of the so-called Reagan revolution. Putting pragmatism ahead of his pride, Velásquez went so far as to submit yet another request for money from LCLAA, the Latino arm of the labor movement that shared a long history of bad blood with Willie and SVREP. He even suggested that LCLAA and SVREP work together (they had never really done so) in strategic places like Denver (where former MALDEF attorney Federico Peña was gearing up for an historic mayoral race) and Los Angeles (where the union group's contacts were particularly strong). With Hank Lacayo, a past foe of Willie's turned SVREP board member, now heading LCLAA, Velásquez believed the project was finally well-positioned to successfully cultivate funding from Latino union leadership. Velásquez also stepped up his private foundation appeals, building on the strength of his participation at the Council on Foundations conference. He succeeded in attracting important new dollars from philanthropies across the country, especially for SVREP's research work and, to a lesser extent, its litigation activity. In addition, to expand the project's capacity to underwrite its field organizing activities (the most difficult area for SVREP to gain institutional support because of donor fears about its directly "political" nature), Willie imposed tough cost savings measures on the organization. These measures, sometimes petty (such as when he imposed stiff financial penalties on his staff for making personal and long distance calls on their office phones), were, for Willie, essential to maximize SVREP's available resources to contend with its evolving opportunities and challenges.

All of these efforts were critically important from Velásquez's standpoint, in order to prepare SVREP for its next generation strategy. But precisely what that strategy would consist of and how to position and structure it were entirely unclear to him. Lacking a clear guidepost and, therefore, a clear target to which he could direct his deep natural passions and talents, Willie floundered momentarily. Then Ronald Reagan came to town to participate in San Antonio's annual Cinco de Mayo celebration and Velásquez's uncertainties about how exactly to position SVREP going forward were quickly put to rest.

On the eve of his trip to San Antonio, President Reagan issued a statement from the White House on the importance of Cinco de Mayo (the May 5 holiday commemorating Mexico's independence from French occupation in the 1860s). The statement previewed the Republican administration's intention to aggressively court Hispanic voters during the coming 1984 national election cycle, reading in part: "May 5 holds an important place for all who value freedom. In Mexico and throughout the hemisphere, we recall the historic victory of the Cinco de Mayo with pride. It demonstrates not only the determination and love of country felt by the Mexican people, but also the heartfelt longing of people everywhere to live in freedom." Reagan's statement and trip to the Southwest represented significant acknowledgments of the region's—and its largely Mexican-American voting base's—growing strategic importance in national politics. Appealing to Mexican cultural and national pride to gain votes in the heavily Hispanic Southwest had never been a Republican priority. Reagan's Cinco de Mayo missive made clear that targeting Mexican-American voters in culturally sensitive ways was now effectively a political necessity.

One of the main proponents of Reagan's trip to San Antonio and of the larger Republican strategy of focusing on the Sun Belt region was Lee Atwater, the brash, young deputy to Ed Rollins, director of the White House Office of Political Affairs. Atwater, a South Carolinian with a deep knowledge of Southern political traditions and a cunning strategist, had just penned a sixty-three page confidential memo to Republican leaders underscoring the emerging political importance of voters concentrated in the Southwest and the significant long-term opportunities for Republicans presented by Hispanic voters in the region. Atwater firmly believed that Hispanic voters, who made up a key bloc in California and Texas, were potential Republican supporters. Cuban voters in Florida had always been staunch Republicans, especially when it came to international affairs, and they had given Reagan their full support in 1980. Yet, from a national perspective, the Cuban-American voting population was not very large. Mexican Americans, on the other hand, were a much larger and very fast growing group. In addition, according to many polls, Mexican Americans had given the president almost a third of their vote in 1980, a marked departure from their historically exclusive ties to the Democratic Party. This combination of factors, coupled with Mexican Americans' tendency to be culturally conservative on issues of religion and family, excited Atwater and his Republican political allies. They clearly seemed to justify expanded investments of time and interest in the Mexican-American community of the Southwest, from Reagan himself on down to the party's most grassroots activists in the region.

When Atwater was helping to plan the Cinco de Mayo visit, he thought long and hard about whom he should ask to introduce the president. It did not take long for him to identify a clear, though somewhat ironic, choice: San Antonio mayor Henry Cisneros, a thirty-five-year-old rising star of the Democratic Party. Atwater had recently met Cisneros when they were both honored by the U.S. Jaycees organization as Outstanding Young Americans. Atwater had been impressed by Cisneros's style and substance, and even though Cisneros was one of the Democratic Party's golden boys, the presidential staffer thought he could count on the mayor to deliver a warm welcome to his president. But, being the ultimate political operative, Atwater was not going to leave anything to chance. "I called up Henry Cisneros and talked to him," he subsequently commented. "Sure enough, Henry understood a good deal when he saw one." The young Democratic mayor agreed to give a cordial and nonpartisan introduction of Reagan. Atwater was ecstatic to have the popular Cisneros join his planned bandwagon for the upcoming presidential event.

On May 5, 1983, in front of a packed crowd of several thousand people, President Reagan stood underneath the scorching Texas sun in La Villita's Plaza Nueva and launched his party's appeal for the heart and soul of Mexican-American voters. Unabashed in his appeal to the assembled audience, the president covered expansive ground in his brief twenty-minute speech. He traded compliments with Mayor Cisneros, announced the creation of a task force to examine economic hardships along the border caused by Mexico's financial crisis, listed his administration's record of appointments of Hispanics, reiterated his tough, but embattled policies for Central America, reflected on the strong ties that bind the United States and Mexico, and praised the patriotism of Hispanic-Americans by citing examples of Latino military heroes. Reagan's whirlwind remarks were peppered with talk of freedom, liberty, courage, and the need to challenge communism in Cuba, the Soviet Union, and Nicaragua. A small crowd of protestors—both Hispanic and non-Hispanic—gathered on Alamo Street across from the La Villita speech site, mainly to denounce Reagan's Central American policies. Four buses, however, were parked in front of La Villita, shielding the president from most of the hecklers as he arrived at and left the scene. Lost in this group of angry activists was a sign that read, "Hispanic Vote Not For Sale!"

Velásquez witnessed the entire event, full of its Republican political hyperbole and rhetoric. What stood out for him was the powerful and effective use of symbols by the administration. The president was presented in a fiesta-like atmosphere that was carefully orchestrated by the White House advance team. Blaring mariachi music, a Mexican ancestral dance, bilingual Spanish-English signage, and hundreds of U.S. and Mexican flags greeted Reagan's visit. Brightly costumed men and women crowded the stage behind the president in traditional *charro* suits, Mexican dresses, and huge sombreros, producing a perfect photo opportunity for the White House. After his speech, Reagan, beaming with comfort and self-satisfaction, made his way to a vibrantly adorned food booth and sampled a corn tortilla stuffed with refried beans and guacamole. The crowd of immediate onlookers and a few die-hard Reagan supporters roared with approval. After nearly two decades fighting in the trenches, the entire picture seemed frighteningly familiar to Velásquez, a scene SVREP, through its work, had been trying to supplant for years: a benignly negligent Anglo patron coming to collect the votes of his peasants at election time.

Led by Mayor Cisneros, the president was shuttled from the stage into the Village Saloon and Eatery, a nearby restaurant in the plaza, for two short private receptions, one hosted by the city council, which contained a number of prominent local Democrats, the other by the State Republican Party, including nearly two dozen pro-Reagan operatives from the region. Mexican Americans, not surprisingly, were well represented at both receptions. Willie took his place alongside everyone else at the city council sponsored event, waiting for the president, engaging in the obligatory five-second presidential handshake, and wondering what all of this Republican attention to Hispanic concerns might mean during the upcoming national elections. Ironically, he fully expected to learn more about Republican Party strategy later that evening, having been invited by the crafty Lee Atwater to meet with him and another Republican National Party official to discuss shared issues and concerns. Willie was intrigued by Atwater's interest in the Latino vote and surprisingly anxious to learn what the Republicans—who had requested the meeting—might have to say.

Velásquez introduced Atwater and fellow Republican Jim Schivone to his own slice of Mexican culture that evening when they met to discuss Southwestern, Latino, and Republican politics. Willie took them to his usual stomping grounds, the spots he typically reserved for special out-of-town guests. They started at the Esquire bar and ended the evening late and drunk at La Margarita. All the while, they talked politics and history and culture. Atwater, the Southerner, and his Republican sidekick, Schivone, loved it all.

Willie loved the get-together too. What he loved most about the meeting was that the Republicans had asked for it. Velásquez had been taking progressive financial supporters and Democratic political people to the Esquire and the mercado for ages, but conservatives were a rarity on the SVREP entertainment circuit. Now that Republicans were emerging as the dominant party of the 1980s, he knew it was significant that they were coming to SVREP for information and advice. Willie understood this with pride as a clear indicator that his organization and life's work were finally measuring up to his most ambitious expectations. He could only be immensely gratified to have it confirmed by the Republicans themselves that SVREP's work and knowledge were important, indeed essential to them too.

Velásquez also appreciated the Republicans direct straight-ahead approach. Atwater's frankness and insight were qualities Willie rarely saw in party officials, whether Democrat or Republican, and it perfectly complemented his own stylistic inclinations and preferences. In fact, Atwater made no effort to sugarcoat his opinions or his purposes. He was not there to waste time or to make promises he could not keep. At bottom, he wanted to learn about the Hispanic vote and he wanted Willie to know that Hispanic voters were now being seen as a potential gold mine by Republican Party leaders, especially in key Sun Belt states those leaders wanted and increasingly needed to win. After all, winning elections was Atwater's business.

Velásquez, though a Democrat, understood and respected Atwater's approach to politics. As Willie saw it, the Republican vote strategist let you know exactly where you stood at all times; he appreciated that transparency. What Willie did not know was whether the South Carolina native's pragmatic attitude and willingness to sit down with groups like SVREP was a characteristic shared by others at the White House and at the Republican National Committee, or whether it was merely an isolated reflection of Atwater's personal inclinations. In either case, Willie sensed, the Republicans appeared to be contemplating a major push to secure new Latino voters in their camp and, in a deeply ironic way, this promised to increase substantially the stakes and visibility of SVREP's activities moving into the 1984 nationwide elections.

↶ ↶ ↶

As Reagan's Cinco de Mayo trip came to a close, with the White House team rating the event a large success, the president motioned for Atwater. The deputy political chief came to Reagan's side and listened carefully as the septuagenarian reflected on the warmth and liveliness of San Antonio, the style of its young mayor, and how much he had enjoyed the day's festivities. The president, looking puzzled, then confided, "Lee, I just don't understand it. They say we Republicans will never make any inroads into the Hispanic community, but with someone like Henry Cisneros on our side, how can we go wrong?" Atwater fumbled sheepishly for a moment, not knowing how to respond, then quickly replied, "Well, actually, Mr. President, he's a Democrat." Reagan was amazed and perplexed by the revelation in a way that made him unsure whether to react with anger, dismay, or utter glee.

For many Democrats and Latinos who later became aware of this exchange, it symbolized the shallowness of the Republican Party's commitment to recruiting Hispanic voters; for others, it was just another mental gap by the aging President Reagan. The gaffe underscored that even a former governor of the state with the nation's largest Latino population did not know much about America's nearly twenty million Hispanic people. He was hardly alone. Most Americans, in fact, really had very little knowledge about who these fast-growing Hispanics were, what they wanted, or how their evolution might impact American politics and policy making. Few Americans were actually sure what the term "Hispanic" meant anyway—Mexican? Cuban? Puerto Rican? Central American?—and whether this seemingly disparate amalgam of cultures, backgrounds, and agendas could legitimately be called a community, let alone a constituency. For all intents and purposes, Latinos remained a largely unknown quantity across most of the country. With the Republicans' strong declaration of interest to woo Latino voters made fully clear by Reagan's Cinco de Mayo visit to San Antonio in 1983, Willie knew that it was time for SVREP to step up and mobilize around the first ever attempt at a national Latino voter registration and education campaign.

Since the beginning of the year, Velásquez had been searching for a daring new direction for SVREP. Now, he began to see the convergence of important developments that convinced him the time was right to undertake a significant voter promotion effort on the national stage. The growing interest of liberal foundations to support progressive voter mobilization, the expanding interest among Republican political party operatives on the right to seize more Latino votes for their cause, and the raw growth in Hispanic numbers nationwide provided an unprecedented backdrop for historic action, as Willie saw it. The possibilities excited Velásquez in a profound and consuming way. No one could doubt the significant potential impact of a nationwide Latino political participation crusade. Governor Toney Anaya of New Mexico was already moving in this direction in January of 1983. Anaya, the only Latino governor in the country at the time, thought he could facilitate such a movement. Sharing his views with the press on the rationale and possible impact of the proposed effort, the New Mexico governor called for an organized campaign to make voting a top priority of Hispanic Americans during the coming election season, saying, "I see a tremendous response to the idea and everybody seems to be waiting. There's a vacuum. Everybody seems to be waiting for a catalyst. I would like to have [an] organization together soon enough to have some impact on the 1984 presidential election. It's going to take a lot of work, but I can envision this coalition in fact being the group that tilts the scales in a close presidential race." Governor Anaya had a great idea. What he lacked was the infrastructure and a viable implementation strategy to make the idea a reality. Willie, however, was developing in his active imagination a way to bring Anaya's vision to the fore in exceedingly practical ways.

The rough plan was simple, as Willie envisioned it. Midwest Voter Registration and Education Project (MVREP), which Velásquez and SVREP board member Hank Lacayo had recently helped to establish in Ohio, would take on the coalition-driven politics of the country's predominantly Mexican-American and Puerto Rican midsection. SVREP, in turn, would cover its natural, heavily Chicano turf extending along the U.S.-Mexico border. The largely *Boricua*[1] Northeast, finally, would be led by some sort of Puerto Rican community entity that did not exist at the time, other than in a handful of people's imaginations. A Cuban component was not something that Velásquez, the lifelong Democrat, was prepared to give high priority, owing, in part, to his informed certainty that the predominantly Republican Cuban community of the Southeastern United States would refuse to partner in any mobilization that focused significantly on areas where Democrats were most likely to be helped. The predictability of Cuban-American discomfort to collaborate with more progressive Hispanic groups toward expanded Latino voter impact suited Velásquez fine. When push came to shove, the last thing Willie wanted to do was help Reagan and the Republicans in areas where they already had a stronghold.

Willie's decision to position SVREP at the center of an unprecedented national Latino voter registration and education campaign was exactly that, his decision, and no one else's. His inclination to move in this direction was a prime example of Velásquez's charismatic management and leadership style.

---

[1]*Boricua* is an indigenous, Spanish-language reference to individuals of Puerto Rican heritage.

He had developed the idea with little input from other Latino organizations or leaders, voter registration officials, foundation supporters, or SVREP staff members. This was not unusual behavior for him. Indeed, Willie typically followed his instincts and passions before even he himself had concluded precisely where these things might ultimately lead. Organizing the most ambitious Latino-focused voter mobilization the nation had ever witnessed was virtually no different for Velásquez than any other SVREP undertaking, ironically, even though time would tell that the campaign would require much more heavy lifting than the SVREP executive director could possibly have imagined.

The kickoff for the national campaign, which would also serve as a major fund-raising event for SVREP, was set for August 8 and 9 in San Antonio. Velásquez believed that commencing the mobilization effort in early August would give SVREP needed lead time to organize a winning strategy. With over thirteen months before the national election, Willie believed he could galvanize unprecedented Hispanic voter participation in 1984. As it turned out, SVREP needed all that time and more.

For the next several months leading up to the planned August kickoff, SVREP's typical day-to-day routine was placed on hold as the staff—wholly inexperienced in events administration—blindly scrambled to organize the gathering. With just a year and a half to go, at that point, before the 1984 presidential elections, Willie and SVREP had precious little time to raise money, train volunteers, and establish effective strategies at the level of scale and significance they were suddenly called upon to reach. Everyone looked to Velásquez to have answers to questions no one in the national Hispanic community had ever asked before. For a long uncomfortable moment, at the outset, however, Willie had no answers to give. He was immobilized by his own uncertainty about the details, about proper prioritization and sequencing, about what should be the core benchmarks upon which to base the proposed national campaign's implementation. What Willie commanded, rather than attention to the details, was a well-developed sense of finding some way, any way to launch U.S. Latinos onto the American political scene in a manner that would inspire widespread recognition and respect.

As soon as Willie started to verbalize his vision for the official kickoff, his staff stepped in admirably to fill in the details, to draw and color between the lines in ways that moved the effort forward, notwithstanding the fact that no one on the staff or anywhere else had organized such an effort before. With Velásquez screaming out directives from the recesses of his office, the SVREP headquarters quickly reached a feverish pitch that would not subside until well after the August conference was over. By the end of May, newspaper and magazine articles on the Hispanic vote began to mention that SVREP was planning what would be "the largest voter registration project among Hispanics in history." These public pronouncements, largely lost against the backdrop of other stories, nevertheless put pressure on project staff to produce, and raised the stakes and the need for Willie to devise a more specific plan. The ambitious goal of the national Latino registration campaign was to increase the number of Hispanic registered voters in the United States by one million individuals, from 3.4 million in 1980 to 4.4 million by November of 1984. Owing to the campaign's lofty numerical target, Velásquez realized early on that it would require strong bipartisan support. He also understood that by increasing Hispanic interest and predisposition to vote, the major political parties would ultimately be afforded new opportunities to secure a significant emerging swing vote, which could decide key elections. He wanted the Republicans and Democrats to show their respect for the Latino population and to advance his own and SVREP's interests by each sending a key national player to San Antonio to offer their party's message for Latino voters. The audiences for these speeches would be top Latino Republican and Democratic leaders and nonpartisan community activists from across the country. As Willie envisioned it, the conference participants would consider presentations by the major party leaders, attend seminars on the objectives and mechanics of the proposed national campaign, and begin plotting strategies to support nonpartisan, Hispanic-focused registration and education drives during the upcoming presidential election season. SVREP, which historically shunned media attention, especially in English-speaking outlets, was now actively committed to ensuring that the proceedings and the campaign would receive maximum mainstream press coverage. In order to advance and refine this rough envisioned outline, Velásquez assembled an impressive national planning committee, a group of twenty top Hispanic leaders from across the United States.

The planning committee met on the morning of June 21 at the Gunter Hotel in downtown San Antonio, just a few blocks away from SVREP's headquarters. The participants, almost all old Mexican-American community activists and Democratic Party leaders who Willie had known for years, included Raúl Yzaguirre, president of the National Council of La Raza; Pablo Sedillo, director of the Secretariat for Hispanic Affairs of the National Catholic Conference; longtime civil rights advocate Dr. Blandina Cárdenas; Rubén Valdez, SVREP's board chairman and the former Speaker of the Colorado House of Representatives; San Antonio Mayor Henry Cisneros; New Mexico Secretary of State Clara Padilla-Jones; Los Angeles Deputy Mayor Grace Montañez; Harry Pachón, director of the National Association of Latino Elected Officials (NALEO); and Tony Bonilla, president of the League of United Latin American Citizens (LULAC). Juan Andrade, head of the Midwest Voter Registration and Education Project (MVREP) was also invited. In addition, Velásquez asked two leading Puerto Rican community representatives to participate on the campaign's national planning committee: Jack Olivero, president of the Puerto Rican Legal Defense and Education Fund, and Luis Núñez, president of the National Puerto Rican Coalition, both of whom had been recently working to develop a Puerto Rican-focused voter registration outfit in the Northeast. They too, therefore, attended the San Antonio meeting in June. Willie rounded out the planning group and June meeting list with two Republicans: Hector Barreto, president of the U.S. Hispanic Chamber of Commerce, and Catalina (Cathy) Villapando, a native of San Marcos, Texas, who worked for the Texas Republican Party and was also a SVREP board member.

Willie opened the planning committee session by welcoming everyone to San Antonio and moved quickly to the topic at hand, telling his guests, "Mexican Americans [and other Hispanics] in this country are now poised to make excellent political advances [during] the balance of . . . the eighties." After reviewing the recent gains Latinos had made in registration and turnout, primarily in the Southwest, Velásquez then pointed out the clear, emerging potential for Latinos to significantly influence national elections and politics. Willie, never one to mince words, put the key questions flowing from his initial observations before the committee leaders right away. "[An essential] question before us, quite simply," he stated, "is whether we have the capability to mobilize our people to have a major impact in the upcoming elections. Perhaps as importantly," Velásquez continued, "is the question of whether we can educate the nation at large about the significance of the [Hispanic] vote so as to create [a political environment] conducive to government being responsive to our needs." Answering his own questions from SVREP's perspective, Willie concluded his opening remarks expressing the firmly held view that "both of these goals can be reached and more readily than we think."

SVREP had conducted more than five hundred registration campaigns since it opened its doors in 1974, Willie reminded his colleagues; MVREP had already supported more than thirty projects in its first year of operation alone. These efforts, as Velásquez saw things, had begun to suggest that Hispanics could indeed be a critical swing vote in important races. Latinos, after all, had been the key support group that helped to elect Governors Mark White of Texas and Toney Anaya of New Mexico in 1982 and Chicago Mayor Harold Washington in 1983. Without the full backing of Latinos, each of these men would have lost, Velásquez argued. What was needed now to build on these victories, he asserted, was precisely the sort of orchestrated national effort he hoped the campaign would produce, based on significant regional mobilizations that could be organized and coordinated by groups like SVREP and MVREP.

Velásquez informed the planning committee that SVREP and MVREP were chartered to work in more than twenty states and together could support nearly three hundred registration drives leading up to the presidential election. SVREP alone could organize nearly two hundred such drives in the heavily Hispanic and Native-American states of Texas, California, New Mexico, Arizona, Colorado, Utah, Washington, Oregon, Idaho, Montana, Nevada, Wyoming, and Oklahoma. To cover these states and campaigns, Velásquez reported, SVREP would require some $1.3 million in revenues, an amount three times larger than the organization's entire 1982 budget. With Willie's encouragement, MVREP projected that it could sponsor some one hundred registration drives in the states of Illinois, Ohio, Michigan, Indiana, Wisconsin, Minnesota, Kansas, Iowa, Nebraska, and Missouri. According to Juan Andrade, the group's director, MVREP could successfully undertake this work for a price tag estimated at $510,000, a massive increase as well in its own budget, amounting to almost three-and-a-half times its current revenues.

Velásquez mitigated potential concerns about SVREP's and MVREP's organizational and fund development capacities to achieve their ambitious goals by underscoring, for the first time, specifically and concretely, how success would be achieved in the campaign. "The foundation upon which we build our political clout [must be] hard-nosed, no-nonsense field organization in all the major cities where [Hispanics] are important," he asserted. In practical terms, this meant ramping up and employing as never before the proven methods SVREP had developed in the field over its lifetime—door-to-door canvassing, locally driven campaigns, coordinator training, political and demographic analysis of each site, voter education through the Spanish media, and litigation, if needed. In addition, drawing from more recent lessons and innovations in the field, Velásquez proposed to mobilize and build on the work of regional planning committees that would bring Latino leaders together in key target areas to shape local campaign strategies and priorities. In total, Willie envisioned mobilizing twenty thousand Hispanic volunteers throughout the country, knocking on doors, walking the streets, doing whatever they could to advance the campaign's goal of registering one million more Latino voters. Velásquez felt genuinely confident that if all of this was accomplished the proposed campaign would be a smashing success that would enable Hispanics to make a "quantum leap" in national political influence.

The steering committee members listened closely to Willie's thinking and plans, which they ultimately endorsed with little question or contention. They fundamentally bought into Willie's package of ideas and spent most of their time focusing on how best to support the campaign, including ways to assist its financing. After a quick lunch, the leaders reconvened at a press conference to publicly announce their plans for the national campaign. San Antonio Mayor Henry Cisneros introduced the planning committee members and predicted that the sheer numbers of Hispanics in many states would play a critical role in the future of American politics and government. The three main speakers at the press briefing were Velásquez, Rubén Valdez, and Raúl Yzaguirre (the National Council of La Raza president who had now put aside his unhappy history with MVREP's Andrade in the broader community's interest to endorse the national effort). The three spokesmen highlighted the nonpartisan campaign's goals: one million more Hispanic registered voters by November 1984 (for a total of 4.4 million), twenty thousand volunteers recruited to go door-to-door registering voters, and $2 million in contributions raised to make it all happen. They also declared August 8 and 9 as the official dates for the campaign kickoff and reported plans to expand their steering committee to include a total of two hundred national Latino leaders by the effort's commencement. Senator Ted Kennedy of Massachusetts, an icon in the Hispanic community, was reported as already having accepted the committee's invitation to speak at the August kickoff event; Vice President George Bush was reported as also having been invited. Though Bush had not yet committed to participate at the kickoff, Velásquez was certain that he would, based on his recent conversations with Lee Atwater who had assured Willie that the vice president would do everything possible to attend. Yzaguirre closed the press conference by elaborating on Cisneros's opening remarks: "This is probably one of the most important things that has ever happened in the Hispanic community," the NCLR leader observed. "We're talking about making a mark, making a difference in American politics."

The planning committee, having successfully convened in June, never met again before the August 8 and 9 kickoff and that didn't bother Willie at all. He never counted on the group playing a truly substantive role in the actual organization of the conference or the follow-up campaign itself. He wanted the committee members merely to validate the effort, advise as requested, spread the word among other Latino leaders, and raise needed funds. Velásquez, in fact, wanted, indeed needed, to be solely at the center of this work's development, which to him represented the logical culmination of everything he and other Hispanic rights and justice leaders had forever been striving for politically.

Planning for the August 8–9 kickoff event proceeded at the SVREP office, with staffers redoubling their efforts to keep up with Willie's ever-dynamic forward movement and periodic mood swings. As Willie anticipated, though only at the eleventh hour, Vice President Bush's staff confirmed that he would attend the August convening in San Antonio. Everything and everyone in Willie's world lurched forward in relation to the planned kickoff event. Now, what had just been ideas and passions in Velásquez's own heart and soul, what had merely been words in discussion at national benefactor's convenings and late-night bar discussions with political party operatives, and what had been little more than press conference conjecture among Latino leaders in June—all of it was suddenly moving clearly into the realm of the real and the possible. Standing on the brink of a potentially transformational moment in U.S. Latino history, Willie could only hope that it would all continue to unfold as he envisioned it going forward in his mind's eye.

Chapter 19

THE SOUTHWEST VOTER REGISTRATION and Education Project had achieved much over the years to connect important local issues to grassroots voter registration drives that encouraged more Latinos to participate in community affairs. Willie would often tell audiences that when SVREP commenced operations in 1974, and in the years immediately following, drainage and getting neighborhood streets paved were the most important issues facing Mexican Americans in San Antonio. In every other Latino community of the Southwest, similar local issues were prevalent. It was the job of SVREP field organizers to find out what those issues were and to rally the community around efforts to address them through increased voting and civic engagement. Velásquez explained the need for this initial generation of organizational strategy in clear historical terms that put in stark perspective the fundamental challenge facing Hispanic voters, election after election: "The money used to come [to Hispanic communities] for presidential elections to get [our] people to the polls, but the biggest complaints of Mexicans were local. People were voting for Roosevelt, Truman, Kennedy, and Johnson, but the streets didn't get paved."

By the early 1980s, thanks to SVREP's hard work, this dynamic began to shift as Hispanic voters across the Southwest began to assert themselves. Willie described this shift and its implications, saying, "Now the money is being spent on those local elections that Mexicans view as important. People are seeing the streets paved and better schools. [Now that] they see things getting done, they [are beginning to] start registering and voting more." With this transformation, Velásquez surmised, Latinos were increasingly poised to move to another level of political involvement: concern for issues beyond the local neighborhood. This evolutionary change in circumstance had significant implications for SVREP's work, as Willie saw it. It spoke to the need to supplement the project's well-established body of work at the local level with efforts to address important issues of the day extending beyond any given grassroots circumstance. According to Velásquez, "Perhaps the most important single change [that needs to be factored into our work today] is that we can now think of having impact on elections other than local. We are not going to abandon local level registration drives for impact on local issues. What we are doing is recognizing that issues, like unemployment, are more and more the result of U.S. public policy decisions not easily impacted at the local city hall."

Willie's analysis along these lines significantly informed his push to commit SVREP to lead the most ambitious voter mobilization effort Hispanic Americans had ever undertaken during the 1984 national election cycle. It also explained his impulse to push for high-level White House support of the national campaign concept, most immediately in the form of Vice President George Bush.

Air Force Two touched down on San Antonio soil at Kelly Air Force Base on Tuesday, August 9, 1983, with plenty of time to enable the vice president to keynote the kickoff luncheon for the National Hispanic Voter Registration Campaign. The invitation-only event encouraged Bush to offer a major address on Hispanic issues for the 1984 presidential contest. All things considered, Willie was extremely pleased to have the vice president lead the charge for the Reagan administration. For the SVREP leader, Bush's participation substantially elevated the drive's national newsworthiness and significance in key opinion leader circles. In addition, Velásquez had confidence that the relatively moderate Republican vice president was simply more in sync with the needs and perspectives of SVREP's core constituents than most of his party colleagues. After all, Willie would always remind people that George Bush was a Texan (even if he had been born on the East Coast). He had also been an effective early critic of the "voodoo economic policies" proposed by Ronald Reagan during the 1980 Republican Party presidential primaries—policies that Hispanics and other poorer American groups were now mostly lamenting as the nation contended with deep recessionary pressures under the new president's watch.

As the vice president walked down the steps of Air Force Two, waving at the people there to meet him, carrying his speech in his right hand, Willie prepared to join him for the fifteen-minute limousine ride to the Gunter Hotel. After exchanging a firm handshake and brief pleasantries, the two men discussed Bush's upcoming luncheon address, and Velásquez explained the philosophy and goals of the National Hispanic Voter Registration and Education Campaign. Willie informed the vice president that he would be providing the Republican Party perspective on the issues, while Massachusetts Senator Ted Kennedy would be presenting the Democratic Party point of view later that evening. Vice President Bush began to review his prepared remarks as Willie briefed him, but reached a point where he became confused by the language his staff had incorporated in his speech. He showed the confusing speech passage to Willie and asked him if it made any sense to him. The passage concerned the administration's policy position on bilingual education and according to Willie it was a "politically perfect" statement, because it sounded as though the nation's Republican leadership supported bilingual education, although nothing in the text actually said so in so many words.

Willie quickly told the vice president that SVREP had recently interviewed nearly a thousand Mexican-American and Latino adults in San Antonio, Texas and East Los Angeles, California, as well as 147 Mexican-American community and political leaders representing twenty-five counties in four Texas regions: South Central, Coastal Bend, Rio Grande Valley, and the Panhandle area. When asked about their stance on bilingual education, SVREP found almost universal concurrence among the various survey respondents. Most believed it was a good idea to have bilingual education in the schools. SVREP found that 93 percent of Mexican Americans in San Antonio, Texas, 87 percent in East Los Angeles, California, and 96 percent of the Texas Mexican-American community leaders polled all strongly supported bilingual education. Vice President Bush, the moderate Republican who had been an early sponsor of bilingual education legislation years before in his political career and who had seen up close the advantages of people speaking two languages in Texas—Spanish and English—was open to and intrigued by SVREP's findings; to him, they made sense. While he might disagree with many Hispanic leaders and advocates on the specifics of how bilingual instruction should be administered, Bush did not have a problem with publicly stating that the Reagan administration supported bilingual education. In fact, he was well aware that within days President Reagan would be going on record with that position at the annual national convention of the American GI Forum Hispanic veterans organization.[1] His own prepared text for the San Antonio Campaign kickoff, however, did not establish the administration's favorable position on bilingual education, at least not clearly enough for the vice president. At Bush's invitation, Willie took the copy of the vice president's speech and penned three additional sentences onto the text that left no doubt as to its meaning. "Let me make this crystal clear—we are for bilingual education," Velásquez wrote. "Good bilingual programs make it possible to phase into the English-speaking mainstream," he added. Then, in conclusion, he incorporated the critical statement: "We are pledged to this end," which effectively bound the administration to go beyond mere policy pronouncements in the bilingual education arena. The vice president gratefully accepted each of these suggestions and used them later that afternoon when he addressed the National Hispanic Voter Registration Campaign

---

[1]The Vice President's participation at the San Antonio kickoff event and President Reagan's plans to address the American G.I. Forum, as well as Latino business leaders, during early August was part of an orchestrated Republican strategy to appeal to Hispanic voters with an eye to the 1984 election campaign.

assembly at the Gunter Hotel. Upon arriving at the hotel, Bush's staff coordinated with SVREP staffers to adjust the official press release highlighting the vice president's remarks on bilingual education. Using white-out liquid paper solution and an old typewriter, the SVREP staff altered and re-xeroxed the White House release for circulation to the national media assembled in San Antonio. Many journalists noted the obvious variation in text font and had to be reassured by Bush team members of its validity.

Upon entering the hotel, Vice President Bush confidently strolled into the Crystal Ballroom where a crowd of three hundred greeted him, consisting largely of active Republicans who had received free tickets to his scheduled luncheon address. Bush received a long standing ovation as he was escorted to the head banquet table to be formally introduced by Velásquez. In his introduction of the vice president (which some in the audience interpreted as a slap at President Reagan), Willie called Bush "the most respected person in the administration." "He is the one we look to," Velásquez asserted. "He is the one we have high expectations of. He is a man the Hispanic community looks to as a statesman."

The vice president went on to deliver the Republican Party and Reagan administration vision for the national Hispanic community. Interrupted by applause a dozen times during his speech, the former Texas congressman enumerated various Republican policy accomplishments and pending policy goals important to SVREP and the broader Latino community: extending the Voting Rights Act; serving as a watchdog on racist gerrymandering and redistricting; championing robust economic recovery, growth, and opportunity through tax and regulatory reforms; increasing minority small business loans; and, last but not least, supporting bilingual education. Bush's remarks demonstrated particular concern about issues of fairness and access in the nation's electoral processes. "This administration is doing its part," he asserted, "[to ensure] that Hispanics have the opportunity to participate—and participate fully—in the political process. We signed into law the longest extension of the Voting Rights Act in history, which, among other things, extends the bilingual provisions in that law for another twenty-five years." The vice president went on to say: "[We] will not rest while any American is denied an equal voice. We will remain constantly vigilant in putting down any attempt at gerrymandering or fancy line drawing that would dilute minority representation."

When it came time to deliver the portion of the vice president's speech related to bilingual education, Bush spoke with sensitivity to Latino concerns about the administration's possible inclination to defund the federal program. "I was an early original sponsor of the bilingual education legislation," he told the audience. "In times of tremendous deficits," he went on, "there is always a fight over funds; but our president and this vice president remain firmly committed to bilingual education." Then, using Willie's words and leaving no room for confusion, Bush emphasized the administration's bilingual education policy position, on cue. If there were any doubts about the Reagan administration's official stance in this area, the vice president, with Willie's help, ironically, made clear that even the conservative leadership in the White House now accepted bilingual education as a permanent fixture of U.S. domestic policy.

Vice President Bush concluded his remarks by underscoring his personal knowledge of the region and the issues affecting Mexican Americans and Hispanics as a whole. Acknowledging that most Hispanic voters traditionally supported Democratic candidates, but citing the lack of change or improvement in Latino communities as a serious, continuing problem, Bush lamented the Democratic Party's near monopoly hold on the U.S. Latino community. "I know what the voting patterns are," the vice president reported. "I've been in Texas since 1948. I wasn't born yesterday," he went on, warning Latino America of the dangers inherent in overreliance on the Democratic Party. "Look at one-party domination if you want to find people that are taken for granted. Look at one-party states if you want to find discrimination in voting or in districts. Why should it be assumed that every [Hispanic] voter is going to vote for [only one] party?" Bush then asked. "This president, President Reagan, and this vice president are not writing off any Americans" in terms of the upcoming elections, he assured the audience, as most of those in attendance registered their wholehearted approval. Bush then closed his remarks, asserting that the 1984 campaign would finally pose a fundamental choice for the American people: "a choice . . . between the shrinking vision of America held by the [Democratic] pessimists or the expansive vision—the expansive reality—we [Republicans] are building right now." The Republicans in the crowd rose for another standing ovation. The Democrats politely applauded and waited for their turn later that evening.

Velásquez observed Bush's remarks with quiet pride. Whether or not the Republican leader's comments resonated with most Hispanic Americans, Willie was gratified that a substantive Republican Party and Reagan-Bush administration position had been offered directly to Latino leaders for their consideration. It was exactly this type of elevated dialogue that Velásquez was hoping to infuse into Latino political culture.

In fact, Willie understood entirely that Bush's presence and remarks were driven by raw Republican self-interest. Without significant Hispanic support in key states across the Southwest, Republican candidates would simply become less electable given the changing demographics of the region. In turn, Republicans desperately needed radical changes to occur in the region's redistricting landscape in order to enhance their candidates' election prospects. On this set of points, ironically, Republican interests converged in unanticipated ways with SVREP's agenda to challenge existing malapportionment on behalf of Latino candidates. For different reasons, both the Republicans and progressive Hispanics thus shared a stake in challenging Democratic Party establishment leaders who largely controlled the status quo.

A photo appearing in newspapers across the country the next day manifested Willie's deep satisfaction with the Bush luncheon event. It showed the vice president sharing a private joke with Velásquez that resulted in the SVREP founder bursting into a hearty, barrel-chested, mouth-wide-open laugh that said "everything is working out just fine." In fact, the newspaper photo later caused many of Willie's closest Democratic friends to wonder half-jokingly whether Velásquez had allowed himself to become too chummy with the Republican vice president. Willie reassured his Democratic allies in the form of a subsequent letter to Al Thomson, an aide to Senator Kennedy, in which he included a copy of the photo and the explanation: "The vice president made me laugh because of his candor. What he actually told me was—'Don't think you [Democrats] are fooling me one bit, you bastard.'—As you can see, I [appreciated] his sense of humor."

The vice president's suggestion that the National Hispanic Voter Registration Campaign was little more than a front for the Democratic Party to expand its grip on Hispanic voters was not entirely unfounded. In fact, the balance of the kickoff convening in San Antonio amounted to an unprecedented coming together of Democratic Party leaders intent on mobilizing Latino Americans to challenge the Republican administration and its party's unfolding dominance in national policy making by registering and voting in larger numbers as proud liberals. The dinner following Vice President Bush's opening luncheon address and the entire next day highlighted Democratic Party leaders and issues to an extent that could leave no doubt about SVREP's—or the larger Latino community's—left-leaning tendencies.

The list of speakers featured to provide the Democratic perspective on Hispanic voter empowerment read like a who's who of contemporary liberal-democratic politics in the region and the nation. New Mexico Governor Toney Anaya, the only Hispanic chief of state in the land at the time, served as master of ceremonies. Presenters included San Antonio Mayor Henry Cisneros; San Antonio City Councilwoman María Antonietta Berriozabal; and Texas Governor Mark White.

Governor Anaya opened the Democratic portion of the conference by thanking Willie and SVREP for inviting him to be "on the ground floor of a project [that would] transform American politics." The governor then quickly set the stage for Senator Ted Kennedy's forthcoming keynote address by invoking the words and spirit of his late brothers, Robert F. Kennedy, who he called a great friend of Hispanics and other historically disenfranchised American groups, and John F. Kennedy, about whom Anaya commented, "We Hispanics still remember him with love and admiration. We are all familiar with the living rooms of many of our brothers and sisters in the barrios of the Southwest, in the homes of people living in poverty, people who some might argue have no reason at all to believe in politicians—and right there, next to the picture of our true savior, Jesus Christ, hangs a picture of President Kennedy . . . because he offered us hope."

Governor Anaya then went on to address important substantive issues germane to the conference, including his intention to work with SVREP and other anchor Hispanic rights groups to achieve four broad objectives during the 1984 campaign season that would build on the spirit of JFK's and RFK's legacies in Hispanic communities across the United States: "First, to unify Hispanic political organizations into a cohesive force [that could help to finance and elect] candidates who [are] sympathetic to the needs of [Spanish-speaking] people"; "Second, to help in voter registration and get-out-the-vote efforts" targeted to Hispanics; "Third, to sensitize [the major party] presidential candidates" to Hispanic issues and needs; and, "Fourth, to [educate] Hispanic Americans . . . on the need to be [more] involved politically." In closing, Anaya reflected on the impending political potential of Hispanic voters, saying, "The hands that historically have picked the lettuce in this country and the hands that have historically picked the cotton are the hands that can pick the next president of this country." The crowd broke out in loud applause.

As the proceedings unfolded and the various Democratic speakers approached and left the podium, anticipation mounted regarding the culminating keynote address to be delivered by Senator Kennedy. The large banquet setting at the Gunter Hotel proved to be surprisingly inadequate to accommodate the overflow crowd, which had been packed into the ballroom at tables nearly touching each other in order to make room for all who wanted to attend. Long buffet service lines and remarks from the multiplicity of pre-keynote speakers pushed the program late into the evening by the time the Massachusetts senator arrived. But the enthusiastic participants were happy to be part of this culminating moment of the gathering. Rising to the podium to introduce Kennedy, dressed in a simple *guayabera* shirt and donning a tiny United Farm Workers' pin on his lapel, was César Chávez. Chávez, the most well-known and respected Hispanic leader in the country, was welcomed with thundering applause and a standing ovation by the conference delegates, many of whom, like Willie Velásquez, could trace their earliest political awakenings to the farmworker movement he had led. Unlike the towering politicians who preceded him, the smallish Chávez was nearly hidden as he spoke from behind the podium, but his voice and presence focused and magnetized all in attendance. The iconic labor and community leader immediately took on the Reagan administration, criticizing those of its policies that had particularly adversely impacted Latinos. Recalling the infamous grape boycott of the 1970s, Chávez reminded the delegates that while

Republicans like Richard Nixon and Ronald Reagan appeared on television defiantly eating scab-harvested grapes, the Kennedy's were supporting the striking farmworkers. As the crowd urged Chávez on with applause and approval, the erstwhile activist recalled the progressive public service history of the Kennedy family, observing, "Through their service, through their commitment, and through their sacrifice, they have reached the hearts and the minds of our people like no one else. Their words, their deeds, and their style [have] captured our souls like no one else." With that, Chávez welcomed Senator Kennedy to the podium to deliver his keynote remarks. The meeting hall—chockful of believers—exploded with another standing ovation.

With the crowd already on its feet and on his side, Kennedy wasted no time in bringing the now Democrat-dominated assembly to a frenzy. Over the next half-hour, the liberal senator's speech would be interrupted more than thirty times by deafening applause, raucous cheers, and shouts of "Viva Kennedy", harking back over two decades to the successful presidential campaign of his brother, JFK, and more recently, to his own failed presidential bid in 1980.

Kennedy began by mercilessly blasting the Reagan administration, dubbing it "the most anti-Hispanic administration in modern history." Referring to Vice President Bush's speech, just hours before in the same room, he said, "Now from what I'm told about that lunch, you liked the things you were eating a whole lot better than the things you were hearing." He then went after President Reagan for what he described as a disingenuous attempt to recruit Hispanic voters, saying, "Mr. Reagan himself came to Texas on Cinco de Mayo and explained how much he appreciated Hispanics. But Hispanics need deeds, not words. And it is not enough to visit a plaza every once in awhile, to put on a sombrero, and to eat a taco or a tamale. I am less concerned about whether the president eats Mexican food and more concerned about the Mexican-American families who don't have enough to eat." The audience roared with laughter and approval at these remarks.

Turning to substance and policy specifics, Kennedy proceeded to offer something approximating a point-by-point response to Vice President Bush's earlier conference remarks as a way to establish his party's felt superiority relative to Latino voter appeal. The senator's list of concerns included tax cuts for the rich, budget cuts for the poor, and social security cuts for the elderly. On the number one issue of concern to Latinos, unemployment, Kennedy remarked, "We are told that we have just rounded the corner of prosperity. But there is no prosperity for the 12.3 percent of Hispanic voters who are out of work—a figure one and a half times the national average." With respect to poverty, the senator pointed out that no Republican could honestly claim "there is . . . prosperity for the 30 percent of Hispanic families who live and barely survive below the poverty level—twice as high as the national average." And then, in one of his most memorable and quoted lines of the night, Senator Kennedy added, "The president and his advisers keep saying that they care about the poor. And as I have responded before, there is one piece of evidence for this: Ronald Reagan must love poor people, because he is creating so many more of them." The audience erupted one more time, even louder than before.

Two other key issues raised by Kennedy in his remarks were bilingual education and the Voting Rights Act. In the first instance, the senator challenged Vice President Bush's earlier conference statement that the Reagan administration supported bilingual education, stating, "If Mr. Reagan really cares about Hispanics, then let him restore the 32 percent reduction he has proposed for bilingual education. . . . And let me tell you how we can pay for a bilingual program: we can stop the [administration-supported] MX which is a missile without a mission and a weapon without a home. The cost of one MX missile equals the entire federal budget for bilingual education for two years—and I would rather spend our resources teaching our children how to read than developing another warhead to read enemy defenses." Then, concerning the Voting Rights Act, Kennedy asserted, "Last year, we blocked the Reagan administration's plan to undermine the Voting Rights Act. We gathered support from an overwhelming majority of the Senate and the House— and forced the president to sign a strong bill."

Senator Kennedy went on to challenge the Hispanic leaders in the crowd: "In the final analysis, our success or failure in 1984 will also depend on you and the work you do in this voter registration project. . . . Your community does not have an army of lobbyists and a vast treasury for campaign contributions. But you have something that matters even more—your vote can be a clear and powerful voice in 1984. This voter registration project can and should elect the next president of the United States. Your goal is to register a million new Hispanic voters—more than enough to change the outcome in three of the six most recent national elections."

Kennedy closed the proceedings by bringing a poignant personal message that was close to home, given his audience that evening, "In closing, let me say a few words to all of you here—and through you, to all who share the Hispanic heritage" the senator remarked. "As I look back on the last two decades, I am more grateful than words can say that you have stood with me and with my brothers. You have given us your help and your hearts. I like to think there is a special tie between your community and my family." The senator recalled his unsuccessful 1980 presidential run, stating, "Among the happiest memories of my [campaign] are a visit at sundown to the Old Town Plaza in Albuquerque; a hopeful hour at the health clinic in East Los Angeles; a busy afternoon at the market in Spanish Harlem; the incredible rally which lifted all our spirits at El Mercado here in San Antonio during the Texas primary in 1980. I can never forget any of that—or all that went on in the years before." Senator Kennedy then concluded with the words: "Fifteen years ago and more, on his visits to migrant camps and barrios, my brother Robert came to regard you as truly his brothers and sisters. In 1960, my brother Jack knew that he never could have won if it had not been for the Hispanics who registered voters and walked precincts and created an organization known as '¡Viva Kennedy!' For us, you have always been there to say '¡Viva Kennedy!' So I have come here to say once again that I will always be there with you in the causes that we share. ¡A la victoria!" The assembled campaign supporters erupted one final time with another standing ovation and robust applause as cries of "¡Viva Kennedy!" "¡Viva Southwest Voter!" and "¡Viva la causa!" rang throughout the ballroom.

As Senator Kennedy's remarks came to a close and the conference ended, Willie and the SVREP staff let out a deep, collective sigh of relief. The National Hispanic Voter Registration Campaign kickoff was finished. All in all, the conference had been a huge success that positioned Hispanics in the national political discourse in a way that was both significant and unprecedented. These had been Velásquez's objectives from the outset. Now he had pulled it off, at least, that is to say, from the standpoint of commencing the campaign from a position of legitimacy and strength. Of course, only the heavy lifting of campaign implementation that lay ahead would reveal whether, in fact, Willie's ambitious aims would finally be realized beyond flowery partisan promises and appeals to Latino leaders.

Simultaneously, Willie and SVREP understood they faced a key challenge—balancing the overriding interest and focus on the potential of the Hispanic electorate as a key swing vote in the presidential election by the national media, both major political parties, and a group of progressive funders against SVREP's ongoing emphasis on long-term political empowerment for Latinos. For many journalists, party leaders, and grant-makers, it was all about the 1984 presidential contest. For Willie and SVREP, it was still about a grassroots strategy that went well beyond the next presidential election. From this point forward, Willie and SVREP would have to respond and react to a set of growing national expectations that they could not control while they continued to pursue the successful approach that had gotten them this far: locally based voter registration and education efforts.

In order to achieve the ambitious aims of the National Hispanic Voter Registration Campaign, Velásquez and SVREP would have to work closely and seamlessly with the Midwest Voter Registration and Education Project and a still-evolving and as yet unnamed Northeast-focused effort being organized by the National Puerto Rican Coalition. This would prove to be an inherently elusive and complicated task owing in large measure to natural tensions created, on one hand, by SVREP's relative dominance and experience in the field compared to the other two groups, and, on the other hand, by the Midwest and Northeast partners' limited capacity and alternative ideas of how best to achieve the campaign's objectives.

In fact, prior to launching the campaign, Willie consulted only very sparsely with his Midwest and Northeast partners. These contacts enabled SVREP, MVREP, and the National Puerto Rican Coalition principals to reach general agreements on the broad outline and aims of the campaign. It left many of the details of organizing such an effort, however, untreated and, consequently, unclear. Both MVREP and the Puerto Rican Coalition began to surface concerns and occasional differences in approach relative to SVREP as the campaign unfolded and its pressing requirements became more evident.

One of the early wake-up calls for SVREP's partners revealed itself when Willie, again with little partnership consultation, publicly announced the following regional registration targets for the campaign: SVREP would register 681,000 Hispanics in California, Texas, Arizona, Colorado, New Mexico, and eight other states in the Southwest; MVREP would be responsible to register 69,000 Hispanics across a ten-state swath of the Midwest that would cover Illinois, Ohio, Michigan, Indiana, and Wisconsin, among other targets; and the Northeast organization being assembled by the Puerto Rican Coalition would register 215,000 Latino voters mainly in New York, Massachusetts, New Jersey, Pennsylvania, and Connecticut. As Velásquez saw it, then, the Southwest, Midwest, and Northeast contingents would produce 965,000 of the one million new Hispanic voters he proposed to register to vote for the 1984 elections. These were highly ambitious targets to be sure. SVREP had never in its history approximated such large numbers in its prior drives; nor had MVREP. And the Northeast organization contributing to the campaign did not even yet really exist. Expecting a brand-new entity to produce nearly a quarter of a million newly registered voters right out of the box was manifestly optimistic.

Despite these ambitious projections, moreover, Willie still lacked 35,000 new registrants to complete the million-person campaign goal. To make up the shortfall, he unilaterally decided to include traditionally conservative Hispanics in Florida as a campaign target population. But even as Willie— and by extension the National Hispanic Voter Registration Campaign—was setting public goals for a Southern strategy, in fact the campaign did not have a voter registration partner to work with in the region.

SVREP's partner organizations in the campaign became quickly concerned about Willie perhaps getting too far ahead of them, although often as a result of divergent sensitivities. Puerto Rican community leaders in the Northeast were especially concerned about the huge expectations Velásquez's campaign targets had committed them to meet, just as they were establishing an organization to manage the work. MVREP, for its part, had its own concerns about Willie's projections—namely that they were too low for the Midwest. Being further along in its development than the Puerto Rican group, the Midwest partner wanted desperately to establish itself as a legitimate voter mobilization entity in its own right, comparable to SVREP. Consequently, though respectful of Willie for his role in facilitating MVREP's development, the organization's leaders tended frequently to want to put their own mark on the campaign, often in ways that at least initially contradicted Velásquez's vision. In the end, Willie brought both groups along with varying levels of success, in most respects less through concretization in planning and coordination than through the magic of his inspiration and people skills.

Louis Nuñez, president of the National Puerto Rican Coalition, which had taken the lead to seed the new Northeast voter promotion organization upon which the campaign's efforts around New York would be based, was convinced early on that Velásquez was pushing too fast and too far to have a hope of achieving success. Willie addressed Nuñez's concerns by flying to Washington and meeting with Puerto Rican leaders involved in the campaign, to walk them through an approach that would enable them to win. Building on SVREP's extensive field experience, Velásquez matter-of-factly focused the Puerto Rican leaders on the importance of strategic research relative to achieving effective voter registration and mobilization. The Northeast group received high marks from Willie for having already engaged leading community policy researchers, such as Juan Cartagena, Harry Pachón, and Angelo Falcón as supportive technical advisors. The SVREP executive director explained the importance of solid research capacity in the following terms: "Research, ladies and gentlemen, is *crucial*. . . . If you are going to win, you've got two choices. You can take up a year's supply of *velas* (votive candles) at Our Lady of Guadalupe [Church and hope for the best,] or you can study the situation and really mobilize yourself. But you're not going to do it by chance. There's no way that you're gonna get lucky. No way in the world. So you'd better study."

Willie then went on to advise the Northeast leaders to use research as a narrowing mechanism that could help to guide them in the right direction by clarifying the best and highest uses of their limited resources, saying, "Right now you want to register Puerto Ricans, and you're starting from point scratch. . . . You can do all kinds of things. But as you start getting data, it starts narrowing [your focus] and it makes some of the things [you might have been considering] look silly. . . . Things that seemed like viable options. [Good research] narrows it down, so that it [finally] makes pretty good sense what you [end up with]."

Velásquez further instructed the Puerto Rican leaders concerning the essential advantages of conducting relatively stealth campaign efforts beyond the radar of the mainstream media. Building on all of SVREP's early lessons, he told the East Coast principals to be very wary of arousing unnecessary opposition among non-minorities by overexposing themselves and their aims in the public domain. "We don't want to do what happened too much [to African Americans during the 1960s] in the South," he warned his Puerto Rican counterparts, explaining further, "Selma (Alabama) was a great [public] victory for blacks all over the world, but it was a *terrible* thing for the blacks in Selma [because, initially at least, it motivated a backlash resulting in] a 100 percent Anglo registration. All that publicity [thus produced] many, many years of blacks not winning in Selma. We do not want to do that. We are not going to arouse the other side."

Next, Willie focused the Northeast project leaders' attention on the importance of working in coalitions and of winning elections. "Coalitions don't work in life, except in politics," he asserted, informing the Puerto Ricans that SVREP had learned over the years that the best way to support successful registration drives was to assemble strong local coalitions of proven leaders and organizations that were willing to work hard, long hours, going door to door to mobilize Hispanic voters and elect friendly candidates. Communities that could not put together local coalitions were places where voter registration campaigns usually failed, according to Willie, either because they didn't have enough person power to physically maximize local impact or because the absence of broad-based support undermined their perceived relevance—and hence their credibility—on the ground, in the community.

Velásquez's presentation to the Puerto Rican leaders of the Northeast was particularly emphatic on the central import of building on coalitions to win elections. SVREP had learned over the years, somewhat to its surprise, Willie informed his listeners, that even where Latinos comprised a large popular majority, community-based coalitions were necessary to elect Latino and/or Latino-friendly candidates. The moral of the story, as Willie interpreted it for his audience, was, "you don't want to have a voter registration drive. You want to win an election. . . .The whole idea is that you are building a voter registration drive that is nothing but a dry run for election day. . . . The whole process, ladies and gentlemen, is [best understood as] a six-week campaign on how to win an election."

Velásquez closed his pep talk by imploring the Puerto Rican leadership group to build its work first and foremost around local leadership, paid staff support that could help to organize and direct large pools of volunteers, and a keen responsiveness to grassroots priorities and issue concerns. One of the most crucial lessons SVREP had learned since its inception, Willie told the assembled leaders, was the critical importance of focusing efforts as closely as possible on the local conditions and issues that directly touched people's lives in a real way. Though the emerging campaign had positioned itself as a nationally focused effort, Willie thus somewhat counter intuitively counseled the Puerto Rican leaders to focus their work on grassroots concerns in the Northeast. To underscore the logic of his point, Velásquez reminded his audience, "[Most] Hispanics . . . want to [elect] their first city councilman in history. A congressman or a president is going to have a somewhat marginal effect on them. . . . Concentrate on those races that are important to the people locally. They'll reward you."

Willie then concluded by specifically warning the Puerto Rican leaders to avoid the seduction of focusing on having an impact on the 1984 presidential race, rather than expanding local and regional Latino community political participation and representation. "[You] ought to have a registration drive," he told them. "But I don't think you ought to say you're doing it to have impact on the 1984 elections. You should say . . . we're going to do it because the Puerto Rican people deserve it, because we as leaders say it needs to be done, and [because we want to] impact local elections. Second, we're gonna do it because it's right that we organize our people, [and] that we [participate in electing more representative and more responsive] state [officials], city council [persons], [and] school board [members]—that's the basic philosophical point."

Willie's no-nonsense "here's how you do it" approach was exactly what the Puerto Rican group wanted—and needed—to hear. After listening to Willie, the assembled Northeastern leaders spent the rest of the day developing their strategy, focusing on the specific political research concerns, trainings, and coalition-building efforts that would guide them in their work.

A month later, an expanded organizing committee consisting of Louis Nuñez, Robert McKay, Miriam Cruz, Angelo Falcón, Ramón Velez, Millie Torres, and John Jack Olivero met with Willie at the Puerto Rican Legal Defense and Education Fund offices in New York City. The meeting resulted in an agreement to establish and christen the Northeast campaign organization as the National Puerto Rican/Hispanic Voter Participation Project. The National Puerto Rican Coalition, led by Nuñez, played an especially key early role serving as fiscal agent and program sponsor for the Northeast project and raising $300,000 in private foundation funding (with considerable assistance and support from Velásquez) to commence field activities.

Nuñez and Velásquez increasingly communicated and coordinated efforts toward getting the Northeast campaign off the ground. But throughout, Nuñez, inherently more cautious and methodical by nature than the SVREP executive director, raised concerns about Willie and the national campaign moving more aggressively than he felt was wise and practical. "There is . . . a possible danger," Nuñez wrote to Velásquez at one point early in the partnership, "that in [your] desire to build a national network . . . we might find ourselves very much a junior partner." Underscoring the Puerto Rican leader's caution was the concern, also expressed to Willie in writing, that "your intention [to launch the] national campaign, to my mind, may be too early for us."

Nuñez, a seasoned veteran of both successful and unsuccessful Hispanic empowerment strategies over the years, remained concerned throughout much of the campaign about the lack of more specific (versus more general) partnership guidelines, decision-making protocols, and divisions of labor. "I have always felt that the process of coalition-building in the Hispanic world has been replete with general calls for working together toward a common goal without identifying any specific project in which we can work together," he wrote to Willie.

Velásquez was simply not temperamentally predisposed to tackle Nuñez's concerns with deeper attention to details and specifics. Instead, he continued to push efforts in the Northeast forward by the sheer force of his human touch. By being available to Puerto Rican leaders throughout the campaign, by inspiring them with relentless insights about the core purposes and the people behind their efforts, and by reassuring them with humor and lessons from SVREP's long experience in the field, Willie simply did not allow Nuñez and his Puerto Rican community partners to be dragged or slowed down by overfocusing on perceived negatives and uncertainties.

In the end, Willie's charismatic qualities prevailed. The Northeast group developed quickly with his intermittent guidance and support. By the end of 1983, the group officially went public, announcing its formalization and goals at a well-attended presentation led by Willie and Miriam Cruz, president of the Equity Research Corporation and the first chairperson of the National Puerto Rican/Hispanic Voter Participation Project. The announcement, which coincided with the National Puerto Rican Coalition's annual conference at the Hyatt Regency in Washington, D.C., ensured a broad audience of community leaders and opinion shapers who Willie knew would be essential campaign allies.

In early 1984, Luis Cabán, an adviser to Nuñez who had been directing a federal Housing and Urban Development contract for the Puerto Rican Coalition, was hired as the first president of the National Puerto Rican/Hispanic Voter Participation Project. Cabán, who had deep experience working in various Puerto Rican and Hispanic communities but was a newcomer to the voter registration field, jumped straight into the position and spent the early months of 1984 working feverishly to establish the new voter registration organization. With considerable support from project organizing committee members, Cabán was quickly able to secure 501(c)3 and 4945(f) tax-exempt designations from the IRS for the new effort. Soon thereafter, Cabán officially opened the doors of the National Puerto Rican/Hispanic Voter Participation Project in Union, New Jersey, just seven months shy of the November general elections. Cabán and the National Puerto Rican/Hispanic Voter Participation Project were finally ready for action. Velásquez was ecstatic, even though primaries had already been held in several key Northeast campaign target states and the New York and Pennsylvania primaries were then only days away. Only New Jersey, of the original six states the Northeast leaders initially targeted, had an upcoming primary that the project could reasonably hope to impact, but even that was only two months away. By any measure, Cabán and his project partners had their work cut out for them. As Willie saw things, however, the national campaign was now truly underway with the Northeast's organizational consolidation.

ᔕ ᔕ ᔕ

A week after the National Hispanic Voter Registration Campaign kickoff in San Antonio, Juan Andrade of MVREP sent Willie notification that his organization would be creating its own, larger voter registration goals for the Midwest in order to expand that region's contribution to the campaign's overall target to register one million new Hispanic voters during 1984. Instead of the roughly 70,000 new registrants Velásquez had publicly committed MVREP to produce, Andrade now informed Willie that the Midwest group would seek to register as many as 200,000 Latino voters. The substantially increased registration goal would be announced at a November conference in Chicago, according to the MVREP leader.

Andrade was optimistic about MVREP's capacity to deliver such numbers based on significant campaign victories that his organization had experienced recently in the region. Willie, though respectful—and even humorous—in his response to Andrade, was dubious. "On reflection, it is pretty evident that we did not do a good job on explaining your role," Velásquez wrote back to Andrade. Then, seeking to find common ground, he went on to write, "Look at it on the bright side, now you get the chance to return the favor at your November conference. After your convention we should be even and maybe we ought to have a beer to discuss our long-term strategy."

Andrade's optimism about delivering greater numbers than Willie had projected for Midwest Voter was not entirely unfounded. In fact, during the prior year, MVREP's work had directly or indirectly achieved significant gains for Latino communities and candidates across the nation's central states. In Lansing, Michigan, María Velásquez was elected as a county commissioner and Tony Benavidez was elected to a seat on the city council as a result of MVREP's efforts. In Illinois, Joe Berrios was similarly elected to the state legislature, one of the first Hispanics in Illinois history to serve in the lower house, and Miguel Santiago became the second Hispanic elected to the Chicago city council.

In addition to these landmark victories, MVREP's optimism was enhanced by various narrow defeats in the region in races that pundits had not thought would involve close contests. For example, Joe Estrada, in Detroit, lost a bid to become the first Hispanic state legislator in Michigan by only 127 votes; Ed Dávila, in Cleveland, also lost a closely contested state legislative race that would have made him the first Hispanic legislator in Ohio; and María Flores of Wisconsin narrowly lost a state senate race in that state. To Andrade, these defeats were actually victories for demonstrating that Hispanics could run competitive races in areas where their overall numbers were low.

Andrade's belief in MVREP's growing vote-producing capacity was especially heightened in the wake of numerous regional contests that involved no Hispanic candidates, but where Latino voters played a pivotal role in the outcome, such as: Bob Karr's sixth congressional district race in Michigan; Jim Blanchard's bid for the governor's office in Michigan; Dick Celeste's governor's race in Ohio; Lane Evan's upset congressional victory over incumbent Ken McMillan in Illinois; and Tony Earl's victory in Wisconsin for governor. And, in Chicago, where Harold Washington was elected the first African-American mayor in the city's history, Hispanics were an essential component of Washington's coalition.

At the end of the day, Andrade and other Midwest Hispanic leaders were simply convinced that their time in the sun had come; they wanted desperately to put their work and their issues on the national political map in a significant and unprecedented way. Various historical factors accounted for this urge. Though Latinos had long been present in the Midwest—as railroad and factory workers, as migrant laborers and meatpackers—until now, their concentration in numbers had never been such that it elevated them as a palpable voice in regional governance. Midwest Hispanic leaders now saw MVREP's early successes, however, as a way to gain a level of power and recognition that had long been desired but never before thought possible. The idea of producing nearly a quarter of a million new Latino voters during the 1984 presidential election cycle was simply too exciting for MVREP's leaders to pass over in this context. So was the idea of assembling a major conference that would attract some of the region's most important political actors for the purpose of announcing the organization's intentions during the upcoming campaign cycle.

MVREP's regional conference, dubbed the Midwest Hispanic Political Leadership Conference, was scheduled for Friday and Saturday, November 11–12, 1983, at the McCormick Center Hotel in Chicago. In an open letter from Andrade to Hispanic leaders in the region, the MVREP leader set the tone for the upcoming gathering. "The Midwest Voter Registration and Education Project, a nonpartisan organization, is very proud to be a sponsor of this historic event," he wrote. "The tendency is to believe that such a conference has been long overdue, [and] our sense [too] is that [it] has been a long time coming. . . . Hispanics in the Midwest have been building at the local level for years in the ten-state region. The time is now right to bring it all together, and that is what this conference is all about." Andrade went on to point out in his letter that the Hispanic vote had recently influenced the 1982 gubernatorial races in Michigan, Illinois, Nebraska, and Wisconsin. He also declared the new goals for the National Hispanic Voter Registration Campaign's Midwest effort during the 1983–1984 election cycle—to hold one hundred voter registration campaigns and to register fully 200,000 new Hispanic voters in the region. Andrade then closed by saying, "We want to make a political statement to this country that in the Midwest we have Hispanic political leadership which can and ought to be recognized and acknowledged."

In a letter to Willie a week and a half before the conference, Andrade updated the SVREP leader (and MVREP board member) on how plans for the event were shaping up. In language that expressed both jubilation and trepidation, Andrade reported that MVREP leaders had never before brought together such a wide array of political heavyweights and, more importantly, had never brought together such a broad collection of Midwestern Hispanic leaders. The Texas-born Ohio transplant knew that the conference would have to be first-rate in order for MVREP and the national campaign to succeed going forward; he felt the pressure, to be sure. But beneath Andrade's anxieties was a strong underlying confidence that the conference was destined to make an historical contribution to the cause. Closing his letter to Velásquez, the MVREP leader wrote, "I am convinced that we have entered into a new beginning in which the collective Hispanic leadership of the Midwest can and will continue to come together in unity and strength and interface with Hispanic leaders from other parts of the country in addressing the very important issues of the day. This conference will serve to link all segments of Hispanic leadership together as we seek to expand our role in influencing the politics of this country in an effective and responsible manner."

MVREP's regional leadership conference, like the National Hispanic Voter Registration Campaign kickoff before it, turned out to be a massive success. Some eight hundred Hispanic leaders from across the ten-state Midwestern region attended, more than double the number of participants that Andrade and his staff had originally anticipated. The list of dignitaries and presenters was long and included: New Mexico Governor Toney Anaya; Illinois U.S. Senator Charles Percy; California U.S. Senator and Democratic presidential candidate Alan Cranston; Chicago Mayor Harold Washington; Democratic presidential candidate Jesse Jackson; and other Hispanic political leaders such as New Mexico Secretary of State Clara Jones; Philadelphia

Judge Nelson Díaz; White House Hispanic Liaison Catalina Villapando; U.S. Civil Rights Commission Director Linda Chávez; and Midwestern Hispanic political leaders such as Michigan board of education member Dr. Gumesindo Salas; Illinois cabinet member Rose Mary Bombela; and Cook County Commissioner Irene Hernández. The momentum created at the conference was contagious and it sent delegates back to their home states primed to do the hard work of achieving the National Hispanic Voter Registration Campaign's ambitious objectives. As one Hispanic leader prophetically observed, looking back on the event's importance, "I think Midwest Voter started a prairie fire."

SVREP's Velásquez was genuinely pleased by MVREP's exceptional accomplishment in moving the national campaign forward through its wildly successful regional conference. Now, with viable campaign components operating in both the Northeast and the Midwest, he could focus on his own efforts at SVREP. With still a year to go before the fall 1984 election, most of the National Hispanic Voter Registration Campaign's main backers felt undeniable enthusiasm about the campaign's prospects for success. Willie, on the other hand, realized that there was still much work to be done for the campaign even to have a hope of succeeding. He also knew that one year's time would pass quickly and that the clock was already ticking. The seasoned Velásquez thus took a deep breath and steadied himself for what would become one of the epic political mobilizations in modern American history.

Chapter 20

THE ENTHUSIASM AND ENERGY CREATED by the National Hispanic Voter Registration Campaign kickoff was transferred to the field as SVREP moved quickly to build on its momentum. In the first twenty-five days following the national kickoff, Willie and his colleagues organized twenty-five voter registration campaigns. For reasons of strategy and impact maximization, these efforts were especially concentrated in California and Texas, the two largest states in the Southwest. California received special attention, accounting for fully seventeen of the twenty-five registration campaigns that SVREP supported to commence its national campaign work. The California cities targeted by SVREP included San Francisco, San Diego, Sacramento, Santa Ana, Pomona, Delano, Rich Grove, Earlimont, Greenfield, McFarland, Bakersfield, Shafter, Castroville, Salinas, Stockton, Gilroy, and Hollister. While almost all of these local drives were centered in Latino neighborhoods and districts, SVREP also supported efforts to help increase Chinese-American registration in San Francisco and Filipino-American voter mobilization in Salinas. In Texas, SVREP focused its efforts on New Braunfels, Dallas, Brownsville, and Beeville. Special attention was also directed to Houston where SVREP's organizing activities included a strong African-American component, as well as a Mexican-American one. In addition to SVREP's campaign work in California and Texas, it also supported registration drives in Yuma and Phoenix, Arizona, as well as a local organizing project in Longmont, Colorado.

Initial field response to the national campaign was robust across the Southwest, producing unprecedented Latino community and leadership interest. In Dallas, for example, SVREP's local partner group assembled an impressive fifty-five-person steering committee and registered six hundred new Hispanic voters over one of its first weekends in operation, with still more than nine months to go before the fall general election. In San Francisco, SVREP helped to register more than three thousand individuals, after twenty-seven different organizations joined its local coalition there and almost one hundred volunteers went door-to-door in Latino and Asian neighborhoods signing up prospective new voters. What was especially impressive about SVREP's mobilization in the Bay Area was that no Latino candidates were on the upcoming ballot at either the local or the state level. There and elsewhere, it seemed, SVREP was experiencing early campaign success purely on the heightened adrenaline building within Hispanic and other minority communities relative to the potential for increased voting to expand their power and access in public governance.

Targeted cross-site trainings, more strategic technical assistance, and increased research capacity helped to support SVREP's activities in the field in unprecedented ways. Much more sophisticated data accumulation and analytical capabilities developed by the project's research department proved to be especially helpful to SVREP and its local partners. Now, for the first time, SVREP had the ability to provide precinct-census tract- and block-level demographics to its partners in the field, such that they could radically improve their targeting and impact.

For the balance of 1983 and moving into the 1984 primary season, SVREP's work continued at a blistering pace. Between July 1, 1983 and May 5, 1984, the date of the Texas primary, SVREP sponsored over one hundred voter registration drives across the region. It organized seventy-four campaigns alone during the first five months of 1984. In the midst of this frenzied period, Willie made important strategic adjustments. For example, in Texas, he decided to refocus many of SVREP's efforts on the major metropolitan areas. In the near past, the dire circumstances and low participation of Hispanics in rural areas led Willie to commit a higher amount of SVREP's resources, both for voter registration and litigation work, to the state's lesser-populated regions. Now, owing to SVREP's interventions, the combined impact of large numbers of local drives and litigation tools that effectively attacked racist gerrymandering and at-large electoral systems had begun to push rural voter registration levels among Hispanics in Texas beyond those of Mexican Americans living in large urban centers.

Preliminary studies conducted by SVREP showed Texas rural Hispanic voter registration rates that ranged from over 65 percent in Bee County to nearly 88 percent in Dimmit County. By contrast, Hispanic voter rates actually declined during this period in larger cities across the state, especially in the cities where Latinos comprised significant potential voting blocks. In San Antonio, SVREP's own headquarters city, Hispanic voter registration levels, which had reached 62 percent just three years earlier, had dropped to only 54 percent. El Paso, the state's most heavily Hispanic large city, saw its Latino voter registration levels dip from 42 percent to 37 percent during roughly the same period.

Houston, one of the fastest growing cities in the country, let alone Texas, had the largest bloc of unregistered Hispanics in the state and the lowest Hispanic voter registration rate of any major metropolitan area in the nation. The city's large Hispanic population had risen from just over 186,000 in 1970 (or just under 11 percent of the metropolitan total) to nearly 370,000 in 1980 (or slightly more than 15 percent of all Harris County residents). However, of the Hispanic voting-age population residing in Houston, barely 29 percent was registered to vote at the outset of 1982 and the turnout rate during the statewide primary held in May of that year was a paltry 8 percent. The two previous Texas primary seasons were not that much better for Latinos in that city with only 15 percent of Houston Hispanics voting in 1978 and just over 18 percent casting ballots in 1980. These turnout levels were anywhere from 11 percent to almost 14 percent lower than the average voting levels of other Texas Hispanics. With an estimated 158,000 potential Hispanic voters not registered to vote, Houston became a top priority for SVREP during the 1983–1984 election cycle.

In addition to refocusing SVREP's efforts on key metropolitan areas with the heaviest Hispanic population concentrations, Velásquez initiated other changes designed to increase the National Hispanic Voter Registration Campaign's success prospects. He expanded SVREP's formal ties to organized labor groups by engaging the consulting services of Henry Santiestevan, the former United Auto Workers leader, who, a decade earlier, had secured the first charitable contributions that eventually led to SVREP's creation. Santiestevan worked hard to expand SVREP's labor funding base and also to encourage more coordinated voter registration and mobilization efforts between the project and leading labor networks in the field.

Willie's inclination to bolster both SVREP's and the National Hispanic Voter Registration Campaign's capacities to achieve their ambitious goals during this period also resulted in other important strategic alliances extending beyond organized labor groups seeking to promote voter participation. In fact, Velásquez and his staff collaborated extensively with other important voter promotion groups through the 1984 election cycle. These groups— most of them newer organizations—included Project Vote!, the Texas Women's Vote Project, the Churches' Committee for Voter Registration/Education, the National Student Campaign for Voter Registration, and the Citizens' Leadership Foundation. Through these alliances, Willie sought to increase field-wide attention to Latino voter interests in exchange for access to his knowledge and networks.

The inclination to partner with other groups was nothing new for Velásquez or SVREP, however the scale of project collaboration in the national field increased dramatically during the 1983–1984 election season as Willie pushed hard to advance the National Hispanic Voter Registration Campaign's objectives. Willie's involvement in the larger national voter registration and education field at this time was complemented by an unprecedented increase in leadership and funding interest related to voting in low-income minority and other historically marginalized communities across the nation. Spurred by influential donor groups, like the Ad Hoc Funders' Committee on Voter Registration and Education, liberal Democratic Party efforts such as the Missing Half (which was driven by significant individual donors like Frank Weil and Richard Dennis), and more targeted efforts such as the Citizens' Participation Project which focused exclusively on voter registration activities in minority communities (with the support of wealthy individuals like moderate Republican David Rockefeller, Jr.), the national voter mobilization arena had never before been so robust and crowded.

Willie was well aware that the net effect of all of these efforts emerging simultaneously was the development of an unprecedented voter promotion movement that could only help to advance Latino and other minority community interests across the nation. It was an historic moment and Velásquez knew he had to seize it. He had to do his part to ensure that Hispanics and comparable groups would be an integral element of the national push to expand American democracy. To accomplish these things would require Willie to free up more time and money than he had ever been called on to produce in the past.

During this period, therefore, Willie dropped off a number of nonprofit boards on which he had been serving, including the San Antonio-based Centro del Barrio and the National Rural Coalition, and he stopped accepting speaking engagements unrelated to the national campaign in order to commit all of his time and energies to the national campaign's goals. Building on past practice, he also borrowed another $10,000 from the Center for Community Change instead of waiting for promised foundation grant funds to arrive. He wanted to avoid breaking the national campaign momentum building at the local level by ensuring seamless financing to as many grassroots drives as possible, rather than risking their inertia or demise simply on account of distribution delays. Velásquez's focus on the national campaign and SVREP's related coalition-building efforts paid especially large dividends in his home state of Texas.

On Cinco de Mayo, 1984, for the third primary election in a row, Texas Mexican Americans turned out to vote at a rate that was significantly higher than the rest of the state. According to SVREP voter studies, some 26 percent of all registered Mexican Americans voted in the Republican and Democratic Party primaries compared to a turnout figure of just over 20 percent for the rest of the state in the Democratic primary and just under 20 percent for non-Hispanics overall. In the Democratic Party primary, SVREP estimated that Mexican Americans cast fully 16.5 percent of the total Democratic vote statewide, though they made up only 14.5 percent of the eligible voting age population in Texas.

During the six weeks leading up to the registration deadline just prior to the Texas primary, SVREP ran voter registration campaigns in forty-four key areas of the state and added nearly 85,000 new voters to increase the number of Hispanic registered voters in Texas to approximately 950,000. With the November general elections still six months away, SVREP had a legitimate opportunity to raise the number of Hispanic registered voters in Texas past the one million mark.

A hotly contested U.S. Senate primary helped to increase voter motivation in Latino and other minority communities of the state when three Democratic candidates finished in a dead heat with approximately 31 percent of the vote going to conservative Democratic Congressman Kent Hance, who had been predicted to finish last, liberal state Senator Lloyd Doggett, and former Congressman Bob Krueger, who had been the front-runner throughout the campaign, but actually finished third in the vote tally, some 1,600 votes behind Hance and 1,300 votes behind Doggett. It was the closest three-person race in modern Texas history, and the razor-close proximity of the candidates' vote totals would require a runoff election between the top two contenders, Hance and Doggett. SVREP exit polls found that Doggett and Krueger had received almost the same amount of support from the Mexican-American community, with each garnering just over 45 percent of the Hispanic vote. Hance, on the other hand, had received less than 10 percent of the Mexican-American vote, owing mainly to community perceptions that the conservative Democrat from Lubbock was anti-immigrant.[1]

The runoff produced yet another unbelievably close race in which Doggett edged out Hance by a mere 509 votes out of nearly 980,000 cast. The Doggett victory was significant for Hispanic voters. According to SVREP research data, Mexican Americans provided the winning margin for the progressive state senator's victory. Texas Hispanic Democrats gave Doggett over 75 percent of their votes, while Hance received less than 25 percent. Without the massive support of the Mexican-American community, Doggett simply could not have won.

Willie's emphasis on mobilizing urban Hispanic voters was a monumental factor in Doggett's favor, it turned out. Hance actually won most of the counties and rural areas in Texas (201 of the 254 counties), but Doggett was able to hold on in the state's major urban areas in places like Houston and Dallas, as well as in Hispanic South Texas in cities such as San Antonio, El Paso, Laredo, Corpus Christi, Brownsville, and McAllen. As had been the case in

---

[1]The major factors accounting for such perceptions were Hance's opposition to amnesty for illegal aliens, which he made his top campaign issue, and a series of anti-immigrant ads that he ran during the primary season. Hispanic advocacy groups, such as the American G.I. Forum, the Mexican-American Democrats, and SVREP, denounced Hance's policy position and supporting ads as nothing less than divisive and offensive to the Hispanic community.

the prior primary race, Mexican Americans turned out at a substantially higher level than the rest of the state with approximately 18 percent of Hispanic voters participating compared to an overall 13 percent turnout rate statewide.

〜 〜 〜

With an ever-growing number of Mexican Americans registering and voting in Texas and at higher levels of relative participation than other groups, Willie gained new optimism and confidence that the political rules of the Southwest and the nation were finally changing. In this set of developments, Velásquez could see the onset of a combination of factors that were increasingly positioning Hispanic Americans as legitimate players in American civic culture. Expanded Latino voting capacity, as Willie saw it, was now making possible the unprecedented ascendance of nationally influential Hispanic elected officials. People like San Antonio Mayor Henry Cisneros (who Vice President Walter Mondale was seriously considering as a potential running mate in 1984), New Mexico Governor Toney Anaya, and Denver Mayor Federico Peña were exemplars of this reality. Increased Latino voting power, made possible in recent years through SVREP's work and that of the other leading Hispanic advocacy groups, was the major factor supporting such leaders' emergence. Where expanded Hispanic voting power was not producing new Latino political leaders, moreover, it was increasingly helping to determine the outcome of key contests involving non-Latino candidates, such as in the case of liberal State Senator Lloyd Doggett's surprise victory over the more established U.S. Representative Kent Hance during the 1984 Democratic primary race in Texas. Developing Latino potential as a critical swing vote in such elections could only portend increased Hispanic political influence in America.

Willie was not alone in his estimation that a critical sea change was underway in American political life. For many observers, what was happening in Hispanic communities to excite and mobilize unprecedented numbers of new voters was part of an ongoing transformation in U.S. democracy, whose roots extended back to the women's suffragist and black civil rights movements of prior decades. Now, buoyed by new infusions of Latino, Native-American, Asian-American, and other groups that were hungry to break past historical barriers to civic participation, the voting rights movement in America seemed to be primed for a momentous breakthrough. With demographers predicting, moreover, that culturally diverse Americans would comprise a growing and potentially dominant role in U.S. society during coming decades, the stakes involved in capturing Hispanic and other new voters were suddenly elevated to new heights during this period.

Progressive civil rights activists were especially excited by the prospects of challenging the key protagonists of the Republican Reagan Revolution by promoting increased minority voting, which they believed would advance liberal Democrats in the 1984 national elections. Many private foundation executives saw themselves in this camp and substantially increased their grant-making attention to the voting rights field, accordingly. The result was an unprecedented infusion of foundation investment in the nonprofit—and supposedly nonpartisan—voter promotion arena, and arguably the largest organized effort to increase the number of registered voters in American history.

The Ad Hoc Funders' Committee, the main anchor of liberal-left foundation voter promotion strategy and funding during this period, tracked 125 different groups of all shapes and sizes receiving 427 grants from 85 foundations totaling $6.6 million for voter registration and education work during the 1984 election cycle. With this support, a range of geographical- and issue-based public interest organizations from all across the country jumped into the voter registration business, many for the first time. These groups included the Alabama Coalition Against Hunger; the Catholic Diocese of Cleveland; the Montana Alliance for Progressive Policies; the Buck's County (PA) Housing Group; North Carolinians for Effective Citizenship; Citizens Against Nuclear War; and Wider Opportunities for Women.

Most of the progressive funding invested in the voter promotion field, however, was limited to a relatively small concentration of a dozen organizations, comprising the most established registration and education networks. SVREP and its National Hispanic Voter Registration Campaign partners, MVREP and the National Puerto Rican/Hispanic Voter Participation Project, constituted an important aspect of this group of twelve. The other nine organizations in the national leadership mix were the American Citizenship Education Project; the Churches' Committee for Voter Registration Education; the Citizens' Leadership Foundation; the Human SERVE Fund; the League of Women Voters Education Fund/Women's Vote Project; the National Coalition on Black Voter Participation/Operation Big Vote; the National Student Campaign for Voter Registration; Project Vote!; and the Voter Education Project. Together, these groups received some $4.7 million of the $6.6 million that foundation donors committed to voter mobilization activities during the 1984 national campaign cycle.

In addition to providing direct support to leading progressive voter promotion groups, private donors also supported important ancillary activities that were designed to help progressive political candidates and activate liberal voters. They created a technical assistance entity called the Future Fund, a one-man outfit, staffed by attorney Frank Smith, whose primary role was to provide political intelligence to wealthy, progressive individuals so that they could complement their charitable gifts with IRS section 501 (c) 4 investments that would not be so heavily regulated as "soft" dollars raised by non-profit groups under the tax code provisions governing 501 (c) 3 contributions. They also heavily supported a national media campaign called the American Citizenship Education Project, which was designed to urge increased voting among minorities, low-income people, women, and youth.

In 1984, the American Citizenship Education Project, with pro bono support from the Advertising Council of America and Mingo-Jones advertising, produced and distributed eighteen thirty-second public service announcements to every radio and television station in the country, as well as to 2,700 newspapers and magazines with the largest regional and national circulations. In total, the project produced media industry donations totaling approximately $4 million in production services and $30 million in airtime and advertising space, including at least eighty-four spots on network television, many of which were aired during prime time.

The unprecedented mobilization of liberal foundations and voter groups during 1983 and 1984 augured well for progressive Latino interests by offering SVREP and its national campaign partners access to needed new monies and media visibility. But the real benefits of this upswing in field support were ultimately mitigated by several factors. To begin, little of the expanded financial support made available to Latino and other progressive voter promotion groups was provided early in the campaign cycle where it could find more optimal impact. Many groups, like SVREP and its campaign partners, thus found themselves experiencing real financial hardships—and even deep budget deficits—precisely as need and interest related to their work was burgeoning across the nation. By the time many of these groups received major funding for their voter mobilization activities, it was simply too late for them to translate it into net gains in the number of progressive registered voters in their respective regions of focus. In addition, much to the liberal left's surprise and dismay, profoundly conservative tendencies were consolidating within the American body politic during this period. Such tendencies, which characterized many Latino, Anglo, and other American voter constituencies, simply overwhelmed many of the liberal cause's capacities to compete with their conservative counterparts on fund-raising and voter engagement. Leal Stegall of the Windom Fund, one of the progressive grant-makers behind the development of the Future Fund, later summed up the field's dilemma by saying: "[W]e knew [that] for every $100,000 we could scratch up, [the conservatives could raise] $10 million like that . . . we knew we were as smart as [the Right was] . . . and we did have successes. . . . [W]e also knew it was David and Goliath, but what else could we do?"

In fact, the liberal organization and leaders of the 1984 voter mobilization strategy to contest the Reagan Revolution could do little more than work and hope as hard as they ever had in order to have a chance to succeed. They forged ahead valiantly and produced an energy and excitement in grassroots communities across the land that had not been seen since John F. Kennedy's 1960 presidential campaign. Unfortunately, notwithstanding heroic actions and important gains in the field, their efforts amounted to a formidable uphill battle.

The three groups comprising the National Hispanic Voter Registration Campaign were simultaneously buoyed and hindered by these circumstances. For the National Puerto Rican/Hispanic Voter Participation Project, the youngest of the three groups, having only officially opened its doors in April of 1984, the final seven months of the election season comprised its entire voter registration campaign. Luis Cabán, the organization's first president, frantically tried to develop a strategy to achieve the national campaign's lofty objectives for the Northeast with painfully little funding and a small staff of only three co-workers. Quickly recognizing that he was facing a no-win situation relative to the Northeast project's target to register 215,000 voters, Cabán turned to Willie constantly for advice and even traveled to San Antonio with his wife to spend time learning directly from the SVREP executive what he should and should not do. Velásquez shared all that he had gleaned from SVREP's experiences with Cabán, including all of the relevant data that his research department had recently produced on the state of Latino voting issues. Willie's accessibility and insights left a lasting impression on the upstart Puerto Rican voting advocate, as was the case in so many other circumstances where the SVREP leader would offer advice. "Willie prepared me for the job and I turned to him for guidance on everything—a plan of action, the location of our group, demographic information, and how to get support in the Puerto Rican community for this type of work," Cabán would later reveal. "But one of the things I remember most about Willie," he would go on to say, "was his ability to memorize data, especially numbers. He reminded me of an old bookie I knew from the South Bronx, 'Bollita,' who had 80 to 90 customers and he'd remember everyone's numbers and how much they had paid. Willie was the same way when it came to voter statistics."

While Velásquez's inspiration and tactical advice were essential to Cabán during the Northeast project's start-up phase, even these formidable assets could not help the Puerto Rican group's executive director to square Willie's proposed target of more than 200,000 new Puerto Rican voters with reality. Cabán soon realized that Velásquez's numbers simply had to be radically revised in a downward direction. Time was just too short and organizational staffing too thin for the Northeast project even to promise 50,000 new voters. Cabán accordingly revised the Northeast project's projected registration target down to a mere 46,200 newly registered Puerto Rican voters. Working as hard as he knew how to make even this substantially downsized target work, the Northeast project executive spent three-quarters of his time on the road during the 1984 registration season. Supported only by a field coordinator, a communications specialist, and an administrative assistant,

Cabán did the best he could to encourage the campaign's success. Sadly, all of his hard work was not enough to overcome the formidable time, staffing, and resource constraints that weighed him down. In addition to the razor-thin time line he was working on and his considerable limitations in staff capacity, Cabán was seriously immobilized by painful delays in promised funding. Fully half of the Northeast project's approved grant resources did not arrive until September 1984, a mere two months before the November election. The other half was only released in early October, less than thirty days before voters went to the polls and only a week or so before many states in the region officially closed their registration windows.

As a result of funding delays, Cabán had to cut the project's planned registration drives in half, targeting and completing only fifteen campaigns instead of thirty. In the end, the Northeast project registered a mere 12,000 new voters, slightly more than a quarter of its revised goal, and dramatically less than the unrealistic 215,000 target assigned to it by Willie at the San Antonio kickoff for the National Hispanic Voter Registration Campaign one year prior to the election. Leaders of the Northeast project were naturally disappointed not to be able to produce a stronger showing; however, their efforts were not without impact. In Philadelphia, two Latinos were elected for the first time to key offices in that area, one to the city council and the other to the state legislature. Similarly, in Buffalo, New York, a Latino was elected as an at-large judge, also making history and demonstrating the significantly growing potential of Hispanic voters and candidates in the region.

The Midwest Voter Registration and Education Project's contributions to the national campaign were slightly greater than originally anticipated by Velásquez. While Willie had assigned an arbitrary number—69,000—as the goal for the Midwest component of the National Hispanic Voter Registration Campaign, MVREP's director, Juan Andrade established a far more ambitious target for his ten-state region: registering 200,000 Latino voters and sponsoring a hundred voter registration campaigns during the 1983–1984 cycle, with most of these drives being scheduled during May and November 1984, and fully half of the projected registration pool—100,000 individuals—being new Hispanic voters.

Andrade projected that it would cost roughly $650,000 to achieve the campaign's Midwest goals. Early in the process, he expressed optimism that even more money might be raised, leading to more than the campaign's target of one hundred registration drives and perhaps as many as 200,000 new Latino voters across the region. But MVREP was quickly forced to scale back its plans to match more closely its realities—a small staff, only two years of experience in the field, a large geographic area to cover, and the still uncertain prospect of securing foundation resources to see the job through.

In the end, MVREP was able to raise only 80 percent of its projected

$650,000 campaign budget, falling short by more than $100,000. Like the Northeast project, moreover, its funding dilemmas were compounded by the fact that many of the support grants that it was able to secure came to it far too late in the campaign cycle to be used as effectively as would have been the case had these monies come sooner.

As a result, MVREP ran only sixty-two voter registration campaigns during the 1983–1984 election period and registered only about 160,000 voters across the ten-state Midwestern territory, roughly half of them newly registered individuals preparing to vote for the first time. In effect, Velásquez's early forecast for MVREP's campaign capacity to produce new Hispanic registrants had been exceeded, but only slightly, by about 10,000 voters.

Still, despite falling far short of its own ambitious goal to register 100,000 new Hispanic voters, MVREP's work helped significantly to augment Latino visibility in the region during the entire political campaign season. The organization's highly successful regional conference in early October 1984 drew leading figures from both the Democratic and Republican parties, including Illinois Attorney General Neal Hartigan, Ohio Secretary of State Sherrod Brown, Republican National Committee official Rudy Becerra, and Joan Mondale, the wife of presidential candidate Walter Mondale. The successful bipartisan leadership conference demonstrated that MVREP's efforts were helping to put Latinos on the Midwest's political map.

In addition, MVREP's campaign efforts helped to position Hispanic groups and issues in critically important ways, often for the first time, in states like Kansas, Missouri, Minnesota, and Nebraska, by focusing not merely on registration drives, but also regional leadership development and public education activities. In addition to its registration successes during 1983–1984, for example, MVREP produced twenty demographic and political profiles of Hispanic voters in these and other states, including a first-time political opinion survey of Midwestern Hispanic leaders. It also sponsored a comprehensive analysis of Midwestern Hispanic voter attitudes and opinions, and organized seven state conferences attended by some five-hundred Midwestern Hispanic leaders on the nuts and bolts of running local voter registration campaigns.

Willie and SVREP faced the same core challenges experienced by their National Hispanic Voter Registration Campaign partners during the 1984 election cycle: a political calendar that was slipping away and critical short-term funding uncertainty. Funding concerns were especially acute. At the outset of the campaign in August 1983, Willie had projected that SVREP would conduct at least 185 registration campaigns, but during the next year, owing to funding delays and the failure of some funds even to materialize, SVREP experienced a roller-coaster ride that required constant adjustment of its campaign commitments.

By the late spring of 1984, SVREP's numbers had been optimistically adjusted upwards to more than two-hundred registration campaigns for the 1983–1984 biennial, as Willie, true to form, pushed toward the outer limits of what he hoped would come to pass. But within a few short months, reality finally caught up with Velásquez and SVREP. By the summer, it had become painfully clear that there simply would not be enough money or time to meet the two-hundred-plus registration drive goal; indeed, even achieving the project's initial goal of 185 campaigns would be a challenge.

Serious downward adjustments would have to be made to align SVREP's projections more accurately with its real life constraints. Begrudgingly, Velásquez responded. The ninety-five voter registration drives Willie proposed to run from early May through November 1984 were reduced to sixty-eight in late July and then again to a grand total of forty-three campaigns by the summer's end.

SVREP's funding challenges had a devastating overall impact on the National Hispanic Voter Registration Campaign during the final stretch of the 1984 elections, as Willie shared with his board and financial contributors in August: "The practical consequences are that our goal of 1,000,000 additional Hispanic voters is now in jeopardy." Under report headlines entitled "Bad News," "More Bad News," and "Field Operation Cutbacks," Willie proposed to mitigate SVREP's losses by targeting its few remaining dollars to support last-minute drives in twenty-five cities that had been cut and to undertake at least three-week drives in those places, instead of the seven-week campaigns SVREP had originally planned. Velásquez closed his August report by taking responsibility for the overly ambitious plans he had originally set for SVREP and the national campaign, stating, "It is quite evident that we set our goals too high. There simply are not enough resources to do the number of campaigns we planned. The bottom line is that we will do 185 campaigns as promised in August 1983 (at the national campaign kickoff) [. . . and] in the next few days [if] we get some help, we will wind up doing about 195 or so campaigns."

During the balance of the election season, Willie pulled no punches on the fund-raising front. He called, harassed, and cajoled virtually every possible source of funding to generate new support or free up grants that had been approved but not yet paid out. The gentile benefactors were not accustomed to such brazen pressure from a grantee and several tried to fend him off. But Velásquez was relentless and unabashed. He simply would not take no for an answer. His raw determination made a difference, in the end.

During September and October, a number of SVREP's key supporters responded positively to Willie's personal pleas to get more resources into the field. SVREP brought in nearly $115,000 during September alone and by the end of the 1984 voter registration season, that figure had increased to nearly

$475,000. The list of financial backers who stepped in to assist included the Citizens' Participation Project; the Field Foundation; The Youth Project; the New World Foundation; the Columbia Foundation; and the Needmor Fund. With this late fund-raising surge, SVREP was miraculously able to revise its national campaign registration plans back up to 194 drives. In addition, it organized two highly successful registration events at the back end of the campaign called "Leadership Walks" to maximize its registration impact, just days before the official voter registration deadline in Texas.

On a parallel track, SVREP deepened its voter education efforts by publishing first-time reports about Hispanic voters and the issues of major concern to them. In a multi-part series about the Mexican-American electorate edited by SVREP's research director Dr. Bob Brischetto and University of Texas at Austin professor Rodolfo de la Garza, the project made available demographic data on where Mexican Americans get their political information, a description of Mexican-American political participation and ideology, and an analysis of Mexican-American political opinions and their implications.

By developing and disseminating these unprecedented reports in coordination with the national campaign, Velásquez sought to infuse the election season with some degree of expanded media and public attention to Hispanic concerns. In doing so, he insisted that media, public observers, and especially political candidates and parties, who wanted to better understand the Hispanic vote, think about Latino community opinion in expansive, rather than narrow terms. "We are not asking for preferential treatment," Willie commented to the press upon the series' release, "but [merely want to be respected] as a constituency that is very much an integral part of [the American] body politic. We feel our needs ought to be clearly addressed by those who want our vote. These reports graphically illustrate our current circumstances. Policy makers ought to know this, and if they . . . don't do anything [about it], we ought to know this too."

By the time the November 6, 1984, elections finally arrived, Willie was exhausted. He had thrown everything he had into the effort to make the National Hispanic Voter Registration Campaign a smashing success. He had done everything he knew how to give his campaign partners a fighting chance to hit their ambitious registration goals. He had pushed foundation benefactors as hard as humanly possible to provide needed support for this work. He had put the Republican and Democratic parties on notice that the Hispanic vote could no longer be taken for granted.

SVREP's efforts to make Willie's dreams and claims real were monumental. During the 1983–1984 election cycle, SVREP ended up sponsoring 197 voter registration campaigns, a dozen more than it had initially targeted as its Southwest regional goal at the National Hispanic Voter Registration Campaign kickoff. It ran effective campaigns in twelve states: Arizona, Cal-

ifornia, Colorado, Idaho, Kansas, Montana, New Mexico, Oklahoma, South
Dakota, Texas, Utah, and Wyoming. And, in addition to targeting Hispanic
neighborhoods, SVREP also canvassed a considerable number of American-
Indian communities and a handful of predominantly black and Asian voter
districts. All of these efforts combined to make the 1983–1984 election cycle
the most successful in the project's brief ten-year history, to date. In East Los
Angeles, SVREP's work resulted in the addition of nearly fifty-thousand new
Hispanic voters and the mobilization of over six hundred volunteers and seventy community organizations. In Houston and El Paso, SVREP's efforts in
partnership with the progressive Industrial Areas Foundation produced thirty
thousand and twenty-two thousand new Latino voters, respectively.

All told, SVREP's campaign efforts directly engaged some 7,170 volunteers, with over three thousand of these individuals serving on local steering committees and 885 different community organizations contributing to
the various local coalitions. In order to support this work, project staff provided more than four thousand on-site training hours to local groups and
more than eighteen hundred public service announcements, posters, bumper
stickers, wall charts, and door hangers carrying the message that had now
become SVREP's official motto: "Su Voto Es Su Voz" (Your Vote is Your
Voice). Significantly, nearly one thousand Hispanic leaders helped to lead the
seventeen regional planning committees SVREP established during the campaign. During the campaign, SVREP also produced targeted demographic
information for each registration drive, more than eighty county profiles, and
nearly a dozen reports related to Hispanic voting issues.

By any reasonable measure, SVREP had achieved historic successes
during the campaign. But none of these proved to be a cause for celebration
for Willie, as things turned out. Always one to be impatient and to expect
more than the possible, Velásquez focused largely on what might have been,
rather than on the campaign's historical and many important accomplishments. SVREP's final registration total of over 430,000 new Hispanic voters
was far short of its unrealistic campaign goal of over 680,000. Coupled with
the results of MVREP's and the Northeast project's drives, SVREP's actual
registration total revealed that the National Hispanic Voter Registration Campaign had achieved only about one-half of its ambitious goal to register one
million new Hispanic voters. Yet never before had Hispanic Americans registered in such significant numbers and never had an Hispanic-focused voter
mobilization effort been able to register so many *new* Latino voters; still, for
Willie, the campaign's results could only be equated with disappointment.

The election outcome revealed that SVREP would not be alone in its
despair among progressive groups when all the votes were counted on election day 1984. In the country's most lopsided electoral college victory in history, the conservative incumbent president, Ronald Reagan, carried every

state but the Democratic challenger Walter Mondale's home base of Minnesota and the District of Columbia on his way to a 525 to 10 electoral college triumph. Reagan received fully 59 percent of the popular vote to Mondale's mere 41.

A suffocating silence emerged as Velásquez and other liberal and progressive leaders took in the blow that had just been dealt them. "Four more years! Four more years!" shouted an enthusiastic crowd of Reagan loyalists as the victorious president appeared to claim his re-election victory at the posh Century Plaza Hotel in Los Angeles, California. "I think that's just been arranged," the president deadpanned before network television cameras. The Reagan supporters were as animated in victory as those on the left were muted in defeat. Velásquez and his people were simply stunned.

Willie had hoped all along that the national campaign would position Hispanic Americans with greater political clout, no matter which political party might prevail, by making the election competitive and alerting Democrats and Republicans alike to Hispanic-Americans' growing electoral force. But, in a landslide, Willie knew better than most that the minority vote, no matter what its overall size, simply would not factor significantly with the victors when the final outcome was never in question. It was beside the point, and, in this case, the point was that Ronald Reagan had breezed his way into a second term despite all the grand talk on the American political left of massive, grassroots voter registration efforts that were going to change the face of American politics.

For Willie, therefore, the most expansive voter registration and education gains that Hispanic Americans had ever achieved were not enough. Even as unprecedented numbers of Hispanics went to the polls, many for the first time with the national campaign's encouragement, and as large contingents of Hispanics were elected to office, many again for the first time, SVREP's founder could only contemplate what might have happened if only he and others could have done just a little bit more. Then, without taking much more time to lament the national campaign's results, the ever-relentless Velásquez directed his staff to redouble its focus on the project's ongoing efforts to leverage essential gains for local Hispanic groups in the Southwest. Less than one month following the national elections, therefore, on December 5, 1984, SVREP announced that it was planning to sue the city of Alvin, Texas, a town of sixteen thousand people because its at-large city council election scheme discriminated against Mexican Americans. Three weeks later, on December 28, SVREP filed yet another at-large city council suit against the city of Floydada, Texas, an even smaller municipality with a total population of only forty-one hundred, pressing the powers that be there to give the locality's 40 percent minority population a fair chance at winning a spot on the town's all-white city council.

Chapter 21

DESPITE THE SHORTCOMINGS OF THE National Hispanic Voter Registration Campaign, the 1983–1984 election period was the most productive in SVREP's history. Willie was ready to build on whatever he could coming out of that experience and boldly wanted to move the organization forward in new directions. Yet he was faced with reluctant benefactors who now wanted to slow down and take stock of what had happened in the most recent round of elections. The Reagan landslide had severely deflated many liberal-progressive supporters and many wanted to rethink their funding strategies relative to minority voter empowerment. More foundation money had been poured into progressive and minority-focused voter registration and education efforts in the 1984 election cycle than during any other period in American history. But had this strategy worked? The question on the table quickly became: Who did a better job of getting their people registered and to the polls—the liberals or the conservatives?

Traditionally, the Democratic Party and its supporters held the advantage over their Republican counterparts when it came to grassroots voter mobilization activities. But as Thomas Edsall of the *Washington Post* reported, for the first time in recent political history, the Republican Party defeated the Democratic Party at its own game—grassroots organizing, voter registration, and get-out-the-vote efforts. In an article published just two weeks before the November election, Edsall raised tough questions about the lofty aims liberal benefactors and Democratic Party leaders harbored. "Could the liberal-left coalition be revived with a massive voter registration campaign?" Edsall contemplated. "Could newly enfranchised poor people, blacks and Hispanics halt the Reagan revolution?" These were the main notions at the heart of Democratic leaders' dreams of unseating Ronald Reagan and his conservative colleagues in Congress and in statehouses across the land. "That dream attracted millions of dollars and mobilized thousands of people during the past year," the *Post* reporter went on, "but by all indications, it is a dream that will not come true." Perhaps most deflating for the progressive left, Edsall concluded, was that "the Republican Party succeeded in putting together [a massive] registration campaign which, backed up by a drive to mobilize fundamentalist white Christians, produced more new GOP voters than Democrats in such states as Florida and California, and matched liberal/Democratic efforts in many other states."

೧ ೧ ೧

In fact, as Edsall and other leading commentators reported in their assessment of the Reagan landslide, the Democratic Party as a whole had failed to register new voters. According to the experts, "The cash-poor Democratic Party depended on a decentralized collection of liberal and left-wing, technically 'nonpartisan' organizations to do its work mobilizing the electorate. . . . The Republican Party, in contrast, ran a highly centralized, party-financed program putting at least $10 million into voter registration in 28 key states." The Mondale campaign, it turned out, actually rejected the grassroots voter registration path, even though a 250-page study produced internally by aides concluded that it should do otherwise, stating, "The only way Mondale can win is by pitching his appeal to the white working class and minorities, not the middle class." Mike Ford, Mondale's field director, went further, saying that "[a] Mondale victory is nearly impossible with the current electorate. . . . We must consider dramatic and perhaps high-risk strategies." Ford pushed accordingly for upwards of $12 million to be spent on registering 5 to 6 million new black, Hispanic, and union voters to alter the current electorate and to give Mondale a fighting chance at victory. His recommendations were rejected, however, and the Democrats never mounted a serious voter registration drive.

Instead, the Mondale team relied almost exclusively on the decentralized, foundation-dependent nonpartisan efforts of groups such as SVREP. There was an unspoken hope that somehow this disconnected set of activities would create the expanded electorate that Mondale and the Democratic Party needed to defeat Reagan and the GOP. The Republicans, on the other hand, left little to hope or chance. Rather, building on the strategic insights of people like Lee Atwater, they committed substantial party resources to voter promotion while simultaneously encouraging independent efforts in support of their cause. Thus, at the same time that the National Hispanic Voter Registration Campaign was announcing its intention to register one million new Hispanic voters in time for the 1984 general election, the American Coalition for Traditional Values, consisting of an umbrella group of fundamentalist Christian groups such as the Moral Majority and the Christian Voice, was declaring its goal of registering two million evangelical Christians in twenty-five states, knowing full well that this effort would supplement the voter mobilization work of the Republican Party.

After the election, Willie feared that SVREP and other groups like it would be punished for not accomplishing the heady and unrealistic goal of defeating a sitting president. The response of liberal foundation benefactors to the election outcome would be especially decisive in this connection. Velásquez knew that financial resources in support of the field would decrease during 1985–1986 because it was a non-presidential election cycle, but by how much was anyone's guess. In the end, private benefactors would rely on a global assessment of grantee performance in the area of voter registration and education in order to draw conclusions about the value of continued investments in this work. Sadly for Willie and others in the field, however, the resulting assessment—though highly favorable to SVREP—would do little to inspire the liberal funding community's continued enthusiasm to fund progressive voter registration groups.

Even before the November general elections, the Ad Hoc Funders' Committee had already started surveying foundations and voter registration groups about its interest in critically evaluating grassroots voter registration and education activities that took place during 1983–1984, particularly those involving low-income and minority populations, women, and youth. Committee leaders argued that a voter registration study would serve as a useful and timely planning tool for improving and expanding electoral participation, as well as identifying performance criteria and long-term staff and resource needs for the field in ways that would greatly improve the capacities of local and national organizations. Most benefactors supported the concept of a post-election assessment along these lines and, accordingly, participated in its development. In total, forty-five benefactors and seventeen grantees, including SVREP, MVREP, and the National Puerto Rican/Hispanic Voter Participation Project, helped to inform the post-1984 evaluation protocol, which concentrated on the activities and impacts of twelve organizations considered to be the leading groups in the nation, including SVREP. What no one could predict as the review got underway was the considerable divisiveness that would result from this seemingly harmless investigation.

ᑴ ᑴ ᑴ

In fact, members of the Ad Hoc Funders' Committee ended up supporting two major evaluations of the 1983–1984 campaign cycle's outcomes. The New York-based group, Interface, completed the first large evaluation of the presidential campaign in July 1985, entitled "Expanding Voter Participation: An Assessment of 1984 Nonpartisan Voter Registration Efforts," with support from a collection of twenty-five different members of the Ad Hoc Funders' Committee. The second evaluation, completed in September 1986, by the consulting firm of Hamilton, Rabinovitz & Alschuler for the New World and Norman Foundations, focused more narrowly on the campaign role and impact of 4945(f) organizations—nonprofit groups whose primary focus was voter registration activity in at least five states over multiple election periods. The Interface report was the more influential of these two studies and the only public evaluation of the 1983–1984 election period. In it, SVREP was deemed the top voter registration organization in the country. The Interface reviewers concluded that "Southwest [had] become a force of major conse- quence in the development of long-term political empowerment of the Mexi- can American community" because of its structure and administrative system, its effective strategies including research and litigation, its focus on long-term goals, local elections, and effective communication—all of this in the context of holding politicians to high standards. The report went on to attribute SVREP's effectiveness to Willie's unrelenting leadership, as well as the com- prehensive nature and quality of its work. Clearly, the report acknowledged, there were other progressive voter registration groups that were providing top- notch performance in the areas of voter registration, education, and get-out- the-vote campaigning. Some of them were even better than SVREP at specif- ic aspects of their work. But, at the end of the day, in the studied judgment of the Interface reviewers, SVREP alone offered a full complement of strategies, approaches, and services that were necessary to make a significant, lasting impact. In short, SVREP was the closest thing to a full-service, progressive voter registration and education organization that existed in the United States.

The Interface report ultimately drew criticism from both foundation offi- cials and several of the other voter registration groups profiled for a variety of methodological and substantive reasons, but, even with all of its deficien- cies, the report was important to SVREP, precisely because it turned out to be the only evaluation of the progressive voter promotion field to be shared publicly, and because it gave private foundation leaders more information, however incomplete and controversial, about what had occurred in the field during the 1983–1984 national election cycle. Most benefactors looking at the field at this time thus came to see SVREP at the top of the pack, the leader in a cohort of organizations that was striving somewhat unevenly to make democratic processes more accessible to the disadvantaged.

Based on prior experiences, the accomplishments achieved during 1983–1984 were noteworthy—SVREP, for example, recorded its most pro- ductive year to date—but the national progressive voter registration commu- nity was nevertheless trounced by more well-organized and well-funded con- servative groups. A large part of the problem rested at the doorstep of liberal and progressive leaders themselves.

One major challenge was the Ad Hoc Funders' Committee's own lack of cohesion. Extremely diverse in terms of participants and ideology, it attract- ed a large number of newer benefactors intent on using the committee plat- form merely to add a voter registration component to advance work in specific issue areas they were already supporting, such as children's rights, environmental advocacy, and nuclear disarmament. For these new donors, voter registration became a new tool to use in ongoing policy and issue battles specific to their substantive priorities. It increased opportunities, as these grant-makers saw it, to leverage expanded public support for their causes and thus to affect national policy-making. Nevertheless, the committee's structure and composition posed difficulties for grantee groups like SVREP that ultimately had severe negative consequences for their ability to be successful. Largely divergent funding calendars and strategic considerations, for example, resulted in substantial delays and unevenness in the distribution of needed resources to the field. As a result, practitioner groups were often left with huge gaps in needed funding and an inability to plan effective campaigns, owing to chronic uncertainty.

The Funders' Committee was also a victim of its own internal politics, which often had more to do with idiosyncratic institutional and personal agendas than the needs of poor, minority voters. As Lynn Walker of the Ford Foundation would later comment, "The limited funding, the diverse agendas, and the matching requirements established by some of the funders meant that the Funders' Committee [was] not necessarily conducive to the most reasoned, fair, collegial exchanges. It was conducive to politicking."

            ෴ ෴ ෴

A related set of challenges concerned competition between many of the nation's leading voter registration groups—and others—for access to voter mobilization funds during the 1983–1984 campaign season. The Ad Hoc Funders' Committee favored steering most of its support to IRS 4945(f)-designated intermediary groups. For many committee members, particularly those that were new to voter registration funding, placing their resources with a 4945(f) intermediary group such as SVREP seemed to be a sensible thing to do. Both legally and practically, 4945(f) organizations operating at the national or regional level offered the easiest way to support impact work at a level of economy and scale that made the investment worthwhile, while at the same time avoiding many of the potential political entanglements that discouraged most grant-makers from supporting voter registration work more directly at the grassroots level. Much to committee members' surprise, however, not all of the leading organizations in the field were 4945(f)-designated. For example, long-standing African-American rights groups such as the NAACP, the National Urban League, the Southern Christian Leadership Conference, and the National Coalition for Black Voter Participation/Operation Big Vote faced initial difficulties securing committee support because they did not have 4945(f) status when committee funds began to be dispersed at the outset of the campaign season. Newer groups, on the other hand, such as Project VOTE! and Human SERVE, that were also working predominantly in African-American neighborhoods but were led or heavily influenced by whites, did have 4945(f) status and were able to receive committee support immediately. In the end, most of the black-led groups sought and were granted 4945(f) status, but virtually all of them suffered from the time delay and perceptions of racial favoritism on behalf of "white" organizations. Addressing the inherent tensions and conflicts that such circumstances created as a result of competitive jockeying for scarce resources and attention proved to be more than an occasional drain on committee members' time and focus.

The unhappy consequence of the progressive left's bitter defeat at the polls in November 1984 and resulting donor self-reflection was a deep grant-making freeze for voter registration organizations across most of the foundation funding world. By early 1985, voter registration and education grants from all but a small handful of Ad Hoc Funders' Committee members were placed on hold, and by 1986, even the relatively well-funded SVREP began to suffer as a result. As early as November of 1985, SVREP was facing a deficit of more than $200,000 for the year. Velásquez's final monthly report for 1985 showed that, unfortunately, the financial crisis had actually gotten worse. As 1986 and a string of highly contested local elections loomed, Willie became unusually concerned. Writing to his board, he stoically reported: "From November 1984 to October 1985 SVREP received less than 40 percent of our total projected budget. . . . In order to maintain a high level of activity during this time, we used up all of our reserves, including every available monetary resource at our disposal. 1986 begins in a couple of weeks. In order to take advantage of hot local elections in March, April, and May, SVREP needs to make commitments to local campaigns by February 1, 1986." Velásquez projected a drastically reduced number of voter registration campaigns for the first quarter of 1986, but as the new year approached, no one, including Willie, was sure how or where the money would be found, even for a radically scaled-down workload projection that barely resembled the SVREP of just one year prior. The SVREP leader responded by quietly taking out a personal loan against his family's property and securing a $40,000 line of credit for SVREP at a local bank. He also selectively reached out yet again to his closest funding allies for help.

SVREP's dire financial straights were exacerbated by Willie's growing fatigue, as well as inadequate organizational systems and management. When Velásquez's old friend, Dick Boone of the Field Foundation, sent two fund-raising consultants to the aid of SVREP, Willie spent little time with them. The consultants' final report proposed several important changes in SVREP's fund-raising approach. The proposals included improving teamwork, shoring up traditional fund-raising activities, customizing SVREP's generic monthly reports to benefactors to provide them with more useful information, developing a contingency plan to contract and expand according to the cyclical nature of voter registration work and funding, and diversifying SVREP's fund-raising base, focusing especially on Hispanic donors.

SVREP had overcome major financial challenges in the past, most of the time through the sheer energy of its founding father, but the current impasse was taking a heavy toll on Velásquez. Not only did he fear insolvency, he feared that his life's work would also be washed away by the looming onslaught of conservative dominance across America. The purging of nearly 100,000 Hispanic voters in Texas by the Republican administration of Governor William P. Clements, Jr. meant that the Latino voter registration rate in Willie's home state would drop for the first time since SVREP was founded in 1974. Much to Velásquez's dismay and chagrin, at the very moment that SVREP needed to step up its efforts in Texas to counter the wholesale purging of Latino voter rolls, he was being forced to cut back its work in Texas by fully a third. "Unless we are able to increase the number of campaigns in a dramatic fashion," Willie warned his board and benefactors, "Hispanic registration will drop, further setting us back."

Resulting substantive and financial worries caused Velásquez's work and health to suffer. He fell behind on his commitments. He gained weight. He lost weight. He lost focus. In a rare moment of personal reflection, Willie confided to Ford Foundation consultant Harry Wexler in a letter, "The interesting thing to me [is] how these financial problems [have] chipped away at my efficiency." On reflection, Velásquez concluded that he was suffering from burnout after almost two decades of nonstop involvement in the Chicano political movement. He could not have been more correct. Now, Willie would have to decide whether he still had the fire to pursue his lifelong dream of helping to create a more powerful Hispanic electorate that would elevate democracy across America, or whether his health and sanity simply required that he do something else. The choice was simple for Velásquez. Politics was his life and SVREP was his purpose. He would redouble his efforts to continue promoting Latino political empowerment, and to that end he would now strive harder than ever to implant SVREP's work in the American imagination.

One of Willie's great motivations to continue was his burning conviction that SVREP had an especially critical role to play in ensuring that elected officials across the Southwest—including Hispanic elected officials—would be held accountable to the policy interests and needs of the region's emerging Hispanic electorate. His thinking in this regard was highly advanced relative to other national Latino community leaders who were still primarily focused on just getting candidates elected to office, and especially Hispanics. Velásquez, however, was fixed not merely on the quantity of Latino electoral representation, but also on its quality. He had been increasingly concerned for some time about the question of how Hispanic officials might best be encouraged to raise leadership standards in the public domain; but one incident in particular during the 1984 campaign cycle had helped especially to concretize his sentiments on the topic of leadership accountability in elected office. The incident involved a confrontation between Willie and popular San Antonio city council member Bernardo Eureste. Willie's unanticipated run-in with Eureste effectively crystallized the SVREP leader's growing belief that Hispanic leaders and voters needed to become far more demanding of their elected officials, even when those officials were themselves Hispanic.

↪ ↪ ↪

By the mid-1980s, as SVREP and other Hispanic rights groups successfully helped the Latino community to increase its voting power and turnout, Anglo elected officials began to court the Hispanic vote themselves. Some Latino leaders and organizations welcomed the attention and were seduced by the campaign promises made by these candidates, but Willie continued to withhold judgment until he heard their positions on the salient issues. During Democrat Mark White's campaign for Texas governor in 1982, for example, Hispanic leaders remained silent, willing to put aside some of their political differences in order to court favor with White and his team, while Willie questioned White's stances on important voting rights issues. Velásquez understood the practical choices being made by these Hispanic politicos, but he disagreed with their tactics. The Mexican-American community would not be strengthened, in his judgment, if Hispanic leaders did not stand up and challenge any political candidate or elected official, friend or foe, on issues important to the Latino community. Popular or not, politically risky or not, Willie continued to speak out, even when his friends advised otherwise. It was the type of politics he felt Hispanics had to learn and live if they were going to raise the level of political discourse in the Southwest. "The great number of votes we can deliver," Velásquez argued, "should require of potential candidates a much stronger presence at the local level when we need their help."

Over the course of a decade, SVREP had been playing a major role in changing the political environment in the Southwest so that Mexican-American political candidates could have a fair shot at getting elected to office, and it was working—Hispanic candidates were finally winning races. But with these victories came the need for community accountability and Willie now challenged the Hispanic community to hold its own elected officials to high standards of responsiveness. Velásquez was convinced that the Latino community had to focus on the quality of leadership and responsiveness it received from its elected officials, pure and simple. It did not matter to him if the elected official was white, black, brown, or any other color. What did matter was what each elected official did to improve the overall condition for Hispanics. Willie had hinted at this approach in the past, but by 1984 it had become a central tenet of his politics. The days of merely amassing Hispanic political clout through raw numbers were being supplanted by a sense of obligation to raise political performance standards in the Southwest and to appropriately use the political power that the Mexican-American community was investing in Hispanic and non-Hispanic candidates alike. In one of the nastier political battles of his career, Willie would be challenged to apply his logic in this area in practice just as he and SVREP were entering the final stretch of the National Hispanic Voter Registration Campaign.

In the late summer of 1984, SVREP was in the midst of its busiest voter registration cycle to date. During this period, Willie, as pressed as he had ever been with the approaching conclusion of the 1984 national campaign cycle, was recruited to join the finance committee of the San Antonio-based Guadalupe Cultural Arts Center, one of the premier Latino nonprofit arts groups in the nation. Founded in 1980, the Guadalupe Center grew out of an effort in the late 1970s called PAN—the Performance Artists Nucleus—to become a multidisciplinary arts group committed to preserve, develop, and promote Chicano and other indigenous arts. Rolando Ríos, SVREP's litigation director, was serving as the organization's board chair, and it was he who desperately sought out and convinced Velásquez to bring his fund-raising expertise to the table on behalf of the center. Willie was an avid fan of the arts, but more so in the traditional sense—classical music, opera, and the fine arts. Nevertheless, he also cherished contemporary Chicano artistic exploration and creation of the sort that flourished at Guadalupe, and, because of his relationship with Ríos, he was willing to spread himself even thinner by accepting the invitation to join the center's finance committee.

Shortly after Willie joined the committee, the Guadalupe Center and its major city council patron, the fiery and combative Bernardo Eureste, became embroiled in a battle. Eureste, known to his constituents as "Bennie," was San Antonio's fifth district councilman, representing a Southwest district that was predominantly Mexican American and poor. Eureste had first been elected in 1977 when San Antonio officially moved from an at-large to a district form of local government. A controversial yet extremely popular councilman, Eureste won his first council race with 63 percent of the vote. He was re-elected in 1979, capturing 68 percent of the vote, and was voted back to office in 1981 for a third term with fully 81 percent of the vote. Eureste was so powerful that he even survived a 1983 public scandal that would have easily destroyed a lesser politician. Late one evening, in February 1983, Eureste was approached and threatened by three young men as he sat in his 1978 Volvo with a twenty-three-year-old intern, Kerry Pruett, at the Brackenridge Park golf course. An inebriated Eureste fled the scene to seek help after being pulled out of his car by the young men, leaving Pruett behind to be molested by the attackers. Two months later, Eureste was re-elected yet again.

Eureste, an assistant professor of social work at Our Lady of the Lake University, had built a reputation for being a straightforward, outspoken progressive elected official and, in four short years, he had carved out his own slice of city power by forcefully staking out a leadership position in the arts funding world. As one local newspaper article described him in August of 1981, "Love him or hate him—he is actually one of those people who can inspire either of the two extremes—City Councilman Bernardo Eureste has emerged as a leading figure in the San Antonio city arts scene." Up until 1977, the council had not included funding for Hispanic arts organizations in its budgets. In 1977–1978, Hispanic arts groups, for the first time, received city support totaling $26,000. By 1980-1981, largely due to Eureste's campaigning, funding for Hispanic arts, under the banner of the San Antonio Consortium for Hispanic Arts, dramatically increased to $316,000. Only four years later, Eureste was able to push city funding aimed at Hispanic arts organizations over the one million dollar mark, to $1,099,510, with the Guadalupe Cultural Arts Center receiving the most significant amount—$588,504—of the total. Thus, in the short span of seven years, Eureste led the charge to put Hispanic arts funding on the city budget map, taking Latino arts groups from zero funding to an annual allotment exceeding one million dollars and positioning the Guadalupe Center as one of San Antonio's and the region's leading cultural organizations.

Eureste, a self-proclaimed "champion of the underdog," effectively solidified his own political power base through his funding of the arts. In the process, he had placed the Guadalupe Cultural Arts Center at the top of his pyramid. The historic Guadalupe Theater, located in the heart of the city's Westside on the corner of Brazos and Guadalupe Streets, had been built in 1940 and had served as a perennial entertainment center for San Antonio's Westside Mexican-American community until the 1960s when it hit hard times and eventually closed in 1970. Eureste persuaded the city to buy the land where the theater was located and helped to raise over one million dollars for its redevelopment. The Guadalupe Theater subsequently reopened as the Guadalupe Cultural Arts Center, a 410-seat performance facility in March 1984. Then, in a dramatic and unexpected reversal, just months after its opening, Eureste, now chair of the city's arts committee, declared open war on the center and its leadership for alleged political and fiscal irregularities, which he asked city officials to investigate. Eureste also accused the center's leaders of artistic elitism and guaranteed that he would do everything possible to make sure the Guadalupe Cultural Arts Center's $500,000 allocation in the 1984–1985 city budget would be zeroed out.

In an interview for an article in the *San Antonio Light* newspaper, the

Westside councilman all but lost it when asked about his intention to pursue retribution against the center's leadership, stating, "If I can't [cut their budget], I'll get those sons of bitches some way. . . . They've exceeded their mandate. They're a seedbed for political activity," Eureste continued. "If they want to play games like this, I'm the expert at playing games. If they're a city-funded agency in my district, there's only one person who plays politics there. Me. Period. As long as I keep getting re-elected . . . I control things. Not them." The angry councilman then closed by saying, "I didn't fight for my council seat to be some patsy. You're going to see the real political shit of the Westside fly in the next few weeks. Is this war? Shit yes!"

Eureste argued that an "infestation of Cuban sympathizers" was the major reason why the Guadalupe Center had to be reigned in. Using McCarthyite tactics, he accused several Center staff members of being communists merely because they had traveled to Cuba on behalf of Latino Cine Festival officials to review Cuban films that might be included in the international film competition. "They've got more people going to Cuba than the State Department," Eureste lamented. He also objected to the Center's involvement in a recent Walk for Peace in Central America campaign that some of its staff members helped to support on behalf of progressive interests concerned about U.S. efforts to squelch the Sandinista movement in Nicaragua and similar indigenous groups in the region.

For those being attacked by Eureste, and for others who closely followed the arts in San Antonio, the councilman's actions could be explained in simple terms. The newly crowned king of the Hispanic cultural scene in San Antonio had stepped over the line from supporter to controller and it now appeared that he would punish any and all who would not heed his arbitrary demands. Responding to Eureste, the Center's board chair, Ríos, and its executive director, Pedro Rodríguez, publicly asserted, in fact, "that City Councilman Eureste [had] sought a variety of political favors from Center officials [over the years] as a condition for his continued support." The alleged improprieties included pressure from Eureste to buy a block of $50 tickets for an upcoming political fund-raiser aimed at retiring the councilman's campaign debts and demanding that Center staff find and pay for entertainment to support various Eureste-sponsored fund-raising events. Center officials furthermore asserted that the councilman had tried recently to involve himself in Guadalupe's day-to-day operations by insisting that its leaders fire three staffers Eureste did not like. At the end of the day, the Center leaders asserted, it was simply no longer possible or appropriate to continue seeking to accommodate Eureste's increasing expectations.

In the heat of the conflict, Rolando Ríos reached out to his boss and friend, Willie Velásquez, to help him and the Center. This was no longer about organizational fund-raising and finance. Instead, it was becoming a good old-fashioned, hard-nosed political street fight, and Ríos wanted Willie's stature and political savvy by his side. It was a tough, even painful decision for Velásquez to reach, but one that he had to make in Ríos's favor given his sense of loyalty to the SVREP litigation director and his own conscience.

Willie had long been a strong supporter of Eureste. He respected Bennie's academic achievements and his role as a leading San Antonio social worker and professor. He admired the hard work and long hours Eureste put in as a council member, spending up to twelve hours a day on a job that barely paid him (council members received $20 per meeting and were covered for some expenses). He liked Bennie's progressive views and his deep commitment to speak out on subjects that other council members were often afraid to address. Willie recalled the key role Bennie had played, moreover, in helping Massachusetts senator Ted Kennedy to win important Hispanic votes in South Texas during the 1980 presidential primaries, despite the overwhelming odds favoring then-president Jimmy Carter, the more moderate, incumbent candidate. He was partial to Eureste's brand of Mexican nationalism and thought highly of his ability to get things done, especially in arts and culture. He even saw the councilman as something of a role model, as someone to look up to, rough edges and all, someone who put the interests of his constituents at the top of his political agenda and who stood up for people who were typically forgotten.

But now, Velásquez knew that Eureste had become corrupt and that he was no longer fulfilling his legitimate role and obligations. Now Willie was watching Bennie trying to destroy the very Chicano arts institution that he had helped to create. As Willie contemplated how he could help Ríos and the Guadalupe Cultural Arts Center, Eureste caught wind of the SVREP leader's intention to intervene in the conflict on the center's behalf. The result was an explosive confrontation between the two men.

On Thursday evening, August 23, in the midst of the 1984 general election campaigns, Willie dragged his overworked body home and went to bed, only to be jolted awake by a late-night call from none other than Councilman Eureste. Bennie, phoning from a local bar, said he called because he had heard Willie was going to write a public letter attacking him and supporting the Guadalupe Cultural Arts Center staff and board. They agreed to discuss the issues face to face on the following day at Willie's office, when the call went sour. "Willie," Eureste said before hanging up, "if you go after me I'll have no choice but to go after you." Willie, already on edge owing to the pressures mounting around the National Hispanic Voter Registration Campaign, had no patience for veiled threats from a business relation who had woken him and his family in the middle of the night. The councilman's comments immediately triggered an ugly exchange between the two strong-willed leaders, who loudly threatened each other, yelled some more, and then abruptly ended their call.

Willie, edgy but still in control, struggled to comprehend what had just happened when the phone rang again. Thinking it was Eureste calling back, Velásquez rushed to answer the call in time to hear an anonymous voice begin a tirade against a backdrop of club music and conversation. The voice on the other end of the line threatened Willie, telling him that he better be careful or some unfortunate accident just might take place. Willie yelled and cursed at the unknown caller who quickly hung up. With his blood boiling, Willie slammed the phone receiver down and furiously began pacing in his room. His wife, Janie, and all three of their children, Carmen, Catarina, and Guillermo, were now awake. They had all heard Willie's screaming and cursing. Frightened, and not knowing what to do, they tried unsuccessfully to calm Willie down.

Soon after, the phone rang one more time, and Janie and the children begged Willie not to answer. Ignoring their pleas, he instantly picked up the receiver. The nameless caller was on the line for a second time, surrounded again by the sounds and noises of San Antonio nightlife. "If I were you, Willie, I'd look out for my wife and kids," the harassing voice now warned. Willie was beside himself. It was one thing to be dragged into a political dog-fight in which he might be targeted by an adversary, but to have his family dragged into the fracas was entirely unacceptable. Willie violently lashed out at the unknown caller, to which the caller coldly replied that he and others would soon be coming after Willie. Velásquez responded forcefully, saying that he would be waiting for the caller and all his partners as the phone harshly went dead, the dial tone angering Willie even more.

Janie, not knowing exactly what to do, immediately phoned Rolando Ríos and begged him to talk to Willie and calm him down. Ríos, now himself fearing retaliations against his own family, did his best to respond but with little persuasiveness or impact. Velásquez calmly listened to Ríos and nonchalantly told him not to worry. Meanwhile, Willie called his sister, Stella, and told her that he was sending Janie and the kids over to spend the night at her house. He then called his brother, Ralph, and told him to join him immediately at the Velásquez's residence, promising to explain later.

With Janie and the Velásquez children safely out of harm's way, Willie anxiously awaited Ralph's arrival. Ralph soon arrived on the scene and Willie explained the situation. The two brothers rearranged furniture throughout the Velásquez living room and opened the front door so that Willie, sitting in a large, black leather chair facing the street, could see and stare down Eureste and anyone else who might dare to threaten him and his family. Willie chain-smoked in the chair while Ralph, armed with a tire iron, sat across the front room surveying the outside of the house and waiting to see if any prospective adversaries would actually show up. For nearly two hours, the Velásquez brothers sat patiently and quietly, readying themselves for whatever might come. Then, in the wee hours of the morning, a car turned onto Velásquez's street and slowly drifted to the curb straight across from the open entrance to Willie's home. Several men in the car stared Willie down. Willie, in return, did not flinch, but waited for them to make the first move. The nameless faces rolled down their windows, fired off some warning shots from a handgun, and quickly made off again in the darkness. The exchange lasted only seconds, but it was clear to Willie that Eureste and his people simply had passed the point of no return. They would have to be stopped and held accountable.

Janie and the kids returned home around five in the morning still nervous and sleepless. Willie, also operating without sleep, made his way to the office for his scheduled nine o'clock appointment with Eureste. The councilman and a group of "concerned citizens" were waiting for Willie in the SVREP library when Velásquez arrived. Willie went into the library, alone, and quietly closed the door behind him. Eureste delivered his standard inflammatory version of what was going on at Guadalupe, his comments filled with innuendo about so-called commies and Sandinista-lovers who had infiltrated the Center's board and staff ranks. The assembled supporters of the councilman claimed to be outraged at Willie's conduct, even though he had not yet even taken any public position related to the Guadalupe Cultural Arts Center conflict. Willie responded calmly yet firmly by telling Bennie that he was wrong, that he had stepped over the line and forgotten what he was elected to do, that he was now acting like a "boss man," and that there would be no backing down by Willie Velásquez, at least from criticizing him for the unfounded and self-centered attacks Eureste was leveling daily against the Guadalupe Center staff and board. After some emotional exchanges and name-calling, the meeting ended. No physical confrontation took place, but the discussion was certainly heated; and it left no doubt about whether Willie would finally take on the councilman publicly. In effect, Velásquez and Eureste were now formally engaged in a political duel.

A week later, on Friday, August 31, 1984, the *San Antonio Light* carried an open letter from Velásquez to Eureste. Willie recalled the admiration and respect that the councilman had until recently inspired among many of his Mexican-American contemporaries, but accused him of no longer being guided by ideals of honesty and fair play. "Today you have become a person who willingly tramples on the rights of others and disregards the most elementary norms of civilized conduct in your struggle to win the next election," Velásquez wrote. He then proceeded to remind his readers that as "Mexican Americans enter the arena of national politics, we have a responsibility to develop a political ethic whose standards of personal integrity are of the highest order." Willie further went on to add that "Mexican Americans will not make a contribution of lasting worth to our country if we decry the unjust actions of others while condoning, through our silence . . . outrageous disregard for truth and common decency in our own backyard." Velásquez had spent the week weighing his words, upset with Eureste both because of the corrupt elected official he had become and because he had tried to drag Willie's family into their political squabble. Nonetheless, Willie knew this story was bigger than any of the players—even bigger than San Antonio politics itself. The true issue concerned the budding political responsibility of the Mexican-American voting public. It was a prime example of what Willie felt the growing Mexican-American electorate had to stand up to. And Willie's responsibility, as he saw it, was to point out the egregious actions of elected officials, particularly when it was hurting the interests of the Hispanic community. As far as Velásquez was concerned, the Eureste-Guadalupe Cultural Arts Center battle was a visceral symbol of the type of politics that Mexican Americans should no longer tolerate. Even though there was no joy in doing battle with one's friends, it was something that Willie was now convinced that serious Latino community leaders had to start doing more often. Five days later, Eureste answered Willie's letter in the same newspaper employing the petty and bombastic political style he had cultivated in recent years, defending his position and repeating his accusations of left-wing infiltration at the Guadalupe Center.

Velásquez's public debate with the wayward Councilman Eureste underscored how far from reason and integrity the Westside elected official had veered. The two men's open letters to the community left no room for disagreement. Velásquez was clearly the voice of reason and responsibility. The point was not lost on San Antonio's most significant political players. Following Velásquez's and Eureste's public exchange in the *Light* newspaper, San Antonio Mayor Henry Cisneros and his key city council supporters stepped in and disbanded the city's arts committee headed by Eureste, stripping him of the powerful platform he had built over the past seven years. The council then created a new committee, excluding Eureste, tasked with the mission of deciding which arts organizations the city would fund over the long run. The *San Antonio Light*'s opinion page editors applauded the mayor and the city council on the action, commenting, "We congratulate Mayor Henry Cisneros on his move Thursday night to dismantle the platform Councilman Bernardo Eureste has been using for his unholy war against the Guadalupe Cultural Arts Center."

Willie was among the most prominent and respected voices that added integrity to the effort to check Bennie Eureste's power, but it was the combined weight of Mayor Henry Cisneros, Councilman Frank Wing, State Representatives Frank Tejeda and Frank Madla, and a number of other key community leaders that finally brought Eureste's actions to the public's attention and disapproval. Ultimately, it was the people in turn who decided Eureste's fate, as Walter Martínez defeated the four-term incumbent in the spring of 1985, handing Eureste a devastating loss that permanently ended his career as a public official.

Velásquez was not happy about playing a role in the demise and eventual defeat of his former friend. If anything, he felt disappointed that Eureste had not been able to return to being a true champion of the underdog, someone who put the interests of his constituents before his own. But now it was too late to revive either Eureste's reputation or his political career. The once powerful council member's defeat in the spring elections of 1985 did, however, make Willie proud. He saw a primarily low-income Mexican-American electorate stand up and declare its refusal to be represented by someone who did not live up to high community standards for responsible elected representation. This, in large measure, is what Velásquez had been working his whole life to make possible.

In a personal letter to Arturo Eureste, Bennie's brother and a longtime supporter of Willie and SVREP, Velásquez wrote, "[M]y objectives were based on principle. I know you may no longer consider me a friend, however you must know that a politician's success depends on quality advice from disinterested individuals whose concern is the public weal." It would always be easier to attack Anglo officials for their neglect of Hispanic community rights, but if Hispanics wanted to have any credibility, Willie believed, they had to be even tougher on their own politicians. The next stage of the Hispanic political movement would not be one of merely electing someone because of the color of their skin, the ethnic card they carried, or the familiar-sounding last name they brought to the ballot. It had to be about raising standards of public responsiveness and supporting individuals who most respected and represented the interests of the Latino community.

Willie knew very well that this worldview might not win him friends among minority nationalists who felt public officials of color should be supported by their people no matter what the cost. He knew that he would likely be attacked by others, moreover, as a self-appointed moral arbiter for the Hispanic community. But Velásquez took little time to worry about any of those possible reactions to his position. His message was simple and clear: Hispanic community issues and needs were infinitely more important than the petty personal or career interests of any elected official and especially any Latino politician who no longer had the community at the center of his or her interest. Following his heated encounter with Councilman Eureste, these sentiments would profoundly anchor Velásquez's public agenda and communications, not only at home in San Antonio, but also wherever he traveled across the nation for the rest of his life.

రా రా రా

When Willie emerged from his post-election crisis in early 1985, he urgently began seeking additional firepower for SVREP. He decided that it was time to switch strategies and to focus on the next stage of the Latino political movement—one in which Hispanics would move from political impotence to the responsible exercise of political power. Velásquez and SVREP would not be satisfied if unresponsive, morally and politically bankrupt Anglo elected officials were replaced with similarly styled Mexican Americans. Willie wanted to increase Latino political power and influence *and* to raise the level of political discourse and democratic standards. His expanded vision for SVREP included the creation of a membership-based League of Hispanic Voters, a Research Institute, and a focus on holding elected officials who represented Latino communities accountable to their Hispanic constituents.

With approximately 2.7 million Hispanics registered to vote in the Southwest by 1985, along with over 2,800 Hispanic elected officials now spread across the region, a rapidly expanding Latino population, and increasing coverage of the Hispanic electorate by the mainstream media, Willie strongly believed that Hispanics in the Southwest had arrived. "We now have political power and have to write a new set of rules based on power as opposed to powerlessness," Velásquez argued. "We need to concern ourselves with the principles that will guide us in making these rules because we are in the process of setting standards for the [Hispanic] entry into U.S. politics as major players." Willie's new themes—having power as opposed to being powerless, holding elected officials accountable to the Hispanic community, building a sophisticated base of political support throughout the Southwest, and developing an Hispanic political agenda—were replacing the predominant focus of the last decade. The first ten years of SVREP's history were about gaining power. The next ten years would concentrate, Velásquez now hoped, on how that power could be used to better the condition of Hispanics.

Willie began implementing his expanded vision by trying to create a League of Hispanic Voters under which individual members would pay annual dues and come together periodically to discuss and advocate issues crucial to the Southwest Hispanic community. Velásquez envisioned building the League into a strong membership lobby and a means of transforming SVREP into a more financially stable institution. He envisioned the league enabling a large number of Mexican-American (and other Latino) professionals—lawyers, doctors, and businesspeople—to join forces with government officials, community activists, and others who had been involved in Hispanic politics, to build a new Latino political agenda. Velásquez also hoped that the Hispanic professionals who became active in this work would serve as bridge builders between their non-Latino professional counterparts and the Hispanic community at large, in ways that would ultimately help to translate grassroots Latino values into mainstream public policy and institutional practice.

The League of Hispanic Voters was considered an intriguing concept when Willie pitched it to SVREP board members and financial supporters in the fall of 1985, but in the end, too many unanswered questions about SVREP's core work and still unfinished business remained. For influential board members such as Vilma Martínez, former head of the Los Angeles-based Mexican American Legal Defense and Educational Fund, and others who had strong California connections, SVREP still had grassroots mobilization work to do in California first—work along the lines of what it had begun to do so well in Texas and other parts of the region—before it transformed itself into a membership-based lobbying group. Benefactors simply wanted to see SVREP consolidate its now-challenged programmatic and fiscal status before striking out in wholly new directions. SVREP's directors and benefactors were not outright opposed to the idea of SVREP becoming a membership-based group. They were chiefly concerned with the question of timing. Above all else, most just wanted to see SVREP apply its proven formula—solid research, inclusive and powerful local coalitions, door-to-door voter registration, substantial voter education, and legal tools—more deeply in the field.

In fact, California was undeniably the most strategically important location requiring breakthroughs of the sort SVREP had achieved elsewhere. With nearly 1.2 million Hispanic registered voters but a Latino cohort of elected officials smaller than in both Texas and New Mexico, the Golden State clearly needed more of SVREP's presence. After considerable debate, Willie begrudgingly accepted the need to step back from the league concept and to focus instead on strategies to strengthen SVREP's field impact, especially in key geographical locations of strategic importance to Hispanic Americans, such as California. But Velásquez knew that to achieve continuing relevance and impact across the region, SVREP could not simply focus on doing more of the same work that it had always done. It was clear that Mexican-American community leaders and activists were growing tired of simple voter registration drives. They now wanted to develop and implement an Hispanic political agenda. Most were increasingly looking for ways to tie effective research to the building of that agenda. Willie had also been thinking about how to integrate such research into SVREP's work.

On December 19–21, 1984, just six weeks after the general elections, SVREP held a planning retreat at which Velásquez formally introduced the concept of creating a Southwest Voter Research Institute. As SVREP Research Director Bob Brischetto described it: "The Southwest Voter Research Institute [would operate] on the premise that political mobilization of Mexican Americans must be organized around issues rather than candidates or parties." Willie had actually considered creating an institute as early as 1977, based loosely on the African-American-focused Joint Center for Political Studies, which specialized in research on black political issues and the training of minority elected officials. But lack of time and resources prevented SVREP from moving on the idea.

In 1982, SVREP's Brischetto revived the subject and suggested creating a researcher-practitioner think tank as part of SVREP's ongoing research agenda. The following summer, Brischetto began working on the concept and by the summer of 1984, he and Andy Hernández, now SVREP's deputy director, presented it to the board. SVREP's board members liked the notion of adding practical research to the project's existing platform of voter engagement activities. Shortly after the November election, SVREP's legal director, Rolando Ríos, thus filed articles of incorporation with the Texas secretary of state for a new SVREP-affiliated entity that would "support and conduct nonpartisan research, technical assistance, training, educational and informational activities to advance the exercise and effectiveness of political participation by Mexican Americans and other minority group members, and to assist members of such groups elected or appointed to public office to [serve] effectively."

Five weeks later, Willie, his staff, and a handful of outside guests convened to hammer out the details of the new Southwest Voter Research Institute. Its mission, argued Velásquez, should be to conduct research that would help to mobilize the collective political power of Mexican Americans. This meant applied, action-oriented research that would finally make a difference in people's lives. "We don't want to get involved with anything that doesn't have historical consequences," Velásquez proclaimed. The institute would identify the major concerns facing Hispanic voters and communities, study these issues in-depth, and then recommend policy solutions for consideration by the public, the media, and elected officials. In this way, the institute would become a preferred information center for the growing number of individuals and organizations interested in Mexican-American voters and the key issues affecting their communities.

As Brischetto described it, the institute would focus on research targeting grassroots voter registration and mobilization efforts, election returns analysis, and research that supported voting rights litigation. It would also cover local, state, and national budget and policy issues that were important to the Hispanic community and conduct public opinion polls. The institute would also develop public policy trainings and host conferences, using its research arm to bring together elected officials of Latino districts to formulate more informed and viable public policy responses to needs in the Hispanic community of the Southwest.

To help SVREP develop the institute along these lines, Willie invited Ed Dorn, deputy director for research at the Joint Center for Political Studies, whose primary audience was the country's 5,700 African-American elected officials. Dorn shared the Joint Center's successes and challenges and outlined a number of the key questions SVREP would have to answer in order to proceed effectively. Velásquez and his staff also sought the expertise of Bob Greenstein, executive director of the Center on Budget and Policy Priorities, an increasingly influential progressive research and advocacy group specializing in fiscal policy issues affecting low- and moderate-income Americans. Greenstein suggested that SVREP could play a much needed role through the proposed institute to inform and mobilize Hispanic constituencies on key federal revenue and spending issues, such as proposed budget cuts, tax reforms, and program modifications affecting job training, welfare, and Medicaid—areas in which Latinos were still effectively invisible in national policy discourse, even though they were heavily impacted.

Willie also invited numerous other experts to help SVREP define a policy research agenda for the new institute, including: Carl Hohman of the Urban Coalition; Jim Browne of the Field Foundation; Ruby Martin, an African-American activist who also did foundation consulting work; Raúl Yzaguirre, president of the National Council of La Raza; and David Cohen of the Advocacy Institute.

After garnering critical feedback from these experts and a general endorsement of the institute concept, Velásquez and SVREP spent the next eight months redefining institute planning at four two-day staff retreats. In addition, Willie invested heavily in efforts to gain support for the institute from leading Hispanic elected officials, which he received in most instances without difficulty. The SVREP executive's keen interest in developing the institute with attention to every critical detail was the product both of his personal conviction in the essential importance of the proposed new entity's work and his practical recognition that, with an effective funding freeze on voter registration activity in place in the aftermath of the 1984 elections, SVREP's evolving institute strategy might offer the only window for the organization to capture major new grant funds for the foreseeable future.

Beginning in the fall of 1985 and throughout most of 1986, Velásquez pressed hard to secure funding for the Southwest Voter Research Institute. In solicitation letters to potential supporters, Willie described the institute as possibly the most significant initiative that SVREP had ever pursued. He stressed that it had the backing of influential politicians such as San Antonio Mayor Henry Cisneros, Denver Mayor Federico Peña, New Mexico Governor Toney Anaya, California State Senator Art Torres, California Assemblywoman Gloria Molina, and a dozen and a half other leading Latino elected officials across the Southwest. He underscored his assertion that Hispanics had moved from powerlessness to power and now had a responsibility to exercise that power intelligently. Willie also suggested a critical new rationale for the institute's work focusing on the strategic importance for the country as a whole to benefit from a fuller integration of Latino groups in public problem solving, arguing, "[W]e must begin thinking in terms of all of us, not just Hispanics. I firmly believe that America must view Hispanic political efforts as being good for our nation and not just a scramble by an interest group to get its share of the pie. Indeed, if we are not able to convince ourselves and our fellow citizens of this fact, we can expect a grim future of limited success and few advances."

Velásquez concluded his appeal to benefactors on behalf of the institute by stressing the growing relevance and importance of national politics to Mexican-American and other U.S. Hispanic groups, stating, "Whereas previously . . . elections seemed [to us] like a genteel game of musical chairs among a small elite without much discussion, [today they are] settled in the open marketplace of ideas among a much expanded electorate. What this means is that elections are now brawling affairs in the good old American tradition. And they are brawling precisely because they are important and [our] people now care." This was the democratic world that SVREP had helped to create and it was this hustling, bustling, changing political environment that Willie wanted to see recognized by foundations in the form of support for his evolving new research project.

On November 20, 1985, William A. ("Bill") Díaz, a Latino program officer at the heavily endowed and widely respected Ford Foundation, began a series of exchanges with Willie to assess the Southwest Voter Research Institute's prospects for foundation funding. Velásquez understood well that Ford Foundation support for the institute would provide an immense vote of confidence in the concept that could only help to encourage other private donors to follow suit. Díaz was interested, but needed ambiguities cleared up before the foundation would be willing to invest.

First, the Ford program officer wanted to know how the new institute would position itself in relationship to the growing number of Hispanic public policy research and advocacy organizations in existence, such as the National Council of La Raza, the National Puerto Rican Coalition, the Tomás Rivera Center, and, in particular, the National Association of Latino Elected Officials (NALEO). Second, Díaz was concerned about the long-term sustainability of the new institute. SVREP was proposing an initial budget of nearly $645,000 to support the institute and was asking the Ford Foundation to fund fully half that level—$322,000, an amount that Díaz knew was unrealistic given the entire package of Hispanic programs the foundation was already committed to supporting. Willie would have to show more clearly how the institute would survive financially over time, building on a broader range of funding sources. Finally, Díaz was worried, given the uncertain climate surrounding future voter registration funding opportunities, that the institute could unwittingly provide an easy way for benefactors to simply refocus their support to safe research projects on minority voting issues, rather than remaining engaged in the more political and controversial world of grassroots voter mobilization. The foundation officer keenly intuited that one of the reasons Velásquez and SVREP might be developing the institute was to tap funding sources that were more interested in research than organizing. The downside of the strategy, however, as Díaz aptly surmised, was that SVREP's gamble could severely compromise its ability to raise dollars for the project's traditional staple of activities.

Velásquez had answers at the ready. First, he asserted, the institute would position itself differently than the other Hispanic public policy groups because its agenda would be driven by grassroots networks of SVREP partners built over eleven years in more than two hundred local sites and thirteen states. It was this network, currently organized around the project's eighteen regional planning committees and over two thousand Hispanic community and political leaders, that continued to ask for more public policy research and that had been pushing Velásquez and SVREP to therefore develop the institute concept now rather than later. The other Hispanic public policy groups, for the most part, did not have a built-in grassroots constituency like SVREP, Willie informed Díaz. For Velásquez, this was a key distinction. The institute's programs would be led by political practitioners who were close to the pulse of the Hispanic community, while other Hispanic public policy groups were directed by scholarly researchers who were relatively removed from the day-to-day realities of Latino neighborhoods.

The institute would be different from the National Association of Latino Elected Officials (NALEO), Velásquez argued, because NALEO did not support the sort of political mobilizing or organizing work that SVREP did, and because the Hispanic elected officials who affiliated themselves with NALEO did not have the deep connections and relationships that were shared, by contrast, among the Latino politicians who were actively involved with SVREP. The years of conducting voter registration and education campaigns in the trenches had bonded these public officials and taught them a number of practical lessons. When SVREP brought these leaders together in regional planning committees to share strategic insights, resources, and frustrations, strong associations of Hispanic community and political leaders began to form that had not existed beforehand. Because of their grassroots connections and positions of authority, Velásquez believed, these Hispanic elected officials would be well positioned to effectively utilize the sort of applied research the SVREP institute planned to develop. Willie underscored the importance of this point for Díaz by reminding the Ford Foundation executive, "[I]t really doesn't matter very much to have a series of reports on public policy questions if no one reads them or is in a position to act upon them." According to Willie, SVREP's proposed institute would serve as a critical new vehicle for elected officials to build on in translating knowledge into effective action on important public policy questions relating to Latino groups.

Velásquez addressed Díaz's concerns about potential downside costs to SVREP's core program work posed by the new institute by arguing that SVREP's voter registration and education work would remain vital as states with smaller Hispanic populations emerged to comprise the next logical frontier for Hispanic political mobilization. "The initial stages of this era are [already upon us]," Willie explained, "because there are very few districts left where Hispanics are the majority and we have no representation." As a result, Velásquez astutely observed, "The vast bulk of [our] work in the future will be in districts where Hispanics are a small percentage of the population. Sophisticated approaches, buttressed by sound, sensible research will be indispensable to our success in these districts. The significant contests in the future, therefore, will depend on our ability to attract the support of citizens who do not happen to be of our ethnic background."

Willie was less convincing to Díaz (and others in the funding world) concerning the institute's potential for financial viability, largely because it was premised on a vision of hope, strong leadership, and a promise of quality work, rather than deep analysis and consultation in the philanthropic field. It was never Willie's style to answer the question of long-term financial support by researching and listing potential funding partners who would be targeted for the institute or any other aspect of SVREP's work for that matter. Velásquez's game plan was simply to approach SVREP's extant family of supporters, both those who had been funding the project for the better part of a decade, as well as more recent donors, to ask each of them to become charter investors in this new endeavor.

In addition to the Ford Foundation, which had been steadily supporting SVREP's registration and education work in recent years through its Social Justice Program, Willie also targeted the Rockefeller Foundation and Carnegie Corporation as crucial prospective anchor investors in the institute. Like Ford, both Rockefeller and Carnegie had become erstwhile benefactors of SVREP's core work in recent years, and both had established interests related to public policy research. Ford's Díaz, recognizing the possible advantages of encouraging coordination among these leading funding institutions, suggested that Willie meet soon with representatives from Ford, Rockefeller, and Carnegie, in order to consolidate discussions around a possible omnibus proposal from SVREP that all three benefactors might entertain simultaneously. Díaz, accordingly, organized the proposed meeting on May 12, 1986, at the Ford Foundation offices in New York. Velásquez joined the Latino program officer, as well as Bruce Williams of the Rockefeller Foundation and Bernard Charles of Carnegie Corporation for a lengthy discussion related to institute funding.

Based on this input, Velásquez agreed to identify appropriate academic and corporate representatives as potential board members to augment his original list of institute board members, which the benefactors considered overly weighed in favor of elected officials. In due course, Velásquez proposed the addition of several new individuals to serve on the institute board, including Jonathan Moore, director of the Institute of Politics at Harvard's John F. Kennedy School of Government; Jesse Aguirre, vice president of Anheuser Busch; Luis Nogales, CEO of UPI, Inc.; Emilio Nicolás, president of the Spanish International Network; Francisco Lorenzo, president of Continental Airlines; Howard Friedman, chair of the American Jewish Committee; Herman Gallegos of the Human Resources Corporation; and Tomás Arciniega of the University of California at Bakersfield. At the strong encouragement of the foundation donors, Willie also proposed adding two key layers to the institute governance structure, namely, a research advisory committee consisting primarily of prominent Hispanic scholars and a compliment of advisory panels to oversee specific policy topics on which the institute's work would touch.

Velásquez's dialogue with Ford continued in June, this time with an expanded number of staff representing the foundation's policy and justice programs, including Díaz, Shepard Forman, Mora McLean, Henry A. J. Ramos, and Lynn Walker. The foundation officers, though generally interested in being helpful to SVREP, raised key questions about the proposed institute. From Willie's standpoint, these questions were legitimate but inconvenient. As he saw things, the questions were focused more on minutiae rather than big-picture strategy. He needed and wanted to gain the Ford staff's full and enthusiastic endorsement of the institute concept, but time was passing and Velásquez was feeling the weight of SVREP's growing financial pressures by the minute.

SVREP had to be kept afloat and the nascent institute was increasingly incurring start-up costs. The two entities needed a significant infusion of money, plain and simple; and they each needed help very soon (in effect, disaster was already waiting in the wings and Velásquez knew it). Under pressure to address these brutal realities, Willie wrote Díaz on July 25, 1986, and somewhat desperately proposed a "bare-bones budget of $122,594 to operate the Southwest Voter Research Institute for the remainder of the calendar year." Velásquez urged Díaz and his Ford colleagues to contribute $85,000 of this budget to help initiate three major research projects: a data-bank of demographic and political information for key counties in Arizona, California, Colorado, New Mexico, and Texas; polls of Latino voters in California and Texas to be administered in conjunction with the 1986 midterm elections; and selected studies of public policy issues that would have a major impact on Hispanic communities during coming years.

Richard Dennis, a Chicago-based progressive philanthropist, had already committed $10,000 to the institute for SVREP to use for these purposes during the second half of 1986, but, otherwise, the donor community to this point seemed more interested in asking questions rather than in writing checks in response to Velásquez's pleas for institute start-up support. The Ford Foundation seemed to offer SVREP's best hope to provide the major portion of the money needed to get the institute off the ground and to keep SVREP alive. Now, approaching the hottest weeks of the summer and having pitched Ford the best deal he could offer under the circumstances, all Willie could do was wait and hope for a favorable foundation response.

Chapter 22

DESPITE SVREP'S CONTINUING FUNDING woes, Willie faced the second half of 1986 feeling optimistic about the future. His conversations with the Ford Foundation and other key benefactors on starting up the Southwest Voter Research Institute were moving forward. Much to Willie's great relief, within a few months Ford would commit $135,000 to help initiate the institute's work; other major donors would follow suit thereafter. In addition, Velásquez's plans to increase the project's presence in California were progressing. Unfortunately, movement on both fronts was at a much slower pace than expected, and Willie was forced to hustle for interim support resources and helpful West Coast alliances wherever he could find them. Sadly, the pressures weighing down on the SVREP founder forced him to increasingly rely on intermediary funding from groups like the Citizens' Participation Project (CPP) and political money from individuals like U.S. Senator Alan Cranston, the Democratic majority whip from California. In the end, however, these seemingly logical allies would fail to deliver to SVREP, and the resulting impact on the project's work and standing would be devastating, particularly in California.

⌐ ⌐ ⌐

CPP was the brainchild of Tom Wahman of the Rockefeller Brothers Fund. It was set up during the 1984 national election to target wealthy individuals through direct mail appeals in order to raise funds for voter registration groups working in low-income and minority communities. Over $345,000 was raised and distributed to the field during CPP's inaugural year of activity. In its initial iteration, CPP operated without staff. The absence of staff enabled the new organization to avoid overhead expenses and to maximize its responsiveness to voter mobilization leaders and groups. In fact, CPP's board of directors, which handled all allocation decisions, was nominated in part by grassroots voter registration leaders themselves. Willie, for example, nominated former United Auto Workers leader Henry Santiestevan and National Council of La Raza President Raúl Yzaguirre, both of whom were appointed to serve; SVREP received $78,000 from CPP for its 1984 campaign efforts.

In preparation for the 1986 midterm elections and its second disbursement cycle, CPP decided to hire a full-time director. Velásquez nominated Rick Hernández, a longtime SVREP supporter, for the position. But one of the CPP board members, Frank Weil from the Norman Foundation family, who had both personally donated and raised big money for progressive voter registration causes in recent years, nominated his wife, Denie Weil, as an unpaid volunteer and agreed to resign if necessary to avoid a conflict of interest. Several board members knew Denie Weil from her prior work at the German Marshall Fund and were intrigued by the idea of saving additional administrative costs by bringing her on. She thus became the first executive director of CPP.

Weil had never run an organization before, but was considered by her supporters to be solid, intelligent, competent, and capable. Most believed that she would run CPP like a good foundation program officer. Her detractors described her as a Radcliffe graduate with a combative style and a lack of experience working closely with minority-led grassroots organizations.

The Citizens' Participation Project, like many other funding entities that had supported progressive voter registration work during 1983–1984, was now rethinking how it could best allocate its limited resources for greater traction in future elections. Following the Reagan landslide of 1984, and unprecedented Republican success at the grassroots level, Frank Weil and other board members wanted to build more accountability into the CPP funding process. They wanted to emphasize hard results and to prioritize payments based on where those results were being maximized on the ground. Under Denie Weil, therefore, the Citizens' Participation Project decided to change its past practice of awarding lump sum payments to grantee groups, which it had done in the first disbursement cycle of 1983–1984, and instead opted to pay organizations in installments based on performance. This meant that groups, such as SVREP, would be given a portion of their funding up front and then would have to fill out reporting forms that detailed their field activities and impact before they could be approved to receive additional grant payments.

Willie considered the lengthy, bureaucratic nature of the new reporting requirements outrageous. SVREP had proven its effectiveness time and time again for more than a decade, most recently in public evaluations underscoring its most productive year to date. No one had ever asked for that amount of detailed documentation before, not even SVREP's largest benefactors. At one point, Willie complained to Rob Stein, head of the nonprofit organization AmericaVotes, "For Christ's sake, the Ford Foundation gives me four times the amount [that CPP does] and they asked for two [page reports . . .] this lady

gives me $50,000 and she's asking for twenty pages. It's crazy. It's insane!".
CPP's new reporting requirements meant more than mere inconvenience
for SVREP. Velásquez believed he had a firm commitment from CPP to support the project to take on a substantial amount of new work in California in
time for the November 1986 elections. The expanded work in California was
an essential deliverable for Willie in light of growing pressure from his board
to concentrate greater SVREP focus in that key electoral state for Latino and
progressive causes. But CPP's new funding strategy made it virtually impossible for SVREP to carry out work in the Golden State using CPP funding
without risking compromising delays from one report-payment period to the
next. Willie began to criticize the new procedural regime at CPP, arguing that
it promised to create more harm than good for the progressive cause by
undermining field continuity and employee retention.

Disagreement over procedure became a deadlock. The information CPP
was asking for was designed to show that its grantee groups were doing what
they said they would do and were doing it well, but as Velásquez saw it Weil
and her staff simply had no practical concept of what it meant to run a large
number of voter registration campaigns simultaneously across a sweeping
geographical region in a very short period of time. What they wanted to promote in theory was fine, Willie believed, but not at all practical without forcing leading groups in the field to literally divert resources from actual registration activity to information collection and reporting. The proposed CPP
approach, which could only add to the field's administrative costs at the
expense of dollars in action on the ground, was anathema to Velásquez's philosophy of limiting back-office costs as much as possible, precisely in order
to invest principally (and directly) in campaigns.

Both Velásquez and Weil were stubborn. Their personalities clashed and
made an amicable resolution difficult. Many observers essentially endorsed
Willie's position that Weil and her staff just did not understand how minority voter empowerment work was done on the ground effectively. Jim
Browne, of the Field Foundation, for example, later commented,
"[Velásquez] felt misunderstood. CPP was asking [SVREP and Willie] to
prove how good they were at being technicians when they were community
builders, not number counters." CPP board member Raúl Yzaguirre, who was
talking to Velásquez on a daily basis during the standoff with Weil, would
later similarly reflect, "Velásquez felt he was being asked to jump through
hoops by people who knew a lot less about voter registration than he did."
But others saw the tensions between Velásquez and Weil differently. CPP
board member Peter Edelman, for example, would subsequently comment,
"Nobody had ever done to Willie what she did to Willie. That is to say,
nobody had ever really questioned him. Denie's style is not smooth. She's
not a sweet person in the way she operates. It was an accident waiting to hap-

pen because a fair amount of what he was angry about were questions that she was asking that were legitimate questions that nobody had ever asked him before . . . questions about what he did with the money."

The conflict between benefactor and nonprofit organizations was particularly complex in the case of SVREP and CPP, according to Colin Greer of the New World Foundation, because "it was a cultural conflict between a white woman of wealth and a Latino male filled with dignity and pride." Weil herself eventually admitted some of this was at play and had been for her with other minority-led groups as well, when she reflected in an interview that "[a] white middle-class woman running this kind of organization always has some tension when the predominant constituency is lower-income minority groups."

The impasse between Velásquez and Weil did not ultimately prevent the two organizations from continuing to do business. It merely made for a complicated and less-than-optimal partnership between the two groups. In fact, CPP awarded SVREP a significant $100,000 donation for the 1986 campaign season. In order to honor this commitment, CPP, paying in multiple installments, sent SVREP $10,000 on July 21 and another $45,000 on August 20; but then, on December 15, Weil informed Willie that she was not going to send any more money until SVREP provided the reporting documentation CPP now required as a matter of policy. Three days later, on December 18, Velásquez returned a check for $10,000 to Weil, saying that SVREP would no longer accept money from organizations that were not satisfied with its work. He suggested that if CPP wanted more information on how SVREP's grant money was spent it should send a staff person to San Antonio to check things out on site. "Perhaps then you can get an idea of . . . our embarrassment at having to tell groups we formed that we didn't have funds to open their projects in time," Willie tersely stated, adding, "You and your staff can then get an idea of what it feels like to still owe funds to local projects months after the campaigns are over." Four days later, on December 22, Weil sent another $10,000 check to replace the one Velásquez had returned and said that CPP had enormous respect for Velásquez and SVREP's work. But in a reply on Christmas Eve 1986, Velásquez told Weil to reread his last letter, coldly reiterating that he did not expect CPP to send any money if it had any doubts about the integrity and impact of SVREP's work.

Eventually, Weil did send a consultant to visit Velásquez and SVREP. The consultant was able to reconstruct enough information to show that indeed there had been successful voter registration campaigns where SVREP had said there had been; but the consultant also found data sorely lacking on the precise number of people registered through SVREP's efforts, and recommended remedial efforts by Velásquez to correct the deficiency. CPP knew well, however, that Willie would be disinclined to do so, and found it easier merely to send SVREP a final installment of $45,000 in April of 1987 to fulfill its $100,000 commitment to SVREP for 1986–1987. Weil said that she hoped this would help to clear things up and lay the groundwork for a smoother working relationship between SVREP and CPP. But, while SVREP and CPP would continue to collaborate in the future, Willie and Denie Weil would never reconcile their differences.

In the end, the demise of the working relationship between SVREP and the Citizens' Participation Project had less to do with issues of form and process in the administration of grants than it did with the substantive question of who most appropriately controlled how work should be conducted in the field. It was Willie's righteous indignation that the focus of the field should not be on bureaucratic bean counting, but rather on proven grassroots empowerment strategies that informed his challenge to CPP over how voter registration should be done in Latino communities and who should broker these decisions. This critical set of considerations would also shape a colossal confrontation between Velásquez and Alan Cranston, one of the nation's most powerful and influential Senate leaders, during 1986 and 1987.

In the spring of 1986, just months before his re-election campaign against twelfth district Silicon Valley Congressman Ed Zschau, Alan Cranston, the seventy-one-year-old senior senator from California and the number two man in the Senate Democratic leadership, called SVREP to express his respect for its important work and to ask whether it was planning on doing any voter registration work that year in California. Velásquez told him yes, SVREP's board had recently voted to make California the organization's top priority and that he wanted to open a permanent office there. Over the course of several subsequent conversations and meetings, Senator Cranston agreed to help raise the $250,000 Velásquez estimated an expanded voter registration capacity would cost for California. A gentleman's agreement was sealed with a handshake and talk of working together in an historic partnership to mobilize California's growing Hispanic voting population.

Neither side, Willie nor Cranston, denied that the senator approached SVREP and they agreed to raise money for the organization's efforts in California. Unfortunately, Velásquez and Cranston quickly disagreed over the nature and amount of the senator's commitment. Based on his earlier conversation with Cranston, Velásquez informed his staff that the senate leader had favorably listened to SVREP's plans for California and agreed to raise the full $250,000 that would be needed for significant work there during the 1986 elections. Senator Cranston, however, later recalled that he had only agreed to *help* raise funds for SVREP and had never committed to a specific amount. Rob Stein of AmericaVotes, who worked closely with both men, subsequently speculated on the origins of their clear miscommunication, stating, "Cranston [was] an expansive enough kind of talker and thinker that it's very possible . . . Velásquez [was entirely reasonable to think he had a specific commitment from him,] even though Alan believed that he didn't actually make the commitment for a specific amount. But there was no doubt [the senator] *had* agreed to help raise money for [SVREP]."

Alan Cranston had been a lifelong supporter of democracy projects and attempts to expand the electorate, but it was a 1985 *New York Times* article on voter registration that rekindled his interest in this work and convinced him to call Rob Stein, one of the people highlighted in the article, to discuss voter registration issues. Stein had founded an organization in 1983 called The Forum Institute, which was intended to serve as a neutral meeting ground for progressive groups that needed a space to gather, share information, and collaborate on projects. Stein and others served as consultants to foundations and individual philanthropists who met there. In its first two years of existence, The Forum Institute focused on challenging conservative efforts to reduce public funding for national legal services and advancing the disarmament agenda of the anti-nuclear movement. It then became deeply engaged in efforts to increase funding for progressive voter registration efforts in 1984, especially including the Citizens' Participation Project and Frank Weil's Missing Half project. But in the bitter, cash-poor aftermath of the 1984 general elections, with no more money left to pursue additional work in the field, The Forum Institute pulled out of voter registration completely. Stein and others who had been helping to run The Forum Institute's voter promotion activities began planning to wind down and close operations. By September 1985, Stein was the last person remaining in the office, his days built increasingly around plotting a new professional focus. Then, out of nowhere, he received Cranston's phone call.

Cranston and Stein spoke about the voter registration crisis in America for more than forty minutes. The discussion renewed Stein's passion to remain involved in voter registration work. It also inspired him to draft an informative essay for Cranston that he called "The Fourth Dimension." The paper focused on three traditional ways that people become politically motivated—through political parties, individual candidate campaigns, and political action committees—and it suggested an emerging fourth dimension: the voter registration, education, and mobilization efforts of the nonprofit sector. Included in Stein's essay was an analysis of how the nonprofit political right-wing and Republican Party operatives were able to coordinate fund-raising efforts during both the 1980 and 1984 elections to capture large amounts of money from wealthy conservative donors. Stein's analysis also included investigative evidence that the Republicans and their wealthy benefactors had plans to do even more collective harm to their counterparts on the left in upcoming elections, building on the allied activities of conservative nonprofit organizations.

The senator was surprised and shocked by Stein's report. He had no idea that Republicans had been decimating the Democrats through such tactics. He invited Stein to continue their conversation, and the two men indeed met several times in October and November of 1985. Reflecting on the Right's effective coordination of voter promotion efforts involving both party and nonprofit campaign investments, Cranston told Stein, "They're doing it (the Republicans and the right-wing), so we need to do it as well." Accordingly, Cranston wasted no time supporting efforts to raise new money for liberally-oriented nonpartisan voter registration work in late 1985 and 1986, concentrating especially on the Center for Voter Education and Participation, which had only recently received its tax-exempt status to conduct voter promotion activities in California. In October 1985, admitting his own political self-interest in supporting this work, Cranston penned a direct mail letter for the California Center that listed his re-election bid as one of four issues of great national significance in the upcoming 1986 elections.

In December 1985, Cranston, now the Senate's minority whip, called a meeting of his House and Senate colleagues. He told them that Republican Party committees were outspending Democrats for electoral purposes by a margin of nearly 6 to 1 ($100 million for the Republicans, $18 million for the Democrats) and that ultraconservative and religious right nonprofit groups were greatly outspending their moderate and progressive counterparts when it came to voter registration, education, and mobilization efforts ($30 million for the Right and $6 million for the Left). At Cranston's behest, the Democrats agreed to form a committee to raise funds for progressive voter registration groups and asked Stein to manage the efforts. Stein accepted. In January 1986, the unincorporated committee led by a combination of leading House and Senate Democrats was named AmericaVotes.[1]

AmericaVotes selected two groups—the Citizens' Participation Project and The Forum Institute—to manage the allocation of funds raised by committee members. The reason for this, Stein would subsequently reveal, was "to separate the fundraisers from the allocators . . . and to insulate the political leadership from . . . groups [that] would try to bring political pressure to get the money for themselves." Its goal for 1986 was to raise $5 million in contributions of $50,000 to be distributed to voter registration groups work-

---

[1]Democratic leaders participating in the work of AmericaVotes included, among others, senators like Frank Lautenberg of New Jersey, George Mitchell of Maine, and Paul Simon of Illinois (in addition to Cranston), as well as leading House members like Tony Coehlo of California and Bill Richardson of New Mexico.

ing in up to twelve states. Following an initial test run to gain preliminary donor commitments in April 1986, the committee began to implement a full fund-raising schedule in May.

Through this work, Senator Cranston became a leading figure in raising funds for liberal voter mobilization efforts across the country; it was in this context that the California senator called Willie Velásquez in the spring of 1986 to link his efforts with those of SVREP. After several exchanges between the SVREP director and the senator, Cranston and Stein informed Willie that SVREP would receive support for its California expansion through the Citizens' Participation Project and The Forum Institute.

The directive to work through the committee's funding arms, rather than the senator himself, represented a departure from Willie's initial understanding with Cranston; but Velásquez believed he had every reason to trust the senator. They were both liberal progressive politicos with decades of community and political experience between them. They knew what the political stakes were. The U.S. senator from California committed to raising national voter registration funds for SVREP and the Mexican-American voter registration leader focused on expanding SVREP's presence in the Golden State in ways that would ultimately benefit Cranston. The timing and complementary agendas fit perfectly.

Shortly after Cranston promised Willie that he would deliver funds for SVREP's California efforts, he asked Stein to meet with Velásquez in order to develop an appropriate partnership strategy for the coming campaign season. But the meeting ended up having a significantly different slant than that, with the emphasis being more on committee fund-raising challenges. Stein alluded for the first time to certain potential complications: they were having difficulty raising money, and he had no idea when or how much the final sum would be. Nevertheless, he reiterated Cranston's commitment to doing what he could to get SVREP something.

Meetings like these made Velásquez angry and nervous. He knew that SVREP was not the only voter registration organization that interested Cranston and Stein in 1986, but he was also aware from his discussions with both men that it was among the very few groups to which Cranston had personally committed himself to raise money. Thus, while Stein's sudden hesitation was unsettling to Willie, he still remained confident that Cranston would honor his commitments to SVREP. Accordingly, he moved quickly when Stein directed him to submit a funding request to CPP as soon as possible, in May. Velásquez was encouraged to send a funding proposal to CPP, notwithstanding his personal differences with Denie Weil, for pragmatic reasons. CPP had just received several large donations as a result of Cranston's fund-raising and had much more money to allocate compared to the still financially strapped Forum Institute. As Stein recalled years after the fact,

"When the crunch happened, which was in June and July of [1986], everybody was freaking out—the foundations were not pouring money in, our fund-raising efforts [were slow getting] organized. . . . [It just so happened that our first big [infusion] came in to CPP, so that was *the place* that had the money. Of the existing vehicles, the Forum didn't have much, [only] around $50,000. [By contrast,] CPP [suddenly had] $400,000."

As early as September of 1985, SVREP was beginning to actively inform its political and financial supporters that California was its highest priority state and would be through at least the 1988 election cycle. There was even talk of the project opening a full-time California branch office in early 1986 with an increased number of field staff. Though continuing tough financial times ultimately made it impossible for SVREP to open its proposed California office during this period, Velásquez's fund-raising pact with Senator Cranston convinced him to move forward with his plans to dramatically increase SVREP's California profile.

Yet, in the end, Willie was badly disappointed. The funding he expected to materialize through Cranston was both too late to arrive to be very useful and nowhere near the $250,000 level he believed he was promised by the senator. As a result, SVREP was abruptly forced to shut down a number of voter registration campaigns that it had organized in California on the basis of Cranston's promises. It also had to abandon plans to initiate even more drives in other parts of the state. In all, fully half of SVREP's envisioned registration campaigns for California had to be discontinued or cancelled—from seventy-one to forty-three. The California campaign, moreover, was not the only one to suffer owing to Cranston's failure to deliver. In fact, Velásquez had to tap into money set aside for other Southwestern areas to complete what work could be salvaged in California. This resulted in cutbacks in SVREP's planned work with Latino groups in Colorado and Nevada, as well as with a number of American-Indian campaigns SVREP was managing in Idaho and South Dakota. "The most important lesson we have learned," Velásquez commented bitterly in his August 1986 report to board members and benefactors, "is that we cannot let our guard down. In talking to [community leaders], we must strictly adhere to our rule of not proposing action unless the funds are in the bank. The funding prospects looked so good in California that we went out on a limb, only to discover that the good intentions were not matched by capability to raise funds. Unfortunately, there is no respite from the need to undertake an extensive program and raise funds at the same time. [In the future,] SVREP will simply rely on the methods we've used in the past and be careful to distinguish a call to action from a siren's song."

The reduced number and shortened period of voter registration campaigns in California were not a complete disaster for SVREP. Velásquez did reestablish old political ties and he made contact with many new leaders and organizations. In addition, the regional planning committee established for California became better organized and positioned to jump quickly into action for the 1988 national campaign cycle. But these were small gains in relation to what had been lost in California during 1986, and Velásquez was livid that he had allowed himself to depend on Cranston and CPP. His involvement with these liberal gatekeepers as a means to expand SVREP's reach in California had largely produced failures. The wholesale cancellation of planned registration campaigns, the inability to pay local coalitions even the pittance in cost compensation that SVREP typically provided, and the late start in so many operational sites that were trained and ready to act, resulted in a significant loss of personal and organizational credibility in California, as Willie saw it. "SVREP has been greatly damaged by this affair," Velásquez later wrote to Pat Hewitt, one of the fund-raising consultants sent by the Field Foundation to assist SVREP. "As you know, previous evaluations show that we have always paid every campaign on time and [for] the full amount contracted. In this case, virtually no drive began on time and a large number have not been fully reimbursed."

In an enraged letter to CPP's Weil, Velásquez made clear the hardships liberal leaders had created for him and his organization by their failure to deliver promised financial backing during this period, stating, "SVREP had never defaulted on any commitment in the field. Not even a penny. This year we defaulted on $22,614.30 in California alone. . . . If it weren't for our Chicano banker who turned hot checks into a long-term loan, SVREP would have closed its doors." The larger state of voter registration funding notwithstanding, Velásquez experienced these failures personally. "My word has been destroyed," he wrote in additional correspondence to Weil, promising to pass along his pain in a way that would help her feel some of it too: "I will make sure you understand how bitter I am that the years I have dedicated to this work and the reputation I have earned among our people as a man of integrity whose word was his bond, no longer holds true in California because we were not able to comply with the contracts we signed with the local groups." Not only was Velásquez ashamed of having broken promises, but he would now also have to live with the humiliation of his misplaced dependency on Cranston as a money broker for SVREP's California efforts.

In the end, SVREP received only $55,000 from CPP and a mere $20,000 from The Forum Institute, the two organizations from which Velásquez had expected to receive a total of $250,000 just to expand work in California. In the same year, Cranston won re-election by a paltry 3 percent out of the nearly 7.2 million votes cast in California. The Democrats also regained control of the U.S. Senate. But, when all was said and done, it was actually Cranston, more than Willie, who turned out to be the big loser.

Velásquez ultimately complained privately to Senator Cranston, who apologized and explained that his group had experienced unanticipated difficulties raising money for voter registration during 1986. What the senator did not tell Velásquez, though, was that he had led the charge to raise $4.1 million from seventy-five wealthy donors under the umbrella of AmericaVotes, and that his re-election campaign had been the primary beneficiary. Only a *Wall Street Journal* article written years later would publicly surface just how disingenuous Cranston had been with Willie relative to his inability to raise voter registration funds during 1986. The article underscored that Cranston's benefactors had in fact generated millions of dollars for Democratic registration during that midterm election year, and that Cranston himself had done extremely well to capture many of those dollars for his own re-election. According to the *Journal* report, "By far the biggest chunk of tax-deductible money—$600,000 according to [an internal campaign] memo—aided Senator Cranston's [own] re-election. [One Cranston aide] said it seemed to be the difference between victory and defeat." In fact, Cranston won his re-election by less than 105,000 votes in 1986. After the fact, Rob Stein of AmericaVotes claimed that "the combined efforts of the party and the tax-exempt groups got at least 160,000 voters to the polls [for Cranston during the 1986 campaign]," adding, "Campaign officials believe that [these votes] were indispensable ingredients for [Cranston's] victory." "Indispensable" was arguably an understatement. As it turned out, in fact, some of the same liberal donors who contributed to Cranston's nonpartisan voter registration efforts also donated approximately $300,000 of nondeductible money directly to the California Democratic Party for a statewide get-out-the-vote effort, largely on the California senator's behalf.

The 1986 election cycle turned out to be a banner year for Alan Cranston's voter registration fund-raising efforts. Significant gifts were secured through the senator's efforts, including $400,000 from Joan Kroc of the McDonald's hamburger fortune to the Citizens' Participation Project and $100,000 from Hollywood producer and department store heir Frederick Field to the Western Center for Voter Education and Participation (formerly known as the California Center), which had been formed by Cranston through a direct mail appeal. Painfully little of this money, however, was routed to SVREP.

Another contributor to Cranston's tax-exempt voter registration activities was Michael Milken from the Wall Street securities firm, Drexel Burnham Lambert. Later, after Milken's highly publicized federal securities fraud conviction and the collapse of the junk-bond market, Cranston sided with Drexel on the Banking Committee against legislation to curb the purchase of high-risk bonds by federally insured thrifts, and joined other California lawmakers in petitioning the Securities and Exchange Commission to preserve Drexel's junk-bond operation in California. This kind of personal intervention on behalf of wealthy and corrupt individuals and corporations was exactly the kind of political conduct that SVREP detested and sought to challenge. From late 1986 through 1987, SVREP struggled to survive. Juan Andrade and MVREP loaned SVREP $7,500 at the end of 1986 to bolster its operational cash flow. Velásquez himself wrote a personal check to the same end a year later for $5,000, and his mother for $3,000. The New World Foundation granted SVREP an emergency loan of $10,000 during this same period. In the spring of 1987, the Field Foundation sent SVREP $50,000—but restricted the money to be used to diversify its funding base, rather than for programs. The financial strain on Willie and SVREP was so intense that the organization never even held a board meeting during 1987.

Velásquez and the staff of SVREP did everything they could to keep a much smaller budgeted organization active in the region and to deliver high-quality work in a reduced number of sites. SVREP thus undertook ninety-six voter registration campaigns across ninety-two cities and eleven American-Indian reservations in fiscal year 1986–1987. Upholding its previous commitments, but at a highly reduced level, the staff had taken on forty-nine voter registration campaigns in California. Unfortunately, many of these drives were tainted by the funding shortfalls created by Willie's dependence on Senator Cranston. Only two new at-large election lawsuits were filed by SVREP during this period, one which was favorably settled and one which was still pending at the outset of 1988.

ᔕ ᔕ ᔕ

Willie had no doubt been left feeling disgusted by Senator Cranston for his part in creating these hardships for SVREP, but the conflict between Velásquez and the senior senator from California reached new levels of intensity in the months following the 1986 campaign, when it came to light that Cranston's son, Kim, and Marshall Ganz, the veteran community and labor organizer who was the architect behind the California Democratic Party's get-out-the-vote effort in 1986, intended to set up their own voter registration and community organizing training outfits in California. As Rob Stein recalls it, "The political operatives felt that there hadn't been much quality work done in 1986 on the voter registration side in California, either amongst blacks or Hispanics. And [Kim, Marshall, and others in their network] felt that they could do better, so they wanted to create a capacity to deal with this problem. . . . When I first heard about it, I thought it was going to be a funding vehicle for California that would [help to finance] viable Latino, black, Asian, and issue groups." But what Alan Cranston, his son Kim, and their partners actually had in mind was something far less friendly to minority-led voter registration organizations.

On July 10, 1987, the Center for Participation in Democracy (CPD) was incorporated by Kim Cranston with the long-term goal of "contributing to the growth of democracy in American public life by increasing citizenship participation, especially by members of communities where such participation has been low." CPD was structured to undertake massive voter registration drives in minority and low-income communities, to conduct campaign skills training to teach citizens how to be effective participants in democracy, and to run naturalization programs for immigrants. The organization ambitiously set a goal of registering 1,000,000 new California voters in time for the 1988 general elections.

On the same day, the Monterey Leadership Training Institute (MLTI) was established with Kim Cranston designated as president. The MLTI, which listed CPD as one of a few potential clients, defined its mission as "contributing to a restoration of democratic participation in American public life by revitalizing democratic organizations through the development of the leadership for and practice of effective organizing." MLTI was designed to recruit, train, and develop organizers; further the philosophy and practice of organizing; and provide training, educational and technical assistance services on organizing to a variety of civic, labor, government, community, and political groups.

In short, MLTI would train organizers for CPD. In turn, CPD would carry out allied voter registration campaigns in California. From this point forward, Senator Cranston revised his voter registration fund-raising pitch, adding CPD—along with The Forum Institute and the Citizens' Participation Project—to his short list of potential donor recipient organizations.

When Velásquez found out that Cranston had set up his own nonprofit voter registration efforts in California run by the senator's son Kim, he exploded. Not only had Cranston failed to live up to his pledge to raise substantial amounts of funding for SVREP's work in California, but also he had now created his own competing vehicle that had grassroots voter registration as one of its top priorities. The 1988 presidential election season would reveal just how much of a conflict of interest Cranston's new organization posed, relative both to his ethical duties as a public official and his earlier representations to Willie concerning his respect for SVREP's work. As Charles Babcock reported in the *Washington Post* in an early 1990 article, "Just like before the 1988 presidential election, Ganz and Kim Cranston shifted from their tax-exempt work to run the state Democratic Party's get-out-the-vote drive. A recent California Democratic Party brochure credited [Senator] Cranston and the 'nonpartisan' CPD with aiding the Dukakis-Bentsen campaign's grassroots efforts in the state."

The Cranstons' move to develop CPD and MLTI was the last straw for Velásquez. He felt as if all the work he and SVREP had done over the past thirteen years was being cast aside at the whim of a few powerful white politicians who possessed tons of money and who felt that they could do whatever they wanted. To add insult to injury, CPD even stole away several former SVREP coordinators by offering them fancy titles and large salaries. Willie saw Cranston's actions, and those of his son and their allies, as nothing more than an elite power play meant to take control of the nonprofit (and nonpartisan) voter registration and education process and as a direct slap at minority-led groups such as SVREP that wanted to pursue a true long-term community empowerment strategy.

At the Campaign for Full Political Participation's voting rights conference in Texas in October 1987, Velásquez publicly confronted Senator Cranston. The senator was not completely surprised. He had been apprised of Velásquez's anger by staff and field allies a day earlier. Nevertheless, he was not expecting Velásquez to come after him in public. In his remarks to conference participants, Senator Cranston urged them to work with and donate money to efforts by elected officials, Democratic presidential candidates, and labor and business leaders to promote greater turnout in key contests during the upcoming 1988 campaign season. Velásquez stood up during the question-and-answer period following the senator's speech and pointedly attacked Cranston. He criticized the senate leader's proposed mobilization strategy because it drained money away from groups such as SVREP who concentrated on local as opposed to national elections. Velásquez reminded Cranston of the importance of local elections in developing the responsible civic participation of minorities. "For us to revert to brokering Mexicans for elections that are important for some national plan," Velásquez asserted, "would be turning back on some important lessons. We are going to refuse any help that puts us in the position of being modern *patrones* delivering so many Mexicans on the hoof." Cranston responded obliquely, reiterating his respect for all the different voter registration efforts in progress and suggesting that no one group could do it all. But the forcefulness of Velásquez's remarks caused a buzz in the room and the crowd began to side with Willie's calls for political decisions to be determined locally. MVREP's director, Juan Andrade, subsequently remembered Willie's public challenge to Cranston was particularly impressive and also revealing of his deep anger toward the senator, commenting in an interview that "his thoughts were never better collected. He knew exactly what he wanted to say and he knew exactly how he wanted to say it and he did it very, very articulately. Yet, at the same time, it was hard to disguise the bitterness that he felt. You could see the bitterness, the resentment, in his eyes, in his face, in his mannerisms, the way he used his hands, the way he pointed his finger at Cranston. You could see how strongly he felt about it." Andrade was not the only conference participant who Willie impressed. A few days after the Texas gathering's conclusion,

Velásquez received a letter from a San Diego woman who wrote, "During the last session of the conference and your response to the proposed Cranston legislation, I believe that the most of us present stopped breathing. For me, everything became suddenly and finally clear, because we too are victims. In San Diego, the Cranston machine, operated by his son and Marshall Ganz, is poised to roll right over our grassroots efforts in voter registration with a program that lacks credibility and a track record of success."

Within weeks of Velásquez's public attacks on Cranston, attempts were made to patch up the conflict. After a few meetings, the senator again promised that he would try to raise money for SVREP, but Velásquez remained highly skeptical. Rob Stein believed that Cranston's instinct was to "work it out." Kim Cranston's response was the same. For both Cranstons, the situation with SVREP was all a huge misunderstanding. For Velásquez, it had become a blood war over minority political self-determination.

Velásquez knew that he could not compete against the Cranstons with their vast pool of resources and influential friends. In its first year, with no track record at all, Cranston's CPD raised almost $1.5 million dollars to work in just one state—California. Cranston's group did an impressive job in getting the numbers nailed down, bolstering California's liberal voter rolls through the use of technology and low-paid organizers. Estimates for the 1988 campaign season ranged from 250,000 to 350,000 newly registered voters, below CPD's overly ambitious goal of one million, but far more than any other group had ever been able to produce in California. Still, Willie and other Latino leaders were unimpressed. Were numbers alone the answer, they asked, to the lack of Latino political power in California? They were a good start, Velásquez acknowledged, but they were not enough. As Willie saw it, strong research, legal firepower, the surfacing of key local issues, and the ability to help communities direct their own political destinies—all of this and more had to be developed as a package if Latinos were going to become active, empowered citizens who made a meaningful contribution to American politics. None of these extra but necessary components, however, were being delivered by Cranston's Center for Participation in Democracy. From Velásquez's perspective, the reason for this was plain: Cranston's group was motivated by one thing—delivering bodies to the Democratic Party on election day. A different mission drove SVREP: helping to create an empowered Latino electorate that delivered its power to the political parties and candidates who responded most to their particular issues and concerns.

Eventually, Cranston became the victim of his own self-dealing. The senator's claims—"we're having a tough time raising voter registration dollars"—turned out to be manifestly false. In fact, Cranston had raised an extremely large amount of money for voter registration efforts. In 1987–1988, according to the *Washington Post*, the senator successfully solicited an estimated $7 million for tax-exempt nonpartisan voter registration efforts, a near doubling of his fund-raising total during 1986.

But this time, the senator's fund-raising efforts tied him to undeniable political wrongdoing, as it came to light that some $850,000 that Cranston had solicited came from ultraconservative financier Charles Keating. Keating, head of the Lincoln Savings & Loan Corporation, would later be indicted and found guilty on charges of securities fraud in one of the nation's most celebrated political and banking scandals ever. Nearly half of Keating's contribution to Cranston's cause went to the Center for Participation in Democracy, the voter registration group headed by Cranston's son, Kim; another $325,000 went to The Forum Institute; and $125,000 went to USA Votes, the Democratic fund-raising group Cranston helped to form as AmericaVotes in 1986. Subsequently it was disclosed that Cranston and a small handful of other Senate members inappropriately sought to intervene on Keating's behalf when he and Lincoln Savings came under federal criminal investigation through the Securities and Exchange Commission.

On February 27, 1991, the Senate Select Committee on Ethics found "substantial credible evidence" of ethics violations by Senator Cranston because of his dealings with Keating. The committee found grounds to believe that Cranston had engaged in an impermissible pattern of conduct in which fund-raising and official activities were substantially linked, citing various instances in which Cranston solicited funds from Keating while inappropriately helping Keating to negotiate with federal thrift regulators. Shortly after this information was made public, both The Forum Institute and the Center for Participation in Democracy shut down their operations. The largest casualty, however, was Senator Cranston himself. When the scandal broke, Cranston lost his Democratic Party number two spot in the Senate. Soon thereafter, the aging senator announced that he would not seek re-election in 1992. After twenty-four years in the U.S. Senate and nearly five decades in California politics, the seventy-eight-year-old senior senator from California had been effectively forced to relinquish his seat and his power. Velásquez might have rejoiced over these developments, but, owing to the most unexpected of circumstances, he would never even have the opportunity to see them play out.

Chapter 23

As 1987 BEGAN, WITH THE CALIFORNIA-Cranston-CPP debacle still a source of hardship for SVREP, Velásquez received a call from an old friend that drew him directly into the 1988 presidential campaign. Nick Mitropoulos, who had served as the associate director of the Institute of Politics at Harvard's John F. Kennedy School of Government when Velásquez was an Institute Fellow, was now helping Massachusetts Governor Michael Dukakis to prepare for a White House bid in 1988. Velásquez had befriended Mitropoulos at Harvard in the fall of 1981. They instantly hit it off and were very much alike: fiercely charismatic, extremely proud of their immigrant roots, and political masterminds who never tired of analyzing and dissecting the latest campaigns and issues.

Velásquez had also met Dukakis at Harvard after the liberal incumbent Democrat lost his initial governorship in 1978 to conservative Democrat challenger Edward J. King. Governor Dukakis was teaching at Harvard's Kennedy School of Government, reflecting on his mistakes, and planning a political comeback when Willie arrived at Harvard. Dukakis and Mitropoulos, both sons of Greek immigrants, spent a great deal of time together during that period and after Dukakis regained the Massachusetts governorship in 1982, Mitropoulos joined his administration as personnel director. By 1987, with Dukakis contemplating a race for the presidency, Mitropoulos had established himself as the governor's closest aide.

Mitropoulos told Willie early on that the governor was considering entering the presidential race and asked him to be part of an important group that Dukakis was assembling to counsel him. Velásquez naturally agreed to serve and was officially added to an impressive list of Dukakis advisors that included former Iowa Senator John Culver; media magnate and activist Norman Lear; and former Vice President Walter Mondale. In January and February 1987, Governor Dukakis quietly met one-on-one with these individuals and consulted with groups of other top Democratic leaders.

Velásquez accordingly came to the Boston statehouse on January 19, 1987 to meet with Dukakis, Mitropoulos, and John Sasso, the man who managed the governor's comeback campaign in 1982 and now served as his chief secretary. The governor probed Velásquez about Southwestern and Texas politics and the Hispanic electorate—Who were they? What did they believe in? What issues are important to them? What types of candidates did they typically support? What motivated them? Where were they concentrated? What would it take to get their support? Velásquez eagerly responded and impressed Dukakis and his campaign managers, all of whom hoped that he would continue to be a source of information and counsel.

Willie was also impressed with Dukakis. Unlike many politicians who Velásquez had met over the years, Dukakis appeared to be a man of substance who spoke Spanish and understood immigrants' concerns. And because of his connection to Mitropoulos, Velásquez believed the governor was being skillfully advised. It was still early in the presidential season and Willie knew that he had to be careful about any public appearance of partisanship, but he instantly felt positive about Governor Dukakis and the governor's potential as a possible Democratic nominee. He told Mitropoulos to call him whenever he had questions and that he would be happy to help in any way he could.

ᔐ ᔐ ᔐ

Back at home in San Antonio, Willie was recharged by the conversation with Dukakis and infused with a renewed sense of civic activism. The first issue of the upcoming national campaign season to grab his attention was the growing English-Only movement spreading across the country—an effort to convince states to adopt English as their official language and to outlaw other languages, typically Spanish, from being used in any official capacity within the state. Four states had already passed such resolutions and had designated English as their official language; another thirty-seven states were considering similar proposals. Beginning in March 1987, Velásquez threw himself into the middle of the English-Only debate, not only because of its potential impact on bilingual ballots and Spanish voter registration and education materials, but also because in his judgment it constituted a politics of discrimination against Hispanics and immigrants.

SVREP announced that it would host a series of public debates on policy issues of concern to the Latino community. The first topic would be "English-Only" with Louis Zaeske, chairman of the American Ethnic Coalition arguing in favor of the English-Only advocacy effort and Velásquez arguing for "English-Plus."

Velásquez saw the case for English-Plus as a fundamental issue of citizenship. He believed that as many citizens as possible had to be brought into the political process in order to strengthen American democracy. In real terms, this meant using Spanish voter registration and education materials and ballots to encourage, rather than discourage, the nation's growing Latino population—much of it consisting of naturalized immigrants whose first language was Spanish—to participate more actively in public elections. He also believed that use of the Spanish language and media in voter registration campaigns throughout the Southwest would ultimately help to elevate Latino standing and relevance in America's evolving global leadership role. As Willie saw things, Latinos in the United States needed to be proud of their native tongue because it was already positively changing America and would continue to do so in the near future. In an increasingly global society, he argued, America needed individuals who could not only speak other languages, but also and ever more importantly, who could understand and work with other cultures. Hispanics, Velásquez believed, would serve as role models for the rest of the country, demonstrating to their fellow citizens in the most positive ways what it meant to be a new American in a rapidly integrating world.

Drawing on these fundamental convictions, Velásquez warned Americans against using immigrants as scapegoats. "They [English-Only proponents] object to bilingual education; they are for English-Only because we are immersed in a long, sustained unemployment period," Velásquez argued, "that gives life to something that always lurks beneath the psyche of American society—xenophobia." Velásquez reminded audiences of laws that were passed in the late nineteenth and early twentieth centuries outlawing the use of German in certain parts of the United States, commenting, "We have to understand that these issues create emotions, and emotions create momentum that sweeps up even good people." Willie went on to observe that the normally liberal *New York Times* had itself "editorialized in favor of these (anti-German language) laws." By extension, he cautioned, similarly draconian measures and otherwise responsible champions now stood ready to make Latino immigrants and the language of their heritage subjects of a modern-day witch-hunt that would finally do America little good.

The English-Only debate simultaneously brought out Velásquez's patriotism, ethnic nationalism, and moral indignation. He described Spanish as an integral part of American culture, a culture that existed in many parts of America even before the creation of the United States. At the core of the argument, for Velásquez, was the notion of striking a balance for the benefit of all Americans. He believed that as a matter of human and constitutional rights, Hispanics should be protected and allowed to speak in their native tongue in all aspects of the nation's public affairs. At the same time, he insisted that it was incumbent upon Hispanics to become more literate in every language, including especially English. Falling back on Spanish would be as much a fault as those who promote English-Only and would isolate Hispanics from the riches of American life, he argued.

Over the course of a year, Velásquez appeared in the English and Spanish media and engaged in a half-dozen English-Only debates. Willie had always believed that public debate was an essential democratic tool to create a more active and engaged Latino electorate that would leave its mark on American policy and history. This was the kind of public debate that Velásquez sought to stimulate through the Southwest Voter Research Institute, where studies and data would be used to surface and assess important issues of the day, such as English-Only policy proposals.

Velásquez further bolstered his activism during this period by focusing as well on U.S. foreign policy in Latin America, which he saw as a significant factor in the creation of expanded immigrant and refugee flows to the United States, and a growing impediment to Latin American political self-determination. Willie had always believed that the connection between Latinos in the United States and Latinos in Latin America needed to be made more concretely from both a cultural as well as a political perspective. As a young man, his first passion had been international diplomacy and he spent much of the 1980s increasingly trying to deepen the relationship between his work on one side of the border with the other. In July 1984, Velásquez agreed to serve as an advisory board member of the Central American Peace Campaign, a group of grassroots and national activist organizations that had been recently formed to oppose U.S. military intervention in Nicaragua, El Salvador, Guatemala, and other parts of Central America. Willie assisted the campaign in various ways, including agreeing to distribute a report to Latino political and community leaders through SVREP's networks entitled "Changing Course: A Blueprint for Peace in Central America and the Caribbean." The report had been completed by a cadre of progressive Central American scholars to offer a sharp contrast to recommendations for U.S. action proposed in the Reagan White House-endorsed Kissinger Commission Report. However, in the end, SVREP's heaviest period of voter registration activity in its history forced Willie's side interest in Central American issues to take a constant back seat to the organization's primary mission: domestic politics. Graciela Sanchez, a former SVREP staffer who had taken her fierce passion and dedication to Central American issues, tried to get Willie more actively involved, but it just wasn't the right time. As the end of the decade neared, however, and Willie observed what was happening in Central and South America, he could no longer permit himself to remain disengaged.

౬ఇ ౬ఇ ౬ఇ

By May 1987, Velásquez was actively corresponding with members of the National Democratic Institute for International Affairs (NDI), a nonprofit group aligned with the Democratic Party whose mission was to encourage democratic development efforts throughout the world by assisting individuals and organizations outside of the United States to become effective participants in budding democracies. Leticia Martínez, assistant to NDI's president, J. Brian Atwood, suggested Velásquez's name as a potential political development expert for an upcoming project in Nicaragua.

The following month, Velásquez accepted an invitation from NDI to join the organization's executive vice president, Ken Wollack, and Frank Greer, a Democratic media and political consultant, on a trip to Chile designed to bolster ongoing democracy-building efforts in that nation. Just a year earlier, in May 1986, the National Democratic Institute had cosponsored an international conference on transition to democracy issues in Caracas, Venezuela, that included participation by representatives of Venezuela's major political parties. Now, eleven leading Chilean opposition leaders who had recently signed a national accord calling for the political and economic democratization of Chile agreed to convene under NDI's auspices, along with representatives from Argentina, Spain, Uruguay, and Venezuela, for regional pro-democracy talks. Velásquez would be traveling to Chile to offer his gritty American experiences, the nuts and bolts of grassroots democracy, to the coalition of Chilean opposition leaders who were desperately seeking help as they prepared for an upcoming presidential plebiscite.

Willie touched down in Chile in July 1987 and felt as though he had stepped back in time and was once again an international relations student of Professor Ludwig Mai or a summer intern for the State Department. Velásquez, the consummate community activist, who was always too busy to write anything down, including his speeches, was mesmerized by what he saw and heard, and recorded copious notes throughout his travels in Chile. He grilled participating delegates about their political histories and philosophies, asking many of the same questions he would ask local Hispanic leaders in America—What do Chileans believe? How do they get their political information? What role does the church play in Chilean politics? What obstacles do Chileans face in trying to participate politically? He was moved by the vivid stories of what these people had faced and the staunch commitment to democracy they carried with them along their way, against all odds. He was humbled by the opportunity to work side-by-side with the Chilean opposition leaders and to develop with them grassroots action plans to mobilize new voters for the impending elections.

One month later, in late August 1987, Dr. Charlie Clements, a Vietnam veteran pilot turned Quaker and peace activist, invited Velásquez to Honduras, Nicaragua, and Costa Rica. Clements had recently spent a year providing medical treatment for civilians wounded behind rebel lines in the war-torn Guazapa region of El Salvador. His story had been memorialized in the 1986 Academy Award-winning short documentary, "Witness to War." Now Clements was focused on doing all that he could to open the eyes of America, and especially its most influential leaders, to the atrocities taking place in

Central America side-by-side with the burgeoning seeds of peace. Clements had come to find Willie through Antonio González, a former National Student Voter Registration staffer who had operated out of SVREP's offices during the 1984 elections and was now working on Central American issues. Clements, the peace activist, was seeking González's help to find some Latino leaders to join a congressional delegation Clements was taking to Central America. In response, González convinced Velásquez to be a part of one of the first international delegations to visit Central America after five presidents in the region had signed onto the recent Arias Peace Plan. Willie joined Texas State Representative Al Luna, chairman of the Mexican American Legislative Caucus; Democratic Congressmen Nick J. Rahall, a Lebanese American who represented West Virginia's fourth district, and Jim Olin, a retired vice president of General Electric who represented Virginia's sixth district; and various congressional aides on the trip. The weeklong excursion made a strong impact on Willie. Once again, as in Chile, he soaked up everything he heard and saw, and took voracious notes on conversations he had with workers, government officials, politicians, business people, and journalists. But this trip differed in important respects from his previous journey to Chile. In Chile, Velásquez had been brought in as a political advisor whose grassroots expertise was needed by the Chilean opposition. In Honduras, Nicaragua, and Costa Rica, by contrast, Velásquez and his fellow travelers were on hand to observe, learn, and experience the working and living conditions of an international region under siege.

Willie's observations in Central America brought many salient political issues forward in a way that he had not experienced, even with all of the reading, thinking, and politicking he had done back home in Texas. In the same way that Velásquez had been changed as a college student when he first experienced the plight of the farmworkers and their strike efforts, his trip to Central America was transformative. He returned determined to get SVREP involved. His growing ties to the region, along with the devastation he saw there, convinced Velásquez that he had a responsibility—and a unique opportunity—to engage Latino Americans in the Central American political debate.

Willie felt that all Hispanics faced a growing imperative to get involved in international issues, especially those with which the Latino community in America had historical and cultural ties. He envisioned Hispanic Americans across the country becoming more and more connected to what was happening south of the border. In the best-case scenario, Velásquez believed, Latinos in the United States could help to raise the level of national discussion concerning Latin American issues, beyond partisan grandstanding. Along these lines, he hoped that Hispanic Americans would eventually come to engage their countries of origin in ways similar to how the American Jewish community engaged in political dialogue on issues crucial to Israel.

Upon returning to the United States from the Clements tour of Central America, Velásquez and the other members of the delegation harshly criticized U.S. involvement in the region, denouncing the U.S.-backed Nicaraguan counterrevolutionary insurgent force known as the Contras (and comparable American-supported paramilitary groups there) as "mercenaries paid for by this country without popular support." To substantiate this criticism, Willie pointed out that polls showed Hispanics were opposed to aiding the Contras by a margin of two-to-one. In October, Velásquez wrote a letter to the U.S. House Speaker, Texas Congressman Jim Wright who had recently broken ranks with the Reagan administration on Central American policy, to underscore his own and other Hispanic leaders' commitment to Latin American reform politics, in which he reported, "In September, State Rep. Al Luna and I took a trip with Congressmen Olin and Rahall to Central America. I consider this trip a departure point for the long-term involvement of Hispanic leaders in U.S.-Latin America policy."

Willie knew realistically that it would not be easy to galvanize the U.S. Latino population to weigh in politically on Central American concerns, given other more immediate domestic community priorities. But, now convinced of the import of the issues for U.S. Latinos and Central Americans alike, the SVREP leader concluded that he and other Hispanic political voices simply had to try in every way possible to help translate U.S. Hispanic opposition to U.S. policy in Central America into improvements in America's role in that part of the world. The plan to that end was for Velásquez and Texas State Representative Luna to make presentations on their Central America findings to groups of Hispanic community leaders and local public officials, encouraging them in turn to lobby their congressional representatives for policy change in the region. The strategy was essentially designed to spur grassroots public support for Speaker Wright and the Central American Peace Plan in ways that would help to undermine the Reagan administration's Contra Aid policy and create space for democratic alternatives in Nicaragua and surrounding nations.

Velásquez had already been asked by Nicaraguan Vice President Sergio Ramírez to organize another trip to the region consisting of U.S. Hispanic leaders who would have the chance to inspect the peace process in action. Based on these developments and his own strong feelings on the issues, Willie decided that over the long-term, the Southwest Voter Research Institute would house a special Latin America Project. As he presented the concept to Speaker Wright and others, "The goal would be to educate, through seminars, training sessions, and delegations, a broad group of Hispanic leaders on U.S.-Latin America relations and related policy issues." Similar to the significant challenges posed to Latinos by the emerging English-Only debate, Willie fundamentally believed that U.S. Central America policy constituted another critical issue that required the Southwest Voter Research Institute's resource prioritization and advocacy.

In order to see his vision through, Willie insisted that Antonio González, who was now working for the Mexican American Legislative Caucus in Texas, run the institute's newly forming Latin America Project. "This is too important to leave to the *gringos*," Velásquez told the young organizer upon recruiting him to help staff the institute. As usual, the SVREP founder was convincing in making his case. Accordingly, in October 1987, González was back at SVREP, this time at the Institute, and charged by Velásquez to make the Latin American Project a reality. Willie told González that he wanted to provoke raucous debate on Central America among Hispanic leaders. He wanted polling and educational efforts done. He wanted Latino delegations sent to Latin America to experience firsthand what was taking place. He wanted Hispanics serving as Central American election observers. And, eventually, he wanted SVREP to be able to transfer and to customize the voter registration, education, and mobilization strategies and techniques that it had mastered over the past thirteen years in the United States to Central American nations struggling to realize their democratic promise.

In January 1988, Willie and the Institute hosted an international fact-finding mission, leading a team of Southwestern Latino leaders to Nicaragua and Costa Rica. The delegation, headed by former New Mexico Governor Toney Anaya, included: Velásquez; Texas State Representative Eddie Cavazos; Mario Obledo, past president of the League of United Latin American Citizens and chairman of the National Rainbow Coalition; Professor Avelardo Valdez, former president of the National Association for Chicano Studies; and Linda Yáñez, an immigration attorney for Brownsville, Texas. Antonio González and Bob Brischetto of the Southwest Voter Research Institute staff, and Alfredo Cruz of National Public Radio also participated in the fact-finding trip. The goal of the delegation was to survey the workings of the Arias Central American Peace Plan firsthand and then to offer observations, both to the Congressional Hispanic Caucus and to U.S. Latino rights groups, that would help to stimulate expanded public policy conversation about American engagement in Central America.

Immediately upon returning to the United States, the Institute's delegation held a roundtable discussion on what its members had seen and heard, in particular regarding American policy toward Nicaragua and the Central American Peace Plan. Velásquez suggested that Hispanics had a special responsibility to offer viable alternatives to current U.S. foreign policy in Latin America, arguing, "We need to understand that with [our] growth of power there is also [a necessary] growth of responsibilities. And one big part of [this] is that as we grow in power, we simply must get involved with foreign policy questions."

On February 2, 1988, the eve of a key House vote on whether to approve

$36.25 million in aid to the Nicaraguan Contra rebels, Velásquez and three other members of the Southwest Voter Research Institute delegation—Anaya, Obledo, and Cavazos—traveled to Washington, D.C. to present a joint statement to the Congressional Hispanic Caucus at a Capitol Hill press conference. After lobbying four hundred of the nation's most influential Hispanic political leaders to voice their opposition to the aid, most of whom did, the congressional appropriations bill was narrowly defeated by a margin of 219–211.

౿ ౿ ౿

On May 9, 1988, Willie turned forty-four years old, but rather than celebrating at home in the traditional way, he hopped onto a plane and flew to the East Coast to give a keynote speech and to meet with some of his funding partners. Ralph Neas, the head of the Leadership Conference on Civil Rights, had invited Velásquez to speak at a Leadership Conference gathering celebrating the 200th anniversary of the Constitution. Two years earlier, in 1985, the Leadership Conference had presented its Hubert H. Humphrey Civil Rights Award for unique contributions to the advancement of civil and human rights to Willie. Being the largest coalition of civil rights organizations in the country, Velásquez knew he would run into a lot of old friends at the convening and he looked forward to catching up with his fellow activists.

Willie did in fact see a number of his longstanding civil rights allies and colleagues at the event; but what they saw as he found them one by one in the crowd was startling and disturbing: a pale, weak, and wasting man who looked much older than his forty-four years and nothing like the forceful, macho Velásquez many had known for nearly two decades. Willie struggled through his speech on Hispanics and the use of political power and barely made it through the evening's formalities. When the program concluded, he immediately found his way upstairs to his hotel room and crawled into bed. There would be no customary late-night rollicking political conversations at the bar this evening for Velásquez. He was in severe pain.

The next day, Jim Browne of the Field Foundation picked Willie up at his hotel and they drove to the D.C. National Airport to fly to New York for a later meeting with Dick Boone, the Field Foundation CEO. Velásquez, still in pain, shuffled behind Browne, unable to keep up. He barely made it up the two-and-a-half flights of stairs at the Field Foundation offices and had to stop along the way to catch his breath. Boone told Velásquez upon greeting him that he looked terrible and needed to do something about it. It was a recurrent ulcer, Willie surmised, that was giving him stomach pains. It ran in his family. Every few years, he told Boone, his ulcer would force him to see a doctor. Boone told him it looked like it was time to go back to his physician again, and soon. Velásquez promised to do so as soon as he returned home to

San Antonio.

Back home, Willie's pain was unremitting. Velásquez, who rarely admitted that he was suffering at any level, informed his wife, Janie, that he was not feeling well. She could see that Willie was in terrible pain and looking unusually exhausted. Janie prepared herself for the couple's usual exchange in which she would tell him he needed to see a doctor. He would respond that he was too busy and did not have the time, but if he could just get some medicine, he would be fine. Janie would then try again and Willie would cut her off, and that would be the end of the conversation. Notwithstanding the painful predictability of this routine, Janie forged ahead hoping that somehow things might be different this time. In fact, something *was* different this time. "Willie," Janie gently told him, "I think you need to see a doctor." Velásquez paused, moved slowly, and answered, "I think you're right."

Two days later, Velásquez went to his doctor's office for a physical exam, but because of his history of peptic ulcer disease, the severe abdominal pain he was experiencing, and the added symptoms of great weight loss, fatigue, and signs of depression, he was immediately sent to the hospital for a battery of tests. The pain associated with his ulcer had been so severe that Willie had sought medical treatment for it three times in the last five years—August 1983, October 1984, and September 1986. These three occasions just happened to coincide with key moments for SVREP and Willie: the kickoff of the national Hispanic Voter Registration Campaign; the closing of SVREP's most active voter registration period; and Willie's realization that he was burning out and needed to do something to shake himself from the malaise that had set in for a year and a half after the 1984 elections (a time when foundation voter registration support was, for all practical purposes, frozen and on hold and SVREP was struggling financially). This would be his fourth visit to the doctor in the past five years. Two days later, the results returned. He was diagnosed with kidney cancer.

Additional tests revealed the extent of Willie's cancer. A large tumor in his kidney had now spread to his left lung and his lymph nodes. Doctors from both the Santa Rosa Hospital and the University Health Science Center in San Antonio advised Velásquez on treatments and possibilities. But the news was bad in every case. Willie was told that he likely had only six months to a year to live. After twelve days at the Santa Rosa Hospital, Velásquez was moved to Houston's M.D. Anderson Medical Center, a top cancer treatment center where he would seek further advice on what, if anything, could be done to prolong his life.

Willie's reaction to his terminal cancer was mixed. He shifted from denial to stoicism; from holding court, as he always had, talking politics, deconstructing the latest presidential campaign moves, and joking about his condition, to weeping and regretting the time he had not spent with his children, asking for special permission to go see his son, Guillermo, play soccer one last time. Privately, he talked about the unfinished business he still needed to complete: providing for Janie and the kids, fixing and paying for his house, advancing Governor Dukakis's presidential campaign, making sure that SVREP was moving ahead, and writing a book.

San Antonio Mayor Henry Cisneros, through his connections at Harcourt, Brace & Jovanovich publishing company, was trying to arrange a book deal for Velásquez. Cisneros and others believed that it was crucial for the story of Willie and SVREP to be told. But Velásquez resisted. The past was the past. He did not want to write about everything that happened in the past. He wanted rather to talk about the future. His book would be a series of essays on the future of Latino politics.

Velásquez had also been talking to Governor Dukakis's campaign leadership about becoming the Massachusetts governor's deputy campaign manager now that he had won the Democratic Party's presidential nomination. Willie had stayed in touch with the Dukakis campaign throughout the primary season and had helped José Villarreal, an attorney who had been working with SVREP, get placed on the Dukakis team. Willie saw this opportunity as the first partisan-paid political consulting job he would ever have after more than two decades slugging it out for 'Mexicans' on the nonpartisan, nonprofit side. The medical diagnosis that foreshadowed his impending passing made for bittersweet fantasies of what might have been for the SVREP founder, if only he had not become ill.

Those closest to Velásquez—his family and the SVREP staff in particular—automatically assumed that if anyone was going to live longer than expected if would be Willie, and many seemed to convince themselves that he would be with them for at least a few more years. When the word got out that Velásquez had cancer and was hospitalized, a torrent of well-wishers—people who had known him for decades as well as recent acquaintances—made their way to San Antonio to see the man they loved. Ernie Cortés, one of the country's top community organizers who worked for the Industrial Areas Foundation, described his last visit with Velásquez in the following terms: "When I arrived [at the hospital] I was taken aback. Everything about Willie seemed abnormally normal. He was his usual self, talking about politics. People kept coming in and out. He was virtually holding court. We began to talk politics; we praised our favorite heroes, denounced our favorite villains, and agreed to disagree on which was which. Throughout it all, his spirit seemed strong, although his body had been clearly wrecked by the cancer. I remember him even praising his doctor, a generosity of spirit I would not have sustained at that moment. He seemed to be able to talk sensibly about his illness, so much so that I found it hard to accept that he had less than six months to live." Willie half-jokingly told one friend that he was glad it was cancer, "It was a relief. I thought I was burning out." To another visitor, he quipped, "I thought I could no longer exercise because I was getting old; I was glad to learn it was only because I had cancer." Even at his eleventh hour, this was vintage Velásquez.

Willie continued to receive nonstop visitors, and while it lifted his spirits to reconnect with parts of his life that he had forgotten or put aside, it also wore him out, though he tried not to show it. At the M.D. Anderson Hospital and Tumor Institute, top cancer doctors tried everything they could. Because the cancer had invaded his lymph nodes and spread throughout his body, it could not be removed. Instead they performed an embolization aimed at freezing the tumor inside him to control the bulk of the cancer. They sent Willie back to San Antonio to rest at home with his family before beginning chemotherapy.

Back home in San Antonio, visitors continued to descend upon Willie with Janie emotionally and practically unable to take matters in hand. Velásquez's strength continued to deteriorate to the point where he could no longer get up and down the stairs. He now slept downstairs on a mattress on the floor to avoid the fatigue of climbing. He could no longer shave, eat, or go to the bathroom, and he suffered increasingly from shortness of breath. Velásquez was quickly becoming incapacitated. On June 13, Willie was readmitted to Santa Rosa Hospital in response to serious heart palpitations. His long history of smoking probably added chronic obstructive pulmonary disease to his list of ailments. He was transferred to the hospital's intensive care unit. Two days later, shortly after midnight on Wednesday, June 15, 1988, at 12:55 a.m., at the age of forty-four, Willie Velásquez died. His last words, according to his brother George, were *qué bonito es el nuevo mundo* (The new world is so beautiful).

Janie was not by his side. She never had the chance to say good-bye. She had been too weak the entire month he had been dying and instead of staying in the room with him when his condition worsened, she allowed Willie's extended family to convince her to wait outside because it was all going to be fine. She would never forgive herself for making that choice.

᷈ ᷈ ᷈

More than twenty-three hundred mourners attended Willie's rosary on the night of Friday, June 17. Andy Hernández, now SVREP's soon-to-be-appointed leader and Velásquez's longtime friend, eulogized him, saying in part, "Willie was more than a leader; he was a champion of our people. He stood for what we are, for our dreams and our aspirations. Willie has left us, but we will never be left without him. His life and words will stay with us for decades to come."

The funeral mass the next day was part celebration, part SVREP political organizing event, and in every way, Mexican. Held at St. Mary's Catholic Church, Velásquez's parish in downtown San Antonio across the street from SVREP's headquarters offices, nearly one thousand mourners packed themselves into the church to say farewell to one of the country's most influential builders of American democracy. Another thousand people quietly assembled outside of the church, unable to gain seating in the overflowing house of worship.

Inside the church, local, county, and state elected officials from throughout the Southwest, most of them Hispanic—a substantial number of whom owed their success to Velásquez and SVREP—joined forces with Latino community activists and voter registration colleagues from all over the country to honor Velásquez's life and work. From his home state of Texas, top state Democratic Party officials attended, including Land Commissioner Garry Mauro; Railroad Commissioner John Sharp; Agriculture Commissioner Jim Hightower; Attorney General Jim Mattox; and State Treasurer Ann Richards. SVREP staff worked the crowd handing out "Su voto es su voz" (Your Vote is Your Voice) lapel and bumper stickers. The back of the funeral mass program contained a reproduction of a SVREP poster entitled "La Esperanza del Futuro" (The Hope of the Future), featuring a young Latino staring out with the tagline reading: *Nuestros hijos merecen una vida mejor. Regístrese y vote. Su voto es su voz.* (Our children deserve a better life. Register and vote. Your vote is your voice.)

Fourth Court of Appeals Justice Al Chapa sang "Ave Maria" as mourners walked in and were escorted to pews. The commemorative mass began with *mariachis* dressed in royal-blue Mexican uniforms playing a moving rendition of the classic Mexican song, "Sin Ti" (Without You). Janie, who announced in advance of the funeral that she did not want people to wear black, wore a simple, white Mexican dress. The children, Carmen, Catarina, and Guillermo also wore white outfits. Seated up front in the church with Willie's family was another friend of Velásquez's, Governor Michael Dukakis, the Democratic Party's presidential nominee who Willie was supposed to have introduced at the Texas state Democratic Party convention in only a few short days. The governor had rearranged his schedule to be at the funeral mass and to visit privately with Janie and the Velásquez family in order to pay his last respects.

The mass was cooperatively led by Bishop Ricardo Ramírez of Las Cruces, New Mexico, who had served as a SVREP volunteer in the organization's early years; Father Bill Davis, a progressive political cleric and Velásquez's parish priest, who was known to harbor Central American immigrants in his basement; and Father Virgilio Elizondo, the internationally renowned theologian and rector of San Fernando Cathedral. Velásquez was remembered by Bishop Ramírez as being "well-rooted in the hope and aspiration of his people," someone of great integrity. He compared Willie's life and work to that of a comet, "Once in a rare moment in the world's history, the Lord raises a man such as this, kind of like a comet that doesn't appear very often but flies through the sky in a shining and brilliant light, but always only for a brief moment." Father Davis added, "Willie Velásquez walked around to tell them [Latinos] how beautiful they were, how gifted they were, and that the country belonged to them." Dukakis also spoke, in Spanish and English, reminding mourners that Willie had changed the world because he understood that great victories require great efforts—"his greatest victories are in the hundreds of thousands of people he helped to empower throughout this land," the presidential candidate observed. "Above all," the governor continued, "he loved this country. He believed in it. He understood it. And all he asked from it was a fair share of the American dream for himself, and for every American, no matter who they are or where they come from or what the color of their skin is."

Only a few weeks later at the Democratic National Convention in Atlanta, Georgia, Massachusetts Governor Michael Dukakis, the Democratic presidential nominee, honored and paid tribute to Willie in his acceptance speech, once again delivering his remarks in both Spanish and English:

> And when a man named Willie Velásquez can register thousands of his fellow citizens as voters . . . [and] can bring new energy and new ideas and new people into courthouses and city halls and state capitols all across the Southwest . . . we are all enriched and ennobled.

Thousands of people, some in groups, others by themselves, lined the procession route from St. Mary's Catholic Church through the Westside of San Antonio to the burial ground at San Fernando Cemetery. Many onlookers silently lifted their fists in salute to the man who had helped them to gain political power and respect in the American political system.

Henry Cisneros offered the final eulogy of the day at Willie's graveside. The mayor—one of Velásquez's generational contemporaries—talked about the large gains made in the number of Hispanic elected officials since Velásquez and SVREP had begun their work. Because of him, Cisneros said, "not only had Hispanics in the United States entered the country's mainstream political life, but because of [Willie] there is hope." His death and funeral made front-page news for days throughout much of Texas and the Southwest; some local television stations carried his funeral live. As word of Velásquez's death spread, other prominent American political figures from both parties offered their praise, including President Reagan, Vice President George Bush, the Reverend Jesse Jackson, and U.S. Senator Lloyd Bentsen. *Washington Post* national political columnist David Broder began his tribute to Willie this way: "The obituaries began with the formal name, William C. Velasquez. They quickly shifted to Willie. That was as it should have been, for there was an infectious, irresistible informality to the man who was mourned across America last week when he died in his home city of San Antonio at the absurd age of 44." Broder added, "I feel as if it were a death in the family. It is, in fact, a loss to the nation, and his spirit, I hope, will continue to inspire the far-from-complete struggle for enfranchisement of millions of Hispanic Americans."

A week after Willie's burial, it was time to get back to work in very changed circumstances. SVREP marked the transition by moving into new offices. SVREP now faced the daunting and inevitable question of how it would survive without Velásquez. At the office, Andy Hernández, now Willie's successor and the first staff professional Willie ever hired at SVREP, moved into unknown territory with a huge burden on his shoulders—living up to his predecessor's legacy. Historically, Hernández had been the buffer between Velásquez and the rest of the SVREP staff; the staff would laugh and joke with him about Velásquez and his directives. What would happen now when Andy directed them to do things? Could SVREP make it without Velásquez? Only time would tell whether and, if so, how SVREP would find its way forward without its founder.

Life for Janie and the children had also been thrown into absolute disarray by Willie's passing. Velásquez had always been the one to make the children tow the line and to galvanize the family's energy to move in a particular direction. Janie was still in shock and at present could not manage her own life, let alone the lives of her three children. The children—none of them yet even teenagers—were lost in understanding the significance of their father's passing. The question of how the family would support itself in Willie's absence loomed overhead. Sadly, Velásquez's financial juggling on behalf of SVREP over the years, including his inclination to borrow from personal loans on his family's home to help the organization through tough times, left Janie and the Velásquez children with virtually nothing but significant debt.

After nearly one thousand voter registration drives in over two hundred communities across the Southwest and beyond, eighty-five successful voting rights lawsuits, a doubling of the number of Hispanic elected officials from just over fifteen hundred in 1974 to over thirty-three hundred in 1988 and, most importantly, a doubling of Latino registered voters to five million in 1988, Willie Velásquez, a hero of grassroots Latino politics, was dead at the age of forty-four. His name was still unknown to many Hispanics and most Americans when he died, but Willie would not have cared. He was more concerned to ensure that his Mexican-American brothers and sisters knew themselves and their democratic rights as Americans and lived up to their civic responsibilities as a fully activated people in the nation's governance.

It was Willie's dedication to his people's political self-determination that made him important to the country, not only to Hispanics. Near the end of his life, Willie talked more and more about a new responsibility Latinos had, now that they had democratically earned their political power.

But in the end, it was just another classic American immigrant story with a twist for Willie: "Probably what is happening politically to Mexicans in the Southwest has happened before to other immigrant groups. There are, of course, differences in that we are not arriving at Ellis Island and are not European whites. Indeed, there is much more emotion in our immigration than previous ones from Europe. We are immigrating to San Antonio, El Paso, Tucson, Albuquerque, Los Angeles, San Diego, and San Francisco—to many, our ancestral homeland where Chicanos were formed as a race. Secondly, Mexican Americans are unusual immigrants in that some of us have been here for over four hundred years with deep emotional ties to the land."

Willie continued, "What we are seeing in the Southwest is only the most recent chapter in a long-running drama that is U.S. history. This quite simply is the way America has always treated 'foreigners.' The process has worked surprisingly well. What Mexicans are therefore enduring is what many other groups have already gone through. We are not asking that the process be changed. Indeed, it is the very firestorm of acrimony and contention that has transformed the rough iron of immigrants into the polished steel of leaders."

And for Willie this new story of the Hispanic immigrant would, in the end, be a success story. "What do I say then about the future? It's the past. Whatever immigrant groups have done in the past, whatever has been their contribution, the Mexicans are going to do the same thing. And I bet you that when it comes time to add it all up and say, well, were the Mexicans up to it? I'll bet you that we will make the same contribution that all the others did."

But Willie wanted more. Doing what others had done before Hispanics had power was not enough. He wanted Latinos to raise the bar, to shoot for something better. "No longer can we just think of striving to elect another Mexican to office. We must now tenaciously adhere to the proposition that Mexican-American candidates for office should subscribe to the highest standards of the American political tradition. If the candidates seeking the Mexican-American vote are of shady character, they should be denied our vote, and if they are in an elected position they should be kicked out of office. If the Mexican-American candidates seeking our vote stand foursquare for apple pie and motherhood but have no opinion on the important public policy questions facing our country, they should be treated the same way."

❧ ❧ ❧

At the same time that Velásquez was battling the cancer that finally consumed him, a political documentary on Hispanics was airing across the nation on Spanish television. When the focus turned to Mexican-American politics, an elderly woman from Cuero, Texas was featured. The journalist covering the story asked the woman to describe what she was doing in her community. She had never held a job outside the home. She had raised ten children and thirty grandchildren, but now she was out in the streets going door-to-door registering Mexicans to vote. Why? Because, she said, it was crucial to make sure that her children and grandchildren got a fair chance in society. "You know," she said, looking straight into the camera, her voice elevated with pride, "*su voto es su voz*." "Your vote is your voice." It was Velásquez and SVREP's signature. It was the Hispanic population's political brand. And it would not disappear anytime soon, as long as there existed unnamed heroes like the grandmother from Cuero who could pick up the democratic baton and show America a glimpse of all that she was and could become in the future. For Willie Velásquez, this was the essence and embodiment of the struggle.

Epilogue

PRESIDENT BILL CLINTON AWARDED THE Presidential Medal of Freedom—the highest honor given to civilians in the United States, posthumously to Willie Velásquez on September 29, 1995, at a White House ceremony. Seven years after dying of cancer at just forty-four years of age, Velásquez became only the fifth Hispanic ever to win the award, joining the father of modern Puerto Rico, Luis Muñoz Marín, the first governor of the commonwealth of Puerto Rico who received the award from President Lyndon Johnson in 1963; Dr. Héctor P. García, the founder of the American G.I. Forum veterans' organization, who was given the honor by President Ronald Reagan in 1984; Luis Ferré, a successful businessman, former governor of Puerto Rico and advocate for Puerto Rican statehood, who was presented the award by President George H. W. Bush in 1991; and César Chávez, the founder of the United Farm Workers Organization (UFWO), who, like Velásquez, received the award posthumously from Clinton in 1994.

President Harry Truman created the Presidential Medal of Freedom in the 1940s to honor exemplary service to the country in time of war. In 1963, President John F. Kennedy broadened its purpose by extending the award to civilians who had made remarkable contributions to America in peacetime.

On the eve of receiving the nation's highest honor, Willie Velásquez also received official praise and recognition from his congressman, Henry B. González. It was the first time the erstwhile González had publicly acknowledged his former protégé and the work of SVREP since the congressman and Willie had become bitter political rivals in the late 1960s and early 1970s. At a time when there were still only at tiny handful of Hispanic congressmen in the United States, González had befriended Willie, the St. Mary's University college student, and become his first political mentor. González had even helped to secure a summer job at the State Department for Velásquez, the budding, "want to be" diplomat who was studying international relations before there existed any affirmative action programs recruiting Mexican Americans to Washington, D.C. Willie, who during the early '60s had led the congressman's initial re-election efforts among college students, had even accompanied González's daughter to her senior prom.

The split began when Willie volunteered to work for César Chávez and the UFWO, and González sternly warned him to avoid getting too heavily involved in radical and leftist politics. The division worsened when Willie left his graduate studies, rejected a promising possible career in the Foreign Service, and deepened his progressive engagements by officially going to work as an organizer for the farmworkers in Texas. The two men became fundamentally disconnected when Willie became intimately involved with the early organizing work of the radical La Raza Unida organization (before it became an independent political party); and, then, later, progressive groups like the Mexican American Youth Organization (MAYO); the Mexican American Unity Council (MAUC, the first Mexican-American community development corporation in the country); and the Southwest Council of La Raza (now known as the National Council of La Raza).

The congressman and Velásquez both played their respective roles: González, the senior federal official who did not want young, inexperienced radicals receiving foundation dollars and creating potential power centers in defiance of established rules and conventions in his district (or elsewhere); and Willie, the Chicano civil rights activist who was seeking to fill a void, along with his generational compatriots, created by González and other establishment officials who, as they saw things, had not done enough for grassroots Chicanos. When the conflicts between González and Velásquez reached a high point, the liberal stalwart congressman took to the floor of the U.S. House of Representatives and began a series of seething, personal attacks aimed at Willie and other Chicano activists. The Congressman's assault eventually led to the rewriting of American tax laws governing private foundation-supported, nonprofit lobbying activities and to Willie's resignation as the first executive director of MAUC.

As the years passed, Congressman González eventually made peace with most of the Chicano activists who had branded him a sellout during the heady days of the Chicano civil rights movement. Typically, both sides would admit that they had been carried away by the highly charged political times and agreed to put it all behind them. But González and Willie never reconciled. The split between them had been too deep and too personal. Neither typically proud and stubborn man had ever been willing to budge when it came to admitting his role in destroying their once close relationship.

When Willie suddenly died and political tributes in his memory began pouring in from all over the country, from the lowest ranking local Mexican-American elected official to the president of the United States, there was one major politician who did not jump on the bandwagon: Congressman Henry B. González. *San Antonio Light* political columnist Rick Casey reflected on González's silence on the occasion of Willie's passing, saying, "At least González was consistent. He didn't say anything good about Willie when he was alive and he wasn't about to start now that he was dead."

But eight years after Willie's death, upon the White House's announcement of his posthumous Presidential Medal of Freedom, Congressman González did finally have something good to say about the promising young college man who had strayed from the political path the longtime elected official had paved for him. "Willie Velásquez had the good fortune to come along when there were great efforts under way to build new sources of empowerment among the disadvantaged," Congressman González wrote in a widely circulated press release. "He had the good sense and the energy to recognize and capitalize on the opportunity—and so was able to create a movement that added [significantly] to the resources and political capability of Hispanics. His was an enormous contribution, and this [presidential] recognition [is] well-deserved."

Janie, Willie's widow, responded to Congressman González's kind words by saying she regretted that Willie and the congressman had never reached out to one another to put the conflicts of the past behind them. "I'm glad he (González) is saying that, and I welcome it," she commented to the local San Antonio press. "It's good for us and the rest of [our] family that [Willie] is finally [being] recognized for the work he [did]. There is no [rancor] on our part because there are [still] too many things to think about and too many things to do in our community [that require our continuing focus]," she added. Then, closing with a final reflection on the relationship that had existed between Velásquez and González during Willie's lifetime, Janie commented, "Willie was not a radical. He believed in the basic rights granted to every American. While the two didn't get along, he (Willie) would [often] say 'You gotta admit he (González) votes right!'"

The White House award ceremony, originally scheduled for Thursday, September 28, 1995 at 1:30 p.m. had to be unexpectedly postponed at the last minute and rescheduled for Friday morning, September 29, owing to new developments affecting the Middle East peace process and President Clinton's consequent need to attend to related negotiations. Because of the unanticipated scheduling change, the Mayflower Hotel reception planned in Willie's honor as a post-ceremony affair became a pre-ceremony celebration. Hosted by longtime Velásquez friend Jesse Aguirre and his corporation, Anheuser Busch, hundreds of SVREP friends and family members gathered to remember the struggles and accomplishments Willie and SVREP had seen during nearly twenty years' time. Antonio González was now president of both SVREP and the SVREP Institute, having replaced Willie's point man, Andy Hernández, the initial SVREP staff hire who had taken over after Willie's death and ably led the two organizations until 1994. President Clinton had publicly announced his plans to honor Willie at the Congressional Hispanic Caucus Institute's annual Hispanic Heritage dinner on September 27, 1995, saying, "I wish he (Willie) could be here tonight to see how much he has helped citizenship to bloom among Hispanic Americans throughout this country."

Janie and the Velásquez kids—Carmen, Catarina, and Guillermo, now young adults, stayed at the Mayflower Hotel to prepare for the White House ceremony. Willie's mother, Mary Louise; his sister, Stella, and her daughter, Feliz; Willie's uncle Gene; and close Velásquez friend, Robbie Greenblum also made the trip from San Antonio to attend the White House ceremony.

On the day of the ceremony, military men in dress whites escorted Janie and the extended Velásquez family members to special gold seats in the yellow-draped East Room of the White House. Various Washington luminaries sat to the right of the presidential stage, while family and friends of the medal winners were placed to the left of the podium. As the large room filled, numerous people who had known Willie and supported SVREP's work over the years emerged—Congressman John Lewis, who shared his experiences leading the African-American-focused Voter Education Project with the young Willie; Housing and Urban Development Secretary Henry Cisneros, the former mayor of San Antonio, Texas, who had been a longtime supporter of SVREP and who had delivered the final eulogy at Willie's burial; Transportation Secretary Federico Peña, who earlier in his political career had benefited from SVREP's efforts by becoming the first Hispanic mayor of Denver, Colorado; and Peter Edelman, who had served as a board member of the Citizens' Participation Project and was a perennial backer of Willie's and SVREP's work. To each of these important American leaders, Willie had been a friend and an inspiration.

President Clinton opened the fifty-minute ceremony by welcoming guests and setting the tone for the event with the words: "We are here today to celebrate people who have always been for change, and who have changed America for the better, but who have done it based on the enduring values that make this country great—the belief that we have to give all of our citizens the chance to live up to the fullest of their God-given capacities; the conviction that we have to do everything we can to strengthen our families and our communities; the certainty that when the chips are down, we have to do what is good and right, even if it is unpopular in the short run; [and] the understanding that we have the obligation to honor those who came before us by passing better lives and brighter opportunities on to those who come after."

President Clinton then went on to present twelve individuals upon whom the nation's highest honor was being bestowed on this occasion. They included Peggy Charen, founder of the anti-violence Action for Children's Television organization; Joan Ganz Cooney, creator of the Children's Television Workshop and shows such as Sesame Street and The Electric Company; William T. Coleman, an African American who served as transportation secretary under President Ford and was now chair of the NAACP Legal Defense and Education Fund; John Hope Franklin, a prominent African-American historian who had spent his career documenting the history of the South and the role of blacks in the country's development; U.S. Court of Appeals Judge Leon Higginbotham, an African-American civil rights attorney and professor at Harvard's John F. Kennedy School of Government who had spent his life fighting for civil rights; U.S. District Judge Frank Johnson who was responsible for several landmark decisions in the areas of desegregation, voting rights, and civil liberties—including the 1956 ruling that declared the Montgomery, Alabama segregated bus system unconstitutional; Dr. C. Everett Koop, former Surgeon General of the United States; former Wisconsin Senator Gaylord Nelson, the father of Earth Day, for his commitment to environmental activism; James Rouse, an urban developer who had created the Enterprise Foundation to help revitalize America's inner cities; and Hollywood studio executive Lew Wasserman for his countless humanitarian efforts, especially on behalf of the blind. The final two medals presented by Clinton were awarded posthumously to Walter Reuther, the former president of the United Auto Workers, and to Willie.

President Clinton spoke eloquently about Willie at the very close of the program, saying:

> His name was William C. Velásquez, but everyone knew him as Willie. Willie was and is now a name synonymous with democracy in America. Through the organization he founded, the Southwest Voter Registration and Education Project, he nearly doubled Hispanic voter registration, and dramatically increased the number of Latino-elected officials in this nation. His appeal to the Hispanic community was simple, passionate, and direct—"Su voto es su voz"—your vote is your voice.
>
> The movement he began here at home went on to support democracy abroad in El Salvador, Nicaragua, and Mexico, and in South Africa. From the farm fields of California where he organized workers with César Chávez, to the halls of Harvard where he taught politics, Willie Velásquez was driven by an unwavering belief that every American should have a role in our democracy and a share in the opportunities of our great nation.
>
> Willie Velásquez died too young. He was just 44 when he passed away in 1988. But in his vibrant life, he restored faith in our ideals and in ourselves. And no person in modern America who has run for public office wherever Hispanic Americans live has failed to feel the hand of Willie Velásquez. He made this a greater country, and we're honored that his wife is here with us today.

As Janie listened to the president's remarks she knew that he had made several minor mistakes describing Willie's life—Willie worked for the United Farm Workers in Texas, not California, and his international work had extended beyond Central America to Chile, but not to South Africa. Still, she could not help being moved and overwhelmed by the thoughtful and dramatic close that Clinton had prepared to recognize Willie. She knew in her heart and soul that Willie himself would have been made to feel proud by Clinton's remarks and that he would have especially resonated with the president's final thoughts, which he shared before the official reading of each award recipient's citation. For, in closing, the president captured in precise terms all that Willie had stood for and fought to make a reality for his own generation, that of his children, and others to come in the future relative to the promise of democracy. According to Clinton:

The miracle of American life is that this cycle [of civic leadership and heroism] can be repeated over and over again with each succeeding generation; and that with each succeeding generation, we make freedom a little more real and full to all Americans. I ask all of you to think about that. You couldn't help feeling, when you heard these stories, that this is a very great country. And we do not have to give in to our lesser selves. We do not have to be divided. We do not have to achieve less than we can. If we will follow these examples, we will make sure that in the next century, this country will be all it was meant to be for all of our citizens.

Following the conclusion of Clinton's formal remarks, an African-American military aide read through each individual citation as the president presented the recipients with their medals, in turn. When Willie's name was announced, Clinton presented the Presidential Medal of Freedom to a beaming, upbeat Janie. "I could not stop smiling," Willie's widow commented after the ceremony. "It was like I was in a dream. It was such an honor to be up there with all those people and to know that the president recognized [Willie's] efforts. [My husband] believed in leaving this world better than how you found it. I think he would be proud to see how far we've come. This is not just our medal. It's for everyone, especially everyone in San Antonio."

Willie's official medal citation was as he would have wanted it: plain, simple, and to the point. He would have undoubtedly appreciated its matter-of-fact tenor and its focus on the continuing legacy of his life's work. In its entirety, the citation elegantly read:

Willie Velásquez labored throughout his career to infuse American public life with the vibrant Hispanic heritage. With vision and the skills he developed as a member of César Chávez' farm worker movement, Velásquez founded the Southwest Voter Registration and Education Project in 1974. His untiring efforts nearly doubled Hispanic voter registration and dramatically increased the number of Latino elected officials in this country. Though cancer took him from us too soon, Willie Velásquez' legacy lives on in all who seek to make our democracy truly representative of America's diversity.

Additional titles in our
Hispanic Civil Rights Series

Message to Aztlán
Rodolfo "Corky" Gonzales
ISBN 1-55885-331-6

A Gringo Manual on How to Handle Mexicans
José Angel Gutiérrez
ISBN 1-55885-326-X

Eyewitness: A Filmmaker's Memoir of the Chicano Movement
Jesús Salvador Treviño
ISBN 1-55885-349-9

Pioneros puertorriqueños en Nueva York, 1917–1947
Joaquín Colón
ISBN 1-55885-335-9

The American GI Forum: In Pursuit of the Dream, 1948–1983
Henry A. J. Ramos
Clothbound, ISBN 1-55885-261-1
Trade Paperback, ISBN 1-55885-262-X

Chicano! The History of the Mexican American Civil Rights Movement
F. Arturo Rosales
ISBN 1-55885-201-8

Testimonio: A Documentary History of the Mexican-American Struggle for Civil Rights
F. Arturo Rosales
ISBN 1-55885-299-9

They Called Me "King Tiger": My Struggle for the Land and Our Rights
Reies López Tijerina
ISBN 1-55885-302-2

Julian Nava: My Mexican-American Journey
Julian Nava
Clothbound, ISBN 1-55885-364-2
Trade Paperback, ISBN 1-55885-351-0

César Chávez: A Struggle for Justice / César Chávez: La lucha por la justicia
Richard Griswold del Castillo
ISBN 1-55885-364-2

Memoir of a Visionary: Antonia Pantoja
Antonia Pantoja
2002, 384 pages, Clothbound
ISBN 1-55885-365-0, $26.95

Black Cuban, Black American
Evelio Grillo
2000, 134 pages, Trade Paperback
ISBN 1-55885-293-X, $13.95

Hector P. García: In Relentless Pursuit of Justice
Ignacio M. García
2002, 256 pages, Clothbound
ISBN 1-55885-387-1, $26.95

A Chicano Manual on How to Handle Gringos
José Angel Gutiérrez
2000, 134 pages, Trade Paperback
ISBN 1-55885-396-0